MARKETING
Canadian Insights and Applications

D1511657

MARKETING
Canadian Insights and Applications

Frederick G. Crane
QMA Consulting Group Limited

E. Stephen Grant
University of New Brunswick

Steven W. Hartley
University of Denver

Represented in Canada by:

McGraw-Hill Ryerson Limited

IRWIN

Toronto · Chicago · New York · Auckland · Bogotá · Caracas · Lisbon · London
Madrid · Mexico · Milan · New Delhi · San Juan · Singapore · Sydney · Tokyo

McGraw-Hill
  A Division of the McGraw-Hill Companies

MARKETING: CANADIAN INSIGHTS AND APPLICATIONS

1 2 3 4 5 6 7 8 9 0 QD/QD 9 1 0 9 8 7
ISBN 0-256-19520-X

Senior sponsoring editor: *Evelyn Veitch*
Developmental editor: *Elke Price*
Marketing manager: *Gary Bennett*
Project supervisor: *Gladys True*
Production supervisor: *Laurie Sander*
Designer: *Crispin Prebys*
Prepress Buyer: *Jon Christopher*
Compositor: *Carlisle Communications, Ltd.*
Typeface: *10½/12 Times Roman*
Printer: *Quebecor Printing Book Group/Dubuque*

Library of Congress Catalog number 96-77931

http://www.mhcollege.com

To Doreen (I keep you forever in my heart); to Erinn, Jacquelyn, and Brenna (you are my pride and joy); to my parents (for your love and simplicity); and to God who continues to bless me.

F.G.C.

To my beautiful wife, Kimberly and my supportive parents, Ernest and Treva. Thank you for your constant understanding and encouragement.

E.S.G.

To the Student

"Why are textbook prices so high?"

This is by far the most frequently asked question heard in the publishing industry. There are many factors that influence the price of your new textbook. Here are just a few:

- **The Cost of Instructor Support Materials**   Your instructor may be making use of teaching supplements, many of which are provided by the publisher. Teaching supplements include videos, colour transparencies, instructor's manuals, software, computerized testing materials, and more. These supplements are designed as part of a learning package to enhance your educational experience.
- **Developmental Costs**   These are costs associated with the extensive development of your textbook. Expenses include permissions fees, manuscript review costs, artwork, typesetting, printing and binding costs, and more.
- **Author Royalties**   Authors are paid based on a percentage of new book sales and do not receive royalties on the sale of a used book. They are also deprived of their rightful royalties when their books are illegally photocopied.
- **Marketing Costs**   Instructors need to be made aware of new textbooks. Marketing costs include academic conventions, remuneration of the publisher's representatives, promotional advertising pieces, and the provision of instructor's examination copies.
- **Book Store Markups**   In order to stay in business, your local bookstore must cover its costs. A textbook is a commodity, just like any other item your bookstore may sell, and bookstores are the most effective way to get the textbook from the publisher to you.
- **Publisher Profits**   In order to continue to supply students with quality textbooks, publishers must make a profit to stay in business. Like the authors, publishers do not receive any compensation from the sale of a used book or the illegal photocopying of their textbooks.

We at Irwin/McGraw-Hill Ryerson Limited hope you will find this information useful and that it addresses some of your concerns. We also thank you for your purchase of this new textbook. If you have any questions that we can answer, please write to us at:

McGraw-Hill Ryerson Limited
College Division
300 Water Street
Whitby, Ontario   L1N 9B6

About the Study Guide

Why not make reviewing and exam preparation a snap? Put marketing concepts to work! A comprehensive study guide, entitled *Study Guide for use with Marketing: Canadian Insights and Applications,* prepared by E. Stephen Grant, Frederick G. Crane, and Erica Michaels, is available from your campus bookstore.

It's specially designed for this text and puts key chapter material at your fingertips. Term and definition checks, and quick recall exercises make your study time count.

Check your campus bookstore or ask the manager to place an order today.

Preface

Today, dramatic changes ranging from the increased importance of building relationships with customers to the globalization of industries and markets to advances in technology are creating a new arena for the marketing discipline. Combining these changes with the sophisticated perspectives that students bring to the classroom can create an exciting and relevant learning experience. *Marketing: Canadian Insights and Applications* is both a contemporary and student-oriented text. It emphasizes and demonstrates many of the new developments in marketing, and utilizes an innovative pedagogical approach that encourages readers to become active participants in the learning process. It is our hope that this text will help you to develop the understanding and skills necessary to participate successfully in the complex and evolving marketing environment of the future.

Pedagogical Features

This textbook is designed to involve you in the study of marketing by encouraging you to think about your personal experiences as a consumer and by asking you to take the role of a marketing decision maker. Examples of contemporary people and organizations and their marketing decisions appear in chapter opening vignettes, while extended examples are included throughout the chapters. Each chapter also contains Marketplace Application and Ethics Insight boxes that allow you to examine and discuss marketing actions taken by various organizations.

Learning Objectives appear at the beginning of each chapter, and Learning Objective Reinforcement summaries appear at the end of each chapter. This book reinforces major concepts as they are introduced in each chapter through the use of Learning Checks. At the end of each major chapter section, Learning Checks pose two to three questions to test your recall and understanding of material you have just covered. Each chapter also closes with a listing of Key Terms and Concepts as well as end-of-chapter questions. Finally, you will have an opportunity to further apply what you have learned by examining and studying the end-of-chapter application cases and the longer end-of-text cases. We believe all these pedagogical features will allow you to learn about, understand, and integrate the many marketing topics covered in the text as well as provide you with an opportunity to apply in a real way, this newly found knowledge.

Text Organization

Marketing: Canadian Insights and Applications is divided into six parts. Part 1, Understanding Contemporary Marketing, contains four chapters. Chapter 1 examines what marketing is, and what it is not. The chapter takes a close look at what defines a market-driven organization and outlines seven imperatives for marketing success. Chapter 2 highlights marketing's role in the organization. The relationship between strategic planning and marketing management is also clearly outlined. Following Chapter 2, an example of an actual marketing plan can be found in Appendix A. Chapter 3 analyzes the evolving marketing environment, while Chapter 4 discusses the importance of marketing ethics as an integral component of contemporary marketing.

Part 2, Understanding Buyers and Markets, first describes how ultimate consumers make buying decisions (Chapter 5), then outlines organizational buyer behaviour in Chapter 6. The role of marketing research and information technology in understanding buyers and markets is examined in Chapter 7. Following Chapter 7, Appendix B provides sources of marketing information and business assistance available in Canada. Finally, Chapter 8 examines the importance of market segmentation.

Part 3, Understanding Products, examines the new product process (Chapter 9) as well as product management (Chapter 10). Part 4, Understanding Pricing and Distribution, includes chapters on pricing (Chapter 11 and Appendix C on Financial Analysis of Marketing); marketing channels, wholesaling, and logistics management (Chapter 12); and retailing (Chapter 13).

Part 5, Understanding Integrated Marketing Communications, contains four chapters to cover this important topic. Chapter 14 provides an overview of integrated marketing communications. Chapter 15 examines Advertising and Public Relations. Chapter 16 deals with Sales Promotion and Direct Marketing Communications. Finally, Chapter 17 covers Personal Selling and Sales Management.

Part 6, Understanding the Expanded Settings for Marketing, devotes separate chapters to marketing topics of increasing importance in today's business environment: Global and International Marketing (Chapter 18), and Services and Nonprofit Marketing (Chapter 19).

The text also includes short end-of-chapter application cases as well as more comprehensive end-of-text cases. A detailed glossary and three indexes (author, company and product, and subject) complete the book. We genuinely hope that you will enjoy this book and discover the challenge and excitement of marketing.

Supplemental Resource Materials

The supplemental resource materials accompanying this text are the ones specifically requested by both inexperienced and experienced instructors. The comprehensive and integrated package of high-quality instructional supplements includes the following:

Instructor's Manual. The Instructor's Manual includes lecture notes, transparency masters, a discussion of the Marketplace Application and Ethics Insight boxes, answers to the end-of-chapter questions, and teaching notes for both end-of-chapter and end-of-text cases. The Instructor's Manual also contains additional cases with accompanying teaching notes.

Computerized Test Bank. Our Test Bank has been developed to provide an accurate and exhaustive source of test items for a variety of examination styles. Irwin/McGraw-Hill's test generation software includes advanced features that allow the instructor to create and customize up to 99 versions of each test.

Videos. A series of videos also accompanies the text. Many of the videos correspond to specific cases found in the text, while others accompany the additional cases found in the Instructor's Manual.

Study Guide. The Study Guide enables students to learn and apply marketing principles instead of memorizing facts for an examination. The guide includes application exercises, matching terms to definitions, matching concepts to examples, recognition and identification exercises, and chapter recall tests.

Acknowledgments

Creating a new textbook requires the support and assistance of many people. We are grateful to the numerous reviewers and case authors who contributed to the development of this text. They include:

Cynthia A. Arbeau, University of New Brunswick, Saint John
Serge Carrier, John Abbott College
Jim Coughlin, Sir Sandford Fleming College
W. Ross Darling, University of New Brunswick
Henry Klaise, Durham College
Laurel Ladd, Champlain College
George Low, Texas Christian University
Ken Parr, Selkirk College
Shelley M. Rinehart, University of New Brunswick, Saint John
Gerald Smith, Humber College
Michael P. Whalen, Nova Scotia Agricultural College
Brian Wrightson, Northern Alberta Institute of Technology
Deborah Zizzo, University of Oklahoma

The Canadian business community also provided us with valuable information to help us illustrate marketing in action. We sincerely thank all those who have helped make this text a reality. Finally, we would like to acknowledge the professional efforts of the Irwin/McGraw-Hill Ryerson Limited staff. Successful completion of our book and its many supplements required the attention and commitment of many editorial, production, marketing, and research personnel. Thanks to Gladys True; Keri Johnson; and the rest of the production team. Also, special thanks is extended to Elke Price, our developmental editor, and to Evelyn Veitch, our sponsoring editor. Evelyn deserves much credit for playing a central role in championing this new book. You have our sincere gratitude.

Finally, we would like to thank our families for being there for us throughout this project. This book is for you.

Brief Contents

Contents

Understanding Contemporary Marketing

1

The Marketing Process

A SHOPPING TRIP TO A CYBERSPACE MALL

Some consumers no longer wander grocery aisles, struggle to open plastic produce bags, or wait in line at the register. With just a few computer keystrokes, from the comfort of their home, they can buy a week's worth of food and have it delivered to their door. All they do is put the groceries away.

Along the information superhighway, you can spend money as though you're at the mall. Not only can you shop while sitting in your own little world, wearing sweats and sipping a Clearly Canadian beverage, you don't even have to talk to anyone. With just some clicks or keystrokes, and a credit card at your side, you can skim through consumer cyberspace, hopping among dozens of online "virtual malls" and hundreds of catalogues and retail sites. You can get a pizza delivered within an hour, or overnight have a new denim shirt arrive at your doorstep.

There are two ways to shop in cyberspace. If you subscribe to a commercial online service such as Prodigy or Compuserve, you have access to their online malls, membership shopping programs, and online retailers. Or you can venture onto the Internet, a system that links an estimated 30 million computers around the globe. There, you can take your pick from online malls ranging in size from four to 600 tenants, and shop in stores as familiar as Pizza Hut or as unusual as Condom Country.

But some shoppers find that online consuming isn't as easy as it sounds. Online shoppers can't squeeze the bread, pick out their own vegetables, and try on the clothing they might like to buy. Sometimes access to the malls is difficult and cumbersome, and when the links are down you can't go shopping at all. Some researchers suggest that while there is a lot of browsing going on in cyberspace, it hasn't translated into the sales anticipated by many businesses. Still, new businesses are flooding the Internet and setting up sites on the World Wide Web. MCI which launched its marketplace—MCI online mall—counted 1 million visits to its Web site the first week the mall was launched. But MCI, like many other businesses, is keeping mum about its online sales.

Whether it is doing business in cyberspace or in a storefront location in downtown Toronto, a company's success depends on the subject addressed in this book: marketing. In this chapter and the ones that follow, you will feel the excitement of marketing. You will see why some companies have succeeded in business while others have failed. You will also meet many of the men and women who work hard to create and provide you with the products you use every day.

This text seeks not only to teach you marketing concepts, but also to demonstrate the many real-world applications of marketing. Our goal is to provide you with marketing knowledge that should make you a better consumer, help you in your career, and enable you to be a more insightful and responsible citizen. We also hope that somewhere in these pages you may find the inspiration to pursue a rewarding marketing career.

MARKETING: WHAT IT IS AND WHAT IT IS NOT

Right now we want you to take your very first marketing test. We know you are probably saying, What a way to start off the book! But don't get stressed out. There's just one question and it's the only time that we'll ever ask you "not" to think before you answer. Quickly and honestly: What is the first word that comes to mind when you hear the word marketing?

We're going to make an educated guess and predict that most of you will answer advertising, selling, or common sense. In our classes, we have asked thousands of other students this same question and found these to be the most typical answers. But *marketing is not advertising*. Although advertising is one of the most visible aspects of marketing, it is but one small element of marketing. *Marketing is not selling*. In fact, some experts believe that effective marketing can reduce the need for selling. *Marketing is not merely common sense*. While good marketers are often perceptive and intuitive, these traits alone are not sufficient for making successful marketing decisions. Effective marketing requires intimate knowledge and understanding of consumers and competition that goes beyond simple common sense.

We are very much aware of misconceptions about marketing, including many negative ones. But marketing is not hucksterism; it is not about selling unwanted things and taking the customer's money. Nor is marketing about manipulating, fooling, or tricking the customer.[1] In order for you to fully appreciate marketing, you will need to understand it (1) as a process and (2) as an organizational philosophy. This book will emphasize marketing as a process, but it will also provide you with some insight into marketing as a philosophy that "drives" very select and high-performance organizations.

Marketing as a Process

Marketing as a process occurs on two levels: micromarketing and macromarketing. **Micromarketing** is how an individual organization directs its marketing activities and allocates its resources to benefit its customers. This process contrasts with **macromarketing**, which involves the aggregate flow of a nation's goods and services to benefit society.[2] Macromarketing focuses on the overall efficiency and effectiveness of an economy's marketing system. Macromarketing, as it relates to the impact of marketing activities on society, will be discussed briefly in this book, but our main focus will be on micromarketing.

At the micromarketing level, **marketing** as a process can be defined as "planning and executing the conception, pricing, communications, and distribution of products to create exchanges that satisfy individual and organizational objectives."[3] This definition stresses the importance of beneficial exchanges that satisfy the objectives of both those who buy and those who market products—whether they be individuals or organizations. In this text, we use the word product in a generic way. A **product** is anything that is offered to a market for acquisition, use, or consumption and satisfies an individual or organizational need. It includes goods, services, ideas, places, and people. A **market** is made up of potential consumers with the desire and ability to buy a specific product. We will return to these concepts later in the chapter.

The **exchange,** or trading of things of *value* between buyer and marketer so that each is better off than before, is a central concept in the marketing process. In order to create beneficial exchanges, the marketing process focuses on (1) discovering and (2) satisfying consumers' real needs. More than ever before, organizations are concerned with providing value (customer value) and in building and sustaining customer relationships (relationship marketing). The concepts of customer value and relationship marketing are so important that they will be discussed throughout the text.

Marketing as an Organizational Philosophy

Every organization has a particular philosophy that directs or drives the way it does business. The philosophy may be found in a formal mission statement or in an organizational document that spells out the basic function or purpose of the organization, or it may be informally communicated through the values and actions of top management. The organizational philosophy focuses the energies of all parts of the organization toward particular activities or outcomes. In terms of organizational philosophies, there are really only three types of organizations: (1) product-driven, (2) sales-driven, and (3) market-driven.

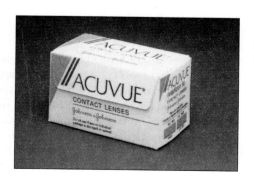

Rollerblades and Acuvue Contact Lenses are examples of products offered to a market.

Automakers were once product-driven; not anymore!

    The central concern for a **product-driven organization** is making and creating products. Product-driven organizations believe in the theory that "a good product will create its own demand." Marketing plays a secondary role in such organizations. Organizational energy is spent on improving production efficiency, gaining wide distribution coverage, or developing new products when supply for existing products exceeds consumer demand. Product-driven organizations tend to be internally focused and pay little attention to consumers' real needs. For years, many automakers focused on creating cars and then tried to sell them to consumers. Rarely were consumers asked what they wanted before the cars were built. Today many high-tech companies follow this same approach, assuming that consumers will buy any new "gadgets" that are produced and made available in the marketplace.

In simple terms, a **sales-driven organization** emphasizes the role of the sales force to find consumers for the goods that it produces best, given its existing resources. Sales-driven firms tend to believe that any product can be sold if enough selling effort is used. In sales-driven organizations, the job is to sell whatever the firm produces.

Many product-driven firms, in particular, become more sales-driven when they reach overcapacity. In other words, when supply exceeds demand, a product-driven firm will shift some of its focus to a selling effort.

In this case, the firm's objective is to sell what it has rather than to make what it can sell! The focus is on making the "immediate" sale, trying to fit the customer to the product, as opposed to having what the customer truly wants or needs. Many makers of "unsought goods"—products that consumers do not normally think of buying such as insurance or funeral plots—also tend to be sales-driven. Door-to-door and telemarketing companies that sell anything from light bulbs to vacation packages are also likely to be sales-driven organizations.

In a **market-driven organization,** customer needs are paramount; they form the basis upon which the organization is built. These organizations seek to discover and satisfy customer needs with a totally integrated organizational effort. Market-driven organizations focus their energy on serving their customers' needs and on building customer relationships that will result in long-term profitability for the firm.

Market-driven organizations are designed so that everyone is involved in marketing, from the receptionist to the board of directors. In essence, everyone's job is focused around discovering and satisfying customer needs. All departments (e.g., production, operations, finance, marketing) are highly integrated, share information about customers, and determine how to best serve customer needs. The entire organization's energy is focused on the customer. The guiding principle in such organizations is simple: If your job does not involve serving the customer directly, then your job is supporting the person who does.

Organizations that embrace a market-driven philosophy do not view marketing as a simple business function designed to generate revenue. To the contrary, market-driven organizations emphasize long-term customer relationships. In these organizations, marketing is less about products and more about people and the social processes that link marketplace participants together in ongoing relationships.

A CLOSE LOOK AT THE MARKET-DRIVEN ORGANIZATION

Before we begin our detailed look at marketing as a process, let's take a close look at what characterizes the market-driven organization. Obviously, we believe in marketing as an organizational philosophy and advocate it as the premise upon which an organization is built. Examining what typifies the market-driven organization will help

FIGURE 1–1   The Non-market-driven vs. the Market-driven Organization.

NON-MARKET-DRIVEN ORGANIZATION	MARKET-DRIVEN ORGANIZATION
• Profit is viewed as the sole purpose of the business	• The purpose of the business is to attract and retain customers, profitably
• Emphasis is on the firm and product (internal focus)	• Emphasis is on discovering/satisfying customers' needs (external focus)
• Marketing is a last-in-line function	• Marketing is a first-in-line function
• Marketers are responsible for marketing activities	• Everyone in the organization is involved in marketing
• Customer has residual input into new product process	• Customer is an active partner in the development and adaptation of products
• Emphasis is on telling and selling the customer (monologue)	• Emphasis is on talking with and listening to the customer (dialogue)
• Focus is on short-term, single transactions, or making the sale	• Focus is on building long-term customer relationships

set the context for your understanding of the marketing process, the central focus of this text. In Figure 1–1 we show the major differences between a non-market-driven and a market-driven organization. We illustrate a rather stark contrast between the two types of organizations. But for some organizations moving toward a market-driven philosophy, the differences presented here would be less pronounced.

A non-market-driven organization tends to place its concern for profit before the needs of the customers it wishes to attract. Such organizations' failure to recognize that their assets are of little value without the existence of customers. In contrast, while profits are important for a market-driven organization, they are viewed primarily as a "scorecard" for how well the organization performs in terms of attracting and retaining customers. In short, for the market-driven organization, profit is is seen as the reward for creating and keeping satisfied customers.

In an effort to attract and retain customers, the market-driven organization realizes it must focus its energy on discovering customer needs and satisfying them. The non-market-driven organization focuses on itself and the products it produces. This internal focus is in contrast to the market-driven organization, which looks outwardly; that is, it possesses an external (customer) focus. The market-driven organization is also proactive, evaluating and anticipating the changing needs of its customers.

The organization that is not market-driven often views marketing as a last-in-line function. In other words, marketing is called upon after the fact, to "get rid of product." A market-driven organization, on the other hand, sees marketing as a first-in-line function. For this organization, marketing dictates production and all other business activities undertaken by the organization.

In a non-market-driven organization, the marketing department is told to go off and "do" marketing, while everyone else in the organization is off the hook in terms of marketing responsibilities. In market-driven organizations, marketing is all-pervasive. Everyone is involved in marketing; it is part of their job descriptions. John F. Welch, Jr., CEO of General Electric, suggests that at GE "every effort of every man and woman in the company is focused on satisfying customers' needs."[4] Even if an employee does not deal directly with a customer, that employee is still responsible for supporting the individuals who do work with the customers.

Organizations that are not market-driven tend to develop products first, and then ask what their customers think. More alarming is that many of these organizations will focus their efforts on changing the customers' minds to fit the new product—practicing a "any colour as long as it's black" type of marketing. In contrast, market-driven organizations develop products in partnership with customers and change their products to fit the customer—practicing the "tell us what colour you want" type of marketing. As we will see in later chapters, one of the reasons for the high failure rate of new products is not plugging the customer into the marketing process from the onset.

Because non-market-driven organizations often neglect the customer as the central focus of their business, they have a tendency to simply "tell and sell" the customer. For them, mass media utilizing one-way communication is the preferred mode of conducting business. Market-driven organizations, on the other hand, engage in "dialogue," talking with and listening to the customer. Seeking and using customer feedback clearly separates a market-driven organization from a non-market-driven one.

Lastly, non-market-driven organizations focus on the single transaction or "simply making the sale." Conversely, market-driven organizations view the sale as just the beginning of the relationship between buyer and seller. Energy is focused on building a long-term relationship that is mutually beneficial to both parties. Experts suggest that market-driven organizations have an ongoing relationship focus, making long-term commitments to maintaining and sustaining a relationship with customers by providing quality, value, service, and innovation.[5]

LEARNING CHECK

1. In a non-market-driven organization, marketing is viewed as a _____ function while in a market-driven organization it is seen as a _____ function.

2. Who is responsible for marketing in a market-driven organization?

THE SCOPE OF THE MARKETING PROCESS

Now that you know something about marketing as an organizational philosophy and what characterizes a market-driven organization, let's get back to our discussion of marketing as a process.

Marketing today affects every person and organization. To understand this, let's analyze (1) what a market is, (2) who markets, (3) what is marketed, (4) who benefits from marketing, and (5) how, specifically, consumers benefit from marketing.

What Is a Market?

As you read earlier, a market is made up of potential consumers with the desire and ability to buy a specific product. People who are aware of their unmet needs may have the *desire* to buy the product, but that alone isn't sufficient. People must also have the *ability* to buy; that is, they must have the authority, time, and money.

A market is made up of either ultimate consumers, organizational buyers, or both. **Ultimate consumers** are people who use the goods and services purchased for a household. In contrast, **organizational buyers** are units such as industrial firms, wholesalers, retailers, or other entities that buy goods and services for their own use or for resale. The terms *consumers, buyers,* and *customers* may each be used interchangeably when referring to ultimate consumers and organizational buyers. In this book, you will be able to tell from the example whether the buyers are ultimate consumers or organizational buyers. To get an understanding of the importance of buyers or customers and why they are the focus of the marketing process, read the Marketplace Application box.

MARKETPLACE APPLICATION

The Importance of Customers

To help motivate employees to serve the customers well, L.L. Bean Inc. displays the following poster prominently around its offices. This poster was developed in the late 1880s when L.L. Bean marketed almost exclusively to male customers. Thus, there is no gender bias intended here.

WHAT IS A CUSTOMER?

A Customer is the most important person ever in this office in person or by mail.

A Customer is not dependent on us . . . we are dependent on him.

A Customer is not an interruption of our work . . . he is the purpose of it. We are not doing a favour by serving him, he is doing us a favour by giving us the opportunity to do so.

A Customer is not someone to argue or match wits with. Nobody ever won an argument with a Customer.

A Customer is a person who brings us his wants. It is our job to handle them profitably to him and to ourselves.

1. What do you think of this definition of a customer?
2. Does L.L. Bean appear to be market-driven based on this definition?

SOURCE: Store poster from L.L. Bean Inc., Freeport, Maine.

Who Markets?

Every organization markets! It's obvious that **business firms**—privately owned organizations that serve customers in order to earn profit—market their offerings. These firms may be involved in manufacturing (e.g., Alcan, Chrysler Canada, Global Furniture), retailing (e.g., The Bay, Canadian Tire, Wal-mart), or in providing services (e.g., Air Canada, Canada Trust, Much Music Network). **Nonprofit organizations**—organizations that operate without the intent of earning profit (e.g., charities, hospitals, and government agencies)—also engage in marketing. For example, Canadian colleges and universities use marketing to attract good students, faculty members, and donations while government agencies use marketing to encourage us to quit smoking or to stay fit.

Finally, even individuals market themselves. Certainly entertainers and politicians market themselves. And when you graduate, one of your toughest tasks will be to market yourself to prospective employers. For simplicity, in the rest of the book the terms *company, corporation, firm,* and *organization* will be used to refer to both business and nonprofit operations.

What is Marketed?

Recall that our definition of a product includes goods, services, ideas, places, and people. *Goods* are physical objects, such as toothpaste, cameras, or computers, that satisfy consumer needs. *Services* are activities, deeds, or other basic intangibles offered for sale to consumers in exchange for money or something else of value (e.g., airline trips, financial advice, or telephone calls). In Canada, we spend more money on services than goods, and most Canadians are employed by organizations that market services. Services marketing is such an important new area of marketing that we carefully examine it in Chapter 19.

Some individuals or organizations market ideas. *Ideas* are thoughts about certain actions or causes (e.g., don't drink and drive). Places, such as countries, provinces,

New Brunswick being marketed as a vacation spot.

cities, or towns are often marketed as tourist destinations or as suitable sites to establish businesses. People, such as politicians, celebrities, and prospective employees are also marketed. Some of these goods, services, ideas, places and people—such as lawn mowers, dry cleaning, annual physical examinations, New Brunswick as a vacation spot, and a Celine Dion concert—may be bought or accepted by individuals for their own use or enjoyment. Others, such as high-volume office copiers and vending machine repair services, are bought by organizations. Finally, the products marketed in today's shrinking globe are increasingly likely to cross a nation's boundaries and involve exports, imports, and global or international marketing (Chapter 18).

Who Benefits?

In our free-enterprise society there are three specific groups that benefit from effective marketing: consumers who buy, organizations that market, and society as a whole. First, true competition between products and services in the marketplace ensures that we consumers can obtain (1) the best products and services available (2) at the lowest price. Providing the maximum number of choices leads to the consumer satisfaction and quality of life that we have come to expect from our economic system.

Organizations that provide need-satisfying products with effective marketing actions—for example McDonald's, Apple, BMW, and the Royal Bank—have blossomed, but this competition creates problems for the ineffective competitors that often go out of business. Effective marketing actions result in rewards for organizations that serve consumers and in millions of marketing jobs.

Finally, effective marketing benefits the whole country. It enhances competition, which in turn both improves the quality of products and services and lowers their prices. This makes the country more competitive in global or international markets, and provides jobs and a higher standard of living for its citizens.

The marketing and
purchase of golf clubs;
meeting the requirements
for the marketing
process.

How Do Consumers Benefit?

In simple terms, consumers benefit from the marketing process by receiving basic value. Marketing creates value by providing consumers with the right goods or services, at the right place, and at the right time. As we will see later in this chapter, successful marketers will be the ones who can create and deliver the best overall value to their customers.

Requirements for the Marketing Process to Occur

For the marketing process to occur, at least four factors are required: (1) two or more parties (individuals or organizations) with unsatisfied needs, (2) a desire and ability on their part to be satisfied, (3) a way for the parties to communicate, and (4) something to exchange.

Two or More Parties with Unsatisfied Needs. Suppose you had an unmet need—a desire for a new set of golf clubs that would improve your game—but you didn't know that such a product existed. Also unknown to you was that several new sets of game-improving clubs were on display at your local sporting goods store, waiting to be bought. This is an example of two parties with unmet needs; you, with your need for the golf clubs, and your sporting goods store owner, needing someone to buy the newly designed clubs.

Desire and Ability to Satisfy These Needs. Both you and the sporting goods store owner want to satisfy your respective unmet needs. Furthermore, you have the money to buy the product and the time to go to the store. The store owner has not only the desire to sell the new golf clubs but also the ability to do so, since the clubs are currently in stock.

LEARNING CHECK

1. Products include goods, _____, ideas, _____, and people.

2. When you go to your dentist you are buying what type of product?

3. What are the three groups that benefit from effective marketing?

A Way for the Parties to Communicate. The marketing transaction of buying the new golf clubs will never occur unless you are aware that the product exists and know where to buy them. Similarly, the store owner won't stock the product unless there's a market of potential consumers near the store who are likely to buy. When you see an ad for the new golf clubs, this communication barrier between you (the buyer) and the sporting goods store (the seller) is overcome.

Something to Exchange. Marketing occurs when the transaction takes place and both the buyer and seller exchange something of value. In this case, you exchange your money for the store's new golf clubs. Both of you have gained something and also given up something, but you are both better off because you have each satisfied your unmet needs. You have the opportunity to use the new golf clubs to help improve your game, but you gave up some money; the store gave up the golf clubs but received money, which enables it to remain in business. While this example focuses on one single exchange, remember that the new emphasis in marketing is on developing long-term relationships with customers over time.

Discovering and Satisfying Consumer Needs Through the Marketing Process

Ultimately, the marketing process involves (1) discovering and (2) satisfying consumers' real needs. Figure 1–2 shows the process of discovering consumer needs and satisfying them. As you can see, in an effective organization this process is continuous: Consumer needs trigger product concepts that are translated into actual products that stimulate further discovery of consumer needs. The importance of discovering consumers' needs and satisfying them is so critical to understanding the marketing process that we look at each of these two steps below.

Discovering Consumer Needs. The first step in the marketing process is discovering the needs of prospective consumers. Sounds simple? Well, it's not. In the abstract,

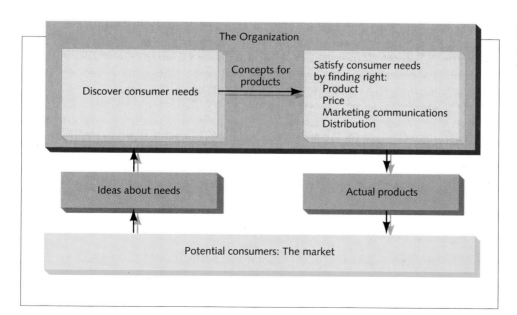

FIGURE 1–2
The marketing process: discovering and satisfying consumer needs.

FIGURE 1–3
Clinique's basic marketing
strategy.

TARGET MARKET	Upper income, well-educated professionals (men and women) who are health- and appearance conscious
MARKETING MIX	
Product	High-quality cosmetics and facial/body care items
Price	High (premium) priced
Marketing Communications	Targeted magazine advertising, and personal selling to consumers in stores
Distribution	Upscale department stores and specialty shops

discovering needs looks easy, but when you get down to the specifics, problems crop up. Thousands of products fail in the Canadian marketplace every year. Two major reasons are that in each case the firm either failed to carefully examine consumers' needs or simply misread them.

It is frequently very difficult to get a precise reading on what consumers need, especially when they are confronted with revolutionary ideas for new products. In order to reduce the risk of product failure, marketers must carefully scrutinize the consumers to understand what they really need. The marketer must also study industry trends and examine competitors' products. One way for marketers to better understand consumers' needs is to talk with and listen to consumers. Through dialogue and active participation of both parties, buyer and seller, marketing effectiveness can be improved.

Satisfying Consumer Needs. After properly discovering consumer needs, the firm must begin the task of satisfying those needs. Since the organization cannot satisfy all consumer needs, it must concentrate its efforts on certain needs of a specific group of potential consumers. This is the **target market,** one or more specific groups of consumers toward which an organization directs its marketing efforts. Selecting target markets to satisfy involves the process of **market segmentation,** or aggregating prospective buyers into groups, known as *market segments,* that (1) have common needs and (2) will respond similarly to a specific marketing offer. After evaluating those market segments, an organization will select a segment or segments to pursue—its target market. The marketing offer, designed to appeal to the target market and to satisfy its needs, is called the **marketing mix.**

The marketer constructs the marketing mix by making decisions in four basic areas: *product* (development of a good, service, or idea to satisfy the consumer's needs), *price* (what is exchanged for the product), *marketing communications* (a means of communicating between buyer and seller, and *distribution* (a means of getting the product into the consumer's hands).[6] Selecting a target market and developing a marketing mix to satisfy that market's needs is called a **marketing strategy.** Figure 1–3 shows the basic marketing strategy developed by Clinique. The selection of target markets and

LEARNING CHECK

1. An organization can't satisfy the needs of all consumers so it must focus on one or more specific groups of potential consumers, which is its _____.

2. What are the four marketing mix elements?

FIGURE 1–4
Factors influencing the marketing process.

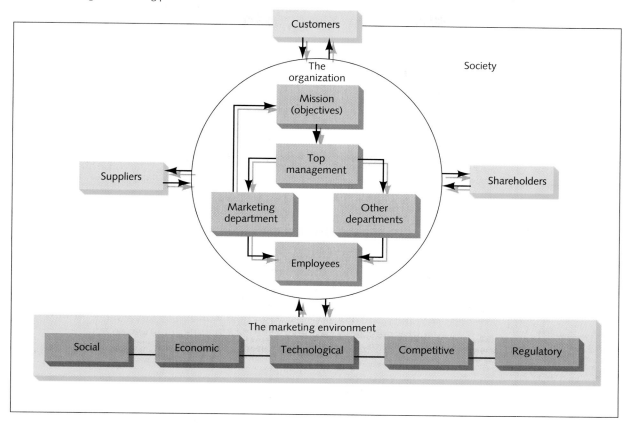

the proper blending of marketing mix elements in order to produce successful marketing strategies will be discussed more carefully throughout the book.

Factors Influencing the Marketing Process

Although the marketing process focuses on discovering and satisfying consumer needs, countless people, groups, and other forces interact to shape it (Figure 1–4). Foremost is the organization itself, whose mission determines what business it is in and what objectives it seeks. Within the organization, top management is responsible for achieving these objectives. The marketing department works closely with other departments and employees to help provide the customer-satisfying products required for the organization to survive and grow.

Figure 1–4 also shows the key people, groups, and forces outside the organization that influence the marketing process. In addition to customers, two groups with an important stake in the organization's success are its shareholders (or, if the organization is nonprofit, representatives of groups it serves) and its suppliers. The **marketing environment**—social, economic, technological, competitive, and regulatory forces, at home and abroad—also shape the organization's marketing process. While this external marketing environment is largely beyond the control of the organization, it is a source of opportunities to be capitalized on and threats to be avoided or managed. The marketing environment is covered in detail in Chapter 3.

FIGURE 1–5
Possible marketing roles
in an organization.

ROLE/POSITION	RESPONSIBILITIES
Vice President of Marketing	Organizes and manages the overall marketing activities of the organization
Advertising Manager	Develops and implements ad campaigns with inhouse staff, or works with an outside advertising agency to produce an ad program
Marketing Researcher	Conducts market or customer studies in order to help the organization effectively market its products (services)
Sales Manager	Organizes, manages, and evaluates the sales force
Product (Service) Manager	Develops and/or manages the products (or services) the organization markets
Distribution Manager	Manages the distribution system including storage, inventory control, and transportation for products

Finally, an organization's marketing decisions are affected by, and in turn often have an important impact on, society as a whole. The organization must strike a continual balance among these individuals and groups, whose objectives sometimes conflict. For example, it is not possible to simultaneously provide the lowest-priced and highest-quality products to customers and pay the highest prices to suppliers, highest wages to employees, and maximum dividends to shareholders.

Your Possible Role in the Marketing Process

Within a particular organization, there are a variety of formal marketing roles that you may play in the marketing process. Figure 1–5 shows just some of these possible roles. You may be part of a new-product team involved in the design of new products, or work as product manager responsible for the growth of existing products. You may play a role conducting consumer or marketing research, spending time studying what people buy and why they buy, or collecting marketing information on competitors. You could also be responsible for the advertising campaign your company is running.

You might be involved in selecting stores to carry your company's products, or managing the sales force that sells the products. Finally, you may not actually work in a formal marketing position. Remember that in market-driven organizations, all employees are involved in the marketing process. So while you may work in accounting or production, you will probably work closely with or provide support for others who develop and execute the marketing activities involved in the marketing process.

SEVEN IMPERATIVES FOR MARKETING SUCCESS

The marketplace, on a global basis, is experiencing rapid changes. On one hand, organizations are faced with ever-increasing levels of foreign and domestic competition. On the other hand, organizations are experiencing a growing number of extremely demanding consumers who are asking, What have you done for me lately? After evaluating major trends in the market, we have established seven imperatives that the market-driven organization should follow in order to ensure its success in the future. We

FIGURE 1–6
Seven imperatives for
marketing success.

1. Have a global outlook.
2. Commit to quality.
3. Deliver customer value.
4. Innovate continuously.
5. Embrace technology.
6. Practise relationship
   marketing.
7. Act ethically and responsibly.

believe that truly market-driven organizations will embrace these imperatives and, inevitably, will dominate the industries in which they compete. The imperatives are shown in Figure 1–6. Let's talk briefly about each of them.

Have a Global Outlook

Whether they like it or not, most organizations find themselves competing in a global arena. Today, markets for many products and services are global in scope rather than local, regional, or national. Advances in travel, communications, and technology, as well as freer trade among nations have helped create this highly competitive global environment. It is not a time for companies to look inwardly. Organizations with a global outlook view the world as a potential marketplace and are prepared to search for opportunities around the globe. They also recognize that if they don't go after foreign markets, foreign competition will surely come after theirs.

As we will discuss in detail in Chapter 18, there is a difference between companies that are engaged in **international marketing,** marketing across national boundaries, and those companies that can truly be considered global corporations. A **global**

Coca-Cola is a global
corporation.

Chrysler Canada's Focus on Quality has made its minivans the leader in its category.

corporation is a business firm that looks at the entire world as one market and conducts research and development, manufacturing, and marketing activities wherever they can best be done. Such firms have a truly global focus—national boundaries and regulations are largely irrelevant. A global corporation runs its business and makes its decisions on the basis of all possible choices in the world, not simply favouring domestic options because they are convenient.

There are very few firms in Canada or the United States that can be considered global corporations. Ford and Coca-Cola are two examples of companies that function on a global dimension. But many Canadian firms, large and small, are engaged in international marketing activities. They may not operate on a truly global scale, but do have a global outlook. Ganong Brothers, a candy manufacturer, operates production facilities in New Brunswick and Thailand, and markets its product in more than a half-dozen countries. Sico, a paint manufacturer in Quebec, also markets in Mexico and Vietnam. Even small Christmas tree farmers in Nova Scotia market their products as far away as South America.

Most Canadian firms will never achieve true global corporation status, but they can still possess a global outlook and seek opportunities in international markets. Over 95 percent of the world's population lives outside of Canada. The markets outside our country are substantial and many are growing faster than comparable markets at home. Many Canadian companies recognize this fact. Even many new small businesses (firms with fewer than 20 employees) start their operations with a global outlook. For example, upstart Canadian Iceberg Vodka Corp. of Newfoundland targeted Los Angeles as its first market. The company sells vodka made with, you guessed it, iceberg water, and has secured a distribution agreement that will see 750,000 cases being shipped to L.A. over the next six years. In Chapter 18, we will discuss strategies for successfully competing in the global or international marketing arena.[7]

Commit to Quality

Quality has become a watchword for many organizations. To be truly effective, an organization must focus on quality as defined by the customer. In this case, **quality** can be defined as the features or characteristics of the product itself that bear upon its ability to satisfy customers' needs. To the customer, there are many dimensions to quality, such as performance, features, reliability, durability, or serviceability. Organizations

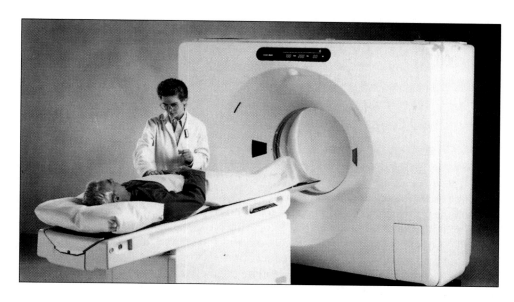

GE's medical systems division offers CAT scanners from $350,000 to over $1 million each, tailored specifically to the imaging needs of its hospital customers.

must determine which of these dimensions are important to the customer and commit to providing quality on those dimensions.

Some companies concentrate on meeting or exceeding certain standards or specifications established internally—without input from the customer. For example, one fast-food company set a standard of serving a customer in under 90 seconds, assuming it was making a commitment to "quality service" to the customer. However, while speed of service was important to the customer, the quality of the food was even more important. Unfortunately, in an effort to deliver the food quickly, the company compromised on food quality and lost business. So the lesson is simple: Find out which dimensions of quality are most important to the customer and deliver on those dimensions.

Research shows that companies that can provide quality products or services "as defined by the customer," can create strong customer loyalty. Evidence also shows that a commitment to quality improves profitability in two ways. First, improved quality increases productivity and reduces costs. Second, companies that produce high-quality products or services can usually charge more than their competitors.

Deliver Customer Value

Customer value is a related but much broader concept than quality. **Customer value** can be defined as the combination of benefits received by customers that includes quality, price, convenience, on-time delivery, and both before- and after-sale service. In general, marketers who place increased emphasis on quality will increase the customer's perception of value. However, marketers must also focus on delivering "overall value" to the customer, of which quality will be a component.

For example, BMW believes it makes a quality automobile, as do most of its customers. But BMW knows that if you buy one of its cars, and your dealer does not deliver it when promised, or if the dealer was rude or indifferent to you during the buying process, then your perception of the "value" of owning a BMW is diminished. This is why a quality product, by itself, does not guarantee marketing success; overall customer value must also be delivered.[8]

Toyota is one of the leaders in the innovation game.

Like quality, there are many dimensions to customer value, and marketers must deliver on the dimensions most important to the customer. Two management experts believe organizations can be successful by focusing on one of three customer value strategies: (1) provide customers with reliable offerings at competitive prices and with the most convenient delivery; (2) tailor product offerings to the exact demands of your customers; or (3) provide customers with leading-edge offerings that enhance use by customers to make competitors' offerings obsolete.[9]

Innovate Continuously

In an effort to stay ahead of competitors, and in order to provide customers with better value, market-driven organizations must strive to find ways to improve their existing products, develop new products, and deliver increased levels of customer service. Many market-driven firms have embraced the Japanese practice of *kaizen,* or "continuous improvement." Firms that practice kaizen are permanently dissatisfied with even exemplary performance. In other words, they are always seeking ways to do better. At Toyota, for example, employees generate about three million ideas a year for improving some aspects of their products or company, and Toyota implements about 90 percent of them. In this way, Toyota continues to outperform many of its competitors in the automotive market. Some experts believe that the organizations that win the innovation game will be the market leaders of tomorrow.[10]

Embrace Technology

Technological change spares few markets. Advances in technology can create new markets, while forever altering or destroying others. It creates new products and renders others obsolete (e.g., CDs vs. LPs or record albums). Technology can also change the way companies do business. For example, computerized checkout scanners in the supermarket allow retailers to monitor which products are selling and at what price. Hand-held computers are being used by companies like Frito-Lay to allow delivery people to monitor in-store sales promotions and send sales reports directly to company headquarters. Avis and Hertz use hand-held computers to speed up the return of rental cars. Benetton gathers information on consumer purchases electronically and sends it instantly over high-speed fibre-optic lines for analysis. Compusearch, a market analysis company, offers a variety of desktop marketing information systems that help Canadian companies select proper business locations, segment markets, and evaluate market opportunities. MarketMath, Compusearch's premier desktop system, is purpose-built software designed to help marketers answer the questions, "Who are my customers, where do they live, and how can I reach them?"

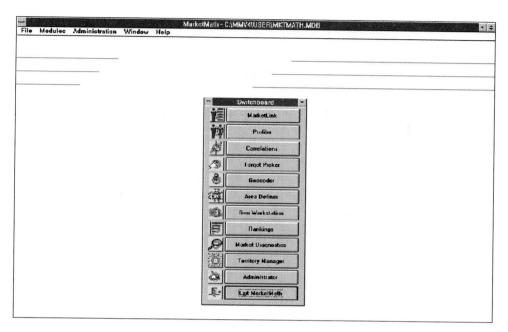

MarketMath is a modular Windows-based desktop system that gives marketers the capability to profile, geocode, analyze their trade areas, rank territories or areas, write reports, and so forth.

Advances in technology must be viewed as opportunities and not threats to an organization. Technological advances should be used to help develop the right products and to reach the right consumers at lower costs. New technologies can improve product quality, production processes, distribution, communications, pricing techniques, and marketing research. Cellular phones, fax machines, notebook computers, on-line databases, and decision-support systems are all part of the arsenal of the market-driven organization. From desktop personal computers to satellites in space, technology improves decision making, keeps the organization close to the customer, and enhances the level of customer service. Organizations that openly embrace and seek out technological advancements improve their chances of success in the marketplace.[11]

Practise Relationship Marketing

As we mentioned earlier in this chapter, market-driven organizations view the sale as just the beginning of the relationship between themselves and their customer. Marketing success will be based largely on how well an organization can build and solidify relationships with their customers. **Relationship marketing** is defined as an organization's effort to develop a long-term, cost-effective link with individual customers for mutual benefit.[12]

The goal of relationship marketing is to retain loyal customers over time by demonstrating a personal commitment to do whatever is necessary to satisfy the customer. Relationship marketing requires that the marketer do three things: (1) connect with the customer on a personal level, (2) converse with the customer, and (3) cultivate a meaningful relationship with the customer over time. Providing value and demonstrating respect and appreciation to the customer are vital elements in relationship marketing.

In order to successfully build relationships with customers, a firm also needs to develop a good working relationship with organizations that assist it in the marketing process. This includes suppliers, distributors, advertising agencies, and

ETHICS INSIGHT

The Body Shop's Community Trading Policy

When Anita Roddick founded The Body Shop in 1976, her idea was the ultimate in simplicity: to offer naturally based cosmetic products, created without the use of animal testing, and to make them available in a variety of sizes to suit every customer's needs. Today it's a little more complex than that.

As part of The Body Shop's policy for Trading with Communities in Need ("Community Trade"), Anita Roddick searches the globe for indigenous communities who can provide ingredients or accessory items to enhance her company's extensive product offering—from Brazil nut oil for shampoos, conditioners, and body lotions to scrub mitts woven out of cactus fibers. The goal of Community Trade, formerly known as "Trade Not Aid," is to help create livelihoods and to support sustainable development by sourcing items directly from socially and economically marginalized producer communities. The Body Shop pays First World prices for Third World products in countries such as Brazil, Nepal, Ghana, and Bangladesh. In doing so, it believes it helps local communities acquire the tools and resources to support and sustain themselves.

1. How do The Body Shop's Community Trade projects affect its customers, employees, owners, and suppliers?

2. The Body Shop makes a conscious decision to pay First World prices for Third World products in order to help communities in developing nations. Is it unethical for other companies not to do the same?

market research firms. Applying relationship marketing in this manner creates a *network organization,* a loose and flexible coalition of partners that are focused on the customer.[13]

Happy and satisfied employees are also needed if relationship marketing efforts with customers are to be successful. Relationship marketing applied internally really becomes relationship management. Cooperation and teamwork within the organization are encouraged and emphasized. Efforts are made to develop the "people skills" of the employees and all departments are organized and integrated to achieve one goal: to keep the customer satisfied.

Today, more organizations recognize the importance of managing a long-term relationship with customers. Moreover, the development and use of databases has helped facilitate the art and practice of relationship marketing. The organizations that focus on relationship marketing and not on just making and selling products are likely to become the market leaders in their field.[14]

Act Ethically and Responsibly

Ethics are the moral principles and values that govern the actions and decisions of an individual or a group. Ethics serve as guidelines on how to act rightly and justly when

Green marketing.

faced with moral dilemmas. Many marketing decisions go beyond legal dimensions to include ethical ones.

Social responsibility means that organizations are part of a larger society and are accountable to that society for their actions. Specifically, social responsibility refers to the obligations that organizations have to (1) the preservation of the ecological environment and (2) society in general.

Companies must recognize that while ethical and socially responsible behaviour often comes with a price tag, the price for unethical and socially irresponsible behaviour is often much higher. Companies can "do well by doing good" because the company behind the product is important to many consumers. An organization with good corporate character and substance can attract customers.

Similarly, ecologically sensitive organizations are often the preferred choice of customers. More frequently, organizations are getting involved in *green marketing*—efforts to produce, market, and reclaim ecologically or environmentally sensitive products.

At the same time, socially responsible efforts on behalf of society are becoming more common. A formal practice is *cause-related marketing (CRM),* which occurs when the charitable contributions of a firm are tied directly to the customer revenues produced through the marketing of one of its products. This distinguishes CRM from a firm's standard charitable contributions, which are outright donations. Many Canadian firms such as Bank of Montreal engage in CRM for causes such as raising money for children's hospitals.

LEARNING CHECK

1. What is (a) international marketing and (b) a global corporation?

2. Quality can be defined as _____ .

3. What is customer value?

LEARNING OBJECTIVE REINFORCEMENT

1. Define marketing and understand it as a process and as an organizational philosophy. Marketing as a process occurs on two levels: micromarketing and macromarketing. Micromarketing examines how an individual organization directs its marketing activities and allocates its resources to benefit its customers. Macromarketing involves the aggregate flow of a nation's goods and services to benefit society. At the micromarketing level, marketing as a process can be defined as planning and executing the conception, pricing, communications, and distribution of products to create exchanges that satisfy individual and organizational objectives. Organizations that embrace marketing as an organizational philosophy seek to discover and satisfy customer needs with a totally integrated organizational effort.

2. Describe the characteristics of a market-driven organization. In a market-driven organization, the entire organization's energy is focused on the customer. The purpose of the business is to attract and retain customers, profitably. The emphasis is on discovering and satisfying customers' needs. Marketing is seen as a first-in-line function and everyone in the organization is involved in marketing. The customer is an active partner in the development and adaptation of products. The organization focuses on communicating and building long-term relationships with the customer.

3. Understand the scope of the marketing process. Marketing affects every person and organization. Markets consist of consumers (ultimate consumers and organizational buyers) with the desire and ability to buy products. Goods, services, ideas, places, and people are marketed. Consumers who buy, organizations that market, and society as a whole benefit from effective marketing.

4. Know what is required for marketing to occur. For the marketing process to occur, at least four factors are required:

(1) two or more parties (individuals or organizations) with unsatisfied needs, (2) a desire and ability on their part to be satisfied, (3) a way for the parties to communicate, and (4) something to exchange.

5. Explain the two critical steps in the marketing process: (1) discovering and (2) satisfying consumers' real needs. The first step in the marketing process is discovering the needs of prospective consumers. To do this, marketers must carefully scrutinize the consumers to understand what they really need. The marketer must also study industry trends and examine competitors' products. After properly discovering consumers' needs, the firm must begin the task of satisfying those needs. Since the organization cannot satisfy all consumer needs, it must concentrate its efforts on certain needs of a specific group of potential consumers, called the target market—one or more specific groups of consumers (market segments) toward which an organization directs its marketing efforts.

6. Understand the marketing mix and the marketing environment. In order to satisfy the consumers in the target market, an organization must develop a marketing mix, or an overall marketing offer, designed to appeal to the target market and to satisfy their needs. The marketing mix consists of product, price, marketing communications, and distribution dimensions. The marketing environment consists of social, economic, technological, competitive, and regulatory forces, at home and abroad, that shape the organization's marketing process.

7. Outline the seven imperatives for marketing success. There are seven imperatives that the market-driven organization should follow in order to ensure its success in the future. These are: (1) have a global outlook, (2) commit to quality, (3) deliver customer value, (4) innovate continuously, (5) embrace technology, (6) practise relationship marketing, and (7) act ethically and responsibly.

KEY TERMS AND CONCEPTS

micromarketing p. 5
macromarketing p. 5
marketing p. 5
product p. 5
market p. 5
exchange p. 5
product-driven organization p. 6
sales-driven organization p. 7
market-driven organization p. 7

ultimate consumer p. 9
organizational buyer p. 9
business firm p. 10
nonprofit organization p. 10
target market p. 14
market segmentation p. 14
marketing mix p. 14
marketing strategy p. 14
marketing environment p. 15

international marketing p. 17
global corporation p. 17–18
quality p. 18
customer value p. 19
relationship marketing p. 21
ethics p. 22
social responsibility p. 23

CHAPTER QUESTIONS AND APPLICATIONS

1. Do you think that cyberspace malls will eventually replace traditional shopping malls? Why or why not?

2. Find an example of a product-driven organization, a sales-driven organization, and a market-driven organization. Explain why you have classified them in this manner.

3. There is an old saying that states, "If you build a better mousetrap, people will beat a path to your door." Given what you now know about marketing, do you think this is a true statement?

4. What is the target market and the marketing mix for your college or university?

5. In developing a marketing mix for your college or university, what forces in the marketing environment you would consider important to analyze and evaluate?

6. Interview someone who works in a marketing position. Ask this person for his or her definition of marketing. Also, ask this person what marketing activities he or she is involved with on a routine basis. Write up a brief report.

7. If you were to select one organization in Canada that you would like to work for, what organization would it be and why?

8. Do you think organizations are more or less ethical than they were 20 years ago. Explain.

9. Do you think Canadian products, in general, are better than, comparable to, or not as good as Japanese products? Explain your answer with some examples.

10. Of the seven imperatives for marketing success cited in the book, which one, in your opinion, is the most critical for organizations to embrace?

ADVICE FOR DOING CASE ANALYSIS

Short cases are presented at the end of each chapter. These cases are designed to help illustrate the material discussed in the text, to improve your reasoning skills, and to facilitate class discussions. At the end of the text there are longer cases designed to improve your ability to make marketing decisions.

All the cases are contemporary and cover situations faced by a range of organizations and individuals involved in marketing. Each case ends with a series of questions designed to help you focus your attention on key issues confronting the organizations and individuals in the case. The case-ending questions also help you examine the organization's or individual's response to the issues, and provide you with an opportunity to take the position of marketing decision maker. You should be able to answer these questions by analyzing the case and using the material in the appropriate chapter to which the case relates.

In doing case analysis, keep this advice in mind:

- Read all the case material carefully and thoroughly.
- Examine and understand all important data that is presented, including any tables and figures.
- Use the case-ending questions to help focus your analysis.
- Determine the key issues or problems outlined in the case. Most cases have one central problem. Generally, all other issues are an outgrowth of that central problem.
- Do not confuse symptoms with problems. For example, if sales have dropped, this may be only symptomatic of an underlying or real root problem.
- Do not make unrealistic or unsupported assumptions.

- Develop a draft list of your responses to the case-ending questions.
- Be sure to identify the central problem and make a list of possible alternative courses of action that could be considered to solve that problem.
- Your list of alternative courses of action should also include the advantages and disadvantages (pros and cons) of each. Generally, two or three alternatives should be considered.
- Clearly state why you believe one course of action is the most appropriate for the organization or individual to take. Use your analysis to support your decision.
- Some instructors will want you to answer the case-ending questions and present those answers in class. Others may ask for a traditional case analysis report. Such a report will generally include: (1) case situation, (2) problem or issue statement, (3) alternative courses of action, and (4) recommendation for action. In doing a traditional case analysis report be sure that you have also answered the case-ending questions in your report.
- Be sure to write clearly. Make sure your response is logical and well-connected.
- Be sure to avoid "case rehash." Do not simply discuss or present the obvious facts in the case; do *real* analysis.
- Do not be afraid to present your answers in a convincing and confident manner.

APPLICATION CASE 1–1
DR. HOWARD

Dr. Andy Howard graduated near the top of his class from one of the best medical schools in Canada. He was looking forward to a successful career as a family practitioner. He had decided early on that he would return to practice in his hometown of Welchville, so shortly after graduation he headed home. He knew there were other physicians practicing in the town of 20,000, but he felt he could easily start and build his own practice given his solid medical training.

Dr. Howard soon found ample office space to lease in a downtown professional building. The office complex was home to some other physicians and it also contained a ground floor pharmacy. He felt this location was ideal for his practice, so he signed a five-year lease. In short order he equipped his office, hired office staff, and had his name listed on the office building directory in the lobby. His office telephone number was assigned and oper-

ational. However, the new telephone directory would not be out for five months, so both his white and yellow page listing would not appear until that time. Until then, he felt that prospective patients who knew he was back in town would simply call and request his telephone number from the operator.

The weekend before he opened his office Dr. Howard had dinner at a friend's home. His friend was a business professor at the local college. He told Dr. Howard that a few other physicians had left Welchville in recent years because they were unable to build their practices. He suggested that Dr. Howard should be a little more aggressive in letting people know he was back in town and looking for patients.

Dr. Howard responded by saying that he wasn't selling used cars and that people would always need good medical care. He suggested that the notion of marketing was unseemly to him. Moreover, even if he wanted to do some marketing, the medical profession tightly regulated the scope and nature of all marketing activities that could be undertaken by physicians. For example, physicians could not advertise on television or radio, and they could not use direct mail. Print ads were allowed but only if they took the form of public announcements such as the commencement or closing of a practice. Name, telephone number, and location were about the only things that could be listed in the print announcements. Dr. Howard believed that when people found out he was in town, he would have no problem obtaining patients. He expected to be proven correct on Monday morning.

QUESTIONS
1. Would you say Dr. Howard is product-driven, sales-driven, or market-driven? Explain.
2. What type of product is Dr. Howard offering to prospective customers?
3. For the marketing process to occur, the text states that at least four factors are required. What are they? Are the requirements met in this case?

APPLICATION CASE 1-2
THE CANADIAN-AMERICAN TOURIST IMBALANCE

For many years the number of Canadian tourists visiting the United States has far exceeded the number of Americans who visit Canada. The imbalance reached about 7 million tourists in both 1991 and 1992. But by 1995, things were improving: 12.9 million American tourists visited Canada while 14.6 million Canadians visited the United States (an imbalance of 1.7 million). While this helped bring Canada's travel trade imbalance down, the deficit was still a worrisome $3.55 billion.

The Canadian government wants to reduce or eliminate this travel–trade imbalance. It's not a matter of Canadian pride but the travel deficit that is the motivating factor. A marketing campaign designed to bring the travel–trade numbers into balance is being considered. The Canadian government is looking for your assistance with this campaign.

QUESTIONS
1. Who would be your primary target market(s) for your "vacation in Canada" marketing campaign?
2. What would be the best way to reach these target market(s)?
3. What message would you use to appeal to your primary target market(s)?

FOODSERVICE

AND

HOSPITALITY

CANADA'S HOSPITALITY BUSINESS MAGAZINE

CHAPTER 2

Marketing's Role in the Organization

AFTER READING THIS CHAPTER YOU WILL BE ABLE TO:

1. Understand the concept of strategic planning and marketing's role in that process.

2. Define the terms, mission statement, objectives, and growth strategies.

3. Explain the alternative growth strategies available to an organization.

4. Understand the planning, implementation, and control phases of marketing management.

5. Outline what is included in a good marketing plan.

6. Explain the alternative ways to organize the marketing management effort and the role of a product manager.

7. Understand the procedures used to control and evaluate the marketing plan.

McDONALD'S: THE RIGHT BLEND OF PLANNING AND EXECUTION

In 1955 Ray Kroc bought seven restaurants owned by Richard and Maurice McDonald. Kroc liked their fast-food concept and had a plan for its future success. He would expand the business by selling franchises, and adhere to rigid standards of quality, service, cleanliness, and value (QSC&V). In short, Kroc planned to offer his customers clean restaurants, friendly service, and quick, good-tasting meals at reasonable prices.

One person who believed in the McDonald's system was George Cohon, chairman, president, and CEO of McDonald's Restaurants of Canada. Chicago-born Cohon had been a lawyer before he came to Canada and opened a McDonald's franchise in 1968. Within a few years he and a partner had opened 14 stores.

By 1986, through successful planning and execution Cohon had turned Canada into the most mature and successful of McDonald's international ventures. Consumers from Newfoundland to British Columbia now have the opportunity to enjoy McDonald's fare. But while Cohon was pleased with McDonald's expansion across Canada, he believed that Russians were also yearning for a helping of QSC&V. He made plans to bring the McDonald's concept to Moscow. His planning paid off: Cohon successfully opened the first McDonald's restaurant in Moscow in 1990. A major processing facility designed to supply the 20 restaurants planned for the city was also completed. By 1995, McDonald's had opened its third restaurant, as well as an office tower, in Moscow, and the corporation is currently expanding into St. Petersburg.

In little more than 40 years, the McDonald's system of fast-food restaurants has become a global business phenomenon—the largest food-service organization in the world. McDonald's Corporation currently has over 14,000 outlets in more than 70 countries ringing in $23 billion in annual systemwide sales. Most experts agree, McDonald's is a market-driven success story. It had a plan for growth, and executed it efficiently and effectively.

This chapter introduces you to marketing's role in the organization. It describes strategic planning and marketing's role in that process. It also outlines how market-driven organizations plan, implement, and control marketing efforts that allow them to grow and prosper in a dynamic marketplace. Lastly, it introduces you to many of the important aspects of marketing that are detailed in the chapters that follow.

STRATEGIC PLANNING

All organizations must look ahead and develop strategies that will meet changing conditions in the markets in which they compete. Yet many organizations operate without formal strategic plans. In new organizations, managers are often too busy for planning. In small businesses, owner/managers generally assume that only large organizations need formal planning.[1] In organizations that have been around for a long time, many managers argue that they have done well without formal planning, so why start now?

Formal planning can provide many benefits to all types of organizations, large and small, new and old. It encourages management to take stock, to look closely at where the organization has been, where it is now, and where it is heading. It forces the organization to look outwardly and to evaluate its objectives and policies in light of the marketing environment. It also helps the organization anticipate, prepare, and respond to sudden environmental changes.

Strategic planning is the process by which an organization examines its capabilities and the changing marketing environment in order to identify its mission, objectives, and strategies for growth. As you can see in Figure 2–1, strategic planning sets the stage for the rest of the planning in the organization. First, the organization defines its overall purpose or mission. It then determines specific objectives that guide the entire organization. Next, it decides which growth strategies will allow it to achieve its objectives. Usually a document, called the organization's strategic plan, emerges from this process. In turn, managers must develop detailed marketing and other departmental plans that support the organization's strategic plan. Marketing plans, in particular, are designed to support the organization's strategic plan with more detailed planning for specific marketing opportunities.

Marketing's Role in Strategic Planning

Much overlap exists between overall organizational strategic planning and marketing planning. Marketing discovers consumer needs and the organization's ability to satisfy them; these same factors guide the organization's mission and objectives. Most organizational strategic planning deals with marketing variables—market potential, market growth—and it is sometimes difficult to separate strategic planning from marketing planning. In fact, many market-driven organizations simply refer to their strategic planning as "strategic marketing planning."[2]

Marketing plays a key role in the organization's strategic planning in three basic ways. First, marketing provides a basic philosophy—the market-driven philosophy—which suggests the organization's overall strategy should focus on satisfying customer needs. Second, marketing provides inputs into strategic planning by helping to identify attractive market opportunities and by assessing the organization's capabilities to ex-

FIGURE 2–1 Steps in strategic planning.

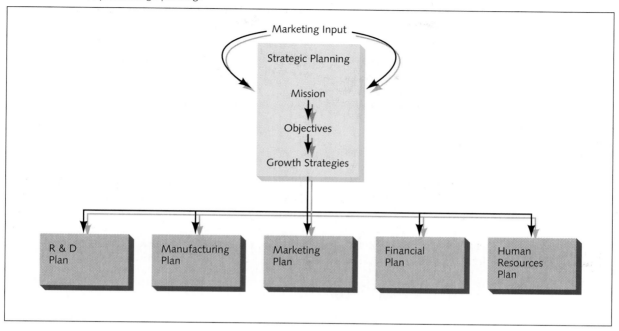

ploit those opportunities. Third, marketing plays an integrative role to help ensure that all departments work together to satisfy customer needs. So while an organization's marketing plan flows logically from the the overall strategic plan, marketing plays a critical role in the development of the organization's strategic plan. Helmut Maucher, chairman of Switzerland's Nestlé, with sales of over $67 billion last year, suggests the company owes its success to marketing. According to Maucher, marketing starts at the very top of the organization.[3]

The Organization's Mission

In order to be successful, an organization must have a defined purpose or **mission.** In the beginning an organization may have a clear mission, but over time its mission may become unclear as the organization grows. Or the mission may remain clear, but employees may no longer be committed to it. Or the mission may remain clear, but may not be the best choice given changes in the marketing environment.

Successful organizations continuously ask themselves questions that will help validate, clarify, or renew their mission. What business are we in? Who is our customer? What do customers need? What business should we be in? These simple-sounding questions are often very difficult to answer, but nonetheless they must be answered.

In an effort to do so, many organizations develop formal mission statements. A **mission statement** is a statement that defines the organization's purpose—what it wants to accomplish. The mission statement also defines what type of customer the organization wishes to serve, the specific needs of customers, and the means or technology by which it will serve these needs. In essence, the mission statement clarifies the nature of existing products, markets, and functions the organization presently provides.

At Nestlé, marketing
starts at the top.

The mission statement affects the organization's growth prospects by establishing guidelines for selecting opportunities in light of the organization's capabilities, customer needs, competitors' actions, and changes in the marketing environment. Many companies have also established "corporate core values or guiding principles" that reinforce their mission statement and help clarify it to employees and customers (Figure 2–2).

Organizational Objectives

The second step in the strategic planning process is to translate the mission statement into **objectives**—specific, measurable goals the organization seeks to achieve and by which it can measure its performance. For our purposes, the terms goals and objectives mean the same thing. The mission actually leads to a hierarchy of objectives, with organizational objectives determining the scope and nature of the objectives set at the departmental levels, including the marketing level. To illustrate, consider that organizational objectives for business firms tend to focus on profit growth, earnings per share, return on investment, or stock price. Improving profits, for example, is often a major organizational objective. One way profits can be improved is by increasing sales. Thus, at the marketing level, sales growth then becomes a marketing objective.

LEARNING CHECK

1. What is strategic planning?

2. What is an organization's mission statement?

3. Which is more specific, an organization's mission statement or its objectives?

DOW CHEMICAL CANADA INC.'S CORE VALUES

Long-term profit growth is essential to ensure the prosperity and well-being of Dow employees, stockholders, and customers. How we achieve this objective is as important as the objective itself. Fundamental to our success are the core values we believe in and practice.

Employees are the source of Dow's success. We treat them with respect, promote teamwork, and encourage personal freedom and growth. Excellence in performance is sought and rewarded.

Customers will receive our strongest possible commitment to meet their needs with high-quality products and superior service.

Our products are based on continuing excellence and innovation in chemistry-related sciences and technology.

Our conduct demonstrates a deep concern for ethics, citizenship, safety, health, and the environment.

source: Courtesy of Dow Chemical Canada Inc.

FIGURE 2–2
Example of core values (Dow Chemical Canada Inc.).

Identifying the Organization's Growth Strategies

Growth strategies are the general approaches used by organizations to achieve growth objectives. The basic strategic alternatives involve limiting organizational operations to existing products and markets or expanding into new ones. Figure 2–3 presents four growth strategies, with examples from McDonald's Corporation. It is important for you to remember that any organization can pursue one or a combination of the four, even at the same time.[4]

A **market penetration** strategy represents a decision to pursue growth with existing products within existing markets. To do so, McDonald's needs to either persuade current customers to purchase more of its products or attract competitors' customers. This typically requires a variety of marketing mix actions such as increased advertising, sales promotion, or lower prices.

A **market development** strategy involves marketing existing products in new markets. The new markets might be different market segments in the same geographic area

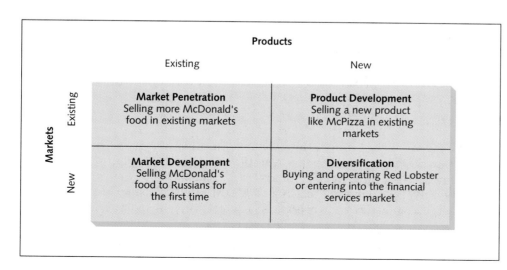

FIGURE 2–3
Alternative growth strategies.

How does McDonald's achieve growth? See the text.

or the same target market in different geographic areas. McDonald's expands geographically by opening new restaurants, such as their expansion into Russia.[5]

A **product development** strategy calls for developing new products in existing markets. McDonald's has actively pursued this strategy by expanding its product offering to include breakfast items, salads, and pizza. One concern with this strategy is the possibility of **product cannibalism**—a firm's new product gaining sales by stealing them from its other products. For example, pizza was added to McDonald's menu to increase overall sales, not to take away from sales of hamburgers.

A final strategy is diversification. **Diversification** requires the organization to expand into new products and new markets. This is the riskiest growth strategy because the organization cannot use its expertise in its current markets or with its current products. There are, however, varying degrees of diversification. *Related diversification* occurs when new products and markets have something in common with existing operations. For example, McDonald's could buy out and operate Red Lobster restaurants. In this case, it remains in the restaurant business. *Unrelated diversification* means that the new products and markets have nothing in common with existing operations. In this case, McDonald's might diversify into completely new business areas such as financial services.

SWOT Analysis

Establishing a clear mission, setting realistic objectives, and selecting appropriate growth strategies are difficult tasks for any organization. One way to do so is through the use of a **SWOT analysis.** The acronym SWOT refers to a simple, effective technique an organization can use to appraise its internal strengths and weaknesses and external opportunities and threats. A SWOT analysis allows an organization to examine the critical factors that can have a major effect on its future. All departments within the organization usually participate in the process. In market-driven organizations, the marketing department plays a central role by providing analysis of the marketing environment and the organization's ability to compete. Through a SWOT analysis, an organization can find a match between available opportunities and its unique resources and special skills. These resources and skills are often referred to as the organization's **distinctive competencies**.

It is these distinctive competencies that form the basis for the organization's **sustainable competitive advantage**—a strength, relative to competitors, to be used in the markets the organization serves or the products it offers. The two basic types of competitive advantage are price and superior performance. The organization can offer the customer value either by being the low-price provider or by offering superior performance (e.g., more benefits such as better product quality or better customer service) that justify higher prices. The marketing department is largely responsible for providing the organization with the information and analysis necessary to determine its competitive advantage.

By conducting a SWOT analysis, the organization can build on vital strengths, correct glaring weaknesses, exploit significant marketing opportunities, and avoid disaster-laden threats.[6] Figure 2–4 shows what is examined when conducting a SWOT analysis at the organizational level. You should also know that a SWOT analysis is a tool that can be used not only at the organizational and departmental levels, but at the product level as well.

LEARNING CHECK

1. When McDonald's Restaurants of Canada opened up new restaurants in Moscow, what growth strategy was it following?

2. What does the acronym SWOT stand for?

3. Define sustainable competitive advantage.

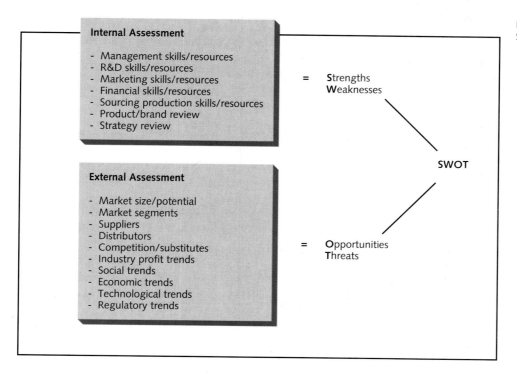

FIGURE 2–4
SWOT analysis.

MANAGING THE MARKETING EFFORT

With the organization's mission, organizational objectives, and growth strategies identified and determined, it is now the responsibility of the marketing department to ensure that marketing efforts are undertaken that will achieve the organization's objectives. This responsibility, called **marketing management,** is the process of planning, implementing, and controlling the organization's marketing effort (see Figure 2–5). Those involved in marketing management must determine marketing objectives, decide how to meet those objectives, and ensure that the plans are carried out effectively. Let's talk about each of these three important phases of marketing management, namely: marketing planning, marketing implementation, and marketing control.

MARKETING PLANNING

Marketing planning involves deciding on marketing strategies that will help an organization achieve its overall organizational objectives. The essential output of the marketing planning process is to produce a plan of action that will achieve these objectives. This plan of action is generally committed to writing and is called a **marketing plan**. The actual format, design, and structure of a marketing plan will vary from organization to organization, but every marketing plan should at least include:

- A review of the marketing situation.
- Specific and measurable marketing objectives.
- Marketing strategy, with identified target markets and marketing mix being offered.
- Marketing budget, including projected sales and expenses.
- Description of the marketing organization responsible for the marketing effort.
- Description of how the plan will be controlled and evaluated.

Figure 2–6 shows a format for a marketing plan that could be used by almost any organization. In Appendix A you will find an actual example of a marketing plan developed by an organization. Let's talk briefly about each of the elements contained in the marketing plan.

FIGURE 2–5
The phases of marketing management.

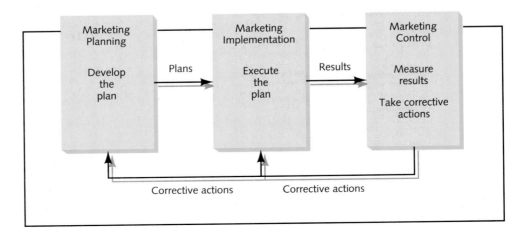

FIGURE 2–6
The marketing plan.

Marketing Situation
Marketing Objectives
Marketing Strategy
  Target Market
  Positioning
  Marketing Mix
    • product
    • price
    • marketing communications
    • distribution
Marketing Budget
Marketing Organization
Control

Marketing Situation

The first section of the marketing plan provides a description of the marketing situation, including market size, growth, market segments, competition, and other factors in the marketing environment that are relevant to the development and execution of the plan. A review of the current marketing strategy and the marketing mix used by the organization is also provided.

Much of the analysis found here has usually served as input for developing the organization's strategic plan (i.e., part of the SWOT analysis). This section also provides a brief summary the organization's mission, organizational objectives, and growth strategies developed as part of the strategic planning process. This is done to ensure that the marketing plan is consistent with and reinforces the organization's strategic plan.

Marketing Objectives

Marketing objectives, as mentioned earlier, should flow directly from the organizational objectives set by the organization. The most common marketing objectives include: sales, stated in terms of units sold or dollars, and market share. **Market share** is the ratio of sales revenue of the firm to the total sales revenue of all firms in the industry, including the firm itself. Other, more specific objectives are also defined at the marketing mix level. Examples include: levels of brand awareness to achieve through advertising, numbers of distributors carrying and stocking the product, and lowest prices compared to direct competitors.

Marketing Strategy

A marketing strategy is the basic "game plan" or means for achieving the marketing objectives which, in turn, will mean attainment of the organizational objectives. It outlines the target markets sought, intended positioning, and specific details of the marketing mix designed to appeal to the target market.

Target Market. As you know from Chapter 1, the target market (selected market segments) is the group of consumers toward which the organization directs its marketing effort. The proper selection of a target market is central to the success of an organization's marketing plan. The actual process of selecting target markets will be discussed in detail in Chapter 8.

MARKETPLACE APPLICATION

Expos Tweak Their Marketing Mix

In an attempt to boost attendance, the Montreal Expos decided to tweak their marketing mix for the 1997 season. Their objective is to raise attendance in 1997 to two million, from the estimated 1.7 million in 1996. The team also wants to boost season ticket sales from 6,000 to 10,000 over the next three years. The club added $500,000 to its $1.5 million advertising budget to market advance sales of tickets for the 1997 season. In addition, Expos fans attending games in 1997 will pay among the lowest prices of all Major League Baseball venues, with reductions on 33,800 of the stadium's 46,000 seats. The price of some $19 seats, for example, will be slashed to $10. The club is also selling new 13-game, partial season ticket packages. The Expos feel that by reducing prices they can increase the volume of tickets sold. Research showed that price was an important consideration for baseball fans, and other clubs have successfully increased attendance by dropping their ticket prices. The Expos suggest that, ultimately, more fans in the seats will help the team increase its payroll in order to better attract and keep top players. The Expos will also try to change fans' negative perceptions of the team, including that it trains players in the minors, but loses them to better-paying clubs, and that it tends to trade its best players for lower-paid ones.

1. Do you think lower ticket prices will bring more fans out to see the Expos?
2. What other aspects of the marketing mix should the Expos try to tweak?

SOURCE: Adapted from Michael McCullough, "Expos Slashing Prices in 1997 Marketing Plan," *Marketing*, August 5, 1996, p. 2.

Positioning. Once an organization has determined its target market, it must now decide what "position" its offering will occupy in the market. **Product positioning** refers the place the product occupies in the consumers' minds relative to competitors. If an offering is perceived to be exactly like another product on the market, the consumer may have no reason to buy it. Marketers, then, plan positions that distinguish their products from competing offerings. For example, Wal-Mart positions itself as the low-price leader, Canon positions its photocopiers as the most reliable, Volvo positions its cars as the safest, and Coca-Cola positions diet Coke as the best tasting diet soft drink on the market.

Volvo positions its cars as the safest.

An organization must consider its identified competitive advantage in order to build an effective position in the market. Simply put, the organization's competitive advantage forms the basis for any intended positioning. Once the organization has chosen a desired position, it must take appropriate steps to deliver and communicate that position to the target market. An important part of this process is developing the appropriate marketing mix to support and reinforce the positioning. The concept of positioning is discussed in detail in Chapter 8, but now let's turn to a discussion of the marketing mix.

Marketing Mix. With the target market selected and the positioning determined, the overall proper marketing mix to be offered to the target market must be developed. The marketing mix will consist of everything the organization can do in order to influence demand for its products. Developing and executing a successful marketing mix involves detailed decision making, such as selecting when and where to use sales promotion, determining advertising messages, setting final prices, or choosing which outlets to carry the product. These decisions, called **marketing tactics,** are the detailed, day-to-day operational decisions essential to the overall success of a marketing strategy. Figure 2–7 shows the four marketing mix elements and their components. These must be combined in a cohesive manner in order to develop an effective marketing mix.

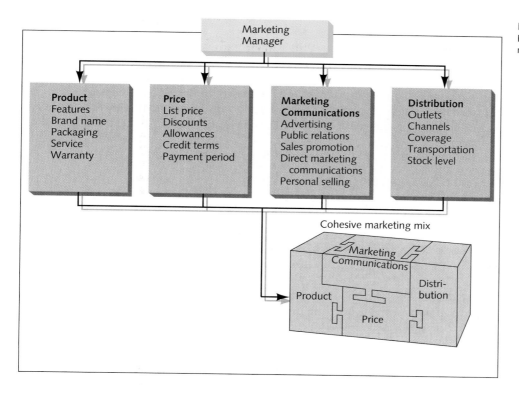

FIGURE 2–7
Elements of the marketing mix.

Marketing Budget

Next, the marketing plan must spell out the sales, expenses, and profit levels that can be expected as a result of the marketing plan. The organization normally establishes a sales forecast, which indicates what it expects to sell under specified conditions for the marketing mix (e.g., at what price and with what level of marketing effort) and certain environmental factors such as reaction by competition. The concept of forecasting demand and sales is discussed in Chapter 7. The budget also includes a statement of expenses, margins, and profits, sometimes at different estimated sales levels, in order to account for possible changes in the marketing mix or environmental factors. The budget aspect of the plan is designed to show management that revenues should exceed expenses and result in increased profits under the strategy and marketing mix conditions specified in the plan.

Marketing Organization

The marketing organization is responsible for developing and converting marketing plans into reality. The marketing plan spells out who is responsible for planning, implementing, and controlling the variety of marketing activities that are part of the marketing plan. In a small business, one person might be responsible for planning, implementing, and controlling the entire marketing effort. In large organizations, on the other hand, many individuals are involved in planning and carrying out specific marketing activities. Large organizations can organize their marketing efforts in several ways. Under the marketing implementation section that follows shortly, we will discuss the types of marketing organizations that can be established to manage a firm's marketing effort. We will also discuss the role a product manager plays in some organizations.

Control

The control section of the plan outlines the controls that will be used to monitor the progress of the marketing plan. Typically, the objectives are carefully spelled out, thereby allowing those responsible for the marketing plan (1) to compare the results of the marketing plan with the marketing objectives to identify deviations and (2) to act on these deviations—correcting negative deviations and exploiting positive ones. We will discuss the control phase of the marketing management effort in greater detail later in this chapter.

Requirements of an Effective Marketing Plan

It has been said that, "Plans are nothing; planning is everything." In other words, it is the process of careful planning that focuses an organization's efforts and leads to its success. The plans themselves, which change with events, are often secondary. Effective planning and plans are inevitably characterized by identifiable objectives, specific strategies or courses of action, and the means to execute them.

Measurable, Achievable Objectives. Ideally, objectives should be measurable in terms of *what* is to be accomplished, by *when.* This means, where possible, objectives should be quantified: "Increase market share from 15 percent to 20 percent by December 1998" is preferable to, "Maximize market share given our available resources."

Measurable objectives also provide a benchmark with which to compare results to determine when corrective action is required. Finally, to motivate the people in the organization whose job it is to reach the objectives, the established objectives must be achievable. Unrealistically difficult objectives will not motivate marketing personnel.

A Base of Facts and Valid Assumptions. The more a marketing plan is based on facts and valid assumptions rather than guesses, the less uncertainty and risk are associated with executing it. Using marketing research to verify assumptions increases the chance of successfully implementing a plan. Schwinn Bicycle Company neglected to do proper research and failed to see the changing preferences of its consumers, from 10-speed bicycles to mountain bikes. As a result, Schwinn's market share dropped from 25 percent to 5 percent.[7]

Simple but Clear and Specific Plans. Effective execution of plans requires that the doers understand what, when, and how they are to accomplish their tasks. Superfluous elements in a plan should be dropped so that the remaining ones are as straightforward as possible, thereby preventing misunderstandings.

Complete and Feasible Plans. Marketing plans must be complete in the sense that all the marketing mix factors were considered and key ones were incorporated into the plans. Marketing resources must also be adequate to make the plans feasible.

Controllable and Flexible Plans. Few plans are carried to completion without a hitch. Results of marketing actions are compared with the measurable, targeted objectives to discern problem areas and trigger new, corrective actions. Marketing plans must provide for this control, which in turn allows replanning—the flexibility to update original plans.

LEARNING CHECK

1. The process of planning, implementing, and controlling the organization's marketing effort is called _____.

2. The essential output of the marketing planning process is to produce a plan of action called a _____.

3. What are marketing tactics?

MARKETING IMPLEMENTATION

The implementation phase of marketing management has emerged in the 1990s as a key factor in the success of a marketing plan. While marketing planning is no doubt an important part of the marketing management effort, the organization must properly implement the marketing plan in order to be successful.

Organizing for Marketing

As we mentioned earlier, the marketing plan must spell out who is responsible for planning, implementing, and controlling the variety of marketing activities that are part of the marketing plan. In a small business, it may be one person. In large organizations, groups of people are generally responsible for the marketing management efforts. Basic issues in organizing for the marketing effort include (1) understanding how line versus staff positions and divisional groupings interrelate to form a cohesive organization and (2) the role of the product manager in some organizations.

Line versus Staff and Divisional Groupings. Although simplified, Figure 2–8 shows the organization of Pillsbury's Prepared Dough Products business unit in detail and highlights the distinction between line and staff positions in marketing. People in *line*

Products from Pillsbury's line of prepared dough products.

FIGURE 2–8   Organization of the Pillsbury Company's Prepared Dough Products business unit.

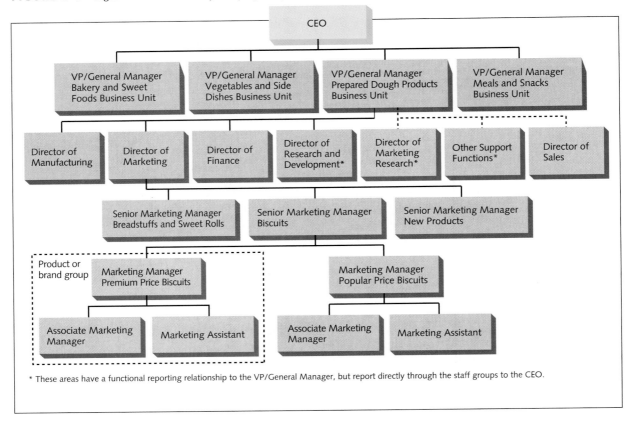

* These areas have a functional reporting relationship to the VP/General Manager, but report directly through the staff groups to the CEO.

positions, such as the director of marketing and senior marketing managers have the authority and responsibility to issue orders to the people who report to them, such as marketing managers and assistants. In the organizational chart, line positions are connected with solid lines.

Those in *staff positions* (shown in dotted lines) have the authority and responsibility to advise people in line positions but cannot issue direct orders to them. For example, the directors of R&D, marketing research, and sales advise the vice president/general manager of the Prepared Dough Products business unit but do not report directly to that person. Instead, they report directly to other vice presidents (not shown in this organizational chart) who issue them orders.

Most organizations use divisional groupings—such as product line, functional, geographical, or market-based groups—to implement marketing plans. Three of these groupings appear in some form in the organizational chart in Figure 2–8. At the top of the organization, Pillsbury organizes by *product line groupings,* in which a unit is responsible for specific product offerings. For example, Pillsbury has four main product lines: bakery and sweet foods, vegetables and side dishes, prepared dough products, and meals and snacks. These product line groupings reflect a Pillsbury reorganization that grouped products by the way consumers think about them, rather than by the distribution system they use (dry grocery, frozen, and refrigerated foods).

The Prepared Dough Products business unit is organized by *functional groupings:* manufacturing, marketing, and finance. These represent the different business activities within a firm. Pillsbury also uses *geographical groupings* for its more than 500 field sales representatives. Each director of sales has several regional sales managers reporting to him or her, such as western, eastern, and so on. Regional sales managers, in turn, have district managers reporting to them (although for simplicity these are not shown in the chart).

A fourth method of organizing a company is to use *market-based groupings,* which assigns responsibility for a specific type of customer to a unit. When this method of organizing is combined with product offerings, the result is a *matrix organization.* Xerox, for example, "turned the traditional vertical organization on its side" and focussed on specific product and market combinations.[8]

A relatively new position in consumer products firms is the *category manager* (e.g., senior marketing manager in Figure 2–8). Category managers have profit-and-loss responsibility for an entire product line—all biscuit brands, for example. They attempt to reduce the possibility of one brand's actions hurting another brand in the same category. The popularity of category management among packaged goods manufacturers has increased as supermarket buyers have become responsible for purchasing, merchandising, and marketing entire categories.[9]

Role of Product Manager. The key person in the product or brand group shown in Figure 2–8 is the manager who heads it. This person is often called the *product manager* or *brand manager,* but at Pillsbury he or she carries the title *marketing manager.* This person and the assistants in the product group are the basic building blocks in the marketing organization of most consumer and industrial product firms. The function of the product manager is to plan, implement, and control the plans for the products for which he or she is responsible. This responsibility includes six primary tasks:[10]

1. Develop strategies for the product that will achieve sales and market share objectives.
2. Prepare marketing plans, sales forecasts, and budgets.
3. Work with outside agencies to develop marketing communications campaigns.
4. Develop support for the product from the firm's sales force and distributors.
5. Gather continuous marketing research information on customers, noncustomers, dealers, competitors, the product's performance, and new opportunities and threats.
6. Find ways to improve existing products and create new ones.

Many organizations are finding that the traditional ways of organizing the marketing effort are not as effective as they once were. The rapidly changing marketplace has created a need for even quicker and more effective implementation of marketing plans. Many organizations are now experimenting with new ways to organize and implement marketing efforts. One new strategy is the trend toward "boundaryless organizations," sometimes called "virtual corporations," in which technology, information, managers, and managerial practices are shared across traditional organizational structures. These organizations emphasize adaptability by taking advantage of information technology and acting in unison, as Peter Drucker suggests, like a symphony orchestra. Organizations such as GE, Kodak, and Hallmark Cards are trying these new structures in the hopes of improving the way marketing plans are implemented.[11]

Improving Marketing Implementation

No magic formula exists to guarantee effective implementation of marketing plans. In fact, the answer seems to be equal parts of good management skills and practices.

Managerial skills that contribute to successful implementation include an ability to interact with people inside and outside the company; a capacity to budget time, people, and money; an ability to track or monitor marketing activities; and an affinity for creating communication networks within the organizational structure. Important management practices include moving decisions as far down the organization as possible, setting deadlines, and rewarding individuals for successful implementation. Combining these skills and practices suggests some guidelines for improving plan implementation.

Communicate Objectives and the Means of Achieving Them. Those marketers called on to implement plans need to understand both the objectives sought and how they are to be accomplished. For example, everyone in Domino's Pizza—from president Tom Monaghan to telephone order takers, make-line people, and drivers—is clear on what the firm's objective is: to deliver tasty, hot pizzas without delay to homes of customers who order them by telephone. All personnel are trained to perform their respective jobs to help achieve that objective.

A popular mechanism for helping members in any organization achieve its objectives is the use of cross-functional teams. A *cross-functional* team is a team of employees from various functions (e.g., people from R&D, operations, finance, production, and marketing) who are mutually accountable to a common set of performance objectives. Motorola Inc., for example, used cross-functional teams to develop handheld cellular phones that were superior to competitive products manufactured in Japan. Successful cross-functional teams typically have fewer than 10 members, a common purpose or focus, and a good mix of skills.[12]

Have a Responsible Champion Willing to Act. Successful plans, such as the plans for Sony's MiniDisc and Chrysler's Dodge Viper, almost always have a *plan champion* who is able and willing to cut red tape and move forward.[13] Such people have the uncanny ability to move back and forth between big-picture strategy questions and specific details when the situation calls for it. Diffused responsibility in marketing plans at best can mean important delays and at worst can result in disaster when team members don't know who is responsible for decisions.

Reward Successful Plan Implementation. When an individual or team is rewarded for achieving an organizational or marketing objective, it has maximum incentive to see a plan implemented successfully because it has personal ownership and a stake in that success. For instance, drivers delivering Domino's pizza take their job seriously because it may lead directly to their owning a franchise in a few years.

Take Action and Avoid "Paralysis by Analysis." In their book, *In Search of Excellence,* Thomas J. Peters and Robert H. Waterman, Jr., warn against "paralysis by analysis," the tendency to excessively analyze a problem instead of taking action. To overcome this pitfall, they call for a "bias for action" and recommend a "do it, fix it, try it" approach.[14] They conclude that perfectionists finish last, so getting 90 percent perfection and letting the marketplace help in the fine tuning makes good sense in implementation.

For example, Chris Haney and Scott Abbott, the Canadian inventors of the Trivial Pursuit® game, took an afternoon to develop the basic concept for the game. Then they formed a company, Horn Abbot Ltd., to manufacture and sell the game, completed development, and test-marketed the product. By making prompt decisions and avoiding

Saturn: Successful implementation through communication.

paralysis by analysis, these entrepreneurs created the biggest-selling adult game in Canada.[15]

Foster Open Communication to Surface any Problems.

Successful implementation of a plan often lies in fostering a work environment that is open enough that implementers are willing to speak out when they see problems, without fear of recrimination. In an open work environment, the focus is placed on trying to solve the problem as a group rather than finding someone to blame. Solutions are solicited from anyone who has a creative idea to suggest—from the janitor to the president—without regard to status or rank in the organization.

The Saturn automobile is an example of participatory management and improved communications leading to a successful product. Saturn avoided some of the common communication problems of large organizations by creating a management–labour partnership in which all decisions are reached by consensus, including selection of suppliers, the advertising agency, and dealers. Employees are also encouraged to put forth any ideas to improve the product and their working environment.

Schedule Precise Tasks, Responsibilities, and Deadlines.

Successful implementation requires that people know the tasks for which they are responsible and the deadline for completing them. To implement the tasks required to carry out its marketing plans, the Royal Canadian Mint prepares *action item lists* that have three columns: the task, the name of the person responsible for accomplishing the task, and the date by which the task is to be finished. Related to action item lists are formal *plan schedules* which show the relationships through time of the various plan tasks.

Proper scheduling of a plan involves identifying the main tasks, determining the time required to complete each task, arranging the activities to meet the deadlines, and assigning responsibilities to complete each task. The key to scheduling is to distinguish tasks that must be done sequentially from those that can be done concurrently. In many cases, scheduling several marketing tasks concurrently often reduces the total time required for implementation.

MARKETING CONTROL

Ideally the quantified objectives in the marketing plan have been accomplished by the marketing actions taken during marketing implementation and measured as results in the control phase of the marketing management process (Figure 2–9). A marketing manager then compares the objectives to the results using *management by exception,* which means identifying results that deviate from plans to diagnose their causes and take new actions.

Often, results fall short of plans and corrective action is needed. For example, after 50 years of profits Caterpillar accumulated losses of $1 billion. To correct the problem, Caterpillar focussed its marketing efforts on its core products and reduced its operating costs substantially. At other times, the comparison of objectives and results shows that performance was far better than anticipated, in which case the marketing manager tries to identify the reason and move quickly to exploit the unexpected opportunity.

Marketing Audit

Marketing control is an especially difficult and important problem in today's organizations. A major tool that can be used in the control phase of the marketing management process is the marketing audit. A **marketing audit** is a comprehensive, unbiased, periodic review of an organization's marketing management efforts designed to identify new problems and opportunities that warrant a plan of action to improve performance.[16]

FIGURE 2–9   Marketing control.

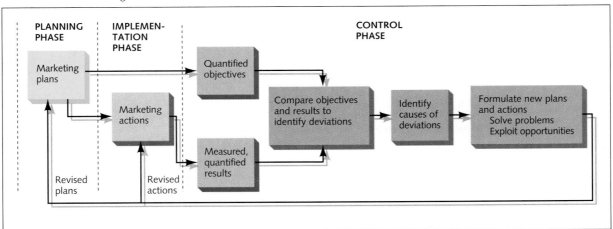

Most organizations undertaking a marketing audit use a checklist of questions such as the one shown in Figure 2–10. The checklist usually focuses on the marketing mix factors designed and executed by the organization.

Two important areas of analysis that are conducted during the marketing audit are a sales analysis and a profitability analysis. *Sales analysis* involves using the organization's sales records to compare actual results with sales objectives, and identify areas of strength and weakness. Often a *sales component analysis* (also called microsales analysis) is performed. A sales component analysis traces sales revenues to their sources, such as specific products, sales territories, or customers. Computers can easily produce the breakdowns necessary to perform this level of analysis.

Profitability analysis enables the organization to measure the profitability of its products, customer groups, sales territories, channels of distribution, and even order sizes. This leads to decisions to expand, maintain, reduce, or eliminate specific products, customer groups, or channels.[17] An important type of profitability analysis is a *contribution margin analysis,* which monitors controllable costs and indicates the contribution to profit of specific marketing factors.

For a meaningful marketing audit to occur, the individuals or team conducting it must have free rein to talk to managers, employees, salespeople, distributors, and customers, as well as have access to all pertinent internal and external reports and memoranda. The audit needs to involve top management and those directly responsible for marketing management efforts in order to ensure that resulting action recommendations have their support.

TARGET MARKET

1. Who are our current and potential customers?
2. Where are they located?
3. Why do they buy our product/services?

MARKETING MIX

Product

1. Do we have the right products (services)?
2. Should some products (services) be eliminated?
3. Should some products (services) be modified?
4. Which products provide the most profit?
5. Are there opportunities to develop new products?

Price

1. Are current pricing policies working?
2. Given our prices, are we offering good value to our customers?
3. How do our prices compare with competitors?

Marketing Communications

1. Are we using the right message to communicate to the customer?
2. Are we using the right communications tools?
3. Are we consistent with our message?
4. Are we communicating with the customer at the right time?
5. Is the budget adequate?

Distribution

1. Are we using the right channels to reach our customers?
2. Do we have adequate market coverage?
3. Do we have good relationships with our channel partners?

FIGURE 2–10
Marketing audit questions.

ETHICS INSIGHT

Be Careful What You Measure

In the marketing control phase of the marketing management process, results of marketing efforts are measured and quantified. Traditionally, organizations have focused on measuring financial results such as sales revenue or profitability. However, organizations that focus narrowly on these measures of performance tend to encourage efforts that ignore other important marketing objectives. In today's competitive environment, other performance measures such as customer satisfaction, order response time, or employee motivation deserve to be part of the measurement process. Part of the difficulty in using multiple performance measures is that improvement along one dimension might lead to a decline on another dimension. For example, an organization might be able to increase sales levels but not maintain customer service or customer satisfaction levels. Or, an organization might hold the line on salary increases but push its employees harder to increase market share. In doing so, the organization might lower employee satisfaction with their jobs and increase turnover. Many organizations are attempting to use both financial and nonfinancial indicators of performance. Ford, for example, now examines its overall performance by exploring three key dimensions of their operations: people, products, and profits. The problem for many organizations is what to measure and the weight that should be attached to the measures.

1. How would you deal with this problem?
2. When should financial measures have a lower priority than other performance dimensions?

LEARNING CHECK

1. What is a marketing audit?

2. What is the difference between a sales analysis and a profitability analysis?

LEARNING OBJECTIVE REINFORCEMENT

1. Understand the concept of strategic planning and marketing's role in that process. Strategic planning is the process by which an organization examines its capabilities and the changing marketing environment in order to identify its mission, objectives, and strategies for growth.

2. Define the terms mission, objectives, and growth strategies. An organization's mission is its defined purpose—what it wants to accomplish. When the mission is often committed to writing it is called a mission statement. Objectives are specific, measurable goals an organization seeks to achieve and by which it can measure its performance. Growth strategies are the general approaches used by organizations to achieve growth objectives.

3. Explain the alternative growth strategies available to an organization. Four specific growth strategies available to an organization are: (1) market penetration, (2) market development, (3) product development, and (4) diversification.

4. Understand the planning, implementation, and control functions of marketing management. After the organization's mission, organizational objectives, and growth strategies have been identified and determined, it is the responsibility of the marketing department to ensure that marketing efforts are undertaken that will achieve the organization's objectives. This responsibility, called marketing management, is the process of planning, implementing, and controlling the organization's marketing effort. Those involved in marketing management must determine marketing objectives, decide how to meet those objectives, and ensure that the plans are carried out effectively.

5. Outline what is included in a good marketing plan. A organization's marketing plan, or plan of action, should include: (1) a review of the current market situation, (2) specific and measurable marketing objectives, (3) marketing strategy, including the target market, intended positioning, and the nature of the marketing mix to be offered, (5) marketing budget, including projected sales and expenses, (6) description of the marketing organization designed to execute the plan, and (7) description of how the plan will be controlled and evaluated.

6. Explain the alternative ways to organize the marketing management effort and the role of a product manager. In a small organization one person may be responsible for the entire marketing management effort. In larger organizations, the effort may be organized in several ways: by product line groupings, functional groupings, geographical groupings, or market-based groupings. The role of the product manager is to plan, implement, and control the plans for the products for which he or she is responsible.

7. Understand the procedures used to control and evaluate the marketing plan. Ideally the quantified objectives in the marketing plan have been achieved through marketing implementation and measured as results in the control phase of the marketing management process. A marketing manager then compares the objectives to the results using management by exception, which means identifying results that deviate from plans to diagnose their causes and take new actions. A procedure used to control and evaluate the marketing plan is the marketing audit, which might include an evaluation of the overall marketing mix being used by the organization.

KEY TERMS AND CONCEPTS

strategic planning p. 30
mission p. 31
mission statement p. 31
objectives p. 32
growth strategies p. 33
market penetration p. 33
market development p. 33

product development p. 34
product cannibalism p. 34
diversification p. 34
SWOT analysis p. 34
distinctive competencies p. 35
**sustainable competitive
    advantage** p. 35

marketing management p. 36
marketing plan p. 36
market share p. 37
product positioning p. 38
marketing tactics p. 38
marketing audit p. 46

CHAPTER QUESTIONS AND APPLICATIONS

1. Suppose you headed up General Motors Canada. Develop a simple SWOT analysis for the company based on what you know about its cars and external environmental factors.

2. Many Canadian liberal arts universities traditionally have offered an undergraduate degree in liberal arts to full-time 18–22-year-old students. How might such a university use the growth strategies shown in Figure 2–3 to grow and prosper in the 1990s?

3. What are some of the problems a firm might experience if it uses product development as a growth strategy?

4. If you selected a growth strategy of market penetration, that is, selling more products in existing markets, which marketing tactics could you use to execute the strategy?

5. Of the four growth strategies discussed in the text, which has the most risk for an organization?

6. In Pillsbury's organizational chart in Figure 2–8, where do product line, functional, and geographical groupings occur?

7. Why are quantified objectives in the marketing planning phase of the marketing management process important for the control phase?

APPLICATION CASE 2–1
OTIS ELEVATOR

Otis Elevator serves two closely related markets: (1) the design, manufacture, and installation of elevators, escalators, and moving sidewalks, and (2) the subsequent service of the equipment. Otis competes with technological leadership (they were first to incorporate microprocessor controls to dispatch elevator cars according to load), high reliability due to superior quality, and a superior service force. These attributes offer significant benefits to customers who are willing to pay a premium for Otis equipment and service.

Elevator sales are very cyclical, going up or down depending on the building cycle. Servicing of the elevators, however, is both stable and profitable. Manufacturers often take low margins on the sale of the elevator to lock up the initial elevator service contract. This means they usually win 60 to 80 percent of the service contracts for new elevators they have installed. However, as a building ages and competition for tenants increases, the cost of service looms larger to the building owner and subsequent contracts are likely to be given to the lowest bidder. Most low bidders are local companies offering an "acceptable" speed of response to a call for service, especially during the sensitive, "trapped in-an-elevator" emergency.

QUESTIONS

1. What would be a clear and meaningful mission statement for Otis elevator?
2. How can Otis regain an edge over the small local service companies that compete on a low price dimension?

APPLICATION CASE 2–2
ROLLERBLADE, INC.

When Rollerblade, Inc., was founded in the 1980s, it was the only manufacturer of in-line skates in the world. It had not only introduced this new product, it was responsible for creating the entire industry (and sport) of in-line skating. Today, however, it faces fierce competition. On one hand, several companies, such as Bauer, are attempting to take away Rollerblade's leadership role in the category by marketing similar premium-quality, high-priced skates. In fact, in Canada, Bauer is now the number one brand in terms of sales and market share. On the other hand, more than 30 other companies are competing with Rollerblade by selling lower-priced skates through mass merchandising chains like Wal-Mart, Kmart, Zellers, and Sears. Rollerblade, Inc., has historically avoided these types of outlets in favour of specialized sporting goods stores.

The original target market for in-line skates was active adults between the ages of 18–35 years of age. However, the target market has expanded to include children and mature adults. Skaters use in-line skates for many different reasons: racing, fun, exercise, street hockey, complex acrobatics, and even transportation to and from work or college. The popularity of in-line hockey is a major reason for growth in the category in Canada. Rollerblade now offers a variety of in-line skate designs targeted at different market segments. In addition, Rollerblade offers a complete line of clothing accessories. Rollerblade, Inc., is also the industry leader in terms of safety and technological advances. In fact, it holds more than 185 patents for its in-line skating products.

QUESTIONS

1. Construct a simple SWOT analysis for Rollerblade, Inc.
2. Outline what you believe should be the basic marketing mix used by Rollerblade, Inc., in order to compete in this new marketing arena.
3. Rollerblade believes significant opportunities exist in global or international markets. Which countries or regions should be priority targets for Rollerblade, Inc.? Why?

The Marketing Plan: A Case Example

In Chapter 2, we provided a format for a marketing plan that could be used by almost any organization. As identified in Figure 2–6, the major sections in the marketing plan include the marketing situation, marketing objectives, marketing strategy, budget, organization, and control. These major sections should not be viewed as a rigid format for all marketing plans, but rather as an approach to structuring a marketing plan in an integrated manner. Marketing plan authors should view marketing plan development as a creative exercise because the exact format used and the issues address must vary to fit the situation.

The plan included in this appendix is for SELFHELP Crafts' Saint John, N.B., retail outlet. SELFHELP is in a unique position of being both a retail outlet and a nonprofit "help" agency which operates with humanitarianism as its primary mission.

This marketing plan was developed to increase awareness of SELFHELP's mission and to improve the financial position of its retail store located in the Trinity Royal area of Saint John, N.B. Note that the authors of this plan have adapted the marketing plan format to fit the needs of this organization's situation.

If this marketing plan is used as an assignment in class please forward any suggestions or solutions you propose to the SELFHELP Crafts location nearest your area. While some of the issues presented here are location-specific, the majority can be applied to SELFHELP retail outlets around the world. Address locations can be found on the SELFHELP web site referred to in the body of the plan. Thank you for your cooperation.

SELFHELP Crafts
Saint John, New Brunswick
MARKETING PLAN

BACKGROUND

The Organization

SELFHELP Crafts of the World is a nonprofit organization established as an alternative trading organization for Third World artisans. SELFHELP ensures that the artisans are paid fair market value for their crafts as defined by the domestic economy within which they reside.

SELFHELP Crafts began in 1946, operating from the basement of a Mennonite Central Committee worker. In the early 1960s SELFHELP Crafts became an official program of the

Source: This plan was prepared by Professor Shelley M. Rinehart and Cynthia A. Arbeau, University of New Brunswick, Saint John, for classroom discussion rather than to illustrate either effective or ineffective handling of an administrative situation. The authors wish to thank the following individuals for their help in data collection and the development of a comprehensive marketing communications plan for SELFHELP Crafts' Saint John retail outlet: Sonya Ebbett, Angela Price, Janelle Shillington, Nicole Theriault, and Tanya Vanier.

Mennonite Central Committee, the service, relief, and development agency of North American Mennonite and Brethren in Christ churches.

Today SELFHELP Crafts operates a number of retail outlets throughout Canada and the United States. These retail stores are operated on a nonprofit basis, managed by a Board of Directors and staffed primarily by volunteers. The crafts are also sold on a consignment sales basis in locations where SELFHELP does not operate a retail outlet, as well as through organized relief sales.

SELFHELP Crafts has purchased products from over 50,000 artisans representing more than 140 producer groups in 33 countries. In 1994, SELFHELP Crafts' retail sales, through stores, consignment sales, and Mennonite Central Committee relief sales, totalled over $11 million (for more information on SELFHELP Crafts of the World visit their web site at http://www.mennonitecc.ca/mcc/selfhelp/).

The Saint John Retail Outlet

SELFHELP Crafts began retail operations in Saint John, New Brunswick, during the latter part of 1988. It was only the second retail outlet to be established east of Ontario.

Saint John is New Brunswick's largest city, with a population base in excess of 150,000 people. As Canada's first incorporated city, Saint John boasts a culturally diverse and history-rich environment (for more information on Saint John visit its web site at http://www.city.saint-john.nb.ca).

During its first year of operation, the Saint John outlet of SELFHELP Crafts reached sales of over $180,000. First year sales far exceeded expectations, and, as a result, SELFHELP Crafts was forced to relocate in order to increase their retail space. The new store front was close to the original location, still in the Trinity Royal area of the city, an area where building owners were encouraged to maintain the heritage of their properties. Walking tours also made the Trinity Royal area attractive to tourists.

MARKET SITUATION

The Market

SELFHELP Saint John is located in the Trinity Royal district of the uptown area. The uptown area employs over 11,000 people. In addition, uptown attracts large numbers of tourists and general shoppers from throughout the city and surrounding area. The fact that this is an historic preservation site ads to the culturally diverse underpinnings of SELFHELP Crafts.

Saint John has a labour force of approximately 62,000 people, 75 percent of whom are employed in white collar occupations. Saint John and the surrounding area boasts a population of 180,000 people, with over 125,000 residing in the metro area. An in-store survey indicates that the majority of SELFHELP patrons come from the West and North sides of the city, from outside city limits, or are in town temporarily.

Growth

During its first year in business, the Saint John outlet of SELFHELP Crafts achieved sales in excess of $180,000. However, since 1989 SELFHELP Saint John has experienced a fairly consistent decline in sales, falling to just over $100,000 in 1995. Total retail sales for Saint John were just over $483 million in 1995.

This trend is not surprising, given that real personal disposable income per capita in Canada has not recovered from the past recessionary period. Figures in the second quarter of 1995 indicate that disposable income is still running over 5 percent below its peak in 1989. As a result, consumer spending in Canada is growing at a modest rate of 2.2 percent per year.

Total retail sales in Canada increased slightly, from just over $172 billion in 1989 to $211 billion in 1995. Results for the retail industry in New Brunswick showed a similar pattern, moving from a total of just over four billion in 1989 to approximately five billion in 1995.

Segments

Given the mission of the SELFHELP organization, the market for SELFHELP Crafts Saint John is quite broadly defined. The primary goal is to increase general awareness throughout Saint John and the surrounding area such that volunteers can be easily recruited; educational services are requested through schools, churches, and other organizations; and sales at the retail outlet are increased.

The primary target markets do, however, vary by focus. With respect to volunteer recruitment the focus is on individuals residing within the Saint John area who are 16 years of age and over. Educational services are targeted toward individuals throughout Saint John and the surrounding areas who are of school age and beyond. Results from an in-store survey suggest that patrons of the retail outlet are primarily between the ages of 25 and 54 and are mostly female.

Competition

While all nonprofit organizations compete for the consumer's charitable dollar, SELFHELP Crafts operates within a slightly different environment. Still functioning as a nonprofit organization, SELFHELP operates within the retail industry and is thus in competition with others in the retail trade, as well as other nonprofit agencies operating in the region.

Being located in the Trinity Royal district of Saint John has its advantages in terms of attracting patrons; however, it is also one of the most heavily "stored" areas of the city. Approximately 600 shops and services are located in the uptown core, with another 100 stores located in malls and shopping centres throughout the city. The Trinity Royal district in particular focuses on the tourist trade with a large percentage of shops offering antiques, handicrafts, and giftware.

Internal Environment

Strengths. The fact that SELFHELP Crafts is a nonprofit organization positively impacts consumer perceptions of the retail outlet and the products it sells. Being run by a Christian organization further strengthens the positive perceptions the majority of consumers hold.

The uniqueness of the product and organization is another strength that SELFHELP Crafts should capitalize on. Having many personal contacts throughout the world enables SELFHELP Crafts to carry a wide assortment of diverse goods, while at the same time maintaining fairly low prices. In addition, the high rate of turnover in the product line carried by the store encourages customers to come in and browse, looking for the latest products to hit store shelves.

SELFHELP's Board of Directors consists of 12 individuals from different walks of life. The diversity, education, and experience of the board constitute a wealth of resources from which SELFHELP is able to benefit. This is also true of the approximately 35 volunteers who staff the store on a weekly basis.

The volunteers are themselves a strength of the organization. The individuals staffing the store are there because they want to be, not because they have to be for monetary reasons. This makes a difference in terms of commitment and enthusiasm when dealing with customers. It also enables SELFHELP Crafts to keep prices down while still covering expenses.

Weaknesses. One of the most pressing problems SELFHELP is forced to deal with is a lack of financial resources. The lean budget makes it difficult for SELFHELP to compete effectively with other for-profit organizations operating within the Trinity Royal area and beyond. While free or reduced cost marketing communications is available, the timing and/or placement is not always suitable to SELFHELP's target audience.

Recently the Prince William Street area has seen an influx of bar and pub-type establishments. This has caused a huge increase in late night pedestrian traffic, vandalism, and litter. While uptown merchants have expressed their concern to city officials, nothing has been done as yet. A number of merchants have expressed their concern for early morning consumers who are forced to step over broken glass and the like to get in to the retail outlets. A number of Trinity Royal retailers fear that they will be forced to relocate to nearby malls if this issue is not dealt with.

Another problem specific to the uptown area is a lack of available and convenient parking for those wishing to shop in the Trinity Royal area. Although over 800 metered, on-street parking spaces are located in the uptown area, along with an additional 3500 spaces in area parking garages, many consumers still complain about the lack of parking. Cost is also a factor, given that area malls provide free parking for their patrons.

Perhaps the most troublesome weakness of SELFHELP Saint John is its lack of a strategic plan for the future. As of yet very little research has been done to measure public awareness or examine consumer trends. Although some marketing communication activities have been undertaken, very little has been done to measure their effectiveness. In fact, a recent in-store survey suggests that the majority of patrons were made aware of SELFHELP through word of mouth or by walking past the store. Very few were even aware that a broadcast media campaign was under way.

A lack of financial resources only serves to compound SELFHELP's problems. There is no money available to conduct comprehensive market research, to engage in major media campaigns, or to pay staff. Having a strictly volunteer labour force sometimes makes scheduling and task assignment difficult.

External Environment

Opportunities. North American society is based on a number of core values which influence behaviour within the culture. One of these core values is humanitarianism, the urge to help others less fortunate than oneself. This core value has grown in importance over the past few years as evidenced by the widespread support of "help" agencies around the world.

SELFHELP is in a unique position of being both a retail outlet as well as one of these "helping" agencies. Being a nonfprofit organization also lends SELFHELP the opportunity to engage in free marketing communications activities and to take advantage of a number of offers not extended to similar for-profit businesses, such as free internet services, reduced cost banking, and free advertising services.

Being located in the downtown core of Saint John also affords SELFHELP Crafts the opportunity to take advantage of the high volume of walk-by traffic afforded the area. With a high concentration of services and a revitalization effort within Trinity Royal, the uptown area enjoys a heavy flow of pedestrian traffic, both tourists and Saint John citizens, in the spring and summer months.

SELFHELP Crafts of the World is also celebrating its 50th birthday this year. This presents the Saint John store with a theme for celebration and a good twist for a public relations and publicity campaign to be based on.

Threats. Being a nonfprofit organization is not without its disadvantages. Given the low margin within which SELFHELP must operate, any decline in traffic or sales has a detrimental effect on store operations. In addition, the small amount of capital available for marketing communications activities severely disadvantages the retail operation compared to its for-profit counterparts.

A related issue revolves around competition between nonprofit organizations, an issue traditionally thought to be nonexistent. As government and institutional support for agencies declines, the competition for funding, donations, volunteers, board members, and customers increases.

SELFHELP is in the unique, and perhaps not enviable, position of competing not only with other nonprofit organizations but also with for-profit organizations meeting similar consumer needs. In the uptown area alone there are 600 retail shops and services, many of which are in direct competition with SELFHELP Crafts. In a time of reduced consumer discretionary income this competition becomes exceedingly intense.

The Saint John climate also represents a considerable threat to pedestrian traffic through-out the winter months. The shops in Trinity Royal are not connected to the city's pedway system. This forces consumers to migrate to major shopping malls to avoid inclimate weather. This severely hampers SELFHELP's ability to capitalize on increased consumer traffic during the holiday season.

Perhaps even more troublesome is the impending issue of a name change for SELFHELP Crafts. At a time when the Saint John store is struggling to increase awareness of its existence and purpose, the plans to change the name of the organization creates an even greater challenge.

SELFHELP CRAFT'S MISSION

The mission of SELFHELP Crafts is to glorify God by serving people; to help the poor in obedience to the teaching of Jesus; to be signs of God's continuing love and care. The production and marketing of handicrafts is one way to meet human need around the world.

SELFHELP CRAFT SAINT JOHN'S OBJECTIVES

SELFHELP Crafts Saint John's primary objective is to increase awareness within Saint John and the surrounding communities such that the objectives of increased volunteer participation, use of educational services, and retail sales can be realized.

This will become more of a challenge over the next 12 months given that the organization is about to initiate a name change for their retail outlets. This also represents an opportunity for SELFHELP Saint John in terms of a theme for marketing communications efforts. It may also aid in endeavours to obtain some publicity for the store.

The new name will be "Ten Thousand Villages." It is believed that the name successfully suggests handicrafts and overseas-sourced products as its main line of business. The name will be given final acceptance by the Mennonite Central Committee in late June or early July. Corporate operations will institute the changes in September and retail outlets will be asked to make the shift beginning in the first quarter of 1997. However, due to the nonprofit nature of the organization, retail outlets will be permitted to implement the name change when they are financially able to do so.

THE PLAN

Marketing Objectives

Primary Objective: Increase awareness of the existence and purpose of SELFHELP Crafts through an increased community profile, increased store traffic, more visible educational activities, and more aggressive recruitment and training of volunteers.

Retail Sales. Store sales, including revenue from sales held off of the retail premises, are down nearly 30 percent from year one. This is especially disturbing since neighbouring businesses operating within the same industry report that their sales have remained steady or have increased slightly over the same time frame.

Objective: Increase retail sales by 10 percent (target: 1997 sales of $130,497).

Educational Activities. Currently there appears to be an "ebb and flow" pattern in terms of bookings for educational talks, and school and store visits. This results in scheduling problems for the volunteers who may be asked to be in two places at once. What is needed is a more proactive method of booking talks and visits so that schedules can be finalized well in advance.

Objective: Pre-book one educational activity, or school or store visit per week, two during weeks containing special holidays.

Volunteers. Currently the store is run by one paid, part-time store manager and staffed exclusively by volunteer labour. On a typical day six volunteers are needed to staff the store, three people per shift. This schedule requires approximately 35 volunteers, working one shift per week, to maintain the current store hours of 9 AM–5 PM Monday through Wednesday plus Saturday, and 9 AM–8 PM Thursday and Friday. Scheduling is sometimes difficult since less than 50 percent of the volunteer roster is actually active.

Objective: Increase number of active volunteers from 48 to 75 to alleviate scheduling difficulties.

Marketing Strategy

Target Markets. While there will be some overlap, each objective of SELFHELP Crafts focuses on a slightly different segment of the general population base of Saint John.

Retail sales
The SELFHELP Crafts retail outlet services the general retail shopper. However, given its nonprofit status and humanitarian position within the community, it attracts several different subsegments of the overall retail consumer market:

- The browser, tourist, or citizen who happens to walk along Prince William Street.
- The general retail shopper, either browsing or shopping for a special occasion.
- The cost-conscious consumer.
- The "individualistic" consumer who searches for unique purchases for him or herself or others.
- The humanitarian consumer who purchases the "gift that gives twice."
- The uptown employee responsible for office gift purchases.
- U.S.-based corporate level research indicates, however, that the typical SELFHELP consumer is between 25 and 50 and is female.

Educational activities
One of the primary goals within the mission statement of the SELFHELP organization is to provide education to those interested in learning about the global village in which we all live. Again, the target market for SELFHELP is very broad:

- Individuals school age and up.
- Institutions with similar goals or an education-based mission (i.e., schools, clubs, and churches).
- Teachers and other educators who may incorporate some of SELFHELP's information into their overall plan.

Volunteers
SELFHELP Crafts Saint John cannot function successfully without a good base of volunteers to draw upon. Many skills are necessary to run the retail outlet and the education services efficiently and effectively. Therefore, volunteer recruitment should target the broad-based population rather than identifying narrowly defined segments:

- All individuals age 16 years and older.
- Make use of the services provided by the volunteer centre, both in terms of recruitment and training of volunteers.

Positioning. SELFHELP Crafts is first and foremost a nonprofit, humanitarian organization. The fact that the SELFHELP organization operates retail outlets is secondary to its primary focus on aid and education. As a result, SELFHELP must be given a unique position in the marketplace where the primary focus is on its nonprofit humanitarian status.

Marketing Mix

Market research

SELFHELP Crafts Saint John suffers from a lack of community awareness. In addition, the retail outlet suffers from a lack of information regarding consumer demographics and buying characteristics.

Activities:
- Solicit students from the local university to direct and participate in market research activities:
- Develop and administer a public awareness survey.
- Develop in-store surveys to create consumer profiles.
- Develop and administer surveys to develop a profile of educational services users.
- Develop and administer surveys to profile volunteers and their interests to allow for better matching of individuals to tasks.
- Collect consumer information at point of purchase to develop a computerized consumer database for later direct mail campaigns.

Place. Since its inception, SELFHELP Crafts Saint John has been located in the Trinity Royal district of the city of Saint John. This location is advantageous in that it is central for Saint John citizens and is also attractive to tourist traffic. However, as mentioned previously, as of late, businesses within this district have been the victims of vandalism, vagrancy, and public displays of emotion and drunkenness.

Activities:
- Investigate the possibility of relocation to Market Square, part of the city's pedway system, or to a major mall in the suburbs of the city.
- Take advantage of mall kiosks or moveable carts which are available free of charge to nonprofit organizations.
- Continue to have a presence on the docks for the arrival of fall cruise ships while still encouraging tourists to visit the store.

Product. SELFHELP Crafts actually markets three separate and distinct products: retail goods, educational services, and volunteerism.

Retail goods
- The mix of products is relatively stable across all SELFHELP outlets and is determined based on availability and self-sufficiency status of the worker groups involved. Once a worker group becomes self-sufficient, SELFHELP no longer carries its products. While individual stores can request certain items, the product line is primarily determined at the head office in New Hamburg, Ontario.
- The unique aspect of products purchased at SELFHELP is that the goods have both intrinsic and extrinsic reward value. Not only do consumers purchase a product, they also purchase a sense of well-being through helping others less fortunate than themselves.

Educational services
- SELFHELP offers a unique educational experience in that it provides not only information, but it also has a multitude of visual aids and, in some cases, is able to relate actual experiences in foreign countries or teach the craft of certain regions.
- Educational services are offered both in-house and on-the-road.
- Volunteers use items from the store during their presentations.

Volunteerism
- SELFHELP Crafts offers volunteers the opportunity to work in a unique retail setting and the opportunity to interact with a wide range of individuals.
- SELFHELP Crafts also provides volunteers with the opportunity to participate in training seminars, gain valuable work experience, and educate themselves on the economic and cultural climates of Third World countries and the global village in which we all reside.

Price. Price refers to the total value given in exchange for a product or service. The concept of price will vary across the products offered by SELFHELP Crafts.

i. Retail products
- Price is determined by SELFHELP Crafts of the World and is uniform across the retail outlets. Goods are priced prior to being shipped to retail stores. Price is determined based on fair market value plus 30 percent markup. This markup is used to cover the costs associated with running the retail outlet.

ii. Educational activities
- An opportunity cost exists for groups in terms of the time they give up to listen to a talk given by SELFHELP volunteers. In this respect, our talks must yield more valuable information than the alternatives available to the consumer.

iii. Volunteers
- Opportunity costs also exist for volunteers who must give up their time to work with SELFHELP. The intrinsic reward structure must be set up such that volunteers perceive their service as worthwhile and the benefits as desirable. Training and experience may also reward volunteers for their time and effort.

Marketing Communications. The marketing communications plan consists of five basic elements: advertising, sales promotion, personal selling, publicity, and public relations. It is important that these elements be integrated such that a consistent and comprehensive image is presented to the consumer. The message must be clear and easily understood.

i. Advertising
- While SELFHELP Crafts has engaged in a number of broadcast and print media campaigns, the effectiveness of these activities has never actually been measured. As a result, trial campaigns should be initiated on a limited basis with measurement mechanisms in place. Only those activities that prove to be effective should be repeated.
- It should be noted that reduced rates and special packages are available to nonprofit groups, but they sometimes are less effective due to non-peak placement.

Activities:
- Broadcast
    Radio (all have nonprofit packages available):
    - K100 FM (music from the 70s, 80s, and 90s)
    - C98 FM (light rock)
    - CHSJ AM (country)
    Television
    - Cable 10 community programming
    - ATV lively notes
    - General public service announcements
- Print
    Newspaper
    - *Telegraph Journal* (morning weekday daily)
    - *Evening Times Globe* (Monday–Saturday evenings)
    - The *Buyer Flyer* (business card size ad free)
    - Periodic local newspaper inserts
    - Local publications (tourist information packets, etc.)
- Internet
    - Freenet of Saint John offers free web site construction and display to all nonprofit organizations within the Saint John area.

ii. Sales promotion
- Sales promotion activities are fast becoming one of the major expenditures within a marketing communications budget. Much more easily targeted and measurable, sales

promotions are an effective and efficient means of marketing a good, service, or organization.
- Because SELFHELP Crafts is governed by the Mennonite Central Committee, it is somewhat limited in terms of the activities it is able to engage in to market its cause. Games of chance are prohibited and Sunday business hours are forbidden. As a result, SELFHELP Saint John is unable to participate in some of Trinity Royal's sales promotional programs. However, while Sunday selling is not permitted, SELFHELP Saint John typically participates in Sunday hours for browsers only. Consumers are encouraged to return on Monday to purchase the items they are interested in, and most do. In fact, many customers have voiced their appreciation of the fact that the SELFHELP store observes Sunday as a "day of rest."
- One of the most successful campaigns SELFHELP Saint John has participated in was the Pewter Christmas Ornament Campaign, 1995. Limited numbers of pewter replicas of historic Saint John sites were available at designated retail outlets in the uptown core. A fee was paid to be a distributor of the ornaments. Interestingly, November, the month that the ornaments were sold, was the only month that SELFHELP Crafts Saint John did not record decreased sales compared to the same period in 1994.

Activities:
- Participate in the 1996 Christmas ornament campaign.
- Continue to participate in Trinity Royal Days, Loyalist Days, Festival By The Sea, and Sidewalk Sales hosted by the city.
- In conjunction with advertising activities, offer customers discounts for mentioning ads.
- Host "by invitation only" store parties for which mailouts are sent based on zip codes.
- Host a "50th birthday" celebration for SELFHELP Crafts of the World, offering cake and special events throughout an entire week.

iii. Personal selling
- Personal selling is ultimately the responsibility of the volunteers. Given that education is a primary goal of SELFHELP Crafts, volunteers must be knowledgeable about the crafts carried in the store, their origins, and a little about the culture of the artisans who produced the goods.
- Since the majority of staff members are volunteers, all motivation to sell is based on intrinsic rewards. Coupled with the lack of homogeneity of backgrounds of volunteers, it is difficult to manage the personal selling function.

Activities:
- Conduct in-house training seminars for volunteers to educate them with respect to producer groups, countries, products, and cultures.
- Take advantage of the three-hour personal selling training sessions available through the volunteer centre at a minimal cost.

iv. Publicity
- Publicity is the element of the marketing communications mix relied on most heavily by nonprofit organizations. While publicity enjoys high credibility of message, the lack of control with respect to what is said when and where can be problematic for the nonprofit organization. However, given the small budget SELFHELP Crafts is forced to work with, the use of publicity as a channel of marketing communications is extremely important.

Activities:
- Notify all media of 50th birthday celebrations through press releases and personal phone calls.
- Notify all media of the name change for SELFHELP Crafts of the World, making sure that the reasoning behind the change is fully explained.
- Plans are currently underway for SELFHELP Saint John to be featured on a local broadcast cooking show. Food stuffs sold at the store will be used to prepare the meal for that day's show.

v. Public relations
- Given its position as a nonprofit humanitarian organization, it is important that SELF-HELP Crafts maintain a positive corporate image and act as a responsible citizen.
- SELFHELP Crafts should also continue its involvement in community activities, such as the annual Tree Decorating Campaign, in which trees are donated by businesses and then auctioned off to raise money for the local hospital.
- SELFHELP Crafts Saint John must be more proactive, becoming increasingly involved in the community thus increasing awareness within the Saint John community and surrounding areas.

vi. An integrated approach to marketing
- It is suggested that SELFHELP Crafts Saint John adopt a "theme" approach to guide all marketing activities. That is, every month a producer group will be chosen and all marketing communications activities will centre around that producer group's products and culture. The theme can also centre around special events such as the 50th birthday celebrations, Mother's Day, Christmas, etc. To ensure the success of this strategy, SELF-HELP Crafts Saint John must inform the public of what activities it is currently engaging in and what they can expect in the future. An efficient method to disseminate this information is through the use of internet services and the *Buyer Flyer.*

Budget.
- As was stated previously, retail margin is set at 30 percent. This revenue must cover all expenses incurred by the retail outlet including rent, maintenance, capital expenditures, and marketing communications campaigns.
- Forecasted financial statements follow based on pessimistic, most likely, and optimistic projections for 1997 retail sales levels (See Exhibits I, II, and III).

Organization. As with any nonprofit organization, all policy and budget allocation decisions are Board responsibilities. The implementation of any recommendations is typically the responsibility of the store manager and the volunteers.

i. Board responsibilities
- Monitoring of all control and evaluation mechanisms.
- Recruitment of students to perform market research.
- Recruitment of volunteers.
- Training of volunteers (customer service, personal selling).
- The development and coordination of educational services.
- Direction of marketing communications activities.

ii. Management responsibilities
- Supervision of volunteers.
- Direction of marketing communications activities.
- Promoting more active personal selling among volunteers.
- Monitoring of market research activities.
- Daily store operations.

iii. Volunteer responsibilities
- Implementation of marketing communications activities.
- Participation in training programs to improve selling and service skills.
- Engaging in market research activities.
- Staffing of kiosks and cruise ship displays.
- Delivery of educational services.

Controls
Desired outcomes:
- Increase retail sales by 10 percent over 1995 figures.
- Increase number of active volunteers to 75.

- Pre-schedule one educational activity or store visit per week, two during weeks containing special holidays.

Measures:
- Analyze sales figures on a monthly basis and relate changes to marketing communications activities occurring during the same time period.
- Analyze volunteer participation and relate changes to appreciation activities, training sessions, and recruitment activities.
- Monitor educational services bookings resulting from a more proactive approach to soliciting requests.
- Each marketing communications activity will have an associated measure such that effectiveness can be accurately monitored (discount coupons attached to print ads).
- If trends do not indicate that objectives will be met after six months of operation, undertake a review and make any necessary adjustments to the strategic plan.
- Compare actual figures with objectives for sales, education, volunteers, and community awareness.

Income Statement		
Year Ending Feb 29/97		
Assume 0% increase over last year sales		
Sales		$118,633.60
Cost of Goods Sold		$ 83,070.75
Gross Margin		$ 35,562.85
Other Income		$ 3,677.14
Total Income		$ 39,239.99
Operating Income		
Rent	$13,200.00	
Electricity	$ 2,475.28	
Depreciation	$ 1,996.16	
Marketing Communications Expense	$ 1,000.00	
Market Research	$ 500.00	
Cash Over/Cash Short	$ 266.60	
Losses	$ 944.78	
Maintenance/Supplies	$ 2,322.69	
Telephone	$ 492.39	
Travel	$ 603.20	
Bank Charges	$ 808.72	
Wages	$15,278.78	
Insurance	$ 789.51	
Miscellaneous	$ 1,013.72	
Total Expenses		$ 41,691.83
Net Income		($ 2,451.84)

EXHIBIT I
SELFHELP

EXHIBIT II
SELFHELP

Income Statement
Year Ending Feb 29/97
Assume 10% increase over last year sales

Sales		$130,496.96
Cost of Goods Sold		$ 83,070.75
Gross Margin		$ 47,426.21
Other Income		$ 3,677.14
Total Income		$ 51,103.35
Operating Income		
Rent	$13,200.00	
Electricity	$ 2,475.28	
Depreciation	$ 1,996.16	
Marketing Communications Expense	$ 1,000.00	
Market Research	$ 500.00	
Cash Over/Cash Short	$ 266.60	
Losses	$ 944.78	
Maintenance/Supplies	$ 2,322.69	
Telephone	$ 492.39	
Travel	$ 603.20	
Bank Charges	$ 808.72	
Wages	$15,278.78	
Insurance	$ 789.51	
Miscellaneous	$ 1,013.72	
Total Expenses		$ 41,691.83
Net Income		$ 9,411.52

EXHIBIT III
SELFHELP

Income Statement
Year Ending Feb 29/97
Assume 5% increase over last year sales

Sales		$124,565.28
Cost of Goods Sold		$ 83,070.75
Gross Margin		$ 41,494.53
Other Income		$ 3,677.14
Total Income		$ 45,171.67
Operating Income		
Rent	$13,200.00	
Electricity	$ 2,475.28	
Depreciation	$ 1,996.16	
Marketing Communications Expense	$ 1,000.00	
Market Research	$ 500.00	
Cash Over/ Cash Short	$ 266.60	
Losses	$ 944.78	
Maintenance/Supplies	$ 2,322.69	
Telephone	$ 492.39	
Travel	$ 603.20	
Bank Charges	$ 808.72	
Wages	$15,278.78	
Insurance	$789.51	
Miscellaneous	$ 1,013.72	
Total Expenses		$ 41,691.83
Net Income		$ 3,479.84

The Evolving Marketing Environment

THE NEED FOR VIGILANCE

In 1985, just two years after the book *In Search of Excellence* reported on 43 of the "best-run" organizations in North America, 14 of the 43 organizations were in financial trouble. Today, most of the 43 either no longer exist or have lost their status as well-run organizations. The reason, according to most experts, was their failure to anticipate and respond to change.

For almost 100 years, Avon Products focused on the Avon Lady as its key to success. By the 1980s, however, sales, profit, and stock value had declined sharply. The firm had lost sight of its customers and had failed to recognize key trends, namely the exodus of women from the home and into the workplace. With more women in the workplace, there were fewer potential customers at home when Avon came calling. The company also had problems recruiting and retaining its sales representatives, losing them to the workplace as well.

Fortunately, unlike some companies, Avon realized that it had to respond to the changes it hadn't anticipated if it was to survive. The company revamped its distribution system and encouraged its representatives to sell at the workplace. Selling at the office now accounts for over one-third of Avon's sales. Realizing its domestic markets were maturing and highly competitive, the company began entering new foreign markets where there were more women at home—and less competition for their products. This allowed Avon to recruit representatives more easily and to continue to utilize the successful at-home selling strategy that had built the company.

One thing marketers can be certain of is that the marketplace will continue to change and evolve. Consumers change, competition changes, and other forces like technology create change. Organizations must accept change as inevitable and be prepared to respond accordingly. Organizations that do not know how to anticipate and adapt to change will not survive. Scientist Buckminster Fuller once said, "You don't fight forces, you use them." This should be a new marketing axiom for market-driven organizations wanting to achieve prosperity in the future. This chapter describes how the environment for marketing has changed and will change in the years to come.

THE MARKETING ENVIRONMENT

As we mentioned in Chapter 1, the marketing environment consists of social, economic, technological, competitive, and regulatory forces, at home and abroad, that shape the organization's marketing process. While this external marketing environment is largely beyond the control of the organization, it is a source of both opportunities to be capitalized on and threats to be avoided or managed.

Market-driven organizations continually acquire information on events occurring outside their organizations in order to identify and interpret potential trends that can impact on their business. This process is called **environmental scanning.** Market-driven organizations use environmental scanning to determine which forces in the marketing environment will serve as accelerators or brakes on the marketing process. Figure 3–1 illustrates the major environmental forces that can affect the marketing activities of an organization.

In conducting an environmental scan, the organization must focus on identifying trends that may offer new marketing opportunities as well as those that may change the demand for its existing products or services. The organization must use this information in planning its strategies for growth. A firm conducting an environmental scan of Canada in the 1990s might uncover key trends such as those listed in Figure 3–2. Trends for each of the five environmental forces are presented. Although the list of trends is far from complete, it reveals the breadth of an environmental scan—from

FIGURE 3–1   Environmental forces affecting the organization, its suppliers, and its customers.

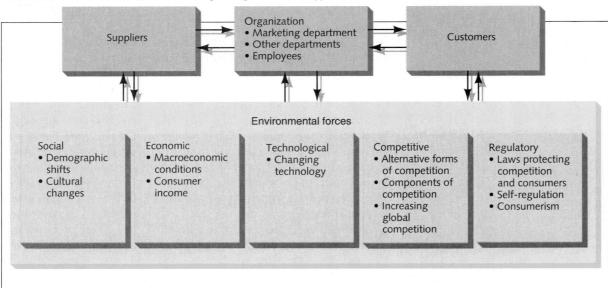

FIGURE 3–2 An environmental scan of Canada in the 1990s.

ENVIRONMENTAL FORCE	TREND IDENTIFIED BY AN ENVIRONMENTAL SCAN
Social	• Growing number and importance of older Canadians • Continuing population shifts to urban areas • Desire for "high-tech and high touch" (gadgets plus human interaction) • Greater desire for value and customer service • Greater role for women in jobs and purchase decisions • Growing ethnic diversity
Economic	• Concern that Canadian government deficit can trigger inflation • Increased number of Canadian firms looking to foreign markets for growth • Continuing decline in real per capita income of Canadians • Less consumer acceptance of debt
Technological	• Increased use of computer databases and networks • Major breakthroughs in biotechnology and superconductivity
Competitive	• More employment in small, innovative firms • Downsizing and restructuring of many corporations • Reduced economies of scale resulting from flexible manufacturing • More international competition from Europe and Asia
Regulatory	• Less regulation of Canadian firms competing in international markets • More protection for firms owning patents • Greater concern for ethics and social responsibility in business • Renewed emphasis on self-regulation

identifying changes in our population, to technological breakthroughs that may change the way companies do business. These trends can also affect consumers and the organizations that serve them. These trends and others are covered as we examine the key environmental forces described in the following pages.

SOCIAL FORCES

The **social forces** in the marketing environment include the characteristics of the population, its values, and its behaviour. Changes in these forces can have a dramatic impact on the marketing strategies planned by organizations.

Demographics

Demographics is the study of the characteristics of a human population. These characteristics include size, growth rate, geographical distribution, age, gender, marital status, education, ethnicity, income, and so forth.

Population Size and Growth. The world population stands at close to 5.5 billion and is expected to reach 6 billion by the year 2000. China and India rank one and two, respectively, as the countries with the largest populations. Over 95 percent of the growth in the world population will take place in developing countries, while population growth in developed countries—particularly the United States and Canada—will be much slower. The population of Canada is currently 28 million, and the population growth rate is expected to average only about 1 percent per year from now to 2000.[1]

Some demographers predict that without increases in immigration, Canada's population will actually start to decline by 2010.[2] This trend indicates that Canadian businesses faced with possible shrinking markets at home might be well advised to seek opportunities in other countries. However, the size of populations in other countries does not tell the whole story. An environmental scan must also examine income trends in various countries in order to determine the size of "markets." The key is to determine which countries offer the best market potential given their growth in population and income.

Urbanization. An important trend in many countries is the growth in urban populations. The concentration of people in major urban centres means marketers can reach large market segments efficiently and effectively. In Canada, close to 80 percent of the population is urban.[3] Just five **census metropolitan areas (CMAs),** geographic labour market areas having a population of 100,000 persons or more, account for about 40 percent of our population. These CMAs are Toronto, Montreal, Vancouver, Ottawa, and Edmonton. Some experts believe that "hyperurbanization" is likely to occur in most countries, including Canada. It is predicted, for example, that most Canadians will be located in seven or eight city-states by 2010, within easy reach of most marketers.[4]

Age Waves. Because age affects the needs, values, and purchasing habits of consumers, tracking consumers by age groupings is also part of an environmental scan. The size, habits, and relative purchasing power of various age groups is closely examined in an environmental scan.

A fast-growing age segment in Canada is the over-50 group. This group, sometimes called the **mature market,** represents close to 30 percent of the population and controls much of the accumulated wealth in this country. *Accumulated wealth* is the value of net assets accumulated by households in the form of real property, financial securities, deposits, and pension assets. Developed nations such as Canada and the United States have seen growth in the mature market.

However, relatively young populations exist in other countries such as Mexico and China. While the median age of the population in Canada will be over 40 by 2010, it will be under 27 in Mexico. In fact, on a global basis, the **youth market,** consumers aged 10–19, represents 25 percent of the world's population. Many companies that market on a global basis have found this group to be very similar worldwide in terms of its values. For example, Coca-Cola has successfully marketed to this group using the same basic appeal (i.e., "Coke is The Real Thing.").

Other major age cohorts or groupings being tracked by marketers include **baby boomers,** people born between 1946 and 1964, and **Generation X,** people aged 20–29. One in three Canadians is a baby boomer. The boomers are a diverse group with different lifestyles, income, and education levels. However, as a group boomers buy more and save less than do other age groups. They are prime targets for consumer electronics, household services, second cars, and luxury goods. But as the boomers age, their attitudes and needs are also changing. Many marketers have recognized these changes and have responded accordingly.

Members of Generation X (often called Xers), represent about 15 percent of the Canadian population. They have attitudes and opinions that are much different from their baby boomer parents. They are generally pessimistic about their future economic prospects and are not prone to extravagance. Many still live at home and will be entering their peak earning years by the year 2000. Currently, Xers are important targets for mar-

MARKETPLACE APPLICATION

The Boomers and the Xers

The postwar baby boomers are aging. The older ones are entering their fifties, and the youngest are already in their thirties. They're slowing down, having children, and settling into home ownership. While they are reaching their peak earning and spending years, they are also reevaluating their lives, the purpose and value of work, and their relationships with others. Their communities and their families have become more important than the outside world. Convenience and comfort are important to them. They are also more interested in life-enhancing experiences than material possessions per se. More than ever before, they now look for quality products that are both aesthetically pleasing and personally satisfying. Stability and moderation are important watchwords for the aging boomers in terms of the way they live, eat, and spend.

Members of Generation X grew up in an era of increased divorce rates, economic recession, and corporate downsizing. These factors and others have influenced their outlook on life. They are somewhat cynical, dislike hypocrisy and self-importance, and they especially hate hype. If a product doesn't fulfill a real need rather than a mere desire for status—watch out! Xers

also dislike advertising that is stupid, misleading, offensive, or boring. They are cautious about spending their money and are generally savvy shoppers. They care about the ecological environment and like to do business with socially responsible organizations. Quality of life and job satisfaction are important to them. Experts predict Xer women will continue to work, but will not sacrifice their personal lives or families to the degree that boomer women did. For the Xer, there will be a continued emphasis on leisure activities and family entertainment, economical and functional clothing, quality day care and home offices. Over the next 10–15 years, Xers will displace the boomers as the primary target for a broad range of product categories. But marketing to this group will be different than marketing to the boomer.

1. Do you think these descriptions of baby boomers and Generation X are accurate?

2. How should an organization market to an Xer?

SOURCE: Adapted in part from "What Xers Cross Out," *Marketing*, April 17, 1995.

keters of clothing, entertainment, and food away from home. In order to clearly understand the differences between boomers and Xers, read the Marketplace Application box.

Family. The types of families in Canada are changing in both size and structure. The average family size in Canada is 3.1 persons, but this figure is expected to decline by the year 2000. As for structure, in 1971 one in three Canadian families consisted of the once-typical husband working outside the home, wife raising children scenario. Today, only one in seven families falls into this category. The dual-income family is the norm in Canada, representing over 60 percent of all husband–wife families.

About 50 percent of all first marriages in Canada end in divorce. The majority of divorced people eventually remarry, giving rise to the **blended family,** in which two previously separate families are merged into one unit. Hallmark Cards specially designs cards and verses for such blended families. Still, many people do not remarry, and single-parent families represent close to 15 percent of all family units in Canada.

Ethnic Diversity. While we often think of Canada as largely consisting of French and English Canadians, close to 3 out of 10 Canadians are neither of French nor British descent. While the majority of the non-British, non-French population is of European descent, there has been growth in other ethnic groups and visible minorities. In fact, close to 70 percent of all immigrants to Canada today are classified as *visible minorities,*

Benetton is one company that recognizes ethnic diversity in Canada.

primarily people from China, Southeast Asia, Africa, and India. Hong Kong Chinese and Southeast Asians are the fastest-growing ethic groups in Canada, representing close to 3 percent of the Canadian population. Visible minorities are projected to represent close to 18 percent of the Canadian population—or over 5.5 million Canadians—by 2001.[5]

Much of the ethnic population can be found in the major metropolitan areas, such as Toronto, Vancouver, Montreal, Calgary, and Edmonton. Close to 20 percent of the populations in those areas register their native tongue as something other than English or French. Marketers have recognized the growing ethnic diversity in Canada. Many companies, such as the Royal Bank, Benetton, Ultramar, and Bell Canada, are putting "ethnic faces" in mainstream advertising. Many other companies, such as Cantel and American Express, devote marketing efforts to specifically cater to these ethnic groups by advertising in their language and providing personnel who speak their language.

Culture

A second social force, **culture,** incorporates the set of values, ideas, and attitudes of a homogeneous group of people that are transmitted from one generation to the next. Culture includes both material and abstract elements. Therefore, monitoring cultural trends, while difficult, is important for effective marketing. We will deal with noteworthy cultural trends in Canada in this section. Cross-cultural analysis needed for successful global or international marketing is discussed in Chapter 18.

The Changing Roles of Women and Men. One of the most notable changes in Canada over the past three decades has been the change in the roles of women and men in society. These changes have had a significant impact on marketing practices. Distinctions between the traditional gender roles assigned to females and males have become blurred. One of the major trends has been the emergence of women as an integral part of the workforce. Nationally, more than 65 percent of women work outside the home. This figure is expected to rise to close to 75 percent by the year 2000. With more women working outside the home, the number of tasks to do is expanding and the time available to do them is shrinking. This phenomenon is often referred to as **time poverty.** As a result, the male spouse has had to assume certain tasks. More men are shopping for groceries and taking on greater responsibility in child care and house-keeping duties.

Marketers are becoming more aware of the necessity not to stereotype female or male behaviour and preferences. Moreover, in an effort to help consumers overcome their time poverty, many marketers offer greater convenience, such as express lanes at checkouts, longer store hours, drive-through windows, and delivery services.

Changing Attitudes. In recent years, there has been a shift in Canadians' attitudes toward work, lifestyles, and consumption. The Puritan work ethnic of "I live to work" is now redefined by many as "I work to live." Work is now more likely seen as a means to an end—recreation, leisure, and entertainment. Canadian consumers are placing more emphasis on quality of life as opposed to work. This attitude shift has contributed to a growth in sales of products such as VCRs and easily prepared foods.

There also is greater concern for health and well-being, as evidenced by the level of fitness and sports participation in Canada. Firms like Nike and Reebok are profiting from this trend. Additionally, Canadians are more concerned about their diets, especially because of the linkage between diet and health. Growth in sales of no-fat, low-fat and cholesterol-free foods is evidence of this concern. The beverage industry has also seen major changes. Consumers are drinking healthier products, including more bottled water and juices, as opposed to traditional soft drinks.

Value Consciousness. Consumers' attitudes toward consumption have also changed. Conspicuous consumption, which marked much of the 1970s and 1980s, has been replaced by the search for value. Instead of seeking highly visible brands or labels, consumers are more concerned about obtaining the best quality at the best prices. In Quebec, for example, research shows that consumers are prepared to drop their favourite brands for alternatives that offer better value. One of the imperatives for marketing success discussed in Chapter 1 was delivering customer value. Innovative marketers who do this by way of better prices or value-added enhancements will be rewarded. For example, Labatt Breweries launched its lower-cost brew, Wildcat, and has successfully captured market share in the Canadian beer market.

Ecological Consciousness. Canadians' attitudes toward the ecological environment have also changed. There is a growing recognition that today's decisions on the use of earth's resources have long-term consequences to society. A recent study shows that caring for the environment is a pervasive and deeply felt part of social responsibility for 80 percent of the population. This concern for the environment spills over to the marketplace. The same study found that 45 percent of people surveyed said a product's environmental friendliness is an important factor in their purchasing decisions.[6]

As we saw in Chapter 1, many Canadian companies practice green marketing (producing, marketing, and reclaiming environmentally sensitive products). Loblaw's, Canada's largest food distributor, sells a line of environmentally friendly products. Coca-Cola and Pepsi-Cola have introduced bottles made from recycled plastic while Sears Canada recycles its catalogues. Also, Procter & Gamble has introduced Downy Refill liquid fabric softener, which uses 75 percent less packaging material. Black Photo of Markham, Ontario, leads the photofinishing industry in chemical waste management. The environment is factored into everything from product conception to manufacturing, distribution, and sales. These companies have responded to consumers'

concerns and implemented these changes with little or no additional cost to consumers. Ecological considerations are important for consumers and marketers. This topic is discussed further in Chapter 4 in connection with the concept of social responsibility.

LEARNING CHECK

1. What is environmental scanning?

2. A census metropolitan area is _____.

3. What are blended families?

ECONOMIC FORCES

Another component of the environmental scan, the **economy,** pertains to the income, expenditures, and resources that affect the cost of running an organization or a household. We'll consider two aspects of these economic forces: a macroeconomic view and a microeconomic perspective of consumer income.

Macroeconomic Conditions

Of particular concern at the macroeconomic level is the inflationary or recessionary state of a nation's economy, whether actual or perceived by consumers or businesses. In an inflationary economy, the cost to produce and buy products and services escalates as prices increase. From a marketing standpoint, if prices rise faster than consumer incomes, the number of items consumers can buy decreases.

Whereas *inflation* is a period of price increases, *recession* is a time of slow economic activity. Businesses decrease production, unemployment rises, and many consumers have less money to spend. The Canadian economy experienced recessions in the early 1970s, early 1980s, and early 1990s.

Assessing consumer expectations of an inflationary or recessionary economy is an important element of environmental scanning. Consumer spending, which accounts for two-thirds of Canadian economic activity, is affected by expectations of the future. Surveys of consumer expectations are often tracked over time by researchers, who ask questions such as "Do you expect to be better off or worse off financially a year from now?" Pollsters record the share of positive and negative responses to this and related questions to develop an index, sometimes called a consumer confidence or consumer sentiment index. The higher the index, the more favourable are consumer expectations. Many firms evaluate such indexes in order to plan production levels. Chrysler, for example, reduced its planned production level at the onset of the recession in 1991, when consumer confidence in the economy was found to be low.

Consumer Income

The microeconomic trends in terms of consumer income are important issues for marketers, as well. Having a product that meets the needs of consumers may be of little value if they are unable to purchase it. A consumer's ability to buy is related to income, which consists of gross, disposable, and discretionary components.

Orlando, Florida

As consumers' discretionary income increases, so does the enjoyment of pleasure travel.

Gross Income. The total amount of money made in one year by a person, household, or family unit is referred to as **gross income.** Individual, household, or family gross income often varies widely from country to country. For example, average gross individual income in Canada is over $25,000, but in China it is only slightly over $1,000.[7] But gross income disparities are also evident within particular countries. Income in Canada varies by gender, province, education level, profession, and age. For example, men, on average, earn almost twice as much as women in Canada. So while it is important for marketers to examine average gross incomes across particular countries, they must also evaluate the income variances within a given country. For example, the average individual income in Mexico is much lower than the average in Canada. However, the top 20 percent of individuals in Mexico have gross incomes comparable to the Canadian average. Therefore, about 18 million Mexicans with similar gross income as the average Canadian could be possible targets for marketers of many products such as modern consumer electronics.

Disposable Income. The second income component, **disposable income,** is money a consumer has left after paying taxes to use for necessities such as food, shelter, and clothing. Thus, if taxes rise at a faster rate than does disposable income, consumers must economize. There is also a wide variance in the percentage of income spent on necessities by various income groups. For example, families making under $10,000 spend over 60 percent of their disposable income on food, shelter, and clothing, while those making over $60,000 and over spend only 30 percent of their income on such necessities. This leaves the higher income group with much more discretionary income, the third component of income, than the lower income classes.

Discretionary Income. The third component of income is **discretionary income,** the money that remains after paying taxes and necessities. Discretionary income could be used for luxury items such as a vacation at a Hyatt resort. An obvious problem in defining discretionary versus disposable income is determining what is a

Technology continually
makes products obsolete.

luxury and what is a necessity. Observation can be a way to make this determination;
if a family has Royal Doulton china, Rolex watches, and Lexus automobiles, one
could assume that they have, or had, discretionary income. It is also important to note
that a product defined as a necessity in one country may be viewed as a luxury in another. For example, with over 99 percent of all households in Canada owning a television set, TVs are basically considered a necessity here, whereas televisions are a luxury item in China.

There has been a general erosion of spending power for the majority of Canadians
since the mid-1980s. This has led to cutbacks in discretionary purchases and to growth
in demand for no-frill brands, do-it-yourself products and smaller, more efficient automobiles. Real income growth in the future is expected to be slow for most Canadians.
However, the upper 20 percent of income earners (those earning $65,000 or more) will
experience even more expansion of their spending power. This affluent segment is attractive to many marketers. This group accounts for over 45 percent of education expenditures, over 40 percent of savings and financial security expenditures, over 40 percent of recreation spending, and over 40 percent of gifts and charitable contributions in
Canada.

TECHNOLOGICAL FORCES

Our society is in the age of technological change. **Technology,** a major environmental
force, refers to inventions or innovations from applied science or engineering research.
Each new wave of technological innovation can replace existing products and companies. Do you recognize the item pictured above and what product it may replace?

The Future of Technology

Technological change is the result of research, so it is difficult to predict the timing of new developments. But already we are seeing significant advances in technology in biomedicine, computers, robotics, telecommunications, and electronics. Such advances are paving the way for electric cars, miniature supercomputers, smart cars (i.e., computerized navigation systems), personal communications devices, three-dimensional televisions, and cures for many illnesses and diseases.

You may have seen some of the new products that are the result of technological breakthroughs. For example, based on the research by Kodak, electronic or digital imaging may soon eliminate the need for film for cameras. Advances in telecommunications systems have spawned a growing industry in cellular telephones, and now personal communications devices the size of credit cards are on the horizon. Procter & Gamble just released a fat substitute called *Olestra,* which gives the flavour but not the calories or cholesterol of fat. Soon you might be happily frying your french fries in Olestra, and enjoying a healthier version of your favourite ice cream.

Technology's Impact on Marketing

Advanced technology, particularly the development of computers, is having a significant impact on marketing. In the supermarket, computerized checkout scanners allow retailers to monitor which products are selling and at what price level. Hand-held computers are being used by many companies' field personnel in order to monitor sales activities and send reports directly back to headquarters. Customer service, an important ingredient in the marketing of services (Chapter 19), is also helped by computer technology. Both Avis and Hertz use hand-held computers to speed up the return of rental cars. Hertz personnel, for example, meet the driver in the parking lot and complete the entire rental transaction there.

Technology can also help in the development of new products.[8] BMW has developed a Heading Control System that tracks the centre stripe and the line on the right side of the road. If a driver gets too close to either, the car's steering self-corrects. Warner-Lambert Company, manufacturer of Trident gum and Rolaids, has developed a biodegradable plastic by using starch derived from corn, rice, or wheat. This application can be used in a host of products and will be a potential help in reducing solid waste in landfills.

Technological advances are fundamentally changing marketing. Technology is not only helping companies to develop new products, it is also assisting them to get existing products to the right consumers with greater speed and at lower costs. Using everything from desktop personal computers to satellites in space, entire industries are using technology to improve research, reduce costs of production and distribution, control inventory, and stay in closer contact with customers and suppliers. Smart marketers will use technology wisely, to better understand and serve the consumer as well as to build better relationships with them.

COMPETITIVE FORCES

Another component of the environmental scan is competition. **Competition** refers to the alternative firms that could provide a product to satisfy a specific market's needs.

There are various forms of competition, and each company must consider its present and potential competitors in designing its marketing strategy.

Alternative Forms of Competition

There are four basic forms of competition that form a continuum: pure competition, monopolistic competition, oligopoly, and monopoly. Chapter 11 contains further discussions on pricing practices under these four types of competition.

Rice: a commodity representative of pure competition.

At one end of the continuum is *pure competition,* in which every company has a similar product. Companies that deal in commodities common to agribusiness (for example, wheat, rice, and other grains) are often in a pure competition position in which distribution (in the sense of shipping products) is important but other elements of the marketing mix have little impact.

In the second point on the continuum, *monopolistic competition,* many sellers compete with their products on a substitutable basis. For example, if the price of coffee rises too much, consumers may switch to tea. Coupons or frequent sales are marketing tactics often used in monopolistic competition.

Oligopoly, a common industry structure, occurs when a few companies control the majority of industry sales. Because there are few sellers in an oligopolistic situation, price competition among firms is not desirable because it would lead to reduced revenue for all producers. Instead, nonprice competition is common. This means businesses compete on other dimensions of the marketing mix, such as product quality, distribution, and/or marketing communications. Canada is referred to by some economists as the "land of oligopoly" because it has several major industries that can be considered oligopolistic, including the airline industry and the banking industry.

The final point on the continuum, *monopoly,* occurs when only one firm sells the product or service. It has been common for companies providing products and services considered essential to a community—water, electricity, or telephone—to be in a monopoly situation, usually granted by government regulation. Typically, marketing plays a small role in a monopolistic setting because of regulation imposed by the provincial or federal government. Government control usually seeks to ensure price protection for the buyer. Until recently, there was no competition in the long-distance telephone business in Canada, but deregulation has given rise to new entrants such as Unitel and Sprint. Bell Canada and the various provincial telephone companies across Canada now must compete in a different marketing environment—a monopolistic competitive one.

Components of Competition

In developing a marketing strategy, companies must consider the components that drive competition: entry, bargaining power of buyers and suppliers, existing rivalries, and substitution possibilities.[9] Scanning the environment requires a look at all of them. These relate to a firm's marketing mix decisions and may be used to develop a new entrant, create a barrier to entry, or intensify a fight for market share.

Entry. In considering competition, a firm must assess the likelihood of new entrants. Additional producers increase industry capacity and tend to lower prices. A company scanning its environment must consider the possible **barriers to entry** for other firms, which are business practices or conditions that make it difficult for new firms to enter the market.

Barriers to entry can be in the form of capital requirements, marketing communications expenditures, product identity, distribution access, or switching costs. The higher the expense of the barrier, the more likely it will deter new entrants. For example, IBM once created a switching cost barrier for organizations that considered Apple computers because IBM had a different programming language for its machines.

Power of Buyers and Suppliers. A competitive analysis must consider the power of buyers and sellers. Buyers are powerful when they are few in number, switching costs are low, or the product represents a significant share of the buyer's total cost. This last factor leads the buyer to exert significant pressure for price competition. A supplier gains power when the product is critical to the buyer and when it has built up the switching costs.

Existing Competition and Substitutes. Competitive pressures among existing firms depend on the rate of industry growth. In slow-growth settings, competition is more heated for any possible gains in market share. High fixed costs also create competitive pressure for firms to fill production capacity. For example, many Canadian universities are increasing their advertising and public relations activities to fill classrooms, which represent high fixed costs.

Global Competition

The concept of global competition has become a central topic in the environment scan for many Canadian corporations. In Chapter 1, we discussed the importance of having a global outlook as one of the seven imperatives to marketing success. This is because competition is no longer constrained by regional or national boundaries. Many corporations find themselves competing in industries that are truly global in nature.

A **global industry,** or global market, is one in which the competitive positions of organizations in given local or national markets are affected by their overall global positions. In other words, an organization's competitiveness in one country is affected by its competitiveness in other countries and vice versa. Automobile, pharmaceutical, apparel, electronics, aerospace, and telecommunications represent well-known global industries with sellers and buyers on every continent. Other industries that are increasingly becoming global include soft drinks, beer, shaving supplies, ready-to-eat cereals, snack chips, and retailing.

In any industry in which competition is global, there is a possibility of novel forms of competition. One example is the creation of **strategic alliances,** or agreements between two or more independent firms to cooperate for the purpose of achieving common objectives. General Mills and Nestlé created Cereal Partners Worldwide for the purpose of fine-tuning Nestlé's European cereal marketing and distributing General Mills cereals worldwide. This alliance is expected to produce global sales of $1 billion by the year 2000. Molson Breweries and Miller Brewing Company also recently formed a strategic alliance in an attempt of make Molson a mainstream brand in the US market.[10]

The New Look in Canadian Corporations

Increased competition, domestically and globally, has had two important effects on Canadian corporations: (1) the restructuring of corporations and (2) the birth and growth of many small businesses.

Restructuring Corporations. Although the process is known by various names—*downsizing, streamlining,* or **restructuring**—the objective is the same: increase corporate efficiency in order to compete. Restructuring can involve selling off unsatisfactory product lines and divisions, closing down unprofitable plants, and even laying off hundreds or thousands of employees. For example, in an attempt to be more competitive, General Motors has shut down many plants and laid of thousands of its workforce over the past few years. Xerox Canada's restructuring meant large-scale layoffs and a reduction in the internal hierarchy to just four layers.

The results of restructuring are painful for those laid off, and remaining employees find their jobs far different, sometimes doing two jobs instead of one. Often restructuring also results in far different employment opportunities for those entering the workforce, and far greater problems for restructured organizations in gaining loyalty from their employees.[11]

Restructuring frequently happens fast. It often involves a *corporate takeover,* meaning the purchase of a firm by outsiders, or a cooperative merger of two or more companies. Many firms have been restructured as a result of takeovers or mergers. Kraft and General Foods merged to create Kraft-General Foods Canada, and as a result many employees were terminated or reassigned. But this merger does give the new company more marketing and distribution clout in the Canadian market.

Startup and Growth of Small Business. One effect restructuring has on corporations is their increased reliance on **outsourcing**—contracting work that formerly was done in house by employees in marketing research, advertising, public relations, data processing, and training departments to small, outside firms. This has been a factor triggering a major growth in new business startups and in employment in small business. Many economists believe that entrepreneurs in these small businesses are the key to Canadian employment growth in the 1990s.

LEARNING CHECK

1. What is the difference between a consumer's disposable and discretionary income?

2. In pure competition there are _____ numbers of sellers.

3. What does restructuring a firm mean?

REGULATORY FORCES

For any organization, marketing and broader business decisions are constrained, directed, and influenced by regulatory forces. **Regulation** consists of restrictions the provincial and federal laws place on business with regard to the conduct of its activities. Regulation exists to protect companies as well as consumers. Much of the regulation from the federal and provincial levels has been passed to ensure competition and fair business practices. For consumers, the focus of legislation is to protect them from unfair trade practices and ensure their safety.

Protecting Competition and Consumers

Legislation and regulations exist in Canada at all three levels of government—federal, provincial, and municipal—to protect and encourage a competitive environment, which is deemed desirable because it permits the consumer to determine which competitor will succeed and which will fail.

The Competition Act. The key legislation designed to protect competition and consumers in Canada is the **Competition Act,** which replaced the Combines Investigation Act. The Combines Act, in effect since 1923, had been found to be ineffectual. The Competition Act was introduced in two stages in 1975 and 1986. The purpose of the Competition Act is:

> to maintain and encourage competition in Canada in order to promote the efficiency and adaptability of the Canadian economy, in order to expand opportunities for Canadian participation in world markets while at the same time recognizing the role of foreign competition in Canada, in order to ensure that small and medium-sized enterprises have an equitable opportunity to participate in the Canadian economy and in order to provide consumers with competitive prices and product choices.

In essence, the act is designed to protect and to balance the interests of competitors and consumers. The Bureau of Competition Policy, which is part of the federal department of Consumer and Corporate Affairs, is responsible for administering and enforcing the provisions of the act. The act contains both criminal and noncriminal provisions.

Criminal offences under Part VI of the act include conspiracy (e.g., price fixing), bid rigging, discriminatory and predatory pricing, price maintenance, and misleading or deceptive marketing practices such as double ticketing or bait-and-switch selling.

Noncriminal reviewable matters under Part VIII of the act include mergers, abuse of dominant position, refusal to deal, consignment selling, exclusive dealing, tied selling, market restriction, and delivered pricing. The director of the Bureau of Competition Policy refers these matters to the Competition Tribunal under noncriminal law standards. The tribunal was established when the act took effect and is governed by the Competition Tribunal Act. The tribunal adjudicates all reviewable matters under the act.

Consumer and Corporate Affairs Canada is responsible for most of the legislation affecting business practices in Canada. Figure 3–3 lists the more significant federal legislation that protects competition and consumers in Canada. Marketers must also be cognizant of the fact that, in addition to federal laws and regulations, there are many more at the provincial level. Many provinces have their own departments of consumer affairs in order to administer any such legislation and regulations enacted on the provincial government level. Unfortunately, the laws and regulations at the provincial level vary from province to province. A marketer may find it necessary to adapt some aspect of the marketing mix or some broader business practice depending on the province.

For example, in Quebec there are specific laws dealing with store signage, packaging, and labelling. Additionally, advertising directed toward children is prohibited in Quebec. Many provinces, including Quebec, also have consumer protection acts and/or business or trade practices acts.

Self-Regulation

The government has provided much legislation to create a competitive business climate and protect the consumer. An alternative to government control is **self-regulation,** under which an industry attempts to police itself. The Canadian Broadcasting Association, whose members include major television networks and radio stations

FIGURE 3–3
Major federal legislation designed to protect competition and consumers.

Bank Cost Borrowing Act	Fish Inspection Act
Bankruptcy Act	Food and Drugs Act
Bills of Exchange Act	Hazardous Products Act
Board of Trade Act	Income Tax Act
Broadcasting Act	Industrial Design Act
Canada Agricultural Products Standards Act	Maple Products Industry Act
	Motor Vehicle Safety Act
Canada Cooperative Association Act	Official Languages Act
Canada Corporations Act	Patent Act
Canada Dairy Products Act	Precious Metals Marketing Act
Canadian Human Rights Act	Small Loans Act
Competition Act	Standards Council of Canada Act
Consumer Packaging and Labelling Act	Textile Labelling Act
Copyright Act	The Interest Act
Criminal Code	Timber Marking Act
Department of Consumer and Corporate Affairs Act	Trade Marks Act
	True Labelling Act
Electricity Inspection Act and Gas Inspection Act	Weights and Measures Act
	Winding-up Act

across the country, has a code of ethics that helps govern the conduct of its members in terms of protecting the consumer against deceptive trade practices such as misleading advertising. Similarly, the Advertising Standards Council, the self-regulatory arm of the Canadian Advertising Foundation, has established the Canadian Code of Advertising Standards for its members to follow. The members of this organization consist of major advertising agencies that are responsible for allocating the bulk of advertising dollars in Canada (see the accompanying Ethics Insight box). The Canadian Radio–Television Commission, the federal agency responsible for licensing and regulating broadcasting in Canada, is in favour of greater industry self-regulation.

Another well-known self-regulatory group is the Better Business Bureau (BBB). This organization is a voluntary alliance of companies whose goal is to help maintain fair business practices. Although the BBB has no legal power, it does try to use "moral suasion" to get members to comply with its regulations. However, there are critics of self-regulation. These critics complain that there are two basic problems with self-regulation: noncompliance by members and enforcement.

Consumerism

Regulation by government and self-regulation by industry help in protecting the consumer in the marketplace. But the consumer can also play a direct and active role. **Consumerism** is a movement to increase the influence, power, and rights of consumers in dealing with institutions. Modern consumerism in Canada and the United States really began in the 1960s. President John F. Kennedy of the United States, in a speech entitled "Consumer Bill of Rights," outlined four basic consumer rights: (1) the right to safety, (2) the right to be informed, (3) the right to choose, and (4) the right to be heard. Although not passed as laws, these proclaimed rights serve as the basis for modern consumerism. Shortly after President Kennedy's consumer bill of rights was unveiled in the United States, the Canadian government formed the Department of Consumer and Corporate Affairs, making it the agency responsible for protecting consumers and regulating corporate activities.

ETHICS INSIGHT

The Canadian Code of Advertising Standards

The Advertising Standards Council, the self-regulatory arm of the Canadian Advertising Foundation, established the Canadian Code of Advertising Standards for its members to follow. The members of this organization consist of major advertising agencies that control much of the advertising you see and hear in this country. The code is designed to merit and enhance public confidence in advertising. This code of standards, approved by all participating organizations, helps set and maintain standards of honesty, truth, accuracy, and fairness in the marketplace. Advertising prepared by participating agencies must adhere in letter and in spirit to the regulatory clauses.

There are 16 different clauses in this code covering a wide range of issues. These are: (1) accuracy and clarity of advertising; (2) the prohibition of disguised advertising techniques such as subliminal advertising; (3) the banning of deceptive price claims; (4) the proper and genuine use of testimonials; (5) the prohibition of "bait-and-switch" techniques; (6) the use of comparative advertising; (7) the proper use of professional and scientific claims; (8) slimming or weight-loss claims; (9) the offering of guarantees; (10) prohibition of imitation of another advertiser's copy, slogan, or other illustrations; (11) regard for public safety; (12) prohibition of the exploitation of human misery; (13) banning the use of superstition and fears to mislead the public; (14) the imposition of a special responsibility in preparing advertisements to children; (15) advertising to minors; and (16) the standards of good taste and public decency.

1. The underlying principles of the code are meant to ensure that participating organizations act in an ethical manner in preparing and executing advertisements directed toward the Canadian consumer. How are these organizations doing?

2. Have you seen or heard any advertising that you believe to be deceptive or dishonest?

SOURCE: Adapted from the Canadian Code of Advertising Standards (Toronto: Canadian Advertising Foundation, 1986).

Canada also has many independent consumer organizations that advance the cause of consumerism. The Consumers Association of Canada (CAC) is the largest consumer group working on behalf of the Canadian consumer. The CAC serves as a channel for supplying consumers' views to government and industry, providing consumer information, and studying consumer problems and presenting recommended solutions to those problems. In addition to ensuring that the four original consumer rights are protected, the consumer movement of the 1990s also includes consumer demands for environmentally safe products and ethical and socially responsible business practices.

LEARNING CHECK

1. The _____ Act is the key legislation designed to protect competition and consumers in Canada.

2. An alternative to legislation protecting competition and consumers is self- _____.

3. What is consumerism?

LEARNING OBJECTIVE REINFORCEMENT

1. Define environmental scanning. Environmental scanning is the acquiring of information on events occurring outside an organization in order to identify and interpret potential trends that can impact on its business.

2. Outline the major social forces that affect marketing. Major social forces in the marketing environment that affect marketing include demographic factors such as population size and growth, urbanization, aging, changes in family structure, and ethnic diversity. Another major social factor is culture, including changes in the roles of women and men, consumers' attitudes toward work, consumption (value consciousness), and the ecological environment.

3. Explain how macroeconomic conditions and consumer income affect marketing. The inflationary or recessionary state of a nation's economy, whether actual or perceived by consumers or businesses, affects marketing. In an inflationary economy, prices can rise faster than consumer incomes, thus reducing the number of items consumers can buy. In a recessionary economy there is slow economic activity; businesses decrease production, unemployment rises, and many consumers have less money to spend. A consumer's ability to buy is related to income. The total amount of money made in one year by a person, household, or family unit is gross income. Disposable income is the number of dollars left after taxes. Discretionary income is the money consumers have after purchasing their necessities. Marketers have to assess the relative buying power of consumers in given markets, including what their gross incomes are, as well as their disposable and discretionary incomes.

4. Outline the impact of technology on marketing. Technological advances are changing marketing by helping companies develop new products, and assisting them to get existing products to the right consumers with greater speed and at lower costs. Using everything from desktop personal computers to satellites in space, entire industries are using technology to improve research, reduce costs of production and distribution, control inventory, and stay in closer contact with customers and suppliers.

5. Explain the alternative forms of competition that can exist in the marketplace. There are four basic forms of competition that form a continuum: pure competition, monopolistic competition, oligopoly, and monopoly. Pure competition is a situation in which every company has a similar product. With monopolistic competition, there are many sellers that compete with their products on a substitutable basis. Oligopoly is a common industry structure which occurs when a few companies control the majority of industry sales. A monopoly occurs when only one firm sells the product or service. It has been common for companies providing products and services considered essential to a community—water, electricity, or telephone—to be in a monopoly situation, usually granted by government regulation.

6. Understand the regulatory forces that protect competition and consumers in Canada. Regulatory forces consist of restrictions the provincial and federal laws place on business with regard to the conduct of its activities. Much of the regulation is designed to ensure fair competition, and to protect consumers from unfair trade practices and ensure their safety. The key piece of legislation designed to protect competition and consumers in Canada is the Competition Act. In addition to government regulation, industries can police themselves through self-regulation. Consumerism, a movement to increase the influence, power, and rights of consumers in dealing with institutions, also plays a role in regulating the marketplace.

KEY TERMS AND CONCEPTS

environmental scanning p. 66
social forces p. 67
demographics p. 67
census metropolitan areas
    (CMAs) p. 68
mature market p. 68
youth market p. 68
baby boomers p. 68
Generation X p. 68

blended family p. 69
culture p. 70
time poverty p. 71
economy p. 72
gross income p. 73
disposable income p. 73
discretionary income p. 73
technology p. 74
competition p. 75

barriers to entry p. 76
global industry p. 77
strategic alliances p. 77
restructuring p. 78
outsourcing p. 78
regulation p. 78
Competition Act p. 79
self-regulation p. 79
consumerism p. 80

CHAPTER QUESTIONS AND APPLICATIONS

1. Describe the target market for a luxury item such as a Lexus 400. List three or four magazines in which you would advertise to reach this target market.

2. Suggest how the following firms and products might become more environmentally friendly:
   (*a*) Gillette safety razor division.
   (*b*) Kentucky Fried Chicken Restaurants.

(*c*) Hallmark greeting cards.

3. In the Canadian brewing industry, two large firms control most of the beer sales (Labatt and Molson). But they are facing competition from many smaller regional beer makers. In terms of the continuum of competition, how would you explain this change?

4. With the deregulation of the long-distance telephone industry in Canada, how do you think the role of marketing in the industry will change? What elements of the marketing mix are more or less important since deregulation?

5. With time poverty being a concern for many dual-income families, how can marketers help these families balance work and family?

6. What type of impact has a new technology like inexpensive fax machines had on traditional delivery or courier companies? How can these companies respond to this technological threat to their business?

7. Today's consumer is more value-conscious. How could a retail home improvement centre sell the exact same products but still offer the consumer greater perceived value? What specific things could the retailer do?

APPLICATION CASE 3-1
ENERGY PERFORMANCE SYSTEMS INC. (A)

David Ostlie had built his own home furnace to burn dry logs in his garage. The furnace worked so well that David convinced top management in the electric utility for which he worked to scale up the design to prove it could produce cheap, clean electricity in actual power plants. Tests went well and his utility planned to commercialize the technology. But when internal political problems shut down further development, Ostlie took his patent, left the utility, and founded his own company—Energy Performance Systems, Inc. (EPS). The mission of EPS was to commercialize whole-tree energy (WTE) technology. WTE involves producing electricity by growing, harvesting, transporting, drying, and burning whole hardwood trees (trunks, branches, and all) in either (1) retrofitted coal or oil power plants or (2) new power plants.

At first glance the WTE technology and burning wood to produce electricity look like a giant step backward. But three little-known facts make the WTE technology especially appealing: (1) at high temperatures dried wood gasifies quickly, which leads to efficient combustion and virtually no acid-gas emission problems; (2) hardwood tree stands are net emitters of CO_2 and methane during the final quarter of their natural life span, thus contributing to the problems associated with the greenhouse effect rather than reducing them; and (3) much of the hardwood that exists is overage not wanted by the logging, paper, and pulp industries and should be harvested. Hardwood trees here means all broadleaf trees such as birch, maple, and poplar (essentially all trees but conifers).

For many people the thought of harvesting and burning trees suggests decimated forests and more acid rain, air pollution, and global warming. In fact, the reverse is true and significant environmental and agricultural benefits occur. When 70 percent of the moisture content is removed, whole trees gasify and burn to over 1,200 degrees C, resulting in virtually no sul-

fur dioxide, very low nitrogen oxides, no toxic polyaromatic hydrocarbons, and very low particulate emissions. So the WTE process virtually eliminates the emission problems of today's fossil fuel power plants. WTE plants will burn (1) hardwoods that are unsalable (not wanted by other forest product firms); (2) fast-growing energy trees raised on plantations that can be harvested as often as every 8 to 10 years and add agricultural jobs; and (3) waste wood left over by forest product firms. Harvesting overage hardwoods actually stimulates forest regeneration and often provides better habitat for wildlife.

David has demonstrated the technical feasibility of key elements in the WTE process. He hopes to commercialize WTE by having a utility retrofit an existing plant that has emissions problems. With demand for electricity expected to grow over the next two decades, a huge opportunity exists for WTE. "And a technology that reduces pollution, puts moth-balled fossil-fuel plants back in operation, aids forest regeneration and wildlife, helps hold the price of electricity down, and adds a cash crop and jobs, should get a hearing, shouldn't it?" asks Dave Ostlie.

QUESTIONS

1. Conduct an environmental scan for Dave Ostlie and EPS on the whole-tree energy (WTE) technology. For the five environmental forces (social, economic, technological, competitive, regulatory), what are the issues affecting (a) the supply of and demand for electricity, and (b) the pollution and ecological (environmental) concern?

2. As a concerned citizen, (a) what do you see as the key benefits of the WTE technology and (b) what do you see as the potential "show stoppers" for WTE—the critical things that can prevent it from being commercialized and becoming a reality?

APPLICATION CASE 3-2
ASSESSING DEMOGRAPHIC TRENDS

As you read in this chapter, environmental scanning is used by market-driven organizations to identify trends that may offer new marketing opportunities as well as those that may threaten the prosperity of those organizations in the future. One aspect of environmental scanning is studying demographic trends in given markets. Changes in population size, growth rate, age, gender, or other population characteristics need to be examined closely in order to determine if such changes will impact positively or negatively on an organization.

Demographers have identified many trends that they feel will affect the scope and nature of our population in the future. Two trends they have identified are: (1) women are having fewer children and (2) Canadians are living even longer.

Trend # 1—Women are having fewer children. At present, the average female in Canada is having less than 1.7 children during her childbearing years and this number is expected to continue to fall. But according to statisticians, at least 2.1 children per female are needed to ensure that in the long term the number of births in Canada is at least equal to the number of deaths. In short, the fertility rate is below the replacement rate.

Furthermore, the fertility rate is expected to continue to fall to 1.2 children per woman over the next two decades.

Trend # 2—Canadians are living even longer. In 1931, life expectancy from birth in Canada was 62 years for females and 60 years for males. Currently, life expectancy is 80 years for females and 73 years for males. By 2011, life expectancy for females is projected to rise to 84 years and 77 years for males. This differential change in longevity between females and males also means there will be more females than males in the future.

QUESTIONS

1. What will be the overall impact of Trend # 1? Will this trend offer anyone better opportunities in the future?
2. What will be the overall future impact of Trend # 2? What will be the specific social impact of Trend # 2?
3. In addition to the two trends mentioned above, what other demographic trends may heavily impact on the Canadian marketplace in the future?

If you think these questions are tough, wait till your child asks, "Why can't I drink?"

Curiosity about alcohol can start as early as preteen years. Your children will look to you for answers.

"How To Talk About Alcohol" is a free Seagram program designed for parents of preteens by Education Development Center. The easy-to-follow audiocassette and handbook are packed with facts and tips: what your youngsters should know about alcohol, how to reach them, peer pressure and other difficult situations they may face.

Give your children a good start with our preteen program. It's free and it's important.

Seagram Canada

CHAPTER 4

Marketing Ethics

AFTER READING THIS CHAPTER YOU WILL BE ABLE TO:

1. Explain the importance of ethics in marketing.

2. Understand the differences between legal and ethical behaviour in marketing.

3. Identify factors that influence ethical and unethical marketing decisions.

4. Distinguish between the concepts of ethics and social responsibility.

SEAGRAM CANADA: DOING THE RIGHT THING

Why would an organization spend millions of dollars trying to convince people not to abuse its product? Ask Seagram Canada, one of Canada's largest distillers and a leader in the campaign for responsible drinking. Seagram acts on what it views as an ethical obligation to society with its "How To Talk About Alcohol" campaign. Seagram recognizes the need to support meaningful public dialogue and programs to raise community awareness about the responsible use of alcohol. As a leader in this campaign for responsible drinking, Seagram Canada has demonstrated its understanding of one of the seven imperatives for marketing success: *act ethically and responsibly* (see Chapter 1 for a review of the seven imperatives for marketing success).

"How To Talk About Alcohol" is a free Seagram program that goes beyond conventional drinking-and-driving campaigns. It is an educational program designed for parents of preteens. The program includes an easy-to-follow audiocassette and handbook that are packed with facts and tips: what your youngsters should know about alcohol, how to reach them, how to deal with peer pressure and other difficult situations they may face.[1]

This chapter focusses on ethics and social responsibility in marketing. You will see how some organizations recognize that while ethical and responsible behaviour often comes with a price tag, the price for unethical and irresponsible behaviour can be much higher. Increasingly in this marketplace, organizations can "do well by doing the right thing."

NATURE AND SIGNIFICANCE OF MARKETING ETHICS

Recall from Chapter 1 that **ethics** are the moral principles and values that govern the actions and decisions of an individual or a group.[2] They serve as guidelines on how to act rightly and justly when faced with moral dilemmas.

Ethical and Legal Framework in Marketing

A good starting point for understanding the nature and significance of ethics is the distinction between legality and ethicality of marketing decisions. Figure 4–1 helps you visualize the relationship between laws and ethics.[3] While ethics deal with personal and moral principles and values, **laws** are society's values and standards that are enforceable in the courts.[4] This distinction can sometimes lead to the rationalization that if a behaviour is within legal limits, then it is not really unethical. When a recent survey asked the question, Is it OK to get around the law if you don't actually break it?, 61 percent of businesspeople who took part responded yes.[5] How would you answer this question?

There are numerous situations where judgment plays a large role in defining ethical and legal boundaries. Consider the following situations. After reading each, assign it to the cell in Figure 4–1 that you think best fits the situation along the ethical–legal continuum.

1. Assume several companies meet and agree to bid rigging for sealed tendered government contract work. Bid rigging is illegal under the Competition Act, since it eliminates free and open competition.
2. Assume a company sells a computer program to auto dealers showing that car buyers should finance their purchase rather than pay cash. The program misstates the interest earned on savings earned over the loan period. The finance option always provides a net benefit over the cash option. Company employees agree that the program does mislead the buyers but say that the company will provide what the car dealers want as long as it is not against the law.
3. Assume a tobacco company decides to market a smaller package of cigarettes, a package containing 10 cigarettes versus the regular 20 or 25. They suggest

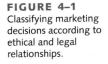

FIGURE 4–1
Classifying marketing decisions according to ethical and legal relationships.

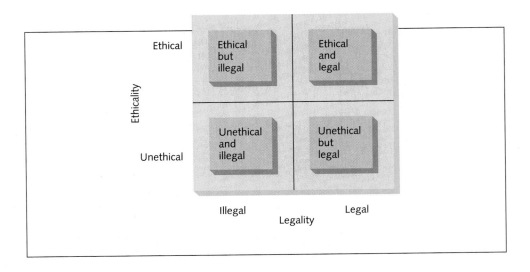

$ MARKETPLACE APPLICATION

Canada's Lobbying Industry Under Attack

The Ottawa-based lobbying business is worth an estimated $100 million a year and includes more than 3,000 registered lobbyists. The federal government recently introduced an ethics package to regulate this lobbying industry and strengthen conflict-of-interest guidelines for cabinet ministers. This action has had mixed reviews.

Among other things, the new regulations mean that the lobbyists will have to disclose their clients' names, the parent company and subsidiaries of any corporate clients, and who is behind any coalition, organization or special-interest group. Penalties for breaching the rules include fines as high as $100,000 and two years in prison.

Dave Miller, a senior consultant with Hill and Knowlton's Ottawa lobbying division, says "it's reasonable and we're perfectly comfortable with the legislation. It will allow us to disclose the required information while still protecting proprietary interests of our clients."

Others, however, feel the new rules don't go far enough. Duff Conacher, coordinator with Democracy Watch, which tracks business and government ethics, says the measures reveal more, but key information is still missing. "We think that lobbyists should state their current and past political activities, as well as their fees and expenditures."

1. Why should groups like Democracy Watch be concerned about the business activities of lobbyists?
2. Should lobbyists be required by law to disclose their current and past political activities, their fees and expenditures? Explain.

SOURCE: Adapted from Gina Brown, "Lobbyists Approve of Feds' New Rules," *Marketing,* July 18, 1994, p. 3.

---

that this offering will provide some of their customers a cheaper alternative. Health officials argue that the smaller, cheaper package will encourage minors to smoke. The company suggests this is not its intention and that stores cannot legally sell cigarettes to minors.

4. Assume a real estate agent sells a high-rise condo unit to a customer, primarily on the basis of the city view from the windows, which the customer loves. The agent knows that in one year another high-rise will be built, effectively blocking the view so important to the customer. The agent decides not to tell the customer, since there is no legal obligation to do so.

Do these situations fit neatly into Figure 4–1 as clearly defined ethical and legal or unethical and illegal practices? Some do while others probably do not.

Current Status of Ethical Behaviour

There has been much discussion over the deterioration of personal morality and ethical standards on a global scale. The news media offer well-publicized examples of personal dishonesty, cheating, and greed. The ethical conduct of business is also coming under closer scrutiny. Most public opinion surveys as well as other research show that most adults believe the ethical standards of business have declined over the years.[6] A recent survey of senior corporate executives confirms this public perception. Two-thirds of these executives think people are "occasionally" unethical in their business dealings, 15 percent believe they are "often" unethical, and 16 percent consider people "seldom" without ethics.[7]

There are at least four possible reasons why the state of perceived ethical business conduct is at its present level. First, there is increased pressure on businesspeople to make decisions in a society characterized by diverse values.[8] Second, there is a growing tendency for business decisions to be judged publicly by groups with different values and interests. Third, the public's expectations of ethical business behaviour have increased. Finally, and most disturbing, ethical business conduct may have declined.

LEARNING CHECK

1. What are ethics?

2. What are four possible reasons for the present perception of the ethical conduct of business?

UNDERSTANDING ETHICAL BEHAVIOUR

Researchers have identified numerous factors that influence ethical behaviour.[9] The framework presented in Figure 4–2 shows the factors that influence ethical decision making by focusing on three variables that affect behaviour: *individual factors, significant others, and opportunity.*

FIGURE 4–2   A framework for understanding ethical behaviour.

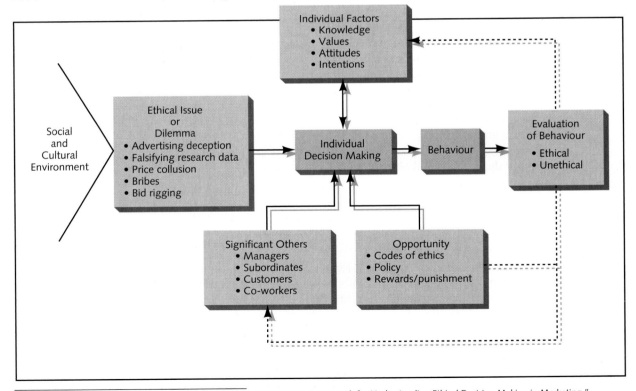

SOURCE: Adapted from O. C. Ferrell and Larry Gresham, "A Contingency Framework for Understanding Ethical Decision Making in Marketing," *Journal of Marketing,* Summer 1985, pp. 87–96.

Individual Factors

Individual factors refer to the moral philosophies or principles that individuals use when deciding between right and wrong. Moral philosophies are learned through a process of socialization with friends, co-workers, and family, and by formal education.

Individuals often make different decisions than others in similar situations. According to developmental psychologist Lawrence Kohlberg, this is because individuals progress through stages of **cognitive moral development.** Kohlberg's model of cognitive moral development suggests that people progress through three distinct phases of moral development. In the first phase, the *preconventional phase,* individuals have a *self focus* and their behaviour is influenced by fear of authority ("obey or pay") or self-interest ("what's in it for me?"). The second phase of moral development is known as the *conventional phase.* Individuals at this phase have a *group focus.* These individuals are influenced by a concern of what others think ("will they approve?") or a sense of duty to society ("it's my duty"). The final phase of moral development is known as the *postconventional phase.* Individuals who have progressed to this phase have a *universal focus.* These individuals' behaviours are influenced by their concern for social standards ("we owe this to our customers") or their belief in universal principles ("we must seek justice and equality for all").[10]

Significant Others

Significant others refers to those who have influence in a work group such as co-workers, subordinates, managers, and customers. Many studies have confirmed that significant others have more impact on a worker's decisions on a daily basis than any other factor in Figure 4–2.[11] For example, a salesperson who associates with other salespeople who steal supplies such as note pads and computer paper from their employer may come to believe that these activities are acceptable. Similarly, an auto mechanic may come to believe that it is acceptable to recommend the installation of unnecessary parts if they are encouraged to do so by their manager.

Opportunity

Opportunity results from conditions that either limit barriers or permit unethical behaviour. An example of a condition that limits barriers to behaviour would be a company policy that fails to punish those who are involved in unethical behaviours, such as accepting bribes or stealing. Sometimes, either knowingly or unknowingly, organizations reward behaviours that are generally considered unethical. For example, an organization may provide bonuses, commissions, or nonfinancial rewards such as sales rewards to those who sell the most product. A reward program such as this may not be intended to reward unethical behaviour, however, it often creates a situation that encourages salespeople to "hard sell" products that customers do not need.

Individual factors, significant others, and opportunity are all influenced by the organization's culture. **Organizational culture** reflects the shared values, beliefs, and purpose of employees that affect individual and group behaviour. The culture of an organization demonstrates itself in the dress ("we don't wear ties"), sayings ("the IBM way"), and the manner of work (team efforts) of employees. **Ethical climate** is an aspect of organizational culture that describes the decision processes used to determine whether dilemmas are ethical or unethical. Factors such as formal codes of ethics and

Competition Heats Up: Ringing the Wrong Numbers

Prior to June, 1992, Bell Canada enjoyed a monopoly for long-distance service in Canada. However, a ruling by the Canadian Radio-television and Telecommunications Commission (CRTC) approved Unitel's proposal for a second long-distance service. As a result, the telephone business in Canada is now competitive and the battle for market share that Canadians have observed in the United States has migrated north.

Marketers involved in this newly competitive telephone business in Canada would do well to take a look at a new study conducted in the U.S. In this study of over 1,000 Americans, New York-based CDB Research & Consulting Inc., found that 78 percent of them are sick of advertising and "hype" about long-distance services. And those with annual incomes of $50,000 or more were even more likely to be tired of it (89%), as were those in the 18-to-34 age range (83%). On top of that, nearly 6 out of 10, or 59 percent of those surveyed, said they were confused about available calling plans.

1. Is it ethical for long-distance service providers to actively participate in the aggressive advertising campaigns that consumers sometimes refer to as "hype?" Discuss.

2. Should government regulators take action to protect Canadian consumers from the "hype" about long-distance services?

SOURCE: Adapted from "Ringing the Wrong Numbers," *Marketing,* April 17, 1995, p. 22.

the ethical actions of top management and co-workers shape the ethical climate within an organization.

Codes of Ethics. A code of ethics is a formal statement of ethical principles and rules of conduct. Ethical codes and committees typically address such issues as contributions to government officials and political parties, relations with customers and suppliers, conflicts of interest, and accurate recordkeeping.[12] Opportunity to behave unethically is reduced if a code of ethics is developed and equitably enforced at all levels in an organization.

A lack of detail, however, is one of the major reasons for the violation of ethics codes. Employees must often judge whether a specific behaviour is really unethical. The American Marketing Association, representing Canadian and American marketing professionals, has addressed this issue by providing a detailed code of ethics, which all members agree to follow. This code is shown in Figure 4–3.

LEARNING CHECK

1. What factors influence ethical behaviour?

2. What is a code of ethics?

UNDERSTANDING SOCIAL RESPONSIBILITY IN MARKETING

As we saw in Chapter 1, acting ethically and responsibly is one of the seven imperatives for marketing success. In this marketplace, acting responsibly often means the organization behaves in a socially responsible manner. Recall that **social responsibility**

CODE OF ETHICS

Members of the American Marketing Association (AMA) are committed to ethical professional conduct. They have joined together in subscribing to this Code of Ethics embracing the following topics:

Responsibilities of the Marketer

Marketers must accept responsibility for the consequence of their activities and make every effort to ensure that their decisions, recommendations, and actions function to identify, serve, and satisfy all relevant publics: customers, organizations, and society.

Marketers' professional conduct must be guided by:

1. The basic rule of professional ethics: not knowingly to do harm.
2. The adherence to all applicable laws and regulations.
3. The accurate representation of their education, training, and experience.
4. The active support, practice, and promotion of this Code of Ethics.

Honesty and Fairness

Marketers shall uphold and advance the integrity, honor, and dignity of the marketing profession by:

1. Being honest in serving consumers, clients, employees, suppliers, distributors, and the public.
2. Not knowingly participating in conflict of interest without prior notice to all parties involved.
3. Establishing equitable fee schedules including the payment or receipt of usual, customary, and/or legal compensation or marketing exchanges.

Rights and Duties of Parties in the Marketing Exchange Process

Participants in the marketing exchange process should be able to expect that:

1. Products and services offered are safe and fit for their intended uses.
2. Communications about offered products and services are not deceptive.
3. All parties intend to discharge their obligations, financial and otherwise, in good faith.
4. Appropriate internal methods exist for equitable adjustment and/or redress of grievances concerning purchases.

It is understood that the above would include, *but is not limited to,* the following responsibilities of the marketer:

In the Area of Product Development and Management

- Disclosure of all substantial risks associated with product or service usage.
- Identification of any product component substitution that might materially change the product or impact on the buyer's purchase decision.
- Identification of extra-cost added features.

FIGURE 4–3
American Marketing
Association Code of
Ethics.

means that organizations are part of a larger society and are accountable to that society for their actions.

Like ethics, agreement on the nature and scope of social responsibility is often difficult to come by, given the diversity of values present in different societal, business, and organizational cultures. Most, however, would probably agree that social responsibility implies that marketing decision makers have some obligation, beyond their individual self-interest, to protect and improve the welfare of society as a whole.[13]

The 1990s have seen an increasing number of Canadian consumers and organizations voicing and demonstrating concern for the environment. Today, more Canadian

FIGURE 4–3
Continued

In the Area of Promotions
- Avoidance of false and misleading advertising.
- Rejection of high pressure manipulation, or misleading sales tactics.
- Avoidance of sales promotions that use deception or manipulation.

In the Area of Distribution
- Not manipulating the availability of a product for purpose of exploitation.
- Not using coercion in the marketing channel.
- Not exerting undue influence over the reseller's choice to handle the product.

In the Area of Pricing
- Not engaging in price fixing.
- Not practising predatory pricing.
- Disclosing the full price associated with any purchase.

In the Area of Marketing Research
- Prohibiting selling or fund raising under the guise of conducting research.
- Maintaining research integrity by avoiding misrepresentation and omission of pertinent research data.
- Treating outside clients and suppliers fairly.

Organizational Relationships
Marketers should be aware of how their behaviour may influence or impact on the behaviour of others in organizational relationships. They should not demand, encourage, or apply coercion to obtain unethical behaviour in their relationships with others, such as employees, suppliers, or customers.

1. Apply confidentiality and anonymity in professional relationships with regard to privileged information.
2. Meet their obligations and responsibilities in contracts and mutual agreements in a timely manner.
3. Avoid taking the work of others, in whole, or in part, and represent this work as their own or directly benefit from it without compensation or consent of the originator or owner.
4. Avoid manipulation to take advantage of situations to maximize personal welfare in a way that unfairly deprives or damages the organization or others.

Any AMA member found to be in violation of any provision of this Code of Ethics may have his or her Association membership suspended or revoked.

SOURCE: Reprinted by permission of The American Marketing Association.

organizations than ever before are demonstrating social responsibility by protecting the environment. Efforts to produce, market, and reclaim ecologically or environmentally sensitive products are known as **green marketing** (sometimes called eco-friendly marketing). The following examples illustrate the practice of green marketing:

- The Grocery Products Manufacturers of Canada has introduced a program known as the *Canadian Industry Packaging Stewardship Initiative,* which is designed to promote responsible waste and product recycling. This program seeks to subsidize curbside recycling programs by charging manufacturers a fee based on the weights of packaging they produce.[14]
- In an effort to reduce the volume of waste experienced with the use of paper plates, Vinnie's Pizza, a single location pizza restaurant, introduced ceramic plates for its eat-in customers.

MARKETPLACE APPLICATION

Enhancing Corporate Image through Cause-Related Marketing

Many Canadian companies are discovering that good corporate citizenship goes hand in hand with effective marketing. Historically, Canadian companies have given little thought to the tie between social responsibility and the subsequent impact on their businesses. Indeed, many simply made donations to causes very quietly, for fear of looking opportunistic or self-serving. Today, however, charitable donations and cause-related marketing (CRM) efforts are often highly visible components of corporate cultures. Corporate philanthropy and CRM are now seen as complements to traditional marketing efforts. Although consumers do not usually choose between products or services solely on the basis of what "causes" a company supports, a company's visible stand or support of a cause may sway the buying decision with all other things—price, performance, perceived value—being equal.

Demonstrating social responsibility through cause-related marketing activities can encourage a new customer to buy as well as solidify relationships with existing customers. Many firms that have tried to build their corporate images solely through advertising and promotion are now finding CRM to be an effective tool in demonstrating the substance and character of a company. Some question the "true" altruism of some companies that engage in CRM activities, since they benefit from such behaviour in terms of enhanced image and customer loyalty. But the fact is, many worthwhile causes do benefit from this form of corporate behaviour, and this should not be diminished simply because the corporation receives residual benefits. It is a win–win situation.

1. What factors may explain the increased visibility of CRM in Canada?

SOURCE: Adapted from A. Mastromartino, "Giving Enhances Corporate Image," *Marketing,* June 28, 1993, p. 31.

- Hewlett-Packard introduced what it calls "new generation" HP LaserJet printers. These printers are designed to have a minimal negative impact on the environment of the office; the communities where they are manufactured, shipped, and used; and the waste disposal site where they eventually go.
- Beaver Foods Ltd. sells a green-coloured coffee mug that is made with recycled material. Printed on the side of this mug is the message "Reduce, Reuse, Recycle." Targeted at eco-friendly oriented coffee and tea drinking customers, this product offers an alternative to non-reusable cups.

Socially responsible efforts on behalf of customers are becoming more common. A formal practice known as **cause-related marketing (CRM)** is an example of this type of effort. This practice occurs when the charitable contributions of an organization are tied directly to the customer revenues produced through the marketing of one of its products.[15] This definition distinguishes CRM from an organization's standard charitable contributions, which are outright donations. CRM programs can demonstrate an organization's social responsibility while accomplishing other marketing objectives by addressing public concerns, satisfying customer needs, and increasing sales and profits. Many organizations have also found that CRM provides another long-term benefit: enhancing corporate image (see the accompanying Marketplace Application). The following examples illustrate the practice of CRM:

- When you purchase Avon's *Flame Pin,* 100 percent of the profits go to Canada's Breast Cancer International Centre to fund research, treatment, prevention, and education in Canada.
- In cooperation with VISA and MasterCard *Ducks Unlimited (DU)* offers a special *DU* credit card, which it promotes with the slogan "Get A Charge Out Of

EcoLogo™ Paper / Papier Éco-Logo™

Environment Canada actively promotes green marketing. This symbol features three stylized doves intertwined to form a maple leaf, representing consumers, industry, and government working together to improve Canada's environment. Companies must be licensed to use the EcoLogo, an official mark of Environment Canada.

Ecological disasters such as the Exxon *Valdez* oil spill have moved environmental concerns to the forefront of corporate planning.

Helping Ducks." A portion of each credit charge purchase is donated to *Ducks Unlimited* for the purpose of preserving wetlands.
• The Bank of Montreal markets its *Project Sunshine* calendars to its customers to raise money for children's hospitals in Canada.

The Social Audit

Converting socially responsible ideas into actions involves careful planning and monitoring of programs. Many companies develop, implement, and evaluate their social responsibility efforts by means of a **social audit,** which is a systematic assessment of a firm's objectives, strategies, and performance in the domain of social responsibility. The development and use of a social audit will depend on the extent to which a company's culture embraces social responsibility as part of its overall mission.

A social audit consists of five steps:[16]

1. Recognition of a firm's social expectations and the rationale for engaging in social responsibility endeavours.
2. Identification of social responsibility causes or programs consistent with the company's mission.
3. Determination of organizational objectives and priorities for programs and activities it will undertake.
4. Specification of the type and amount of resources necessary to achieve social responsibility objectives.
5. Evaluation of social responsibility programs and activities undertaken, and assessment of future involvement.

Attention to the social audit on environmental matters has increased since 1989, when the Exxon *Valdez* oil tanker spilled 11 million gallons of crude oil off the Canadian and American west coast. This spill killed tens of thousands of birds and mammals and fouled 1,000 miles of coastline. Soon after, the Coalition for

Environmentally Responsible Economics drafted guidelines designed to focus attention on environmental concerns and corporate responsibility. These guidelines, called the **Valdez Principles,** encourage companies to:

- Eliminate pollutants, minimize hazardous wastes, and conserve nonrenewable resources.
- Market environmentally safe products and services.
- Prepare for accidents and restore damaged environments.
- Provide protection for employees who report environmental hazards.
- Appoint an environmentalist to their boards of directors, name an executive for environmental affairs, and develop an environmental audit of their global operations to be made available for public inspection.

Numerous companies now embrace these guidelines, and firms such as S. C. Johnson & Sons and Colgate-Palmolive have environmental policy officers.[17] Nevertheless, environmental mishaps still occur.

Turning the Table: Consumer Ethics and Social Responsibility

Consumers also have an obligation to act ethically and responsibly in the exchange process and in the use and disposition of products. Unfortunately, consumer behaviour is spotty on both counts.

Unethical practices of consumers are a serious concern to marketers.[18] These practices include filing warranty claims after the claim period; misredeeming coupons; making fraudulent returns of merchandise; providing inaccurate information on credit applications; tampering with utility meters or tapping cable TV lines; recording copyrighted music, videocassettes, and computer software; and submitting phony insurance claims. The cost to marketers is lost revenue, and prevention expenses are huge.[19] For example, consumers who redeem coupons for unpurchased products or use coupons destined for other products cost manufacturers millions of dollars annually. The record industry loses hundreds of millions of dollars due to illegal recording, and many VCR owners who make illegal copies of videotapes cost producers millions of dollars in lost revenue.

Consumer purchase, use, and disposition of environmentally sensitive products relates to consumer social responsibility. Research indicates that consumers are sensitive to ecological or environmental issues.[20] However, research also shows that consumers (1) may be unwilling to sacrifice convenience or pay potentially higher prices to protect the environment and (2) lack the knowledge to make informed decisions dealing with the purchase, use, and disposition of products.[21]

Consumer confusion over which products are environmentally safe is also apparent, given marketers' rush to produce "green" products. For example, few consumers realize that nonaerosol "pump" hairsprays contribute to air pollution. And "biodegradable" claims on a variety of products, including trash bags, have not proven to be accurate, thus leading to buyer confusion.[22]

Ultimately, marketers and consumers are accountable for ethical and socially responsible behaviour.

LEARNING CHECK

1. What is meant by social responsibility?

2. What is a social audit?

LEARNING OBJECTIVE REINFORCEMENT

1. Explain the importance of ethics in marketing. Ethical behaviour in marketing has come under criticism by the public. There are four possible reasons for this criticism: (1) increased pressure on businesspeople to make decisions in a society characterized by diverse values, (2) a growing tendency to have business decisions judged publicly by groups with different values and interests, (3) an increase in the public's expectations for ethical behaviour, and (4) a possible decline in business ethics. Some organizations recognize that while ethical and responsible behaviour often comes with a price tag, the price for unethical and irresponsible behaviour can be much higher. Increasingly in this marketplace, organizations can "do well by doing the right thing."

2. Understand the differences between legal and ethical behaviour in marketing. While *ethics* deal with personal and moral principles and values that govern the actions and decisions of an individual or a group, *laws* are society's values and standards that are enforceable in the courts.

3. Identify factors that influence ethical and unethical marketing decisions. Numerous factors influence ethical and unethical marketing decisions. There are, however, three factors that are known to have a significant affect on ethical behaviour: *individual factors, significant others,* and *opportunity. Individual factors* refer to the moral principles that individuals use when deciding between right and wrong. Individuals progress through stages of *cognitive moral development,* therefore the moral principles that govern their actions may change as the individual's moral development progresses. *Significant others* refers to those who have influence in a work group such as co-workers, managers, and customers. *Opportunity* results from conditions that either limit barriers or permit unethical behaviour. Often an organization's system of rewards (e.g., commissions and bonuses) and punishments creates situations that encourage or allow unethical behaviour.

4. Distinguish between the concepts of ethics and social responsibility. *Ethics* deal with personal and moral principles and values that govern the actions and decisions of an individual or a group. They serve as guidelines on how to act rightly and justly when faced with a moral issue. Any discussion of ethical practices in marketing will soon lead to the closely related topic of *social responsibility*. Social responsibility means that organizations are part of a larger society and are accountable to that society for their actions. Like ethics, agreement on the nature and scope of social responsibility is often difficult to come by, given the diversity of values present in different societal, business, and organizational cultures.

KEY TERMS AND CONCEPTS

ethics, p. 88
laws, p. 88
cognitive moral development, p. 91
organizational culture, p. 91

ethical climate, p. 91
social responsibility, p. 91–93
green marketing, p. 94
cause-related marketing, p. 95

social audit, p. 96
Valdez Principles, p. 97

CHAPTER QUESTIONS AND APPLICATIONS

1. Why should ethics be a topic of concern in marketing? Isn't it enough to operate within the law?

2. Increasingly in this marketplace, organizations can "do well by doing the right thing." Do you agree or disagree with this statement? Describe one or more situations that support your opinion.

3. The text provides three factors that affect ethical behaviour. Can you name others?

4. What personal guidelines do you apply when deciding what is ethical behaviour for you?

5. Is it ethical to charge one customer a higher price than you charge another for the same product simply because you think that customer will pay it?

6. Codes of ethics are more popular today than ever before. How would you explain this popularity?

7. Cause-related marketing programs have become popular. Identify and describe two such programs that you are familiar with.

8. Do you think that a social audit is a useful assessment tool? Why or why not?

9. The text lists several unethical practices of consumers. Can you name others? Why do you think consumers engage in unethical conduct?

10. When you are at the grocery store you may see people pick grapes or other small items to munch on while they are shopping without telling the cashier or offering to pay for their munchies. Is this behaviour OK?

APPLICATION CASE 4-1
THE TOO-SMALL SAMPLE

It was Monday morning and Roland, the statistician for a small marketing research house, was sitting at his terminal cleaning up the tabulation program for a telephone survey that was currently in the field. Todd, the owner of the firm, walked into Roland's office. "Roland, I just heard from the interviewing service that the data collection for the bank study won't be completed for at least two weeks. I guess we should have pretested the questionnaire. It's taking twice as long to complete the interviews as we estimated. Not only are we going to lose money on this project, but the final report is due in two weeks."

"Oh no!" cried Roland. "We need a week just to edit and code the open-ended questions before data entry can begin. We'll have to beg for time from the bank."

"We can't do that. Remember how I got the project? They had been quoted $30,000 by Jones & Wilson Research and I told them we could do it in half the time and for only 20 grand." There was silence for a few minutes and then Todd added, "I've got an idea. We stop interviewing now with the 352 interviews that are complete and bump the numbers up to 500 with a multiplier, you know, a weighting routine. Roland, you can do that with just a few lines of programming. The bank will never know. Hell, they don't know anything about survey research, much less statistics. The printout will only show the bumped-up numbers and they will never see the programming.

Before Roland could say anything, Todd was walking out of the office saying, "Start doing your magic with the programming now and I'll call the interviewing service. This is great, we'll make money *and* get the job done on time. Go to it, Roland!"

After Todd left his office, Roland said aloud, "Terrific, my first job as a real marketing research statistician and I've got an idiot for a boss." As he reflected on the situation he thought, "Bumping-up the numbers without telling the client is like stealing their money. And even if they are told, I'm not sure if the statistical routines we plan to use will be appropriate for weighted data. I don't know what to do. I guess other companies weight data and I do need this job. But . . ."

QUESTIONS:
1. What are the ethical issues?
2. What alternatives are available to Roland?
3. What actions should be taken?

APPLICATION CASE 4-2
CODE OF ETHICS EXERCISE

Assume the senior administrators at your school have asked you to participate in the development of a code of ethics for the school. As a participant in this process you have been asked to consider:

• Your understanding of ethics.
• Topics and situations that should be addressed.
• How to implement and use the code of ethics.

After giving these issues consideration, please work through the following questions and provide a written summary of your responses:

1. What are your beliefs about personal and professional ethics? Why do people make (un)ethical decisions? How do individuals' ethics, actions, and decisions affect your college experience?
2. What specific ethical issues and dilemmas are common in your school of business? How can those dilemmas be resolved?

3. Can a code of ethics be helpful in your school? How would it be helpful? Could the code have any negative effects? Are there other solutions?
4. Should your school of business develop and implement a code of conduct? Who would write the code? How would you enforce it? What issues should be addressed?
5. In groups of four or five individuals, work through these four questions. After you have developed comprehensive responses, draft a code of ethics for your school. You may consult professional codes of conduct such as the American Marketing Association Code of Ethics which is shown in Figure 4–3.

SOURCE: This exercise was developed by Debbie Thorne, Ph.D., Director of the Center for Ethics at The University of Tampa, Tampa, FL, for educational purposes and has been used in a variety of contexts, including the university classroom, student leadership programs, and professional development seminars. Used with permission.

Understanding Buyers and Markets

PART II

CHAPTER 5

Consumer Behaviour

AFTER READING THIS CHAPTER YOU SHOULD BE ABLE TO:

1. Outline the stages in the consumer purchase decision process.

2. Distinguish between three variations of the consumer purchase decision process: routine, limited, and extended problem solving.

3. List the five situational influences that impact on the consumer purchase decision process.

4. Understand the psychological influences that affect consumer behaviour, particularly purchase decision processes.

5. Identify major sociocultural influences on consumer behaviour and their effects on purchase decisions.

THE CANADIAN SHOPPER

A NEW CREATURE SEEKING VALUE The Canadian shopper of the 1990s is much different than the one who spent in the decadent 1980s. Today's shopper has less money to spend, is more concerned with saving, more circumspect about purchases, and no longer relies on material acquisitions to boost self-image. Many shoppers are now saying they find less joy in buying and are focusing their efforts on attaining what is needed at a good price, rather than making marginal purchases.

The typical Canadian shopper is looking for a wide selection of brands to choose from in order to select the best value. In fact, one study found that only 20 percent of shoppers know the brand they will buy when they enter the store.[1] This indicates that most shoppers are not particularly loyal to one brand over another. Instead they evaluate the alternatives and select the ones that best suit their needs at the price they want.

This purchase decision process takes time and effort. For example, research has shown that the average shopper makes more than 30 product, size, and flavour decisions during a single shopping trip to the grocery store.[2] Still, many shoppers are prepared to make this commitment in their search for value. Marketers who want to be successful must deliver that value.

This chapter examines **consumer behaviour,** the actions a person takes in purchasing and using products and services, and the mental and social processes that precede and follow these actions. Successful marketing begins with understanding how and why consumers behave as they do. This chapter will help answer these questions.

CONSUMER PURCHASE DECISION PROCESS

Behind the visible act of making a purchase lies an important decision process that must be investigated. The stages a buyer passes through in making choices about which products and services to buy is called the **consumer purchase decision process.** This process consists of five stages shown in Figure 5–1: (1) problem recognition, (2) information search, (3) alternative evaluation, (4) purchase decision, and (5) postpurchase behaviour.

Problem Recognition: Perceiving a Need

Problem recognition is the first step in the purchase decision.[3] It occurs when the consumer perceives a difference between his or her ideal and actual situations that is big enough to trigger a decision. This can be as simple as finding an empty milk carton in the refrigerator, noting that your clothes are not in the style that other students are wearing, or realizing that your old car may not be working properly.

In marketing, advertisements or salespeople can activate a consumer's purchase decision process by showing the shortcomings of competing (or currently owned) products. For instance, an advertisement for a new car could stimulate problem recognition because it emphasizes how dependable and maintenance-free it is compared to the old car you may now own.

Information Search: Seeking Value

After recognizing a problem, a consumer begins to search for information, the next stage in the purchase decision process. First, you may scan your memory for previous experiences with products or brands.[4] This action is called an *internal search.* For frequently purchased products such as shampoo, this may be enough. Or you may undertake an *external search* for information.[5] This is especially needed when past experience or knowledge is insufficient, the risk of making the wrong purchase decision is high, and the cost of gathering information is low. The primary sources of external information are (1) *personal sources,* such as relatives and friends whom the consumer trusts; (2) *public sources,* including various product-rating organizations such as *Consumer Reports,* government agencies, and TV "consumer programs"; and (3) *marketer-dominated sources,* such as information from sellers that includes advertising, salespeople, and point-of-purchase displays in stores.[6]

Suppose you are considering buying a new car. You will probably tap several of these information sources: friends and relatives, advertisements, and car dealers. You

FIGURE 5–1 Consumer purchase decision process.

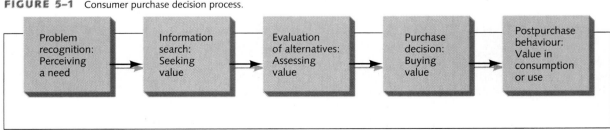

might even study comparative evaluations of new cars published by various automotive-testing organizations such as *Car & Driver.*

Alternative Evaluation: Assessing Value

The information search stage clarifies the problem for the consumer by (1) suggesting criteria to use for the purchase, (2) yielding brand names that might meet the criteria, and (3) developing perceptions of value. All of the factors you might consider when evaluating purchase choices are called **evaluative criteria.** These criteria consist of both the objective attributes of a brand (such as fuel economy) and the subjective ones (such as prestige) that you would use to compare different products and brands.[7] Firms try to identify and capitalize on both types of criteria to create the best value for money sought by you and other consumers.

Considering a new car purchase? How would you go about it?

Consumers often have several criteria for evaluating brands. Knowing this, companies seek to identify the most important evaluative criteria that consumers use when judging brands. For example, the evaluative criteria you might use when evaluating new car choices could include a price under $10,000, a five-year warranty, and good fuel economy. These criteria establish the brands in your **evoked set**—the group of brands you would consider acceptable from among all the brands in the product class of which you are aware.[8]

Your evaluative criteria could result in only a few models in your evoked set. If these brands don't satisfy you, you can change your evaluative criteria to create a different evoked set of models.

Purchase Decision: Buying Value

For a product like a car, the information search process probably involves visiting the dealers, seeing different brands in the showroom or lot, and perhaps taking a test drive. Having examined the alternatives in the evoked set, you are almost ready to make a purchase decision. Two choices remain: (1) from whom to buy and (2) when to buy. The choice of which seller to buy from will depend on such considerations as the terms of sale (e.g., what you'll get on your trade-in, final price, finance package), your past experience buying from the seller, and the dealer's after-sale service policy. Often a purchase decision involves a simultaneous evaluation of both the product attributes and seller characteristics. For example, you might choose the second-most preferred car model from a dealer who offers a better price and free maintenance for three years, over the most-preferred model from a dealer who wants a higher price and doesn't provide free maintenance.

Deciding when to buy is frequently determined by a number of factors. For example, you might buy sooner if one of your preferred brands is on sale or if its manufacturer offers a rebate. Other factors such as store atmosphere, salesperson persuasiveness, and financial circumstances could also affect whether a purchase is made or postponed.

Postpurchase Behaviour: Value in Consumption or Use

After buying a product, the consumer compares it with his or her expectations and is either satisfied or dissatisfied. If the consumer is dissatisfied, marketers must decide whether the product was deficient or consumer expectations too high. Product deficiency may require a design change; on the other hand, if expectations were too high, perhaps the company's advertising or the salesperson oversold the product's features.

Market-driven organizations place great emphasis on delivering customer value in order to ensure satisfaction after the sale. By providing value and satisfaction a firm is able to develop long-term relationships with customers. Nissan Canada, for example, increased its market share by offering 24-hour roadside assistance and a 100 percent satisfaction commitment. Nissan provides customers with toll-free telephone numbers and offers trained staff to handle problems, answer questions, and record suggestions.

In addition to providing value and satisfaction, these efforts also help to alleviate what is called **cognitive dissonance,** the feeling of postpurchase tension or anxiety about the purchase decision. To alleviate cognitive dissonance, consumers often attempt to applaud themselves for making the right choice. So after a purchase you may seek information to confirm your choice by asking friends questions like, "Don't you like my new car?" or by reading ads of the brands you chose. You might even look for negative information about the brand you didn't buy. Firms often use ads or follow-up calls from salespeople in this postpurchase stage to try to convince buyers that they made the right decision. For example, for many years Buick ran an advertising campaign with the message, "Aren't you really glad you bought a Buick?"

Involvement and Problem-Solving Variations

Sometimes consumers don't engage in the five-step purchase decision process. Instead, they skip or minimize one or more steps depending on the level of **involvement**—the personal, social, and economic significance of the purchase to the consumer.[9] High-involvement purchase occasions typically have at least one of three characteristics—the item to be purchased (1) is expensive, (2) can have serious personal consequences, or (3) could reflect on one's social image. For these occasions, consumers engage in extensive information search, consider many product attributes and brands, form attitudes, and participate in word-of-mouth communication. Low-involvement purchases, such as toothpaste and soap, are generally not too involving, whereas stereo systems and automobiles are very involving.

Researchers have identified three general variations in the consumer purchase decision process based on consumer involvement and product knowledge.[10] Figure 5–2 summarizes some of the important differences between the three problem-solving variations.[11]

Routine Problem Solving. For products such as toothpaste and milk, consumers recognize a problem, make a decision, and spend little effort seeking external infor-

FIGURE 5–2 Comparison of problem-solving variations.

Characteristics of Purchase Decision Process	Consumer Involvement High <————————————————> Low		
	Extended Problem Solving	Limited Problem Solving	Routine Problem Solving
Number of brands examined	Many	Several	One
Number of sellers considered	Many	Several	Few
Number of product attributes evaluated	Many	Moderate	One
Number of external information sources used	Many	Few	None
Time spent searching	Considerable	Little	Minimal

mation and evaluating alternatives. The purchase process for such items is virtually a habit and typifies low-involvement decision making. Routine problem solving (RPS) is typically the case for low-priced, frequently purchased products. It is estimated that about 50 percent of all purchase occasions are of this kind.

Limited Problem Solving. In limited problem solving (LPS), consumers typically seek some information or rely on a friend to help them evaluate alternatives. In general, several brands might be evaluated using a moderate number of different attributes. You might use limited problem solving in choosing a toaster, a restaurant for dinner, and other purchase situations in which you have little time or effort to spend. Limited problem solving accounts for about 38 percent of purchase occasions.

Extended Problem Solving. In extended problem solving (EPS), each of the five stages of the consumer purchase decision process is used in the purchase, including considerable time and effort on an external information search and in identifying and evaluating alternatives. Several brands are usually in the evoked set, and these are evaluated on many attributes. Extended problem solving exists in high-involvement purchase situations for items such as CD players, VCRs, automobiles, and investments in stocks and bonds. Firms marketing these products put significant effort into informing and educating consumers. About 12 percent of purchase occasions fall into this category.

Situational Influences

Situational influences are temporary conditions or settings that occur at the time and place of a particular purchase that can affect the decision process. They are neither part of the product nor part of the inherent characteristics of the consumer. Five situational influences can impact on the purchase decision process: (1) the purchase task, (2) social surroundings, (3) physical surroundings, (4) temporal effects, and (5) antecedent states.[12] The purchase task is the reason for engaging in the decision in the first place. Information searching and evaluating alternatives may differ depending on whether the purchase is a gift, which often involves social visibility, or for the buyer's own use. Social surroundings, including the other people present when a purchase decision is made, may also affect what is purchased. Physical surroundings such as decor, music, and crowding in retail stores may alter how purchase decisions are made. Temporal effects such as time of day or the amount of time available will influence the purchase process. Finally, antecedent states, which include the consumer's mood or the amount of cash on hand, can influence purchase behaviour and choice.[13]

Figure 5–3 shows the many influences that affect the consumer purchase decision process. The decision to buy a product also involves important psychological and sociocultural influences, the two important topics discussed during the remainder of this chapter. Marketing mix influences are described throughout the other chapters in the text.

LEARNING CHECK

1. What is the first step in the consumer purchase decision process?

2. The brands a consumer considers buying out of the set of brands in a product class of which she is aware are called the _____.

3. What is the term for postpurchase anxiety?

FIGURE 5–3
Influences on the
consumer purchase
decision process.

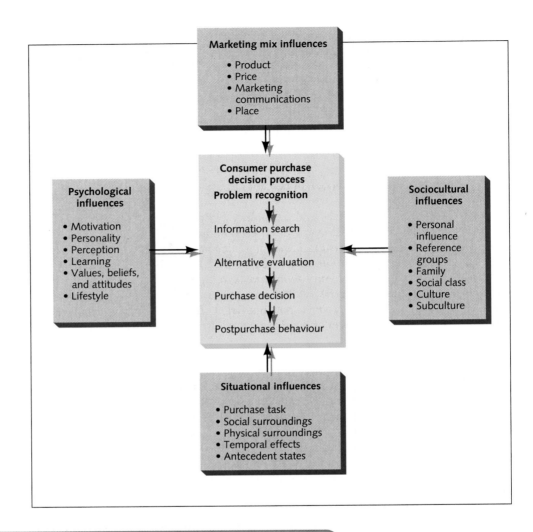

PSYCHOLOGICAL INFLUENCES ON CONSUMER BEHAVIOUR

Psychology helps marketers understand why and how consumers behave as they do. Particularly useful for interpreting buying processes and directing marketing efforts are concepts such as motivation and personality; perception; learning; values, attitudes, and beliefs; and lifestyle.

Motivation and Personality

Motivation and personality are two familiar psychological concepts that have specific meanings and marketing implications.[14] They are both used frequently to describe why people do some things and not others.

Motivation. **Motivation** is the energizing force that causes behaviour that satisfies a need. Because consumer needs are the focus of the marketing process, marketers try to understand and arouse these needs.

A LOT OF TIRES COST LESS THAN A MICHELIN. THAT'S BECAUSE THEY SHOULD.

To everyone out there looking to save a few dollars on a set of tires, let's not mince words. You buy cheap, you get cheap.

There may be a lot of tires out there that cost less than a Michelin.

The only question is, what do you have to give up if you buy one?

Do they handle like a Michelin?

Do they last like a Michelin?

Are they as reliable as a Michelin?

Then ask yourself this: Do you really want to find out?

At Michelin, we make only one kind of tire. The very best we know how.

Because the way we see it, the last place a compromise belongs is on your car.

As a matter of fact, we're so obsessed with quality we make the steel cables that go into our steel-belted radials.

We even make many of the machines that make and test Michelin tires.

And our quality control checks are so exhaustive that they even include x-rays.

These and hundreds of other details, big and small (details that may seem inconsequential to others), make sure that when you put a set of Michelin tires on your car, you get all the mileage Michelin is famous for.

True, there may be cheaper tires. But if they don't last like a Michelin, are they really less expensive?

So the next time someone tries to save you a few dollars on a tire, tell him this: It's not how much you pay that counts. It's what you get for your money.

And then *he'll* know that *you* know that there's only one reason a tire costs less than a Michelin. It deserves to.

MICHELIN
BECAUSE SO MUCH IS RIDING ON YOUR TIRES.

Sometimes firms try to arouse multiple needs to stimulate problem recognition. Michelin combined security needs with parental love/social needs to promote tire replacement.

An individual's needs are boundless. People possess physiological needs for basics such as water, sex, and food. They also have learned needs, including esteem, achievement, and affection. Psychologists point out that these needs are hierarchical; that is, once physiological needs are met, people seek to satisfy their learned needs.

Figure 5–4 shows one need hierarchy and classification scheme that contains five need classes.[15] *Physiological needs* are basic to survival and must be satisfied first. A Burger King advertisement featuring a juicy hamburger attempts to activate the need for food. *Safety needs* involve self-preservation and physical well-being. Smoke detector and burglar alarm manufacturers focus on these needs. *Social needs* are concerned with love and friendship. Dating services and fragrance companies try to arouse these needs. *Personal needs* are represented by the need for achievement, status, prestige, and self-respect. Visa Gold Cards and Rolex watches appeal to these needs. *Self-actualization needs* involve personal fulfillment, such as completing a higher education degree.

Personality. **Personality** refers to a person's consistent behaviours or responses to recurring situations. Although numerous personality theories exist, most identify key traits—enduring characteristics within a person or in his relationship with others. Such traits include assertiveness, extroversion, compliance, dominance, and aggression, among others. For example, cigarette smokers have been identified as having traits such as aggression and dominance, but not compliance.[16] Research suggests that compliant people prefer known brand names and use more mouthwash and toilet soaps. In contrast, aggressive types use razors, not electric shavers, apply more cologne and after-shave lotions, and purchase signature goods such as Gucci, Yves St. Laurent, and Donna Karan as an indicator of status.[17]

Research also suggests that residents of different countries have a *national character*, or a distinct set of personality characteristics common among people of a

FIGURE 5–4
Hierarchy of needs.

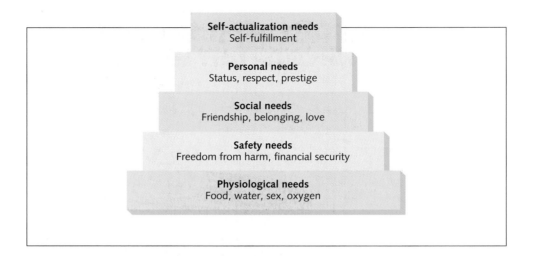

country or society.[18] For example, Americans and Germans are relatively more assertive than Canadians.

Perception

One person sees a Cadillac as a mark of achievement; another sees it as ostentatious. This is the result of **perception**—the process by which an individual selects, organizes, and interprets information to create a meaningful picture of the world.

Selective Perception. Because the average consumer operates in a complex environment, the human brain attempts to organize and interpret information through a filtering process called *selective perception.* The four stages of selective perception are selective exposure, selective attention, selective comprehension, and selective retention. First, consumers do not expose themselves to all information or messages in the marketplace. In other words, there is *selective exposure* to information. For example, you may watch CTV, but not CBC television. In doing so, you do not expose yourself to any information broadcast on the CBC network. Because of selective exposure, marketers must work to determine where consumers are most likely to be exposed to information.

But even if a consumer is exposed to a message, either by accident or by design, she may not attend to that message. In general, with *selective attention,* the consumer will pay attention only to messages that are consistent with her attitudes and beliefs and will ignore those that are inconsistent. Consumers are more likely to attend to messages when they are relevant or of interest to them. For example, you are more likely to pay attention to an ad about a product you just bought, or to an ad for a product you are interested in buying.

Even if a marketer is successful in getting the consumer exposed to a message and to attend to it, the message is of little value if the consumer does not understand it. With *selective comprehension,* consumers interpret information so that it is consistent with their attitudes and beliefs. Thus, the same message may be interpreted differently by different people. Research on the commercials featuring the popular Eveready Energizer Bunny revealed that 40 percent of the people surveyed thought the bunny was powered by Duracell batteries. This is a case of selective miscomprehension and it is quite common in the marketplace.

Is it the Duracell or
Energizer bunny?

Selective retention means that consumers do not remember all the information they see, read, or hear, even minutes after exposure to it. This affects the internal and external information search stage of the purchase decision process. The fact that we don't remember everything we see explains why furniture and automobile dealers often give consumers product brochures to take home after they leave the showroom.

Since perception plays such an important role in consumer behaviour, it is not surprising that the topic of subliminal perception is a popular item for discussion. *Subliminal perception* means that you see or hear messages without being aware of them. The presence and effect of subliminal perception on behaviour is a hotly debated issue. Some evidence suggests that such messages can influence behaviour.[19] If this is the case, it raises another question: If consumers perceive subliminal messages without being aware of them, is it ethical for marketers to create such messages designed to change buying behaviour? (See the Ethics Insight box.)

Perceived Risk. Perception plays a major role in the perceived risk in purchasing a product or service. **Perceived risk** represents the anxieties felt because the consumer cannot anticipate the outcomes of a purchase but believes that there may be negative consequences. Examples of possible negative consequences are the size of the financial outlay required to buy the product (can I afford $500 for those skis?), the risk of physical harm (is bungee jumping safe?), and the performance of the product (will the hair colouring work?). A more abstract form of risk is psychosocial (what will my friends say if I wear that sweater?). Perceived risk affects information search because the greater the perceived risk, the more extensive the external search phrase is likely to be.

Recognizing the importance of perceived risk, companies develop strategies to reduce the consumer's risk and encourage purchases. These strategies and examples of firms using them include:[20]

- Obtaining seals of approval: the Good Housekeeping seal or Canadian Standards Association (CSA) seal.
- Securing endorsements from influential people: Celine Dion and Anne Murray singing the praises of The Bay's fashion labels.
- Providing free trials of the product: samples of new Diet Pepsi.
- Giving extensive usage information: Clairol hair colouring.
- Providing warranties and guarantees: Volkswagen's 10 year, 100,000 mile warranty.

The Ethics of Subliminal Messages

As you read in the text, subliminal perception means that you see or hear messages without being aware of them. Since the first widely known use of subliminal stimulation in advertising came to light in the 1950s, it has become a focus of much debate and controversy. To some, the concept of subliminal messages is a hoax. To others, the possibility of people's being influenced without their knowledge is either an exciting or a frightening concept. When the topic of subliminal messages is discussed by experts, the discussion focuses on two specific issues: First, are subliminal messages a real phenomenon? Second, if they are real, are they effective in influencing a person's attitudes or behaviour?

Conceptually, it is believed that a subliminal message—in the form of words, pictures, or voices—is presented either so rapidly or so faintly that a receiver is not consciously aware of having seen or heard anything. A subliminal message is not invisible, but it cannot be dis-

criminated by conscious perceptual processes. The purported benefit of using subliminal messages is that the message will not be strong enough to arouse a consumer's selective attention and perceptual defense mechanisms, but it will be strong enough to influence them at an unconscious level. In essence, the consumer does not see or hear the message, but it registers.

1. Do you think subliminal messages are a real phenomenon?

2. If such a phenomenon exists, what are the social and ethical questions surrounding its use?

3. Would subliminal advertising be any more offensive than regular advertising?

4. What if audio subliminal devices could control shoplifting; would this use of subliminal messages be appropriate?

Learning

Much consumer behaviour is learned. Consumers learn which information sources to use for information about products and services, which evaluative criteria to use when assessing alternatives, and more generally, how to make purchase decisions. **Learning** refers to those behaviours that result from (1) repeated experience and (2) thinking.[21]

Behavioural Learning. *Behavioural learning* is the process of developing automatic responses to a situation through repeated exposure to it. Four variables are central to how consumers learn from repeated experience: drive, cue, response, and reinforcement.

A *drive* is a need that moves an individual to action. Drives, such as hunger, might be represented by motives. A *cue* is a stimulus or symbol perceived by consumers. A *response* is the action taken by a consumer to satisfy the drive, and a *reinforcement* is the reward. Being hungry (drive), a consumer sees a cue (a billboard), takes action (buys a hamburger), and receives a reward (it tastes great!).

Marketers use two concepts from behavioural learning theory. *Stimulus generalization* occurs when a response elicited by one stimulus (cue) is generalized to another stimulus. Using the same brand name for different products is an application of this concept, such as Tylenol Cold & Flu and Tylenol P.M. *Stimulus discrimination* refers to a person's ability to perceive differences in stimuli. Consumers' tendency to perceive all light beers as being alike led to Budweiser Light commercials that distinguished between types of "lights" and Bud Light.

Cognitive Learning. Consumers also learn through thinking, reasoning, and mental problem solving without direct experience. This type of learning, called *cognitive* *learning,* involves making connections between two or more ideas, or simply observing the outcomes of others' behaviours and adjusting your own accordingly. Marketers also try to influence this type of learning. Through repetition in advertising, messages such as "Anacin is the headache remedy" attempt to link a brand (Anacin) and an idea (headache remedy) by showing someone using the brand and finding relief.

Brand Loyalty. Learning is also important because it relates to habit formation—the basis of routine problem solving. Furthermore, there is a close link between habits and **brand loyalty,** which is a favourable attitude toward and consistent purchase of a single brand over time. Brand loyalty results from the positive reinforcement of previous actions. A consumer reduces risk and saves time by consistently purchasing the same brand over time. For example, if the brand of shampoo you buy gives you favourable results—healthy, shining hair—you are likely to continue to buy that brand.

But there is some evidence that brand loyalty is declining, even for frequently used products.[22] More than ever, consumers searching for the best value will evaluate a wide selection of brands when they purchase instead of automatically buying the same brand every time. Market-driven organizations realize that they must provide the best value to the customer in order to encourage brand loyalty.

Values, Attitudes, and Beliefs

Values, attitudes, and beliefs play a central role in consumer decision making and related marketing actions.

Values. **Values** represent personally or socially preferable modes of conduct or states of existence that are enduring. Values vary by level of specificity. We can speak broadly of the values of Canadian society such as material well-being and humanitarianism. We can also refer to an individual's personal values such as thriftiness and ambition. Society's values shape personal values and these values, in turn, affect an individual's attitudes and beliefs.

Attitudes. An **attitude** is a learned predisposition to respond to an object or class of objects in a consistently favourable or unfavourable way.[23] Personal values affect attitude formation by influencing the importance assigned to specific product attributes. Suppose thriftiness is one of your personal values. When you evaluate cars, fuel economy (a product attribute) becomes important. If you believe a specific car has this attribute, you are likely to have a favourable attitude toward it.

Beliefs. Beliefs also play a part in attitude formation. **Beliefs** are a consumer's subjective perception of *how well* a product or brand performs on different attributes. Beliefs are based on personal experience, advertising, and discussions with other people. Beliefs about product attributes are important because, along with personal values, they create the favourable or unfavourable attitude the consumer has toward certain products and services.

Attitude Change. Marketers use three approaches to try to change consumer attitudes toward products and brands, as shown in the following examples.[24]

1. *Changing beliefs about the extent to which a brand has certain attributes.* McDonald's ran ads to allay consumer concerns about too much cholesterol in its french fries.

2. *Changing the perceived importance of attributes.* 7UP succeeded in building on its positively viewed "no-caffeine" attribute with its "never had it, never will" slogan to build market share.

3. *Adding new attributes to the product.* Chrysler added dual-airbags to its minivans, hoping consumers would perceive this new product attribute favourably.

Lifestyle

Lifestyle is a mode of living that is identified by how people spend their time and resources (activities), what they consider important in their environment (interests), and what they think of themselves and the world around them (opinions).[25] Moreover, lifestyle reflects consumers' *self-concept,* which is the way people see themselves and the way they believe others see them.[26]

The analysis of consumer lifestyles (also called psychographics) has produced many insights into consumers' behaviour. For example, lifestyle analysis has proven useful in segmenting and targeting consumers for new and existing products (Chapter 8).

Lifestyle analysis typically focuses on identifying consumer profiles. Perhaps the best-known example of this type of analysis is the Values and Lifestyles (VALS 2) Program developed by SRI International.[27] The VALS 2 Program has identified eight interconnected categories of adult lifestyles. Although the VALS 2 Program is widely used in the United States, it is American-based and has rarely been used in Canada. However, there are some lifestyle or psychographic systems that have been developed for Canada, the most comprehensive being the Goldfarb Segments.

The Goldfarb Segments. Goldfarb Consultants of Toronto surveyed 1,400 adult Canadians. They asked the respondents approximately 200 questions concerning their activities, interests, and opinions. After analyzing the data, six lifestyle or psychographic segments were identified and labelled the Goldfarb Segments.[28] The six segments were classified according to two broad categories: more traditional and less traditional.

As you can see from Figure 5–5, the more traditional segments, representing 52 percent of the adult population, include the day-to-day watchers, the old-fashioned puritans, and the responsible survivors. The less traditional segments, representing 48 percent of the adult population, include the joiner–activists, the disinterested self-indulgents, and the aggressive achievers. Figure 5–5 highlights selected demographic and behavioural characteristics of each segment.

Many Canadian companies use the Goldfarb Segments to assist them in making successful marketing decisions. Sears Canada, for example, tailors its messages and media campaigns to reach two specific segments, the day-to-day watchers and the joiner–activists. The company believes it must reach these two groups in order to stay competitive in the retail department store market.

LEARNING CHECK

1. The problem of confusing the Energizer Bunny for the Duracell Bunny was an example of selective _____.

2. What three attitude-change approaches are most common?

3. What does lifestyle mean?

FIGURE 5–5 The Goldfarb Segments.

Segment	Percent of Population	Characteristics
MORE TRADITIONAL		
Day-to-Day Watchers	24%	Traditional value structure; prefer the tried and true; research their purchases; satisfied with life as it is.
Old-Fashioned Puritans	16%	Conservative; afraid of change; home and family-oriented; least likely to try new brands; least likely to own credit cards; heavily insured.
Responsible Survivors	12%	Respect the status quo; usually want and seek advice; enjoy self-rewards; very brand loyal; heavy TV viewers.
	52%	
LESS TRADITIONAL		
Joiner–Activists	21%	Non-conformists; dynamic and leading-edge thinkers; quality and convenience-oriented; like new technology; willing to spend; eat out frequently; heavy pleasure trip takers.
Disinterested Self-indulgents	17%	Insular and self-oriented; interested in self-gratification, risk-oriented; impulse purchasers; borrow heavily; heavy lottery ticket buyers; like product innovation.
Aggressive Achievers	10%	Success-oriented; want to be leaders; need to have psyches stroked; love status-signalling products; flaunt material possessions.
	48%	

SOURCE: Goldfarb Consultants, Toronto. Used with permission.

SOCIOCULTURAL INFLUENCES ON CONSUMER BEHAVIOUR

Sociocultural influences, which evolve from a consumer's formal and informal relationships with other people, also exert a significant impact on consumer behaviour. These influences include personal influence, reference groups, the family, social class, and culture and subculture.

Personal Influence

A consumer's purchases are often influenced by the views, opinions, or behaviour of others. Two aspects of personal influence are important to marketing: opinion leadership and word-of-mouth activity.

Opinion Leadership. Individuals who exert direct or indirect social influence over others are called **opinion leaders.** Opinion leaders are more likely to be important for products that provide a form of self-expression. For instance, automobiles, clothing, club memberships, home video equipment, and personal computers are products affected by opinion leaders, but appliances are not.[29]

Identifying, reaching, and influencing opinion leaders is a major challenge for companies. Some firms use sports figures or celebrities as spokespeople to represent their products, such as Wayne Gretzky for Thrifty Rent-a-Car, Sharp, and Coca-Cola, and Doug Gilmore for milk. However, many consumers are starting to question the credibility of celebrity spokespeople, believing most are simply promoting the product for money.[30]

Word of Mouth. People's influencing each other during face-to-face conversations is called **word of mouth.** Word of mouth is perhaps the most powerful information source for consumers, because it typically involves friends viewed as trustworthy. One Canadian study found that 95 percent of people surveyed said they used word of mouth to select a physician, and 70 percent used word of mouth to select a financial institution.[31]

The power of personal influence has prompted firms to promote positive and retard negative word of mouth.[32] For instance, "teaser" advertising campaigns are run in advance of new product introductions to stimulate conversations. Other techniques such as advertising slogans, music, and humour also heighten positive word of mouth. On the other hand, rumours about Kmart (snake eggs in clothing) or McDonald's (worms in hamburgers) have resulted in negative word of mouth, none of which was based on fact. Overcoming or neutralizing negative word of mouth can be difficult and costly.

Delivering customer value and satisfaction is the best way for a firm to ensure positive word of mouth. Consumers do talk to others about their satisfaction or dissatisfaction with their purchases. However, negative word of mouth tends to travel faster and further than positive word of mouth.

For example, studies on automobile purchasing show that satisfied buyers tell eight other people about their experience, but dissatisfied buyers complain to 22 people.[33] Satisfying existing customers not only means repeat business, it also produces positive word of mouth communications between existing and prospective customers.

Reference Groups

Reference groups are people to whom an individual looks as a basis for self-appraisal or as a source of personal standards. Reference groups affect consumer purchases because they influence the information, attitudes, and aspiration levels that help set a consumer's standards.[34] For example, one of the first questions many people ask others when planning to attend a social occasion is, What are you going to wear? Reference groups have an important influence on the purchase of luxury products but not on necessities. In general, reference groups exert a strong influence on the brand chosen when its use or consumption is highly visible to others.[35]

Consumers have many reference groups, but three groups have clear implications to marketers. A *membership group* is one to which a person actually belongs, such as a fraternity, a social club, or the family. Such groups are easily identifiable and are targeted by firms selling insurance, insignia products, and charter vacations. An *aspiration group* is one that a person wishes to be a member of or wishes to be identified with, such as a professional society. Firms frequently rely on spokespeople or settings associated with their target market's aspiration group in their advertising. A *dissociative group* is one that a person wishes to maintain a distance from because of differences in values or behaviours. Believing that motorcycle ownership and usage has a "black leather-jacketed biker" stigma, Honda Motor Company has focussed its marketing efforts on disassociating its motorcycles from this group.[36]

Family Influence

Family influences on consumer behaviour result from three sources: consumer socialization, passage through the family life cycle, and decision making within the family.

Doug Gilmore as a spokesperson for milk.

Consumer Socialization. The process by which people acquire skills, knowledge, and attitudes necessary to function as consumers is **consumer socialization.** Children learn how to purchase by (1) interacting with adults in purchase situations and (2) their own purchasing and product usage experiences.[37] As children mature into adults, brand preferences emerge that may last a lifetime. Thus, many companies are attempting to build relationships with children at a very young age. Several Canadian financial institutions, such as the Canadian Imperial Bank of Commerce (CIBC), have developed specific marketing programs designed to attract young consumers and to keep them as lifetime customers. (See Marketplace Application box.)

Family Life Cycle. Consumers act and purchase differently as they go through life. The **family life cycle** concept describes the distinct phases that a family progresses through from formation to a couple's old age, each phase bringing with it identifiable purchasing behaviours.[38] Figure 5–6 illustrates the traditional progression as well as the contemporary variations of the family life cycle, including the prevalence of single households with and without children.

Young singles' buying preferences are for nondurable items, including prepared foods, clothing, personal care products, and entertainment. These people represent a target market for recreational travel, automobile, and consumer electronics firms. Young married couples without children are typically more affluent than young singles, because usually both spouses are employed. These couples exhibit preferences for furniture, housewares, and gift items for each other. Young marrieds with children are driven by the needs of their children. They make up a sizable market for life insurance, various children's products, and home furnishings.

Single parents with children are the least financially secure of households with children. Their buying preferences are affected by a limited economic status and tend toward convenience foods, child care services, and personal care items. Middle-aged married couples with children are typically better off than their younger counterparts. They are a significant market for leisure products and home improvement items and represent one of the fastest-growing life cycle stages in the 1990s. Middle-aged couples without children typically have a large amount of discretionary income. These couples buy better furnishings, status automobiles, and financial services. Persons in

FIGURE 5–6 Family life cycle.

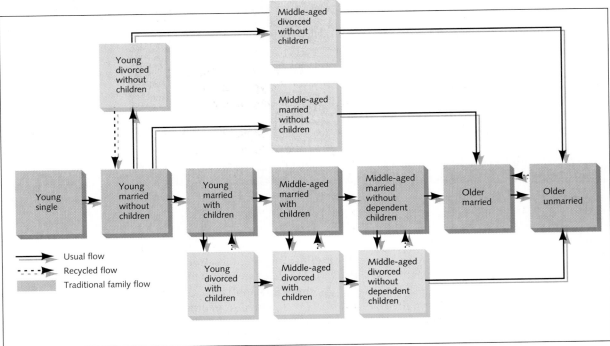

$ MARKETPLACE APPLICATION

Children as a Target Market

Many organizations are directing more of their marketing efforts toward a new target market—children, some as young as three years old. Children are already prime targets for products such as toys, video games, soft drinks, and snack food. But other marketers are now seeing greater opportunities to market to children for three reasons. First, more and more children now possess their own discretionary income and can afford to buy a broader range of products. Second, children also heavily influence many areas of overall family spending. For example, a Canadian study revealed that among young teens living at home, 85 percent influence grocery brand selection, and close to 50 percent even influence family automobile purchases. Third, and most importantly, many marketers are not only interested in children for immediate sales, they want to develop a relationship with them and make them customers for life.

Research indicates that marketing to children can be effective. For example, children have been shown to like advertising and to form their shopping list as a result of advertising. Many advocates would like to see marketing efforts directed at children banned or more heavily regulated. Others insist that children should only be targets for messages that encourage positive social behaviour, such as not smoking and staying away from drugs.

Despite the debate, many companies see children as their primary target market and go to great lengths to appeal to them. The Canadian toy market, excluding video games, is valued at over $1.5 billion. The toy industry uses ongoing research and product testing to develop the toys children want. They even do complex research called "play pattern segmentation" in order to match products to the way children play. Mattel, for example, targeted 14 different play segments with 90 different new dolls.

Other companies see children as a new market and have extended their product lines to appeal to them. For example, Delisle Foods of Quebec developed Petit Danone, a new cheese product for children aged 3 to 12. The company stresses nutrition since the product contains more minerals than its competitors in the category. The product launch included extensive in-store sampling and a teaching kit on healthy eating sent to primary schools in Quebec and Ontario. Delisle also sponsors sports events for children.

1. What is your feeling on marketing to children?
2. What could marketers do to increase their likelihood of success with this target market?

SOURCES: Adapted from Gail Chiasson, "Quebec 13 to 24," *Marketing,* February 20, 1995, p. 13; "Delisle Serves New Cheese Product for Kids," *Marketing,* March 20, 1995, p. 1; David Short, "Advertising and Kids," *Marketing,* February 6, 1995, p. 13; Lara Mills, "The Serious Business of Toys," *Marketing,* February 6, 1995, pp. 11–12.

the last two phases—older married and older unmarried—are a sizable market for prescription drugs, medical services, vacation trips, and gifts for younger relatives. These consumers represent another fast-growing family life cycle stage in the 1990s.

Family Decision Making. A third influence in the decision-making process occurs within the family. Two decision-making styles exist: spouse-dominant and joint decision making. With a joint decision-making style, most decisions are made by both husband and wife. Spouse-dominant decisions are those for which either the husband or the wife is responsible. The types of products and services associated with the decision-making styles are shown in Figure 5–7.[39] However, these tendencies are changing with the rise in dual-income families. Today, 40 percent of all food-shopping dollars are spent by male customers. Women now purchase 70 percent of men's dress shirts and 40 to 50 percent of all condoms purchased.

Roles of individual family members in the purchase process are another element of family decision making. Five roles exist: (1) information gatherer, (2) influencer, (3) decision maker, (4) purchaser, and (5) user. Family members assume different roles for different products and services. Knowledge of who plays which role is important to firms. Increasingly, teenagers are the information gatherers, decision makers, and

FIGURE 5–7   Influence continuum of spouse in family decision making.

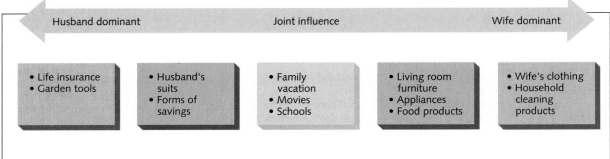

purchasers of grocery items for the family, given the prevalence of working parents and single-parent households. General Mills, Nabisco, Kraft-General Foods, and others advertise on the Much Music television network to reach these teens.

Social Class

A more subtle influence on consumer behaviour than direct contact with others is the social class to which people belong. **Social classes** may be defined as the relatively permanent, homogeneous divisions in a society into which people sharing similar values, interests, and behaviour can be grouped. Occupation, education, and source of income (not level of income) are the key determinants of social class. Research shows that social class influences the type of purchases consumers make and the activities they undertake.

Many researchers classify Canadians into one of five social classes: (1) upper, (2) upper middle, (3) middle, (4) working, and (5) lower. The *upper class* consists of two groups, the "old rich" and the "new rich." The old rich have inherited wealth and have aristocratic status. The new rich are the new social elite—top professionals and corporate leaders. The *upper middle class* consists of successful professionals and business-people, and are generally the best educated in our society. The *middle class* consists of the typical white-collar worker, including small business owners, middle managers, and minor professionals. The *working class* consists of the traditional blue-collar worker. The *lower class* is comprised of working poor, the unemployed, and those on welfare.

No one has developed a completely accurate depiction of the size of each of the five social classes. However, we do know that the middle and working classes represent the bulk of Canadians. By some estimates 70 percent of the population falls into either the middle or working class.[40] Thus, these two classes represent the mainstream market segments that are of interest to most marketers. Furthermore, research shows that the middle class and the working class do differ in many ways, including their lifestyle and consumption behaviour. Figure 5–8 shows some of the differences between the middle and working class.[41]

Culture and Subcultures

As described in Chapter 3, *culture* refers to the set of values, ideas, and attitudes that are accepted by a homogeneous group of people and transmitted to the next generation. Thus, we often refer to Canadian culture, American culture, or Japanese culture. The culture of a country will influence what needs consumers have and how they go about

FIGURE 5–8 Middle and working class differences.

	Middle Class	Working Class
Concept of Time	Future-oriented	Present day-oriented
Homes	Choose a home in a neighbourhood for status	Choose home convenient to work and schools
Sports/Hobbies	Golf, tennis, skiing	Hunting, fishing, bowling
Media Habits	Lighter viewers of TV; watch public broadcasting and late-night shows; listen to FM, jazz, soft rock; read MacLean's	Heavy viewers of TV; watch game shows, and sitcoms; listen to AM, hard rock, and country; read National Enquirer and Reader's Digest
Shopping Habits	Make lists and plan outings; use a variety of information sources; use self-serve outlets	Buy on impulse; use word of mouth; use full-service outlets

satisfying them. Marketers must be sensitive to the cultural underpinnings of different societies if they are to initiate and consummate mutually beneficial exchange relationships with consumers. We saw in Chapter 3 how cultural changes are affecting purchasing patterns in Canada. In Chapter 18, we will see how the process of cross-cultural analysis helps marketers involved in global or international marketing.

Subcultures are subgroups within the larger, national culture that share unique values, ideas, and attitudes setting them apart from that larger culture. Subcultures can be identified by age (e.g., baby boomers vs. Generation X), geography (e.g., Western Canadians vs. Atlantic Canadians), and ethnicity. We will focus here on ethnic subcultures.

An *ethnic subculture* is a segment of a larger society whose members have a common origin and participate in shared activities felt to be culturally significant.[42] Common traits such as customs, language, religion, and values hold ethnic subcultures together. Because of Canada's pluralistic tradition, ethnic groups do not necessarily join the cultural mainstream. Some people have referred to this as a *salad bowl phenomenon,* where a potpourri of people mix but do not blend. This allows for the maintenance of subcultural traditions and values.

French Canadian Subculture. There are approximately 7 million French-speaking Canadians in this country, representing about 25 percent of the population. The overwhelming majority of French Canadians live in Quebec. Research shows that French-speaking Quebecers exhibit different consumption behaviour from the rest of Canadians.[43] For example, French Quebecers link price to perceived value but will pass on a buy rather than buy on credit. They are more willing to pay higher prices for convenience and premium brands, and they give more credence to advertising than the average Canadian. They are cautious of new products and often postpone trial until after the product has proven itself. They do exhibit brand loyalty but will switch for specials. They also prefer convenience and health food stores over food warehouses and local grocery stores.

French Quebecers are more concerned with personal grooming and fashion, and more likely to shop in specialized clothing boutiques. French women in Quebec are big users of perfumed body spray, cologne, and lipstick. They also buy more pantyhose, swimwear, and hair-colouring products, and prefer Japanese cars over domestic.

French Quebec has a higher percentage of wine and beer drinkers and more smokers. However, they do consume less hard liquor than the rest of Canada. There are fewer

Percentage wise, there are more cyclists in French Quebec than the rest of Canada.

golfers, joggers, and gardeners, and the proportion of people who go to movies or entertain at home is also lower. There are, however, more cyclists, skiers, and live theatre fans.

French Quebecers are big buyers of lottery tickets and more likely to subscribe to book clubs, but they make fewer long-distance phone calls. They travel less, whether for business or pleasure. More French Quebec adults hold life insurance policies but they are less likely to have a credit card. They also tend to use credit unions (*caisses populaires*) more than banks.

Some argue that French Quebec can be characterized by a set of values that are traditional, consistent, and relatively static. But changes are evident. While values are still strong about family life, about having children in a marriage, and about giving them religious training, the use of birth control is on the rise and the marriage rate is below the national average.

Marketers must realize that certain products and other elements of the marketing mix may have to be modified in order to be successful in French Quebec. In addition to cultural differences, there are other issues marketers must address. Commercial advertising to children is prohibited and greater restrictions exist for tobacco and alcohol advertising. Provincial regulations also require that labels and packages must be both in French and English, while storefront signage must be in French, not English. Good investigation and analysis of this market is a requirement for all companies wishing to do business there.

Acadian Subculture. Many Canadians assume that French Canadians are basically the same. Even though the majority of French-speaking Canadians do reside in Quebec, there is another special group of French-speaking Canadians who live outside of Quebec. These people are the Acadians, most of whom live in New Brunswick and are proud of their distinctive heritage. The Acadians are often referred to as the "forgotten French market."

Acadians are different from French Quebecers in many ways. In terms of consumption, Acadians are very fashion-oriented and tend to dine out more often than their French counterparts in Quebec. Acadians are also very price-conscious. In addition, they prefer companies that speak to them in their language, which is slightly different than French Quebecois.

Chinese Canadian Subculture. The Chinese Canadian market currently represents about 3 percent of Canada's population, but it is one of the fastest-growing subcultures in Canada. This ethnic group is made up predominantly of immigrants from Hong Kong and Taiwan, and is concentrated in Toronto and Vancouver.

Chinese Canadians have unique values. While most Canadians value straight-line thinking (logic), the Chinese value circular thinking (what goes around comes around). They value work, family, and education. They have different purchasing patterns and often perceive products differently than other Canadians. This group also appreciates companies that speak to them in their language. For example, many firms produce ads in Mandarin or Cantonese and run them in specialty publications such as the *Sing Tao*, a Toronto newspaper for Chinese readers.

The average Chinese-Canadian has a higher income, is better educated, less likely to be unemployed, and significantly younger than the general Canadian population. Because of these characteristics, many firms see Chinese Canadians as a viable target market for a variety of products. For example, the Royal Bank sees them as good prospects for RSP and mutual fund products, while Cantel markets its cellular phones to this group.

Other Ethnic Subcultures. Many other ethnic Canadians can be found in large metropolitan centres or clustered in certain geographic areas. Kitchener–Waterloo has a large German Canadian population, Winnipeg is home to many Ukrainian Canadians, and Toronto has a large number of Italian Canadians. The emerging trend in Canada today is that 70 percent of all immigrants to this country are visible minorities. In addition to Asia, many new Canadians are coming from Africa and India. Marketers must appreciate the fact that these new ethnic Canadians will carry with them distinctive social and cultural behaviour that will affect their buying patterns. Subcultural research and sensitivity can aid organizations in developing effective marketing strategies designed to appeal to these groups.

LEARNING OBJECTIVE REINFORCEMENT

1. Outline the stages in the consumer purchase decision process. There are five steps in the consumer purchase decision process: problem recognition, information search, alternative evaluation, purchase decision, and postpurchase behaviour.

2. Distinguish between three variations of the consumer purchase decision process: routine, limited, and extended problem solving. There are three general variations in the consumer purchase process based on consumer involvement and product knowledge. Routine problem solving involves little or no effort to acquire external information or evaluate alternatives. It is typically used for frequently purchased or low-priced products. Limited problem solving involves the use of moderate information-seeking efforts; several brands might be evaluated using a moderate number of attributes. Extended problem solving involves the consumer going through each of the five stages of the consumer purchase decision process, including taking considerable time and effort to search for and evaluate alternatives.

3. List the five situational influences that impact on the consumer purchase decision process. The five situational in-

fluences are: (1) the purchase task, (2) social surroundings, (3) physical surroundings, (4) temporal effects, and (5) antecedent states.

4. Understand the psychological influences that affect consumer behaviour, particularly purchase decision processes. Psychology helps marketers understand why and how consumers behave as they do. Numerous psychological factors influence a consumer's behaviour including: motivation and personality; perception; learning; values, attitudes, and beliefs; and lifestyle. These concepts are useful for organizations in interpreting buying processes and directing marketing efforts.

5. Identify major sociocultural influences on consumer behaviour and their effects on purchase decisions. Sociocultural influences, which evolve from a consumer's formal and informal relationships with other people, exert a significant impact on consumer behaviour and on purchase decisions. These influences include personal influence, reference groups, the family, social class, and culture and subculture.

KEY TERMS AND CONCEPTS

consumer behaviour p. 103
consumer purchase decision
    process p. 104
evaluative criteria p. 105
evoked set p. 105
cognitive dissonance p. 106
involvement p. 106
situational influences p. 107
motivation p. 108

personality p. 109
perception p. 110
perceived risk p. 111
learning p. 112
brand loyalty p. 113
values p. 113
attitudes p. 113
beliefs p. 113
lifestyle p. 114

opinion leaders p. 115
word of mouth p. 116
reference groups p. 116
consumer socialization p. 117
family life cycle p. 118
social class p. 120
subcultures p. 121

CHAPTER QUESTIONS AND APPLICATIONS

1. Demonstrate your understanding of the five-stage consumer purchase decision process by using your experience in selecting your college or university.

2. Suppose Apple Computer discovers that some prospective buyers still are anxious about buying a personal computer. What strategies might you recommend to the company to reduce the buyers' perceived risk?

3. A Porsche salesperson was taking orders on new cars because he was unable to satisfy demand with the limited number of cars in the showroom and lot. Several persons had backed out of the contract within two weeks of signing the order. What explanation can you give for this behaviour, and what remedies would you recommend?

4. Which social class would you associate with each of the following items or actions? *(a)* tennis club membership, *(b)* an arrangement of plastic flowers in the kitchen, *(c) True Romance* magazine, *(d) MacLean's* magazine, *(e)* formally dressing for dinner frequently, and *(f)* being a member of a bowling team.

5. Assign one or more levels of the hierarchy of needs and motives described in Figure 5–3 to the following products:

(a) life insurance, *(b)* cosmetics, *(c)* the *Financial Post* magazine, and *(d)* hamburgers.

6. With which stage of the family life cycle would the purchase of the following products and services be most closely identified? *(a)* bedroom furniture, *(b)* life insurance, *(c)* a Caribbean cruise, *(d)* a house mortgage, and *(e)* children's toys.

7. "The greater the perceived risk in a purchase situation, the more likely that cognitive dissonance will result." Does this statement have any basis given the discussion in the text? Why?

APPLICATION CASE 5-1
THREE SISTERS CAFE

Three Sisters Cafe is a medium-sized (120 seats), upscale restaurant that had been in business for five years. The owners, three sisters, are happy with the restaurant's performance but would like to do better. They believe their customers like the restaurant and repeat business is very good. In a highly competitive market, however, the sisters feel they must find ways to attract more business. After much discussion and debate, the three sisters decided to hire a local consulting firm to conduct some consumer research. Basically, the three sisters wanted to know (1) the attributes that a licensed sit-down restaurant must possess in order for consumers to patronize an establishment; (2) how well Three Sisters Cafe measured up on those attributes; and (3) consumers' satisfaction and dissatisfaction with Three Sisters Cafe. A telephone survey of restaurant goers was conducted. A person had to have dined out in the last four weeks to be part of the survey. A total of 320 respondents participated. Of this total, 140 had dined at Three Sisters Cafe at least once in the previous four weeks.

CONSUMER RESEARCH FINDINGS

First, consumer awareness levels were obtained for the licensed sit-down restaurants in the area. It was particularly important to examine consumer awareness of a business or brand since awareness is a necessary prerequisite to purchase. A restaurant with low awareness levels may mean consumers will not think of that particular restaurant when they consider dining out. Three Sisters Cafe had an overall awareness score of 60 percent. In other words, 60 percent of consumers surveyed were aware of Three Sisters Cafe. Many of its competitors had lower awareness scores, ranging from 25 percent to 55 percent. One nearby competitor, however, had the highest awareness score at 85 percent.

The consulting firm uncovered the attributes required by consumers in order to patronize a licensed sit-down restaurant. Exhibit 1 depicts what respondents believed to be the "ideal" attributes making up such an establishment. It was derived by examining the percentage of those who, on the dimension under consideration, rated the attributes as "Very Important or Must Have It." The element was considered to be an ideal element if 70 percent or more respondents indicated it to be very important or a must have. There were no differences between users of Three Sisters Cafe and nonusers in terms of the ideal attributes that a restaurant must have in order to patronize.

EXHIBIT 1 Attributes a restaurant must possess and how users rate Three Sisters Cafe on those attributes

	Ideal Attributes (% mentioning as Very Important or Must Have it, all respondents)	Users' Ratings of Three Sisters (% rating it as Very Good/Excellent on that attribute)
Good food	95.0%	66.0%
Atmosphere	90.0	84.0
Efficient service	83.0	82.0
Friendly service	80.0	77.0
Comfortable seating	78.0	87.0
Decor	77.0	92.0
Good prices	76.0	26.0
Table presentation	75.0	85.0
Good wine list	73.0	76.0
	N=320	N=140

Exhibit 1 also shows how Three Sisters Cafe was rated by users on those ideal attributes.

The consulting firm also examined customer satisfaction with Three Sisters Cafe. The analysis revealed that 87 percent of users were satisfied with their experience while 13 percent were dissatisfied. Of those who were dissatisfied, 70 percent stated food quality to be the reason for their dissatisfaction, while 30 percent stated high prices was their reason for dissatisfaction. All three sisters reviewed the findings and wondered about the ratings their restaurant received, as well as the awareness scores and the satisfaction data. They realized the key issue now is what to do with the information?

QUESTIONS

1. Which attributes (evaluative criteria) do you think are most critical in the consumers' assessment of value when selecting a restaurant?
2. What is the relationship between a consumer's awareness of given restaurants and his or her evoked set of choice?
3. What do you think about the consumers' satisfaction levels with Three Sisters Cafe? Do you think this is a problem area they need to address? Why or why not?

APPLICATION CASE 5-2
MY OWN MEALS

Mary Anne Jackson set out to satisfy the need for nutritious and convenient children's meals. Her idea: develop a line of healthy, microwaveable meals for children 2 to 10 years old. As Mary Anne explains, "Being a busy working mother, I knew that there was a need for this type of product in the marketplace." Mary Anne's insight was supported by several socioeconomic trends. For example, most working mothers now have school-age children; about 90 percent of children under the age of 7 eat at McDonald's at least 4 times per month; over 60 percent of homes in Canada have microwaves; and more women continue to enter the workforce. With this evidence, some food industry experience and business education, and a lot of entrepreneurial spirit, Mary Anne founded her own company, My Own Meals, Inc. The company produced a line of five healthy microwaveable meals offered in shelf-stable "retort" packages, which are like flexible cans. Some major food companies quickly noticed her efforts and eventually launched their own products to compete with My Own Meals.

In order to understand how My Own Meals should be marketed, Mary Anne looked carefully at the consumer's purchase decision process. She learned about important characteristics of each stage of the purchase process. In terms of problem recognition, she discovered that today's parents are busier than ever. They face a dilemma between finding time to prepare healthy meals or using fast-food and supermarket alternatives that they do not perceive as nutritious. In terms of information search, she found out that word of mouth was the best form of advertising. This was fortunate since My Own Meals had few resources that could be devoted to marketing communications. Two other important sources of information were public sources, such as the media who featured stories or articles about the new microwaveable meals, and market-dominated sources such as in-store displays and direct-mail coupons.

In terms of alternative evaluation, she found that not all products were in every store or every region, so consumers' choices were limited to the products carried by their grocer. Many first-time buyers had trouble finding the products, particularly shelf-stable offerings, which were located in a grocer's pasta section. Also, some shoppers were hesitant to buy the shelf-stable packages, fearing contamination. Finally, while My Own Meals emphasized the nutritional attributes of its products, Mary Anne found that competitors focused on fun and games, as well as price. In terms of the actual purchase decision, mothers were found to be the decision makers for this purchase, although other family members were likely to be influencers, especially grandmothers.

QUESTIONS

1. What consumer problem does My Own Meals address?
2. What makes Mary Anne Jackson's marketing approach different than the approach used for most children's grocery items?
3. Who has the most influence over postpurchase behaviour for My Own Meals?

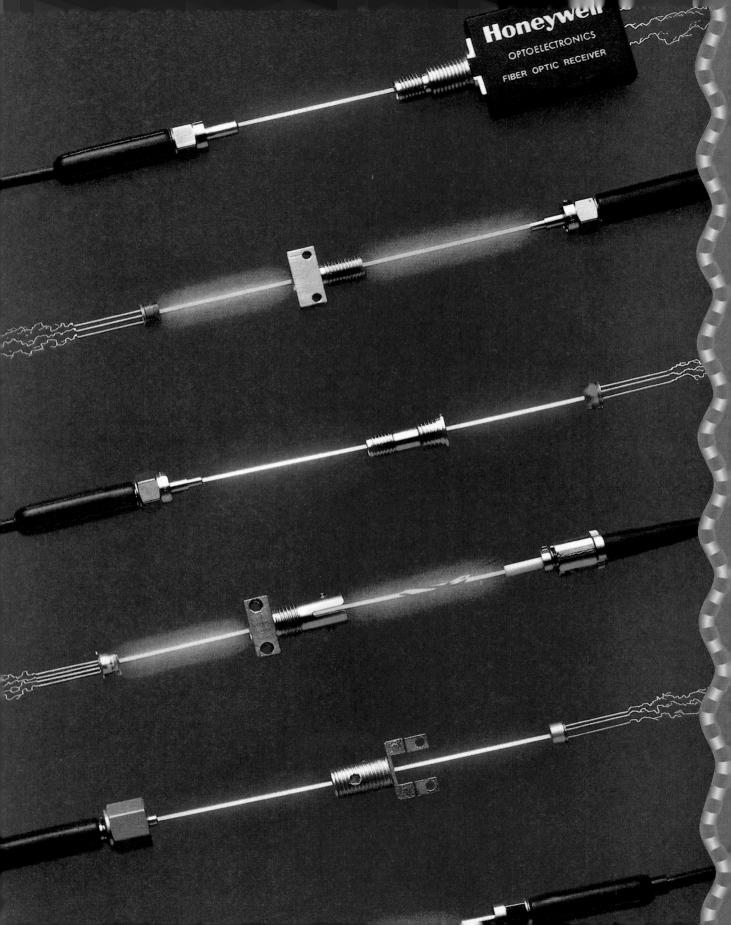

Organizational Buyer Behaviour

COMMUNICATING THROUGH LIGHT

Steve Whitacer views light very differently from most people.

As product manager of fibre optics products at Honeywell, MICRO SWITCH Division, Whitacer is responsible for fibre optic products (like those in the photo opposite) that sense, modulate, and transmit infrared light for the data communications industry. Converting technology into products and bringing those products to market is part and parcel of his typical day.

Marketing fibre optic technology and products is a challenging assignment. Buyer experience with the technology is limited, even though potential applications are numerous in data communications, computer networks, and industrial automation. Honeywell's MICRO SWITCH Division and other suppliers such as Hewlett Packard and Mitsubishi must often convey the benefits of fibre optics technology and specific products through advertising, trade shows, personal selling, and demonstrations. This task often involves communicating with a diverse set of organizational buyers ranging from industrial firms to governmental agencies, throughout the world and in different languages.

It also requires knowing which people influence the purchase decision; what factors they consider important when choosing suppliers and products; and when, where, and how the buying decision is made.

Whitacer believes Honeywell's MICRO SWITCH Division is poised to be a significant player in the multibillion-dollar fibre optics market. Ultimate success will depend on continued product development and effective marketing to an ever-growing number of prospective buyers for fibre optic technology in a globalizing marketplace.[1]

The challenge facing Whitacer of marketing to organizations is often encountered by both small, start-up corporations and large, well-established companies like Honeywell. Important issues in marketing to organizations are examined in this chapter, which deals with the types of organizational buyers, key characteristics of organizational buying, and some typical buying situations that organizations face. The chapter concludes with how organizations can more effectively market to other organizations.

THE NATURE AND SIZE OF ORGANIZATIONAL MARKETS

Steve Whitacer and Honeywell's MICRO SWITCH Division engage in organizational marketing (sometimes called business-to-business marketing, or simply business marketing). **Organizational marketing** is the marketing of goods and services to profit and nonprofit organizations for use in the creation of goods and services that they then produce and market to other organizational customers, as well as ultimate consumers.[2] Because many Canadian business school graduates take jobs in firms that engage in organizational marketing, it is important to understand the fundamental characteristics of organizational buyers and their buying behaviour.[3]

Organizational buyers are units such as industrial firms, wholesalers, retailers, and nonprofit agencies that buy goods and services for their own use or for resale. For example, all these organizations buy pencils and desks for their own use. However, manufacturers buy raw materials and parts that they reprocess into finished goods they sell, whereas retailers resell goods they buy without reprocessing them.

Organizational buyers include all the buyers in the nation except ultimate consumers. They purchase and lease tremendous volumes of capital equipment, raw materials, manufactured parts, supplies, and business services. In fact, because they often buy raw materials and parts, process them, and sell the upgraded product several times before it is purchased by the final organizational buyer or ultimate consumer, the aggregate purchases of organizational buyers in a year are far greater than those of ultimate consumers.

Organizational buyers are divided into three different markets: (1) industrial, (2) reseller, and (3) nonprofit markets.

Industrial Markets

Industrial firms in some way reprocess a good or service they buy before selling it again to the next buyer. This is certainly true of a steel mill, which converts iron ore into steel. It is also true (if you stretch your imagination) of a firm selling services, such as a bank, which takes money from its depositors, reprocesses it, and "sells" it as loans to its borrowers. In fact, there has been a marked shift in the scope and nature of the industrial marketplace.

Service industries are growing and currently make the greatest contribution to Canada's gross domestic product (GDP). Because of the importance of service firms, services marketing is discussed in detail in Chapter 19. Industrial firms and primary industries (e.g., farming, mining, fishing, and forestry) currently contribute about 25 percent to Canada's GDP. Nevertheless, primary industries and the manufacturing sector are important components of Canada's economy. There are close to 40,000 manufacturers in Canada; their estimated value of shipments is over $300 billion.

Reseller Markets

Wholesalers and retailers who buy physical products and sell them again without any reprocessing are **resellers.** There are over 200,000 retailers and over 65,000 wholesalers operating in Canada. In Chapters 12 and 13, we shall see how manufacturers use wholesalers and retailers in their distribution strategies as channels through which their products reach ultimate consumers.

In this chapter, we look at these resellers mainly as organizational buyers in terms of how they make their own buying decisions and which products they choose to carry.

Nonprofit Markets

In Chapter 1, we defined *nonprofit organizations* as organizations that operate without the intent of earning profit (e.g., charities, hospitals, and government agencies). There are thousands of nongovernmental, nonprofit organizations in Canada that make millions of dollars in purchases every year in order to stay operational. Governmental agencies at the federal, provincial, and local levels also buy goods and services in order to carry out their functions and serve constituents. Their annual purchases can vary in size from billions of dollars for a federal government department such as National Defence to thousands of dollars for a local school board. The bulk of the buying at the federal government level is done by the Department of Supply and Services Canada. Most provincial governments have a government services department that does the buying on the provincial level. Hundreds of government departments—including agencies and crown corporations such as CN and the Royal Canadian Mint—must purchase goods and services to operate. The federal government is a large organizational consumer, making purchases of goods and services in excess of $100 billion annually.[4]

Global Organizational Markets

Industrial, reseller, and nonprofit markets also exist on a global scale. In fact, many of Canada's top exporters, including Noranda, Abitibi-Price, and Pratt & Whitney, focus on organizational customers, not ultimate consumers. The majority of world trade involves manufacturers, resellers, and government agencies buying goods and services for their own use or for resale to others. The exchange relationships often involve numerous transactions spanning the globe. Honeywell's MICRO SWITCH Division sells its fibre optic technology and products to manufacturers of data communication systems worldwide, through electronic component resellers in more than 20 countries and directly to national governments in Europe and elsewhere.

MEASURING INDUSTRIAL, RESELLER, AND NONPROFIT MARKETS

Measuring industrial, reseller, and nonprofit markets is an important first step for a firm interested in gauging the size of one, two, or all three markets. This task has been made easier with the publication of the **North American Industry Classification System (NAICS)**.[5] NAICS provides common industry definitions for Canada, Mexico, and the United States, which will help facilitate the measurement of economic activity in the three member countries of the North American Free Trade Agreement (NAFTA). NAICS replaces the Standard Industrial Classification (SIC) system, a version of which has been in place for more than 50 years in the three NAFTA-member countries. The SIC neither permitted comparability across countries nor accurately measured new or emerging industries. Furthermore, NAICS is consistent with the International Standard Industrial Classification of All Economic Activities, published by the United Nations, to facilitate measurement of global economic activity.

FIGURE 6–1
NAICS breakdown illustration (abbreviated).

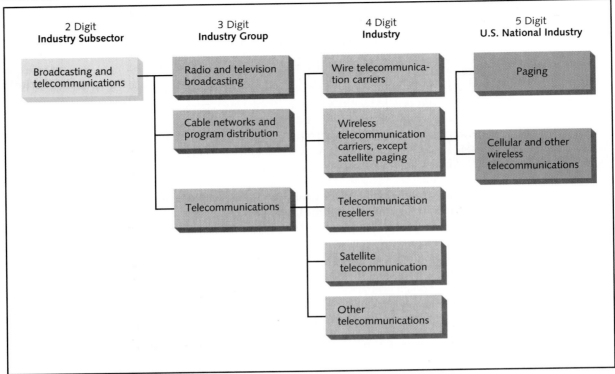

The NAICS groups economic activity to permit studies of market share, demand for goods and services, import competition in domestic markets, and similar studies. Like the earlier SIC system, NAICS designates industries with a numerical code in a defined structure. The first digit of the NAICS code designates a sector of the economy and is followed by a two-digit code signifying a subsector. Subsectors are further divided into three-digit industry groups, four-digit industries, and five digit country-specific industries. Figure 6–1 presents an abbreviated breakdown within the broadcasting and telecommunications industry to illustrate the classification scheme.

The NAICS permits a firm to find the NAICS code for present customers and then obtain NAICS-coded lists for similar organizations. Also, it is possible to monitor NAICS categories to determine the growth in various sectors and industries in order to identify promising marketing opportunities. However, NAICS codes, like the earlier SIC codes, have important limitations. The NAICS assigns one code to each organization based on its major economic activity, so large organizations that engage in many different activities are still given only one NAICS code. A second limitation is that five-digit national industry codes are not available for all three countries because in order to protect the confidentiality of the organizations, the respective governments will not reveal when too few organizations exist in a category.

LEARNING CHECK

1. What are the three main types of organizational buyers?

2. What is the North American Industry Classification System (NAICS)?

MARKET CHARACTERISTICS

- Demand for industrial products and services is derived.
- Few customers typically exist, and their purchase orders are large.

PRODUCT OR SERVICE CHARACTERISTICS

- Products or services are technical in nature and purchased on the basis of specifications.
- There is a predominance of raw and semifinished goods purchased.
- Heavy emphasis is placed on delivery time, technical assistance, postsale service, and financing assistance.

BUYING PROCESS CHARACTERISTICS

- Technically qualified and professional buyers exist and follow established purchasing policies and procedures.
- Buying objectives and criteria are typically spelled out, as are procedures for evaluating sellers and products (services).
- Multiple buying influences exist, and multiple parties participate in purchase decisions.
- Reciprocal arrangements exist, and negotiation between buyers and sellers is commonplace.

OTHER MARKETING MIX CHARACTERISTICS

- Direct selling to organizational buyers is the rule, and physical distribution is very important.
- Advertising and other forms of marketing communications are technical in nature.
- Price is often negotiated, evaluated as part of broader seller and product (service) qualities, typically inelastic owing to derived demand, and frequently affected by trade and quantity discounts.

FIGURE 6–2
Key characteristics of industrial and organizational buying behaviour.

CHARACTERISTICS OF ORGANIZATIONAL BUYING

Organizations are different from individuals, so buying for an organization is different from buying for yourself or your family.[6] True, in both cases the objective in making the purchase is to solve the buyer's problem—to satisfy a need or want. But unique objectives and policies of an organization put special constraints on how it makes buying decisions. Understanding the characteristics of organizational buying is essential in designing effective marketing plans to reach these buyers.

Organizational buying behaviour is the decision-making process that organizations use to establish the need for products and services and identify, evaluate, and choose among alternative brands and suppliers. Some key characteristics of organizational buying behaviour are listed in Figure 6–2 and discussed in the following pages.[7]

Demand Characteristics

Consumer demand for products and services is affected by their price and availability and by consumers' personal tastes and discretionary income. By comparison, industrial demand is derived. **Derived demand** means that the demand for industrial products and services is driven by, or derived from, demand for consumer products and services. For example, the demand for Alcan's aluminum products is based on consumer demand for beer, soft drinks, cars, and cameras. Derived demand is often based on expectations of future consumer demand. For instance, Whirlpool purchases parts for its washers and dryers in anticipation of consumer demand, which is affected by the replacement

Consumer needs and wants provide a derived demand for Alcan's aluminum products.

cycle for these products and by consumer income. As such, forecasting is very important in organizational buying, and it is discussed in Chapter 7.

Number of Potential Buyers

Firms selling consumer products or services often try to reach thousands or millions of individuals or households. For example, your local supermarket or bank probably serves thousands of people, and Quaker Oats tries to reach 9 million Canadian households with its breakfast cereals and probably succeeds in selling to a third or half of these in any given year. In contrast, firms selling to organizations are often restricted to far fewer buyers. Cray Research can sell its supercomputers to fewer than 1,000 organizations throughout the world, and B. F. Goodrich sells its original equipment tires to fewer than 10 car manufacturers.

Buying Objectives

Organizations buy products and services for one main reason: to help them achieve their objectives. For business firms the **buying objective** is usually to increase profits through reducing costs or increasing revenues. Southland Corporation buys automated inventory systems to increase the number of products that can be sold through its 7-Eleven outlets and to keep them fresh. Nissan Motor Company switched its advertising agency because it expected a more effective ad campaign than it was getting to help it sell more cars and increase revenues. To improve executive decision making, many firms buy advanced computer systems to process data. The objectives of nonprofit organizations including government agencies are usually to meet the needs of the groups they serve. Thus a hospital buys a high-technology diagnostic device to serve its patients better, and Employment Canada buys pencils and paper to help run its office so it can assist Canadian workers.

Understanding buying objectives is a necessary first step in marketing to organizations. Recognizing the high costs of energy, Sylvania promotes cost savings and increased profits made possible by its new fluorescent lights to prospective buyers.

Sylvania focusses on buyers' objective of reducing costs to improve profits.

Buying Criteria

In making a purchase, the buying organization must weigh key buying criteria that apply to the potential supplier and what it wants to sell. **Organizational buying criteria** are the objective attributes of the supplier's products and services and the capabilities of the supplier itself. These criteria serve the same purpose as the evaluative criteria used by consumers described in Chapter 5. Seven of the most commonly used criteria are: (1) price, (2) ability to meet the quality specifications required for the item, (3) ability to meet required delivery schedules, (4) technical capability, (5) warranties and claim policies in the event of poor performance, (6) past performance on previous contracts, and (7) production facilities and capacity.[8] Suppliers that meet or exceed these criteria create customer value.

Many organizational buyers today are transforming their buying criteria into specific requirements that are communicated to prospective suppliers. This practice, called **reverse marketing,** involves the deliberate effort by organizational buyers to build relationships that shape suppliers' products, services, and capabilities to fit a buyer's needs and those of its customers.[9] For example, Intel supports its suppliers by offering quality management programs and investing in supplier equipment that produces fewer defects.[10] Harley-Davidson has defined Quality, Cost and Timing (QCT) strategies which its suppliers participate in. These strategies drive ongoing quality improvement, reduce material costs, improve product development times, and deliver components using a JIT schedule. Suppliers performance aimed at specific QCT targets is measured and reported regularly.[11]

With many Canadian manufacturers adopting a "just-in-time" (JIT) inventory system that reduces the inventory of production parts to those to be used within hours or days, on-time delivery is becoming an even more important buying criterion and, in some instances, a requirement.[12] Caterpillar trains its key suppliers at its Quality

The success of Harley-
Davidson motorcycles is
due to continuous quality
improvements with its
suppliers.

Institute in JIT inventory systems and conducts supplier seminars on how to diagnose, correct, and implement continuous quality improvement programs.[13] The just-in-time inventory system is discussed further in Chapter 12.

Size of the Order or Purchase

The size of the purchase involved in organizational buying is typically much larger than that in consumer buying. The dollar value of a single purchase made by an organization often runs into the thousands or millions of dollars. For example, IBM's world-wide purchases of electronic components, subassemblies, and assembly services is in the tens of billions annually. With so much money at stake, most organizations place constraints on their buyers in the form of purchasing policies or procedures. Buyers must often get competitive bids from at least three prospective suppliers when the order is above a specific amount, such as $5,000. When the order is above an even higher amount, such as $50,000, it may require the review and approval of a vice president or even the president. Knowing how the size of the order affects buying practices is important in determining who participates in the purchase decision and makes the final decision and also the length of time required to arrive at a purchase agreement.[14]

Buyer–Seller Relationships

Another distinction between organizational and consumer buying behaviour lies in the nature of the relationships between organizational buyers and suppliers. Specifically, organizational buying is more likely to involve complex and lengthy negotiations concerning delivery schedules, price, technical specifications, warranties, and claim policies. These negotiations can last as long as five years, as was the case in GE's purchase of a $9.5 million Cray Research supercomputer.[15]

Reciprocal arrangements also exist in organizational buying. **Reciprocity** is an industrial buying practice in which two organizations agree to purchase each other's products and services. For example, GM purchases Borg-Warner transmissions, and Borg-Warner buys trucks and cars from GM.[16] Consumer and Corporate Affairs Canada frowns on reciprocal buying because it restricts the normal operation of the free market. However, the practice exists and can limit the flexibility of organizational buyers in choosing alternative suppliers. (Regardless of the legality of reciprocal buying, do you believe this practice is ethical? See the accompanying Ethics Insight box.)

ETHICS INSIGHT

Scratching Each Other's Back: The Ethics of Reciprocity in Organizational Buying

Reciprocity, the buying practice in which two organizations agree to purchase each other's products and services, is frowned upon in many countries because it restricts the normal operation of the free market. Reciprocal buying practices do exist, however, in a variety of forms, including certain types of countertrade arrangements in international marketing. Furthermore, the extent to which reciprocity is viewed as an ethical issue varies across cultures.

Reciprocity is occasionally addressed in the ethics codes of companies. For instance, the Quaker Oats Company code of ethics states:

In many instances, Quaker may purchase goods and/ or services from a supplier who buys products or services from us. This practice is normal and acceptable, but suppliers may not be asked to buy our products and services in order to become or continue to be a supplier.

1. Do you think reciprocal buying is unethical?

SOURCES: Based on N. C. Smith and J. A. Quelch, *Ethics in Marketing* (Homewood, IL: Richard D. Irwin, 1993), p. 796; N. Gilbert, "The Case for Countertrade," *Across the Board*, May 1992, pp. 43–45; and A. J. Dubinsky, M. A. Jolson, M. Kotobe, and C. U. Lim, "A Cross-National Investigation of Industrial Salespeople's Ethical Perceptions," *Journal of International Business Studies*, Fourth Quarter 1991, pp. 651–70.

Long-term relationships are also prevalent. As an example, Shanghai Aviation Industrial Corporation, owned by the government of China, announced a $4.5 billion project to build 150 commercial airliners over 10 years. McDonnell Douglas, Boeing, and Europe's Airbus Industrie all vied for this lucrative, long-term project, with Boeing getting the initial order valued at $2 billion for the delivery of 33 aircraft. Boeing has sold aircraft to the Chinese government since 1972 and cited this factor as being important in getting the order.

The Buying Centre

For routine purchases with a small dollar value, a single buyer or purchasing manager often makes the purchase decision alone. In many instances, however, several people in the organization participate in the buying process. The individuals in this group, called a **buying centre,** share common objectives, risks, and knowledge important to the purchase decision. For most large multistore chain resellers such as Sears Canada, 7-Eleven convenience stores, Zellers, The Bay, or Safeway, the buying centre is highly formalized and is called a *buying committee*. However, most industrial firms or non-profit organizations, particularly government agencies, use informal groups of people or call meetings to arrive at buying decisions.

The importance of the buying centre requires that a firm marketing to organizational customers understand the structure and behaviour of these groups. One researcher has suggested four questions to provide guidance in understanding the buying centre in organizations:[17]

1. Which individuals are in the buying centre for the product or service?
2. What is the relative influence of each member of the group?
3. What are the buying criteria of each member?
4. How does each member of the group perceive our firm, our products and services, and our salespeople?

These ads are directed toward specific people in Honeywell's customer buying centres.

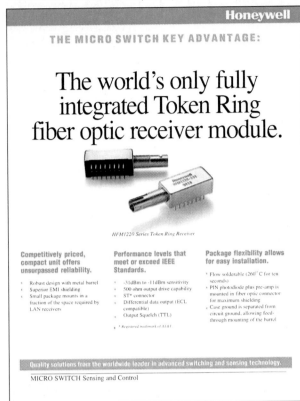

Answers to these questions are difficult to come by, particularly in dealing with industrial firms, resellers, and nonprofit organizations outside Canada.[18] For example, Canadian firms are often frustrated by the fact that foreign buyers such as the Japanese or Chinese "ask a thousand questions" but give few answers, sometimes rely on third parties to convey views on proposals, are prone not to "talk business," and often say yes to be courteous even when they mean no. Firms in the global chemical industry recognize that production engineering personnel have a great deal of influence in Hungarian buying groups, while purchasing agents in the Canadian chemical industry have relatively more influence in buying decisions.

People in the Buying Centre. The composition of the buying centre in a given organization depends on the specific item being bought. Although a buyer or purchasing manager is almost always a member of the buying centre, individuals from other functional areas are included depending on what is to be purchased. In buying a million-dollar machine tool, the president (because of the size of the purchase) and the production vice president or manager would probably be members. For key components to be incorporated in a final manufactured product, individuals from R&D, engineering, and quality control are likely to be added. For new word-processing equipment, experienced secretaries who will use the equipment would be members. Still, a major question in penetrating the buying centre is finding and reaching the people who will initiate, influence, and actually make the buying decision.[19]

Roles in the Buying Centre. Researchers have identified five specific roles that an individual in a buying centre can play.[20] In some purchases the same person may perform two or more of these functions.

Buying centre at work.

- *Users* are people in the organization who actually use the product or service, such as a secretary who will use a new word processor.
- *Influencers* affect the buying decision, usually by helping define the specifications for what is bought. The information systems manager would be a key influencer in the purchase of a new mainframe computer.
- *Buyers* have formal authority and responsibility to select the supplier and negotiate the terms of the contract. The purchasing manager probably would perform this role in the purchase of a mainframe computer.
- *Deciders* have the formal or informal power to select or approve the supplier that receives the contract. Whereas in routine orders the decider is usually the buyer or purchasing manager, in important technical purchases it is more likely to be someone from R&D, engineering, or quality control. The decider for a key component being incorporated in a final manufactured product might be any of these three people.
- *Gatekeepers* control the flow of information in the buying centre. Purchasing personnel, technical experts, and secretaries can all keep salespeople or information from reaching people performing the other four roles.

STAGES IN AN ORGANIZATIONAL BUYING DECISION

As shown in Figure 6–3, the five stages a student might use in buying a CD player also apply to organizational purchases.[21] However, comparing the two right-hand columns in Figure 6–3 reveals some key differences. For example, when a CD player manufacturer buys headphones for its units from a supplier, more individuals are involved, supplier capability becomes more important, and the postpurchase evaluation behaviour is more formalized. The headphone-buying decision illustrated is typical of the steps in a purchase made by an organization.[22] Later in the chapter we will analyze a more complex purchase made by an industrial organization.

TYPES OF BUYING SITUATIONS

The number of people in the buying centre and the length and complexity of the steps in the buying process largely depend on the specific buying situation. Researchers who have studied organizational buying identify three types of buying situations, which they have termed **buy classes.**[23] These buy classes vary from the routine reorder, or **straight rebuy,** to the completely new purchase, termed **new buy.** In between these extremes is the **modified rebuy.** Some examples will clarify the differences:

- *Straight rebuy.* Here the buyer or purchasing manager reorders an existing product or service from the list of acceptable suppliers, probably without even checking with users or influencers from the engineering, production, or quality

FIGURE 6–3   Comparing the stages in consumer and organizational purchases.

Stages in the Buying Decision Process	Consumer Purchase: CD Player for a Student	Organizational Purchase: Headphones for a CD Player
Problem recognition	Student doesn't like the sound of the stereo system now owned and desires a CD player.	Marketing research and sales departments observe that competitors are including headphones on their models. The firm decides to include headphones on its own new models, which will be purchased from an outside supplier.
Information search	Student uses past experience and that of friends, ads, and *Consumer Reports* to collect information and uncover alternatives.	Design and production engineers draft specifications for headphones. The purchasing department identifies suppliers of CD player headphones.
Alternative evaluation	Alternative CD players are evaluated on the basis of important attributes desired in a CD player.	Purchasing and engineering personnel visit with suppliers and assess (1) facilities, (2) capacity, (3) quality control, and (4) financial status. They drop any suppliers not satisfactory on these factors.
Purchase decision	A specific brand of CD player is selected, the price is paid, and it is installed in the student's room.	They use (1) quality, (2) price, (3) delivery, and (4) technical capability as key buying criteria to select a supplier. Then they negotiate terms and award a contract.
Postpurchase behaviour	Student reevaluates the purchase decision, may return the CD player to the store if it is unsatisfactory, and looks for supportive information to justify the purchase.	They evaluate suppliers using a formal vendor rating system and notify supplier if phones do not meet their quality standard. If problem is not corrected, they drop the firm as a future supplier.

control departments. Office supplies and maintenance services are usually obtained as straight rebuys.

- *Modified rebuy.* In this buying situation the users, influencers, or deciders in the buying centre want to change the product specifications, price, delivery schedule, or supplier. Although the item purchased is largely the same as with the straight rebuy, the changes usually necessitate enlarging the buying centre to include people outside the purchasing department.
- *New buy.* Here the organization is a first-time buyer of the product or service. This involves greater potential risks in the purchase, so the buying centre is enlarged to include all those who have a stake in the new buy. The purchase of CD player headphones was a new buy.

The marketing strategies of sellers facing each of these three buying situations can vary greatly because the importance of personnel from functional areas such as purchasing, engineering, production, and R&D varies with (1) the type of buying situation and (2) the stage of the purchasing process.[24] Read the accompanying Marketplace Application Box and suppose you are a sales representative selling a component part to a manufacturer for use in one of its products. How will your sales task differ depending on the purchase (buy-class) situation?

If it is a new buy for the manufacturer, you should be prepared to act as a consultant to the buyer, work with technical personnel, and expect a long time for a buying decision to be reached. However, if the manufacturer has bought the component part from you before, so that it is a straight or modified rebuy, your sales task should emphasize low price and a reliable supply in meetings with the purchasing agent.

How the Buying Situation Affects Buying Centre Behaviour

How does the buy-class situation influence the size and behaviour of the buying centre? Considerable research has examined this question and produced some consistent findings. The research findings are summarized below and illustrate that the buy-class situation affects buying centre tendencies in different ways. This research has important implications for organizational reality that are discussed in the text.

SOURCES: Based on J. M. Bristor, "Influence Strategies in Organizational Buying: The Importance of Connections to the Right People in the Right Places," *Journal of Business-to-Business Marketing*, vol. 1 (1993), pp. 63–98; E. Anderson, W. Chu, and B. Weitz, "Industrial Purchasing: An Empirical Exploration of the Buy-Class Framework," *Journal of Marketing*, July 1987, pp. 71–86; and R. D. McWilliams, E. Naumann, and S. Scott, "Determining Buying Center Size," *Industrial Marketing Management*, February 1992, pp. 43–49.

	Buy-Class Situation	
Buying Centre Dimension	*New Buy*	*Straight or Modified Rebuy*
People involved	Many	Few
Decision time	Long	Short
Problem definition	Uncertain	Well defined
Buying objective	Good solution	Low-price supplier
Suppliers considered	New and present	Present
Buying influence	Technical or operating personnel	Purchasing agent

LEARNING CHECK

1. What one department is almost always represented by a person in the buying centre?

2. What are the three types of buying situations, or buy classes?

THE ORGANIZATIONAL NEW BUY DECISION

New buy purchase decisions are ones where the most purchasing expertise is needed and where both the benefits of good decisions and penalties of bad ones are likely to be greatest. This means that effective communication among people in the buying centre is especially important.[25] Tracing the stages in the buying decision made by an appliance manufacturer highlights some of the important aspects of organizational buying. It also illustrates the challenges involved in marketing to organizations.

An Industrial Purchase: An Electric Motor

Suppose GE decides to design and build a new line of clothes dryers and needs an electric motor, a key component in the dryer. Let's track the five purchasing stages in this new buy situation.

Problem Recognition. After top management in GE's appliance division decides to introduce a new line of clothes dryers, engineering and R&D personnel come up with a workable design that is tested and approved. They meet with the purchasing manager to reach a **make–buy decision**—an evaluation of whether a product or its parts will be purchased from outside suppliers or built by the firm itself. The group concludes that the electric motor in each dryer should be bought, not made.

Information Search. The engineering and R&D personnel need to develop product specifications for the electric motor, which are detailed technical requirements the motor must meet, such as its horsepower, life in hours, and ability to operate at a stated temperature and humidity. Members of the purchasing and production departments then perform a **value analysis** on the electric motor—a systematic appraisal of the design, quality, and performance requirements of the product to reduce purchasing costs. For example, suppose the GE engineers conclude that at least a one-eighth-horsepower motor is needed to power the dryer. The purchasing department would recommend buying a one-fourth-horsepower motor, which is available as a standard item from many vendors, rather than a one-eighth-horsepower motor, which must be made to order at a higher cost.

In its information search, the purchasing department also relies on the technical expertise of vendors in developing appropriate design specifications. Specifications are generally stated in terms of material, dimensions, and performance characteristics rather than brand name to maximize the number of qualified vendors available and to ensure genuine competition among bidders. A variety of other sources may be used by GE during the information search process in order to make an effective purchase decision. These sources could include vendors' salespeople, trade associations, advertising, vendor files, and product literature, as well as the Internet or other computerized data sources.

Alternative Evaluation. The buying centre must develop the necessary buying criteria for the electric motor, which in this case are quality requirements, on-time delivery, and price, in that order. The purchasing manager is given the responsibility to select the supplier and negotiate a contract for motors.

The next step in purchasing is soliciting bids from potential suppliers. This involves selecting the names of vendors from a **bidders list**—a list of firms believed to be qualified to supply a given item—and sending each vendor a quotation request form describing the desired quantity, delivery date, and specifications of the product.

Most purchasing departments maintain a separate bidders list for each general class of items they order. They update these lists continually by adding the names of potential new vendors and deleting the names of unsatisfactory vendors. To further ensure competition, many firms require that at least three bids be solicited for purchases exceeding a specified dollar amount.

Purchase Decision. Unlike the short purchase stage in a consumer purchase (such as buying a bag of potato chips), in organizations the purchase stage covers the period from vendor selection and placing the purchase order until the product is delivered, which often takes months or years. This period frequently involves performing vendor follow-up, expediting the order, and renegotiating the contract terms if specification changes are made after the initial contract is awarded.

How does GE go about buying an electric motor for their clothes dryers? Read the text.

Sometimes contracts are awarded directly to vendors on the basis of the data they provide in the quotation request forms. At other times the purchasing manager may wish to negotiate with one or more bidders, particularly on high-dollar, high-volume items. Eventually the GE purchasing manager selects two vendors and awards each a contract in the form of a purchase order—an authorization for the vendor to provide the items under the agreed-on terms and to bill the purchasing firm.

If the purchased item is of minor value and if no design or delivery changes are made in the order after it has been issued, the purchasing manager rarely follows up on the order. However, vendor follow-up is essential if conditions change or if an item is of high value, in short supply, or crucial to the firm. In the case of the electric motors, they are so critical to producing the new clothes dryers that the purchasing manager periodically checks with the two vendors to see that no problems arise.

Postpurchase Behaviour. When the electric motors are finally delivered, the quality control department tests them to ensure they meet specifications. If they are unsatisfactory, the purchasing manager negotiates with the supplier to rework the items according to specifications or arranges for an entirely new shipment.

Experienced buyers realize that evaluation of purchase decisions is essential. The vendor's performance is evaluated after final delivery of the purchased items. This information is often noted on a vendor rating sheet and is used to update the bidders lists kept by the purchasing department. Performance on past contracts determines a vendor's chances of being asked to bid on future purchases, and poor performance results in a vendor's name being dropped from the list.

LEARNING CHECK

1. What kind of buying situation is GE's purchase of an electric motor?

2. What types of information sources are available to GE in making a purchase decision?

MARKETING TO ORGANIZATIONS MORE EFFECTIVELY

The preceding example of an organizational purchase suggests steps sellers can take to increase their chances of marketing products and services to organizations. Firms marketing to organizations must learn four key lessons to be successful in organizational marketing: (1) understand the organization's needs, (2) get on the bidders list, (3) find the right people in the buying centre, and (4) provide value to the organizational buyer.

Understand the Organization's Needs

As important and obvious as understanding the organization's needs seems, this guideline is violated as often with industrial products as with consumer products. Getting to know the organization's needs can be accomplished in several ways. A firm could simply review what an organization has purchased in the past. For example, a firm wanting to sell to the federal government can examine the "detailed expenditure accounts" of the government to see exactly what it has purchased over the past year. An important aspect of discovering needs is also determining if those needs are being met. To do so, a firm can obtain a copy of the successful bidders lists published by the government in order to determine who is currently supplying the government with goods and services. This information can allow the firm to investigate whether the government was satisfied with the existing goods and services and/or their suppliers. Marketing opportunities may exist where the organizational buyers have experienced some dissatisfaction.

Another way to understand the organization's needs is to *ask*. The firm can simply talk to organizational buyers to discuss their needs. In doing so, a firm may be able to work with potential customers to specifically design products that meet their requirements, rather than wait and hope for orders.

Global Upholstery Co., Ltd., of Downsview, Ontario, has been very successful with this strategy. Global is the sixth-largest office furniture manufacturer in North America, competing with such giants as Steelcase and Haworth. Very often Global will talk to customers to determine their exact requirements and then will make the product. David Feldberg, president of Global, says, "We'll have a customer in, and we'll show them a chair, and they'll say, 'Yeah, but I'd like the back a little bigger.' We say, 'Hold on,' and while we're out to lunch, we make a new chair. There's no way you'll lose a sale when you can do that."[26]

Get on the Bidders List

Understanding an organization's needs is vital, but a firm must also be considered a satisfactory or qualified supplier and get its name on the bidders lists of organizations to which it hopes to market. A firm cannot compete unless its name is on the bidders list. This is often accomplished through personal selling and sending product samples to be tested by the organization. If the product and the supplier meet the organization's specifications, their name will get onto the list. For example, Global Upholstery met the rigid requirements of the Boeing Corporation and was selected to bid on a $20 million contract to refurbish Boeing's headquarters in Seattle, Washington. Global beat out a US competitor, Steelcase, for the contract.[27]

Find the Right People in the Buying Centre

One of the most difficult parts of an industrial salesperson's job is finding the "right" people in the buying centre—the people who influence and make the decision to select the product and supplier. This information is critical to obtain, and it is often readily available. For example, one source that could be used is the *Canadian Trade Index* published by the Canadian Manufacturers Association. It lists Canadian manufacturers, contact people, telephone numbers, and addresses. Using this and other information can help the firm better direct its marketing efforts.

Provide Value to the Organizational Buyer

Obtaining the right or privilege to supply products or services to an organization is a marketing accomplishment. Now, however, the firm must satisfy the organization's needs and provide that customer with value. Providing value leads to repeat business and continued success. Global Upholstery attributes much of its success in providing value to its customers to its commitment to product design. Micheline Sanitar, an interior design consultant, says Global "is a real Canadian success story. When they started out calling themselves 'Global,' it seemed like a silly name, but now it's really appropriate."[28] The company has built a global business based on providing value to its customers. For example, in the low-end steno chair category, Global has been able to outshine its Italian and Chinese competitors by offering a nicer design, better detail, and better quality—all at a price within 10 percent of its competitors.

To sell to the Canadian and US federal governments, Global has to meet demanding quality and durability standards, important ingredients in the concept of customer value. In order to meet these standards, the company created its own testing facility—one of only two manufacturing laboratories in Canada certified to do furniture testing. This investment has paid off for Global. It has built a reputation for providing value and now exports close to 45 percent of its total production, with one-third of its output going to the United States.[29]

LEARNING CHECK

1. Why is getting on the bidders list important to a prospective vendor?

2. How could a firm wanting to market to the federal government discover the needs of that organization?

LEARNING OBJECTIVE REINFORCEMENT

1. Distinguish among industrial, reseller, and nonprofit markets. Organizational buyers are divided into three different markets: industrial, reseller, and nonprofit. Industrial firms in some way reprocess a good or service they buy before selling it again to the next buyer. Resellers buy physical products and resell them again without any reprocessing (e.g., wholesalers and retailers). Nonprofit markets include nongovernmental, nonprofit organizations as well as governmental agencies (federal, provincial, and local) that buy goods and services for the constituents they serve.

2. Recognize key characteristics of organizational buying that makes it different from consumer buying. Many aspects of organizational buying behaviour are different from consumer buying behaviour. Some of the key characteristics are: demand characteristics, number of potential buyers, buying objectives, buying criteria, size of order or purchase, buyer–seller relationships, and multiple buying influences within the organizations.

3. Explain the buying centre concept and the five roles people can play in the buying centre. The buying centre consists of groups of persons within an organization who participate in the buying process and share common objectives, risks, and knowledge important to that process. There are five specific roles that an individual can play in a buying centre: users, influencers, buyers, deciders, and gatekeepers. In some purchases the same person may perform two or more of these roles.

4. Outline the three types of buying situations that organizations face. The three types of buying situations, or buy classes, are the straight rebuy, the modified rebuy, and the new buy. These form a scale ranging from a routine reorder to a totally new purchase.

5. Understand the four key lessons that organizations must learn to be successful in organizational marketing. To market effectively to organizations, a firm must (1) understand the organization's needs, (2) get on the bidders list, (3) reach the right people in the buying centre, and (4) provide value to the organizational buyer.

KEY TERMS AND CONCEPTS

organizational marketing p. 130
organizational buyers p. 130
industrial firms p. 130
resellers p. 130
North American Industry
    Classification System (NAICS)
    p. 131

organizational buying
    behaviour p. 133
derived demand p. 133
buying objective p. 134
organizational buying criteria p. 135
reverse marketing p. 135
reciprocity p. 136
buying centre p. 136

buy classes p. 139
straight rebuy p. 139
new buy p. 139
modified rebuy p. 139
make–buy decision p. 142
value analysis p. 142
bidders list p. 142

CHAPTER QUESTIONS AND APPLICATIONS

1. Describe the major differences among industrial firms, resellers, and nonprofit markets in Canada.

2. Explain how the North American Industry Classification System (NAICS) might be helpful in understanding industrial, reseller, and nonprofit markets, and discuss the limitations inherent in this system.

3. List and discuss the key characteristics of organizational buying that make it different from consumer buying.

4. What is a buying centre? Describe the roles assumed by people in a buying centre and what useful questions should be raised to guide any analysis of the structure and behaviour of a buying centre.

5. Effective marketing is of increasing importance in today's competitive environment. How can firms more effectively market to organizations?

6. A foreign-based producer of men's apparel is interested in the sales volume for such products in Canada. The producer realizes this is a difficult assignment but has given you a sizable fee to find these data. What information source would you examine first, and what kind of information would be found in this source?

7. If many of the federal government's purchases are classified as straight rebuy, how can a new firm wanting to do business with the government break into this market?

APPLICATION CASE 6–1
ENERGY PERFORMANCE SYSTEMS INC. (B)

"What we need," said David Ostlie matter-of-factly, "is just one electric utility to say yes—to try our technology. Then the whole-tree energy technology will speak for itself." David Ostlie is president of Energy Performance Systems, Inc. (EPS), a firm he founded in 1988 to produce clean, cheap electricity by growing, harvesting, transporting, drying, and burning whole hardwood trees in retrofitted or new power plants. The simplicity of whole-tree energy (WTE) technology is a big plus compared to many of the alternative energy technologies being studied around the world.

EPS is based on the WTE technology and owns US, Canadian, and European patents. The WTE technology has been scaled up in four successive tests that have demonstrated the feasibility of large-scale power production from sustained burning of whole trees. Conventional fossil-fuel power plants, the staple for utilities, produce large volumes of CO_2, SO_2, NO_x, and particulate emissions that contribute to air pollution, acid rain, and global warming. The fact that wood contains little or no sulfur, combined with the efficient combustion of WTE technology, virtually eliminates the SO_2 emissions and results in large reductions in NO_x and particulate emissions—and at a lower cost per kilowatt hour produced than fossil-fueled power plants. By burning a renewable biomass—trees—there is no net addition to the CO_2 released into the atmosphere.

Demand for electrical power is increasing. To avoid electrical blackouts, new electrical generating capacity must be added. For Energy Performance Systems Inc., this provides an opportunity either to (1) retrofit existing power plants to use WTE (many that operate infrequently because of pollution problems) or (2) construct new plants to use the new technology. In an electric utility, capacity planners project demand for electricity and assess the utility's ability to supply the demand. The chief executive officer makes the recommendation to add new capacity, a decision reviewed by the board of directors. The vice president of power supply probably recommends the technology to be used and the site for the new power plant.

As Ostlie talked to prospective utility customers about WTE technology, several concerns emerged, including: (1) Can enough heat be generated by burning wood to produce electricity? (2) Can whole trees be loaded, transported, and dried? (3) Are there enough trees available at a reasonable cost to support commercial-size power plants? (4) What are the environmental benefits of WTE? (5) What will it cost to build a retrofitted or new power plant? (6) What will be the cost of electricity produced by a WTE plant? "It's not far away, but we've still got to make that first sale," added Dave Ostlie.

QUESTIONS
1. In a utility's decision whether or not to buy and use the WTE technology (*a*) who comprises the buying centre, and (*b*) what role does each person in the buying centre play?
2. What should be the key elements of EPS's strategy to market WTE to prospective utility buyers?

APPLICATION CASE 6–2
HONEYWELL, INC., OPTOELECTRONICS DIVISION

After several years of developing fibre optic technology, the Optoelectronics Division of Honeywell, Inc., began pursuing commercial applications of this new technology. The task would not be easy because many firms were unfamiliar with fibre optics. Fibre optics is the technology of transmitting light through long, thin, flexible fibres of glass, plastic, or other transparent materials. In its chief commercial applications, a light source emits infrared light flashes corresponding to data. Millions of light flashes per second send streams through a transparent fibre. A light sensor at the other end of the fibre "reads" the data transmitted. Honeywell estimated that sales of fibre optic technology would run into the billions of dollars. About half of the volume would come from telecommunica-

tions, about 25 percent from government or military purchases, and about 25 percent from commercial applications in computers, robotics, cable TV, and other products.

Honeywell executives examined the organizational buying behaviour associated with the adoption of a new technology. The buying process appeared to contain at least six phases: (1) need recognition, (2) identification of available products, (3) comparison with existing technology, (4) vendor or seller evaluation, (5) the purchase decision itself, and (6) follow-up on technology performance. Moreover, there appeared to be several people within the buying organization who would play a role in the adoption of a new technology. For example, top management (such as the president and executive vice presidents) would certainly be involved. Engineering and operations management (e.g., vice presidents of engineering and manufacturing) and design engineers (e.g., people who develop specifications for new products) would also play a major role. Purchasing personnel would also have a say in such a decision and particularly in the vendor-evaluation process.

The role played by each person in the buying decision was still unclear to Honeywell. It seemed that engineering management personnel could slow the adoption of fibre optics if they did not feel it was appropriate for the products made by the organization. Design engineers, who would actually apply fibre optics in product design, might be favourably or unfavourably disposed to the technology, depending on whether they knew how to use it. Top management personnel would participate in any final decision to use fibre optics and could generate interest in the technology if stimulated to do so. In the end, Honeywell's review of organizational buying behaviour led to many questions about how to penetrate an organization's buying centre and how to convince organizations to use fibre optics in their products.

QUESTIONS

1. What type of buying situation is involved in the purchase of fibre optics, and what important buying criteria will be used by organizations considering using fibre optics in their products?

2. Describe the purchase decision process for adopting fibre optics, and state how members in the buying centre for this technology might play a part in this process.

3. What effect will perceived risk have on an organization's decision whether to use fibre optics in its products?

CHAPTER 7

Marketing Research and Information Technology

KNOW YOUR CUSTOMER:

EMBRACING TECHNOLOGY TO COLLECT MARKETING INFORMATION What is multimedia and how can it be used to collect marketing information? Ask Frank O'Hara, president of O'Hara Systems Inc., a Toronto-based interactive multimedia firm specializing in providing marketing solutions. In talking about multimedia, O'Hara stresses the interactive aspect—it's his definition of multimedia. "If it doesn't have an interactive component, it isn't multimedia," he says. Using the interactive aspect of multimedia to its fullest, O'Hara creates products that allow his clients to interact with customers to provide customer services and gather marketing information. By doing so, O'Hara allows his clients to act upon one of the seven imperatives for marketing success: to *embrace technology*. (See Chapter 1 for a review for the seven imperatives for marketing success.)

Case in point: Instead of bikini-clad women on a beach, Labatt Breweries Ltd. is using one of O'Hara's products—an interactive multimedia kiosk in the shape of a beer can—as part of the company's marketing strategy. This system allows Labatt to gather marketing information and, at the same time, reward customers with coupons as thanks for filling out an electronic survey.[1]

This chapter focuses on marketing research and information technology. You will see how quality information is linked to making effective marketing decisions. You will also see how marketing research and information technology can be used by organizations to utilize information to their advantage. Moreover, this chapter will discuss one very important application of the marketing research process—sales forecasting. In today's marketplace, an accurate sales forecast is a valuable piece of marketing information.

THE ROLE OF MARKETING RESEARCH

To place marketing research in perspective, we can describe what it is, some of the difficulties in carrying it out, and how marketing executives can use the marketing research process to make effective decisions.

What Marketing Research Is and Does

Marketing research is the process of defining a marketing problem or opportunity, systematically collecting and analyzing information, and recommending actions to improve an organization's marketing activities. Marketing research should be considered an ongoing process for acquiring routine and nonroutine information, internal as well as external, for marketing decision making.[2]

A Means of Reducing Risk and Uncertainty. Assessing the needs and wants of consumers and providing information to help design an organization's marketing mix to satisfy them is the principal role that marketing research performs. This means that marketing research attempts to identify and define both marketing problems and opportunities, and to generate and evaluate marketing actions.[3] Although marketing research can provide few answers with complete assurance, it can reduce risk and uncertainty to increase the likelihood of the success of marketing decisions.

Marketing research is useful in both problem diagnosis (identifying the cause of a problem) and problem prognosis (determining how to solve the problem). Conducted properly, marketing research can answer any pressing marketing-related question that an executive might have. However, marketing research should not be designed to simply replace an executive's good sense, experience, or intuition but should rather be used in conjunction with those skills.

Judging the Value of Marketing Information. The value of marketing information should be judged by the extent to which it improves the marketing decision-making process. In other words, the marketing executive must ask, by gathering marketing information, will I increase my chances of making the correct decision? Marketing information is generally more valuable in a decision situation when:

- There is a high degree of uncertainty.
- The consequences of a wrong decision are great.
- There are several alternatives and more than one is likely to be selected.

Why Good Marketing Research Is Difficult

First of all, good research requires a clear understanding of the marketing problem to be investigated. Sometimes the nature of the problem appears obvious; other times it is much more difficult to identify and define. Collecting information for an inappropriately identified or poorly defined problem will not be of much help to the marketing executive.

When a marketing researcher must talk to consumers, other problems can arise, such as properly determining who to talk to, deciding what to ask them, and how to ask them. Good marketing research requires great care—especially because of the inherent difficulties in asking consumers questions. For example:

- Do consumers really know whether they are likely to buy a particular product that they have probably never thought about before? Can they really assess its advantages and disadvantages on the spur of the moment?
- Even if they know the answer, will they reveal it? When personal or status questions are involved, will people give honest answers?
- Will their actual purchase behaviour be the same as their stated interest or intentions? Will they buy the same brand they say they will?

When people know they are being measured, the very measurement process itself can significantly affect their answers and behaviours. A task of marketing research is to overcome these difficulties to provide useful information on which marketing executives can act.

CONCEPT CHECK

1. What is marketing research?

2. How can you judge the value of marketing information?

THE MARKETING RESEARCH PROCESS

Marketing researchers should always attempt to conduct research on the basis of the *scientific method,* a process of systematically collecting, organizing, and analyzing data in an unbiased, objective manner. Marketing research must meet two basic principles of the scientific method: reliability and validity. **Reliability** refers to the ability to replicate research results under identical environmental conditions. In other words, if a research project was to be conducted for the second, third, or fourth time, the results should be the same. Marketers need to have reliable information to make effective decisions. If results of a study are not reliable, the research can do more harm than no research at all.

Validity involves the notion of whether or not the research measured what it was intended to measure. In other words, does the research tell marketers what they needed to know? For example, sometimes a poorly worded question can mean different things to different people and the answers can lead to invalid results.

The marketing research process is generally considered to involve five basic steps, as shown in Figure 7–1. The marketing researcher usually proceeds through the five

Step 1	Problem definition
Step 2	Exploratory research
	• Informal fact finding
	• Secondary data search
Step 3	Primary data generation
	• Sampling
	• Qualitative research
	• Quantitative research
Step 4	Data analysis and interpretation
Step 5	Recommendations and implementation

FIGURE 7–1
The marketing research process.

steps in sequence. The research should proceed to successive steps only if a solution to the problem has not been found in the earlier steps. For example, exploratory research very often provides enough insight to solve the problem, thus saving the company from conducting more time-consuming and expensive research.

Step 1: Problem Definition

The first step in the marketing research process is problem definition, or properly defining the scope and nature of the research topic. It is important to point out that while we use the term *problem,* the marketing research process can also be undertaken to explore an *opportunity.* In this text, we will use the term *marketing problem* to include both problems and opportunities. Sometimes the problem is obvious, but in other cases the problem may be more difficult to identify and define. Regardless, the marketing researcher must fully understand and properly identify the problem at hand.

The marketing research process is often initiated by the marketing manager, who will approach the marketing researcher with a problem that requires information for decision making. For example, the marketing manager might ask the researcher to find out why market share for the company's product is dropping in Saskatchewan. But before any actions can be taken, the researcher needs to know what the manager really means by market share. How is it defined and measured? By units? Dollars? Number of customers? Before the researcher can investigate the problem, these questions and many others must be answered.

Proper problem definition is critical, since research based on incorrect problem definition will be a waste of resources. Many researchers agree that when proper problem definition is completed, 50 percent of the marketing research task is already accomplished.

LEARNING CHECK

1. What are reliability and validity?

2. What are the five steps in the marketing research process?

Step 2: Exploratory Research

The next step in the marketing research process involves undertaking some exploratory research. Exploratory research is a preliminary examination of problem-specific information that may provide some insight into possible causes and solutions to the problem. This step helps the researcher determine why or how the marketing problem arose and to further identify some alternatives to solving the problem. While exploratory research appears informal and casual, it is a critical stage of the marketing research process. In many cases, good exploratory research can solve many marketing problems without the need to conduct further, more expensive research.

Exploratory research usually consists of informal fact finding, both from discussions with informed sources inside the firm or customers and/or others outside the firm and from an examination of secondary sources of information. The researcher is scanning for any readily available information that can offer insights into the problem as well as provide ideas about possible approaches and techniques to be applied or avoided in the later stages of the research process.

Secondary Data. Exploratory research almost always involves the use of secondary data. **Secondary data** means existing data not collected specifically for the research project but considered relevant and pertinent to the marketing problem. The researcher will usually first examine any internal documentation that may be relevant to the problem under investigation. This existing information is referred to as *internal secondary data.* Such data include financial statements, research reports, customer letters, sales reports, and customer lists. The researcher may also examine, simultaneously or in sequence, any useful outside information that may exist, or *external secondary data.* The federal government is a key source of such data. These data are made available through Statistics Canada or from local libraries.

In addition to government-supplied data, commercial organizations, trade associations, universities, and business periodicals provide detailed data of value to marketing researchers. A list of external secondary sources of marketing information is given in Appendix B following this chapter.

Advantages and disadvantages of secondary data A general rule among marketing people is to use secondary data first before collecting primary data. Two important advantages of secondary data are (1) the tremendous time savings, since the data have already been collected and published, and (2) the low cost (e.g., most census reports are available for only a few dollars each).

However, these advantages must be weighed against some significant disadvantages. First, the secondary data may be out of date. If you were working on a project in 1997 and you used 1990 census data, the data would already be seven years old. Second, the definitions or categories of information that you find might not be quite right for your research purposes. For example, suppose you are interested in the age group from 13 to 16; many census age statistics appear only for the 10-to-14 and 15-to-19 age groupings. Finally, because the data are collected for another purpose, they may not be specific enough for your needs as a marketing researcher.

But what is critical to remember is that analysis of secondary data may be sufficient to solve the marketing problem and conclude the research process. All too often, marketers skip this stage of the marketing research process and start generating primary data. This is often a time-consuming and costly mistake.

CONCEPT CHECK

1. What are secondary data?

2. What are some advantages and disadvantages of secondary data?

Step 3: Primary Data Generation

When researchers have exhausted all secondary data sources and do not have sufficient information to solve their marketing problems, they will proceed to generate primary data. **Primary data** consist of "new" information that is problem-specific and necessary for the research project. In general, the secondary data research should have at least helped the researcher refine the scope and nature of the problem, as well as filled in some of the information requirements about the problem. The objective at this stage is to proceed with new-information gathering until a sufficient amount of information is obtained to allow the company to make an informed and reasonable decision about the marketing problem.

Primary data can be classified as either qualitative or quantitative. Qualitative data are normally generated, as we shall see, through the use of depth interviews and focus groups. Methods normally used to generate quantitative data include observation, surveys, and experiments. However, these methods, particularly observation and surveys, can also be used to obtain qualitative data. Ultimately, the type of primary data and the method used to generate the data should be driven largely by the type of information that needs to be obtained, as well as by time and cost considerations.

Before discussing the differences between qualitative and quantitative primary data and the methods used to generate such data, we need to discuss the concept of sampling.

Sampling. When primary data are to be generated, the researcher must determine the appropriate population that should be the subject of the research. The *population* is the universe of people, places, or things to be investigated. To define the population or universe correctly, the researcher must know who and what to study as well as where and when. Because of the time and cost involved in conducting a census, however, a research project rarely involves a complete census of every person. Instead, **sampling**—selecting representative elements from the chosen population—occurs.

Sampling techniques fall into two general categories: probability and nonprobability sampling. *Probability sampling* involves precise rules to select the sample such that each element of the population has a specific known chance of being selected. For example, if your college wants to know how last year's 1,000 graduates are doing, it can put their names in a bowl and randomly select 100 names of graduates to contact. The chance of being selected—100/1,000, or 0.10—is known in advance, and all graduates have an equal chance of being contacted. This procedure helps select a sample (100 graduates) that should be representative of the entire population (the 1,000 graduates) and allows conclusions to be drawn about the entire population.

Nonprobability samples, on the other hand, are chosen on the basis of convenience or judgment by the marketing researchers. With nonprobability samples, the chance of selecting a particular member of the population is either unknown or zero. If your college decided just to talk to 100 of last year's graduates who lived closest to the college, many class members would be arbitrarily eliminated. This has introduced a sampling bias, or possible lack of representativeness, which may make it difficult to draw conclusions about the entire population of the graduating class.

When a sample is used instead of a census, marketers need to be concerned with sampling error. *Sampling error* is a measure of the discrepancy between results found researching the sampled group and the results that could have been expected had a census been conducted. In general, large samples, if selected correctly, have lower sampling errors than smaller samples.

Qualitative Research. Very often, because of time and cost constraints, a researcher may elect to conduct only qualitative research when attempting to generate primary data. **Qualitative research** does not allow the researcher to make statistical inferences or quantitative statements. This is because the samples used are often selected on a nonprobability basis and are generally small. But qualitative research can play a valuable role in focusing quantitative research efforts and/or uncovering hypotheses that could be tested in a planned quantitative research activity. In fact, idea or *hypothesis generation* is a major reason for conducting qualitative research.

Focus groups enable a moderator to obtain information from 6 to 10 people at the same time.

Many marketing researchers conduct a two-stage primary data generation procedure. First, qualitative research is conducted. If this does not provide sufficient information to solve the problem, then quantitative research is undertaken. However, the use of qualitative research as a stand-alone method is growing in popularity as marketers learn more about the weaknesses and strengths of secondary research. Qualitative research data are usually obtained through depth interviews and/or focus group sessions.

Depth interviews **Depth interviews** are detailed individual interviews with people relevant to the research project. The researcher questions the individual at length in a free-flowing, conversational style in order to discover information that may help solve the marketing problem being investigated. Sometimes the interviews can take a few hours, and they are often recorded on audio- or videotape.

Focus groups **Focus groups** are informal interview sessions in which 6 to 10 people relevant to the research project are brought together in a room with a moderator to discuss topics surrounding the marketing research problem. The moderator poses questions and encourages the individuals to answer in their own words and to discuss the issues with each other. Oftentimes, the focus group sessions are watched by observers through one-way mirrors and/or the sessions are videotaped. Of course, participants should be informed if they are being observed and/or taped. Focus group sessions often provide the marketer with valuable information for decision making or can uncover other issues that should be researched in a more quantitative fashion.

CONCEPT CHECK

1. What are primary data?

2. What is sampling?

3. Depth interviews and focus groups represent what type of research?

Careful observation of "toy testers" in Fisher-Price's school leads to better products.

Quantitative Research. **Quantitative research** differs from qualitative research because it allows conclusions to be drawn about the population under study through statistical inference. To draw accurate conclusions about a population, either a census must be completed or a representative sample must be used. Quantitative research is typically used to evaluate any hypotheses that may have been generated in the qualitative research stage of the marketing research process. As we stated earlier, the three principal ways to generate quantitative primary data are observation, surveys, and experiments.

In general, *observation* means watching, either mechanically or in person, how people actually behave. In some circumstances, the speed of events or the number of events being observed make mechanical or electronic observation more appropriate than personal observation. Retailers, for example, can use electronic cameras to count the number of customers entering or leaving a store. Marketers can also rely on personal observations to collect primary data. For example, Fisher Price uses its licensed nursery schools to observe children using and abusing toys in order to develop better products. Personal observation is both useful and flexible, but it can be costly and unreliable, especially when different observers report different conclusions in watching the same activities. Also, although observation can reveal what people do, it cannot determine why they do it—why, for example, they are buying or not buying a product.

In order to determine why consumers behave as they do, marketing researchers must ask consumers. This can be accomplished through the use of *surveys*—a method used to generate primary data by asking consumers questions and recording their responses. Surveys can be conducted by mail, telephone, or personal interview. In choosing among the three alternatives, the marketing researcher has to make important trade-offs to bal-

FIGURE 7–2 Comparison of mail, telephone, and personal interview surveys.

Basis of Comparison	Mail Surveys	Telephone Surveys	Personal Interview Surveys
Cost per completed survey	Usually the least expensive, assuming adequate return rate	Moderately expensive, assuming reasonable completion rate	Most expensive, because of interviewer's time and travel expenses
Ability to probe and ask complex questions	Little, since self-administered format must be short and simple	Some, since interviewer can probe and elaborate on questions to a degree	Much, since interviewer can show visual materials, gain rapport, and probe
Opportunity for interviewer to bias results	None, since form is completed without interviewer	Some, because of voice inflection of interviewer	Significant, because of voice and facial expressions of interviewer
Anonymity given to respondent	Complete, since no signature is required	Some, because of telephone contact	Little, because of face-to-face contact

ance cost against the expected quality of the information obtained. (See Figure 7–2). The figure shows that personal interviews have a major advantage of enabling the interviewer to be flexible in asking probing questions or to get reactions to visual materials. In contrast, mail surveys usually have the lowest cost per completed survey of the three data collection procedures. Telephone surveys lie in between in terms of flexibility and cost. See the accompanying Marketplace Application for a discussion of a popular form of personal interview: Mall intercept interviewing.

When marketers decide to use surveys to ask questions, they make several assumptions: (1) that the right questions are being asked, (2) that people will understand the questions being asked, (3) that people know the answers to the questions, (4) that people will answer the questions truthfully, and (5) that the researchers themselves will understand the answers provided. Marketers must concern themselves not only with asking the right questions but also with how to properly word those questions. Proper phrasing of a question is vital in uncovering useful marketing information. Figure 7–3 shows typical problems to guard against in wording questions to obtain meaningful answers from respondents.

Surveys of distributors—retailers and wholesalers in the marketing channel—are also very important for manufacturers. A reason given for the success of many Japanese consumer products in Canada and the United States, such as Sony Walkmans and Toyota automobiles, is the stress that Japanese marketers place on obtaining accurate information from their distributors.[4]

Constructing a survey instrument or questionnaire takes great skill. Moreover, good marketing researchers will always *pretest* the instrument in order to ensure that the questions being asked are the correct ones and are being asked properly. But even properly worded questionnaires may not get good response rates. In fact, a growing concern among market researchers today is the unwillingness of respondents to participate in surveys. Many marketers are looking for ways to improve this situation. For

MARKETPLACE APPLICATION

Changes In Retail Could Impact Mall Intercept Interviewing

For many marketing researchers, mall intercept interviewing (a form of personal interviewing) is second only to telephone surveys in collecting data. The research industry views mall intercepts as an inexpensive alternative to door-to-door interviews. The convenience of using a central location such as a mall has made mall intercept interviewing popular.

Despite the convenience of mall intercept interviewing, marketing researchers may have to reconsider the quality of information collected in this manner. Many retailing experts are predicting major changes in shopping malls for the 1990s and beyond. Shopping malls have seemingly lost their luster among many consumers today. New competitors like Wal-Mart and the category-killer specialty shops (e.g., Toys 'Я' Us) are challenging shopping malls just as malls did to downtown department stores in the 1970s and 1980s. Moreover, these newer competitors are seldom located in malls.

This trend suggests that malls may be losing certain types of shoppers to these non-mall retailers. Mall intercept samples potentially have an over-representation of a particular type of shopper known as the *recreational*

shopper. Recreational shoppers differ from the more value-conscious and convenience-oriented shoppers. For example, recreational shoppers tend to spend more time shopping per trip and usually seek more product information than nonrecreational shoppers by reading more magazines, watching more television, and visiting more stores. Given this trend, marketing researchers need to rethink the appropriateness of using mall intercept interviewing.

1. Should marketing researchers avoid the use of mall intercept samples if they know these samples tend to have an over-representation of recreational-type shoppers? Explain.

2. What effect do you expect the increasing use of "the new media" (e.g., shopping networks, video catalogs, computer shopping services, etc.) will have on the use of mall intercept interviewing?

SOURCE: Adapted from Alan J. Bush and E. Stephen Grant, "The Potential Impact of Recreational Shoppers on Mall Intercept Interviewing: An Exploratory Study," *Journal of Marketing—Theory and Practice,* Fall, 1995, pp. 73–83.

FIGURE 7–3 Typical problems in wording questions.

Problem	Sample Question	Explanation
Leading question	Why do you like Wendy's fresh-meat hamburgers better than competitors' hamburgers made with frozen meat?	Consumer is led to make statement favouring Wendy's hamburgers.
Ambiguous question	Do you eat at fast-food restaurants regularly? ☐ Yes ☐ No	What is meant by word regularly—once a day, once a month, or what?
Unanswerable question	What was the occasion for your eating your first hamburger?	Who can remember the answer? Does it matter?
Two questions in one	Do you eat Wendy's hamburgers and chili? ☐ Yes ☐ No	How do you answer if you eat Wendy's hamburgers but not chili?
Nonexhaustive question	Where do you live? ☐ At home ☐ In dormitory	What do you check if you live in an apartment?
Nonmutually exclusive answers	What is your age? ☐ Under 20 ☐ 20-40 ☐ 40 and over	What answer does a 40-year-old check?

Survey data being collected by personal interview.

mailed questionnaires, there is some evidence to suggest that simply improving the design and format of the instrument itself can improve response rates.

Another method that can be used by marketing researchers to generate primary data is the experiment. An **experiment** is a way of obtaining data by manipulating factors under tightly controlled conditions to test for cause and effect. The interest is in whether changing one of the conditions (a suspected cause) will change the behaviour of what is studied (the effect).

In marketing experiments the suspected cause is often one or more of the marketing mix variables, such as product features, price, or marketing communications

A successful test market led to the national rollout of Shoppers Drug Mart's Life brand cola.

technique used. An ideal effect is usually a change in purchases of an individual, a household, or an entire organization.

Experiments can be conducted in the field or in a laboratory. In *field experiments,* the research is conducted in the real world—for example, in a store, in a bank, or wherever the behaviour being studied occurs naturally. Test marketing is probably the most common form of field experiment. Shoppers Drug Mart used taste tests in the field to determine how consumers felt about its Life brand cola, compared with national brands such as Pepsi and Coke. The tests revealed that 33 percent of the consumers who participated liked Life brand better than the competitive colas. Shoppers Drug Mart then put the product on the shelves of stores in Atlantic Canada to test the market's response to the product. A successful test market there led to a national rollout of the product in Shoppers stores across Canada.[5]

Because marketers cannot control all the conditions in the field, they sometimes turn to a laboratory setting. Laboratories are not the real world but do offer highly controlled environments. Unlike in the field, the marketer has greater control over the factors that may play a role in impacting on the behaviour under investigation.

Ethical Aspects of Collecting Primary Data. Professional marketing researchers have to make ethical decisions in collecting, using, and reporting primary data. Examples of unethical behaviour include failure to report problems with research results because of incomplete data, reporting only favourable but not unfavourable results, using deception to collect information, and breaching the confidentiality of respondents and/or their personal data if anonymity or nondisclosure was guaranteed.[6] Using formal statements on ethical policies and instituting rewards and punishments can increase ethical behaviour in marketing research. The accompanying Ethics Insight shows an example of an ethical issue in marketing research.

CONCEPT CHECK

1. What are the three ways to generate quantitative data?

2. Survey data can be collected by three methods. What are they?

ETHICS INSIGHT

What Is "Truth" in Reporting Survey Results?

Doctors were surveyed to find out what brand of butter substitute they recommend for their patients concerned about cholesterol. The results:

- Recommended no particular brand: 80%
- Recommended brand A: 5%
- Recommended brand B: 4%

No other brand is recommended by more than 2 percent of the doctors. The firm owning brand A runs an ad that states, "More doctors recommend brand A than any other brand."

1. Is this ethical? Why or why not?
2. What kind of ethical guideline, if any, should be used to address this issue?

SOURCE: Adapted from D. S. Tull and D. I. Hawkins, *Marketing Research: Measurement and Method*, 5th ed. (New York: Macmillan Publishing Company, 1990), Chap. 23.

Step 4: Analysis and Interpretation

The purpose of step 4 of the marketing research process is to transform data into valuable information for decision making.

In general, the researcher must evaluate and analyze both the sources and the nature of any secondary data being used, including how they were originally gathered. Relevant secondary data that have been collected are usually condensed and summarized by the researcher with a focus on how they relate to the marketing problem under investigation. If qualitative data have been collected (e.g., through depth interviews or focus groups), the marketing researcher must carefully analyze and interpret this information. However, no statistical interpretations or inferences can be made from such data. Instead, the researcher will analyze the verbatim responses provided by respondents while looking for any general "themes" that may have emerged from the data.

The researcher tabulates the quantitative primary data that have been collected and makes calculations from these data in a statistical manner. The level of analysis conducted on the data depends on the nature of the research and the information needed to provide a solution to the marketing problem. For survey data, frequency analysis is completed; the responses are calculated question by question. The researcher may then wish to identify patterns in the data or examine how some data pertaining to some questions may relate to data obtained from asking other questions.

Cross Tabulations. Probably the most widely used technique for organizing and analyzing marketing data is cross tabulation. A *cross tabulation*, or "cross tab," is a method of analyzing and relating data having two or more variables. It is used to discover the relationships in the data. In order to use cross tabs effectively, the marketing researcher must decide which variables should be paired together.

Figure 7–4 contains the result of cross tabulating a sample of 500 households that participated in a study of potato chip consumption. This cross tabulation relates awareness of a new brand of potato chips to household consumption of potato chips. Although statistical analysis would normally be used to assess the relationships illustrated in Figure 7–4, a quick examination shows that awareness of the new brand increases with consumption rate.

Cross tabs offer a simple format that permits direct interpretation and an easy means of communicating data to management. They have great flexibility and can be

FIGURE 7–4
A cross tabulation relating awareness of a new brand of potato chips to household consumption of potato chips.

CROSS TABULATION—AWARENESS OF NEW BRAND AND HOUSEHOLD CONSUMPTION

		Heavy	Medium	Light	Total
Aware of the New Brand	Yes	70	140	90	300
	No	20	80	100	200
		90	220	190	500

used to summarize observational, survey, and experimental data. Also, cross tabulations may be easily generated on today's personal computers.

Cross tabulations also have some disadvantages. For example, they can be misleading if percentages are used in the cross tabs when there are only a small number of responses to given questions. Also, cross tabulations can hide some relations because each typically shows only two or three variables. By balancing both advantages and disadvantages, researchers probably make more marketing decisions using cross tabulations than any other method of analyzing data.[7] Good marketing researchers who have a solid understanding of all aspects of marketing as well as research are insightful and creative enough to use the proper level of analysis in this phase of the marketing research process.

Step 5: Recommendations and Implementation

At this stage of the process the marketing researcher, often in conjunction with marketing management, must make suggestions for actions that should be taken by the organization that will solve the marketing problem. The potential solution(s) to the problem must be clearly identified. But identification of the potential solution(s) is not enough. Management must then make a commitment to act, to make decisions based on the research and on good judgment and knowledge of the situation. In other words, someone must "make something happen"—see that the solution is implemented. Finally, once implemented, the proposed solution should be monitored to ensure that intended results do occur. The accompanying Marketplace Application identifies some techniques firms use to increase the usefulness of their marketing research.

The Need for Ongoing Marketing Research. In this chapter, we have established why marketers need accurate and insightful information in order to make effective marketing decisions. Unfortunately, many believe that marketing research should be used situationally and for problem-specific reasons. In other words, marketing research should be used only when problems arise, and thus research projects should have a starting point and an end point. But more and more marketers are recognizing the need for continual collection and analysis of marketing information in order to avoid *potential* problems and to uncover possible future marketing opportunities.[8]

When Not to Conduct Marketing Research. Marketing research should not be conducted when the cost of conducting the research is greater than the benefits that will be derived. If the cost of a marketing research project is $25,000 but the impact of a wrong decision on the organization is only $5,000, then the research is not economical. Research should not be conducted when it only supplies redundant information at needless cost. Finally, it should not be conducted if it is unlikely to be both reliable and valid.[9]

MARKETPLACE APPLICATION

Increasing the Value of Marketing Research

Stated in simplest terms, the job of marketing research is to help managers understand the voice of the customer. Unfortunately, in the increasing technical sophistication of many marketing research studies, that voice of the consumer is lost and fails to be translated into better products and product features. For example, only one-half of the market segmentation studies done for six consumer goods companies over a four-year period were useful and helped companies reach strategic business decisions.

Here are some suggestions for increasing the value of marketing research:

- *Keep key executives in touch with customers.* At age 82, J. Willard Marriott, Sr., still reads every complaint card from Marriott customers.
- *Use observation research, not just questionnaire research.* Honda was the first carmaker to install coin trays in its cars. The reason: its founder insisted on it after his first visit to the United States, when he observed the hassle of trying to find change quickly at expressway tollbooths.
- *Try "sequential recycling."* Use small samples to go out and learn a little bit, digest what you learn, and go back out again.
- *Practise "backward marketing research."* Start by identifying the key marketing decisions to be reached, and work back to specify the marketing data and research useful for those decisions.

These ideas can convert marketing research to better products.

1. Why might the voice of the consumer be lost as the result of increasing technical sophistication of many marketing research studies?

SOURCES: Adapted from C. L. Hodock, "The Decline and Fall of Marketing Research in Corporate America," *Marketing Research*, June 1991, pp. 12–22; and A. R. Andressen, "Backward Marketing Research," *Harvard Business Review*, May–June 1985, pp. 176–82.

CONCEPT CHECK

1. What are cross tabs?
2. When would it be appropriate not to conduct marketing research?

INFORMATION TECHNOLOGY IN MARKETING

Since the advent of computers after World War II and the growth of personal computers in the 1980s, management perceptions of the value and use of information have changed significantly. Even the terms have changed: Whereas a decade ago managers talked about separate information systems for marketing, accounting, and the other functional areas, the lines separating information among various departments in a firm are now disappearing. Today, all generally fall under the broader term *information technology,* which involves designing and managing a computer and communication system to satisfy an organization's requirements for information.

Information technology can provide a sustainable competitive advantage in a number of ways: building barriers to entry, increasing switching costs (the cost of changing from one supplier to another), and satisfying customers by providing essential information and databases. Increasingly though, marketing managers are learning that they must embrace information technology, just to enter a market and remain competitive. (See Chapter 1 for a review of the seven imperatives for marketing success.)

Eaton's connects hundreds of its suppliers into its electronic data interchange system (EDI). By embracing this new technology Eaton's is practising strategic partnering. Shown here are Jeff Otis, President of Grand National, an Eaton's supplier, and Tony LaMantia, Senior VP of Eaton's School of Retailing and Strategic Alliances.

Today even the smallest of organizations can efficiently store and organize *internal secondary data*. Moreover, information technology allows these small organizations to be effective at database marketing and enables them to benefit from electronic data interchange (EDI). **Database marketing**—also called *micromarketing*—is an organization's effort to collect demographic, media, and consumption profiles of customers in order to target them more effectively. Database marketing enables marketers to use direct marketing communications—such as direct mail or telemarketing—to reach customers more efficiently. (Direct Marketing Communications is covered in Chapter 16.) **Electronic data interchange (EDI)** is an interactive network that connects manufacturers with suppliers, distributors, and retailers so that they can share information. EDI enables a more efficient marketing process.

Creative use of information technology helps organizations practise *relationship marketing*. For example, a supplier could use *database marketing* to track on computer every order that its retailers make. With this data, special offers to particular retailers who buy or fail to buy certain products could be developed. Such offers could even be communicated via *EDI* to enable retailers to benefit from such offers in a timely manner. Information technology used this way helps to build long-term exchange relationships that are highly valued by all parties involved in the exchange.

When Information Technology Is Needed in Marketing

Not every firm needs information technology to help it make marketing decisions. The need for it is largely determined by the value versus the cost of marketing information, as well as the kinds of decisions a marketing manager makes and how they relate to the information included in the information system.

Trade-Offs: Value versus Cost of Marketing Data. Information and data can be valuable commodities, but they can also be very expensive. The facts and figures that make up marketing information have no value by themselves. Their value comes from being organized and interpreted to help the decision maker reach better decisions.

MARKETPLACE APPLICATION

Nielsen Marketing Research Supplies New Information Services

Nielsen Marketing Research of Markham, Ontario, has identified an increase in retail/supplier partnerships as an opportunity to build new business. As a result, Nielsen now has representatives in Halifax, Montreal, Toronto, and Calgary to offer ongoing advice on category management (where retailers and suppliers work together to maximize off-shelf sales through product positioning and sales promotions).

Nielsen is also enhancing its software program, *Spaceman,* developed by Logistics Data Services Inc., the company's Dallas subsidiary. The software analyzes performance factors such as price, shelf position, and duration of sales promotions. In addition, Nielsen has introduced a database service that predicts the impact of price changes and sales promotions based on historical performances.

Nielsen is also broadening the products its HomeScan division monitors. The HomeScan division employs about 7500 consumers who scan UPC codes off packages in their homes. This service extends Nielsen's reach beyond its traditional avenues of major grocery stores and drug chains. These people are capturing purchase information off products bought in stores typically not served by Nielsen, including warehouse clubs and specialty-merchandise retailers.

1. What factors may account for Nielsen's decision to supply new information services?

2. Do you expect that small independent retailers need or want information services such as the new services now being offered by Nielsen Marketing Research?

SOURCE: Adapted from James Pollock, "Nielsen Boosts Retail Consulting Arm," *Marketing,* February 12, 1995, p. 2.

In practice, a marketing manager sets the priority of the data from most valuable to least valuable in solving a problem, assesses the cost of collecting each kind of data, and stops collecting more data on the list when the cost of collection outweighs their value in improving the decisions. Although these are very difficult guidelines to apply, they stress an important issue: the value of the data must be balanced against their cost of collection and use.

Kinds of Decisions a Marketing Manager Makes. A marketing manager makes two distinctly different kinds of decisions. One type is *structured decisions,* routine and repetitive decisions for which standard solutions exist. A product manager for a grocery products manufacturer may plan dozens of sales promotions (coupons and deals) over a five-year period. For these structured decisions the manager can access the information system to determine what will be the impact on sales of moving the promotion up two weeks or changing a coupon's price allowance.

In contrast, *unstructured decisions* are complex decisions for which there are no cut-and-dried solutions. For example, a department store manager may ask for an assessment of the impact on sales of changing the department's location within the store. Researchers have found that past experience is especially important for marketing managers in making unstructured decisions such as new products, but not as important for structured decisions such as scheduling consumer promotions.[10]

One-time and special reports don't go into an information system. Only the cost-effective, repetitive information is typically included and becomes the database used, with pertinent models to provide the standardized, periodic reports produced by the information system. To see just how information technology is used in a variety of marketing applications, read Application Case 7–1 at the end of this chapter.

Key Elements in an Information System

Today's marketing managers are seeking user-friendly information systems to assist them in their decisions. As shown in Figure 7–5, today's strategic information system that helps a marketing manager develop relationship marketing strategies contains five key elements:

1. *Input devices.* These means of collecting marketing data include in-store and in-home scanners, people meters, and purchase or reservation workstations.
2. *Databases.* The marketing data collected by the input devices are stored in diverse databases containing data on households, products, retailers, media, and sales promotions.
3. *Models.* The models provide hypotheses about the relationships among the data contained in the databases to enable the decision maker to organize, interpret, and communicate the resulting information in order to reach marketing decisions.
4. *Mainframe or minicomputer.* This is today's main means of collecting, processing, and updating the data coming from the input devices, databases, and models. Replacing these older computers are systems of networked microcomputers.[11]
5. *Personal computer.* The PC on the marketing manager's desk serves as an input and output device and a means of querying the system to obtain and analyze the data it contains.

An information system like this permits a marketing manager to reach decisions using *sensitivity analysis,* asking "what-if" questions to determine how changes in a factor like price or advertising affect marketing results like sales revenues or profits.

FIGURE 7–5
Strategic information system for use in today's relationship marketing decisions.

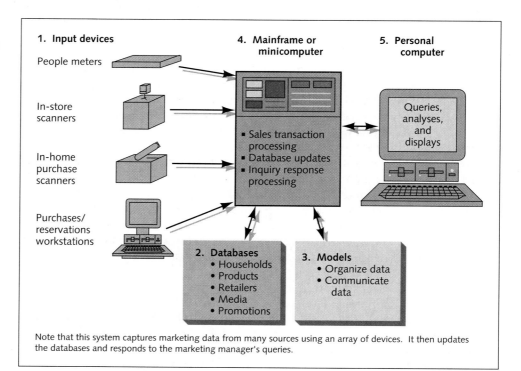

1. **Input devices**
People meters
In-store scanners
In-home purchase scanners
Purchases/ reservations workstations

4. **Mainframe or minicomputer**
- Sales transaction processing
- Database updates
- Inquiry response processing

5. **Personal computer**
Queries, analyses, and displays

2. **Databases**
- Households
- Products
- Retailers
- Media
- Promotions

3. **Models**
- Organize data
- Communicate data

Note that this system captures marketing data from many sources using an array of devices. It then updates the databases and responds to the marketing manager's queries.

SALES FORECASTING

In today's marketplace an accurate sales forecast is a valuable piece of marketing information. This is because overestimating the size of a market may mean wasting research and development, manufacturing, and marketing dollars on new products that fail. Conversely, underestimating market size may mean missing the chance to introduce successful new products. In this section, we will discuss some basic forecasting terms, two major approaches to forecasting, and specific forecasting techniques.

Basic Forecasting Terms

Unfortunately, there are no standard definitions for some forecasting concepts, so it's necessary to take care in defining the terms used.

Market or Industry Potential. The term **market potential,** or *industry potential,* refers to the maximum total sales of a product by all firms to a segment under specified environmental conditions and marketing efforts of the firms. For example, the market potential for cake mix sales to Canadian consumers in 1998 might be 2 million cases— what Pillsbury, Betty Crocker, Duncan Hines, and other cake mix producers would sell to consumers under the assumptions that past patterns of dessert consumption continue and the same level of marketing effort continues relative to other desserts.

Sales or Company Forecast. What one firm expects to sell under specified conditions for the uncontrollable and controllable factors that affect sales is the **sales forecast,** or *company forecast.* For example, Duncan Hines might develop its sales forecast of 1 million cases of cake mix for Canadian consumers in 1998, assuming past dessert preferences continue and so does the same relative level of marketing expenditures between it, Pillsbury, and Betty Crocker.

With both market potential estimates and sales forecasts, it is necessary to specify some significant details: the product involved (all cake mixes, only white cake mixes, or only Bundt cake mixes); the time period involved (month, quarter, or year); the segment involved (Canadian, western region, upper-income buyer, or single-person households); controllable marketing mix factors (price and level of advertising support); uncontrollable factors (consumer tastes and actions of competitors); and the units of measurement (number of cases sold or total sales revenues).

Two Basic Approaches to Forecasting

A marketing manager rarely wants a single number for an annual forecast, such as 5,000 units or $75 million in sales revenue. Rather, the manager wants this total subdivided into elements, such as sales by product line or sales to a market segment. The two basic approaches to sales forecasting are (1) subdividing the total sales forecast (top-down approach) or (2) building the total sales forecast by summing up the components (buildup approach).

Top-Down Approach. The **top-down approach** to sales forecasting involves subdividing an aggregate estimate into its principal components. A shoe manufacturer can use the top-down approach to estimate the percentage of its total shoe sales in a province and develop province-by-province forecasts for shoe sales for the coming year. *Canadian Markets,* published by the *Financial Post,* and *Sales and Marketing Management* magazine are sources that are widely used for top-down forecasting information.

For example, using *Canadian Markets* information, one can determine that Ontario has 36.4 percent of the Canadian population, 42.3 percent of the personal income of Canada, and 38.5 percent of Canadian retail sales. If the shoe manufacturer wanted to use a single factor related to expected shoe sales, it would choose the factor that has been closely related to shoe sales historically, in this case the percentage of Canadian retail sales found in Ontario. The top-down forecast would then be that 38.5 percent of the firm's sales would be made in the province of Ontario.

Buildup Approach. The **buildup approach** sums the sales forecasts of each of the components to arrive at the total forecast. It is a widely used method when there are identifiable components such as products, product lines, or market segments in the forecasting problem.

Figure 7–6 shows how GE's medical technology department uses the buildup approach to develop a sales forecast involving three broad categories of projects or products: work currently under contract that can be forecast precisely, follow-up work that is likely to result from current contracts, and new business that results from GE's proposals for new business, which is difficult to forecast. Each of these three forecasts is

FIGURE 7–6
Buildup approach to a 2-year sales forecast for General Electric's medical technology department.

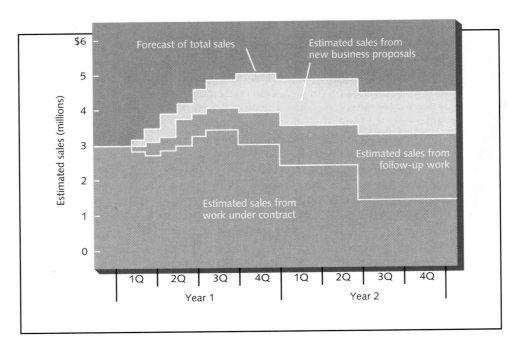

the sum of a number of individual products or projects, which for simplicity are not shown. In turn, forecasts for each of the three kinds of business can be summed to give the total sales forecast for the entire department.

Specific Sales Forecasting Techniques

Broadly speaking, three main sales forecasting techniques are available that can lead to the forecasts used in the top-down and buildup approaches. Ordered from least costly in terms of both time and money to most costly, these are: judgments of the decision maker, surveys of knowledgeable groups, and statistical methods.

Judgments of the Decision Maker. Probably 99.9 percent of all sales forecasts are judgments of the person who must act on the results of the forecast—the individual decision maker. An example is the forecasts of likely sales, and hence the quantity to order, for the 13,000 items stocked in a typical supermarket that must be forecast by the stock clerk or manager.

Surveys of Knowledgeable Groups. If you wonder what your firm's sales will be next year, ask people who are likely to know something about future sales. Four common groups that are surveyed to develop sales forecasts are prospective buyers, the firm's sales force, its executives, and experts.

A *survey of buyers' intentions forecast* involves asking prospective customers whether they are likely to buy the product during some future time period. For industrial products with few prospective buyers who are able and willing to predict their future buying behaviour, this can be effective. For example, there are probably only a few hundred customers in the entire world for Cray Research's supercomputers, so Cray simply surveys these prospects to develop its sales forecasts.

A *sales force survey forecast* involves asking the firm's salespeople to estimate sales during a coming period. Because these people are in contact with customers and are likely to know what customers like and dislike, there is logic to this approach. However, salespeople can be unreliable forecasters—painting too rosy a picture if they are enthusiastic about a new product and too grim a forecast if their sales quota is based on it.

A *jury of executive opinion forecast* involves asking knowledgeable executives inside the firm—such as vice presidents of marketing, research and development, finance, and production—about likely sales during a coming period. Although this approach is fast and includes judgments from diverse functional areas, it can be biased by a dominant executive whose judgments are deferred to by the others.

A *survey of experts forecast* involves asking experts on a topic to make a judgment about some future event. A *Delphi forecast* is an example of a survey of experts and involves polling people knowledgeable about the forecast topic (often by mail) to obtain a sequence of anonymous estimates. A major advantage of Delphi forecasting is that the anonymous expert does not have to defend his views or feel obliged to agree with a supervisor's estimate.

Statistical Methods. The best-known statistical method of forecasting is **trend extrapolation,** which involves extending a pattern observed in past data into the future. When the pattern is described with a straight line, it is *linear trend extrapolation.* Suppose that in early 1987 you were a sales forecaster for the Xerox Corporation and had actual sales revenue figures running from 1980 to 1986 (Figure 7–7). Using linear

FIGURE 7–7
Linear trend extrapolation
of sales revenues of
Xerox, made at the start
of 1987.

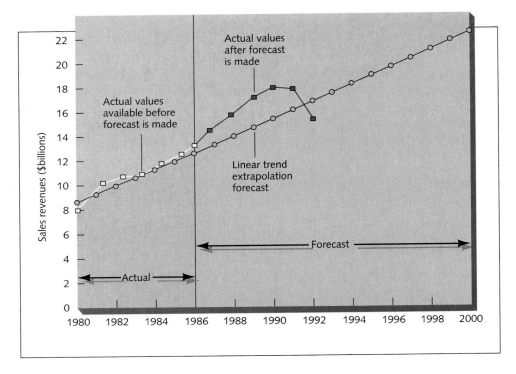

trend extrapolation, you draw a line to fit the past data and project it into the future to give the forecast values shown for 1987 to 2000.

If in 1993 you had wanted to compare your forecasts with actual results, you were in for a surprise—illustrating the strength and weakness of trend extrapolation. Trend extrapolation assumes that the underlying relationships in the past will continue into the future, which is the basis of the method's key strength: simplicity. If this assumption proves correct, you have an accurate forecast. However, if the assumption proves wrong, the forecast is likely to be wrong. In this case your forecasts from 1987 through 1991 were too low. Xerox's aggressive new product development and marketing in the 1980s helped alter the factors underlying the linear trend extrapolation and caused the forecast to be too low. However, in 1992 Xerox encountered serious marketing problems and the linear trend forecast was far too high.

In practice, marketing managers often use several of the forecasting techniques to estimate the size of markets important to them. Also, they often do three separate forecasts based on different sets of assumptions: "best case," with optimistic assumptions, "worst case," with pessimistic ones, and "most likely case," with most reasonable assumptions.

CONCEPT CHECK

1. What is the difference between the top-down and buildup approaches to forecasting sales?

2. What is linear trend extrapolation?

LEARNING OBJECTIVE REINFORCEMENT

1. Understand what marketing research is and why it is used. Marketing research is the process of defining a marketing problem or opportunity, systematically collecting and analyzing information, and recommending actions to improve an organization's marketing activities. The primary goal of marketing research is to assist in marketing decision making by reducing uncertainty.

2. Identify the five steps in the marketing research process. The marketing research process consists of five steps: problem definition, exploratory research, primary data generation, data analysis and interpretation, and recommendations and implementation.

3. Describe how and when to collect secondary data. Secondary data are data that have been recorded prior to the research project and include data internal and external to the organization. Secondary data are normally collected as part of Step 2 (*exploratory research*) of the marketing research process. They are collected as part of the researchers' preliminary examination of problem-specific information that may provide some insight into possible causes and solutions to the problem. Secondary data are collected by examining all possible *internal secondary data* sources (e.g., financial statements, research reports, customer letters, etc.) and *external secondary data* sources, such as Statistics Canada documents and reports prepared by research firms. A list of secondary sources of marketing information is given in Appendix B following this chapter.

4. Describe how and when to collect primary data. Primary data are data that is problem-specific "new" information. Observation, surveys, and experiments are means of collecting information for quantitative research that is normally used for hypothesis evaluation. Primary data are normally collected after the collection of secondary data if it is determined that the secondary data are not sufficient to solve the marketing problem.

5. Understand when information technology is needed in marketing. Not every organization needs information technology to help it make marketing decisions. The need is normally determined by the value versus the cost of marketing information, as well as the kinds of decisions a marketing manager makes and how they relate to the information included in the information system. In today's marketplace, however, many marketing managers are finding that they must utilize information technology in order to remain competitive.

6. Identify two basic approaches to forecasting and three specific sales forecasting techniques. The two basic approaches to sales forecasting are subdividing the total sales forecast (top-down approach) or building the total sales forecast by summing up the components (buildup approach). Ordered from least costly in terms of both time and money to most costly, the three main sales forecasting techniques are judgment of the decision maker, surveys of knowledgeable groups, and statistical methods.

KEY TERMS AND CONCEPTS

marketing research, p. 152
reliability, p. 153
validity, p. 153
secondary data, p. 155
primary data, p. 155
sampling, p. 156

qualitative research, p. 156
depth interviews, p. 157
focus groups, p. 157
quantitative research, p. 158
experiment, p. 161
database marketing, p. 166

electronic data interchange (EDI), p. 166
market potential, p. 169
sales forecast, p. 169
top-down approach, p. 170
buildup approach, p. 170
trend extrapolation, p. 171

CHAPTER QUESTIONS AND APPLICATIONS

1. What are the five steps in the marketing research process? Do marketing researchers usually proceed through the five steps in sequence? When, if ever, should a marketing researcher not proceed to successive steps in this process?

2. The text lists three inherent difficulties in asking consumers questions. Can you name other difficulties? Why do many people refuse to answer questions for marketing researchers?

3. As a way to earn tuition money you are thinking of providing a lawn care service in your hometown. What type of exploratory research data would you collect to determine the feasibility of the venture? You find that the exploratory research didn't answer all your questions so you decide to do a survey to determine whether or not you should invest in this venture. What kind of questions will you ask? Whom do you ask?

4. The text describes several advantages and disadvantages of secondary data. Should marketing researchers assess the quality of this type of data? If so, how can they assess the quality of secondary data?

5. You plan to open a new car rental business. You have drafted a survey you want to distribute to airline passengers. The survey will be left at airports, and respondents will mail questionnaires back in a prepaid envelope. You plan to use the following questions:

a) Do you own your own car or usually rent one?

_____ Yes _____ No

b) What is your age? _____ 21–30 _____ 30–40
   _____ 41–50 _____ 50+

c) How much did you spend on rental cars last year?
   _____ $100 or less _____ $101–$400
   _____ $401–$800 _____ $800–$1,000
   _____ $1,000 or more

d) What is a good daily rental car rate? _____

Use Figure 7–3 to (a) identify the problem with each question and (b) correct it. **NOTE:** With some of the questions, there may be more than one problem.

6. What are the five elements in an information system?

7. In Chapter 1 the practice of relationship marketing was identified as a critical imperative for marketing success. How might marketing researchers use information technology as part of the practice of relationship marketing?

8. Suppose you are the dean of your college's business school responsible for scheduling courses for the school year. (a) What repetitive information would you include in your information system to help schedule classes? (b) What special, one-time information might affect your schedule? (c) What standardized output reports do you have to provide? When?

9. Suppose you are assessing a new business venture for which you have no historical sales records and no particular expertise. This venture is a fitness club that offers dance, aerobics, free weights, and weight machines. Which of these sales forecasting techniques would you use, and why? (a) judgment of decision makers, (b) survey of knowledgeable groups, or (c) statistical methods.

10. Suppose you are to prepare a sales forecast using a top-down approach to estimate the percentage of a manufacturer's total Canadian sales going to each of the 10 provinces. You plan to use a single factor—percentage of Canadian population, percentage of effective buying income, or percentage of retail sales. Which of these three factors would you use if your sales forecast were for each of the following manufacturers, and why? (a) Lantic sugar, (b) Christian Dior dresses, and (c) Sony compact discs.

APPLICATION CASE 7-1
CONSUMERS DISTRIBUTING:
FINDING VALUE IN THE DATA

When Consumers Distributing was founded in 1957, there was little idea that the retail format being introduced then was tailor-made for the age of database marketing. Since that time, fashions have come and gone (and come back again). But the unstoppable march toward realizing the full potential of using individual customer information to market directly to that person has remained.

The seeds of what is only now becoming a mature marketing principle were evident in the late 1950s. Consumers' "catalogue showroom" format combined elements of mail order with bricks-and-mortar shopkeeping. Requiring customers to complete order forms with the details of name, address, and purchases provided a goldmine of information that was not really exploited for many years. That changed in the 1980s when Consumers decided to place that information in a database and begin building the purchase history of its customers going back several years. At that time Consumers' management also moved to systematically fix each component of its operations, including inventory control, stock replenishment, and network communications.

At first the customer database was a valuable asset, but it was only accessible via a mainframe computer. Although a number of applications had been developed for the system—store penetration and trading zones, catalogue distribution, market research—the accessibility issue hampered executions. The mainframe was too time-consuming and expensive to encourage a culture of data usage. In most mainframe environments, the user must complete a work order; have it estimated, approved, and prioritized; line up for a programmer's time; explain the (marketing) query; then likely repeat this entire process when follow-up work is required. All in all, it's a painful exercise that only serves to inhibit creativity and breakthrough into new ways of thinking and doing.

Consumers soon learned that success in database marketing is directly related to the ability to respond on a timely basis with complete and accurate information. Putting personal computers on marketers' desks gave Consumers the tools to query the database dynamically, interactively. With a PC-based or client-server system, the freedom exists to create tables and new relationships in the database—activities that were prohibitive in a mainframe environment.

Now flexible, intelligent data manipulation is fairly routine. Marketers can perform profiling, benchmarking, segmenting into multidimensional layers of information, measuring the true impact of promotions, flyers, and advertising, for example. Probably most rewarding is the ability to follow clues, delving deeper into the data and drawing out a better understanding of the marketplace.

The marketing executives at Consumers believe retailing, like any other sector, is and will continue to be driven by technological innovation that is applied to reduce costs and aggressively compete. Technology is continually delivering more for less, and will lead Consumers into a brighter future.

QUESTIONS

1. What did the marketing executives at Consumers learn about information technology?
2. Has Consumers' PC-based system enabled its marketing executives to be more efficient marketing researchers? Explain.
3. Do you expect that Consumers will have to significantly alter its existing mode of retailing in order to compete with those retailers that have chosen alternative forms of retailing such as home shopping clubs, Internet, etc.?

SOURCE: Adapted from Robert Massoud, "Finding Value in the Data: Consumers Fights the 'Tyranny of Information'," *Marketing,* April 24, 1995, p. 22; Interview with Robert Massoud, manager, direct marketing and database development, Consumers' Distributing Ltd., Used with permission.

APPLICATION CASE 7-2
THE INSTITUTE OF CANADIAN ADVERTISING DISCOVERS THE WORLD WIDE WEB

To further its mandate to provide leadership and education in the age of new media, the Institute of Canadian Advertising (ICA) of Toronto has created its own World Wide Web site. ICA executive VP John Harding says the site will serve a number of functions, such as providing ICA background informa-

tion, a listing of members, information on the process of agency searches, promotion of specific advertising-related books, and dialogue through e-mail.

In the future, Harding hopes to expand the dialogue through a conference forum. Moreover, he would like to make improvements to ICA's web site and explore ways of using the web site as a means of gathering marketing information.

YOUR TASK:

Examine ICA's web site, which is shown below in Figure 1 (or view the latest edition of the web site at http://www.goodmedia.com/ica/) and provide the following:

1. Suggestions for enhancements to the web site. Make sure your suggestions are consistent with ICA's mandate.
2. Ideas for using the web site as a means of gathering marketing information. Be specific. How can the web site be used to gather marketing information that would be of interest to ICA?
3. Now examine each of your ideas for information gathering and identify what type of research (qualitative or quantitative) ICA would be conducting if they were to implement.

SOURCE: Adapted from "Reading All about ICA on the Web," *Marketing,* May 15, 1995, p. 34; Interview with John Harding, executive VP of the Institute of Canadian Advertising. Used with the permission of ICA. This case serves as a basis of discussion rather than an illustration of either effective or ineffective handling of an administrative situation.

FIGURE 1
ICA's web site.

Welcome to the
Institute of Canadian Advertising

Yonge-Eglinton Centre
2300 Yonge Street
Box 2350 - Suite 500
Toronto, Ontario
M4P 1E4

INSTITUTE OF CANADIAN ADVERTISING

More and more advertisers are beginning to realize that membership in ICA makes a significant statement about an advertising agency's sense of responsibility to its clients. Its commitment to achieving the highest creative and business standards. Its focus on education and training, to develop the brightest advertising minds of the future.

Through ICA, our members are kept on the leading edge of the latest trends, rules and technical innovations which are happening at an accelerated pace. And they are committed to adhering to the ICA Code of Ethics, Practices and Obligations, to ensure that a fair and healthy advertising industry flourishes in Canada.

If you are an advertiser and are interested in learning more about our members and the value they can add to your business, please call the Institute of Canadian Advertising at 1-800-567-7422, or send us mail by clicking here:
ica@goodmedia.com.

ICA Fact Sheet:—Mission/Vision/Staff Directory

Benefits of ICA Membership—plus Membership Criteria and Application Procedure

ICA Member Agencies—(The Who's Who of Advertising Agencies)

ICA / ACA Guidebook—Searching for an Advertising Agency: Procedures, tips, and questionnaire

Agency Remuneration—Guidelines for Effective Advertiser/Agency Remuneration

Professional Development Courses: 1996/1997 Educational Programs

Reference Books for Sale: Advertising Works/CASSIES 1

"ALL ADVERTISING PEOPLE BELONG IN AN INSTITUTION"

Sources of Marketing Information, Business Assistance, and Small Venture Financing

This appendix includes a partial list of sources of marketing information, business assistance, and small venture financing available in Canada. Many marketing managers in Canada must concern themselves with data relevant to non-Canadian markets. For this reason, a selection of international sources has also been provided.

A growing number of the information sources listed in this appendix can be accessed on-line or on CD-ROM. With your own personal computer, a modem, and some communications software, you can access thousands of on-line databases. Hence, on-line databases are no longer restricted to huge corporations and reference libraries. When desired, this information can be transferred to the user's own computer. Because of the cost of the telecommunications link to these on-line databases, many of these databases are available on CD-ROMs. Often updated monthly, one CD-ROM can obtain the same amount of information as an entire 20-volume encyclopedia.

SELECTED GUIDES, INDEXES, AND DIRECTORIES

Most of these documents are available or can be accessed through your local public or school library. These guides, indexes, and directories list such things as business associations, organizations, business periodicals, trade shows, and special events which may be of interest to marketing managers.

Indexes of business articles, books and newspapers:

ABI/Inform (available on-line and on CD-ROM)
Business Periodical Index
Canadian Business Index
Canadian News Index
Canadian Periodical Index
Gale Directory of Publication and Business Media
Infoglobe (an on-line service)
The Standard Periodical Directory
Ulrich's International Periodicals Directory

Directories of associations and companies:

Corporate Directory
Dialog (an on-line service)
Directory of Associations in Canada
Dunn & Bradstreet Reference Book
Encyclopedia of Associations
Fraser's Canadian Trade Directory

Scott's Industrial Directories
Thomas Register of American Manufacturers

Directories of conventions and trade shows:

Canadian Industry Shows & Exhibitions: Annual Directory
Conventions & Meetings Canada
Eventline
Trade Shows and Professional Exhibits Directory

SELECTED BUSINESS AND MARKETING PERIODICALS

There are numerous professional, academic, and business magazines and journals that cover a wide range of marketing topics. These publications can be a valuable source of information concerning techniques for solving marketing problems, research methods, current trends, and emerging issues of concern to marketing managers.

Advertising Age
Adweek
American Demographics
Business Horizons
Canadian Business
Canadian Consumer
Forbes
Fortune
Harvard Business Review
Journal of Advertising
Journal of Advertising Research
Journal of Consumer Research
Journal of Marketing

Journal of Marketing Management
Journal of Marketing Research
Journal of Personal Selling and Sales Management
Journal of Public Policy and Marketing
Journal of Retailing
Journal of Small Business
Marketing Magazine
Marketing & Media Decisions
Marketing News
Marketing Research
Profit (formally Small Business)
Sales and Marketing Management

SELECTED CANADIAN TRADE PUBLICATIONS

Trade publications are a good source of information on specific markets and are a well-targeted means of communicating with potential customers. The following list includes a very small sample of the many trade publications that are available in Canada.

Canadian Doctor
Canadian Grocer
Canadian Music Trade
Canadian Jeweller
Construction Canada
Eastern Trucker

Dental Practice Management
Floor Covering News
Hardware Merchandising
Modern Purchasing
Shopping Centre Canada
Transportation Business

NEWSPAPERS AND SPECIAL REPORT SUPPLEMENTS

Across Canada there are numerous newspapers that report general business and marketing information. Most municipal and provincial publications offer a special business section and periodically include a supplement that reports on business issues and trends that are relevant to the readership within the paper's market. The following list includes the newspapers and supplements that provide the widest coverage.

The Globe and Mail
The Financial Post
The Financial Post Magazine
The Report on Business Magazine
The Wall Street Journal (US)

SOURCES OF DEMOGRAPHIC DATA

Statistics Canada is the primary source of demographic data in Canada. Statistics Canada maintains regional offices in St. John's, Halifax, Montreal, Ottawa, Toronto, Winnipeg, Regina, Edmonton, and Vancouver. In addition to regional offices, more than 50 Canadian libraries carry all Statistics Canada publications. A complete listing of Statistics Canada publications is provided in the *Statistics Canada Catalogue* (Catalogue #11–204). This is the best source for finding Statistics Canada publications on any topic. The following list includes a small sample of the Statistics Canada publications that may be of interest to marketing managers.

Market Research Handbook (Catalogue #63–224)
Family Expenditures in Canada (Catalogue #62–555)
Homeowner Repair and Renovation Expenditure in Canada (Catalogue #62–201)
Household Facilities by Income and Other Characteristics (Catalogue #13–218)
Canada Yearbook

In the United States, the Bureau of the Census is a primary source of demographic data. The Bureau's *Census of Population and Housing* provides the most complete demographic and socioeconomic profile of the U.S. population. The Census Bureau has also developed a system, named *Tiger,* that allows marketing managers to access census data by personal computer for about 7 million small geographic areas. In addition to the Census Bureau, the U.S. Department of Commerce supplies reports on economic trends, income, and consumer consumption levels.

SOURCES OF GEOGRAPHIC MARKET AND ECONOMIC DATA

The following documents are useful to market forecasters because they break consumer markets down into geographic markets and provide economic data and projections. Sources marked with an asterisk are sources of U.S. market data.

Annual Retail Trade (Statistics Canada)
Canadian Economic Observer (Statistics Canada)
Canadian Markets (an annual *Financial Post* publication)
Economic Review (National Bank of Canada)
Handbook of Canadian Consumer Markets (Conference Board of Canada)
Survey of Business Attitudes and Investment Spending Intentions (Conference Board of
    Canada)
Survey of Consumer Buying Intentions (Conference Board of Canada)
The Canadian Business Review (Conference Board of Canada)
Survey of Buying Power (a special issue of *Sales and Marketing Management* magazine)*
U.S. Industrial Outlook (U.S. Department of Commerce)*

SOURCES OF ADVERTISING, MEDIA, AND PROMOTION INFORMATION

The following publications provide information on firms operating in the field of advertising, media, and promotions.

Canadian Marketing Gold Book (CMGB Publishing)
Standard Directory of Advertising Agencies (National Register)
Marketing: A Guide to Canadian PR Services (Maclean Hunter)
Marketing: A Guide to Sales Promotion Services (Maclean Hunter)
Marketing: A Guide to Direct Marketing Services (Maclean Hunter)
Marketing: Advertising Agencies of Canada (Maclean Hunter)
National List of Advertisers (Maclean Hunter)

PROFESSIONAL AND TRADE ASSOCIATIONS

Professional and trade associations are often a useful source of information. These organizations are the source of several of the publications cited in this appendix. These organizations generally represent the special needs of their membership and as such they often provide such things as marketing data, educational programs, directories, codes of conduct/ethics, etc.

American Marketing Association
250 South Wacker Drive
Chicago, IL 60606–5819
(312) 648–0536
Website: http://www.ama.org
Toronto Chapter
100 University Avenue
Toronto, Ontario M5W 1V8
(416) 367–3573

Canadian Advertising Foundation
350 Bloor St. E. #402
Toronto, Ontario M4W 1H5
(416) 961–6311

Canadian Advertising Research
    Foundation
175 Bloor St. E South Tower #307
Toronto, Ontario M4W 3R8
(416) 964–3832

Canadian Association of Broadcasters
350 Sparks Street #306
P.O. Box 627 Stn. B
Ottawa, Ontario K1P 5S2
(613) 233–4035
e-mail: CAB-ACR.ca

Canadian Direct Marketing Association
1 Concorde Gate #607
Don Mills, Ontario M3C 3N6
(416) 391–2362

Canadian Federation of Business and
    Professional Women's Clubs
56 Sparks Street #308
Ottawa, Ontario K1P 5A9
(613) 234–7619

Canadian Federation of Independent
    Business
4141 Yonge Street #401
Willowdale, Ontario M2P 2A6
(416) 222–8022

Canadian Institute of Marketing
41 Capital Drive
Nepean, Ontario K2G 0E7
(613) 727–0954

Conference Board of Canada
255 Smyth Road
Ottawa, Ontario K1H 8M7
(613) 526–3280
Website: http://www.Conference Board.ca

Institute of Canadian Advertising
Yonge-Eglinton Centre
2300 Yonge St.
Box 2350—Suite 500
Toronto, Ontario M4P 1E4
Website: http://www.goodmedia.com/ica/

Purchasing Management Association of
    Canada
2 Carlton Street #1414
Toronto, Ontario M5B 1J3
(416) 977–7111

Professional Marketing Research Society
2323 Yonge Street #806
Toronto, Ontario M4P 2C9
(416) 493–4080

Retail Council of Canada
121 Bloor St. E #1210
Toronto, Ontario M4W 3M5
(416) 922–6678

Retail Merchants Association of Canada
1780 Birchmount Road
Scarborough, Ontario M1P 2H8
(416) 291–7903

SOURCES OF BUSINESS ASSISTANCE

There are many sources of business counselling available in Canada. The *Business Development Bank of Canada* (BDC) promotes the establishment of small and medium-sized businesses in Canada. BDC provides a wide range of financial services such as loans, guarantees, and venture capital. BDC also provides a wide range of business counselling services. BDC's *Counselling Assistance to Small Enterprises* (CASE) is specifically designed to provide small-business counselling services. Specific information on BDC services can be obtained by contacting:

Business Development Bank of Canada
5 Plâce Ville Marie
Montreal, QC H3B 5E7
(514) 283–3657

Several other federal programs and organizations offer business assistance. For example, the *Atlantic Canada Opportunity Agency* (ACOA) provides loan guarantees, business counselling, and other such services to businesses wishing to invest in the Atlantic region. For small and medium-sized Canadian businesses interested in the development and use of technology, the *National Research Council* (NRC) provides assistance through its *Industrial Research Assistance Program* (IRAP). Specific information on assistance offered by these organizations can be obtained by contacting:

ACOA (Head Office)
Blue Cross Centre
644 Main Street
P.O. Box 6051
Moncton, NB E1C 9J8
(506) 851–2271

National Research Council Canada
Administrative Services
Montreal Road
Ottawa, ON K1A 0R6
(613) 993–9101
Website: http://www.nrc.ca

Provincial governments also provide assistance services to businesses within their province. Specific information on provincial programs offered can be obtained by contacting the following government departments:

British Columbia

Ministry of Small Business, Tourism and
   Culture
6th Floor 1405 Douglas
Victoria, B.C.
V8W 3C1
(604) 356–6305
Website: http://www.TBC.GOV.BC.ca/
   Homepage.html

Alberta

Alberta Economic Development and
   Tourism
Independent Business and Tourism
   Development
12th Commerce Place
10155 102nd Street
Edmonton, Alberta
T5J 4L6
(403) 427–5267

Saskatchewan

Department of Economic Development
1919 Saskatchewan Drive
Regina, Saskatchewan
S4P 3V7
(306) 787–2232

Manitoba

Manitoba Industry, Trade, and Tourism
Business Resource Centre
5–155 Carlton Street
Winnipeg, Manitoba
R3C 3H8
(204) 945–7738

Ontario

Ministry of Economic Development, Trade
    and Tourism
Small Business Branch
900 Bay Street
8th Floor Hearst Block
Toronto, Ontario
M7A 2E1
(416) 325–6666
Website: http://www.ontario-canada.com

Quebec

Ministry of Industry, Commerce, Science
    and Technology
710 Plâce D'Youville
Quebec City, Quebec
Q1R 4Y4
(418) 691–5950

New Brunswick

Department of Economic Development
    and Tourism
P.O. Box 6000
Fredericton, New Brunswick
E3B 5H1
(506) 453–3984
Website: http://www.gov.nb.ca.

Nova Scotia

Economic Renewal Agency
World Trade and Convention Center
1800 Argyle Street
7th Floor
P.O. Box 519
Halifax, Nova Scotia
B3J 2R7
(902) 424–7583
Website: http://www.gov.ns.ca/ecor/ced/

Prince Edward Island

Department of Industry
Small Business
Shaw Building
P.O. Box 1115
Charlottetown, P.E.I.
C1A 7M8
(902) 368–0771
Website: http://www.gov.pe.ca

Newfoundland

Industry Trade and Technology
P.O. Box 8700
Confederation Building
St. John's, Newfoundland
A1B 4J6
(709) 729–5600
Website: http://www.compusult.nf.ca/ditt/
    ditt.html

Northwest Territories

Department of Economic Development
    and Tourism
Business Development
P.O. Box 1320
Yellowknife, N.W.T.
X1A 2L9
(403) 873–7115
Website: http://www.EDT.GOV.NT.CA

Yukon Territory

Department of Economic Development
211 Main Street
Suite 400
P.O. Box 2703
Whitehorse, Y.T.
Y1A 2C6
(403) 667–5466

There are many other organizations that work on behalf of Canadian entrepreneurs to promote and in some cases train Canadian entrepreneurs. One such organization is the *Canadian Federation of Independent Business* (CFIB). Specific information can be obtained by contacting:

Canadian Federation of Independent Business
1888 Brunswick St., Suite 819
Halifax, NS B3J 3J8
(902) 420–1997
e-mail: obriencfib.ips.ca

SOURCES OF SMALL VENTURE FINANCING

Adequate financing is a major hurdle for most new business ventures. In Canada, banks are the most widely used external source of funds for small business and start-up ventures. Many federal and provincial programs and organizations, however, are very active in providing a wide range of grants and loans to business ventures (see the Sources of Business Assistance section). For additional information on government sources of financial assistance you should review the following publications that are normally available at your school or local library:

> *Government Assistance Programs and Subsidies*
> *Government Financial Assistance Programs in Canada*
> *Industrial Assistance Programs in Canada*

In addition to banks and government sources, venture capital companies are a source of funding for small and medium-sized businesses. Although these venture capitalists often invest in high-risk ventures, they are not generally considered a source of funding for a firm at the idea development or start-up stage of operations. Individuals and organizations at this stage of operations generally rely on private venture capitalists within their community or on one or more of the above-mentioned sources of financial assistance.

For more detailed information on sources of financial information and advice on arranging financing you should review the following publications which may be available at your local library or bookstore:

> Good, Walter S. *Building a DREAM: A Comprehensive Guide to Starting a Business of Your Own*. 2nd ed. Toronto: McGraw-Hill, 1989. (ISBN 007–5525–860)
> Brockhouse, Gordon. *Starting A Business: A Complete Guide to Starting and Managing Your Own Company*. Revised and updated ed. Toronto, Ontario: Key-Porter Books Limited, 1994. (ISBN 1–55013–485–x)

Market Segmentation

REEBOK: PUTTING STYLE AND WINGS ON YOUR FEET

If you are an athlete—of sorts—and your thing is step training, running, or tennis, or if you just like comfortable, stylish shoes, Reebok may have changed what you have on your feet.[1] This is possible because of a very unlikely occurrence in 1979. That's the year when Paul Fireman, a camping equipment distributor, wandered through an international trade fair and saw Reebok's custom track shoes. He bought the North American licence from the British manufacturer and started producing top-of-the-line running shoes.

But Fireman then saw that the running boom had peaked and he needed other outlets for his shoes. In a brilliant marketing decision, Fireman introduced the first soft-leather aerobic dance shoe—the Reebok Freestyle—in 1982. The flamboyant colours of these Reebok designer sneakers captured the attention of aerobic dance instructors and students alike. This colour strategy still helps the sneakers get good display space in stores and attracts a lot of consumer attention.[2]

Today known as Reebok International Ltd., the firm successfully introduced tennis shoes, children's shoes (Weeboks), and basketball shoes in 1984, and walking shoes in 1986. For those who don't want to buy four different pairs of shoes to run, play tennis, shoot baskets, and walk in, Reebok introduced—of course—"cross-trainers" in 1988. This was followed the next year by the $170 Reebok Pump, a high-tech, high-top basketball sneaker with its own built-in air compressor located in the toe of the shoe. The Reebok Step Trainer appeared in 1991. And Reebok is now moving aggressively into the European sports shoe markets.[3]

The Reebok strategy, making shoes designed to satisfy needs of different customers, illustrates successful market segmentation, the main topic of this chapter. It also helps explain why Reebok's sales grew by more than 100,000 percent from the early 1980s to today.

In this chapter we will discuss what segmentation is, approaches used to segment markets, the selection of target segments, and the concept of positioning an offering in the marketplace.

MARKET SEGMENTATION

One of the oldest stories about the need for market segmentation comes from the early automobile industry. Henry Ford developed his Model T, a car he felt would satisfy the needs of everyone. Ford said, "They can have it in any colour, as long as it's black." His strategy was simple: focus on the economies of scale created by mass production and blanket the world with one marketing mix. In short, Ford's was a mass marketing strategy. In contrast, General Motors produced several models of cars, each with different colours, designed to appeal to the needs and preferences of different consumers. This is known as a target marketing strategy, a strategy that enabled GM to become the leading automaker in the world.

Today, most marketers recognize that a single marketing mix will rarely meet the needs of an entire market. Even Coca-Cola, whose slogan was at one time, "One world, One Coke," no longer uses mass marketing. In fact, Coca-Cola now offers a variety of products and tailors marketing mixes to specific segments (e.g., diet Coke for the diet segment, Minute Maid for the noncola segment, and Powerade, a sports drink, for the athletic segment).

Coca-Cola caters to specific segments with different products.

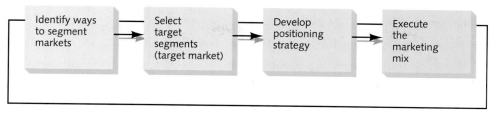

FIGURE 8–1
Process of segmenting, targeting, and positioning.

The fact that people are different is not necessarily comforting for marketers. Indeed, it would be easier for marketers if all people were the same. Still, most marketers concede that the general concept of segmentation is based on an almost unassailable premise: Markets are heterogeneous, and people who differ from one another are likely to have different needs and behave in different ways. Accordingly, market-driven organizations segment markets so they can respond more effectively to the needs of groups of prospective buyers and thus increase sales and profitability. **Market segmentation** involves aggregating prospective buyers into groups that (1) have common needs and (2) will respond similarly to a specific marketing offer or marketing mix. The groups that result from this process are **market segments,** a relatively homogeneous collection of prospective buyers. From these market segments, an organization will pick its target segment(s) or *target market*—segments toward which to direct its marketing efforts.

Figure 8–1 shows the relationship between segmenting a market, selecting target segments (target market), positioning a product in a target segment, and executing the overall marketing mix to appeal to the selected segment(s). It demonstrates that segmentation is, in fact, a means to an end: it attempts to link customer needs to an organization's marketing actions. Let's discuss ways to segment markets, then we will talk about selecting target segments and effective product positioning.

WAYS TO SEGMENT CONSUMER MARKETS

Segmenting markets is not a science—it requires large doses of common sense and managerial judgment. There is no single way to segment a given market. A marketer may have to use several different approaches, alone or in combination, in order to best understand how a market should be viewed. Figure 8–2 outlines the basic ways that consumer markets may be segmented. They include: geographic segmentation; demographic segmentation, psychographic segmentation, and behavioural segmentation.

Geographic Segmentation

When marketers segment markets based on where consumers live, they are using **geographic segmentation.** Using geographic segmentation, a marketer can segment markets by geographic units such as countries, regions, provinces, counties, cities, or even neighbourhoods. Marketers may consider a number of variables when they use geographic segmentation, including population density, population growth, and climate.

An organization may decide to operate in one or two geographic areas, or operate in all areas but pay attention to geographical differences in needs or preferences. For

FIGURE 8–2
Ways to segment
consumer markets.

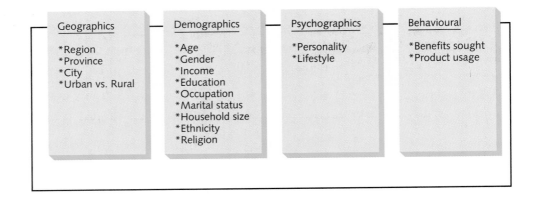

example, Colgate-Palmolive markets either different detergents or the same detergents using different messages in different parts of Canada. Arctic Power, a cold-water detergent, is sold on an energy-cost-saving dimension in Quebec, but as a clothes saver (cold-water washing is easier on clothes) in western Canada.

Demographic Segmentation

One of the most common ways to segment consumer markets is to use **demographic segmentation,** or segmenting a market based on population characteristics. This approach segments consumers according to variables such as age, gender, income, education, marital status, and so forth. Demographic segmentation is a popular way to segment markets for two reasons. First, consumer needs are often tied to demographic characteristics such as age, gender, or household size. Second, demographic information on markets is often easier to locate and measure than other variables used in other segmentation approaches.

Marketers can consider a variety of demographic variables when segmenting markets. Age, for example, can affect what a consumer buys and uses, since people in particular age categories have certain needs and preferences. As we saw in Chapter 3, marketers sometimes examine groups of consumers based on age, such as the mature market (consumers over 50 years of age), baby boomers, Generation X, and the youth market (those under 19 years of age). The mature or over-50 segment is a key segment for health care and personal products; baby boomers are considered a primary market segment for consumer electronics and automobiles, while Generation X and the youth market are major market segments for the fast-food industry.

A marketer can also use gender as a means to segment markets. It seems obvious that men and women differ in terms of product needs and preferences. Some of these differences are directly related to the gender of the consumer. Gender segmentation has long been used by many marketers including those in the clothing, cosmetics, and magazine industries. Family size has also been used by a number of marketers to segment markets. For example, the average family size in Canada is 3.1 persons. Because many families are smaller, they have smaller houses and, thus, smaller kitchens. Knowing this, GE developed and marketed a small microwave that could be hung under a kitchen cabinet. At the same time, GE also recognized that there are larger families out there. As such, GE offers extra-large refrigerators for bigger family units, especially for families at the beginning of their family life cycle.

Very often a single demographic variable may not be sufficient for understanding and segmenting a given market. Thus, many marketers combine a number of demo-

A product directed toward women over 50.

graphic variables that might clearly distinguish one segment from another. For example, when age and gender are combined, the resulting information is more useful in segmenting the face soap market than either variable alone. Some cosmetics companies combine gender, income, and occupation in order to examine market segments for different lines of cosmetic products.

Psychographic Segmentation

Marketers use **psychographic segmentation** when they segment markets according to personality or lifestyle. Researchers have found that people who share the same demographic characteristics can have very different psychographic profiles. As we saw in Chapter 5, personality traits have been linked to product preferences and brand choice. In addition, a person's lifestyle (their activities, interests, and opinions) also affects the types of products and the particular brands of products that may be purchased. Kellogg uses psychographics to segment the cereal market. For example, it identified a health-conscious segment and launched its All-Bran and Nutri-Grain brands to appeal to that segment.

Remember the Goldfarb Segments from Chapter 5? This psychographic segmentation system divides the Canadian market into six major segments (see Figure 8–3). Each segment is profiled and its characteristics are related to purchase behaviour. This allows a marketer to examine the segments most likely to respond to a given marketing mix or to better develop an existing marketing mix. For example, a Canadian frozen-food manufacturer discovered that 80 percent of its customers fell into the disinterested self-indulgent Goldfarb Segment and that convenience was more important to this segment than the taste of the food product. The manufacturer pushed convenience in its advertising and was successful in attracting this market segment.[4]

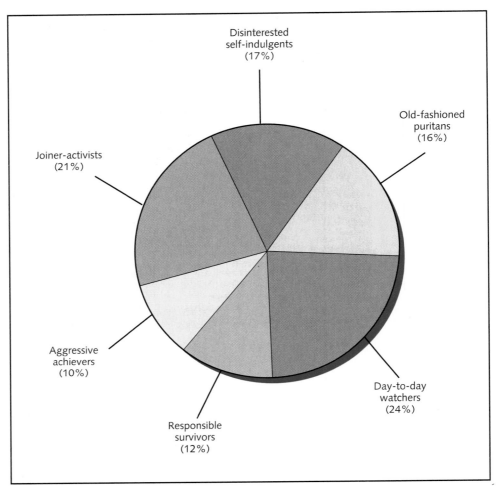

SOURCE: Goldfarb Consultants, *The Goldfarb Psychographic Segments* (Toronto, March 1992). Used with permission.

Behavioural Segmentation

When marketers use consumers' behaviour with or toward a product to segment the market, they are using **behavioural segmentation.** Key behavioural variables used to segment markets include consumer needs for certain product benefits (benefits sought) and product usage.

Benefits Sought. A powerful form of behavioural segmentation is to divide the market according to the benefits consumers seek from a product category. Using benefits sought (or *benefit segmentation*), the marketer examines the major benefits consumers look for in the product category, the kinds of consumers who look

Lactantia PurFiltre for a market segment looking for a fresher, longer lasting milk.

for each benefit, and the major brands that deliver each benefit. For example, Ontario-based Ault Foods examined the fluid milk market and discovered a segment of people who were looking for a fresher-tasting, longer-lasting product and who were prepared to pay a premium price for a product that would deliver those benefits. In response, Ault developed Lactantia PurFiltre milk for this consumer segment.[5]

Product Usage. Another behavioural variable used to segment markets is the consumers' use of the product. Using product usage, a market can be segmented based on four dimensions: (1) User status, (2) usage rate, (3) occasions for use, and (4) degree of brand loyalty.

- *User status.* User status means segmenting consumers into categories such as nonusers, ex-users, potential users, first-time users, and regular users. Marketers may examine user status very closely to determine the size of both current markets and future market potential. Marketers may also find that different marketing efforts are required to attract potential users compared to regular users.
- *Usage rate.* Segmenting based on product usage rate usually involves categorizing users as light, medium, or heavy. Usage rate is often assumed to follow the **80/20 rule,** a concept that suggests that 80 percent of an organization's sales are obtained from 20 percent of its customers. The percentages in the 80/20 rule are not really fixed; rather, the rule suggests that a small fraction of customers

Wendy's attempts to
attract the heavy user of
fast-food restaurants.
Could it be you?

provide a large fraction of sales. For example, while only 20 percent of milk-user households in Canada can be classified as heavy users, this segment is responsible for over 42 percent of all milk consumption.[6] Research also shows that the fast-food market can also be segmented into light, medium, or heavy users. For every $1.00 spent by a light user in a fast-food restaurant, each heavy user spends $5.22.[7] Almost all fast-food restaurants place great emphasis on attracting this heavy-user segment. By the way, college students are a major component of the heavy-user segment for fast-food restaurants. How does it feel to be a target segment?

• *Occasions for use.* Occasions for use means dividing a market based on when consumers make a purchase and/or when they actually use the product. Cereal manufacturers have recognized the majority of cereal eaters consume the product at breakfast. But others consume cereal as a snack in the evening. Some manufacturers are now marketing cereal as a great "anytime snack" in the hope of building up product usage.

• *Degree of brand loyalty.* Some consumers are very loyal to the brands they purchase while others are not. Perhaps you only drink Pepsi or maybe your friend drinks only Coke or Pepsi, while another friend will drink whatever is on sale. Examining loyalty patterns can allow marketers to determine whether or not they simply need to encourage brand-loyals to continue purchasing, or attempt to create more loyalty from brand switchers.

WAYS TO SEGMENT CONSUMER MARKETS

Organizational marketers face many of the same challenges that consumer marketers face in segmenting their markets. Like consumer marketers, organizational marketers use many of the same approaches to segmentation including: geographic segmentation, demographic segmentation, psychographic segmentation, and behavioural segmentation (see Figure 8–4).

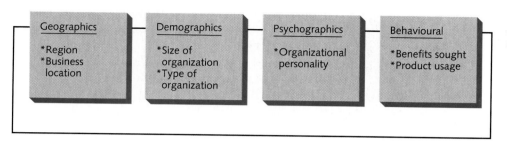

FIGURE 8–4 Ways to segment organizational markets.

Organizational markets can be divided based on geographics (e.g., by country, region, province, city, etc.), as well as by demographics. In the case of organizational markets, the key demographic characteristics are the size and type of organizations operating in the market. For example, a product manager at Panasonic responsible for its Plain Paper Laser Fax, which doubles as a personal copier, answering machine, and autodial phone, might segment the market based on: (1) the number of employees an organization has (e.g., small business with under 20 employees; medium-sized business with 20–49 employees; or a large business with over 50 employees), (2) annual sales volume, (3) number of locations, and (4) type of organization.

The product manager could analyze NAICS code data in order to categorize organizations by the principal product or service they produce. Based on this data, the manager might be able to relate this information to the fax and answering machine needs of these different types of organizations.

What ways might Panasonic use to segment the organizational markets for its Plain Paper Laser Fax? For answers see the text.

Apple segmented
organizational markets
into identifiable
segments.

Psychographic segmentation involves segmenting the market based on the organizations' personalities. Organizations might be categorized by whether or not they are conservative or risk-oriented. Using behavioural segmentation, an organizational market can be divided based on benefits sought (e.g., one segment may be looking for low prices, while another segment wishes to build a relationship with a vendor). Finally, organizational markets can be segmented based on behavioural use of a given product (e.g., user status, usage rate, occasions for use, brand loyalty).

Segmentation of organizational markets allowed Apple Computer to offer different products to meet the needs of different market segments. Using a benefits sought approach, it designed the Quadra line for sophisticated, highly technical users (e.g., engineers, scientists, and large corporations) looking for power and speed; the Peforma line for the "soho" (small office, home office) segment looking for "ease of use"; and the Powerbook laptops for those wanting portability.

A COMPOSITE APPROACH TO SEGMENTATION

In general, most marketers, both consumer and organizational, find it necessary to combine several approaches to segmentation in order to accurately describe and define market segments. Using a composite approach, a marketer may start with geographic and demographic segmentation, which are relatively simple and straightforward ways to segment markets. These approaches provide some insight into the possible location and sizes of market segments for broad product categories, yet they provide little guidance in terms of how individual marketers should position their products or the exact marketing mixes that should be offered. For example, automobile manufacturers know that the 25–44 age segment is a key segment for new automobile purchases. But the specific makes and models of cars as well as the accompanying marketing mix elements desired by this group cannot be gleaned from geographic or demographic information. For this information, contemporary marketers will then turn to psychographic and behavioural segmentation.

Conversely, a marketer may start with behavioural segmentation, particularly a benefits sought approach, since it correlates well with specific brand purchase behaviour. This allows the marketer to determine appropriate product positioning and marketing mix requirements for given segments.[8] Then, working backwards, the marketer can relate particular behavioural segments to various psychographic, demographic, and geographic variables in order to determine sizes of market segments and their locations.

Using a composite approach, a marketer is able to link the types of brands consumers buy and why they buy (psychographic and behaviour segmentation) to who they are (demographics) and to where they are located (geographics). This is an extremely difficult but necessary task if marketers want to have a meaningful basis for segmentation as well as take subsequent, effective marketing actions. By using a composite approach to segmentation, a marketer is more likely to make effective decisions with regard to proper target segment selection.

THE REQUIREMENTS FOR EFFECTIVE SEGMENTATION

As you have seen, there are many ways to segment a market. But the process of segmentation is not always successful. That is, sometimes you don't end up with segments in which marketing can be conducted efficiently and effectively. The most basic test of the usefulness of the segmentation process is whether or not the target segment responds to the organization's marketing mix. To be useful and effective, all market segments must be:

1. *Distinctive.* There must be similarity of needs of potential buyers within a segment, and a difference of needs of buyers among segments. If the needs of the various segments are not different, they should be combined into fewer segments.
2. *Measurable.* The size, purchasing power, and profiles of segments must be measurable. Measurability is enhanced if segments can be defined by concrete variables that are readily identifiable. For example, if age and income are used as variables, organizations can use such data to estimate the size of segments and identify ways to reach them.
3. *Substantial.* Large enough or profitable enough to serve.
4. *Accessible.* Segments must be reachable with a feasible marketing plan.

Segments that meet these criteria can be examined carefully for possible selection as target segments. Let's now deal with the important process of selecting appropriate target segments.

LEARNING CHECK

1. What are some of the ways to segment consumer markets?

2. What is the 80/20 rule?

3. All market segments must meet five basic requirements. What are they?

SELECTING TARGET SEGMENTS

It is now an axiom of marketing that those who properly select target segments are more likely to be successful than those who do not. An organization must take care in choosing its target segments. If it picks too narrow a group of segments, it may fail to reach the volume of sales and profit it needs. If it selects too broad a group of segments, it may spread its marketing efforts so thin that the extra expenses more than offset the increased sales and profits.

There are five criteria that marketers should use in actually selecting target segments:

- *Size.* The estimated size of a segment is an important factor in deciding whether or not it's worth going after. If the segment is too small, why devote any marketing effort toward reaching it?
- *Expected growth.* Although the size of a segment may be small now, perhaps it is growing significantly or is expected to grow in the future.
- *Competitive position.* Is there a lot of competition in a segment now, or is there likely to be in the future? The less the competition, the more attractive a segment is.
- *Cost of reaching a segment.* If a segment cannot be reached with a feasible and cost-effective marketing effort it should be not pursued.
- *Compatibility with the organization's objectives and resources.* Is a segment compatible with the organization's objectives and resources? Does the organization want to serve that particular segment? If so, will it achieve its objectives by doing so?

As is often the case with many marketing decisions, a particular segment may appear attractive according to some criteria and very unattractive according to others. Marketers must use their experience and judgment to balance their findings and select the segments they will target.

MARKET SEGMENTATION STRATEGIES

After evaluating different segments, an organization must determine how to deal with these segments. They could decide to choose to market to all target segments, to market to some of the target segments, or to just one segment. The three basic market segmentation strategies available to an organization are: undifferentiated marketing, differentiated marketing, and concentrated marketing (see Figure 8–5).

Undifferentiated Marketing

A marketer might decide not to distinguish between any segments and go after the market as a whole using one marketing mix. This is called **undifferentiated marketing** (mass marketing). In this case, a marketer assumes that there are more commonalities among the segments than there are differences. The same marketing mix is designed to appeal to the largest number of buyers in all segments. Remember Henry Ford and his Model T automobile? This is a classic case of undifferentiated marketing.

Undifferentiated marketing keeps down production and marketing costs. However, in today's marketplace many marketers question the wisdom of undiffer-

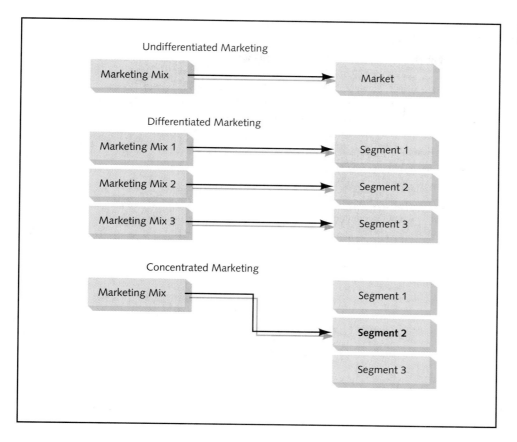

FIGURE 8–5 Market segmentation strategies.

entiated marketing. Remember, segmentation is done because there are usually distinctive differences between consumers. Thus, developing one product or brand to satisfy all consumers can be difficult. Moreover, organizations using undifferentiated marketing often invite heavy competition that will either seek the same segments or attempt to cater to smaller ones seemingly ignored by an undifferentiated marketing approach.

Differentiated Marketing

A **differentiated marketing** strategy means a marketer will target more than one segment and design separate marketing mixes for each. In some cases, unique products may be developed for each segment. In other instances, a common product may be marketed to different segments using unique distribution or marketing communications strategies.

Remember the chapter opener about Reebok? This is an example of differentiated marketing. Reebok offers several products designed specifically to satisfy the needs of different customers in different segments, including athletic shoes for several different sports and fashion footwear for the style-conscious consumer segment. Manufacturing and marketing these different styles of shoes is clearly more expensive than producing one. For Reebok, as for many other companies, differentiated marketing is an effective strategy and it is therefore worth the additional costs. However, an organization that wishes to pursue this strategy should carefully weigh increased sales and profits against increased costs of doing business.

Small businesses often
use a concentrated or
niche marketing strategy.

Concentrated Marketing

A marketer may decide to seek a large share of just one (often smaller but profitable) segment of the total market, tailoring the elements of the marketing mix specifically to attract that segment. Using a **concentrated marketing** strategy, an organization focuses its efforts on serving this segment in creative and innovative ways. This strategy is sometimes called *niche marketing* and is especially appealing to organizations with limited resources. It is often an excellent way for small businesses to get a foothold in the market, especially when faced with larger and more resourceful competitors. Concentrated marketing often allows an organization to achieve a strong market position in the segment it serves because of its knowledge of the segment's needs and the special attention it gives to the segment. However, this strategy can be risky; a change in demand can cause the organization's sales to plummet.

Rapid advances in technology are now allowing many large, undifferentiated marketers to act more like concentrated marketers. Using customer databases, many marketers are now segmenting their larger (mass) markets into smaller, more homogeneous segments and targeting them with specific offers tied to their buying behaviour. Quaker Oats, for example, a large packaged-goods firm that tends to use a somewhat undifferentiated marketing approach, now attempts to build a relationship with every single customer (relationship marketing) through direct marketing communications. Quaker tailors particular offers including coupons and premiums to individual households based on their product usage histories and demographic profiles. In this case, it is a form of segmentation to the extreme. This is known as *individualized* or *customized marketing*.

MARKETPLACE APPLICATION

Women, RRSPs, and Segmentation

Women make up about 42 percent of Canada's registered retirement savings plan (RRSP) contributors and provide 34 percent of the $12 billion in contributions. Women's rising importance as RRSP buyers is increasing as the wage gap between men and women shrinks, and as even fewer women leave money matters to their husbands. Moreover, longer-living women will also inherit a major portion of an estimated $1 trillion in RRSP funds over the next 20 years.

This raises a ticklish question for marketers of financial services: How should you market to women? For the vast majority of Canadian financial services companies, the answer is that you shouldn't. The way to reach women, they argue, is through the marketing efforts used to reach people in general. But a few companies do target women specifically. The RRSP product isn't modified, just the methods used to market the product to women. Some of the strategies are simple—special booklets and seminars, or advertising in media geared to reach the female buyer. These companies are betting that women differ enough from men in their attitudes and preferences that it's worth the investment to treat them as a distinct market segment.

Yet this view is rare. Many companies believe that they adequately address both women and men as part of their overall marketing efforts. They argue that men and women are just not different enough when it comes to

RRSPs to warrant separate and distinct marketing mixes. Moreover, they suggest that there is some indication that women do not want to be treated differently and would find insulting the idea of being targeted as women.

But others argue there are subtle differences—enough to justify treating men and women as separate segments. Research found that women want information at times convenient to their hectic schedules, such as lunchtime seminars or evening visits at home. They also want advice and information without the hard sell. Women also spend more time gathering information before making an investment. North American Life and Trimark Investments are two companies that feel women should be targeted specifically. They have prepared special magazines, booklets, and advertising geared directly to women. They also train their financial advisors on marketing to women.

1. Does it make sense to market to women as a separate segment for RRSPs?

2. Are the differences big enough, and the market large enough to support separate marketing programs for women as a distinctive market segment for RRSPs?

SOURCE: Adapted from Jim McElgunn, "Money, Marketing and Gender," *Marketing*, January 30, 1995, pp. 11, 13.

Factors That Influence Market Segmentation Strategies

Many factors influence the type of market segmentation strategy that should be selected by an organization. They include:

1. *Market sensitivity.* If consumers are not particularly sensitive to product differences, an undifferentiated marketing strategy is appropriate. But if there are many different segments with different product preferences, a differentiated or concentrated approach is a better choice. The accompanying Marketplace Application illustrates the ticklish question of whether or not women should be targeted as a separate segment for RRSPs.

2. *Product variability.* Undifferentiated marketing is more appropriate for uniform or commodity-based products such as oranges or cement. Products that can be varied or modified, such as electronics or automobiles, lend themselves to differentiated or concentrated marketing strategies.

3. *Product life cycle.* If the product is new, a concentrated marketing strategy may be best. If an organization wants to build primary demand for the product, an undifferentiated marketing strategy is appropriate. In the later stages of the product life cycle, differentiated marketing becomes more appropriate.

4. *Organizational size and resources.* If an organization is small and has limited resources, the best strategy is concentrated marketing.

5. *Competitors' strategies.* If major competitors are pursuing undifferentiated marketing, an organization may be best to utilize differentiated or concentrated marketing. If there are many competitors, concentrated marketing may be appropriate.

LEARNING CHECK

1. What are the five criteria used in selecting target segments?

2. Going after the market as a whole using one marketing mix is called a(n) _____ _____ strategy.

3. The most appropriate market segmentation strategy for a small business with limited resources is a(n) _____ strategy.

POSITIONING THE PRODUCT

No matter which market segmentation strategy they use, marketers must follow up by selecting an effective product positioning strategy that will appeal to the selected target segment(s). In simple terms, they must decide how to "position" its offering in those segments. Then they must develop an overall marketing mix that will support that product positioning strategy.

In Chapter 2, we introduced you to the concept of product positioning. **Product positioning** refers to the place the product occupies in the consumers' minds relative to competitors. As you discovered in Chapter 2, an organization must consider its identified competitive advantage before it can build an effective position in the market. It is the organization's competitive advantage that forms the basis for any intended positioning.

Once the desired positioning is determined, the marketer must take steps to communicate that position to the target segment. For example, Duracell believed it had a competitive advantage in the household battery market: a battery that lasted longer than its competitors. It selected a very simple positioning theme: "Duracell, the one that lasts" (more recently it became, "No other battery is longer, stronger"). The company communicated this positioning to the consumer through extensive advertising. Duracell was able to successfully occupy a position in the consumers' minds as the longest-lasting battery—that is, until the Eveready Energizer came along, as we will see later.

The key to effective positioning is to distinguish the product from competitive offerings so that consumers see the value in purchasing it over others available. If a product is perceived to be exactly the same as another on the market, the consumer may have no reason to buy it. It is also important that the organization's marketing plan (including the entire marketing mix) be built to support the chosen positioning.

Given that positioning is a consumer's *subjective evaluation* of the product, the differences between products can be *real* or *perceived*. For example, a Lexus automobile doesn't necessarily have to be objectively a better-quality car than a BMW; the consumer just has to believe that it is. Thus, in many cases, positioning is based on image and not reality. Brewers go to great lengths in positioning their beer brands in the minds of consumers. But in general, most consumers cannot objectively tell the difference in the tastes of various beers, buying instead on the basis of perceived differences.

Approaches to Product Positioning

There are two broad approaches to positioning a product in the market: head-to-head in direct competition with other products, or avoiding direct competition through differentiation. **Head-to-head positioning** means competing directly with competitors on similar attributes in the same target market. In its famous "We're number two, so we try harder" campaign, Avis successfully positioned itself against the number one car rental service, Hertz. Duracell versus Eveready Energizer is another example of head-to-head positioning.

Or, a firm can avoid direct competition through **differentiation positioning,** stressing the unique aspects of the product. This strategy can involve positioning a product on a specific attribute, feature, or benefit. BMW, for example, positions its cars as the "ultimate driving machines" to connote superior handling and driving performance. Crest is positioned as the toothpaste that prevents cavities. A firm can also position its product for a particular usage situation. Arm & Hammer positions its baking soda as the one to use when you need a refrigerator deodorant, and Gatorade is positioned as the beverage to use for replacing body fluids after athletic performances. Companies also follow a differentiation positioning strategy among brands within their own product line to try to minimize cannibalization of a brand's sales or market share.

Product Positioning Using Perceptual Maps

A key to positioning a product effectively is understanding the perceptions consumers have of product categories and brands within those categories. In determining a brand's position and the preferences of consumers, companies obtain three types of data from consumers:

1. Evaluations of the important attributes for a product category or class.
2. Judgments of existing brands with the important attributes.
3. Ratings of an "ideal" brand's attributes.

From these data, it is possible to develop a **perceptual map,** a means of displaying or graphing in two dimensions the locations of products or brands in the minds of the consumers. Marketers can use perceptual maps to see how consumers perceive competing products or brands and then, if necessary, take actions to change the product offering and the image it projects to consumers.

Figure 8–6 shows a perceptual map of many of the brands of beer sold in the Canadian market. A beer maker can examine this perceptual map to determine its brand's current position, and its closest competition, in terms of consumer perceptions. The beer maker also has to assess the size of the segments looking for a beer with the specific characteristics depicted on the map. For example, Kronenbourg appears to be well separated from its competitors. But the question for the marketers of Kronenbourg is how many beer drinkers want a light, bitter beer. If the segment is too small, Kronenbourg might have to reposition itself in order to become a more viable brand.

Repositioning

In a strict sense, most marketers hope that positioning will be a one-time exercise with a new product or brand. But eventually most firms have to reassess their product's positioning. The trigger might be a recognition that the current position is eroding as a

FIGURE 8–6   Positioning of brands of beer in Canadian market.

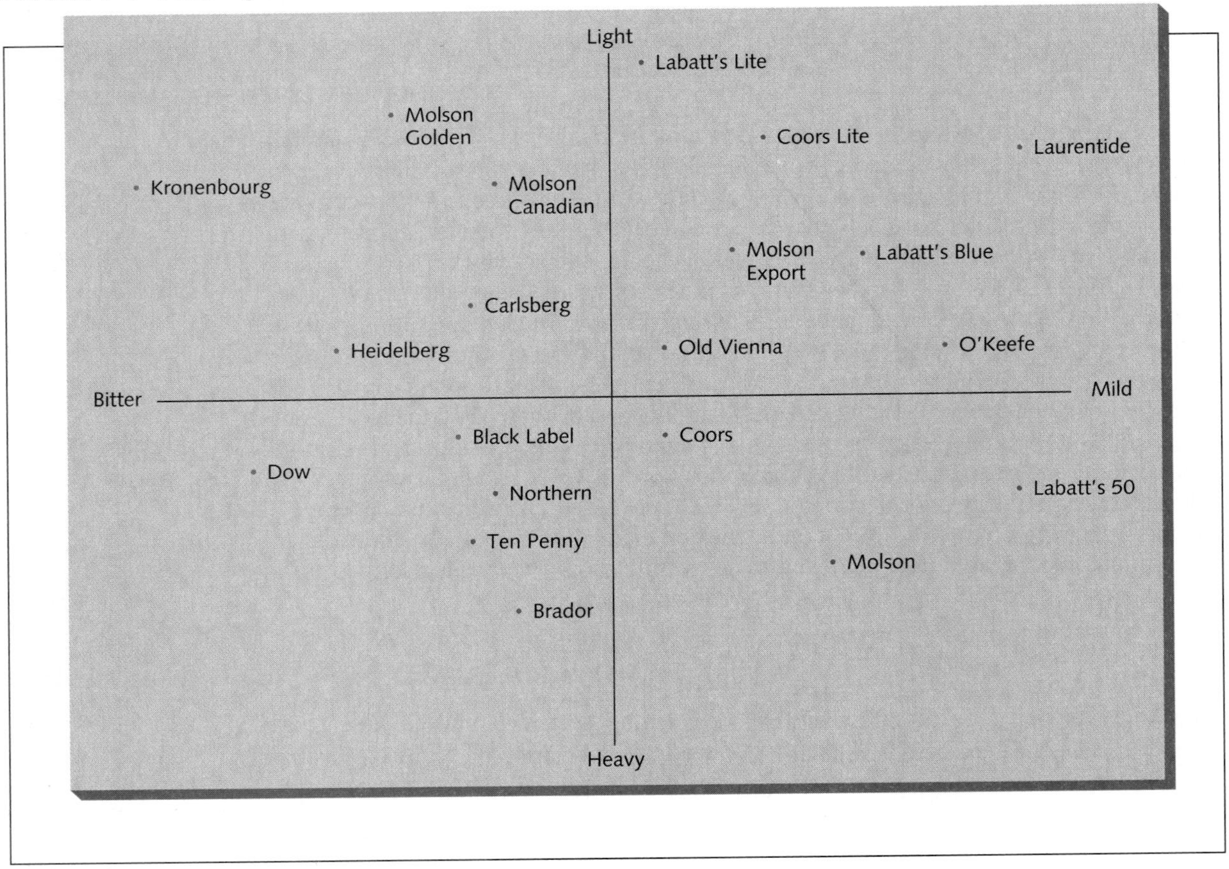

SOURCE: J. E. Brisoux, Université Québec à Trois-Riviéres.

result of competitive pressures, the position is no longer meaningful to customers, or the performance results are unsatisfactory.[9] When a product is **repositioned,** its place changes in a consumer's mind relative to competitive offerings.

Sometimes marketers will attempt to reposition a competitor's product and not their own. This is generally referred to as *repositioning the competition.*[10] This strategy assumes that if a competitor's product can be repositioned, a new product may be able to move in and take over the position once held by that product in the consumer's mind. As we mentioned earlier, Duracell successfully positioned itself as a long-lasting battery. However, Eveready repositioned Duracell batteries, in the minds of many consumers, through its use of the Energizer bunny and its "still going" positioning theme; in doing so, it took over the position once occupied by Duracell. Sometimes repositioning the competition can involve some ethical questions, as discussed in the Ethics Insight box.

LEARNING CHECK

1. What are the two approaches to product positioning?

2. Why do marketers use perceptual maps when making product positioning decisions?

3. What is repositioning?

ETHICS INSIGHT

The Ethics of Repositioning the Competition

The worldwide market for thrombolytics—medicines to break up blood clots in heart attack victims—is valued at $600 million a year. The traditional product used to treat this problem is called streptokinase. But a pharmaceutical firm developed a new product called TPA (tissue plasminogen activator), and attempted to position it as better than streptokinase. The pharmaceutical firm marketed the product aggressively to doctors, convincing them that they should prescribe TPA rather than streptokinase. Subsequent research showed, however, that there was no difference in the effectiveness of the two medicines. Nonetheless, the pharmaceutical firm continued in their attempts to "reposition" streptokinase as an older, less effective treatment.

Doctors did discover, however, that there was a major difference between the products that had nothing to do with effectiveness. The difference was price: TPA cost $2,500 per treatment compared to $220 per treatment for streptokinase. In spite of this cost difference, many doctors did start prescribing TPA over streptokinase.

1. What do you think about this situation?
2. Should a firm be allowed to reposition a competitor's product?
3. If a product is "not" any better than the one it is attempting to reposition, is it ethical to reposition it?

LEARNING OBJECTIVE REINFORCEMENT

1. Explain what market segmentation is. Market segmentation involves aggregating prospective buyers into groups that (1) have common needs and (2) will respond similarly to a specific marketing offer or marketing mix.

2. Understand the ways used to segment consumer and organizational markets. The basic ways to segment consumer and organizational markets include: geographic segmentation (dividing markets based on where consumers live); demographic segmentation (dividing a market based on population characteristics); psychographic segmentation (segmenting markets according to personality or lifestyle); and behavioural segmentation (segmenting markets according to consumers' behaviour with or toward a product). Two key behavioural variables used to segment markets include consumer or organizational needs for certain product benefits (benefits sought) and product usage.

3. Recognize the requirements for effective segmentation. To be useful and effective, all market segments must be: (1) distinctive (similarity of needs of potential buyers within a segment, and difference of needs of buyers among segments); (2) measurable (the size, purchasing power, and profiles of segments must be measurable); (3) substantial (large enough or profitable enough to serve); and (4) accessible (segments must be reachable with a feasible marketing plan).

4. Outline the criteria used in choose target segments. The criteria used to choose target segments include: (1) size, (2) expected growth, (3) competitive position, (4) cost of reaching the segment, and (5) compatability with the organization's objectives and resources.

5. Explain the three basic market segmentation strategies available to marketers. The three basic market segmentation strategies available to an organization are: undifferentiated marketing, differentiated marketing, and concentrated marketing. When a marketer decides not to distinguish between any segments and goes after the market as a whole using one marketing mix, this is called undifferentiated (mass) marketing. A differentiated marketing strategy means a marketer will target more than one segment and design separate marketing mixes for each. A marketer may decide to seek a large share of just one (often smaller but profitable) segment of the total market, tailoring the elements of the marketing mix specifically to attract that segment. This is called concentrated marketing.

6. Understand the concept of positioning products in the marketplace. After a market segmentation strategy is selected, marketers must follow up by selecting an effective product positioning strategy that will appeal to the selected target segment(s). Positioning refers to the place the product occupies in the consumers' minds relative to competitors. The key to effective positioning is to distinguish the product from competitive offerings so the consumers see the value in purchasing it over others available. The product can be positioned head-to-head, directly against a competitor, or it can be positioned away from the competitor, using differentiation.

KEY TERMS AND CONCEPTS

market segmentation p. 187
market segments p. 187
geographic segmentation p. 187
demographic segmentation p. 188
psychographic segmentation p. 189

behavioural segmentation p. 190
80/20 rule p. 191
undifferentiated marketing p. 196
differentiated marketing p. 197
concentrated marketing p. 198

product positioning p. 200
head-to-head positioning p. 201
differentiation positioning p. 201
perceptual map p. 201
repositioning p. 202

CHAPTER QUESTIONS AND APPLICATIONS

1. What ways might be used to segment these consumer markets? *(a)* lawn mowers, *(b)* frozen dinners, *(c)* dry breakfast foods, and *(d)* soft drinks.

2. What ways might be used to segment these organizational markets? *(a)* industrial sweepers, *(b)* photocopiers, *(c)* computerized production control systems, and *(d)* car rentals.

3. If you wanted to segment the market for skis in Canada, how would you go about it?

4. Do a little research: Try to profile the typical National Hockey League fan. How can the NHL use this information in developing its marketing mix?

5. Suppose you want to increase revenues for Wendy's restaurants. What segment(s) of the market would you target and why?

6. Savin entered the photocopier market with a claim that its products were the same as Xerox's, only cheaper. What type of positioning strategy was this?

7. What positions do McDonald's and Wendy's occupy in the fast-food market? What target segments do you think they are reaching?

8. The Canadian Football League has entered the United States market with a differentiation positioning approach. How likely is it that American football fans will embrace this Canadian form of football?

9. Molson Canadian and Labatt Blue are generally considered two mainstream beer brands, appealing to the consumers' preference for middle-of-the-road taste. However, recently, Molson Breweries and Labatt Breweries placed two new offerings on the market, Red Dog and Labatt Copper, respectively. Red Dog is a dark (heavy) beer that is a mix of ale and lager, while Labatt Copper is a dark (heavy) lager. Where do you think the Canadian beer drinker would place these products on the perceptual map shown in Figure 8–6? Do you think they can become viable brands?

APPLICATION CASE 8-1
CANTEL

Cantel is the only Canadian company with a national licence to provide cellular service, in competition with the cellular divisions of regional phone companies. Cantel's cellular network is what is known as "non-wire." It operates in competition with the cellular subsidiaries of the "wire" companies such as Bell Canada, Maritime Tel & Tel, Alberta Government Telephone, and B.C. Tel, all of which also offer conventional telephone services via telephone wires.

A cellular phone uses radio signals instead of wires to transmit calls. The cellular networks are connected to the public wire phone system allowing cellular users to make calls to, or receive calls from, virtually any other phone in the world. As a cellular network service provider, Cantel has erected hundreds of transmitters across the country; each transmitter serves an area called a "cell." As a cellular subscriber uses a phone in a moving car or while walking down the street, a switching computer "hands off" the call from one cell to another without interruption of the call. Cantel's cellular network covers cities and corridors in all

10 Canadian provinces. Today, more than 87 percent of the Canadian population has access to Cantel service.

Besides operating Canada's only nationally licenced cellular company, Cantel also operates a chain of retail service centres and provides paging and data communication services. Cantel directly employs over 2,500 people and has indirectly created thousands of jobs in cellular sales and service. Cantel currently has over 531,000 cellular subscribers and more than 106,000 paging subscribers.

QUESTIONS
1. Segment the market for cellular phone subscribers.
2. Who are the key target segments for cellular phones?
3. How should Cantel position its cellular service in those target segments?

SOURCE: The information in this case was supplied by Rogers Cantel Inc. Used with permission.

APPLICATION CASE 8-2
BERRYMORE FARMS

Berrymore Farms has been experiencing rising costs and falling prices, yet remains one of the more profitable dairy operations in its market. The firm has its full line of milk products in the major chain stores, independent stores, and many institutional outlets like schools and hospitals. While it has been successful maintaining market share, one factor is working against the organization: Research has shown that Canadians are drinking less milk than ever before. The major reasons cited for the decline in milk consumption are the aging population (older people drink less milk) and negative attitudes toward milk (i.e., beliefs that it has too much cholesterol and that it is too fattening).

Berrymore's management wants to increase its volume in a market that is experiencing little or no growth. It currently holds about 40 percent market share while its three other competitors equally share the remaining 60 percent. Berrymore believes the market can best be segmented on the basis of product usage. It has discovered that the market can be divided into three distinctive user categories: (1) light user households, which consume 0–5 litres per week; (2) medium user households, which con-

sume 6–10 litres per week; and (3) heavy user households, which consume 11 litres or more per week. Close to 50 percent of households are considered light users and another 31 percent are medium users. Even though less than 20 percent of households were considered heavy users, they account for over 42 percent of all milk consumed. But while 20 percent of households are considered heavy users, only 10 percent of Berrymore's customers fall into the heavy user category.

The heavy user household is most likely to have a male who primarily uses milk as a drink. These heavy users exhibit different media habits compared to the other groups. In particular, they watch more television than the light and medium users of milk. Heavy users are also more brand loyal than medium or light users and more likely to have home delivery of milk. At this point, only about 25 percent of all households in the market take home delivery of milk, but these households account for over 38 percent of all milk consumed. The average consumption for those households not receiving home delivery is 5.9 litres per week while the average for those receiving home delivery is 9.4 litres per week. At this point, Berrymore has only a small home delivery program and is considering whether or not to expand this component of its business as a way to increase volume and market share.

QUESTIONS

1. If a market is experiencing little or no growth, how is it possible for Berrymore to increase its sales volume in such a market?

2. What conclusions can you make about the heavy user segment?

3. Do you think that Berrymore should expand its home delivery business? Why or why not?

Understanding Process

PART **III**

The New Product Process

WHAT'S NEW?

What do you think about the following new products? Do you think there is a market for them? Would you be interested in buying them? How about a pair of air-conditioned shoes? Each shoe is equipped with bellows in the heel that blow in a gust of cool air with every step. What about a new type of pencil made from recycled newspaper instead of wood? How about an electric carpet designed to heat the floor under your feet? What about a watch that can track your speed down a ski slope? Finally, what about tropical chips made out of real slices of exotic vegetables?

While vacationing in Costa Rica, Toronto's Rob Richards came up with the idea that North Americans might like a potato chip alternative. Back in Canada, he and a partner set up a company, Sursun International Inc., to manufacture REALSLICE Tropical Chips. Instead of using the traditional potato, the would-be snack kings decided to import Costa Rican plantain (a cousin to the banana) and the potato-like tuber, cassava, for their chips.

REALSLICE produces four flavours: original and zesty herb plantain, and original and lemon mesquite cassava. The chips are also kosher. The Loeb food chain is currently selling the 150-gram bags at its stores in Ontario and Quebec. Richards hopes to chip away at the traditional potato chip market, attracting consumers interested in something new and different.

Developing new products to meet consumer needs captures the essence of marketing. Many entrepreneurs start their companies with a product idea and a hope that consumers will embrace that idea. But many companies—new and well-established alike—do not fare well in the new product process. In fact, new product failure is the rule not the exception for most companies. Every year in North America about 15,000–20,000 new products are launched into the marketplace. Experts suggest 80 percent of those are commercial failures. Still, marketers agree that the life of a company often depends on how well it conceives, produces, and markets new products. Thus, marketers keep developing new products, in hopes of a new product success story. Will any of the products just discussed, including REALSLICE Tropical Chips, be successful? The answer depends largely on how consumers respond to the product and its accompanying marketing mix.

In this chapter we discuss the decisions involved in developing and marketing a new product. Chapter 10 covers the process of managing existing products.

DEFINING A PRODUCT

How do we define a product? As you read in Chapter 1, a **product** is anything that is offered to a market for acquisition, use, or consumption and satisfies an individual or organizational need. Products include goods, services, ideas, places, and people. When consumers buy products they are buying a bundle of tangible and intangible attributes that deliver value and satisfaction. Tangible attributes include physical characteristics such as colour or sweetness, and intangible attributes include becoming healthier or wealthier. Hence, the breakfast cereal you eat, the accountant who fills out your tax return, and your member of parliament are all products.

In most cases, the consumer just doesn't buy the core product (the basic value it provides), she also buys product adjuncts (value-added dimensions) that accompany the product, such as customer service. In this highly competitive marketplace many organizations offer similar core products, so increasingly it is the product adjuncts or value-added dimensions of the product that makes the real difference with the consumer. For example, many new hotels offer a basic room at a given price (the core product or service). However, some hotels might include free breakfast, free cheque cashing, and a pool and fitness room. These product adjuncts might entice a consumer to choose one hotel over another. More and more often when organizations develop new products, they consider not only the basic product but what value-added dimensions can accompany the product to increase its likelihood of success. To better appreciate the new product process, let's first define some terms pertaining to products.

Product Line and Product Mix

A **product line** is a group of products that are closely related because they satisfy a class of needs, are used together, are sold to the same customer group, and are distributed through the same type of outlets, or fall within a given price range.[1] Polaroid has two major product lines consisting of cameras and film. Adidas product lines are shoes and clothing. Each product line has its own marketing strategy.

Within each product line is the *product item,* a specific product as noted by a unique brand, size, or price. For example, Downy softener for clothes comes in 300ml and 600ml sizes; each size is considered a separate item and assigned a distinct ordering code, or *stock-keeping unit (SKU).*

Another way to look at products is by the **product mix,** or the number of product lines offered by an organization. Cray Research has a single product line consisting of supercomputers which are sold mostly to government and large corporations. Nabisco

Brands, however, has many product lines, consisting of biscuits, cookies, chocolates, candy, cereal, wines, and pet foods, featuring such brands as Ritz and Dr. Ballards.

Classifying Products

Both the federal government and companies classify products, but for different purposes. The government's classification method helps it collect information on economic activity by business sectors. Companies classify products to help develop appropriate marketing strategies for a wide range of products offered. Two major ways to classify products are by degree of tangibility and type of user.

Degree of Tangibility. Classification by degree of tangibility divides products into one of three categories.[2] First, a *nondurable good* is an item consumed in one or a few uses, such as food products and fuel. A *durable good* is one that usually lasts over an extended number of uses, such as appliances, automobiles, and stereo equipment. As we read in Chapter 1, *services* are activities, deeds, or other basic intangibles offered for sale, such as marketing research, health care, and education. According to government data, growth in services is outpacing the production of both nondurable and durable goods. While services are different in many ways from tangible goods (discussed in Chapter 19), the new product development process outlined in this chapter can be applied to services. Keep this in mind as you read through this chapter.

This classification based on tangibility provides some basic direction for an organization developing its marketing strategy. Nondurable products such as Wrigley's gum are purchased frequently and at relatively low cost. Advertising is used to remind consumers of the item's existence, and wide distribution in retail outlets is essential. Durable products, however, generally cost more than nondurable goods and last longer, so consumers usually deliberate longer before purchasing them. Therefore, personal selling is an important component in durable-product marketing because it assists in answering consumer questions and concerns.

Since services are intangible, the major objective in marketing is to make the benefits of purchasing the service real to consumers. Thus, Norwegian Cruise Line shows the gourmet food offered on its cruise ships. The people who provide the service are often the key to success in marketing services because consumers often evaluate the service by the service provider they meet—the Hertz reservation clerk, the receptionist at the university admissions office, or the nurse in the physician's office. Thus, in developing a new service careful attention must be paid to not only creating the right service concept, but in having the right people to provide it.

Type of User. The second major type of product classification is according to the user. **Consumer goods** are products purchased by the ultimate consumer, whereas **industrial goods** are products used in the production of other products for ultimate consumers. In many instances the differences are distinct; Oil of Olay face moisturizer and Bass shoes are clearly consumer products, whereas DEC computers and high-tension steel springs are industrial goods used in producing other products or services.

There are difficulties, however, with this classification because some products can be considered both consumer and industrial items. A Macintosh computer can be sold to consumers as a final product or to industrial firms for office use. Each classification results in different marketing actions. Viewed as a consumer product, the Macintosh would be sold through computer stores. As an industrial product, the Macintosh might

Services must emphasize
their benefits.

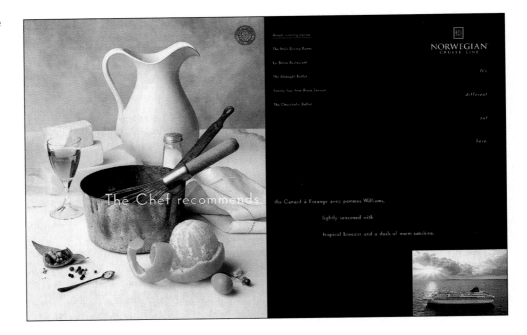

be sold by a salesperson offering discounts for multiple purchases. Classifying by the
type of user focuses on the market and the user's purchase behaviour, which determine
the marketing mix strategy.

CLASSIFYING CONSUMER AND INDUSTRIAL GOODS

Because the buyer is the key to marketing, consumer and industrial product classifica-
tions will be broken down further for discussion.

Classification of Consumer Goods

Convenience, shopping, specialty, and unsought goods are the four types of consumer
goods. They differ in terms of effort the consumer spends on the decision, attributes
considered in purchase, and frequency of purchase.

Convenience goods are items the consumer purchases frequently, conveniently,
and with a minimum of shopping effort. **Shopping goods** are items for which the consumer compares several alternatives on criteria such as price, quality, or style. **Specialty
goods** are items, such as Tiffany silverware, that a consumer makes a special effort to
search out and buy. **Unsought goods** are items that the consumer either does not know
about or knows about but does not initially want. Figure 9–1 shows how the classification of a consumer product into one of these four types results in a stress on different aspects of the marketing mix. Different degrees of brand loyalty and amounts of
shopping effort are displayed by the consumer for a product in each of the four classes.

The manner in which a consumer good is classified depends on the individual. One
person may view a camera as a shopping good and visit several stores before deciding on
a brand, whereas a friend may view cameras as a specialty good and only buy a Nikon.

FIGURE 9–1 Classification of consumer goods.

	Type of Consumer Good			
Basis of Comparison	Convenience	Shopping	Specialty	Unsought
Product	Toothpaste, cake mix, hand soap, laundry detergent	Cameras, TVs, briefcases, clothing	Rolls-Royce cars, Rolex watches	Burial insurance, thesaurus
Price	Relatively inexpensive	Fairly expensive	Usually very expensive	Varies
Distribution	Widespread; many outlets	Large number of selective outlets	Very limited	Often limited
Marketing communications	Price, availability, and awareness stressed	Differentiation from competitors stressed	Uniqueness of brand and status stressed	Awareness is essential
Brand loyalty of consumers	Aware of brand, but will accept substitutes	Prefer specific brands, but will accept substitutes	Very brand-loyal; will not accept substitutes	Will accept substitutes
Purchase behaviour of consumers	Frequent purchases; little time and effort spent shopping; routine decision	Infrequent purchases; comparison shopping, use decision time	Infrequent purchases; extensive time spent to decide and get the item	Very infrequent purchases, some comparison shopping

The product classification of a consumer good can change and is more likely to do so the longer the product is on the market. When first introduced, the Litton microwave oven was unique, a specialty good. Now there are competing brands on the market, and microwaves are a shopping good for many consumers.

Classification of Industrial Goods

A major characteristic of industrial goods is that their sales are often the result of *derived demand;* that is, sales of industrial products frequently result (or are derived) from the sale of consumer goods. For example, if consumer demand for Ford cars (a consumer product) increases, the company may increase its demand for paint-spraying equipment (an industrial product). Industrial goods are classified not only on the attributes the consumer uses, but also on how the item is to be used. Thus, industrial products may be classified as production or support goods.

Production Goods. Items used in the manufacturing process that become part of the final product are **production goods.** These include raw materials such as grain or lumber, as well as component parts. For example, a company that manufactures door hinges used by GM in its car doors is producing a component part. As noted in Chapter 6, the marketing of production goods is based on factors such as price, quality, delivery, and service. Marketers of these products tend to sell directly to industrial users.

Support Goods. The second class of industrial goods is **support goods,** which are items used to assist in producing other goods and services. Support goods include installations, accessory equipment, supplies, and services.

- *Installations* consist of buildings and fixed equipment. Because a significant amount of capital is required to purchase installations, the industrial buyer deals directly with construction companies and manufacturers through sales representatives. The pricing of installations is often by competitive bidding.

Tiffany brand silverware is an example of a specialty good.

- *Accessory equipment* includes tools and office equipment, and is usually purchased in small-order sizes by buyers. As a result, instead of dealing directly with buyers, sellers of industrial accessories use distributors to contact a large number of buyers.
- *Supplies* are similar to consumer convenience goods and consist of products such as stationery, paper clips, and brooms. These are purchased with little effort, using the straight rebuy decision sequence discussed in Chapter 6. Price and delivery are key factors considered by the buyers of supplies.
- *Services* are intangible activities to assist the industrial buyer. This category can include maintenance and repair services and advisory services such as tax or legal counsel. The reputation of the seller is a major factor in marketing industrial services.

LEARNING CHECK

1. Explain the difference between product mix and product line.

2. To which type of good (industrial or consumer) does the term *derived demand* generally apply?

3. A limited problem-solving approach is common to which type of consumer good?

NEW PRODUCTS AND WHY THEY FAIL

New products are the lifeblood of a company and keep it growing, but the financial risks are large. Before discussing how new products reach the stage of commercialization, at which they are available to the consumer, we'll begin by looking at *what* a new product is.

What Is a New Product?

The term *new* is difficult to define. Does changing the colour of a laundry detergent mean it is a new product? Is a new hot-air appliance that cooks like a regular oven but with the speed of a microwave considered new? There are several ways to view the newness of a product.

Newness Compared with Existing Products. If a product is functionally different from existing offerings, it can be defined as new. The microwave oven and the automobile were once functionally new, but in today's world innovation usually consists of modification of an old product rather than a dramatic functional change.

New in Legal Terms. Consumer and Corporate Affairs Canada (CCAC) has determined that a product can be called "new" only for a limited time. Currently CCAC has indicated that 12 months is the longest period of time a product can be called new.

Newness from the Company Perspective. Successful companies are starting to view newness and innovation in their products at three levels.[3] At the lowest level, which usually involves the least risk, is product line extension. This is an incremental improvement of an exciting or important product for the company, such as Honey Nut Cheerios or Gillette Sensor for women—extensions of the basic Cheerios or men's Sensor product line, respectively. At the next level is a significant new step in the innovation or technology, such as Sony's leap from the micro tape recorder to the Walkman. The third level is true innovation, a truly revolutionary new product, like the first Apple computer in 1976. Some people wonder whether Sony's Data Discman—a portable electronic book using a removable disk, which may lead to novels, textbooks, and encyclopedias on disks—could be such an innovation.[4] Effective new product programs in large firms deal at all three levels.

Sony's Data Discman: a revolutionary new product that may replace some books.

Newness from the Consumer's Perspective. A fourth way to define new products is in terms of their effects on consumption. This approach classifies new products according to the degree of learning required by the consumer, as shown in Figure 9–2.

With *continuous innovation,* no new behaviour must be learned. Such products require minimal consumer education. Toothpaste in stand-up tubes, ice beer, and the latest game of Nintendo are examples of continuous innovation. Effective marketing of these products depends on generating awareness and having strong distribution in appropriate outlets.

With *dynamically continuous innovation,* only minor changes in behaviour are required for use. For six years, Ron Zarowitz pushed Chrysler to accept the idea of

FIGURE 9–2   Consumption effects define newness.

LOW DEGREE OF CHANGE IN BEHAVIOUR AND LEARNING NEEDED BY CONSUMER HIGH			
BASIS OF COMPARISON	CONTINUOUS INNOVATION	DYNAMICALLY CONTINUOUS INNOVATION	DISCONTINUOUS INNOVATION
Definition	Requires no new learning	Disrupts consumer's normal routine but does not require totally new learning	Establishes new consumption patterns among consumers
Examples	Sensor and New Improved Tide	Electric toothbrush, compact disc player, and automatic flash units for cameras	VCR, microwave oven, and home computer
Marketing emphasis	Generate awareness among consumers and obtain widespread distribution	Advertise benefits to consumers, stressing point of differentiation and consumer advantage	Educate consumers through product trial and personal selling

Microwave cooking: a discontinuous innovation that has revolutionized some consumption patterns.

built-in, fold-down child seats in their cars. Finally, the seats appeared as a $200 option in the 1992 Chrysler minivans. Chrysler then started selling them as fast as it could make them.[5] Built-in car seats for children require minor amounts of education and changes in behaviour and so the marketing strategy is to educate prospective buyers about their benefits and advantages.

Discontinuous innovation requires the consumer to learn entirely new consumption patterns in order to use the product. This would be seen in such products as the first television set, personal computer, or microwave oven. Hence, marketing efforts involve not only gaining consumer awareness but also educating consumers on both the benefits and proper use of the innovative product. Personal selling and creative marketing communications are often needed for discontinuous innovations. Few new products are discontinuous innovations; most are continuous innovations.[6]

Why Products Fail

Thousands of product failures that occur every year cost Canadian businesses millions of dollars. Some estimates place new product failure rates as high as 80 percent. To learn marketing lessons from these failures, we can analyze why new products fail and then study several failures in detail. As we go through the new product process later in the chapter, we can identify ways such failures might have been avoided—admitting that hindsight is clearer than foresight.

Reasons for New Product Failures.   Many factors contribute to new product failures or are symptoms of them: incompatibility with the firm's objectives and capabilities, competition that is too tough, lack of top management support, and lack of money. However, six factors, often present in combination, are far more fundamental:

1. *Too small a target market.* The market is too small to warrant the R&D, production and marketing expenses to reach it. Kodak invented its Utralife lithium battery and touted it as lasting twice as long as an alkaline battery. However, it was only available in the 9-volt size, which accounts for less than 10 percent of all batteries sold. The small size of the target market forced Kodak to discontinue it.[7]

2. *Lack of real product advantage.* If a new product does not have a clear and significant advantage over existing products, consumers are likely to reject that new product. Several new brands of beer launched into the Canadian market over the past few years have not been successful because beer drinkers did not perceive a significant difference in taste compared to existing brands.[8]

3. *Poor product quality.* R. J. Reynolds developed a smokeless cigarette at an estimated cost of almost $1 billion. But after months of test marketing, the product was killed. The reason is best stated by one employee of a 7-Eleven store: "They're terrible. They're nasty. They're beyond nasty."[9] Similarly, many services fail because of poor service quality, particularly rude or indifferent treatment of customers by the service providers.

4. *No access to market.* Manufacturers of potentially better products sometimes can't make prospective buyers aware of them or gain retail shelf space. Dozens of computer software programs did not succeed in the market because prospective buyers didn't know about them.

5. *Bad timing.* A product is sometimes introduced too soon, too late, or at a time when consumer tastes are shifting dramatically.

6. *Poor execution of the marketing mix.* Mennen's new deodorant, Real, was introduced with a $14 million ad campaign. However, when the customer twisted the dispenser too hard, too much came came out, creating a mess. Also, the name Real gave little indication of the product or its benefits.[10]

To see why this product failed, read the text.

Reasons for New Product Success. Obviously, having a sizable target market, a real product advantage, good product quality, access to market, good timing, and good execution of the marketing mix are prerequisites for new product success. But the greatest differences between those products that succeed and those that don't are:

1. *Having a real product advantage.* As we pointed out in Chapter 2, a competitive advantage can come in the form of either a better price or superior performance.

2. *Having a precise protocol.* This is a statement that identifies a well-defined target market before the product development begins; specifies customers' needs, wants, and preferences; and carefully states what the product will be and do.[11]

Developing successful new products may sometimes involve luck, but more often it involves having a product that really meets a need and has real advantage over competitive products. The likelihood of success is improved by paying close attention to the early steps in the new product process described in the next section of the text.

LEARNING CHECK

1. From a consumer's viewpoint, what kind of innovation would an improved electric toothbrush be?

2. What does "lack of real product advantage" mean as a reason for new product failure?

THE NEW PRODUCT PROCESS

Most organizations, including General Electric, Sony, and Procter & Gamble take a sequence of steps before their products are ready for market. The **new product process** is the sequence of activities a firm uses to identify market opportunities and convert them to a salable good or service.[12] As shown in Figure 9–3, the process consists of seven stages:

1. New product strategy development.
2. Idea generation.
3. Screening and evaluation.
4. Business analysis.
5. Development.
6. Market testing.
7. Commercialization.

Let's look at each step in the new product process in detail.

New Product Strategy Development

For companies, **new product strategy development** involves defining the role for a new product in terms of the firm's overall corporate objectives. This step in the new product process has been added by many companies recently to provide a needed focus for ideas and concepts developed in later stages. 3M, for example, has a corporate objective that a quarter of the division's sales must come from products introduced within the past five years.[13]

Objectives: Identify Markets and Strategic Rules. During this step the company uses the environmental scanning process described in Chapter 3 to identify trends

FIGURE 9–3
Stages in the new product process.

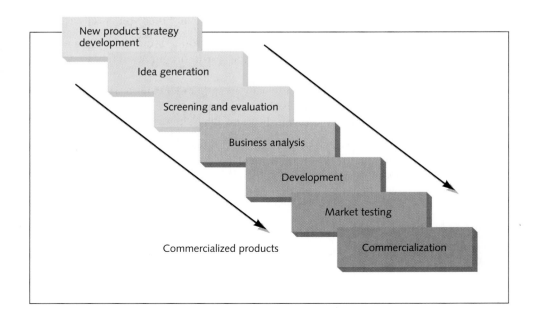

that pose either opportunities or threats. Relevant company strengths and weaknesses are also identified. The outcome of new product strategy development is not new product ideas, but markets for which new products will be developed and strategic roles new products might serve—the vital protocol discussed earlier that separates new product winners and losers.

Proactive and Reactive New Product Strategies. New product strategies can generally be classified as either proactive or reactive. Proactive strategies lead to an allocation of resources to identify and seize opportunities. These approaches include future-oriented R&D, consumer research, entrepreneurial development, or acquisition. In a proactive approach to developing new products, many companies scan the international marketplace, and even other industry sectors, to uncover opportunities. Both Molson and Labatt developed their dry beer on the basis of a new product concept pioneered by leading Japanese brewers. Timex Canada looked to another industry sector for its most recent innovation, the night-light technology in its new IndiGlo watches. Timex discovered the technology, called electroluminescence, being widely used to light car and aircraft dashboards. It took Timex 10 years to adapt the technology for the IndiGlo watch, but it believes it created the first marketable technical breakthrough in the watch industry in the past 15 years.[14]

Reactive strategies involve defensive actions taken in response to a competitor's actions. Many companies often attempt to mirror each other's new products, as in the controversial new beer brand battle between Labatt Ice Beer and Molson Canadian Ice.[15] A similar situation occurred in the Canadian tea market. Thomas J. Lipton, Toronto, launched its freeze-dried Red Rose instant tea in English Canada and its Salada instant tea in Quebec, where Salada is Lipton's top-selling brand. Tetley responded in kind by marketing its new instant tea. Other firms might take a leapfrog approach. For example, Minolta developed the first autofocus camera, but Canon has extended the technology to improve on Minolta's original product.

Labatt's new Ice Beer.

Idea Generation

The development of a pool of concepts for new products, or **idea generation,** must proceed from the results of the previous stages of the new product process. New product ideas are generated by consumers, employees, basic R&D, and competitors.

Customer Suggestions. Procter & Gamble surveyed Japanese parents and found that they changed their babies' diapers far more frequently than Canadian or American parents. In response to this market difference, P&G developed Ultra Pampers, a more absorbent diaper that makes frequent changing less necessary. Today, Ultra Pampers is the market leader in Japan.[16]

Companies often analyze consumer complaints, concerns, or problems to discover new product opportunities. They also pose complaints or concerns to a sample of consumers, who are asked to suggest ways to improve existing products. Bausch & Lomb developed the first alcohol-free mouthwash, Clear Choice, as a result of this kind of research.[17]

Bausch & Lomb, better known for its eye care products, surveyed more than 3,000 consumers to find that the majority didn't realize conventional mouthwash contained up to 21.9 percent alcohol. After making them aware of this fact, Bausch & Lomb asked consumers whether or not it was a concern and if they would be interested in an alcohol-free mouthwash. Many consumers were indeed concerned and did express an interest in an alcohol-free mouthwash product. Clear Choice was developed using purified water-soluble ingredients to perform alcohol's function of binding ingredients. Clear Choice is now vying for a share of Canada's $70 million mouthwash market.[18]

Employee and Co-Worker Suggestions. Employees may be encouraged to suggest new product ideas through suggestion boxes or contests. The idea for General Mills' $250 million-a-year Nature Valley granola bars came when one of its marketing managers observed co-workers bringing granola to work in plastic bags.

In another example, Paul Breedlove, a Texas instruments (TI) engineer, discussed with some co-workers an idea for a hand-held calculator that could talk. They just laughed, so he did some work on the idea and eventually sold them on it. The company still refused to fund the idea because it was "too wild," but Breedlove and his believing co-workers got $25,000 from a special fund TI uses to finance long shots. Breedlove's concept came to market as Speak & Spell, a microprocessor that helps children learn to spell. Its success spawned a family of new products such as Speak & Math and Speak & Read, largely because of the commitment by TI to generate a pool of alternative new product ideas.

3M, a leader in product innovation, has a 15 percent rule that allows anyone in the company to spend up to 15 percent of the workweek on anything he or she wants to. In addition, the company develops grants of up to $50,000 to carry a concept past the idea stage. This approach allowed one employee, Sanford Cobb, to develop a lighting technology with a potential for millions of dollars in sales.[19]

Research and Development Breakthroughs. Another source of new products is a firm's basic research, but the costs can be large. Sony is the acknowledged world leader in new product development in electronics. Sony's research and development breakthroughs have led to innovative products, and its ability to manufacture and market those products has made it a legend in the electronics industry, popularizing VCRs, the Walkman, and—coming soon—the Data Discman.

Sony believes in cross-fertilization among its departments. Its policy of "self-promotion" encourages engineers to seek out interesting projects throughout Sony. If an engineer finds one, she leaves with the boss's blessing. Consultants studying the new product and innovation process say firms need a dual approach to get the most from their R&D: create cultures where new ideas can thrive and have systems that will sift ideas through the development process and get them to market with lightning speed. Sony seems to have done this for four decades.[20]

Competitive Products. New product ideas can also be found by analyzing the competition. A six-person intelligence team from the Marriott Corporation spent six months travelling around staying at economy hotels. The team assessed the competition's strengths and weaknesses on everything from soundproof qualities of rooms to the softness of towels. Marriott then budgeted $500 million for a new economy hotel chain, Fairfield Inns.[21]

Screening and Evaluation

The third stage of the new product process is **screening and evaluation,** which involves internal and external evaluations of the new product ideas to eliminate those that warrant no further effort.

Internal Approach. Internally, the firm evaluates the technical feasibility of the new product idea and whether it meets the new product strategy objectives defined in step 1. Many firms use a scoring system for internal screening and evaluation. The firm establishes screening criteria and then scores a new product idea based on how well it meets the criteria. The specific criteria usually include many of the factors cited earlier for new product failure or success such as size of market, product advantage, and so on. The firms usually establish a minimum score that a product idea must achieve in order to make it through the screening and evaluation process.

External Approach. *Concept tests* are external evaluations that consist of preliminary testing of the new product idea (rather than the actual product) with consumers. Concept tests usually rely on written descriptions of the product but may be augmented with sketches, mock-ups, or marketing literature. Several key questions are asked during concept testing: How does the customer perceive the product? Who would use it? How would it be used?

Frito-Lay spent a year interviewing 10,000 consumers about the concept of a multigrain snack chip. The company experimented with 50 different shapes before settling on a thin, rectangular chip with ridges and a slightly salty, nutty flavour. They successfully introduced the product which they called Sun Chips, in 1991.[22]

A year's worth of consumer interviews went into the development of Sun Chips.

LEARNING CHECK

1. What steps in the new product process has been added in recent years?

2. What are four sources of new product ideas?

3. What is the purpose of the screening and evaluation stage of the new product process?

Business Analysis

Business analysis involves (1) specifying the features of the product and the marketing strategy needed to commercialize it and (2) making necessary financial projections. This is the last checkpoint before significant capital is invested in creating a prototype of the product. Economic analysis, marketing strategy review, and legal examination of the proposed product are conducted at this stage. It is at this point that the product is analyzed relative to its existing synergies with the firm's marketing and technological strengths.

The marketing strategy review studies the new product idea in relation to the marketing program to support it. The proposed product is assessed to determine whether it will help or hurt sales of existing products. Likewise, the product is examined to assess whether it can be sold through existing channels or if new outlets will be needed.

After the product's important features are defined, economic considerations focus on several issues, starting with costs of R&D, production, and marketing. For financial projections, the firm must also forecast the possible revenues from future product sales and forecast market shares. Airwick's new product criteria require a product to be both a specialty and a noncommodity household item. The company also wants a new idea to have potential revenues of $30 million to $100 million annually. Investments are expected to be recouped within two years. These requirements have led the company to discard ideas like plant care items, toilet bowl cleaners, and a fire extinguisher—all in the business analysis stage.[23] In this stage the firm also estimates how many units of the product must be sold to cover the costs of production and projects a return on investment to determine the profitability.

As an important aspect of the business analysis, the proposed new product is studied to determine whether it can be protected with a patent. An attractive new product proposal is one in which the technology can be patented or not easily copied.

Development

Product ideas that survive the business analysis proceed to actual **development**—turning the idea on paper into a prototype. This results in a demonstrable, producible product in hand. Outsiders seldom understand the technical complexities of the development stage, which involves not only manufacturing the product but also performing laboratory and consumer tests to ensure that it meets the standards set. Design of the product becomes an important element.

For example, Liquid Tide, introduced by P&G, looks like a simple modification of its original Tide detergent. However, P&G sees this product as a technological breakthrough: the first detergent without phosphates that cleans as well as existing phosphate detergents.

To achieve this breakthrough, P&G spent 400,000 hours and combined technologies from its laboratories in three countries. The new ingredient in Liquid Tide that helps suspend the dirt in wash water came out of the P&G research lab in Cincinnati. The cleaning agents in the product came from P&G scientists in Japan. Cleaning agent technology is especially advanced in Japan because consumers there wash clothes in colder water (about 70° F) than consumers in Canada (95° F) and Europe (160° F). P&G scientists thought that Liquid Tide also needed water-softening ingredients to make the cleaning agents work better. For this technology it turned to P&G's lab in Belgium, whose experience was based on European water, which has more than twice the mineral content of Canadian wash water.[24]

To see how Liquid Tide was developed, read the text.

The prototype product is tested in the laboratory to see if it achieves the physical standards set for it. Prototypes of disposable consumer goods are also subjected to consumer tests, often in-home placements of a product to see if consumers actually perceive it as a better product after they use it. In a blind test, consumers preferred Liquid Tide nine to one over the detergent of their own choice tested in their washers. Often prototypes undergo rigorous field tests. In developing its Air 180 athletic shoe, Nike had runners test the product. They were asked to run a minimum of 75 km a week and tell how the shoes held up.[25]

Market Testing

In the **market testing** stage of the new product process, prospective consumers are exposed to new products under realistic or simulated purchase conditions to see if they will buy. Often a product is developed, tested, refined, and then tested again to get consumer reactions. The testing may be carried out through either test marketing or purchase laboratories.

Test Marketing. Test marketing involves offering a product for sale on a limited basis in a defined area. This test is done to determine whether consumers will actually buy the product and to try different ways of marketing it. Only about a third of the products test-marketed do well enough to go on to the next phase of the new product process. Market tests are usually conducted in cities that are considered representative of Canadian consumers. *Standard markets* are those test sites where companies sell a new product through normal distribution channels and monitor the results. *Selected controlled markets,* sometimes referred to as *forced-distribution markets,* are those in which the total test is conducted by an outside agency. An outside testing service conducts the test by paying retailers for shelf space, thus guaranteeing distribution in the most popular test markets.

In examining the commercial viability of a new product, companies measure sales in the test area, often with store audits that measure the sales in grocery stores and the number of cases ordered by a store from a wholesaler. This gives the company an indication of potential sales volume and market share in the test area. Although test markets have not been able to predict exact future sales or share, they do help a company by giving an idea of relative product performance and the likelihood of having a loser or a winner.

Market tests are also used to check other elements of the marketing mix besides the product itself, such as price, level of marketing communications support, and distribution. In industrial or business marketing, tests are often used to gain a record of product performance. This experience can then be used as part of the sales presentation when a product is offered elsewhere.

There are difficulties with test marketing, a primary one being how well the results can be projected. The degree to which the test market is representative of the target market for the product is very important. Market tests are also time-consuming and expensive, because production lines as well as marketing programs must be set up. Costs can run over a million dollars, the exact amount depending on the size of the city and the cost of buying media time or space to advertise the product.

Market tests also reveal plans to competitors, sometimes enabling them to get a product into national distribution first or to take actions to disrupt the test markets. When a product can be easily copied by a competitor, test marketing may not be used. Although Hunt-Wesson got its Prima Salsa tomato sauce into the test market first, Chesebrough-Pond's Ragú Extra Thick & Zesty beat it into national introduction. Competitors can also try to sabotage test markets. Pepsi ran Mountain Dew Sports Drink in a test market and Gatorade counter-attacked furiously with ads and coupons. Pepsi pulled the product off the market. With such problems, some firms skip test markets completely or use simulated test markets.

Simulated Test Markets. Because of the time, cost, and confidentiality problems of test markets, manufacturers often turn to *simulated (or laboratory) test markets (STMs),* a technique that simulates a full-scale test market but in a limited fashion. STMs are often run in shopping malls, where consumers are questioned to identify who uses the product class being tested. Willing participants are questioned on usage, reasons for purchase, and important product attributes. Qualified persons are then shown TV commercials or print ads for the test product along with competitors' advertising, and are given money to make a decision to buy or not to buy a package of the product (or the competitors') from a real or simulated store environment. If the test product is not purchased, the consumer may receive it as a free sample. Participants are interviewed later for their reactions and the likelihood of repurchase. On the basis of these reactions, the company may decide to proceed to the last stage of the new product process.[26]

Market testing is a valuable step in the new product process, but not all products can use it. Testing a service beyond the concept level is very difficult because services are intangible and consumers can't see what they are buying. Similarly, market testing of expensive consumer products such as cars or VCRs or costly industrial products like jet engines or computers is impractical.

MARKETPLACE APPLICATION

Labatt Uses Innovative Approach to Test New Beer

Labatt Breweries of Toronto developed two new beers, Labatt X and Labatt Y (one a lager, the other an ale). The company wanted the consumers to have a say in which one would become the new Labatt Copper brand. Labatt decided to ask drinkers to try the products and to vote—via ballots at bars and some beer stores and through an 800 number—on which brew they preferred. The company conducted an extensive advertising campaign to inform consumers about the products and their role in helping Labatt choose the brew that would become Copper. The campaign was set up to look like a political election. The vice-president of marketing for Labatt, Bruce Elliot, appeared in the ads, essentially asking consumers to vote for the "best beer."

The results of the voting were announced during the Superbowl. Over 115,000 votes were cast either by ballot or phone, 56.7 percent of them in favour of the dark lager, Labatt X. Labatt says this approach is the most comprehensive market test undertaken by any brewer. The company said it had committed itself more than a year ago to engage in more dialogue with the consumer. Allowing the consumer to determine which beer should "go to market" was part of that dialogue. Labatt says that Copper is a dark, refreshing beer which it hopes can be positioned as a mainstream brand. It is projecting that Copper will capture 3–5 percent market share of the $10 billion Canadian beer market.

1. What do you think of Labatt's approach to market testing?

2. While over 56 percent voted for Labatt X, Labatt Y did receive over 40 percent of the votes. What might this tell Labatt?

SOURCE: Adapted from Lara Medcalf, "X Marks the Copper Spot," *Marketing,* February 6, 1995, p. 4; and "Labatt Lets Consumers Choose Their Brew," *Marketing,* January 16, 1995, p. 1.

Recently, Labatt Breweries used an innovative approach to test a new brand of beer for the Canadian market. (See the Marketplace Application Box.)

Commercialization

Finally, in the last stage of the new product process, the product is brought to the point of **commercialization**—positioning and launching it in full-scale production and sales. Because of the many steps required for developing a new product, bringing a new concept to this stage involves many delays and significant expense. The cost of commercialization has increased for many consumer product companies as retailers have begun to require special payments. Because space is limited in many stores, particularly supermarkets, many retailers require manufacturers to pay a *slotting fee,* a payment a manufacturer makes to place a new item on a retailer's shelf. A recent study in the grocery industry found that manufacturers paid an average of $5.1 million dollars to get a new product on store shelves.[27]

Getting the new product to market does not guarantee success. The cost of failure can be far more than merely sales the new product failed to make. For example, if a new grocery product does not achieve a predetermined sales target, some retailers require a *failure fee,* a penalty payment by a manufacturer to compensate the retailer for sales its valuable shelf space never made.

Lag from Idea to New Product. The time from idea generation to commercialization can be lengthy: 32 years for the heart pacemaker, 55 years for the zipper, 18 years for instant rice. Companies generally proceed carefully because, at this last stage, commercialization, production, and marketing expenses are greatest. To minimize the financial risk of a market failure of a new product introduction, many grocery product manufacturers use *regional rollouts,* introducing the product sequentially into limited geographical areas to allow production levels and marketing activities to build up gradually.

In recent years, companies have begun to recognize that speed is important in bringing a new product to market. A recent study by McKinsey & Company, a management consulting firm, has shown that high-tech products that come to market late but on budget will earn 33 percent less profit over five years. Yet those products that come out on time and 50 percent over budget will earn only 4 percent less profit.[28] IBM, for example, killed several laptop computer prototypes before commercialization because competitors offered better, more advanced machines to the market before IBM. As a result, some companies—such as Sony, NEC, Honda, Fuji, and Hewlett-Packard—have moved away from the development approach that uses the sequence of stages described in this chapter. A new trend, termed *parallel development* (the simultaneous development of both the product and the production process), is being tried. With this approach, cross-functional new product teams of marketing, manufacturing, and R&D personnel stay with the product from conception to production. The results are significant. Honda has cut car development from five years to three, while Hewlett-Packard has reduced the development time for computer printers from 54 months to 22.[29] Early reports indicate that involving these new product teams early in the product development process also leads to increased success rates for the new products introduced.[30]

How the New Product Process Reduces Failures. Figure 9–4 identifies the purpose of each stage of the new product process and the kinds of marketing information and methods used. Firms that follow the seven stages in the new product process reduce risks and have a better chance of averting new product failures. A look at Figure 9–4 suggests information that might help avoid some new product failures. Although

FIGURE 9–4 Marketing information and methods used in the new product process.

Stage of Process	Purpose of Stage	Marketing Information and Methods Used
New product strategy development	Identify new product niches to reach in light of company objectives	Company objectives; assessment of firm's current strengths and weaknesses in terms of market and product
Idea generation	Develop concepts for possible products	Ideas from employees and co-workers, consumers, R&D, and competitors; methods of brainstorming and focus groups
Screening and evaluation	Separate good product ideas from bad ones inexpensively	Screening criteria, scoring systems, and concept tests
Business analysis	Identify the product's features and its marketing strategy, and make financial projections	Product's key features, anticipated marketing mix strategy; economic, marketing, production, legal, and profitability analyses
Development	Create the prototype product, and test it in the laboratory and on consumers	Laboratory and consumer tests on product prototypes
Market testing	Test product and marketing strategy in the marketplace on a limited scale	Test markets, simulated test markets (STMs)
Commercialization	Position and offer product in the marketplace	Perceptual maps, product positioning regional rollouts

ETHICS INSIGHT

The Cost of New Product Failure

Between 15,000 and 20,000 new products are launched annually in Canada and the United States. Yet very few survive. Most research indicates that new product success is the exception and not the rule. Still, millions and millions of dollars are spent to develop and support new products. Who pays the costs when products fail? First, many companies simply go out of business as a result of new product failure, costing jobs and creating hardship in affected communities. Other companies may survive new product failures but often have to reduce their number of personnel in order to offset the costs of the failure. Very often, prices on a company's existing products go up when their new products fail, and the consumer pays the price. Finally, resources—natural, labour, and monetary—are lost forever as a result of failure.

While new products are often the lifeblood for a corporation, many question the expenditures on new products, especially when the likelihood of new product success is low. Money that might go to improve the quality of employees' work life or to new measures to protect the environment may be siphoned away for new product development. On one hand, companies look to innovation and product improvement to stay ahead of the competition. Consumers are also demanding new and improved products and we know that older products must eventually be replaced by new ones as societal needs change.

1. What are the ethical issues involved in spending scarce resources on new products that may do little to improve society in general?

2. Moreover, and more importantly, should the total costs of failure to the business, employee, consumer, and society be carefully considered when making the decision to develop new products?

using the new product process does not guarantee successful products, it does increase a firm's success rate. Still, many argue that the high rate of product failure carries many costs which give rise to ethical questions about the process. (See the Ethics Insight box for a discussion of this issue.)

New technologies to reduce product failure are being experimented with at this time. One emerging technique is the use of virtual reality (VR). VR is the creation of simulated environments by way of sophisticated computer animation software. VR can create simulations of new products with which the consumer can often interface via a headset or helmet. Consumers can provide instant feedback concerning what they like or do not like about the product, without the need for actual expensive prototypes. Changes can be made within minutes and consumers can evaluate the changes on the spot. Some architectural firms are already using VR. Simulated building designs are created, and customers can provide instant feedback about the design. Xerox uses a type of VR to test the designs of its office workstations. VR is also spawning new products or services itself, such as fantasy trips and the ability to create and manage one's own simulated environment.

VR technology may help reduce new product failure.

LEARNING CHECK

1. How does the development stage of the new product process involve testing the product inside and outside the firm?

2. What is a test market?

3. What is commercialization of a new product?

LEARNING OBJECTIVE REINFORCEMENT

1. Understand the ways in which consumer and industrial products can be classified. Products can be classified by tangibility and by user. By degree of tangibility, products divide into nondurable goods, durable goods, and services. By user, the major distinctions are consumer or industrial goods. Consumer goods consist of convenience, shopping, specialty, and unsought products. Industrial goods are for either production or support.

2. Outline the alternative ways of viewing "newness" in new products. There are several ways to define a new product, such as degree of distinctions from existing products, a time base specified by Consumer and Corporate Affairs Canada, a company perspective, or effect on a consumer's usage pattern.

3. Recognize the reasons for product failure. The failure of a new product is usually attributable to one or a combination of the following six factors: too small a target market, lack of product advantage, poor product quality, no access to market, poor timing, and poor execution of the marketing mix.

4. Explain the seven steps in the new product process. The new product process consists of seven stages. Objectives for new products are determined in the first stage, new product strategy development. This is followed by idea generation, screening and evaluation, business analysis, development, market testing, and commercialization.

5. List where ideas for new products come from. Ideas for new products come from several sources, including consumers, employees, R&D laboratories, and competitors.

6. Explain how new product ideas are screened and evaluated. Screening and evaluation of new product ideas are done internally, usually using a scoring system, and externally, testing the idea with the consumer, usually through concept tests.

7. Understand the concept of market testing. In market-testing new products, companies rely on test markets to see that consumers will actually buy the product when it's offered for sale and that other marketing mix factors are working. Products surviving this stage are commercialized—taken to market.

KEY TERMS AND CONCEPTS

product p. 210
product line p. 210
product mix p. 210
consumer goods p. 211
industrial goods p. 211
convenience goods p. 212
shopping goods p. 212

specialty goods p. 212
unsought goods p. 212
production goods p. 213
support goods p. 213
new product process p. 218
new product strategy development
    p. 218

idea generation p. 220
screening and evaluation p. 221
business analysis p. 222
development p. 222
market testing p. 223
commercialization p. 225

CHAPTER QUESTIONS AND APPLICATIONS

1. Products can be classified as either consumer or industrial goods. How would you classify the following products? *(a)* Johnson's baby shampoo, *(b)* a Black & Decker two-speed drill, and *(c)* an arc welder.

2. Are products like Nature Valley granola bars and Eddie Bauer hiking boots convenience, shopping, specialty, or unsought goods?

3. On the basis of your answer to question 2, how would the marketing actions differ for each product and the classification to which you assigned it?

4. In terms of behavioural effect on consumers, how would a PC, such as a Macintosh or an IBM Aptiva, be classified? In light of this classification, what actions would you suggest to the manufacturers of these products to increase their sales in the market?

5. Several alternative definitions were presented for a new product. How would a company's marketing strategy be af-

fected if it used *(a)* the legal definition or *(b)* a behavioural definition?

6. Test marketing and purchase laboratories are two approaches for assessing the potential commercial success of a new product. On the basis of the strengths and weaknesses of each approach, what methods would you suggest for the following items: *(a)* a new, improved ketchup, *(b)* a three-dimensional television system that took a company 10 years to develop, *(c)* a new children's toy for which the company holds a patent.

7. Concept testing is an important step in the new product process. Outline the concept tests for *(a)* an electrically powered car and *(b)* a new loan payment system for automobiles that is based on a variable interest rate. What are the differences in developing concept tests for products as opposed to services?

APPLICATION CASE 9-1
ORBITZ

You've heard of meals you can drink. Now there's a drink you can eat. A new product called Orbitz is the most psychedelic offering yet from new-age beverage marketers. Clearly Canadian Beverage Corporation, a Vancouver-based company, has launched Orbitz—a textually enhanced drink with scores of flavoured gel spheres floating in the bottle. The company spent more than a year developing a liquid-suspension technology that allows the edible jelly balls to levitate in the drink without settling to the bottom.

Clearly Canadian is calling Orbitz fun in a bottle. But some marketing experts wonder whether a drink that looks like a broken lava lamp will fly. "It's gross," says Simon Williams of the Sterling Group, an industry consulting firm. "It's like, when you drink a glass of milk, do you want to find lumps?"

Yet Orbitz isn't the first of its kind. Companies have been putting things in drinks for years—with little success. New-age beverage rival Mistic Brands launched something similar last year called "Jumpin Gems." But because the jelly balls settled to the bottom, consumers thought the product had gone bad. "I never even drank it," says Michael Weinstein, president of Mistic.

Clearly Canadian says Orbitz is deliberately weird in order to appeal to rebellious teens. The company points to the success of Goldschlager—a spicy liquor with bits of real gold

floating in it—and brands of tequila that have worms in the bottles. Several drinks in Southeast Asia contain bursting malt balls or chunks of fruit.

Clearly Canadian says it's going to let Orbitz drinkers figure out for themselves whether to eat the neon-coloured jelly balls. "It's going to be an adventure," said Jonathan Cronin, Clearly Canadian's marketing director. "They can choose to eat them, drink them, or spit them out." After extensive testing, the company decided to make the balls small enough to fit through a straw—but large enough that they "didn't look like a mistake," Mr. Cronin added.

At $1.29 for a 10-ounce bottle, however, some beverage experts say Orbitz could become yet another new-age fizzle with consumers. "It may be a brief novelty item," said Mr. Williams. "But basically, people are taught not to drink things floating in their glass."

QUESTIONS

1. What type of innovation is Orbitz?
2. Do you think Orbitz will be a commercial success?
3. Outline the reasons why you believe Orbitz will succeed or fail.

SOURCE: Adapted, in part, from Robert Frank, "Yum! It's a Bottle of Soda Filled with Big Lumps of Slippery Jelly," *The Wall Street Journal,* May 16, 1996, B16.

APPLICATION CASE 9-2
WESTERN UNION

Western Union is an established US corporation which has been in operation for over 100 years. Its role in opening the western frontiers of America is well acknowledged in many old western movies. In Canada, its profile is less established. Moreover, times have changed considerably. As communication technology progressed, Western Union shifted its business focus to one of its services, one which was proprietary and with which phones and faxes could not compete: long distance cash transfers. Western Union decided to relaunch this service in Canada even though the service had previously been run by CNCP with no success.

Western Union's Money Transfer product (service) is quite simple. Someone in Red Deer, Alberta for instance, can go to a Western Union agent and, with the aid of Western Union's

worldwide network, send money to a friend or family member in Burma or India within a few minutes. The alternatives—mail, courier, or bank transfers—can take from one or two days to up to two weeks.

Western Union believed the time was right for this service. Research showed that people were sending money to friends and families by a variety of means. Yet, in Canada, there were no high profile players in the money transfer business. Instead there were a number of "mom and pop" shops that offered international money transfers. These local business people marketed "safe, fast service" to their customers' native countries. They used any number of techniques to get the money to its destination, including using their network of friends and acquaintances, finding someone travelling home to act as a courier, or having an "arrangement" with a business partner in the other country. While people were using these mom and pop operations, Western Union believed it had a better way to transfer money. In a world where "fast" meant next day, Western Union had a product where "fast" meant literally within minutes.

QUESTIONS

1. Would you define Western Union's Money Transfer product (service) as new? If so, in what ways could it be defined as new?

2. Examine the six factors that contribute to new product failure discussed in this chapter. If Western Union's money transfer concept was to fail, what would be the most likely causes?

3. Does this new service have a real product advantage over existing products? If so, what is it?

SOURCE: Adapted from Canadian Advertising Success Stories, Cassies II, Canadian Congress of Advertising, 1995. Used with permission.

Product Management

IT TASTES AWFUL— AND IT WORKS

Frank Buckley often hangs up his white smock, packs his bags, and hits the road. Sometimes he guests on a radio program, other times he visits a drugstore in a neighbourhood shopping centre. No matter where he goes, the objective is the same: to build awareness of Missisauga, Ontario-based W. K. Buckley Ltd.

In the 1920s, Toronto drugstore owner William Knapp Buckley, Frank's dad, decided to get into the cough-remedy business. His challenge, if the product was to sell, was to gain retail distribution and shelf space. This is often a difficult task because distributors and retailers generally are hesitant to carry new products. But with almost quiet tenacity, the company slowly and assuredly built consumer awareness, gained distribution, and developed market share.

Over the last decade, the now 75-year-old Frank Buckley has become the marketing spokesperson for the company founded by his father. He appears in a series of quirky ads that make a virtue of the bad taste of Buckley's Mixture to relieve coughs and colds. Eight years ago, the company embarked on its "tastes bad and it works" ad campaign and it struck a resonant chord with consumers. This small Canadian company (less than 25 employees) saw its revenue grow from $3 million to $8 million, and its share of the Canadian cough-remedy market, currently worth $97 million, grow from 2.2 percent to 8.1 percent.

But the company believes the Canadian market is maturing and very crowded. It intends to stay here to defend and build market share, hoping to reach 12–15 percent market share in the next few years. For the long term, however, Buckley believes the company must compete in foreign markets if it wants significant growth. After 75 years, Buckley's Mixture is still a successful player in the Canadian cough-remedy market. But it now hopes to replicate its Canadian strategy in order to achieve success in other countries.[1]

Later in the text, we'll examine Buckley's strategies for entering foreign markets (Chapter 18), but in this chapter we want to deal with effective management of a product. Specifically, we will discuss how successful marketers manage their products and brands over time in an evolving marketplace.

PRODUCT LIFE CYCLE

Products, like people, have been viewed as having a life cycle. The **product life cycle** consists of the stages a product goes through in the marketplace: introduction, growth, maturity, and decline. Figure 10–1 shows two curves—total industry sales revenue and total industry profit—which represent the sum of sales revenue and profit of all firms producing the product.[2] The reasons for the changes in each curve and the marketing decisions involved are discussed in the following pages.

Introduction Stage

The introduction stage of the product life cycle occurs when a product is first introduced to its intended target market. During this period, sales grow slowly and profit is minimal. The lack of profit is often a result of large investment costs in product development, such as the $200 million spent by Gillette to develop the Sensor razor shaving system. The marketing objective for the company at this stage is to create consumer awareness and stimulate trial—the initial purchase of a product by a consumer.

Companies often spend heavily on advertising and other marketing communications tools to build awareness among consumers in the introduction stage.[3] For example, Gillette spent $35 million in advertising alone to introduce the Sensor razor to consumers, while Frito-Lay used a $30 million marketing communications budget to market its Sun Chips multigrain snacks to consumers and retailers.[4] These expenditures are often made to stimulate *primary demand,* or desire for the product class (such as in-line skates or multigrain snack chips) rather than for a specific brand, since there are no competitors with the same product. As competitors introduce their own products and the product progresses along its life cycle, company attention is focused on creating *selective demand,* or demand for a specific brand.

Other marketing mix variables are also important at this stage. Gaining distribution is often a challenge because channel intermediaries may be hesitant to carry a new product. Moreover, in this stage a company often restricts the number of variations of the product to ensure control of product quality. For example, Gillette originally offered only a single version of the Sensor razor.

During introduction, pricing can be either high or low. A high initial price may be used as part of a *skimming* strategy to help the company recover the costs of development, as well as capitalize on the price insensitivity of early buyers. 3M is a master of this strategy. According to a 3M manager, "We hit fast, price high, and get the heck out when the me-too products pour in."[5] High prices also tend to attract competitors more eager to enter the market because they see the opportunity for profit. To discourage

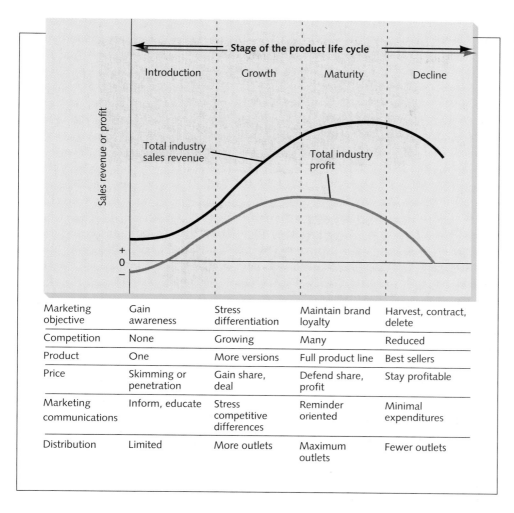

FIGURE 10–1
How stages of the
product life cycle relate to
a firm's marketing
objectives and marketing
mix actions.

	Introduction	Growth	Maturity	Decline
Marketing objective	Gain awareness	Stress differentiation	Maintain brand loyalty	Harvest, contract, delete
Competition	None	Growing	Many	Reduced
Product	One	More versions	Full product line	Best sellers
Price	Skimming or penetration	Gain share, deal	Defend share, profit	Stay profitable
Marketing communications	Inform, educate	Stress competitive differences	Reminder oriented	Minimal expenditures
Distribution	Limited	More outlets	Maximum outlets	Fewer outlets

competitive entry, a company can price low, or use *penetration pricing.* This pricing strategy also helps build unit volume, but a company must closely monitor costs. These and other pricing techniques are covered in depth in Chapter 11.

Several product classes are poised to enter the introductory stage of the product life cycle, or have been only recently commercialized. These include high-definition televisions, electronic-imaging cameras, and electric cars.[6]

Growth Stage

The second stage of the product life cycle, growth, is characterized by rapid increases in sales. It is in this stage that competitors appear. For example, the number of companies selling fax machines went from one in the 1970s to over 25 by the mid-1990s. The result of more competitors and more aggressive pricing is that profit usually peaks during the growth stage. For instance, the average price for a fax declined from $3,300 in 1985 to under $300 by 1996. At this point the emphasis of marketing communications shifts to selective demand, in which product benefits are compared with those of competitors' offerings.

In what stage of the
product life cycle would
you find cellular phones
in Canada? See the text.

Product sales in the growth stage grow at an increasing rate because of new people trying or using the product and a growing proportion of *repeat purchasers*—people who tried the product, were satisfied, and bought again. As a product moves through the life cycle, the ratio of repeat to trial purchasers grows. Failure to achieve substantial repeat purchasers usually means an early death for a product.

Changes start to appear in the product during the growth stage. To help differentiate a company's brand from those of its competitors, an improved version or new features are added to the original design and product proliferation occurs. Changes in fax machines included models with built-in telephones, models that used plain, rather than thermal paper for copies, models that integrate telex for electronic mail purposes, and models that allowed for secure (confidential) transmissions. For Clearly Canadian beverages and Sun Chips, new flavours and package sizes were added during the growth stage, while Gillette added a modified version of its Sensor razor for women.

In the growth stage it is important to gain as much distribution for the product as possible. In the retail store, for example, this often means that competing companies fight for display and shelf space. Expanded distribution in the fax industry is an example. In 1986, early in the growth stage, only 11 percent of office machine dealers carried this equipment. By the early 1990s, more than 60 percent of these dealers carried fax equipment, distribution was expanded to other stores selling electronic equipment, and the fight continues for which brands will be displayed.

Numerous product classes or industries are in the growth stage of the product life cycle. Examples include disposable 35-mm cameras, nonalcoholic beer, and laptop computers. Cellular telephones are in the growth stage in Canada but are appearing to enter the maturity stage in Great Britain.

Maturity Stage

The third stage, maturity, is characterized by a gradual levelling off of total industry sales or product class revenue. Also, marginal competitors begin to leave the market. Most consumers who would buy the product are either repeat purchasers of the item or have tried and abandoned it. Sales increase at a decreasing rate in the maturity stage, as few new buyers enter the market. Profit declines because there is fierce price competition among many sellers and the cost of gaining each new buyer at this stage is greater than the resulting revenue.

Marketing expenses in the maturity stage are often directed toward holding market share through further product differentiation, and price competition continues through rebates and price discounting. Companies also focus on retaining distribution outlets. A major factor in a company's strategy is to reduce overall marketing costs by improving its marketing communications and distribution efficiency.

Stand-alone fax machines for business use entered the maturity stage in late 1990. Sixty-five percent of industry sales were captured by five products at this time (Sharp, Murata, Canon, Panasonic, and Ricoh), reflecting the departure of many marginal competitors. Industry sales growth had slowed, compared with triple-digit average annual dollar increases in the four previous years.

Numerous product classes and industries are in the maturity stage of their product life cycle. These include carbonated soft drinks, personal computers, automobiles, and TVs.

Decline Stage

The decline stage occurs when sales and profits begin to drop. Frequently, a product enters this stage not because of any wrong strategy on the part of the company, but because of changes in the marketing environment. New technology led to video cameras, which pushed 8-mm movie cameras into decline. Similarly, the merging of personal computer and facsimile technology began to replace the stand-alone fax machine in 1993. The decline stage for stand-alone fax machines for business use is projected for the year 2000. Wine coolers, popular in the late 1980s, are now in the decline stage as drinking preferences have changed. Marketing communications support for a product in this stage diminishes, as does investment in major product development. Products in the decline stage tend to consume a disproportionate share of management time and financial resources relative to their potential future worth. To handle a declining product, a company follows one of three strategies: deletion, harvesting, or contracting.

Deletion. Product deletion, or dropping the product from the company's product line, is the most drastic strategy. Since a residual core of consumers still consume or use a product even in the decline stage, product elimination decisions are not taken lightly. When Coca-Cola decided to drop what is now known as Classic Coke, consumer objection was so intense that the company brought the product back.

Harvesting. In a second strategy, harvesting, a company retains the product but reduces marketing support costs.[7] The product continues to be offered, but salespeople do not allocate time in selling, nor are advertising dollars spent. The purpose of harvesting is to maintain the ability to meet customer requests. For example, IBM continues to sell typewriters in the era of word-processing equipment.

Contracting. Some companies operate on a scale that makes it financially unwise for them to carry a product after sales decline below a certain level. However, this same sales level might be profitable for a smaller company, and the larger firm may contract with a smaller company to manufacture the product. In this way its production budget is freed for more profitable items, but the item is still available to customers. An alternative to contracting manufacturing is to contract the marketing: manufacturing efficiencies may allow a company to continue producing a product, but marketing costs may require other companies to sell it.

Some Dimensions of the Product Life Cycle

Some important aspects of product life cycles are their length, the shapes of their curves, and how they vary with different levels of the products.

Length of the Product Life Cycle. There is no exact time that a product takes to move through its life cycle. As a rule, however, consumer products have shorter life cycles than industrial products.[8] For example, many new consumer food products move from the introduction stage to maturity in 18 months. The availability of mass communication vehicles informs consumers faster and shortens life cycles. Also, the rate of technological change tends to shorten product life cycles as new product innovation replaces existing products.

The Shape of the Product Life Cycle. The product life cycle curve shown in Figure 10–1 might be referred to as a *generalized life cycle,* but not all products have the same shape to their curves. In fact, there are several different life cycle curves, each type suggesting different marketing strategies. Figure 10–2 shows the shape of life

FIGURE 10–2
Alternative product life cycles.

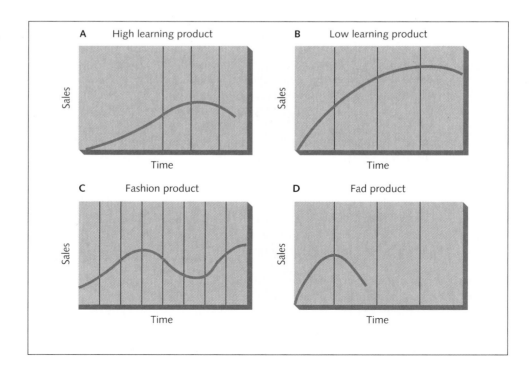

cycle curves for four different types of products: high learning, low learning, fashion, and fad products.[9]

A *high learning product* is one for which significant education of the customer is required and there is an extended introductory period (Figure 10–2A). Products such as home computers have had this type of life cycle curve because consumers have to understand the benefits of purchasing the product or be educated in a new way of performing a familiar task. Convection ovens, for example, necessitate that the consumer learn a new way of cooking and alter familiar recipes.

In contrast, for a *low learning product* sales begin immediately because little learning is required by the consumer and the benefits of purchase are readily understood (Figure 10–2B). This product often can be easily imitated by competitors, so the marketing strategy is to broaden distribution quickly. In this way, as competitors rapidly enter, most retail outlets already have the innovator's product. It is also important to have the manufacturing capacity to meet demand. A recent example of a successful low learning product is Frito-Lay's Sun Chips, discussed earlier. Sun Chips achieved $100 million in sales the first year it was introduced.

A *fashion product* (Figure 10–2C), such as hemline lengths on skirts or lapel widths on sports jackets, is introduced, declines, and then seems to return. Life cycles for fashion products most often appear in women's and men's clothing styles. The length of the cycles may be years or decades.

A *fad,* such as toe socks, pet rocks, Rubik's Cubes, or pogs, experiences rapid sales on introduction and then an equally rapid decline (Figure 10–2D). The life cycle of fads is usually short, and they tend to attract only a small segment of the market. Some companies actually make fads their business. This requires a good understanding of current trends as well as excellent timing—knowing when to get in the market and when to get out.[10]

Fashion products have their own life cycle.

The Product Level: Class, Form, and Brand. In managing a product it is important to distinguish often among the multiple life cycles (industry, class, and form) that may exist. **Product class** refers to the entire product category or industry, such as the total cigarette industry. **Product form** pertains to variations within the class. For example, in the cigarette industry there are filter and nonfilter product forms. A final type of life cycle curve can represent the brand. For example, the entire product class of cigarettes is in the late maturity or decline stage of its life cycle, with filter cigarettes (product form) dominating over nonfilters. Most brands of cigarettes, except new brands, are in the mature or decline stage of their life cycle.

The Life Cycle and Consumers. The life cycle of a product depends on sales to consumers. Not all consumers rush to buy a product in the introductory stage, and the shapes of the life cycle curves indicate that most sales occur after the product has been on the market for some time. In essence, a product diffuses, or spreads, through the population, a concept called the *diffusion of innovation.*[11]

Some people are attracted to a product early, while others buy it only after they see their friends with the item. Figure 10–3 shows the consumer population divided into five categories of product adopters based on when they adopt a new product. Brief profiles accompany each category. For any product to be successful, it must be purchased by innovators and early adopters. This is why manufacturers of new pharmaceuticals try to gain adoption by leading hospitals, clinics, and physicians who are widely respected in the medical field. Once accepted by innovators and early adopters, new products move on to adoption by the early majority, late majority, and laggard categories.

FIGURE 10–3
Five categories and
profiles of product
adopters.

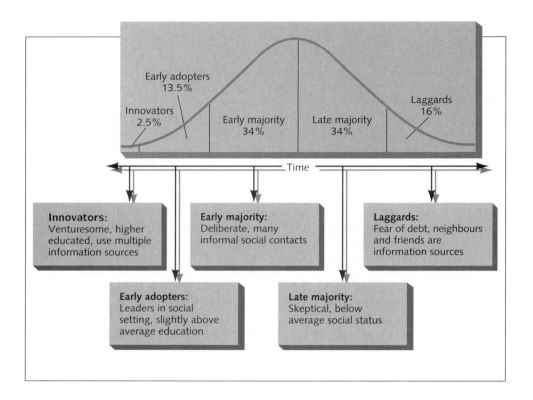

Several factors affect whether a consumer will adopt a new product or not. Common reasons for resisting a product in the introduction stage are usage barriers (the product is not compatible with existing habits); value barriers (the product provides no incentive to change); risk barriers, which can be physical, economic, or social; and psychological barriers, such as cultural differences or image.[12]

Companies attempt to overcome these barriers in numerous ways, such as offering consumers samples or money-back guarantees. When Pepsi-Cola Canada Beverages launched its new version of Diet Pepsi, it provided consumers an incentive to try the product by giving away one million samples of the product during in-store sales promotions.[13]

LEARNING CHECK

1. Advertising plays a major role in the _____ stage of the product life cycle, and _____ plays a major role in maturity.

2. How do high learning and low learning products differ?

3. What does the life cycle for a fashion product look like?

MANAGING THE PRODUCT LIFE CYCLE

An important task for a firm is to manage its products through the successive stages of their life cycles. This section discusses the role of the product manager, the person who is usually responsible for this, and analyzes three ways to manage a product through its life cycle: modifying the product, modifying the market, and repositioning the product.

Role of a Product Manager

As you learned in Chapter 2, a product manager (sometimes called a brand manager) plans, implements, and controls the plans for products for which he or she is responsible. This involves managing existing products through the stages of the life cycle, making modifications or improvements when necessary. The product manager is also responsible for the development of new products. Essentially, anything that relates to the viability of the products, such as advertising or packaging, is part of the product manager's responsibility.

Modifying the Product

Product modification involves altering a product's characteristic, such as its quality, performance, or appearance, to try to increase and extend the product's sales. Christie Brown & Co., the Toronto-based division of Nabisco Brands, launched its 25 percent less-fat Ritz crackers, Oreo, and Fudgee-O cookies hoping to increase its sales to health-conscious consumers. These products followed the successful introduction of the company's fat-reduced Snackwell's products.[14] Another kind of modification is illustrated in Black & Decker's changing the angle on its Phillips screwdriver to prevent the tip from slipping out of the screw.[15]

New features, packages, or scents can be used to change a product's characteristics and give the sense of a revised product. Procter & Gamble revamped Pert shampoo with a new formula that combined a shampoo and hair conditioner in one application. Prior to the modification, Pert's market share was declining. After reformulation, Pert Plus became the top-selling shampoo in an industry with over 1,000 competitors.[16]

A modified shampoo led to a market leader.

But some marketers are not turning to new features, or packages; instead, they are turning to the past to extend the life of their products. Capitalizing on growing adult nostalgia for the past, companies are retromarketing their products. *Retromarketing* is product modification based on consumer nostalgia for brands and packages of yesterday. Old-style packaging and old-fashioned advertising themes are being used to prop up maturing products. Maxwell House coffee used Norman Rockwellesque advertising and a redesign of a 1950s package to revive its brand. Coca-Cola Canada is now using an updated version of its universally recognized contour design bottle for single-serve Coca-Cola Classic and Diet Coke, hoping to appeal to adults who will remember the trademark bottle from their childhood.[17]

Modifying the Market

With **market modification strategies,** a company tries to increase a product's use among existing customers, create new use situations, or find new customers.

Increasing Use. Encouraging more frequent usage has been a strategy of Woolite, a laundry soap. Originally intended for the hand washing of woolen material, Woolite is now marketed for use with all fine clothing items. The Florida Orange Growers Association advocates drinking orange juice throughout the day rather than for breakfast only.

Creating New Use Situation. Finding new uses for an existing product has been the major strategy in extending the life of Arm & Hammer baking soda. This product, originally intended as a baking ingredient, is now being marketed as a toothpaste; a deodorizer for cat litter, carpeting, and refrigerators; and a fire extinguisher.

Finding New Users. To prevent sales declines in wall-to-wall carpeting, carpet manufacturers found new user groups such as schools and hospitals. To expand company sales, Nautilus, a manufacturer of fitness equipment for gyms, recently entered the home market. Commercial accounts represented 95 percent of the company's sales, but the home market has a $1 to $5 billion sales potential.

Repositioning the Product

Often a company decides to reposition its product or product line in an attempt to prevent sales decline. As we saw in Chapter 8, *product repositioning* is changing the place a product occupies in a consumer's mind relative to competitive products. A firm can reposition a product by changing one or more of the four marketing mix elements. Four factors that trigger a repositioning action are discussed in the following.

Coca-Cola's contour bottle; retromarketing in action.

Reacting to a Competitor's Position. One reason to reposition a product is because a competitor's entrenched position is adversely affecting sales and market share. Procter & Gamble recently repositioned its venerable Ivory soap bar in response to the success of Lever 2000, sold by Lever Brothers. Lever 2000, a bar soap that moisturizes, deodorizes, and kills bacteria, eroded P&G's dominance of the bar soap market. P&G responded with its own triple-threat soap called New Ivory Ultra Safe Skin Care Soap. The problem? The new Ivory doesn't float!

Reaching a New Market. Dannon introduced Yop, a liquid yogourt, in France. The product flopped because the French were not interested in another dairy product. When Dannon repositioned Yop as a soft drink for the health-conscious French consumer, sales soared.

Repositioning can involve more than merely changing advertising copy. The New Balance Company changed its product's position as a running shoe for the serious runner to a shoe for the mass market. The distribution strategy was altered from selling only through specialty running stores to selling through discount and department stores as well.

Catching a Rising Trend. Changing consumer trends can also lead to repositioning. From 1980 to 1991 annual per capita consumption of beef fell almost 5 kgs., while consumption of poultry rose by almost 12 kgs. For many years, pork producers positioned their product as similar to beef. Noticing the trend toward poultry, a dramatic repositioning campaign was implemented, changing the focus from beef to poultry with the campaign tag line "Pork: the other white meat" and a nutritional message. Consumer demand for pork is now on the rise.[18]

Changing the Value Offered. In repositioning a product, a company can decide to change the value it offers buyers and trade up or down. *Trading up* involves adding value to the product (or line) through additional features of higher-quality materials. Japanese automakers built their reputations with reliable and affordable cars. Many have since traded up, as evidenced by Honda's Acura, Toyota's Lexus, and Nissan's Infiniti, to compete in the luxury sedan market historically occupied by Mercedes-Benz

ETHICS INSIGHT

Consumers Are Paying More for Less in Downsized Packages

Starkist has reduced the amount of tuna it puts in its cans, but charges the consumer the same price. Procter & Gamble has cut the number of Pampers disposable diapers in its packages while leaving the price the same. The price of Mennen Speed Stick deodorant has not changed but the consumer nows gets less deodorant. Other companies, such as Quaker Oats and Ragu Foods, have allegedly engaged in similar practices.

Consumer advocates charge that "downsizing" packages while maintaining or increasing prices is a sub-tle and unannounced way of taking advantage of consumers' buying habits. Manufacturers argue that this practice is a way of keeping prices from rising beyond psychological barriers for their products.

1. Is downsizing an unethical practice if manufacturers do not inform consumers that the package contents are less than they were previously? Remember, they also always tell you when they are "giving" you more!

and Cadillac. Dog food manufacturers also have traded up by offering super premium foods based on "life-stage nutrition." Mass merchandisers can trade up by adding a designer clothes section to their store, as shown by recent actions by K mart, Sears, and The Bay.

Trading down involves reducing the number of features, quality, or price. For example, airlines have added more seats, thus reducing leg room, and eliminated extras, such as snack service and food portions. Trading down often exists when companies engage in *downsizing*—reducing the content of packages without changing package size and maintaining or increasing the package price. For instance, Fabergé's Brut antiperspirant deodorant spray comes in its regular-size can at the same price, but the content has been reduced by 28 grams.[19] Firms have been criticized for this practice, as described in the accompanying Ethics Insight Box.

LEARNING CHECK

1. How does a produce manager help manage a product's life cycle?

2. What does "creating new use situations" mean in managing a product's life cycle?

3. Explain the difference between trading up and trading down in repositioning.

BRANDING

A basic decision in marketing products is **branding,** in which an organization uses a name, a phrase, a design, symbols, or a combination of these to identify its products and distinguish them from those of competitors. A **brand name** is any word, "device" (design, sound, shape, or colour), or combination of these used to distinguish a seller's goods or services. Some brand names can be spoken, such as Clearly Canadian. Other brand names cannot be spoken, such as the rainbow-coloured apple (the *logotype,* or *logo*) that Apple Computer puts on its machines and in its ads. A **trade name** is a commercial, legal name under which a company does business. The Campbell Soup Company is the trade name of that firm.

FIGURE 10–4
Examples of well-known trademarks.

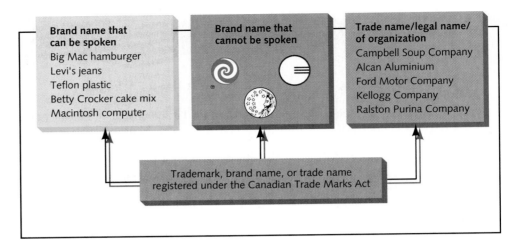

A **trademark** identifies that a firm has legally registered its brand name or trade name so the firm has its exclusive use, thereby preventing others from using it. In Canada, trademarks are registered under the Trade Marks Act with Consumer and Corporate Affairs Canada. A well-known trademark can help a company advertise its offerings to customers and develop their brand loyalty. Figure 10–4 shows examples of well-known trademarks.

Because a good trademark can help sell a product, *product counterfeiting,* or the manufacture of low-cost copies of popular brands by someone other than the original producer, has been a growing problem. Counterfeit products can steal sales from the original manufacturer or hurt the company's reputation.

Trademark protection is a significant issue in global marketing. For instance, the transformation of the Soviet Union into individual countries has meant that many firms, such as Xerox, have had to reregister trademarks in each of the republics to prohibit misuse and generic use ("xeroxing") of their trademarks by competitors and consumers.[20]

The Value of Branding

Branding policy is important not only for manufacturers but also for retailers and consumers. Retailers value branding because consumers shop at stores that carry their desired brands. Some retailers have created their own store brands to further enhance loyalty from their customers. Sears exclusively offers the Kenmore brand for its appliance line and Craftsman as the brand for tools. Canadian Tire offers its Motormaster brand on a variety of its automotive and home care products.

A good brand name is of such importance to a company that it has led to a concept called **brand equity,** an added value a brand name gives to a product beyond the functional benefits provided.[21] This value consists of two distinct advantages. First, brand equity provides a competitive advantage: for example, the Sunkist label implies quality fruit, and Clearly Canadian is known as the leader in the alternative beverage category. A second advantage of brand equity is its ability to endure changes in the marketing environment. Globalization of markets and freer trade means many more brands will be brought to the consciousness of consumers. One brand that will continue to be popular despite these changes is Coca-Cola, the world's best-known brand.[22]

The NHL uses licensing to market its produects.

Consumers, however, may benefit most from branding. Recognizing competing products by distinct trademarks or names allows them to be more efficient shoppers. Consumers can recognize and avoid products with which they are dissatisfied, while becoming loyal to other, more satisfying brands. As discussed in Chapter 5, brand loyalty often eases consumers' decision making by eliminating the need for an external search. Also, the expense of establishing a brand in the marketplace means that some brands are reintroduced years after they apparently died. For example, Buick resurrected its Roadmaster brand in 1993 after the name had been discontinued for about 20 years.

Licensing

Brand equity is evident in the strategy of licensing. **Licensing** is a contractual agreement whereby a company allows another firm to use its brand name, patent, trade secret, or other property for a royalty or a fee. Licensing can be very profitable to a licensor and a licensee. The National Hockey League (NHL) has over 350 licensees worldwide providing thousands of products and receives a percentage of the wholesale price of the products sold. Licensed products for the NHL brought in over $1 billion at retail in 1996, and the NHL expects licensing to increase in the coming years.[23]

Licensing also assists companies in entering global markets with minimal risk. Buckley's, discussed in the chapter opener, entered the Holland market through a licensing agreement.[24] PepsiCo International licensed Elite Foods in Israel to produce and market Frito-Lay's Ruffles potato chips and Cheetos cheese-flavoured corn puffs. These brands now capture 8 percent of the salty-snack market in Israel.[25]

Picking a Good Brand Name

We take brand names such as Dial, Sony, Coke, BMW, and Porsche for granted, but it is often a difficult and expensive process to pick a good name. Five criteria are mentioned most often in selecting a good brand name.[26]

The name should suggest the product's benefits. For example, Accutron (watches), Easy-Off (oven cleaner), Glass Plus (glass cleaner), Cling Free (antistatic cloth for drying clothes), and Tidy Bowl (toilet bowl cleaner) all clearly describe the benefits of purchasing the product.

The name should be memorable, distinctive, and positive. In the auto industry, when a competitor has a memorable name, others quickly imitate. When Ford named

Ruffles and Cheetos are in Israel now, and more PepsiCo snack foods may follow.

a car the Mustang, Pinto, Colt, Maverick, and Bronco soon followed. Similarly, the Thunderbird brand name stimulated the Phoenix, Eagle, Sunbird, and Firebird.

The name should fit the company or product image. Sharp is a name that can apply to audio and video equipment. Excedrin is a scientific-sounding name, good for an analgesic. However, naming a personal computer PCjr, as IBM did with its first computer for home use, neither fit the company nor the product. PCjr sounded too much like a toy and stalled IBM's initial entry into the home use market.

The name should have no legal or regulatory restrictions. Legal restrictions produce trademark infringement suits, and regulatory restrictions arise through improper use of words.

Finally, the name should be simple (such as Bold laundry detergent, Sure deodorant, and Bic pens), and should be emotional (such as Joy and My Sin perfumes). In the development of names for international use, having a nonmeaningful brand name has been considered a benefit. A name such as Exxon does not have any prior impressions or undesirable images among a diverse world population of different languages and cultures.[27]

Branding Strategies

In deciding to brand a product, companies have several possible strategies, including manufacturer branding, reseller branding, or mixed branding approaches.

Manufacturer Branding. With **manufacturer branding,** the producer dictates the brand name using either a multiproduct or a multibrand approach. **Multiproduct branding** is the use of one name for all a company's products. This approach is often referred to as a *blanket* or *family* branding strategy (Figure 10–5).

FIGURE 10–5 Alternative branding strategies.

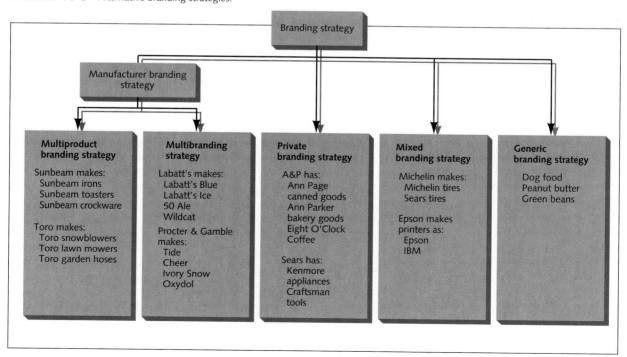

There are several advantages to multiproduct branding. Capitalizing again on brand equity, consumers who have a good experience with the product will transfer this favourable attitude to other items in the product class with the same name. Therefore, this brand strategy makes possible *line extensions,* the practice of using a current brand name to enter a new market segment in its product class. Campbell Soup Company effectively employs a multiproduct branding strategy with soup line extensions. It offers regular Campbell soup, home-cooking style, chunky, and "healthy choice" varieties and more than 100 soup flavours. This strategy can also result in lower marketing communications costs because the same name is used on all products, thus raising the level of brand awareness.

A strong brand equity also allows for *brand extension,* the practice of using a current brand name to enter a completely different product class.[28] For instance, the equity in the Tylenol name as a trusted pain reliever allowed Johnson & Johnson to successfully extend this name to Tylenol Cold & Flu and Tylenol PM, a sleep aid. Fisher-Price, an established name in children's toys, was able to extend this name to children's shampoo and conditioners and baby bath and lotion products.[29]

However, there are some risks to the multiproduct branding approach. Poor performance of one item may have a negative impact on similarly named items in the line. Also, too many uses for one brand name can dilute the image of a product line.

An alternative manufacturer's branding strategy, **multibranding,** involves giving each product a distinct name. Multibranding is a useful strategy when each brand is intended for a different marketing segment. P&G makes Camay soap for those concerned with soft skin, Safeguard for those who want deodorant protection, and Lava for those who desire a strong cleaner. Competing internationally, P&G even uses multiple brand names for the same product. Pert Plus Shampoo is sold as Rejoice in Hong Kong, Pert Plus in the Middle East, and Vidal Sassoon in the United Kingdom. However, international branding strategies do differ. In Japan, where corporate names are important, P&G markets the company's name prominently with the brand name of the product.

Compared with the multiproduct approach, marketing communications costs tend to be higher with multibranding. The company must generate awareness among consumers and retailers for each new brand name without the benefit of any previous impressions. The advantages of this approach are that each brand is unique to each market segment and there is no risk that a product failure will affect other products in the line.

The multibranding approach in Europe is slowly being replaced by **euro-branding,** the strategy of using the same brand name for the same product across all countries in the 12-nation European Community. This strategy has many of the benefits linked with multiproduct branding in addition to making pan-European marketing communications programs possible. But this strategy is not always easily implemented, especially for firms that have been successful using a European multibranding strategy. Changing to a euro-brand strategy takes time and money—and a little reeducating of the consumer, who must look for a once-familiar product with a new name. Growth in North American branding will also be inevitable under NAFTA. Moreover, with globalization of many industries or markets and growing homogenization of consumer needs, the prospects of successful *global* branding increase. A **global brand** would have the same name and positioning in worldwide markets.[30] Coca-Cola is an example of a successful global brand.

Private Branding. A company uses **private branding,** often called *private labelling* or *reseller branding,* when it manufactures products but sells them under the brand name of the wholesaler or retailer. Radio Shack, Loblaws, Canadian Tire, and Shoppers Drug Mart are large retailers that have their own brand names. Consumers often buy private brands over national brands when they perceive that the private brands deliver comparable quality at lower prices (value).[31]

Matsushita of Japan manufactures VCRs for Magnavox, GE, Sylvania, Philco, and some major reseller or retail brands. The advantage to the manufacturer is that marketing communications costs are shifted to the retailer or other company, and the manufacturer can often sell more units through others than by itself. There is a risk, though, because manufacturers' sales depend heavily on the efforts of others.

Mixed Branding. A compromise between manufacturer and private branding is **mixed branding,** in which a firm markets products under its own name and that of a reseller because the segment attracted to the reseller is different from the manufacturer's own market. Sanyo and Toshiba manufacture television sets for Sears, as well as for themselves. This process is similar to that used by Michelin, which manufactures tires for Sears as well as under its own name. A new development in mixed branding strategy has been explored by Polaroid. It is allowing Minolta, a competing camera company, to sell the Spectra Pro instant camera as the Minolta Instant Pro. Minolta has a very strong brand name in cameras, and Polaroid believes the Minolta name will lend positive identification to the high-end camera market.

Generic Branding. An alternative branding approach is the **generic brand,** which is a no-brand product such as dog food, peanut butter, or green beans. There is no identification other than a description of the contents. The major appeal is that the price is up to one-third less than that of branded items. The limited appeal of generics has been attributed to the popularity of private brands and greater marketing communications efforts for manufacturer brand-name items. Consumers who use generics see these products as being as good as brand-name items, and in light of what they expect, users of these products are relatively pleased with their purchases.

PACKAGING

The **packaging** component of a product refers to any container in which it is offered for sale and on which information is communicated. To a great extent, the customer's first exposure to a product is the package, and it is an expensive and important part of the marketing strategy. A grocery product package is especially important because packaging designers using eye cameras have discovered that a typical consumer's eye sweep of a grocery shelf is a mere few seconds. Today's packaging costs run in the billions of dollars, and these costs are inevitably passed on to the Canadian consumer.

Creating Customer Value Through Packaging

Despite the cost, packaging is essential because packages provide important benefits for the manufacturer, retailer, and ultimate consumer.

Communication Benefits. A major benefit of packaging is the information on it conveyed to the consumer, such as directions on how to use the product and the composition of the product, which is needed to satisfy legal requirements of product disclosure. Other information consists of seals and symbols, either government-required

New packaging for
traditional products.

or commercial seals of approval (such as the Good Housekeeping seal or CSA approved).

Functional Benefits. Packaging often plays an important functional role, such as convenience, protection, or storage. Quaker State has changed its oil containers to eliminate the need for a separate spout, and Borden has changed the shape of its Elmer's Wonder Bond adhesive to prevent clogging of the spout.

The convenience dimension of packaging is becoming increasingly important. For example, microwave popcorn has been a major market success.

Consumer protection has become an important function of packaging, as well, including the development of tamper-resistant containers. Today, companies commonly use safety seals or pop-tops that reveal previous opening. Nevertheless, no package is truly tamper resistant.

Another functional value of packaging is in extending storage and *shelf life* (the time a product can be stored before it spoils). New technology allows products requiring refrigeration to be packaged in paper-sealed containers, which dramatically increases their shelf life.

Perceptual Benefits. A third component of packaging is the perception created in the consumer's mind. Procter & Gamble changes the packaging for Clearasil every year, to give the appearance of a new cream, which is important to the target market of teenagers who purchase the product.

A package can connote status, economy, or even product quality. Equally fresh potato chips were wrapped in two different types of bags: wax paper and polyvinyl. Consumers rated the chips in the polyvinyl as crisper and even tastier, even though the chips were identical.[32]

In the past, the colour of packages was selected subjectively. For example, the famous Campbell's soup can was the inspiration of a company executive who liked Cornell University's red-and-white football uniforms. Today, there is greater recognition that colour affects consumers' perceptions. Owens-Corning judged the pink colour of its fibre insulation to be so important that the colour was given trademark status by the courts.

Functional and perceptual aspects of packaging consume an enormous amount of time and research dollars among manufacturers.

Global Trends in Packaging

Companies worldwide are seeing packaging as a way to increase sales of existing brands.[33] Valvoline Motor Oil Company tested 40 variations on its packaging of motor oil before deciding to increase the size and add more colour to the label. But redesigns are not without expense—some packaging changes can cost upwards of $300,000, because of alterations in production equipment. There can also be other risks, such as confusing the consumer.

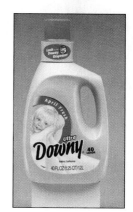

There are two different trends in packaging. One trend involves ecological or environmental sensitivity. Because of the growing concern about solid-waste disposal, packaging is receiving a great deal of attention. Lever Brothers is trying to address these concerns with a test of a "bag-in-box" package for Wisk laundry detergent. Procter & Gamble uses recycled cardboard in 70 percent of its paper packaging, and is packaging Tide and Cheer detergents in jugs that contain 25 percent recycled plastic, Spic and Span liquid cleaner is packaged in 100 percent recycled material, and a similar approach is used by Heinz for its ketchup bottle.

European countries have strict packaging guidelines pertaining to environmental sensitivity. Many of these now exist in the provisions governing trade within the 12-nation European Community.[34] In Germany, for instance, 80 percent of packaging material must be collected, and 80 percent of this amount must be recycled or reused to reduce solid waste in landfills. North American firms marketing in Europe have responded to these guidelines, which has ultimately benefited North American consumers. The history of Procter & Gamble's Downy Refill liquid fabric softener is an example.[35] The product's plastic bottle is reusable, and the refill carton uses 75 percent less packaging material. First introduced in Germany in 1987, the product moved to Canada in 1989, and then to the United States in late 1990. Downy Refill now accounts for 40 percent of Downy sales.

A second trend involves the health and safety concerns of packaging materials. Studies suggest that microwave heating of some packages can lead to potentially cancer-causing agents seeping into food products. The major concern relates to packaging that contains heat susceptors—thin, metallized plastic-film strips that help brown microwavable food. Companies like Du Pont and 3M are working to develop alternatives in anticipation of regulatory changes regarding packaging.[36]

The accompanying Marketplace Application box discusses the marketing role the package will play in the 1990s and beyond.

PRODUCT WARRANTY

A final component for product consideration is the **warranty,** which is a statement indicating the liability of the manufacturer for product deficiencies. There are

MARKETPLACE APPLICATION

The Package: More than a Pretty Face

Packaging today has achieved a legitimate and increasingly important status in the marketing mix. Smart companies are recognizing the value of strategically relevant packaging which addresses their marketing objectives and business realities instead of simple aesthetics. Packaging must do much more than simply look pretty. With nearly twice as many products on the retail shelf, a package must communicate, inspire, and motivate the consumer in a highly competitive visual arena.

For a package to work, most designers believe that it must be "likeable." The package should forge a link between the product and the consumer. It should also pack more visual punch than the competition. In other words, it should stand out. If the package isn't noticed on the shelf, it can't get purchased. But beyond being simply noticed, the package must deliver the right message to the consumer at the point-of-purchase, where research has found that two-thirds of buying decisions are made. In addition to helping to market the product,

the package can make the product easier to use, or with proper copy, make it more understandable to the consumer. Packaging must also keep pace to reflect changes in society, lifestyles, technology, and laws. For example, environmental concerns over excessive packaging will continue to impact on package design. New legislation will require packaged goods companies to undertake packaging audits and draft new ways to further reduce packaging.

The package can be considered today's hot button. A package holds more than a product. It holds a lot of clout. It's the final link in the marketing chain between manufacturer and consumer. The package can and should be a big weapon in an organization's marketing communications arsenal.

SOURCE: Adapted from "Package Designs," *Marketing,* January 16, 1995, p. 8–9; and Jo Marney. "More than a Pretty Surface," *Marketing,* April 10, 1995. p. 25.

various degrees of product warranties with different implications for manufacturers and customers.

The Variations of a Warranty

Some companies offer *express warranties,* which are written statements of liabilities. In recent years the government has required greater disclosure on express warranties to indicate whether the warranty is a limited-coverage or a full-coverage alternative. A *limited-coverage warranty* specifically states the bounds of coverage and, more important, areas of noncoverage, whereas a *full warranty* has no limits of noncoverage. Peugeot is a company that boldly touts its warranty coverage.

With greater frequency, manufacturers are being held to *implied warranties,* which assign responsibility for product deficiencies to the manufacturer. Studies show that warranties are important and affect a consumer's product evaluation. Brands that have limited warranties tend to receive less positive evaluations than full-warranty items.[37]

Consumer and Corporate Affairs Canada is responsible for protecting consumer rights with regard to warranties.

The Growing Importance of Warranties

Warranties are important in light of increasing product liability claims. In the early part of the 20th century the courts protected companies, but the trend now is toward "strict liability" rulings, where a manufacturer is liable for any product defect, whether it followed reasonable research standards or not. This issue is hotly contested between companies and consumer advocates.

Warranties represent much more than just protection of the buyer from negative consequences—they can hold a significant marketing advantage for the producer. Sears has built a strong reputation for its Craftsman tool line with a simple warranty: If you break a tool, it's replaced with no questions asked.

LEARNING CHECK

1. How does a generic brand differ from a private brand?

2. Explain the role of packaging in terms of perception.

3. What is the difference between an expressed and an implied warranty?

LEARNING OBJECTIVE REINFORCEMENT

1. Explain the four stages of the product life cycle. Products have a finite life cycle consisting of four stages: introduction, growth, maturity, and decline. The introduction stage of the product life cycle occurs when a product is first introduced to its intended target market. The growth stage is characterized by rapid increases in sales. At maturity there is a gradual levelling off of total industry sales. The decline stage occurs when sales and profits begin to drop.

2. Outline what marketing actions are required as the product moves through its life cycle. In the introductory stage the need is to create awareness and stimulate trial, as well as establish primary demand for the product class. In the growth stage it is important to differentiate the product from the competitors and gain as much distribution as possible. The emphasis here is to encourage selective demand. In the maturity stage it is important to maintain brand loyalty, or hold market share, while trying to reduce overall marketing costs. The decline stage necessitates a deleting, harvesting, or contracting strategy in order to maintain profitability.

3. Recognize the differences in product life cycles for various products and their implications for marketing decisions. There are various shapes to the product life cycle. High learning products have a long introductory period. Marketers must educate the consumer about the benefits of the product. Low learning products rapidly enter the growth stage. The product is easily imitated by competitors, so the key is to broaden distribution quickly. There are also different curves for fashions and fads. For fashion products, the marketer must recognize that the life cycle may be years or decades. For fads, there are rapid sales increases and then rapid declines. The key is to know when to enter and when to exit. Different product life cycle curves can also exist for the product class, product form, and brand.

4. Understand alternative approaches to managing a product life cycle. In managing a product's life cycle, changes can be made in the product itself or in the target market. Product modification approaches include changes in quality, performance, or appearance. Market modification approaches entail increasing a product's use among existing customers, creating new use situations, or finding new users. Product repositioning can be done by modifying the product, as well as through changes in marketing communications, pricing, or distribution.

5. Define branding and identify the attributes of a successful brand name. Branding occurs when an organization uses a name, a phrase, a design, symbols, or a combination of these to identify its products and distinguish them from those of competitors. A good brand name should suggest the product's benefits, be memorable, fit the company or product image, be free of legal restrictions, and be simple and emotional.

6. Explain the rationale for alternative brand name strategies employed by organizations. Manufacturers can follow one of three branding strategies: a manufacturer's brand, a reseller brand, or a mixed-brand approach. With a manufacturer's branding approach, the company can use the same brand name for all products in the line (multiproduct, or family branding) or can give products different names (multibranding). A reseller, or private, brand is used when a firm manufactures a product but sells it under the brand name of a wholesaler or retailer. A generic brand is a product with no identification of manufacturer or reseller that is offered on the basis of price appeal.

7. Understand the benefits of packaging and warranties in the marketing of a product. Packaging provides communication, functional, and perceptual benefits. Warranties are an important aspect of a manufacturer's product strategy. Warranties do more than protect the buyer, they can offer the company a marketing advantage over competitors.

KEY TERMS AND CONCEPTS

product life cycle p. 234
product class p. 239
product form p. 239
product modification p. 241
market modification strategies p. 241
branding p. 243
brand name p. 243

trade name p. 243
trademark p. 244
brand equity p. 245
licensing p. 246
manufacturer branding p. 247
multiproduct branding p. 247
multibranding p. 247

euro-branding p. 248
global branding p. 248
private branding p. 248
mixed branding p. 249
generic brand p. 249
packaging p. 249
warranty p. 251

CHAPTER QUESTIONS AND APPLICATIONS

1. Several years ago, Apple Computer was one of the first companies to market PCs to the general public. IBM, the giant, had no competing product, but within a short time it announced its PC model. Steven Jobs, the founder of Apple, is said to have exclaimed, "We're glad to see IBM is entering the market." According to the product life cycle, is there any rationale for Jobs's statement?

2. Listed are three different products in various stages of the product life cycle. What marketing strategies would you suggest to these companies? *(a)* Cantel cellular telephone company—growth stage; *(b)* Water Doctor tap-water purifying systems—introductory stage; and *(c)* Acme hand-held manual can openers—decline stage.

3. In many communities the birthrate has dropped substantially, adversely affecting hospitals' pediatric medicine departments. Although pediatrics as a specialty is declining, hospitals still need a complete service mix. As the chief executive of a hospital, what decline strategies would you suggest?

4. It has been suggested that products are intentionally made to break down or wear out. Is this strategy a planned product modification approach?

5. A product manager at GE is reviewing the penetration of trash compactors in Canadian homes. After more than a decade in existence, this product is in relatively few homes. What problems account for this poor acceptance? What is the shape of the trash compactor life cycle curve?

6. For several years Ferrari has been known as the manufacturer of expensive luxury automobiles. The company now plans to attract the major segment of the car-buying market that purchases medium-priced automobiles. As Ferrari considers this trading-down strategy, what branding strategy would you recommend? What are the trade-offs to consider with your strategy?

7. The nature of product warranties has changed as the government reassesses the meaning of warranties. How does the regulatory trend toward warranties affect product development and management?

APPLICATION CASE 10-1
POLAROID CANADA

When Polaroid first introduced instant photography in 1948, it was a remarkable breakthrough in consumer photography. Polaroid prints were of comparable quality to other camera systems of the time, but the unique aspect of Polaroid pictures was that they developed instantly.

Instant photography became very popular with consumers and very profitable for Polaroid. However, in the 1980s the advent of newer technology and a changing and more sophisticated consumer began to change the marketplace. New, compact, fully automatic 35mm cameras provided high-quality prints never before achieved with easy-to-use cameras. Meanwhile, rapidly declining processing time—to as low as one hour—further contributed to the popularity of 35mm cameras. This development began to undermine Polaroid's competitive advantage: immediacy.

In the late 1980s, 35mm cameras and film became the standard in consumer photography for traditional photographic uses. The new 35mm prints forced comparisons with instant pictures and consumers perceived that there was some differences in terms of colour and resolution. In addition, an instant print was typically twice as expensive as a 35mm print. As the photographic marketplace changed, Polaroid remained committed to the instant segment even though instant photography's competitive advantage of immediacy was slowly eroding. With the advent of 35mm point-and-shoot cameras, there was a concern that consumers would be less likely to use Polaroid instant cameras in traditional photographic situations since they now had more camera options.

The key issue facing Polaroid in the 1990s is how to make "instant" important to consumers once again. Polaroid has to begin to reposition the camera and rejuvenate what consumers view as a mature brand.

QUESTIONS
1. How can Polaroid revitalize its instant photography business?
2. Who should Polaroid target?
3. What message should Polaroid communicate to the target(s)?

SOURCE: Adapted from Canadian Advertising Success Stories, Cassies II, Canadian Congress of Advertising, 1995. Used with permission.

APPLICATION CASE 10-2
CLEARLY CANADIAN

Vancouver-based Clearly Canadian Beverages is a major player in the new-age or alternative beverage market. The new-age or alternative beverage market is a catchall that includes "healthful" carbonated or non-carbonated, flavoured waters, and other beverages sold as alternatives to traditional soft drinks. The new-age beverage market is valued at over $1 billion in North America. However, the new-age segment is still very small compared to the traditional soft drink market, which is estimated to be valued at between $45 and $50 billion dollars.

In general, the people who drink new-age beverages are doing so because they offer something different and, in most cases, something lighter, healthier, or more natural. The target consumer for the category was originally thought to be upscale and health-conscious 18–34 year-olds. But many new-age beverage marketers discovered that the market also included maturing baby-boomers as well as a youth segment, including pre-teens.

Clearly Canadian had entered the new-age beverage market relatively early, seeing the trend toward healthier beverages. Its line of quality beverages were clear, contained no caffeine or artificial sweeteners, used only natural flavours, and were packaged in an attractive blue teardrop bottle. The beverages originally came in 23-ounce multi-serving bottles as well as four-packs placed in display racks at all retailers. The company used premium pricing and a network of independent bottlers to ensure the product got on the retail shelf. Marketing communications activities included regional ad campaigns as well as consumer and trade sales promotions including sampling, point-of-purchase displays, and sales incentive programs for its sales representatives.

Clearly Canadian had aggressively pursued a market penetration strategy in North America. That was followed by a market development strategy, during which the company entered several countries or regions including Mexico, the Carribbean, England, Ireland, Japan, and the Middle East. However, by

1994, both growth in the category and company sales started to level off. Some experts suggested that the decline in growth was due to consumers' capricious tastes and the growing competition from other products such as the ready-to-drink iced teas. Others suggested that with the growing number of new brands, these so-called specialty drinks were no longer special enough to command the premium prices being charged by new-age beverage marketers.

But Clearly Canadian continued to expand its market coverage, launched some new flavours, and began using a 200-ml (6 oz) bottle designed to help boost sales in the hospitality industry. Clearly Canadian also launched its own ready-to-drink ice tea and Orbitz, a drink with flavoured gel spheres floating in the bottle designed to appeal to rebellious teens. Still, experts are concerned that the new-age beverage category may see further declines in growth, and so too will Clearly Canadian.

QUESTIONS
1. At what stage in the product life cycle are new-age beverages? Justify your answer.
2. What are the key components of Clearly Canadian's marketing strategy?
3. Outline some ways that can help the company continue to achieve growth in the new-age beverage market.

Understanding Pricing and Distribution

PART IV

11

Pricing

PRICING IN THE DOG-BREEDING BUSINESS

As a professional artist, Kimberly Grant possessed little knowledge about the dog-breeding business. Kimberly purchased Tuffy, a male West Highland White Terrier (Westie) to have only as a pet. She soon realized, however, that Tuffy presented a modest yet exciting business opportunity. To Kimberly's untrained eye, Tuffy's pedigree looked very impressive and it seemed that every groomer and vet that saw him commented on his good looks and the absence of the genetic problems common to Westies.

Discouraged by the quality of Westies seen in his practice, Tuffy's vet encouraged Kimberly to breed Tuffy and offered to help her identify a breeder interested in Tuffy's services. Upon acceptance of this offer of help, Kimberly found herself in the business and soon discovered many unexpected costs associated with this opportunity (kennel club fees, a microchip implant, etc.). This discovery left Kimberly asking a key question: What price should I charge?

Despite Kimberly's business sense, which told her to set a price that would enable her to recover all breeding related costs plus a profit, she learned that in this business she had very little control over price. A competition-based method of pricing, known as *customary pricing,* was being used in this business. In other words, the price of the service is, for the most part, fixed because of an arrangement which is generally accepted within the business. According to this arrangement, Kimberly could expect to receive either first pick of the litter (a form of compensation known as *countertrade* or *barter*) or a payment equal to the market value of one puppy.[1] Kimberly now had an answer to her question.

This chapter covers many important factors that decision makers use in setting prices. The role of price in marketing strategy and a step-by-step procedure organizations use to set prices for products and services are discussed. In addition, an overview of legal and regulatory aspects of pricing is provided.

NATURE AND IMPORTANCE OF PRICE

The price paid for goods and services goes by many names. You pay *tuition* for your education, *rent* for an apartment, *interest* on a bank credit card, and a *premium* for car insurance. Your dentist or physician charges you a *fee,* a professional or social organization charges *dues,* and transportation companies charge a *fare.* In business, a consultant may require a *retainer* for services rendered, an executive is given a *salary,* a salesperson receives a *commission,* and a worker is paid a *wage.* Of course, what you pay for clothes or a haircut is termed a *price.*

What Is a Price?

These examples highlight the many varied ways that price plays a part in our daily lives. From a marketing viewpoint, **price** is the money or other considerations (including other goods and services) exchanged for the ownership or use of a good or service. For example, Shell Oil recently exchanged 1 million pest control devices for sugar from a Caribbean country, and Wilkinson Sword exchanged some of its knives for advertising used to market its razor blades. This practice of exchanging goods and services for other goods and services rather than for money is called *countertrade* (also called *barter*).

For most products and services, money is exchanged, although the amount is not always the same as the list or quoted price. Often the list price is a base amount from which discounts and allowances are subtracted and extra fees are added. Therefore, you need to apply the *price equation* (as shown in Figure 11–1) to each purchase to discover the price per item:

Price = List price − Discounts and allowances + Extra fees

Figure 11–1 illustrates how the price equation applies to a variety of different products and services.

Price as an Indicator of Value

From a consumer's standpoint, price is often used to indicate value when it is paired with the perceived benefits of a product or service. Specifically, **value** can be defined as the ratio of perceived benefits to price (value = perceived benefits/price).[2] This relationship shows that for a given price, as perceived benefits increase, value increases. Also, for a given price, value decreases when perceived benefits decrease. Creative marketers engage in *value-based pricing,* the practice of simultaneously increasing product and service benefits and maintaining or decreasing price.[3]

For some products, price influences the perception of overall quality, and ultimately value, to consumers.[4] For example, in a survey of home furnishing buyers, 84 percent agreed with the statement "The higher the price, the higher the quality." How consumers make value assessments is not fully understood. Nevertheless, innovative companies now recognize that value is more than a low price.

FIGURE 11-1 The price of four different purchases.

Item Purchased	Price	=	List Price	−	Discounts and Allowances	+	Extra Fees
					Price Equation		
New car bought by an individual	Final price	=	List price	−	Quantity discount Cash discount Trade-ins	+	Financing charges Special accessories
Term in college bought by a student	Tuition	=	Published tuition	−	Scholarship Other financial aid Discounts for number of credits taken	+	Special activity fees
Bank loan obtained by a small business	Principal and interest	=	Amount of loan sought	−	Allowance for collateral	+	Premium for uncertain credit-worthiness
Merchandise bought from a wholesaler by a retailer	Invoice price	=	List price	−	Quantity discount Cash discount Season discount Functional or trade discount	+	Penalty for late payment

Price in the Marketing Mix

Pricing is also a critical decision made by a marketing executive, because price has a direct effect on a firm's profits. This is apparent from a firm's *profit equation:*

Profit = Total revenue − Total cost

or

Profit = (Unit price × Quantity sold) − Total cost

What makes this relationship even more important is that price normally affects the quantity sold. Furthermore, since the quantity sold sometimes affects a firm's costs because of efficiency of production, price also indirectly affects costs. So pricing decisions influence both total revenue and total cost, which makes pricing one of the most important decisions marketing executives face.[5]

The importance of price in the marketing mix necessitates an understanding of six major steps involved in the process organizations go through in setting prices (Figure 11–2):

- Identify pricing constraints and objectives.
- Estimate demand and revenue.
- Determine cost, volume, and profit relationships.
- Select an approximate price level.
- Set list or quoted price.
- Make special adjustments to list or quoted price.

The remainder of this chapter will be devoted to discussing these steps in detail.

FIGURE 11–2   Steps in setting price.

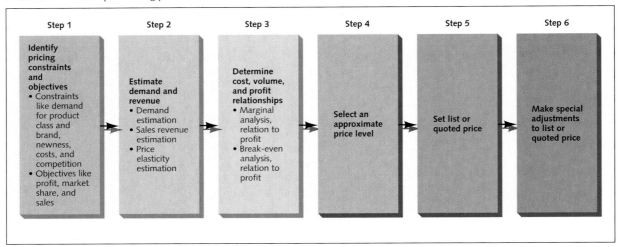

STEP 1: IDENTIFY PRICING CONSTRAINTS AND OBJECTIVES

Let's first review pricing constraints so that we can better understand the nature of pricing alternatives. We will then discuss the variety of pricing objectives that may be set by organizations.

Identifying Pricing Constraints

Factors that limit the latitude of prices an organization may set are **pricing constraints.** Consumer demand for the product clearly affects the price that can be charged. Other constraints on price are set by factors within the organization: newness of the product, whether it is part of a product line, and cost of and flexibility in changing a price. Competitive factors such as the nature of competition and prices set by competitors also restrict the latitude of an organization's ability to set price. Moreover, legal and regulatory factors, which are discussed at the end of this chapter, can limit the latitude of prices an organization may set.

Demand for the Product Class, Product, and Brand.   The number of potential buyers for the product class (cars), product (sports cars), and brand (Dodge Viper) clearly affects the price a seller can charge. The nature of demand is discussed later in the chapter.

Newness of the Product: Stage in the Product Life Cycle.   The newer a product and the earlier it is in its life cycle, the higher is the price that can usually be charged. When NutraSweet was introduced in 1983, it was the only non-artificial sugar substitute that was safe to use, contained few calories, and was sweeter than sugar. The newness of the product coupled with patent protection meant that a premium price of $92 per pound could be charged. However, once its patent expired in December 1992, rivals emerged (such as Johnson & Johnson's sweetener Sucralose), which affected the pricing latitude for NutraSweet. NutraSweet's price per pound in January 1993 was $52.[6]

FIGURE 11–3   Pricing, product, and marketing communications strategies available to firms in four types of competitive markets.

	Type of Competitive Market			
Strategies Available	Pure Monopoly (One seller who sets the price for a unique product)	Oligopoly (Few sellers who are sensitive to each other's prices)	Monopolistic Competition (Many sellers who compete on nonprice factors)	Pure Competition (Many sellers who follow the market price for identical, commodity products)
Price competition	None: sole seller sets price	Some: price leader or follower of competitors	Some: compete over range of prices	Almost none: market sets price
Product differentiation	None: no other producers	Various: depends on industry	Some: differentiate products from competitors'	None: products are identical
Extent of marketing communications	Little: purpose is to increase demand for product class	Some: purpose is to inform but avoid price competition	Much: purpose is to differentiate firm's products from competitors'	Little: purpose is to inform prospects that seller's products are available

Single Product versus a Product Line.   When Sony introduced its CD player, not only was it unique and in the introductory stage of its product life cycle but also it was the *only* CD player Sony sold, so the firm had great latitude in setting a price. Now, with a line of CD player products, the price of individual models has to be consistent with the others based on features provided and meaningful price differentials that communicate value to consumers.

Cost of Producing and Marketing the Product.   In the long run, a firm's price must cover all the costs of producing and marketing a product. If the price doesn't cover the cost, the firm will fail, so in the long run a firm's costs set a floor under its price.

Cost of Changing Prices and Time Period They Apply.   If Sears Canada decides that sweater prices are too low in its winter catalogues after thousands of catalogues have been mailed to customers, it has a big problem. It can't easily inform thousands of potential buyers that the price has changed, so Sears Canada must consider the cost of changing prices and the time period for which they apply in developing the price list for its catalogue items.

Type of Competitive Markets.   The seller's price is constrained by the type of market in which it competes. Economists generally delineate four types of competitive markets: pure monopoly, oligopoly, monopolistic competition, and pure competition. Figure 11–3 shows that the type of competition dramatically influences the latitude of price competition, and in turn the nature of product differentiation and extent of marketing communications. A firm must recognize the general type of competitive market it is in to understand the latitude of both its price and nonprice strategies. For example:

- *Pure monopoly:* Ontario Hydro, an electric power company, receives approval from the public utility commission for the rates it can charge. In most areas of the province, it is the only source of electricity for consumers.
- *Oligopoly:* The few sellers of aluminum (Alcan or Alcoa) or gasoline (Esso or Shell), try to avoid price competition because it can lead to disastrous price

wars in which all lose money. Yet firms in such industries stay aware of a competitor's price cuts or increases and may follow suit. Informative marketing communications that avoids head-to-head price competition is used.

- *Monopolistic competition:* Regional or private brands of peanut butter compete with national brands like Skippy and Jif. Both price competition (regional, private brands being lower-priced than national brands) and nonprice competition (product features, marketing communications) exist.
- *Pure competition:* Hundreds of local grain elevators sell corn, whose price per bushel is set by the marketplace. Within strains, the corn is identical, so marketing communications only informs buyers that the seller's corn is available.

Competitors' Prices. A firm must know or anticipate what specific price its present and potential competitors now charge or will charge. When the NutraSweet Company planned the market introduction of Simplesse® all-natural fat substitute, it had to consider the price of fat replacements already available as well as potential competitors including Procter & Gamble's Olestra.

Identifying Pricing Objectives

Goals that specify the role of price in an organization's marketing and strategic plans are known as **pricing objectives.** Although profit maximization is a common pricing objective, organizations often set sales, market share, unit volume, customer value, and social responsibility objectives which can tie in directly with the organization's pricing policies.

Profit. Three different objectives relate to a firm's profit, usually measured in terms of return on investment (ROI) or return on assets. One objective is *managing for long-run profits,* which is followed by many Japanese firms that are willing to forgo immediate profit in cars, TV sets, or computers to develop quality products that can penetrate competitive markets in the future. A *maximizing current profit* objective, such as during the present quarter or year, is common in many firms because the targets can be set and performance measured quickly. Canadian firms are sometimes criticized for this short-run orientation. A *target return* objective involves a firm like Clearly Canadian or Esso setting a goal (such as 20 percent) for pretax ROI.

Sales. Given that a firm's profit is high enough for it to remain in business, its objectives may be to increase sales revenue. The hope is that the increase in sales revenue will in turn lead to increases in market share and profit. Objectives related to sales revenue have the advantage of being translated easily into meaningful targets for marketing managers responsible for a product line or brand—far more easily than objectives connected with an ROI target, for example.

Market Share. Market share is the ratio of a firm's sales revenues or unit sales to those of the industry (competitors plus the firm itself). Companies often pursue a market share objective when industry sales are flat or declining and they want to get a larger share. In their battle for market share, Pepsi and Coke often use price specials or discounts.

Unit Volume. Many firms use unit volume, the quantity produced or sold, as a pricing objective. These firms often sell multiple products at very different prices and are

MARKETPLACE APPLICATION

H. J. Heinz Pricing Objectives Vary in the Global Ketchup Marketplace

H. J. Heinz Company has been making and marketing ketchup for more than a century. Heinz ketchup, the firm's flagship brand, holds more than 50 percent of the North American ketchup market. About one-half of all ketchup consumed in the world is sold by Heinz.

This seasoned global marketer sells ketchup in over 200 countries. Like other global marketers, Heinz pursues different pricing objectives for its ketchup in different countries. For instance, in those countries where competition is intense and Heinz is not the market leader, the company tends to price its ketchup aggressively with the objectives of building dollar sales, unit volume, and market share. In Japan, Heinz has focused its pricing objective on protecting its profitability. Thus, its ketchup prices are higher than competitors'.

1. Why would Heinz pursue different pricing objectives for its ketchup in different countries?

SOURCES: Based on J. P. Jeannet and H. D. Hennessey, *Global Marketing Strategies,* 2nd ed. (Boston: Houghton Mifflin Company, 1992), p. 430; "Ketchup War Will Be Fought to the Last Drop," *Financial Times,* February 21, 1990, p. 18; "Counting Costs of Dual Pricing in the Run-Up to 1992," *Financial Times,* July 9, 1990, p. 4; and G. Hoover, A. Campbell, and P. J. Spain, eds., *Hoover's Handbook—1991: Profiles of Over 500 Major Corporations* (Austin, TX: The Reference Press, 1991), p. 283.

sensitive to matching production capacity with unit volume. Volume can be increased by employing sales incentives (such as lowering prices, giving rebates, or offering lower interest rates).

Customer Value. Providing customer value may be an important organizational objective. To provide it, many firms will engage in value-based pricing, increasing product or service benefits while maintaining or lowering prices. Others offer "everyday low prices" or specific values, like Wendy's "value menu."

Social Responsibility. A firm may forgo higher profit on sales and follow a pricing objective that recognizes its obligations to customers and society in general. Medtronics followed this pricing policy when it introduced the world's first heart pacemaker. Gerber supplies a specially formulated product free of charge to children who cannot tolerate foods based on cow's milk.[7] Government agencies, which set many prices for services they offer, often use social responsibility as a primary pricing objective.

LEARNING CHECK

1. What do you have to do to the list price to determine the final price?

2. How does the type of competitive market a firm is in affect its latitude in setting price?

STEP 2: ESTIMATE DEMAND AND REVENUE

Basic to setting a product's price is the extent of customer demand for it.

Fundamentals in Estimating Demand

How did *Newsweek* determine the demand curve for its magazine? See the text.

Newsweek conducted a pricing experiment in 11 cities.[8] In one city, newsstand buyers paid $2.25. In five cities, newsstand buyers paid the regular $2.00. In another city, the price was $1.50, and in four other cities it was only $1.00. By comparison, the regular newsstand price for *Time* was $1.95. Why did *Newsweek* conduct the experiment? According to a *Newsweek* executive at that time, "We want to figure out what the demand curve for our magazine at the newsstand is." And you thought that demand curves only existed to confuse you on a test in basic economics!

The Demand Curve. A **demand curve** shows a maximum number of products consumers will buy at a given price. Demand curve D_1 in Figure 11–4 shows the newsstand demand for *Newsweek* under present conditions. Note that as price falls, more people buy. But price is not the complete story in estimating demand. Economists stress three other key factors:

1. *Consumer tastes.* As we saw in Chapter 3, these depend on many factors such as demographics, culture, and technology. Because consumer tastes can change quickly, up-to-date marketing research is essential.
2. *Price and availability of other products.* As the price of close substitute products falls (*Time* for *Newsweek*) and their availability increases, the demand for a product declines.
3. *Consumer income.* In general, as real consumer income (allowing for inflation) increases, demand for a product also increases.

The first of these two factors influences what consumers *want* to buy, and the third affects what they *can* buy.

FIGURE 11–4
Illustrative demand curves for *Newsweek* magazine.

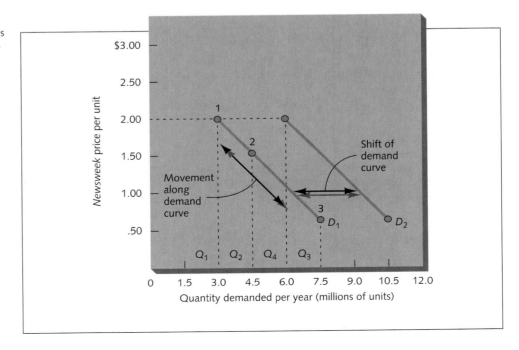

Movement Along versus Shift of a Demand Curve.

Demand curve D_1 in Figure 11–4 shows that as the price is lowered from $2 to $1.50, the quantity demanded increases from 3 million to 4.5 million units per year. This is an example of a movement along a demand curve and assumes that other factors (consumer tastes, price and availability of substitutes, and consumer income) remain unchanged.

What if some of these factors change? For example, if advertising causes more people to want *Newsweek,* newsstand distribution is increased, and consumer incomes double, then the demand increases. This is shown in Figure 11–4 as a shift of the demand curve to the right, from D_1 to D_2. This means that more *Newsweek* magazines are wanted for a given price: at a price of $2, the demand is 6 million units per year (Q_4) on D_2 rather than 3 million units per year (Q_1) on D_1.

Fundamentals in Estimating Revenue

While economists may talk about demand curves, marketing executives are more likely to speak in terms of revenues generated. Demand curves lead directly to three related revenue concepts critical to pricing decisions: **total revenue, average revenue,** and **marginal revenue.** (See Figure 11–5 for definitions.)

Demand Curves and Revenue. Figure 11–6A again shows the demand curve for *Newsweek,* but it is now extended to intersect both the price and quantity axes. The demand curve shows that as price is reduced, the quantity of *Newsweek* magazines sold increases.

Figure 11–6B shows the total revenue curve for *Newsweek* calculated from the demand curve shown in Figure 11–6A. The total revenue curve is developed by simply multiplying the unit price times the quantity for each of the points on the demand curve. Total revenue starts at $0 (point A), reaches a maximum of $6,750,000 at point D, and returns to $0 at point G. This shows that as price is reduced in the A-to-D segment of the curve, total revenues are increased. However, cutting price in the D-to-G segment results in a decline in total revenue.

Marginal revenue, which is the change in total revenue obtained by selling one additional unit, is positive but decreasing when the price lies in the range from $3 to above $1.50 per unit. But below $1.50 per unit, marginal revenue is actually

---

Total revenue (TR) is the total money received from the sale of a product. If:

TR = Total revenue
P = Unit price of the product
Q = Quantity of the product sold

then:

$$TR = P \times Q$$

Average revenue (AR) is the average amount of money received for selling one unit of the product, or simply the price of that unit. Average revenue is the total revenue divided by the quantity sold:

$$AR = \frac{TR}{Q} = P$$

Marginal revenue (MR) is the change in total revenue obtained by selling one additional unit:

$$MR = \frac{\text{Change in } TR}{1 \text{ unit increase in } Q} = \frac{\Delta TR}{\Delta Q}$$

FIGURE 11–5
Fundamental revenue concepts.

FIGURE 11–6

How a downward-sloping demand curve affects total, average, and marginal revenue.

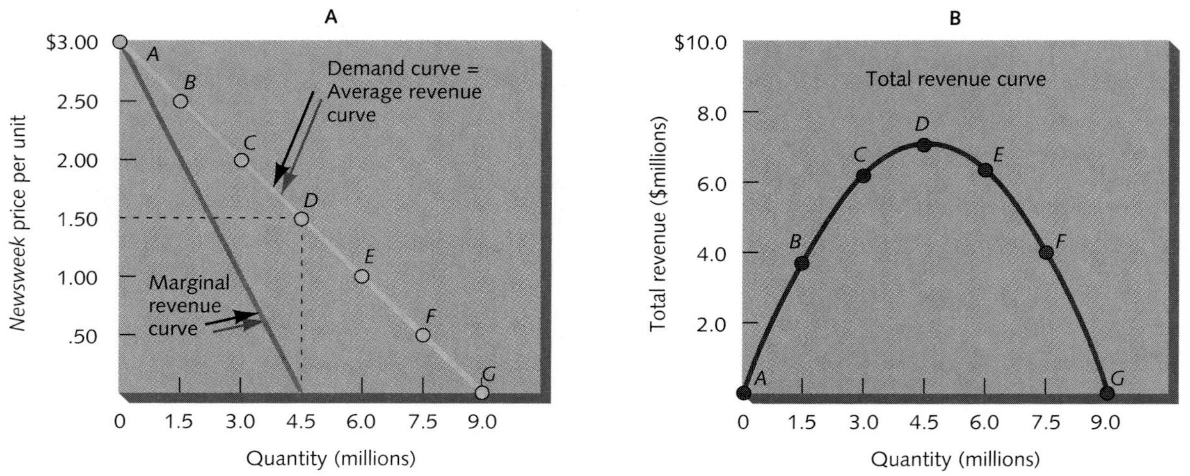

POINT ON DEMAND CURVE	PRICE (P)	QUANTITY SOLD (Q)	TOTAL REVENUE (P x Q)	AVERAGE REVENUE (TR/Q = P x Q/P = P)	MARGINAL REVENUE (ΔTR/ΔQ)
A	$ 3.00	0	$ 0	$ 3.00	$ 3.00
B	2.50	1,500,000	3,750,000	2.50	2.00
C	2.00	3,000,000	6,000,000	2.00	1.00
D	1.50	4,500,000	6,750,000	1.50	0
E	1.00	6,000,000	6,000,000	1.00	−1.00*
F	.50	7,500,000	3,750,000	.50	−2.00*
G	0	9,000,000	0	0	−3.00*

*Not shown in Figure 11-6A.

negative, so the extra quantity of magazines sold is more than offset by the decrease in the price per unit.

For any downward-sloping straight-line demand curve, the marginal revenue curve always falls at a rate twice as fast as the demand curve. As shown in Figure 11–6A, the marginal revenue becomes $0 per unit at a quantity sold of 4.5 million units—the very point at which total revenue is maximum (see Figure 11–6B).

What price did *Newsweek* select after conducting its experiment? They kept the price at $2.00. However, through expanded newsstand distribution and more aggressive advertising, *Newsweek* was later able to shift its demand curve to the right and charge a price of $2.50 without affecting its newsstand volume.

Price Elasticity of Demand. With a downward-sloping demand curve, we have been concerned with the responsiveness of demand to price changes. This can be conveniently measured by **price elasticity of demand,** or the percentage change in quantity demanded relative to a percentage change in price. Price elasticity of demand (*E*) is expressed as follows:

$$E = \frac{\text{Percentage change in quantity demanded}}{\text{Percentage change in price}}$$

Because quantity demanded usually decreases as price increases, price elasticity of demand is usually a negative number. However, for the sake of simplicity and by convention, elasticity figures are shown as positive numbers.

Price elasticity of demand is determined by a number of factors. First, the more substitutes a product or service has, the more likely it is to be *price elastic*. For example, butter has many possible substitutes in a meal and is price elastic, but gasoline has almost no substitutes and is price inelastic. Second, products and services considered to be necessities are *price inelastic*. For example, open-heart surgery is price inelastic, whereas airline tickets for a vacation are price elastic. Third, items that require a large cash outlay compared with a person's disposable income are price elastic. Accordingly, cars and yachts are price elastic; books and movie tickets tend to be price inelastic.

Price elasticity is important to marketing managers because of its relationship to total revenue. For example, with elastic demand, total revenue increases when price decreases, but decreases when price increases. With inelastic demand, total revenue increases when price increases and decreases when price decreases. Finally, with *unitary demand*—where the percentage change in price is equal to the percentage change in quantity demanded—total revenue is unaffected by a slight price change.

STEP 3: DETERMINE COST, VOLUME, AND PROFIT RELATIONSHIPS

The profit equation described earlier in this chapter showed that profit = total revenue − total cost. Therefore, understanding the role of costs is critical for all marketing decisions, particularly pricing decisions.

To determine the role of costs, marketing managers use marginal analysis and break-even analysis. **Marginal analysis** means studying whether revenue received from the sale of an additional product (marginal revenue) is greater than the additional cost of producing and marketing it (marginal cost); if it is greater, an organization can reasonably expand its output of that product.[9] The message of marginal analysis, then, is to operate up to the quantity and price level where total revenue resulting from marketing one additional unit exceeds the increase in the total cost of producing and marketing that unit.

Break-even analysis is a technique that analyzes the relationship between total revenue and total cost to determine profitability at various levels of output. When applying break-even analysis, decision makers are typically interested in the break-even point. The **break-even point** is the quantity at which total revenue and total cost are equal and beyond which profit occurs. Break-even analysis is a useful technique because it allows marketing managers to answer "what-if" questions about the effect of changes in price and cost on profit.[10] Appendix C, which follows this chapter, provides a discussion and illustration of both marginal analysis and break-even analysis.

STEP 4: SELECT AN APPROXIMATE PRICE LEVEL

A key to a marketing manager's setting a final price for a product is to find an "approximate price level" to use as a reasonable starting point. Three common approaches to help find this approximate price level are demand-based, cost-based, and competition-based methods (Figure 11–7). Although these methods are discussed separately, some

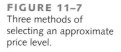
FIGURE 11-7
Three methods of
selecting an approximate
price level.

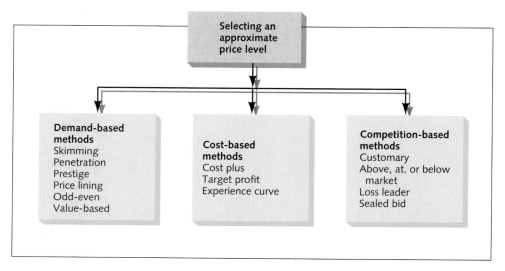

of them overlap, and an effective marketing manager will consider several in searching for an approximate price level.

Demand-Based Methods

Demand-based methods of finding a price level weigh factors underlying expected customer tastes and preferences more heavily than such factors as cost, profit, and competition.

Skimming Pricing. A firm introducing a new or innovative product can use **skimming pricing,** setting the highest initial price that customers really desiring the product are willing to pay. These customers are not very price sensitive, because they weigh the new product's price, quality, and ability to satisfy their needs against the same characteristics of substitutes. As the demand of these customers is satisfied, the firm lowers the price to attract another, more price-sensitive segment. Thus, skimming pricing gets its name from skimming successive layers of "cream," or customer segments, as prices are lowered in a series of steps. The initial pricing of VCRs at more than $1,500 and the Trivial Pursuit game at $39.95 are examples of skimming pricing. Within three years after their introductions, both products were often priced at less than half their initial prices.
Skimming pricing is an effective strategy when:

• Enough prospective customers are willing to buy the product immediately at the high initial price to make these sales profitable.
• The high initial price will not attract competitors.
• Lowering price has only a minor effect on increasing the sales volume and reducing the unit costs.
• Customers interpret the high price as signifying high quality.

These four conditions are most likely to exist when the new product is protected by patents or copyrights, or its uniqueness is understood and appreciated by customers.

Penetration Pricing. Setting a low initial price on a new product to appeal immediately to the mass market is **penetration pricing,** the exact opposite of skimming pricing. The conditions favouring penetration pricing are the reverse of those supporting skimming pricing:

- Many segments of the market are price sensitive.
- A low initial price discourages competitors from entering the market.
- Unit production and marketing costs fall dramatically as production volumes increase.

These conditions exist in the European personal computer market today. A firm using penetration pricing may maintain the initial price for a time to gain profit from its low introductory level or lower the price further, counting on the new volume to generate the necessary profit.

Prestige Pricing. **Prestige pricing** involves setting a high price so that status-conscious consumers will be attracted to the product and buy it. Rolls-Royce cars, diamonds, perfumes, fine china, and crystal have an element of prestige pricing appeal in them and may sell worse at lower prices than at higher ones.

Price Lining. Often a firm that is selling not just a single product but a line of products may price them at a number of different specific pricing points, in a practice called **price lining.** For example, a department store manager may price a line of women's dresses at $59, $79, and $99. In some instances all the items might be purchased for the same cost and then marked up at different percentages to achieve these price points based on colour, style, and expected demand. In other instances manufacturers design products for different price points and retailers apply approximately the same markup percentages to achieve the three or four different price points offered to consumers. Sellers often feel that a limited number (such as three or four) of price points is preferable to 8 or 10 different ones, which may only confuse prospective buyers.[11]

Odd–Even Pricing. Sears offers a Craftsman radial saw for $499.99; Leon's prices a five-piece living room set at $2,499; and K mart has Windex glass cleaner on sale for 99 cents. Why not simply price these items at $500, $2,500, and $1, respectively? These retailers are using **odd–even pricing,** which involves setting prices a few dollars or cents under an even number. The presumption is that consumers see the Sears radial saw as priced at "something over $400" rather than "about $500." In theory, demand increases if the price drops from $500 to $499.99. There is some evidence to suggest this does happen.[12]

Value-Based Pricing. With the growing number of value-conscious consumers, many marketers are using value-based pricing to appeal to this group. **Value-based pricing** involves increasing perceived product or service benefits while maintaining or decreasing prices or simply lowering prices on standard items consumers buy with regularity, such as household supplies and grocery items. It can also take the form of an *"everyday low-price"* (EDLP) retail strategy. Discount merchandisers like Zellers and Wal-Mart have adopted this strategy by attempting to offer the lowest prices possible on a broad selection of products.

Another form of value-based pricing is *bundle pricing*—the marketing of two or more products in a single "package deal" price. For example, Air Canada offers vacation packages that include airfare, car rental, and lodging. Bundle pricing is based on the idea that consumers value the package more than the individual items. Moreover, bundle pricing often provides a lower total cost to buyers and lower marketing cost to sellers.[13]

Cellular telephones were introduced with skimming pricing. Once a very expensive item, many retailers now offer free cell phone hardware as an incentive for air-time packages.

Cost-Based Methods

In cost-based methods the price setter stresses the supply or cost side of the pricing problem, not the demand side. Price is set by looking at the production and marketing costs and then adding enough to cover direct expenses, overhead, and profit (if the organization has set a profit objective).

Cost-Plus Pricing. In **cost-plus pricing** the price setter merely adds an amount—a *markup*—to all costs. Manufacturing and construction firms often apply a variation of this method known as *cost plus percentage-of-cost pricing,* which means they add a fixed percentage to the production or construction cost. Thus, for a house with a construction cost of $100,000 and a builder's fee of 15 percent of construction cost, or $15,000, the final price would be $115,000.

Another variation of cost-plus pricing known as *cost plus fixed-fee pricing* is used by the manufacturers of highly technical, few-of-a-kind products such as navy frigates or satellites. This means that a supplier is reimbursed for all approved costs, regardless of what they turn out to be, but is allowed only a fixed fee as profit that is independent of the final cost of the project.

Managers of retail stores often have such a large number of products that estimating the demand for each product as a means of price setting is impossible. Therefore, they use a form of cost-plus pricing known as *standard markup pricing,* which entails adding a fixed percentage of the cost of items in a specific product class. This percentage markup varies depending on the type of retail store (such as furniture, shoe, or grocery) and on the product involved. High-volume products usually have smaller markups than do low-volume products. For example, the markup in supermarkets such as Loblaws may vary from 10 percent to 23 percent for such items as sugar, flour, and dairy products, whereas the markup on items such as snack foods may range from 27 percent to 47 percent.

An explanation of how to compute a markup, along with operating statement data and other ratios, is given in Appendix C following this chapter.

Target Profit Pricing. In **target profit pricing** the price setter begins with a specific profit objective and then determines a product's price based on the number of units he or she expects to sell. For example, suppose a picture frame store owner wishes to use target profit pricing to establish a price for a typical framed picture and assumes:

- Variable cost is a constant $30 per unit.
- Fixed cost is a constant $30,000.
- A target profit of $10,000 is sought at an annual sales volume of 1,000 units (framed pictures).

The target profit price can be calculated as follows:

$$\text{Target profit price} = \frac{\text{Fixed costs} + \text{Target profit}}{\text{Sales volume in units}} + \text{Variable costs per unit}$$

$$\text{Target profit price} = \frac{(\$30,000 + \$10,000)}{1,000} + 30$$

$$= \$70$$

A primary weakness of target profit pricing is that it ignores customer and demand factors. If demand is less than expected at the target profit price that is set, a loss could occur because there are fewer units over which to spread fixed costs. An explanation of fixed and variable costs is given in Appendix C following this chapter.

Experience Curve Pricing. The method of **experience curve pricing** is based on the learning curve effect, which holds that experience enables greater efficiencies. Organizations adopting experience curve pricing expect lower unit costs because of experience-based efficiency improvements and greater economies of scale as production increases. As a result, many of these organizations experience unit cost reductions of 10 percent to 30 percent each time production and sales double.[14] Since prices often follow costs with experience curve pricing, a rapid decline in price is possible.

This cost-based method of pricing complements the demand-based pricing strategy of skimming followed by penetration pricing. For example, fax machine prices have declined from $1,000 to under $300, and cellular telephones that sold for $4,000 are now offered free of charge when long-term airtime packages are purchased.

Competition-Based Methods

Rather than emphasize demand or cost factors, a price setter can stress what competitors or "the market" is doing.

Customary Pricing. For some products where tradition, a standardized channel of distribution, or other competitive factors dictate the price, **customary pricing** is used. For example, soft drinks offered through standard vending machines have a customary price of one dollar. The dog-breeding services of Tuffy in the Chapter Opener were based on a customary price of first pick of the litter or the market value of a puppy.

Above-, At-, or Below-Market Pricing. For most products it is difficult to identify a specific market price for a product or product class. Still, marketing managers often have a subjective feel for the competitors' price or market price. Using this benchmark, they then may deliberately choose a strategy of **above-, at-, or below-market pricing.**

Among watch manufacturers, Rolex takes pride in emphasizing that it makes one of the most expensive watches you can buy—a clear example of above-market pricing. Manufacturers of national brands of clothing such as Alfred Sung and retailers like Holt Renfrew deliberately set premium prices for their products.

In contrast, a number of firms such as Wal-Mart use a strategy of below-market pricing. Manufacturers of all generic products and retailers who offer their own private brands of products ranging from peanut butter to shampoo deliberately set prices for these products about 8 percent to 10 percent below the prices of nationally branded competitive products such as Skippy peanut butter, Vidal Sassoon shampoo, or Crest toothpaste.

Loss-Leader Pricing. For a special sales promotion many retail stores deliberately sell a product below its customary price to attract attention to it. For example, grocery stores will often use produce or paper goods (e.g., bathroom tissue) as loss leaders. The purpose of **loss-leader pricing** is not to increase sales of the particular product but to attract customers in hopes they will buy other products as well, particularly the discretionary items carrying large markups.

Sealed-Bid Pricing. When the Federal Department of Supply and Services wants to buy a million number 2 wooden pencils for the army, it would probably use **sealed-bid pricing.** The buying agency widely publicizes specifications for the items to inform prospective manufacturers, who are invited to submit a bid that includes a specific price for the quantity ordered.

LEARNING CHECK

1. What is cost-plus pricing?

2. What is experience curve pricing?

3. What is the purpose of loss-leader pricing when used by a retail firm?

STEP 5: SET THE LIST OR QUOTED PRICE

After an approximate price level has been set, a specific list or quoted price must be set in light of all relevant factors.

One-Price versus Flexible-Price Policy

A seller must decide whether to follow a one-price or a flexible-price policy. A *one-price policy* is setting the same price for similar customers who buy the same product and quantities under the same conditions. In contrast, a *flexible-price policy* is offering the same product and quantities to similar customers, but at different prices. Car dealers have traditionally used flexible pricing based on buyer–seller negotiations to agree on a final price. However, flexible pricing carried to the extreme could be a form of price discrimination, a practice prohibited under the Competition Act.

Company, Customer, and Competitive Effects

As the final list or quoted price is set, the effects on the company, customers, and competitors must be assessed.

Company Effects. For a firm with several products, a decision on the price of a single product must also consider the impact on the demand for other products in the line. IBM has an enviable record of assessing the impact of a price change in a mainframe computer on the substitutes (its other mainframe computers) and complements (its peripheral equipment) in its product line. In contrast, IBM has often struggled in its attempts to position its personal computers by price points as new models are added to its line.[15]

Customer Effects. In setting price, retailers weigh factors heavily that satisfy the perceptions or expectations of ultimate consumers, such as the customary prices for a variety of consumer products. Retailers have found that they should not price their store brands 20 to 25 percent below manufacturers' brands. When they do, consumers often view the lower price as signalling lower quality and don't buy.[16] Manufacturers and wholesalers must choose prices that result in profit for resellers in the channel to gain their cooperation and support.

ETHICS INSIGHT

Negative-Option Billing Practices Under Attack

Negative-option billing occurs when customers are charged for optional services unless they specifically decline those services. This practice has been prohibited for some time in the United States by the Federal Communications Commission. In Canada, however, public discussion and initiatives to amend the Consumer Protection Act did not begin until late 1994 when consumers reacted to *Rogers Cablesystems* billing practices for new specialty TV channels.

On January 25, 1995, Joan Smallwood, the minister of consumer services, announced her intention to draft an amendment to the Consumer Protection Act. The amendment would prohibit billing for services not specifically requested. It would also restrict the taking of payment directly from a subscriber's bank account. If the subscriber had opted not to take the new channels, Rogers would have to refund any direct withdrawals used to pay for the extra cable service within 15 days, or

pay a refund of $100 or three times the refund's value, whichever is greater.

While legislation is pending, Rogers has adopted a voluntary set of negative-option guidelines developed by the cable industry in response to negative consumer reaction. These guidelines include a four-month, money-back guarantee if customers are not satisfied.

1. What factors may explain why an organization would practice negative-option billing? (You may wish to refer back to Figure 4–2 in Chapter 4 as a guide for your response to this question).

2. Should negative-option billing be prohibited by law? Why or why not?

SOURCES: Adapted from Michael Burgi, "Cable Billing Practices Under Attack," *Adweek (Eastern Edition),* June 20, 1994, p. 12, and Michael McCullough, "Negative Billing To Go In B.C.," *Marketing,* March 20, 1995, p. 3.

Consideration of the customer can sometimes have serious ethical overtones, particularly in the cable and telecommunications industry (see the Ethics Insight).

Competitive Effects. A manager's pricing decision is immediately apparent to most competitors, who may react with price changes of their own. Therefore, a manager who sets a final list or quoted price must anticipate potential price responses from competitors.

STEP 6: MAKE SPECIAL ADJUSTMENTS TO THE LIST OR QUOTED PRICE

When you receive a quoted price of $5,000 from a contractor to build a new kitchen, the pricing sequence ends with the last step just described: setting the list or quoted price. But when you are a manufacturer of M&M's candies or gas grills and sell your product to dozens or hundreds of wholesalers and retailers in your channel of distribution, you may need to make a variety of special adjustments to the list or quoted price. Wholesalers also must adjust list or quoted prices they set for retailers. Three special adjustments to the list or quoted price are discounts, allowances, and geographical adjustments (Figure 11–8).

Discounts

Discounts are reductions from list price that a seller gives a buyer as a reward for some activity of the buyer that is favourable to the seller. Four kinds of discounts are especially important in marketing strategy: quantity, seasonal, trade (functional), and cash discounts.

Quantity Discounts. To encourage customers to buy larger quantities of a product, firms at all levels in the channel of distribution offer *quantity discounts,* which

FIGURE 11–8
Three special adjustments
to list or quoted price.

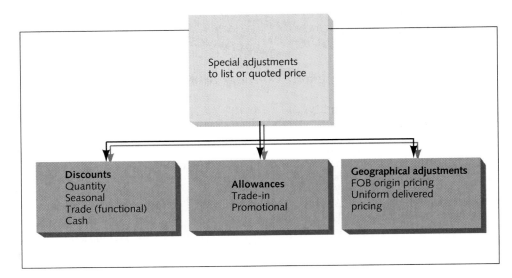

are reductions in unit costs for a larger order.[17] For example, an instant photocopying service might set a price of 10 cents a copy for copies 1 to 25, 9 cents a copy for 26 to 100, and 8 cents a copy for 101 or more. Because the photocopying service gets more of the buyer's business and has longer production runs that reduce its order-handling costs, it is willing to pass on some of the cost savings in the form of quantity discounts to the buyer.

Seasonal Discounts. To encourage buyers to stock inventory earlier than their normal demand would require, manufacturers often use seasonal discounts. A firm like Toro, which manufactures lawn mowers and snow throwers, offers seasonal discounts to encourage wholesalers and retailers to stock up on lawn mowers in January and February and on snow throwers in July and August—five or six months before the seasonal demand by ultimate consumers. This enables Toro to smooth out seasonal manufacturing peaks and troughs, thereby contributing to more efficient production.

Trade (Functional) Discounts. To reward wholesalers and retailers for marketing functions they will perform in the future, a manufacturer often gives trade, or functional, discounts. These reductions off the list or base price are offered to resellers in the channel of distribution on the basis of the marketing activities they are expected to perform in the future.

Traditional trade discounts have been established in various product lines such as hardware, food, and pharmaceutical items. Although the manufacturer may suggest the trade discounts, the sellers are free to alter the discount schedule depending on their competitive situation.

Cash Discounts. To encourage retailers to pay their bills quickly, manufacturers offer them cash discounts. Suppose a retailer receives a bill quoted at $1,000, 2/10 net 30. This means that the bill for the product is $1,000, but the retailer can take a 2 percent discount ($1,000 − 0.02 = $20) if payment is made within 10 days and send a check for $980. If the payment cannot be made within 10 days, the total amount of $1,000 is due within 30 days. It is usually understood by the buyer that an interest charge will be added after the first 30 days of free credit.

Toro uses seasonal discounts to stimulate consumer demand.

USUALLY THE BEST COSTS A LITTLE MORE BUT RIGHT NOW IT COSTS A LITTLE LESS

Regular Price	$1149.95
Pre-season Savings	$ 200.00
Sale Price	**$ 949.95**

2-YEAR LIMITED WARRANTY • TORO LASTS

Model 56125

COMPACT, ECONOMICAL RIDER FOR AVERAGE SIZE YARDS

- Dependable 7 hp Tecumseh engine
- Key-Lectric® starting; five forward speeds
- 25" Whirlwind® deck
- Optional Easy Empty® Catcher

It may seem early to buy a riding mower, but to save $200 you're right on time. During our Toro pre-season rider sale we're taking $200 off the regular price. But you better hurry. Once it's time to mow the lawn, this sale will be over.

Ask us about our Toro-sponsored consumer-credit programs. We make it easy to step up to a Toro.

 **Haven't you done without a Toro long enough?®**

Canadian Tire's cash
bonus coupon.

Retailers also provide cash discounts to consumers to eliminate the cost of credit granted to consumers.[18] These discounts take the form of discount-for-cash policies. For example, Canadian Tire probably has one of the oldest discounts-for-cash concepts in Canada. They offer 3 percent off for cash purchases in the form of cash-bonus coupons that consumers use against their next purchases.

Allowances

Allowances—like discounts—are reductions from list or quoted prices to buyers for performing some activity.

Trade-In Allowances. A new car dealer can offer a substantial reduction in the list price of that new Ford Taurus by offering you a trade-in allowance of $1000 for your 1987 Chevrolet. A trade-in allowance is a price reduction given when a used product is part of the payment on a new product. Trade-ins are an effective way to lower the price a buyer has to pay without formally reducing the list price.

Promotional Allowances. Sellers in the channel of distribution can qualify for *promotional allowances* for undertaking certain advertising or selling activities to promote a product. Various types of allowances include an actual cash payment or an extra amount of "free goods" (such as a free case of pizzas to a retailer for every dozen cases purchased). Frequently, a portion of these savings is passed on to the consumer.[19]

Geographical Adjustments

Geographical adjustments are made by manufacturers or even wholesalers to list or quoted prices to reflect the cost of transportation of the products from seller to buyer. The two general methods for quoting prices related to transportation costs are FOB origin pricing and uniform delivered pricing.

FOB Origin Pricing. *FOB* means "free on board" some vehicle at some location, which means the seller pays the cost of loading the product onto the vehicle that is used (such as a barge, railroad car, or truck). **FOB origin pricing** usually involves the seller's naming the location of this loading as the seller's factory or warehouse (such as "FOB Toronto" or "FOB factory"). The title to the goods passes to the buyer at the point of loading, so the buyer becomes responsible for picking the specific mode of transportation, for all the transportation costs, and for subsequent handling of the product.

Uniform Delivered Pricing. When a **uniform delivered pricing** method is used, the price the seller quotes includes all transportation costs. It is quoted in a contract as "FOB buyer's location," and the seller selects the mode of transportation, pays the freight charges, and is responsible for any damage that may occur, since the seller retains title to the goods until delivered to the buyer.

Multiple-zone pricing (also called corridor pricing) is a form of uniform delivered pricing which is used when an organization divides its selling territory into geographic areas, or zones. The delivered price to all buyers within any one zone is the same, but prices across zones may vary depending on the transportation cost to the zone and other factors such as the level of competition and demand within the zone. This system is used in setting prices on long-distance phone calls and in global price setting. (For a description of this type of global price setting read Application Case 11–2 at the end of this chapter.)

Basing-point pricing involves selecting one or more geographical locations (basing points) from which the list price for products plus freight expenses are charged to the buyer. For example, a company might designate Montreal as the basing point and charge all buyers a list price of $100 plus freight from Montreal to their location. Basing-point pricing methods have been used in the steel, cement, and lumber industries, where freight expenses are a significant part of the total cost to the buyer and products are largely undifferentiated.

Legal and Regulatory Aspects of Pricing

Arriving at a final price is clearly a complex process. The task is further complicated by legal and regulatory restrictions. Chapter 3 described the regulatory environment of companies. Here we elaborate on the specific laws and regulations affecting pricing decisions. Five pricing practices have received the most scrutiny: price-fixing, price discrimination, deceptive pricing, predatory pricing and delivered pricing.

Price-Fixing. A conspiracy among firms to set prices for a product is termed *price-fixing*. Price-fixing is illegal per se under the Competition Act (*per se* means in and of itself). When two or more competitors explicitly or implicitly set prices, this practice is called *horizontal price-fixing*.

Vertical price-fixing involves controlling agreements between independent buyers and sellers (a manufacturer and a retailer) whereby sellers are required not to sell products below a minimum retail price. This practice, called *resale price maintenance* is also illegal under provisions of the Competition Act.

It is important to recognize that a manufacturer's "suggested retail price" is not illegal per se. The issue of legality arises only when manufacturers enforce such a practice by coercion. Furthermore, there appears to be a movement toward a "rule of reason" in pricing cases. This rule holds that circumstances surrounding a practice must be considered before making a judgment about its legality. The "rule of reason" perspective is the direct opposite of the per se rule, which holds that a practice is illegal in and of itself.

Price Discrimination. The Competition Act prohibits *price discrimination*—the practice of charging different prices to different buyers for goods of like grade and quality. However, it is not easy to prove that price discrimination has actually taken place. The

FIGURE 11–9
Five most common
deceptive pricing
practices.

- *Bait and switch.* A deceptive practice exists when a firm offers a very low price on a product (the bait) to attract customers to a store. Once in the store, the customer is persuaded to purchase a higher-priced item (the switch) by means of a variety of tricks, including downgrading the promoted item and not having the item in stock or refusing to take orders for the item.
- *Bargains conditional on other purchases.* This practice may exist when a buyer is offered "1-cent sales," "buy 1, get 1 free," and "Get 2 for the price of 1." Such pricing is legal only if the first items are sold at the regular price, not a price inflated for the offer.
- *Comparable value comparisons.* Advertising such as "retail value $100, our price $85" is deceptive if a verified and substantial number of stores in the market area did not price the item at $100.
- *Comparisons with suggested prices.* A claim that a price is below a manufacturer's suggested or list price may be deceptive if few or no sales occur at that price in a retailer's market area.
- *Former price comparison.* When a seller represents a price as reduced, the item must have been offered "in good faith" at a higher price for a substantial previous period.

Competition Act also covers promotional allowances. To legally offer promotional allowances to buyers, the seller must do so on a proportionally equal basis to all buyers distributing the seller's products. In general, this rule of reason applies frequently in price discrimination cases and is often applied to cases involving flexible pricing practices of firms.

Deceptive Pricing. Price deals that mislead consumers fall into the category of deceptive pricing. Deceptive pricing is outlawed by the Competition Act. Consumer and Corporate Affairs Canada monitors such practices. The five most common deceptive pricing practices are described in Figure 11–9. As you read, it should be clear that laws cannot be passed and enforced to protect consumers and competitors against all of these practices. So it is essential to rely on the ethical standards of those making and publicizing pricing decisions.

Predatory Pricing. Predatory pricing is the practice of charging a very low price for a product with the intent of driving competitors out of business. Once competitors have been driven out, the firm raises its prices. This practice is illegal under the Competition Act. Proving the presence of this practice has been difficult and expensive because it must be shown that the predator explicitly attempted to destroy a competitor and the predatory price was below the defendant's average cost.

Delivered Pricing. Delivered pricing is the practice of refusing a customer delivery of an article on the same trade terms as other customers in the same location. It is a noncriminal offense, but the Competition Tribunal can prohibit suppliers from engaging in such a practice.

LEARNING CHECK

1. Why would a seller choose a flexible-price policy over a one-price policy?

2. Why are trade (functional) discounts used?

3. What are the five most common deceptive pricing practices?

LEARNING OBJECTIVE REINFORCEMENT

1. Understand the importance of price in marketing strategy. Price is the money or other considerations exchanged for the ownership or use of a product or service. Pricing decisions are critical because consumers often use price to indicate value when it is paired with the perceived benefits of a product or service. Pricing is also a critical decision made by marketing executives, because price has a direct effect on a firm's profit. Price has a direct effect on profit because if affects the quantity sold and it has an influence on both total revenue and total cost.

2. Explain a step-by-step procedure organizations can use to set prices. The importance of price in the marketing mix necessitates an understanding of six major steps involved in the process organizations go through in setting prices: identify pricing constraints and objectives; estimate demand and revenue; determine cost, volume, and profit relationships; select an approximate price level; set list or quoted price, and make special adjustments to list or quoted price.

3. Recognize the constraints and objectives a firm has in setting prices. The many factors that limit the latitude of prices a firm may set are pricing constraints. Consumer demand is clearly a constraint that affects the price that can be charged. Other constraints on price are set by factors within the organization: newness of the product, whether it is part of a product line, and cost of and flexibility in charging a price. Competitive factors such as the nature of competition and prices set by competitors restrict an organization's abil-

ity to set price. Legal and regulatory factors also act to limit the latitude of prices a firm may set.

Goals that specify the role of price in an organization's marketing and strategic plan are known as pricing objectives. Although profit maximization is a common pricing objective, organizations often set sales, market share, unit volume, customer value, and social responsibility objectives which can tie in directly with the organization's pricing policies.

4. Distinguish among three methods of selecting an initial approximate price level. Three general methods of finding an approximate price level for a product or service are demand-based, cost-based, and competition-based. Demand-based pricing stresses consumer demand and revenue implications of pricing and include six types: skimming, penetration, prestige, price lining, odd–even, and value-based pricing.

Cost-based pricing methods emphasize the cost aspects of pricing and include three types: cost-plus, target profit, and experience curve pricing. Competition-based pricing methods stress what competitors or the marketplace is doing and include four types: customary; above-, at-, or below-market; loss-leader, and sealed-bid pricing.

5. Describe the five pricing practices that receive the most scrutiny on ethical and legal grounds. The five pricing practices that receive the most scrutiny are price-fixing, price discrimination, deceptive pricing, predatory pricing, and delivered pricing.

KEY TERMS AND CONCEPTS

price p. 260
value p. 260
pricing constraints p. 262
pricing objectives p. 264
demand curve p. 266
total revenue p. 267
average revenue p. 267
marginal revenue p. 267
price elasticity of demand p. 268
marginal analysis p. 269
break-even analysis p. 269

break-even point p. 269
skimming pricing p. 270
penetration pricing p. 270
prestige pricing p. 271
price lining p. 271
odd-even pricing p. 271
value-based pricing p. 271
cost-plus pricing p. 272
target profit pricing p. 272
experience curve pricing p. 273
customary pricing p. 273

above- at-, or below-market
    pricing p. 273
loss-leader pricing p. 274
sealed-bid pricing p. 274
discounts p. 275
FOB origin pricing p. 278
uniform delivered pricing p. 279
predatory pricing p. 280
delivered pricing p. 280

CHAPTER QUESTIONS AND APPLICATIONS

1. How would the price equation apply to the purchase price of (*a*) gasoline, (*b*) an airline ticket, and (*c*) a checking account?

2. What would be your response to the statement, "Profit maximization is the only legitimate pricing objective for the firm"?

3. A student theatre group at a college has developed a demand schedule that shows the relationship between ticket prices and demand based on a student survey, as follows:

Ticket Price	Number of Students Who Would Buy
$1	300
2	250
3	200
4	150
5	100

(a) Graph the demand curve and the total revenue curve based on these data. What ticket price might be set based on this analysis?

(b) What other factors should be considered before the final price is set?

4. Identify and briefly explain the various types of competitive markets.

5. Under what conditions would a camera manufacturer adopt a skimming price approach for a new product? A penetration approach?

6. What are the similarities and differences between skimming pricing, prestige pricing, and above-market pricing?

7. A producer of microwave ovens has adopted an experience curve pricing approach for its new model. The firm believes it can reduce the cost of producing the model by 20 percent each time volume doubles. The cost to produce the first unit was $1,000. What would be the approximate cost of the 4,096th unit?

8. Is it ethical to charge different customers different prices for the same product or service? Is it legal? Discuss.

NOTE: Attempt questions 9 and 10 after reading Appendix C which follows this chapter.

9. Darling Toiletries, Inc., has developed a new cologne it has branded as Rossco Cologne. Unit variable costs are 45 cents for a 3-ounce bottle, and heavy advertising expenditures in the first year would result in total fixed costs of $900,000. Rossco Cologne is priced at $7.50 for a 3-ounce bottle. How many bottles must be sold to break even?

10. Suppose the marketing executives for Darling Toiletries reduced the price of Rossco Cologne to $6.50 for a 3-ounce bottle and the fixed costs were increased to $1,100,000. Suppose further that the unit variable cost remained at 45 cents for a 3-ounce bottle.

(a) How many bottles must be sold to break even?

(b) What dollar profit level would Rossco achieve if 200,000 bottles were sold?

APPLICATION CASE 11-1
PRICING PROBLEMS: PRICING IN A GLOBAL SETTING (A)

More often than not, international pricing is a big headache for marketing managers. Why? Long-proven price structures are collapsing in the European Union, with similar developments imminent in the North American Free Trade Agreement (NAFTA) and the global market in general. Gone are the days when markets were neatly separable, and imports were solely a concern of exotic, high-priced products such as French perfumes or Swiss watches. Today almost every product is affected by the pressures for international pricing adjustments.

A leading manufacturer for consumer products distributed through large local and pan-European retailers recently had its biggest retail customer request that all products be supplied at the lowest European price. The company had to comply, but the 20 percent price decline across Europe resulted in a profit disaster.

Enormous price differentials exist between countries. For identical consumer products, prices typically deviate 30 percent to 150 percent. In some markets, the differentials are more extreme. A certain drug costs exactly five times more in Germany than in Italy. If you live in France but buy your car elsewhere, you can save 24.3 percent on a Citroen, 18.2 percent on a Peugeot, or 33 percent on a Volkswagen Jetta. These differentials are rooted in consumer behaviour, distribution systems, varying market positions, and tax structures—and

they are not going to disappear quickly. Neither the European Union nor NAFTA will settle many price differentials in the foreseeable future.

According to global pricing expert Hermann Simon, "The skill in pricing lies in exploiting differences in customers' willingness to pay. To take full advantage of this . . . we have to study and compare consumers, competitors, and distributors." However, pricing is typically not based on such study but rather it is based on intuition—or experience-driven—and it tends to be chaotically decentralized. Managers devote much more time and energy to costs than to prices, though both are equally important in the making of profit.

QUESTIONS

1. How does this process of price setting differ from the six-step pricing process discussed in this chapter (see Figure 11–2)?
2. How would global price setting be different if country-to-country prices were harmonized by trading block agreements such as NAFTA?
3. What suggestions do you have to improve the price-setting situation described in this case?

SOURCE: Adapted from Hermann Simon, "Pricing Problems in a Global Setting," *Marketing News*, (October 9, 1995), pp. 4, 8.

APPLICATION CASE 11-2
PRICING PROBLEMS: PRICING IN A GLOBAL SETTING (B)

As discussed in Application Case 11–1, more often than not international pricing is a big headache for marketing managers. However, according to global pricing expert Hermann Simon, there are several solutions available for those marketing managers who wish to optimize pricing decisions in a global setting.

The worst, yet easiest solution is to let all prices slide to the lowest common denominator. This is often the worst solution because it can lead to profit disasters. An alternative is to raise prices to the highest level. This is usually unadvisable, as well, because it can mean giving up significant, if not all, market share from some of the low-price countries. In extreme cases this alternative is actually advisable. If, for instance, a very low price in Austria causes a price decline of 10 percent in Germany, it is better to pull out of the Austrian market.

The establishment of an international price corridor (or multiple-zone pricing) is another solution. According to Simon, corridors typically improve profits by 15 percent to 25 percent. Relative to this improvement, the costs of such a system are insignificant. This solution takes into account both the differences between countries and mounting alignment pressures. To be effective, the corridor boundaries have to be determined by the company headquarters and its country subsidiaries. Moreover, no one country should be allowed to set its prices outside those established for the corridor. Countries with lower prices have to raise them; countries with prices above the limit have to lower them.

Hermann Simon advises that price setting under a corridor system should take into account such factors as market data for the individual countries in the corridor, price sensitivities in the countries, parallel imports resulting from price differences, currency exchange rates, and data on competition and distribution.

It is clear that corridors require a stronger centralization of pricing competence. This runs against decentralization tendencies, but if country markets are merging, centralization is a necessary consequence. One country destroying the pricing of a whole region and profiting is unacceptable.

QUESTIONS

1. Is the pricing corridor concept consistent with the six-step pricing process discussed in this chapter (see Figure 11–2)?

2. What role, if any, should cultural difference play when implementing a price corridor system?

3. What are the advantages and disadvantages of centralization in global pricing situations?

SOURCE: Adapted from Hermann Simon, "Pricing Problems in a Global Setting," *Marketing News,* (October 9, 1995), pp. 4, 8.

APPENDIX C

Financial Analysis in Marketing

Basic concepts from accounting and finance provide valuable tools for marketing executives. This appendix describes an actual company's use of accounting and financial concepts and illustrates how they assist the owner in making marketing decisions.

An accomplished artist and calligrapher, Jane Westerlund, decided to apply some of her experience to the picture framing business. She bought an existing retail frame store, The Caplow Company, from a friend who owned the business and wanted to retire. She avoided the do-it-yourself end of the framing business and chose two kinds of business activities: (1) cutting the frame, mats, and glass for customers who brought in their own pictures or prints to be framed and (2) selling prints and posters that she had purchased from wholesalers.

To understand how accounting, finance, and marketing relate to each other, let's analyze the operating statement for her frame shop, some general ratios of interest that are derived from the operating statement, and some ratios that pertain specifically to her pricing decisions.

The Operating Statement

The operating statement (also called an *income statement*) summarizes the profitability of a business firm for a specific time period, usually a month, quarter, or year. The title of the operating statement for The Caplow Company shows it is for a one-year period (Figure C–1). The purpose of an operating statement is to show the profit or loss of the firm and the revenues and expenses that led to that profit or loss.

The left side of Figure C–1 shows that there are three key elements to all operating statements: sales of the firm's goods and services, costs incurred in making and selling the goods and services, and profit or loss, which is the difference between sales and costs.

Sales Elements. The sales element of Figure C–1 has four terms that need explanation:

- *Gross sales* are the total amount billed to customers. Dissatisfied customers or errors may reduce the gross sales through returns or allowances.
- *Returns* occur when a customer gives the item purchased back to the seller, who either refunds the purchase price or allows the customer a credit on subsequent purchases. In any event, the seller now owns the item again.
- *Allowances* are given when a customer is dissatisfied with the item purchased and the seller reduces the original purchase price. Unlike returns, in the case of allowances the buyer owns the item.
- *Net sales* are simply gross sales minus returns and allowances.

285

THE CAPLOW COMPANY
OPERATING STATEMENT
FOR THE YEAR ENDING DECEMBER 31, 1997

Sales	Gross Sales			$80,500
	Less: Returns and allowances			500
	Net sales			80,000
Costs	Cost of goods sold:			
	Beginning inventory at cost		$ 6,000	
	Purchases at billed cost	$21,000		
	Less: Purchase discounts	300		
	Purchases at net cost	20,700		
	Plus freight-in	100		
	Net cost of delivered purchases		20,800	
	Direct labour (framing)		14,200	
	Cost of goods available for sale		41,000	
	Less: Ending inventory at cost		5,000	
	Cost of goods sold			36,000
	Gross margin (gross profit)			44,000
	Expenses:			
	Selling expenses:			
	Sales salaries	2,000		
	Advertising expense	3,000		
	Total selling expense		5,000	
	Administrative expenses:			
	Owner's salary	18,000		
	Bookkeeper's salary	1,200		
	Office supplies	300		
	Total administrative expense		19,500	
	General expenses:			
	Depreciation expense	1,000		
	Interest expense	500		
	Rent expense	2,100		
	Utility expenses (heat, electricity)	3,000		
	Repairs and maintenance	2,300		
	Insurance	2,000		
	Social insurance and Canada Pension	2,200		
	Total general expense		13,100	
	Total expenses			37,600
Profit or loss	Profit before taxes			6,400

The operating statement for The Caplow Company shows:

Gross sales	$80,500
Less: Returns and allowances	500
Net sales	$80,000

The low level of returns and allowances suggests the shop generally has done a good job in satisfying customers, which is essential in building the repeat business necessary for success.

Cost Elements. The *cost of goods sold* is the total cost of the products sold during the period. This item varies according to the kind of business. A retail store purchases finished goods and resells them to customers without reworking them in any way. In contrast, a manufacturing firm combines raw and semifinished materials and parts, uses labour and overhead to rework these into finished goods, and then sells them to customers. All these activities are reflected in the cost of goods sold item on a manufacturer's operating statement. Note that the frame shop has some features of a pure retailer (prints and posters it buys that are resold without alteration) and a pure manufacturer (assembling the raw materials of moulding, matting, and glass to form a completed frame).

Some terms that relate to cost of goods sold need clarification:

- *Inventory* is the physical material that is purchased from suppliers, may or may not be reworked, and is available for sale to customers. In the frame shop, inventory includes moulding, matting, glass, prints, and posters.
- *Purchase discounts* are reductions in the original billed price for reasons like prompt payment of the bill or the quantity bought.
- *Direct labour* is the cost of the labour used in producing the finished product. For the frame shop, this is the cost of producing the completed frames from the moulding, matting, and glass.
- *Gross margin (gross profit)* is the money remaining to manage the business, sell the products or services, and give some profit. Gross margin is net sales minus cost of goods sold.

The two right-hand columns in Figure C–1 between "Net sales" and "Gross margin" calculate the cost of goods sold:

Net sales		$80,000
Cost of goods sold		
Beginning inventory at cost	$ 6,000	
Net cost of delivered purchases	20,800	
Direct labour (framing)	14,200	
Cost of goods available for sale	41,000	
Less: ending inventory at cost	5,000	
Cost of goods sold		36,000
Gross margin (gross profit)		$44,000

This section considers the beginning and ending inventories, the net cost of purchases delivered during the year, and the cost of the direct labour going into making the frames. Subtracting the $36,000 cost of goods sold from the $80,000 net sales gives the $44,000 gross margin.

Three major categories of expenses are shown in Figure C–1 below the gross margin:

- *Selling expenses* are the costs of selling the product or service produced by the firm. For The Caplow Company there are two such selling expenses: sales salaries of part-time employees waiting on customers, and the advertising expense of simple newspaper ads and direct-mail ads sent to customers.
- *Administrative expenses* are the costs of managing the business, and, for The Caplow Company, include three expenses: the owner's salary, a part-time bookkeeper's salary, and office supplies expense.
- *General expenses* are miscellaneous costs not covered elsewhere. For the frame shop these include seven items: depreciation expense (on equipment), interest expense, rent expense, utility expenses, repairs and maintenance expense, insurance expense, and social insurance and Canada Pension.

As shown in Figure C–1, selling, administrative, and general expenses total $37,600 for The Caplow Company.

Profit Element. What the company has earned, the *profit before taxes,* is found by subtracting cost of goods sold and expenses from net sales. For The Caplow Company, Figure C–1 shows that profit before taxes is $6,400.

General Operating Ratios to Analyze Operations

Looking only at the elements of Caplow's operating statement that extend to the right-hand column highlights the firm's performance on some important dimensions. Using operating ratios such as *expense-to-sales ratios* for expressing basic expense or profit elements as a percentage of net sales gives further insights:

Element in Operating Statement	Dollar Value	Percentage of Net Sales
Gross sales	$80,500	
Less: Returns and allowances	500	
Net sales	80,000	100%
Less: Cost of goods sold	36,000	45
Gross margin	44,000	55
Less: Total expenses	37,600	47
Profit (or loss) before taxes	6,400	8%

Westerlund can use this information to compare her firm's performance from one time period to the next. To do so, it is especially important that she keep the same definitions for each element of her operating statement. Performance comparisons between periods are more difficult if she changes definitions for the accounting elements in the operating statement.

She can use either the dollar values or the operating ratios (the value of the element of the operating statement divided by net sales) to analyze the firm's performance. However, the operating ratios are more valuable than the dollar values for two reasons: the simplicity of working with percentages rather than dollars and the availability of operating ratios of typical firms in the same industry, which are published by Dun & Bradstreet and trade associations. Thus, Westerlund can compare her firm's performance not only with that of *other* frame shops but also with that of *small* frame shops that have annual net sales, for example, of under $100,000. In this way she can identify where her operations are better or worse than other, similar firms'. For example, if trade association data showed a typical frame shop of her size had a ratio of cost of goods sold to net sales of 37 percent, compared with her 45 percent, she might consider steps to reduce this cost through purchase discounts, reducing inbound freight charges, finding lower-cost suppliers, and so on.

Ratios to Use in Setting and Evaluating Price

Using The Caplow Company as an example, we can study four ratios that relate closely to setting a price: (1) markup, (2) markdown, (3) stockturns, and (4) return on investment. These terms are defined in Figure C–2 and explained in the following.

Markup Both markup and gross margin refer to the amount added to the cost of goods sold to arrive at the selling price, and they may be expressed either in dollar or percentage terms. However, the term *markup* is more commonly used in setting retail prices. Suppose the average price Westerlund charges for a framed picture is $80. Then in terms of the first two definitions in Figure C–2 and the earlier information from the operating statement:

Element of Price	Dollar Value
Cost of goods sold	$36
Markup (or gross margin)	44
Selling price	$80

The third definition in Figure C–2 gives the percentage markup on selling price:

$$\text{Markup on selling price (\%)} = \frac{\text{Markup}}{\text{Selling price}} \times 100$$

$$= \frac{44}{80} \times 100 = 55\%$$

FIGURE C–2 How to calculate selling price, markup, markdown, stockturn, and return on investment.

Name of Financial Element or Ratio	What it Measures	Equation
Selling price ($)	Price customer sees	Cost of goods sold (COGS) + Markup
Markup ($)	Dollars added to COGS to arrive at selling price	Selling price − COGS
Markup on selling price (%)	Relates markup to selling price	$\dfrac{\text{Markup}}{\text{Selling price}} \times 100 = \dfrac{\text{Selling price} - \text{COGS}}{\text{Selling price}} \times 100$
Markup on cost (%)	Relates markup to cost	$\dfrac{\text{Markup}}{\text{COGS}} \times 100 = \dfrac{\text{Selling price} - \text{COGS}}{\text{COGS}}$
Markdown (%)	Ability of firm to sell its products at initial selling price	$\dfrac{\text{Markdowns}}{\text{Net sales}} \times 100$
Stockturn rate	Ability of firm to move its inventory quickly	$\dfrac{\text{COGS}}{\text{Average inventory at cost}}$ or $\dfrac{\text{Net sales}}{\text{Average inventory at selling price}}$
Return on investment (%)	Profit performance of firm compared with money invested in it	$\dfrac{\text{Net profit after taxes}}{\text{Investment}} \times 100$

and the percentage markup on cost is obtained as follows:

$$\text{Markup on cost (\%)} = \frac{\text{Markup}}{\text{Cost of goods sold}} \times 100$$

$$= \frac{44}{36} \times 100 = 122.2\%$$

Inexperienced retail clerks sometimes fail to distinguish between the two definitions of markup, which (as the preceding calculations show) can represent a tremendous difference, so it is essential to know whether the base is cost or selling price. Marketers generally use selling price as the base for talking about "markups" unless they specifically state they are using cost as a base.

Retailers and wholesalers that rely heavily on cost-plus pricing (discussed in Chapter 11) often use standardized tables that convert markup on selling price to markup on cost, and vice versa.

Markdown. A *markdown* is a reduction in a retail price that is necessary if the item will not sell at the full selling price to which it has been marked up. The item might not sell for a variety of reasons: the selling price was set too high or the item is out of style or has become soiled or damaged. The seller "takes a markdown" by lowering the price to sell it, thereby converting it to cash to buy future inventory that will sell faster.

The markdown percentage cannot be calculated directly from the operating statement. As shown in the fifth item of Figure C–2, the numerator of the markdown percentage is the total dollar markdowns. Markdowns are reductions in the prices of goods that are purchased by customers. The denominator is net sales.

Suppose The Caplow Company had a total of $700 in markdowns on the prints and posters that are stocked and available for sale. Since the frames are custom made for individual customers, there is little reason for a markdown there. Caplow's markdown percent is then:

$$\text{Markdown (\%)} = \frac{\text{Markdowns}}{\text{Net sales}} \times 100$$

$$= \frac{700}{\$80,000} \times 100$$

$$= 0.875\%$$

Other kinds of retailers often have markdown ratios several times this amount. For example, women's dress stores have markdowns of about 25 percent, and menswear stores have markdowns of about 2 percent.

Stockturn Rate. A business firm is anxious to have its inventory move quickly, or "turn over." Stockturn rate, or simply stockturns, measures this inventory movement. For a retailer a slow stockturn rate may show it is buying merchandise customers don't want, so this is a critical measure of performance. When a firm sells only a single product, one convenient way to measure stockturn rate is simply to divide its cost of goods sold by average inventory at cost. The sixth item in Figure C–2 shows how to calculate stockturn rate using information in the operating statement:

$$\text{Stockturn rate} = \frac{\text{Cost of goods sold}}{\text{Average inventory at cost}}$$

The dollar amount of average inventory at cost is calculated by adding the beginning and ending inventories for the year and dividing by 2 to get the average. From Caplow's operating statement, we have:

$$\text{Stockturn rate} = \frac{\text{Cost of goods sold}}{\text{Average inventory at cost}}$$

$$= \frac{\text{Cost of goods sold}}{\dfrac{\text{Beginning inventory} + \text{Ending inventory}}{2}}$$

$$= \frac{\$36,000}{\dfrac{\$6,000 + \$5,000}{2}}$$

$$= \frac{\$36,000}{\$5,500}$$

$$= 6.5 \text{ stockturns per year}$$

What is considered a "good" stockturn varies by the kind of industry. For example, supermarkets have limited shelf space for thousands of new products from manufacturers each year, so they watch stockturn carefully by product line. The stockturn rate in supermarkets for breakfast foods is about 17 times per year, for pet food is about 22 times, and for paper products is about 25 times per year.

Return on Investment. A better measure of the performance of a firm than the amount of profit it makes in a year is its ROI, which is the ratio of net income to the investment used to earn that net income. To calculate ROI, it is necessary to subtract income taxes from profit before taxes to obtain net income, then divide this figure by the investment that can be found on a firm's balance sheet (another accounting statement that shows the firm's assets, liabilities, and net worth). While financial and accounting experts have many definitions for "investment," an often-used definition is "total assets."

    For our purposes, let's assume that Westerlund has total assets (investment) of $20,000 in The Caplow Company, which covers inventory, store fixtures, and framing equipment. If she pays $1,000 in income taxes, her store's net income is $5,400, so her ROI is given by the seventh item in Figure C–2:

$$\text{Return on investment} = \text{Net income} / \text{investment} \times 100$$
$$= \$5,400 / \$20,000 \times 100$$
$$= 27\%$$

If Westerlund wants to improve her ROI next year, the strategies she might take are found in this alternative equation for ROI:

$$ROI = \text{Net sales / investment} \times \text{Net income / net sales}$$
$$= \text{Investment turnover} \times \text{Profit margin}$$

This equation suggests that The Caplow Company's ROI can be improved by raising turnover or increasing profit margin. Increasing stockturns will accomplish the former, whereas lowering cost of goods sold to net sales will cause the latter.

Marginal Analysis and Profit Maximization

Marginal analysis means studying whether revenue received from the sale of an additional product (marginal revenue) is greater than the additional cost of producing and selling it (marginal cost); if it is greater, a firm can reasonably expand its output of that product. Four cost concepts are important in marginal analysis: total cost, fixed cost, variable cost, and marginal cost (Figure C–3).

Marginal analysis is central to the concept of maximizing profits. In Figure C–4A, marginal revenue and marginal cost are graphed. Marginal cost starts out high at lower quantity levels, decreases to a minimum through production and marketing efficiencies, and then rises again as a result of the inefficiencies of overworked labour and equipment. Marginal revenue follows a downward slope. In Figure C–4B, total cost and total revenue curves corresponding to the marginal cost and marginal revenue curves are graphed. Total cost initially rises as quantity increases but increases at the slowest rate at the quantity where marginal cost is lowest. The total revenue curve increases to a maximum and then starts to decline, as shown in Figure C–4B.

The message of marginal analysis, then, is to operate up to the quantity and price level where marginal revenue equals marginal cost (MR = MC). Up to the output quantity at which MR = MC, each increase in total revenue resulting from selling one additional unit exceeds the increase in the total cost of producing and marketing that unit. Beyond the point at which MR = MC, however, the increase in total revenue from selling one more unit is less than the cost of producing and marketing that unit. At the quantity at which MR = MC, the total revenue curve lies farthest above the total cost curve and they are parallel.

- *Total cost (TC)* is the total expense incurred by a firm in producing and marketing a product. Total cost is the sum of fixed cost and variable cost.
- *Fixed cost (FC)* is the sum of the expenses of a firm that are stable and do not change with the quantity of product that is produced and sold. Examples of fixed costs are rent on a building, executive salaries, and insurance.
- *Variable cost (VC)* is the sum of the expenses of a firm that vary directly with the quantity of product that is produced and sold. For example, as the quantity sold doubles, the variable cost doubles. Examples are the direct labour and direct materials used in producing a product and the sales commissions that are tied directly to the quantity sold. As mentioned above:

    TC = FC + VC

- Variable cost expressed on a per unit basis is called *unit variable cost (UVC)*. *Marginal cost (MC)* is the change in total cost that results from producing and marketing one additional unit:

$$MC = \frac{\text{Change in TC}}{\text{1 unit increase in Q}} = \frac{\Delta TC}{\Delta Q}$$

FIGURE C–3
Fundamental cost concepts.

FIGURE C–4
Profit maximization
pricing.

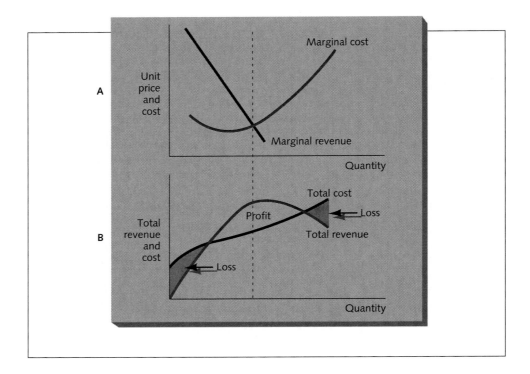

Break-Even Analysis

Marketing managers often employ a simpler approach for looking at cost, volume, and profit relationships. *Break-even analysis* is a technique that analyzes the relationship between total revenue and total cost to determine profitability at various levels of output. The *break-even point (BEP)* is the quantity at which total revenue and total cost are equal and beyond which profit occurs. In terms of the definitions in Figure C–3:

$$BEP_{Quantity} = \frac{Fixed\ cost}{Unit\ price\ -\ Unit\ variable\ cost}$$

Calculating a Break-Even Point.   Assume, for example, Jane Westerlund wishes to determine the number of oval picture mats she must sell to cover her fixed cost associated with the machine needed to manufacture oval-shaped mats. Jane estimated a fixed cost (FC) of $2,000 (for equipment and interest on a bank loan) and a unit variable cost (UVC) of $1 per mat (for labour, matting paper, and other variable cost). If the price (P) is $2 per oval mat, her break-even quantity is 2,000 mats:

$$BEP_{Quantity} = \frac{FC}{P\ -\ UVC} = \frac{\$2,000}{\$2\ -\ \$1} = 2,000\ mats$$

Figure C–5 shows that the break-even quantity at a price of $2 per oval mat is 2,000 mats, since at this quantity total revenue equals total cost. At less than 2,000 mats, Jane incurs a loss; and at more than 2,000 mats, she makes a profit. Figure C–6 shows a graphic presentation of the break-even analysis, called a break-even chart.

FIGURE C–5 Calculating a break-even point.

Quantity Sold (Q)	Price per Mat (P)	Total Revenue (TR) (P × Q)	Unit Variable Cost (UVC)	Total Variable Costs (TVC) (UVC × Q)	Fixed Cost (FC)	Total Cost (TC) (TVC + FC)	Profit (TR − TC)
0	$2	$ 0	$1	$ 0	$2,000	$2,000	$−2,000
1,000	2	2,000	1	1,000	2,000	3,000	−1,000
2,000	2	4,000	1	2,000	2,000	4,000	0
3,000	2	6,000	1	3,000	2,000	5,000	1,000
4,000	2	8,000	1	4,000	2,000	6,000	2,000
5,000	2	10,000	1	5,000	2,000	7,000	3,000
6,000	2	12,000	1	6,000	2,000	8,000	4,000

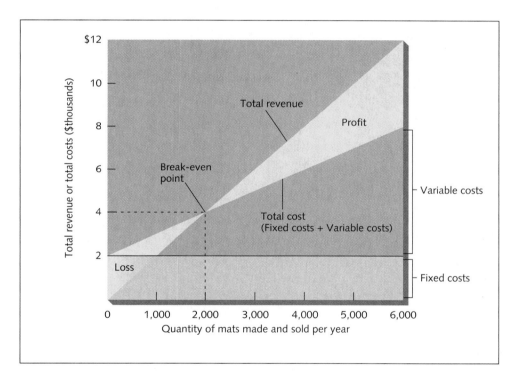

FIGURE C–6
Break-even analysis chart.

Good news for those who worry about their packages just as much as we do.

Presenting GroundTrac from UPS. The ideal delivery service for anybody who would like to know just where on the ground their delivery actually is.

This computerized service option lets you track your ground packages to every address in the forty-eight states, from the day of pickup to the day of delivery.

So now you can obtain such important shipping information as daily status, the scheduled day and time of delivery, as well as delivery verification. And you can do so 24 hours a day, seven days a week, simply by calling us toll-free at 1-800-457-4022.

All of which means you can keep an eye on your long-distance or high-value shipments, even if they're 2,000 miles away.

What's more GroundTrac not only keeps you in touch with your packages, but your money as well.

Immediate delivery confirmation via telephone can help shorten your company's billing cycle, thereby improving cash flow.

For detailed information about GroundTrac and a complete rate chart, just call your UPS account executive.

After all, worrying if your important package arrives on time isn't your job. It's ours.

We run the tightest ship in the shipping business.

CHAPTER 12

Marketing Channels, Wholesaling, and Logistics Management

AFTER READING THIS CHAPTER YOU WILL BE ABLE TO:

1. Explain marketing channels and why intermediaries are needed.

2. Recognize differences between marketing channels for consumer and industrial products and services.

3. Describe the functions performed by intermediaries.

4. Describe factors considered by marketers when making a channel choice.

5. Explain the distinction between physical distribution management and logistics management.

6. Understand the importance of logistics management.

7. Explain the key logistics functions of transportation, warehousing and materials handling, order processing, and inventory management.

UPS's "NEW THINKING" PROVIDES RETAILERS WITH SUPERIOR SERVICE

Dramatic cost savings are possible when efficient transportation systems and information technology are substituted for inventory. Moreover, the best retail concept, products, and marketing communications strategies of a firm may be hurt by a poor system of product distribution. This is why a growing number of Canadian retailers are picking up the telephone to call 1-800-PICK-UPS. United Parcel Service (UPS) is capable of transporting thousands of items from thousands of different suppliers so that they reach the right store aisle, in perfect condition, on time, and in exactly the right quantities. This level of product distribution service enables UPS's retail customers to prosper in today's demanding retail environment.

How do they do it? UPS has adopted a "new thinking" approach to helping Canadian retailers. This approach to distribution management is implemented with the aid of (1) advanced bar coding to speed ordering, receiving, and tracking, (2) a new electronic billing system that eliminates paper invoices, and (3) a seamless North American network to expedite inbound shipments from suppliers located all across the continent. What's more, UPS works with Canadian retailers to implement distribution solutions that are compatible with the retailers' existing technology and processes.[1]

This chapter focuses on marketing channels of distribution and their importance in the marketing mix. It also describes factors that influence the choice and management of marketing channels, including channel conflict and legal considerations. Finally, it describes the concept of logistics management, as well as how firms use logistics systems to balance distribution costs against the need for effective customer service.

NATURE AND IMPORTANCE OF MARKETING CHANNELS

Reaching prospective buyers, either directly or indirectly, is a prerequisite for successful marketing. At the same time, buyers benefit from distribution systems used by firms.

Defining Marketing Channels of Distribution

You see the results of distribution every day. You may have purchased Lay's potato chips at the 7-Eleven store, your lunch at McDonald's, and Levi's jeans at Sears. Each of these items was brought to you by a marketing channel of distribution, or simply a **marketing channel,** which consists of individuals and firms involved in the process of making a product or service available for use or consumption by consumers or industrial users.

Marketing channels make possible the flow of goods from a producer, through intermediaries, to a buyer. Intermediaries go by various names (Figure 12–1) and perform various functions. Some intermediaries actually purchase items from the seller, store them, and resell them to buyers. For example, Nabisco produces cookies and sells them to food wholesalers. The wholesalers then sell the cookies to supermarkets and grocery stores, which in turn sell them to consumers. Other intermediaries such as brokers and agents represent sellers but do not actually take title to products—their role is to bring a seller and a buyer together. Century 21 real estate agents are examples of this type of intermediary. The importance of intermediaries is made even clearer when we consider the functions they perform and the value they create for buyers.

Rationale for Intermediaries

Few consumers appreciate the value created by intermediaries; however, producers recognize that intermediaries make selling goods and services more efficient because they minimize the number of sales contacts necessary to reach a target market. Figure 12–2 shows a simple example of how this comes about in the personal computer industry. Without a retail intermediary (such as Computerland), IBM, Apple, Compaq, and Epson would each have to make four contacts to reach the four buyers shown who are in the target market. However, each producer has to make only one contact when

FIGURE 12–1 Terms used for marketing intermediaries.

Term	Meaning
Middleman	Any intermediary between manufacturer and end user markets
Agent or broker	Any intermediary with legal authority to act on behalf of the manufacturer
Wholesaler	An intermediary who sells to other intermediaries, usually to retailers; usually applies to consumer markets
Retailer	An intermediary who sells to consumers
Distributer	An imprecise term, usually used to describe intermediaries who perform a variety of distribution functions, including selling, maintaining inventories, extending credit, and so on; a more common term in industrial markets, but may also be used to refer to wholesalers
Dealer	An even more imprecise term that can mean the same as distributor, retailer, wholesaler, and so forth

SOURCE: Adapted from F. E. Webster, Jr., *Marketing for Managers* (New York: Harper & Row, 1974), p. 191. Copyright © 1974 by F. E. Webster, Jr. Reprinted by permission of HarperCollins Publishers.

FIGURE 12–2 How intermediaries minimize transactions.

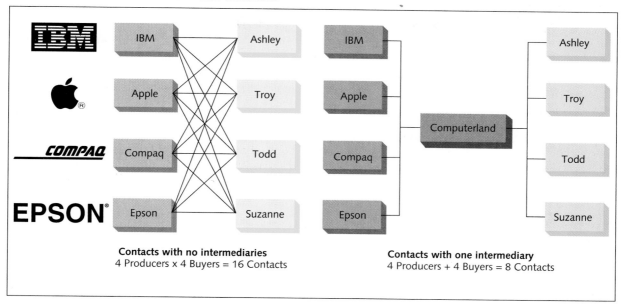

Contacts with no intermediaries
4 Producers × 4 Buyers = 16 Contacts

Contacts with one intermediary
4 Producers + 4 Buyers = 8 Contacts

FIGURE 12–3 Marketing channel functions performed by intermediaries.

Type of Function	Description
Transactional functions	*Buying.* Purchasing products for resale or as an agent for supply of a product
	Selling. Contacting potential customers, demonstrating products, and soliciting orders
	Risk taking Assuming business risks in the ownership of inventory that can become obsolete or deteriorate
Logistical functions	*Assorting.* Creating product assortments from several sources to serve customers
	Storing. Assembling and protecting products at a convenient location to offer better customer service
	Sorting. Purchasing in large quantities and breaking into smaller amounts desired by customers
	Transporting. Physically moving a product to customers
Facilitating functions	*Financing.* Extending credit to customers
	Grading. Inspecting, testing, or judging products and assigning them quality grades
	Marketing information and research. Providing information to customers and suppliers, including competitive conditions and trends

SOURCE: Based on F. E. Webster, Jr., *Industrial Marketing Strategy* (New York: John Wiley & Sons, 1979), pp. 162–63.

Computerland acts as an intermediary. Equally important, the total number of industry transactions is reduced from 16 to 8, which reduces producer cost and hence benefits the consumer.

Functions Performed by Intermediaries. Intermediaries make possible the flow of products from producers to buyers by performing three basic functions (Figure 12–3). Most prominently, intermediaries perform a transactional function that involves buying, selling, and risk taking because they stock merchandise in anticipation of sales.

Intermediaries perform a logistical function evident in the gathering, storing, and dispersing of products. Finally, intermediaries perform facilitating functions, which assist producers in making goods and services more attractive to buyers.

All three groups of functions must be performed in a marketing channel, even though each channel member may not participate in all three. Channel members often negotiate about which specific functions they will perform. Sometimes conflict results and a breakdown in relationships among channel members occurs.

Value Created by Intermediaries. Consumers also benefit from intermediaries. Having the goods and services you want, when you want them, where you want them, and in the form you want them is the ideal result of marketing channels. In more specific terms, marketing channels help create value for consumers.

LEARNING CHECK

1. What is meant by a marketing channel?

2. What are the three basic functions performed by intermediaries?

CHANNEL STRUCTURE AND ORGANIZATION

A product can take many routes on its journey from a producer to buyers, and marketers search for the most efficient route from the many alternatives available.

Marketing Channels for Consumer Goods and Services

Figure 12–4 shows the four most common marketing channels for consumer goods and services. It also shows the number of levels in each marketing channel, as evidenced

FIGURE 12–4
Common marketing channels for consumer goods and services.

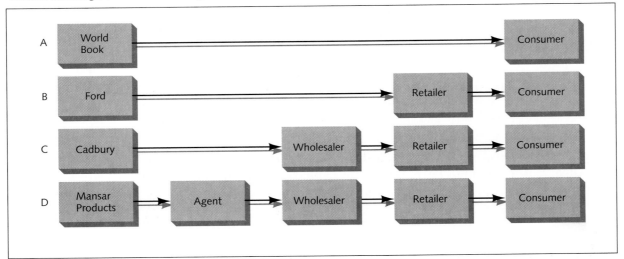

by the number of intermediaries between a producer and ultimate buyers. As the number of intermediaries between producer and buyer increases, the channel is viewed as increasing in length. Thus the producer → wholesaler → retailer → consumer channel is longer than the producer → consumer channel.

Channel A represents a **direct channel,** because a producer and ultimate consumers deal directly with each other. Many products and services are distributed this way. A number of insurance companies sell their financial services using a direct channel. Because there are no intermediaries in a direct channel, the producer must perform all channel functions.

The remaining three channel forms are **indirect channels,** because intermediaries are inserted between the producer and consumers and perform numerous channel functions.

Channel B, with a retailer added, is most common when a retailer is large and can buy in large quantities from a producer or when the cost of inventory makes it too expensive to use a wholesaler. Manufacturers such as GM, Ford, and Chrysler use this channel, and a local car dealer acts as a retailer. Why is there no wholesaler? So many variations exist in the product that it would be impossible for a wholesaler to stock all the models required to satisfy buyers; in addition, the cost of maintaining an inventory would be too high.

Adding a wholesaler as in channel C is most common for low-cost, low-unit value items that are frequently purchased by consumers, such as candy, confectionery items, and magazines. For example, Cadbury sells its line of candy bars to wholesalers in case quantities; then they can break down (sort) the cases so that individual retailers can order in boxes or much smaller quantities. Channel D, the most indirect channel, is employed when there are many small manufacturers and many small retailers. An agent is used to help coordinate a large supply of the product. Mansar Products, Ltd., is a Belgian producer of specialty jewellery that uses agents to sell to wholesalers, which then sell to many small retailers.

Marketing Channels for Industrial Goods and Services

The four most common channels for industrial goods and services are shown in Figure 12–5.[2] In contrast with channels for consumer products, industrial channels typically are shorter and rely on one intermediary or none at all because industrial users are fewer in number, tend to be more concentrated geographically, and buy in larger quantities (see Chapter 6).

Channel A, represented by IBM's large, mainframe computer business, is a direct channel. Firms using this channel maintain their own sales force and are responsible for all channel functions. This channel arrangement is employed when buyers are large and well defined, the sales effort requires extensive negotiations, and the products are of high unit value and require hands-on expertise for installation or use.[3]

Channels B, C, and D are indirect channels with one or more intermediaries to reach industrial users. In Channel B an *industrial distributor* performs a variety of marketing channel functions, including selling, stocking, and delivering a full product assortment and financing.[4] In many ways, industrial distributors are like wholesalers in consumer channels. Ingersoll-Rand, for example, uses industrial distributors to sell its line of pneumatic tools.

Channel C introduces another type of intermediary, an *agent,* who serves primarily as the independent selling arm of producers and represents a producer to industrial

FIGURE 12–5
Common marketing channels for industrial goods and services.

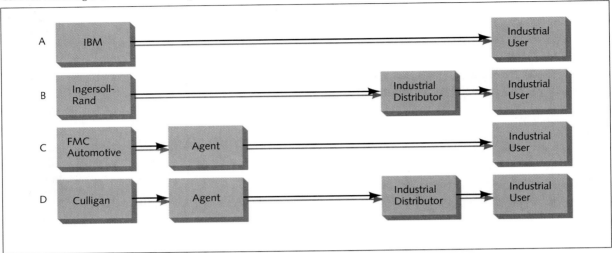

users. For example, FMC Automotive, a producer of auto parts, has an agent call on industrial users rather than employ its own sales force.

Channel D is the longest channel and includes both agents and distributors. For instance, Culligan, a producer of water treatment equipment, uses agents to call on distributors, who sell to industrial users.

Multiple Channels and Strategic Alliances

In some situations producers use **dual distribution,** an arrangement whereby a firm reaches different buyers by employing two or more different types of channels for the same basic product.[5] For example, GE sells its large appliances directly to home and apartment builders but uses retail stores to sell to consumers.

A recent innovation in marketing channels is the use of **strategic channel alliances,** whereby one firm's marketing channel is used to sell another firm's products. An alliance between Pepsi-Cola and Thomas J. Lipton Company is a case in point. Lipton relies upon Pepsi-Cola's extensive bottling network to distribute Lipton Original, a ready-to-drink iced tea sold only in bottles.[6] Strategic alliances are very popular in global marketing, where the creation of marketing channel relationships is expensive and time-consuming.[7] For example, General Motors distributes the Swedish Saab through its dealers in Canada. And Kraft General Foods uses the distribution system of Ajinomoto, a major Japanese food company, to market its Maxwell House coffee in Japan.

A Closer Look at Wholesaling Intermediaries

As we have seen, channel structures for consumer and industrial products assume various forms based on the number and type of intermediaries. Knowledge of the roles played by these intermediaries is important for understanding how channels operate in practice.

MARKETPLACE APPLICATION

How to Get a Job with a Wholesaler

A big problem confronting every college graduate is where to seek employment. The possibilities are many, including the manufacturing, retailing, service, and nonprofit sectors. However, in these traditional areas competition for jobs is keen. Hence, students seeking jobs in the traditional areas are discouraged.

Most graduates do not consider wholesalers as possible targets of employment. Jobs in these enterprises do not seem to offer much glamour. However, some very desirable job opportunities are found in firms located in medium and small cities. Job seekers should look for the substance—the job—and not be detoured by the lack of glamour.

What strategies should marketing majors employ in qualifying for and getting these jobs? One prerequisite is to realize that many wholesalers value practical experience. Students who pursue these positions are advised to accumulate part-time or summer experiences in wholesale operations or with related firms such as retailers, transportation carriers, and producers. Students should enroll in pragmatically oriented courses such as

personal selling, sales management, physical distribution, advertising, and computer applications.

In dressing for interviews, job seekers should be flexible. Some firms operate in an informal atmosphere, and jeans and a T-shirt may be more appropriate than a suit. This is not necessarily the case in all wholesale units of course. Often the atmosphere of formality is customary in an industry. Jewelry wholesalers, for instance, pursue a more formal dress code than do those in the oil field supplier industry.

1. How might a job seeker go about discovering the atmosphere of formality that is customary in an industry?

2. Develop a strategy that will improve your chance of finding a job with a wholesaler upon your college graduation.

SOURCE: Adapted from Robin T. Peterson, "Wholesaling: A Neglected Job Opportunity for Marketing Majors," *Marketing News,* January 15, 1996, p. 4

The terms *wholesaler, agent,* and *retailer* have been used in a general fashion consistent with the meanings given in Figure 12–1. However, on closer inspection a variety of specific types of intermediaries emerges. Figure 12–6 shows a common classification of intermediaries that engage in wholesaling activities—those activities involved in selling products and services to those who are buying for the purpose of resale or business use. Intermediaries engaged in retailing activities are discussed in detail in Chapter 13.

Merchant Wholesalers. Merchant wholesalers are independently owned firms that take title to the merchandise they handle. They go by various names, including industrial distributor (described earlier). About 80 percent of the firms engaged in wholesaling activities are merchant wholesalers.

Merchant wholesalers are classified as either full-service or limited-service wholesalers, depending on the number of functions performed. Two major types of full-service wholesalers exist. *General merchandise* (or full-line) *wholesalers* carry a broad assortment of merchandise and perform all channel functions. This type of wholesaler is most prevalent in the hardware, drug, and clothing industries. However, these wholesalers do not maintain much depth or assortment within specific product lines. *Specialty merchandise* (or limited-line) *wholesalers* offer a relatively narrow range of products but have an extensive assortment within the product lines carried. They perform all channel functions and are found in the health foods, automotive parts, and seafood industries.

FIGURE 12–6
Types of wholesaling
intermediaries.

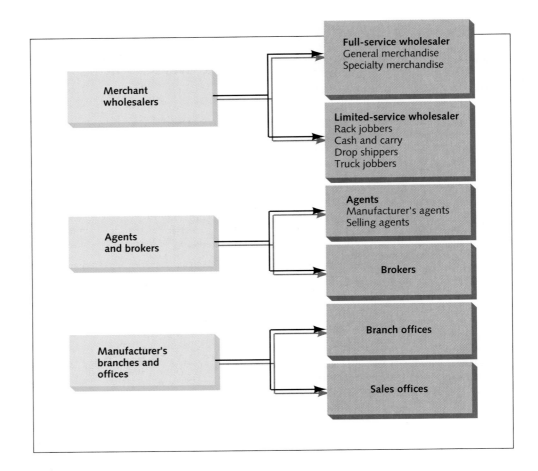

Four major types of limited-service wholesalers exist. *Rack jobbers* furnish the racks or shelves that display merchandise in retail stores, perform all channel functions, and sell on consignment to retailers, which means they retain the title to the products displayed and bill retailers only for the merchandise sold. Familiar products such as hosiery, toys, housewares, and health and beauty aids are sold by rack jobbers. *Cash-and-carry wholesalers* take title to merchandise but sell only to buyers who call on them, pay cash for merchandise, and furnish their own transportation for merchandise. They carry a limited product assortment and do not make deliveries, extend credit, or supply market information. This wholesaler is common in electric supplies, office supplies, hardware products, and groceries. *Drop shippers,* or *desk jobbers,* are wholesalers who own the merchandise they sell but do not physically handle, stock, or deliver it. They simply solicit orders from retailers and other wholesalers and have the merchandise shipped directly from a producer to a buyer. Drop shippers are used for bulky products such as coal, lumber, and chemicals, which are sold in extremely large quantities. *Truck jobbers* are small wholesalers that have a small warehouse from which they stock their trucks for distribution to retailers. They usually handle limited assortments of fast-moving or perishable items that are sold for cash directly from trucks in their original packages. Truck jobbers handle products like bakery items, dairy products, meat, and tobacco.

Agents and Brokers. Unlike merchant wholesalers, agents and brokers do not take title to merchandise and typically provide fewer channel functions. They make their profit from commissions or fees paid for their services, whereas merchant wholesalers make their profit from the sale of the merchandise they own.[8]

Manufacturer's agents and selling agents are the two major types of agents used by producers. *Manufacturer's agents,* or *manufacturer's representatives,* work for several producers and carry noncompetitive, complementary merchandise in an exclusive territory.[9] Manufacturer's agents act as a producer's sales arm in a territory and are principally responsible for the transactional channel functions, primarily selling. They are used extensively in the automotive supply, footwear, and fabricated steel industries. By comparison, *selling agents* represent a single producer and are responsible for the entire marketing function of that producer. They design marketing communications plans, set prices, determine distribution policies, and make recommendations on product strategy. Selling agents are used by small producers in the textile, apparel, food, and home furnishing industries.

Brokers are independent firms or individuals whose principal function is to bring buyers and sellers together to make sales. Brokers, unlike agents, usually have no continuous relationship with the buyer or seller but negotiate a contract between two parties and then move on to another task. Brokers are used extensively by producers of seasonal products (such as fruits and vegetables) and in the real estate industry.

Manufacturer's Branches and Offices. Unlike merchant wholesalers or agents and brokers, manufacturer's branches and offices are wholly owned extensions of the producer that perform wholesaling activities. Producers will assume wholesaling functions when there are no intermediaries to perform these activities, customers are few in number and geographically concentrated, or orders are large or require significant attention. Wholesaling activities performed by producers are conducted by means of a branch office or sales office. A *manufacturer's branch office* carries a producer's inventory, performs the functions of a full-service wholesaler, and is an alternative to a merchant wholesaler. A *manufacturer's sales office* does not carry inventory, typically performs only a sales function, and serves as an alternative to agents and brokers.

Vertical Marketing Systems

The traditional marketing channels described so far represent a loosely knit network of independent producers and intermediaries brought together to distribute goods and services. However, new channel arrangements are emerging to improve efficiency in performing channel functions and achieving greater marketing impact. For example, **vertical marketing systems** are professionally managed and centrally coordinated marketing channels designed to achieve channel economies and maximum marketing impact.[10] Figure 12–7 depicts the major types of vertical marketing systems: corporate, contractual, and administered.

Corporate Systems. The combination of successive stages of production and distribution under a single ownership is a *corporate vertical marketing system.* For example, a producer might own the intermediary at the next level down in the channel. This practice, called *forward integration,* is exemplified by Polo/Ralph Lauren, which manufactures clothing and also owns apparel shops.[11] Other examples of forward

FIGURE 12-7 Types of vertical marketing systems.

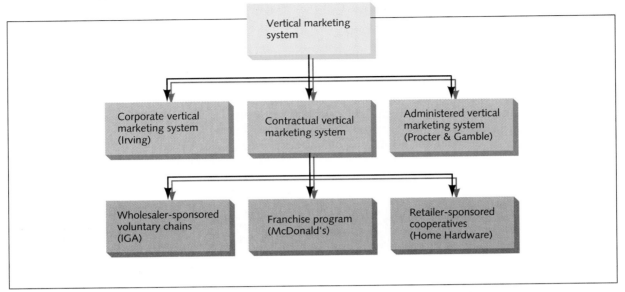

integration include Goodyear and Singer. Alternatively, a retailer might own a manufacturing operation, a practice called *backward integration.* For example, Safeway supermarkets operate their own bakeries.

Contractual Systems. Under a *contractual vertical marketing system,* independent production and distribution firms integrate their efforts on a contractual basis to obtain greater functional economies and marketing impact than they could achieve alone. Contractual systems are the most popular among the three types of vertical marketing systems and are estimated to account for about 40 percent of all retail sales.

Three variations of contractual systems exist. *Wholesaler-sponsored voluntary chains* involve a wholesaler that develops a contractual relationship with small, independent retailers to standardize and coordinate buying practices, merchandising programs, and inventory management efforts. With the organization of a large number of independent retailers, economies of scale and volume discounts can be achieved to compete with chain stores. IGA stores represent wholesaler-sponsored voluntary chains. *Retailer-sponsored cooperatives* exist when small, independent retailers form an organization that operates a wholesale facility cooperatively. Member retailers then concentrate their buying power through the wholesaler and plan collaborative promotional and pricing activities. An example of a retailer-sponsored cooperative is Home Hardware.

The most visible variation of contractual systems is **franchising,** a contractual arrangement between a parent company (a franchisor) and an individual or a firm (a franchisee) that allows a certain type of business to be operated under an established name and according to specific rules.

Administered Systems. In comparison, *administered vertical marketing systems* achieve coordination at successive stages of production and distribution by the size and influence of one channel member rather than through ownership. For example, Procter

& Gamble, given its broad product assortment ranging from disposable diapers to detergents, is able to obtain excellent cooperation from supermarkets in displaying, promoting, and pricing its products.

LEARNING CHECK

1. What is the difference between a direct and an indirect channel?

2. Why are channels for industrial products typically shorter than channels for consumer products?

3. What is the principal distinction between a corporate vertical marketing system and an administered vertical marketing system?

H&R Block represents a successful service provider that uses a vertical marketing system known as franchising.

CHANNEL CHOICE AND MANAGEMENT

Marketing channels not only link a producer to its buyers, but also provide the means through which a firm implements various elements of its marketing strategy.[12] Therefore, choosing a marketing channel is a critical decision.

Factors Affecting Channel Choice and Management

The final choice of a marketing channel by a producer depends on a number of factors that often interact with each other. Some of these factors are shown in Figure 12–8 and will now be discussed.

Environmental Factors. The changing environment described in Chapter 3 has an important effect on the choice and management of a marketing channel. For example, advances in the technology of growing, transporting, and storing perishable cut flowers have allowed some retailers to eliminate flower wholesalers and buy direct from flower growers around the world. Technological advances have also made it possible to market personal computers that require less training for users, thus enabling the broadened distribution of these products.

Consumer Factors. Consumer characteristics have a direct bearing on the choice and management of a marketing channel. Determining which channel is most appropriate is based on answers to fundamental questions such as: Who are potential customers? Where do they buy? When do they buy? How do they buy? What do they buy? These answers also indicate the type of intermediary best suited to reaching target buyers. For example, Ricoh Company, Ltd., studied the serious (as opposed to recreational) camera user and concluded that a change in marketing channels was necessary. The company terminated its contract with a wholesaler who sold to mass merchandise stores and began using manufacturer's agents who sold to photo specialty stores.

Product Factors. In general, highly sophisticated products such as large scientific computers, unstandardized products such as custom-built machinery, and products of high unit value are distributed directly to buyers. Unsophisticated, standardized products with low unit value, such as table salt, are typically distributed through indirect channels. A product's stage in the life cycle also affects marketing channels. Figure 12–9 shows the dominant retail marketing channel for personal computers since their introduction in the 1970s.[13]

Company Factors. A firm's financial, human, or technological capabilities affect channel choice. For example, firms that are unable to employ a sales force might use manufacturer's agents or selling agents to reach wholesalers or buyers.

FIGURE 12–8   Many factors affect channel choice.

Environmental Factors	Product Factors
• Economic	• Perishability
• Regulatory	• Value
• Technological	• Size
	• Life Cycle

Consumer Factors	Company Factors
• Location	• Resources
• Buying behaviour	• Product mix

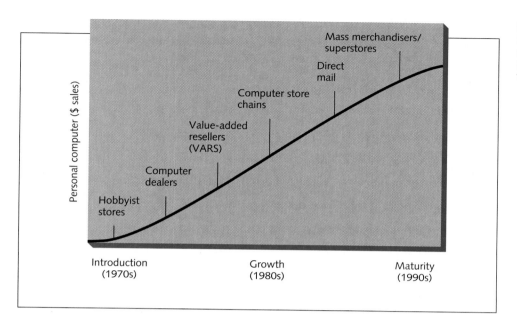

FIGURE 12–9
Dominant retail
marketing channel for
personal computers over
the PC life cycle.

Company factors also apply to intermediaries. For example, personal computer hardware and software producers wishing to reach business users might look to value-added resellers such as Micro Age, which has its own sales force and service staff that calls on businesses.

Channel Design Considerations

Recognizing that numerous routes to buyers exist and also recognizing the factors just described, marketing executives typically consider three questions when choosing a marketing channel and intermediaries:

1. Which channel and intermediaries will provide the best target market coverage?
2. Which channel and intermediaries will best satisfy buyer requirements?
3. Which channel and intermediaries will be the most profitable?

Target Market Coverage. Achieving the best target market coverage requires attention to the density and type of intermediaries to be used at the retail level of distribution. Three degrees of distribution density exist: intensive, exclusive, and selective. **Intensive distribution** means that a firm tries to place its products and services in as many outlets as possible. Intensive distribution is usually chosen for convenience products or services—for example, chewing gum, automatic teller machines, and cigarettes.

Exclusive distribution is the extreme opposite of intensive distribution, because only one retail outlet in a specified geographical area carries the firm's product. Exclusive distribution is typically chosen for specialty products or services—for example, automobiles, some women's fragrances, men's suits, and yachts. Sometimes manufacturers sign exclusive distribution agreements with retail chain stores.

Selective distribution lies between these two extremes and means that a firm selects a few retail outlets in a specific area to carry its products. This is the most common form of distribution intensity and is usually associated with shopping goods or services such as Seiko watches.

Satisfying Buyer Requirements. A second consideration in channel design is gaining access to channels and intermediaries that satisfy at least some of the interests buyers might want fulfilled when they purchase a firm's products or services. These interests fall into four categories: information, convenience, variety, and attendant services.

Information is an important requirement when buyers have limited knowledge or desire specific data about a product or service. Properly chosen intermediaries communicate with buyers through in-store displays, demonstrations, and personal selling. Computer stores originally grew in popularity as a source for small computers because they provided such information. Similarly, direct sales firms such as Amway, Avon, and Tupperware have been able to identify the unique information needs of Japanese women and successfully communicate the benefits of their products and method of selling.[14]

Convenience has multiple meanings for buyers, such as proximity or driving time to a retail outlet. For example, 7-Eleven stores, with hundreds of outlets nationwide, satisfy this interest for buyers, and candy, tobacco, and snack food firms benefit by gaining display space in these stores. For other consumers, convenience means a minimum of time and hassle.

Variety reflects buyers' interest in having numerous competing and complementary items to choose from. Variety is evident in both the breadth and depth of products and brands carried by intermediaries, which enhances their attraction to buyers. Thus, a manufacturer of men's ties would seek distribution through stores that offer a full line of men's clothing.

Attendant services provided by intermediaries are an important buying requirement for products such as appliances that require delivery, installation, and credit. Therefore, Whirlpool seeks dealers that provide such services.

Profitability. The third consideration in designing a channel is profitability, which is determined by the margins earned (revenues minus cost) for each channel member and for the channel as a whole. Channel cost is the critical dimension of profitability. Costs include distribution, advertising, and selling expenses associated with different types of marketing channels. The extent to which channel members share these costs determines the margins received by each member and by the channel as a whole.

Global Dimensions of Marketing Channels

For the answer to how Schick became the razor and blade market share leader in Japan read the text.

Marketing channels around the world reflect traditions, customs, geography, and the economic history of individual countries and societies. Even so, the basic marketing channel functions must be performed. But differences do exist, and these are illustrated by highlighting marketing channels in Japan.

Intermediaries outside Western Europe and North America tend to be small, numerous, and often owner-operated. Japanese marketing channels tend to include many intermediaries based on tradition and lack of storage space. As many as five intermediaries are involved in the distribution of soap in Japan, compared with one or two in North America.[15]

Understanding marketing channels in global markets is often a prerequisite to successful marketing. For example, Gillette attempted to sell its razors and blades through company salespeople in Japan as it does in North America, thus eliminating wholesalers traditionally involved in marketing toiletries. Warner-Lambert Company sold its Schick razors and blades through the traditional Japanese channel involving wholesalers. The result? Gillette holds 19 percent of the Japanese razor and blade market and Schick holds 70 percent.[16]

Channel Relationships: Conflict, Cooperation, and Law

Unfortunately, because channels consist of independent individuals and firms, there is always potential for disagreements concerning who performs which channel functions, how profits are allocated, which products and services will be provided by whom, and who makes critical channel-related decisions. These channel conflicts necessitate measures for dealing with them. Sometimes they result in legal action.

Conflict in Marketing Channels. Channel conflict arises when one channel member believes another channel member is engaged in behaviour that prevents it from achieving its goals.[17] Two types of conflict occur in marketing channels: vertical conflict and horizontal conflict.

Vertical conflict occurs between different levels in a marketing channel—for example, between a manufacturer and a wholesaler or retailer or between a wholesaler and a retailer. Three sources of vertical conflict are most common. First, conflict arises when a channel member bypasses another member and sells or buys products direct. Second, disagreements over how profit margins are distributed among channel members produce conflict. A third conflict situation arises when manufacturers believe wholesalers or retailers are not giving their products adequate attention. For example, H. J. Heinz Company found itself in a conflict situation with its supermarkets in Great Britain when supermarkets promoted and displayed private brands at the expense of Heinz brands.[18]

Horizontal conflict occurs between intermediaries at the same level in a marketing channel, such as between two or more retailers (Zellers and Kmart) or two or more wholesalers that handle the same manufacturer's brands. Two sources of horizontal conflict are most common. First, horizontal conflict arises when a manufacturer increases its distribution coverage in a geographical area. For example, a franchised Cadillac dealer in Toronto might complain to GM that another franchised Cadillac dealer has located too close to its dealership. Second, dual distribution can cause conflict when different types of retailers carry the same brands. For instance, Revlon's Charlie perfume can be found in drug stores, department stores, and discount stores, which may lead to complaints by any one of the retailers.

Securing Cooperation in the Channel. Conflict can have destructive effects on the workings of a marketing channel, so it is necessary to secure cooperation among channel members. One means is through a **channel captain,** a channel member that coordinates, directs, and supports other channel members. Channel captains can be producers, wholesalers, or retailers. Sears and Wal-Mart are retail channel captains because of their number of outlets and purchasing volume.

A firm becomes a channel captain because it is typically the channel member with the power to influence the behaviour of other members.[19] Some organizations use channel power to gain concessions from other channel members. For example, manufacturers are often expected to pay supermarket chains allowances, in the form of cash or free goods, to stock and display products. Some manufacturers call these allowances "extortion," as described in the Ethics Insight.

Legal Considerations. Sometimes channel conflict produces legal implications. Therefore knowledge of legal restrictions affecting channel strategies and practices is important. Some of these restrictions were described in Chapter 11, namely price-fixing and price discrimination. However, other legal considerations unique to marketing channels warrant attention.

ETHICS INSIGHT

The Ethics of Channel Power

How firms acquire and use power in marketing channels has often prompted legal restrictions. Nevertheless, power gained through the economic strength, expertise, identification with others, and legitimate rights of channel members can be used in numerous ways.

Recently some supermarket chains have demanded slotting allowances from manufacturers, paid in the form of money or free goods, to stock and display products. The allowances, which can range from $100 for a single store to upwards of $25,000 for a supermarket chain, have been labelled "ransom" and "extortional allowances." Supermarket operators see these allowances as a reasonable cost of handling business for manufacturers.

1. Is the practice of charging slotting allowances unethical behaviour?

SOURCES: Based on J. A. Siguaw and K. Douglas Hoffman, "The Role of Slotting Allowances in Retail Channel Relationships: Review and Propositions," *American Marketing Association Educators' Proceedings* (Chicago: American Marketing Association, 1992), pp. 494–95; L. Therrien, "Want Shelf Space at Supermarkets? Ante Up," *Business Week*, August 7, 1989, pp. 60–61; and C. Donahue, "Conflict in the Aisles," *Adweek's Marketing Week*, September 4, 1989, pp. 20–21.

In general, suppliers do have the right to choose the intermediaries that carry or represent their products. However, suppliers can run into legal difficulty if their actions violate the Competition Act. The Competition Act looks seriously at cases in which a channel arrangement adversely affects consumers by eliminating or lessening competition. *Refusing to deal* with a customer who can meet the usual trade terms offered by the supplier is an example of an action that could be deemed to adversely affect that customer. Other actions that are not necessarily illegal, but in practice could be deemed to violate the Competition Act include:

- *Exclusive dealing,* which exists when a supplier requires channel members to sell only its products or restricts distributors from selling directly competitive products.
- *Tied selling,* which occurs when a supplier requires a distributor purchasing some products to buy others from the supplier. These arrangements often arise in franchising.
- *Resale or market restrictions* refer to a supplier's attempt to stipulate to whom distributors may resell the supplier's product and in what specific geographic territories they may be sold.
- *Dual distribution* is a situation where a manufacturer distributes through its own vertically integrated channel in direct competition with wholesalers and retailers that also sell its products.

These practices could be subject to review under the Competition Act if such restrictions were deemed to be restraining or lessening competition.

LEARNING CHECK

1. What are the three degrees of distribution density?

2. What are the three questions marketing executives consider when choosing a marketing channel and intermediaries?

3. What is meant by exclusive dealing?

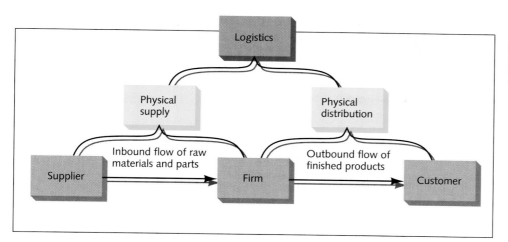

FIGURE 12–10
Relation of physical supply, physical distribution, and logistics to a manufacturing firm's operations.

LOGISTICS MANAGEMENT

Marketing managers often use **physical distribution management** to mean organizing the movement and storage of a finished product until it reaches the customer. *Logistics* implies a broader view and attempts to coordinate both inbound flow of raw materials and the outbound flow of finished product. Because these two flows are not simply mirror images of each other, we prefer to discuss the broader term of logistics, or *logistics management*. **Logistics management** is organizing the cost-effective flow of raw materials, in-process inventory, finished goods, and related information from point of origin to point of consumption to satisfy *customer requirements*.[20]

Figure 12–10 demonstrates the relation of physical supply, physical distribution, and logistics to the operations of a manufacturing firm. This chart shows how the firm receives its physical supply in the form of raw materials and parts from its suppliers, converts these into finished products, and then engages in the distribution of these products to its customers. Note that these concepts also apply to nonmanufacturing firms, such as retailers and wholesalers, for which the inbound activities include the finished goods that are resold to customers without physical modification.

Increasing Importance of Logistics Management

Several factors account for the trend of increased emphasis on logistics management. There has been a large growth in the differentiation of products in order to respond to customer demands. The effect of this increased product differentiation is that inventory control has become more complex, and thus there are many more things to keep track of. Consider, for example, that L.L. Bean carries approximately 5,000 different products. However, when each product is divided by size, colour, etc., L.L. Bean must track 54,000 separate items.[21] In today's environment, the increasing costs of carrying inventory make it clear that inventories cannot grow unchecked. Thus, while firms are under pressure to provide high levels of customer service by having many items available, they need to control the cost of such service.

OBJECTIVES OF THE LOGISTICS SYSTEM

The objectives of a logistics system are to minimize relevant logistics costs while delivering maximum customer service. To realize these objectives, marketing managers need to balance total logistics cost factors against customer service factors.

Total Logistics Cost Concept

Total logistics cost includes expenses associated with transportation, materials handling and warehousing, inventory, stockouts (being out of inventory), and order processing. A more complete list of decisions that are associated with the flow of product and make up total logistics cost includes:

- Traffic and transportation.
- Warehousing and storage.
- Packaging.
- Materials handling.
- Inventory control.
- Order processing.
- Customer service level.
- Plant and wholesale site locations.
- Return goods handling.

Many of these costs are interrelated so that changes in one will impact the others. For example, as a firm attempts to minimize its transportation costs by shipping in larger quantities, it will also experience an increase in inventory levels. Larger inventory levels will increase inventory costs but should also reduce stockouts. It is important, therefore, to study the impact on all of the logistics functions when considering a change in one.

Figure 12–11 provides a graphic example of this interrelatedness. As the number of warehouses increases, inventory costs rise and transportation costs fall. In Figure 12–11, having 10 warehouses will create the net effect of minimizing the total costs of the logistics system. This means the cost curve is minimized at a point where neither of the two individual cost elements is at a minimum but the overall system is.

FIGURE 12–11
How total logistics cost varies with number of warehouses used.

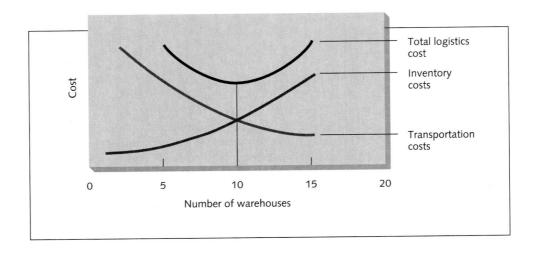

Customer Service Concept

If logistics is a *flow,* the end of it—or *output*— is the service delivered to customers. However, service can be expensive. One firm found that to increase on-time delivery from a 95 percent to a 100 percent rate tripled its total logistic costs. This is because higher levels of service often require more inventory to reduce stockouts, more expensive transportation to improve speed and lessen damage, and double or even triple checking of orders to ensure correctness.

Within the context of logistics, **customer service** is the ability of a logistics system to satisfy users in terms of (1) time, (2) dependability, (3) communications, and (4) convenience.[22] A firm's goal should be to provide its desired level of customer service while controlling logistics costs. Customer service is now seen not merely as an expense, but as a strategic tool for increasing customer satisfaction and sales. As suggested by Figure 12–12, a logistics manager's key task is to balance these four customer service factors against total logistics cost factors.

Time. In a logistics setting, time refers to **lead time** for an item, which means the lag from ordering an item until it is received and ready for use. This is also referred to as **order cycle time** or *replenishment time.* The various elements that make up the typical order cycle include recognition of the need to order, order transmittal, order processing, documentation, and transportation. A current emphasis in logistics is to reduce lead time and to make the process of reordering and receiving products as simple as possible, often through electronic data interchange (EDI).

Dependability. Dependability is the consistency of replenishment. This is important to both intermediaries and consumers. It can be broken into three elements: consistent lead time, safe delivery, and complete delivery. Studies indicate that dependability is a key element in customer service.[23] Consistent service allows planning (such as appropriate inventory levels), whereas inconsistencies create surprises. While surprise

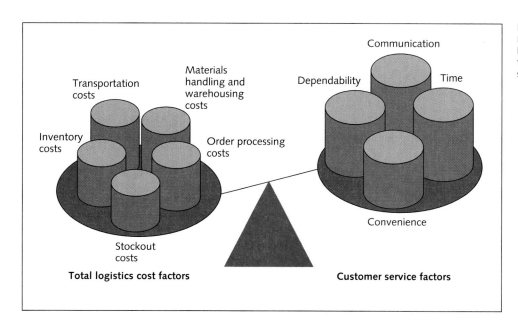

FIGURE 12–12
Logistics managers balance total logistics cost factors against customer service factors.

Communication

Transportation costs

Materials handling and warehousing costs

Dependability

Time

Inventory costs

Order processing costs

Stockout costs

Convenience

Total logistics cost factors

Customer service factors

The objectives of a logistics system are to minimize costs while delivering maximum customer service.

delays may shut down a production line, early deliveries can be as troublesome because of the problems of storing extra inventory.

Communication. Communication is a two-way link between buyer and seller that helps in monitoring service and anticipating future needs. Status reports on orders are a typical example of improved communication between buyer and seller. The increased communication capability of transportation carriers has enhanced the accuracy of such tracing information and improved the ability of buyers to schedule shipments.

Convenience. The concept of convenience for a logistics manager means that there should be a minimum of effort on the part of the buyer in doing business with the seller. Is it easy for the customer to order? Does the buyer have to buy huge quantities of the product? The seller must concentrate on removing unnecessary barriers to customer convenience.

Customer Service Standards

Firms that operate effective logistics systems usually develop a set of written customer service standards. These serve as objectives and provide a benchmark against which results can be measured. Note that the examples in Figure 12–13 suggest customer service standards will differ by type of firm.

LEARNING CHECK

1. What is a current strategy adopted by firms attempting to squeeze costs from their logistics system while delivering customer service?

2. What ways do key customer service factors differ between a manufacturer and a retailer?

FIGURE 12–13 Examples of customer service standards.

Type of Firm	Customer Service Standard
Wholesaler	At least 98% of orders filled accurately
Manufacturer	Order cycle time of no more than 5 days
Retailer	Returns accepted within 30 days
Airline	At least 90% arrivals on time
Trucker	A maximum of 5% loss and damage per year
Restaurant	Lunch served within 5 minutes of order

KEY LOGISTICS FUNCTIONS

Logistics includes four key functions: transportation, warehousing and materials handling, order processing, and inventory management. These functions need to be carefully coordinated to provide desired levels of customer service at an affordable cost.

Transportation

Transportation provides the movement of goods necessary in a logistics system. There are five basic modes of transportation: railroads, motor carriers, air carriers, pipelines, and water carriers. Figure 12–14 summarizes the relative advantages and disadvantages of these basic modes of transportation.

Warehousing and Materials Handling

Warehouses may be classified in one of two ways: storage warehouses and distribution centres. In *storage warehouses* the goods are intended to come to rest for some period of time, as in the aging of products or in storing household goods. *Distribution centres,* on the other hand, are designed to facilitate the timely movement of goods.

Distribution centres not only allow firms to hold their stock in decentralized locations but are also used to facilitate sorting and consolidating products from different plants or different suppliers. Some physical transformation can also take place in distribution centres such as mixing or blending different ingredients, labelling, and repackaging. The success of many retailing chains such as Wal-Mart and Zellers is due to sophisticated distribution centres that serve their retail outlets.[24]

Materials handling, which involves moving goods over short distances into, within, and out of warehouses and manufacturing plants, is a key part of warehouse operations. The two major problems with this activity are high labour costs and high rates of loss and damage. Common materials handling equipment includes forklifts, cranes, and conveyers. Recently, materials handling in warehouses has been automated by

FIGURE 12–14 Advantages and disadvantages of five modes of transportation.

Mode	Relative Advantages	Relative Disadvantages
Rail	Full capability Extensive routes Low cost	Some reliability, damage problems Not always complete pickup and delivery Sometimes slow
Truck	Complete pickup and delivery Extensive routes Fairly fast	Size and weight restrictions Higher cost More weather-sensitive
Air	Fast Low damage Frequent departures	High cost Limited capabilities
Pipeline	Low cost Very reliable	Limited routes (accessibility) Slow
Water	Low cost Huge capacities	Slow Limited routes and schedules More weather-sensitive

using computers and robots to reduce the cost of holding, moving, and recording the inventories of stores.

Order Processing

There are several stages in the processing of an order, and a failure at any one of them can cause a problem with the customer. The process starts with transmitting the order by a variety of means such as computer or electronic data interchange (EDI). This is followed by entering the order in the appropriate databases and sending the information to those needing it. For example, a regional warehouse is notified to prepare an order. After checking inventory, a new quantity may need to be reordered from the production line, or purchasing may be requested to reorder from a vendor. If the item is currently out of stock, a back order is created and the whole process of keeping track of a small part of the original order must be managed. In addition, credit may have to be checked for some customers, all paperwork associated with the order must be prepared, transportation must be arranged, and a confirmation of the order must be sent.

Inventory Management

Inventory management is one of the primary responsibilities of the logistics manager. The major problem is maintaining the delicate balance between too little and too much. Too little inventory may result in poor service, stockouts, brand switching, and loss of market share; too much leads to higher costs because of the money tied up in inventory and the chance that the inventory may become damaged or obsolete. Note that the management of a firm's inventory level often depends on the level of service of vendors such as the reliability of transportation carriers or the order cycle of suppliers.

One major area of change in inventory management is the concept of *electronic data interchange (EDI),* which we first discussed in Chapter 7. EDI is an interactive network that connects manufacturers with suppliers, distributors, and retailers so that they can share information. EDI enables retailers such as Wal-Mart and Canadian Tire to establish working relationships with vendors like Procter & Gamble to improve inventory management efficiency.

EDI permits a **just-in-time (JIT)** inventory control system. With such a control system, very low inventory levels are maintained but stock is constantly being ordered and delivered as it is being sold. When parts are needed for production, they arrive from suppliers "just in time," which means neither before nor after they are needed. JIT is used in situations where demand forecasting is reliable, such as when supplying a production line, and in situations where information technologies such as EDI enable quick and accurate information with respect to inventory needs. The many potential benefits of JIT can serve as a source of competitive advantage. The potential benefits of JIT inventory control include:

- Decreased investment in inventory and storage space.
- Faster inventory turnover.
- Improved production scheduling and product quality.
- Fewer stockouts.
- Higher levels of customer satisfaction.

For JIT to work properly, suppliers must be able to provide fast, reliable deliveries or there will be failures relative to customer service. Consequently, with JIT the supplier assumes more responsibility and risk for inventory and on-time delivery than does the buyer. Ideally, to reduce these risks suppliers move closer to the user. This is easier in a smaller country like Japan, but more difficult in a country like Canada, the second largest country in the world. But some supply companies are able to locate near major buyers. For example, automotive parts suppliers often locate close to the automobile manufacturers in order to exploit JIT. If suppliers cannot locate near their customers, then reliable transportation is critical for JIT to be effective. Canadian Tire uses its private truck fleet to move its over 40,000 product items to its stores nationwide on a timely basis.

LEARNING CHECK

1. What are the basic trade-offs between the various modes of transportation?

2. What type of inventory should use storage warehouses and which type should use distribution centres?

3. What are the strengths and weaknesses of a just-in-time system?

LEARNING OBJECTIVE REINFORCEMENT

1. Explain marketing channels and why intermediaries are needed. A marketing channel of distribution consists of the individuals and firms involved in the process of making a product or service available for use or consumption by consumers or industrial users. Few consumers appreciate the value created by intermediaries; however, producers recognize that intermediaries make selling goods and services more efficient because they minimize the number of sales contacts necessary to reach a target market.

2. Recognize differences between marketing channels for consumer and industrial products and services. In contrast with channels for consumer products, industrial channels typically are shorter and rely on one intermediary or none at all because industrial users are fewer in number, tend to be more concentrated geographically, and buy in larger quantities.

3. Describe the functions performed by intermediaries. Intermediaries make possible the flow of product from producers to buyers by performing three basic functions. The most prominent function is a *transactional function* that can involve buying, selling, and risk taking. Intermediaries also perform a *logistical function* that can include gathering, storing, sorting, and transporting products. Finally, intermediaries can perform a *facilitating function* by providing financing, grading services, and marketing information and research.

4. Describe factors considered by marketers when making a channel choice. The final choice of a marketing channel by a producer depends on a number of factors that often interact with each other. These factors include: (1) environmental factors (economic, regulatory, technical), (2) consumer factors (location, buyer behaviour), (3) product factors (perishability, value, size, life cycle), and (4) company factors (resources, product mix). In addition to these factors, marketing executives typically consider three questions when choosing a marketing channel and intermediaries: (1) What channel and intermediaries will provide the best target market coverage? (2) Which channel and intermediaries will best satisfy buyer requirements? and (3) Which channel and intermediaries will be the most profitable?

5. Explain the distinction between physical distribution management and logistics management. Physical distribution management means to organize the movement and storage of a finished product until it reaches the customer. Logistics management implies a broader view of distribution and attempts to coordinate both the inbound flow of raw materials and the outbound flow of finished product.

6. Understand the importance of logistics management. There has been a trend of increased emphasis on logistics management because of (1) increasing costs of carrying inventory, (2) a growing complexity of inventory control as the result of a growth in the differentiation of products (into sizes, colours, etc.), and (3) high consumer and industrial buyer expectations with respect to product availability.

7. Explain the key logistics functions of transportation, warehousing and materials handling, order processing, and inventory management. Logistics includes four key functions: (1) transportation, (2) warehousing and materials handling, (3) order processing, and (4) inventory management. These functions need to be carefully coordinated to provide desired levels of customer service at an affordable cost.

KEY TERMS AND CONCEPTS

marketing channel p. 296
direct channel p. 299
indirect channels p. 299
dual distribution p. 300
strategic channel alliances p. 300
vertical marketing systems p. 303
franchising p. 304

intensive distribution p. 307
exclusive distribution p. 307
selective distribution p. 307
channel captain p. 309
physical distribution management
　p. 311

logistics management p. 311
total logistics cost p. 312
customer service p. 313
lead time p. 313
order cycle time p. 313
just-in-time (JIT) p. 316

CHAPTER QUESTIONS AND APPLICATIONS

1. A distributor for Celanese Chemical Company stores large quantities of chemicals, blends these chemicals to satisfy requests of customers, and delivers the blends to a customer's warehouse within 24 hours of receiving an order. How is this distributor creating value?

2. Suppose the president of a carpet manufacturing firm has asked you to look into the possibility of bypassing the firm's wholesalers (who sell to carpet, department, and furniture stores) and selling direct to these stores. What caution would you voice on this matter, and what type of information would you gather before making this decision?

3. What type of channel conflict is likely to be caused by dual distribution, and what type of conflict can be reduced by direct distribution? Why?

4. Suppose 10 firms in an industry wish to reach 10,000 potential customers by selling to them direct. How many sales contacts would be required in this industry if each firm called on each customer? How many sales contacts would be required if an intermediary were placed between the firms and potential customers?

5. Comment on this statement: The only distinction among merchant wholesalers and agents and brokers is that merchant wholesalers take title to the products they sell.

6. How do specialty, shopping, and convenience goods (see Chapter 9) generally relate to intensive, selective, and exclusive distribution? Give a brand name that is an example of each goods-distribution matchup.

7. Describe the conditions that favour each of the following types of distribution: (a) intensive, (b) selective, and (c) exclusive.

8. Name some cases when extremely high service levels (e.g., 99 percent) would be warranted.

9. Name the mode of transportation that would be the best for the following products: (a) farm machinery, (b) cut flowers, (c) frozen meat, and (d) coal.

10. The auto industry is a heavy user of the just-in-time concept. Why? What other industries would be good candidates for its application? What do these industries have in common?

APPLICATION CASE 12–1
BENETTON: BUILDING A GLOBAL NETWORK

In today's competitive retail environment, cooperation with supply network partners is integral to successful strategy implementation. Moreover, the structuring of an organization's logistics system with supplier cooperation can be the principal means of achieving competitive advantage. Benetton, with over 4,000 stores and several billion dollars in sales, is an organization that has built a strong global supply network with supplier cooperation. Through its network of 350–400 subcontractors who produce almost exclusively for Benetton, and approximately 80 independent agents, Benetton delivers product to a chain of investor–owner stores.

Benetton subcontracts close to 95 percent of its manufacturing, distribution, and sales activities, keeping only raw material purchases and cutting and dyeing in-house. These activities are retained in-house to provide a measure of central control. As the largest wool purchaser in the world, the company reaps significant economies in central buying. Benetton also centralizes technical research, production planning, and product development.

Benetton provides the following services to its subcontractors: production planning, raw materials in exact production quantities, materials requirement planning, quality control technical assistance, technical documents, and financial aid for leasing or buying equipment. The subcontractors, in exclusive supply relationships to Benetton, enjoy a guaranteed market and a high level of capacity utilization.

Benetton encourages its managers to become involved in the subcontracting system through ownership of subcontractors or directorships in subcontractor firms. The company also buys equity positions in subcontracting firms. This method of organizing subcontracting allows flexibility and low costs.

The partners in Benetton's network recognize that trust and cooperation facilitate relationship stability and long-term association. The longevity reduces the risk of opportunism in the outsourced activities in Benetton's logistics system. Opportunism, such as subcontractors raising prices in tight capacity situations, is counter-productive because it harms cooperation and reduces trust.

QUESTIONS

1. How has Benetton applied the imperatives for marketing success to its system of doing business? (Refer back to the discussion of seven imperatives for marketing success in Chapter 1.)
2. From a supplier perspective, is there a downside to entering into contractual relations with Benetton?
3. Discuss why a clothing retailer must have a sophisticated logistics system to be competitive.

SOURCE: Adapted from Joseph R. D'Cruz and Alan M. Rugman, "Developing International Competitiveness: The Five Partners Model," *Business Quarterly*, Winter 1993, pp. 60–72.

APPLICATION CASE 12–2
HERE'S THE DEAL: MULTI-LEVEL DISTRIBUTION

While sharing a morning coffee break, co-workers John Dennison and Gail Shanks were discussing a new business opportunity that was presented to John the previous evening. John was extremely excited about this opportunity that his trusted friend, Brian Dorsey, had offered him.

John Dennison: Well, Gail, this time next year I could retire from this place. My friend Brian just offered me a very exciting business opportunity that is sure to be a major money maker. He calls it the distribution system of the future. It's called multi-level marketing. I don't even have to sell products. All I need to do to make money and generate wealth is sign up other investors. I make a percentage on each item my investor sells. But it gets even better because in a short period

of time my investors find other investors and this thing begins to take off. The more investors, the more money I make. I can't lose because this is such a great concept.

Gail Shanks: I know you are excited, John, but I think you should be very careful. This sounds like one of those pyramid selling schemes that is illegal in Canada. My dad was investigating an opportunity like this one a few years ago but his accountant advised him not to get involved. According to Dad's accountant, pyramid selling is illegal because the promoters of these schemes exaggerate earnings potential, force purchase of inventory without the ability to return items, and require that you purchase product in order to remain qualified for their plan.

John Dennison: What? There are those who accept some risk and then there are those who find a fault with every opportunity. I trust Brian because he has been a good friend of mine for more than a decade. He would never ask me to invest in an illegal venture.

Gail Shanks: Perhaps Brian doesn't know that this could be an illegal venture or maybe this is a legit scheme. But if I were in your shoes, I would be very cautious.

QUESTIONS:

1. Should John invest in this business opportunity? Why or why not?
2. What questions should John ask of Brian?
3. How could John confirm the information supplied by Gail?

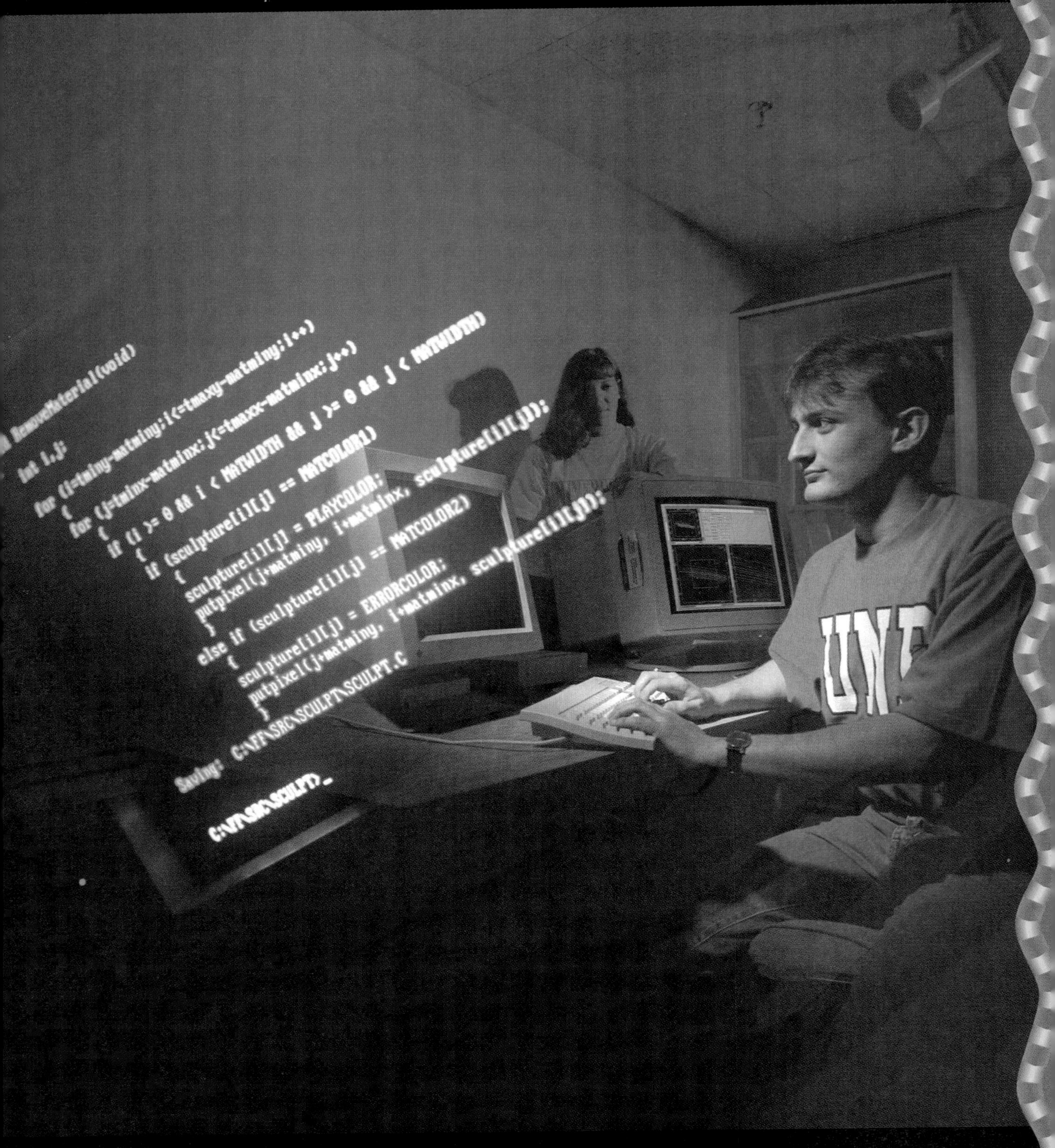
RemoveMaterial(void)
int i,j;
for (i=tminy-matminy;i<=tmaxy-matminy;i++)
{
for (j=tminx-matminx;j<=tmaxx-matminx;j++)
{
if (i >= 0 && i < MATWIDTH && j >= 0 && j < MATWIDTH)
{
if (sculpture[i][j] == MATCOLOR1)
{
sculpture[i][j] = PLAYCOLOR;
putpixel(j+matminy, i+matminx, sculpture[i][j]);
}
else if (sculpture[i][j] == MATCOLOR2)
{
sculpture[i][j] = ERRORCOLOR;
putpixel(j+matminy, i+matminx, sculpture[i][j]);
}
Saving: C:\FF\SRC\SCULPT\SCULPT.C
UNF

Retailing

AFTER READING THIS
CHAPTER YOU WILL BE
ABLE TO:

1. Understand the value
created by retailing.

2. Describe the life cycle of
retail stores.

3. Explain the impact of
future challenges in Canadian
retailing.

THE CHANGING FACE OF RETAILING: FROM STORE FRONT TO CYBERSPACE

In the channel of distribution, retailing is where the customer meets the product. **Retailing** includes all activities involved in selling, renting, and providing goods and services to ultimate customers for personal, family, or household use.

There have been many changes in Canadian retailing in recent years and many more changes will occur over the remainder of this century and into the next. The "old way" of retailing is being challenged because of such factors as new technologies, changing demographics, and increased competition. For those retailers willing to accept and respond to these challenges, there are many new and exciting opportunities.

One trend in retailing is the growth in the nonstore concept of electronic retailing. Banks, airlines, hotels, and auto rentals are enabling customers to open accounts, pay bills, and select among a choice of products and services from their homes through various new technologies such as the Internet and cable TV. Although still at an early stage of development, the Internet already offers shoppers the ability to skim through consumer cyberspace, hopping among dozens of online "virtual malls" and hundreds of catalogues and retail sites. Some retail analysts are predicting very rapid growth in electronic retailing. Whether such growth becomes a reality is uncertain, but the stage has been set with the development of the World Wide Web and a growing number of potential shoppers entering cyberspace every day.

What is the World Wide Web and how can it be used in retailing? Ask Keith Dunphy, founder and president of THE NET IDEA, a Nelson, B.C.-based company specializing in Internet access and services. Dunphy helps retailer and non-retailer clients find their way onto the information superhighway and the powerful new Internet tool known as the World Wide Web (often just called "the Web" or "WWW"). According to Dunphy, *the Web* is an Internet service that lets users retrieve text and graphics from various cyberspace sites. Dunphy helps his retail clients create a presence on *the Web* by creating graphic identifiers that are commonly called "home/pages" or "Web pages." By doing so, Dunphy allows his retail clients to instantly communicate a wide range of information as well as sell goods and services to anyone in the world who has a personal computer and a modem and uses one of the many services now providing Internet access.[1]

This chapter explains the nature and scope of retailing in the Canadian environment. First we will talk about the value of retailing and its economic impact. Then we will review the many variations of retailing, identify how a retail store may position itself, describe actions the store can take to develop a retailing strategy, and discuss the changing nature of retailing and future challenges in retailing.

THE VALUE OF RETAILING

Retailing is an important marketing activity. Not only do producers and consumers meet through retailing activities, but retailing also creates customer value and has a significant impact on the economy. Retailing's economic value is represented by the people employed in retailing, as well as by the total amount of money exchanged in retail sales.

Consumer Value Offered by Retailing

As intermediaries in a channel of distribution, retailers create value for consumers. As discussed in Chapter 12, retailers, like other intermediaries, create value by performing three basic functions: a transactional function (buying, selling, and risk taking), a logistical function (gathering, storing, and dispersing of products), and a facilitating function (assisting producers in making goods and services more attractive to consumers). In more specific terms, retailers can create value for you as a consumer by having the goods and services you want, when you want them, where you want them, and in the form and quantity that you want them.

Having 15,000 representatives across Canada, as Mary Kay Cosmetics does, puts the company's products close to the consumer. By providing financing or leasing and taking used cars as trade-ins, Saturn facilitates purchase. Many supermarkets offer convenient locations and are open 24 hours. These supermarkets offer consumer value by having goods and services available where and when consumers want them. These are just a few examples of how retailers provide value to consumers. In addition, many retailers provide consumer value by offering entertainment, recreation, or information.[2]

Economic Impact of Retailing

Retailing is important to the economy as a whole. Retail sales in Canada are estimated to reach $249 billion in 1999. The retail sector also employs over 1.8 million people in Canada, or approximately 15 percent of the total employed labour force.[3] Just three major retail categories—food stores, motor vehicle dealers, and clothing and shoe stores—represent 55 percent of the total retail trade in Canada.

The magnitude of retail sales is hard to imagine. Some of Canada's top retailers such as the Hudson's Bay Company, Zellers, and Kmart Canada each had sales in the billions in 1996. Their sales levels surpass even the GNP of several small nation–states.

The Value of Cross-Border Retailing. There is much debate over the relative impact that cross-border shopping has on the Canadian economy. Some believe the value of retail trade is declining in Canada as a result of Canadians' shopping in the United States. However, estimates show that only about 2 percent of total Canadian retail trade is lost to cross-border shopping. Moreover, some experts believe that cross-border shopping has actually improved the scope and nature of retailing in Canada. Canadian retailers, in an effort to keep customers on this side of the border, have become more efficient and better able to offer increased value to their customers.[4]

The cross-border concept involves more than just customers crossing the Canadian–U.S. border. Retailers on both sides are crossing the border looking for market opportunities. White Spot restaurants of British Columbia has recently expanded south into Washington, hoping to attract cross-border shoppers and residents of northern Washington by capitalizing on the spillover of radio and TV advertising that airs on southwestern British Columbia stations. At the same time, some American retailers are heading north. Major U.S. chains such as Toys "Я" Us and The Gap have set up shop in Canada. For a discussion of the entry of U.S. retailers into Canada, read the Marketplace Application box later in this chapter.

One of the biggest cross-border moves in recent history has been the entry of Wal-Mart into the Canadian market. The $55- to $60-billion-a-year retail juggernaut moved north by acquiring 120 Woolco stores in 1994. Undoubtedly the arrival of U.S. firms in Canada will create some market disruption for domestic companies. But consumers benefit from such cross-border retail expansions by having increased store and product choices, and possible new employment opportunities.

The Value of Global Retailing. Retailing also adds value to the world economy. A study on global retailing found that the top 100 retailers in the world took in more than $1 trillion (U.S.). These global retail companies operate almost 185,000 stores and have their head offices based in 15 countries. The top 100 global retailers had average sales of approximately $10 billion, profits of $240 million, and more than 1,900 outlets. Just the top 10, including U.S.-based Wal-Mart and Kmart, as well as Swiss-based Metro/Kaufhof International, had total sales of over $271 billion.[5]

LEARNING CHECK

1. When a Mary Kay representative brings products into a potential buyer's home, how is value being provided?

2. Two measures of the importance of retailing in the Canadian economy are _____ and _____.

CLASSIFYING RETAIL OUTLETS

For manufacturers, consumers, and the economy, retailing is an important component of marketing that has several variations. Because of the wide number of alternative forms of retailing, it is easier to understand the differences among retail institutions by recognizing that outlets can be classified in several ways:

- **Form of ownership:** Who owns the outlet.
- **Level of service:** The degree of service provided to the customer.

FIGURE 13–1   Classifying retail outlets.

Method of Classification	Description of Retail Outlet
Form of ownership	Independent retailer Corporate chain Contractual system • Retailer-sponsored cooperative • Wholesaler-sponsored voluntary chain • Franchise
Level of service	Self-service Limited service Full service
Merchandise line	Depth • Single line • Limited line Breadth • General merchandise • Scrambled merchandising
Method of operation	Store retailing Nonstore retailing

- **Merchandise line:** How many different types of products a store carries and in what assortment.
- **Method of operation:** The manner in which services are provided—how and where the customer purchases products.

Within each method of classification there are several alternative types of outlets, as shown in Figure 13–1 and explained in the following pages.

Form of Ownership

Independent Retailer. One of the most common forms of retail ownership is the independent business, owned by an individual. The neighbourhood dry cleaner or florist is often an independent retailer. The advantage of this form of ownership for the owner is that she can be her own boss. For customers, the independent store often provides a high level of personal service.

Corporate Chain. A second form of ownership, the corporate chain, involves multiple outlets under common ownership. If you've ever shopped at The Bay, Zellers, Eaton's, or Loblaws, you've shopped at a chain outlet.

In a chain operation, centralization in decision making and purchasing is common. Chain stores have advantages in dealing with manufacturers, particularly as the size of the chain grows. A large chain can bargain with a manufacturer to obtain good service or volume discounts on orders. Consumers also benefit in dealing with chains because there are multiple outlets with similar merchandise and consistent management policies.

Contractual System. Under contractual systems, independently owned stores band together to act like a chain. The three kinds described in Chapter 12 are retailer-sponsored cooperatives, wholesaler-sponsored voluntary chains, and franchises. One retailer-sponsored cooperative is Guardian Drugs or Uniprix, which consists of neighbourhood pharmacies that all agree with several other independent pharmacies to buy their prod-

Many independent stores, such as neighbourhood grocery stores, form alliances in the form of retailer-sponsored cooperatives.

ucts from the same wholesaler. In this way, members can take advantage of volume discounts commonly available to chains and also give the impression of being a large chain, which may be viewed more favourably by some consumers. Wholesaler-sponsored voluntary chains such as Independent Grocers' Alliance (IGA) try to achieve similar benefits.

As noted in Chapter 12, in a franchise system an individual or a firm (the franchisee) contracts with a parent company (the franchisor) to set up a business or retail outlet. McDonald's, Holiday Inn, and H&R Block all involve some level of franchising. The franchisor usually assists in setting up the store, selecting the store location, advertising, and training personnel. The franchisee pays a one-time franchise fee and an annual royalty, usually tied to the store's sales.

Franchising is attractive because of the opportunity for people to enter a well-known, established business where managerial advice is provided. Also, the franchise fee may be less than the cost of setting up an independent business. The International Franchise Association recently reported that franchising is one of the strongest segments of the economy and the source of over 160,000 new jobs each year.[6]

Franchise fees paid to the franchisor can range from as little as $3,000 for a Domino's Pizza franchise to $50,000 for a TGI Friday restaurant franchise.[7] When the fees are combined with other costs such as real estate and equipment, however, the total investment can be substantial. By selling franchises, an organization reduces the cost of expansion but loses some control. A good franchisor, however, will maintain strong control of the outlets in terms of delivery and presentation of merchandise.

Level of Service

Even though most customers perceive little variation in retail outlets by form of ownership, differences among retailers are more obvious in terms of level of service. Three levels of service exist: (1) self-service, (2) limited service, and (3) full service.

Self-Service. Self-service is at the extreme end of the level-of-service continuum, because the customer performs many functions and little is provided by the outlet. Home building supply outlets, discount stores, and catalogue showrooms are often self-service. Warehouse stores, usually in buildings several times larger than a conventional store, are self-service with all nonessential customer services eliminated. Price Club/Costco Warehouse Club is an example of the no-frills, self-service approach.

Limited Service. Limited-service outlets provide some services, such as credit, merchandise return, and telephone ordering, but not others, such as custom making of clothes. Department stores are typically considered limited-service outlets.

Full Service. The full-service retailer provides a complete list of services to cater to its customers. Specialty stores are among the few stores in this category. Holt Renfrew has set the standard for full service among Canadian retailers. The store typically has 50 percent more salespeople on the floor than similar-sized stores.

Merchandise Line

Retail outlets also vary by their merchandise lines, the key distinction being the breadth and depth of the items offered to customers (Figure 13–2). **Breadth of product line** refers to the variety of different items a store carries. **Depth of product line** refers to the assortment of each item a store carries—for a shoe store, for instance, running shoes, dress shoes, and children's shoes.

Depth of Line. Stores that carry a considerable assortment (depth) of a related line of items are limited-line stores. Black's Photography stores carry considerable depth in

FIGURE 13-2 Breadth versus depth of merchandise lines.

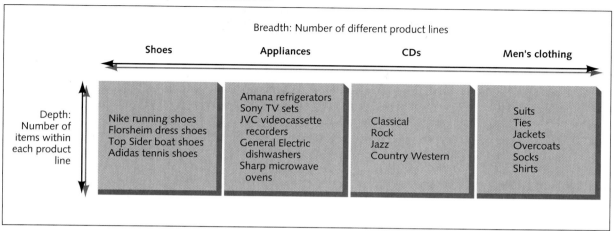

photography equipment, supplies, and services. Stores that carry tremendous depth in one primary line of merchandise are single-line stores. Victoria's Secret carries great depth in women's lingerie. Both limited- and single-line stores are often referred to as *specialty outlets.* Specialty store growth is strong in Canada, including specialty clothing, gift, and coffee stores, such as Starbucks. These specialty outlets usually provide consumers with knowledgeable staff and personal attention.[8]

Specialty discount outlets focus on one type of product, like electronics, business supplies, or party goods, at very competitive prices. These outlets are referred to in the trade as *category killers* because they often dominate the market. Toys "Я" Us, for example, controls 20 percent of the toy market.

Breadth of Line. Stores that carry a broad product line, with limited depth, are referred to as *general merchandise stores.* For example, a large department store carries a wide range of different types of products, but not unusual sizes. Traditionally, outlets carried related lines of goods. Today, however, **scrambled merchandising**—offering several unrelated product lines in a single store—is common. The modern drugstore, such as Shoppers Drug Mart, carries food, camera equipment, magazines, paper products, toys, small hardware items, and pharmaceuticals. Department stores repair automobiles, provide travel planning, and sell insurance.

Scrambled merchandising is convenient for consumers because it eliminates the number of stops required on a shopping trip. However, for the retailer this merchandising policy means there is competition between very dissimilar types of retail outlets, or **intertype competition.** A local bakery may compete with a department store, a discount outlet, or even a gas station. Scrambled merchandising and intertype competition make it more difficult to be a retailer.

A form of scrambled merchandising, the **hypermarket,** has been successful in Europe since the late 1960s. Hypermarkets are large stores (over 200,000 square feet) offering a mix of 40 percent food products and 60 percent general merchandise. Prices are typically 5 to 20 percent below discount store prices. The general concept behind the hypermarkets is simple: "one-stop" shopping. Hypermarkets have not been popular in North America. Only a few outlets have been opened, and none have met with much success. Consumers find the stores too big. The competitive environment is also too tough; wholesale clubs beat hypermarkets on price, category killers beat them on selection, and discounters beat them on location.

Searching for a better concept, some retailers have opened superstores, which combine a typical merchandise store with a full-size grocery outlet. Superstores run about 100,000 to 150,000 square feet, about half the size of a hypermarket.

In addition to superstores, there are also oversized (large-format) store concepts opening in Canada, including large-format specialty outlets. IDOMO Furniture, for example, opened a 120,000-square-foot store offering a wider and more upper-market range of furniture than its major competitor, IKEA. IDOMO's store provides a supervised video room for kids, atriums, showroom galleries, and a restaurant that cooks gourmet pizza in a wood-burning stove.[9]

Method of Operation

Retail outlets have begun to vary widely in the way their products are provided, and in their method of operation. Classifying retail outlets by method of operation means dividing these outlets into store and nonstore retailing.

Store Retailing. Traditionally, retailing meant that the consumer went to the store and purchased a product—which is store retailing. Most of the retailing examples discussed earlier in the chapter, such as corporate chains, department stores, and limited- and single-line specialty stores, involve store retailing.

Nonstore Retailing. Viewing retailing as an activity limited to sales in a store is too narrow an approach. Nonstore retailing occurs outside a retail outlet, through a direct channel and direct marketing approach, such as mail order, vending machines, video-tex, Internet, or teleshopping.

Few areas of retailing have grown as rapidly during the past decade as mail-order retailing. Mail-order retailing is attractive because it eliminates the cost of a store and clerks. Mail-order retailing with catalogues is big business in Canada. A Canadian study shows that close to 60 percent of adult Canadians make a catalogue mail-order purchase in a given year.[10] The Canadian market has already attracted some U.S. catalogue retailers such as L.L. Bean.

For the answer to how L.L. Bean has reduced catalogue postage costs and increased response rates, read the text.

As the growth in mail-order retailing begins to slow, two trends will emerge. One is specialization, or niche catalogues, which reduce postage costs and increase response rates by focusing on a very narrow line of products. L.L. Bean has already developed individual catalogues for fly fishing devotees and hunters. The second trend is toward selling through or opening retail stores. Traditional catalogue retailers are now moving into store retailing in an effort to reach noncatalogue shoppers. There are some threats to the continued success of mail-order retailers. One concern is market saturation. Another is the rising cost of postage, which reduces the profitability of this form of retailing.

Nonstore retailing also includes vending machines, which make it possible to serve customers when and where stores cannot. Vending machine sales in Canada are estimated at over $450 million.[11] Typically, small convenience products are available in vending machines. Two trends, however, signal likely continued growth for vending sales. First, improved technology will soon allow vending machines to accept credit cards. This change will permit more expensive items to be sold through this form of retailing.[12] Second, there is a movement toward smaller vending units that can be installed in the workplace. Coca-Cola has developed a small desktop vending unit, while Pepsi-Cola has invented its own version.[13] In the future, few locations will be immune

ETHICS INSIGHT

Pop Goes the Principles

The Toronto Board of Education recently signed a deal with Pepsi-Cola Canada that gives the bottler sole vending machine access to the city's public schools in exchange for a $1.14 million payment. Many have no problems with Pepsi making the deal. Pepsi was presented with a marketing opportunity to reach close to 90,000 students, its primary market, and it outhustled its competitors to clinch the deal.

The controversy centres on whether or not there should have been a deal in the first place. Some argue that our schools should be exempt from the marketing battleground. Some suggested that boards of education should not be initiating deals to give marketers even higher profiles than they already have in our hypercommercialized society.

However, some ask, What's the problem with the deal? Kids are already exposed to thousands of ads daily. Most of the kids wear brand images on their clothing and shoes, so what's one more message? And besides, it raises a little extra money to help cash-poor schools.

1. Faced with economic hard times, should school boards sign deals like this as an option over closing cafeterias or laying off teachers?

2. Is the school board, in essence, renting access to the minds of its students?

SOURCE: Adapted from an editorial by W. Gooding, "Pop Goes the Principles," *Marketing*, January 31, 1994, p. 23.

to vending machine deployment. As the accompanying Ethics Insight box points out, our schools may become the new vending machine battleground.

Another form of nonstore retailing is a type of electronic retailing known as *videotex*. Videotex is an interactive information system in which data and graphics are transmitted through telephone lines or coaxial cables and displayed on a television or computer monitor. Shoppers operate videotex systems with a keyboard connected to a television set or a keypad linked to a personal computer.

In Canada, New Brunswick-based NBTel, has been a pioneer in videotex technology. NBTel's investment in its multimedia system (a broadband network) will allow business and residential customers to use their television screen, PCs, and multimedia kiosks to access such services as video on demand, games on demand, home shopping, and home banking, as well as an array of health, educational, business, and information services. NBTel's CallMall service, which is available on the Vista 350 computerized telephone system carried over an existing narrowband network, is another example of videotex. The Vista 350 system enables customers to receive weather reports, check lotto numbers, complete banking transactions, shop by phone, and receive special offers from local merchants.[14]

An alternative form of videotex is *Internet retailing*. Several companies have entered this form of retailing in recent years. One of the largest is Prodigy, where for approximately $9.95 per month a customer can have access to a computerized database of products. Prodigy has merchandise from stores like Sears, catalogue retailers, and manufacturers such as Xerox and Sony. Travel reservations, stock transactions, and encyclopedia searches can also be made via this Internet service provider's system. Prodigy charges retailers up to $25,000 to sign up for the service, and there is an ongoing fee of approximately one-third of the retailer's gross margin.[15] Recently, Southam Inc. of Ontario has launched a Canadian version of Prodigy.

Another form of electronic nonstore retailing is *teleshopping*. Teleshopping enables the shopper to sit at home and tune in to a television show on which products are

Modems allow computer users access to many types of information and services.

displayed. This form of nonstore shopping experienced rapid growth during the early 1990s. The United States has two major networks, the Home Shopping Network and QVC, while Canada has one major network, the Canadian Home Shopping Network, which reaches over 6 million Canadian households, 24 hours a day, seven days a week.

LEARNING CHECK

1. Centralized decision making and purchasing are an advantage of _____ownership.

2. Would a shop for big men's clothes carrying pants in sizes 40 to 60 have a broad or a deep product line?

3. What are some examples of nonstore retailing?

RETAILING STRATEGY

This section identifies how a retail store may position itself and describes specific actions the store can take to develop a retailing strategy.

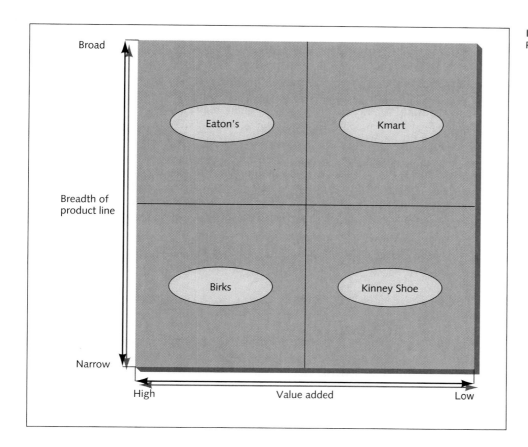

FIGURE 13–3
Retail positioning matrix.

Positioning a Retail Store

The four classification alternatives presented in the previous section help determine one store's position relative to its competitors.

Retail Positioning Matrix. The **retail positioning matrix** is a matrix developed by the MAC Group, Inc., a management consulting firm.[16] This matrix positions retail outlets on two dimensions: breadth of product line and value added. As defined previously, breadth of product line is the range of products sold through each outlet. The second dimension, *value added,* includes elements such as location (as with 7-Eleven stores), product reliability (as with Holiday Inn or McDonald's), or prestige (as with Birks).

The retail positioning matrix in Figure 13–3 shows four possible positions. An organization can be successful in any position, but unique strategies are required within each quadrant. Consider the four stores shown in the matrix:

1. Eaton's tends to have high value added and broad product line. Retailers in this quadrant pay great attention to store design and product lines. Merchandise often has a high margin of profit and is of high quality. The stores in this position typically provide high levels of service.
2. Kmart has low value added and a broad line. Kmart and similar firms typically trade a lower price for increased volume in sales. Retailers in this position focus on price with low service levels and an image of being a place for good buys.

3. Birks has high value added and a narrow line. Retailers of this type typically sell a very restricted range of products that are of high status quality. Customers are also provided with high levels of service.

4. Kinney has low value added and a narrow line. Such retailers are specialty mass merchandisers. Kinney, for example, carries attractively priced shoes for the entire family. These outlets appeal to value-conscious consumers. Economies of scale are achieved through centralized advertising, merchandising, buying, and distribution.

Keys to Positioning. To successfully position a store, it must have an identity that has some advantages over its competitors yet is recognized by consumers. A company can have outlets in several positions on the matrix, but this approach is usually done with different store names. Hudson's Bay Company, for example, owns The Bay department stores (with high value added and a broad line) and Zellers stores (low value added and a broad line).

Retailing Mix

In developing retailing strategy, managers work with the **retailing mix,** which includes the goods and services, physical distribution, and communications tactics chosen by a store (Figure 13–4).[17] Decisions relating to the mix focus on the consumer. Each of the areas shown is important, but we will cover only three basic areas: pricing, store location, and image and atmosphere. The communications components are discussed in Chapters 14 through 16.

Retail Pricing. In setting prices for merchandise, retailers must decide on the markup, markdown, and timing for markdowns. As mentioned in Appendix C following Chapter 11, *markup* refers to how much should be added to the cost the retailer paid for a product to reach the final selling price.

Discounting a product, or taking a *markdown,* occurs when the product does not sell at the original price and an adjustment is necessary. Often new models or styles force the price of existing models to be marked down. Discounts may also be used to increase demand for complementary products.[18] For example, retailers might reduce the price of cake mix to generate frosting purchases.

Although most retailers plan markdowns, many retailers use price discounting as part of their regular merchandising policy, with some now using an everyday low pricing (EDLP) strategy. Emphasizing consistently low prices and eliminating markdowns or sales has been a successful strategy for some retailers, including Home Depot and Zellers.

A final issue, timing, involves deciding when to discount the merchandise. Many retailers take a markdown as soon as sales fall off to free up valuable selling space and cash. However, other stores delay markdowns to discourage bargain hunters and maintain an image of quality. There is no clear answer, but retailers must consider how the timing might affect future sales.

Off-price retailing is a retail pricing practice that is most commonly found in clothing sales. **Off-price retailing** is the selling of brand-name merchandise at lower-than-regular prices.

There is a difference between the off-price retailer and a discount store. Off-price merchandise is bought by the retailer from manufacturers with excess inventory at prices below wholesale prices, while the discounter buys at full wholesale price but takes less of a markup than do traditional department stores. Because of this difference

FIGURE 13–4 The retailing mix.

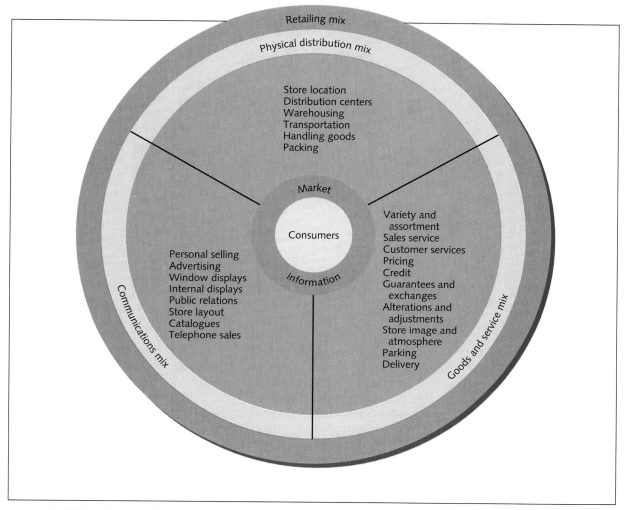

SOURCE: Adapted from W. Lazer and E. J. Kelley, "The Retailing Mix: Planning and Management," *Journal of Retailing,* vol. 37, Spring 1961, pp. 34–41. By permission of The American Marketing Association.

in the way merchandise is purchased by the retailer, selection at an off-price retailer is unpredictable, and consumers must be willing to search or hunt for what they want at different off-price retailers or at different times.

There are two growing variations of off-price retailing. One is warehouse clubs. These large stores, often larger than 100,000 square feet, offer no elaborate displays and minimal customer service. They require an annual membership fee (usually $25) for the privilege of shopping there.

The most popular warehouse clubs include Sam's Wholesale Club and Price Club/Costco Warehouse Club.

A second variation of off-price retailing is the factory outlet store. These outlets include companies that market clothing and shoes, such as Bass shoes, Ralph Lauren, and Levi's. Consumers can save up to 50 percent off suggested retail prices. Manufacturers use the stores to clear merchandise and to reach consumers who focus on value shopping.

The West Edmonton
Mall, the largest variation
of a regional shopping
centre.

Store Location. A second aspect of the retailing mix involves deciding where to locate the store and how many stores to have. Most stores today are near several others
in one of five settings: the central business district, the regional centre, the community
shopping centre, the strip, or the power centre.

The **central business district** is the oldest retail setting, the community's downtown area. Until the regional outflow to suburbs, it was the major shopping area, but
the suburban population has grown at the expense of the downtown shopping area.

Regional shopping centres are the suburban malls of today, containing up to 100
stores or more. The typical drawing distance of a regional centre is over 5 to 10 miles
from the mall, and could be as high as 50 miles. The largest variation of a regional shopping centre is the West Edmonton Mall in Edmonton, Alberta. The shopping centre is
a conglomerate of 800 stores, six amusement centres, 110 restaurants, and the 355-
room Fantasyland Hotel.[19]

A more limited approach to retail location is the **community shopping centre,**
which typically has one primary store (usually a department store outlet) and often
about 20 to 40 outlets. Generally, these centres serve a population of about 100,000.

Not every suburban store is located in a shopping mall. Many neighbourhoods
have clusters of stores, referred to as a **strip location,** to serve people who are within
a 5- to 10-minute drive and live in a population base of under 30,000. Gas station, hardware, laundry, and grocery outlets are commonly found in a strip location.

A new variation of the strip shopping location is called the **power centre,** which is
a huge shopping strip with multiple anchor (or national) stores. Power centres are seen
as having the convenient location found in many strip centres and the additional power
of national stores. These large strips often have two to five anchor stores and often contain a supermarket, which brings the shopper to the power centre on a weekly basis.[20]

Retail Image and Atmosphere. Deciding on the image of a retail outlet is an important retailing mix factor that has been widely recognized and studied since the late

1950s. Pierre Martineau described image as "the way in which the store is defined in the shopper's mind, partly by its functional qualities and partly by the aura of psychological attributes."[21] In this definition, *functional* refers to the mix elements such as price ranges, store layouts, and breadth and depth of merchandise lines. The psychological attributes are the intangibles, such as a sense of belonging, excitement, style, or warmth. Image has been found to include impressions of the corporation that operates the stores, the category or type of store, the product categories in the store, the brands in each category, and the marketing activities of the store.[22]

Closely related to the concept of image is the store's atmosphere, or ambiance. Many retailers believe that sales are affected by layout, colour, lighting, and music in the store, as well as by how crowded it is. In addition, the physical surroundings that influence customers may affect the store's employees.[23] In creating the right image and atmosphere, a retail store tries to identify its target audience and what the target audience seeks from a buying experience so the store will fortify the beliefs and emotional reactions buyers are seeking.[24]

Many stores are spending considerable time and money to create the right image and atmosphere for their customers. For example, Southland Canada, operator of 7-Eleven stores across the country, is sprucing up its image. In addition to remodelling its stores, 7-Eleven is offering customers a 100 percent satisfaction guarantee.[25]

LEARNING CHECK

1. What are the two dimensions of the retail positioning matrix?

2. A shopping centre with up to 100 other stores is a(n) _____ centre.

THE CHANGING NATURE OF RETAILING

Retailing is the most dynamic aspect of the channel of distribution. Stores like factory outlets show that new retailers are always entering the market, searching for a new position that will attract customers. The reason for this continual change is explained by the retail life cycle concept.

The Retail Life Cycle

The process of growth and decline that retail outlets, like products, experience is described by the **retail life cycle.**[26] Figure 13–5 shows the retail life cycle and the position of various current forms of retail outlets on it. Early growth is the stage of emergence of a retail concept, with a sharp departure from existing competition. Market share rises gradually, although profits may be low because of start-up costs. In the next stage, accelerated development, both market share and profit achieve their greatest growth rates. Usually multiple outlets are established as companies focus on the distribution element of the retailing mix. In this stage some later competitors may enter. Wendy's, for example, appeared on the hamburger chain scene almost 20 years after McDonald's had begun operation. The key goal for the retailer in this stage is to establish a dominant position in the fight for market share.

FIGURE 13–5
The retail life cycle.

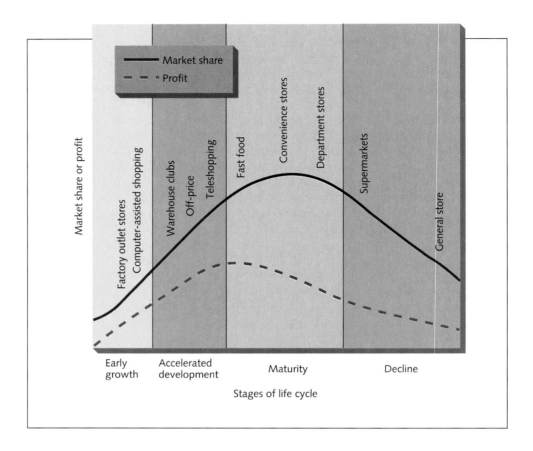

The battle for market share is usually fought before the maturity phase, and some competitors drop out of the market. New retail forms enter in the maturity phase, stores try to maintain their market share, and price discounting occurs. In the early 1990s, the major fast-food chains like Wendy's and McDonald's began to aggressively discount their prices. McDonald's introduced its "value menu," while Wendy's followed with a kid's Value Menu. The challenge facing these retailers is to delay entering the decline stage, in which market share and profit fall rapidly.

Figure 13–6 shows how many of today's retail institutions evolved. It shows the difficult challenge facing today's retailers: The time retail forms take to move from early growth to maturity is decreasing, so there is less time for a retailer to achieve profitability. Department stores took 100 years to reach maturity, whereas warehouse clubs are expected to reach maturity in five years. As a result, retailers must continually modify their mix to avoid early decline.

FUTURE CHALLENGES IN RETAILING

As noted in the introduction to this chapter, retailing in Canada is in a constant state of change. The following sections address four trends that are, in part, responsible for this state of change: information technology, changing demographics, increasing competition,

FIGURE 13-6 The evolution of today's retail institutions.

Institutional Type	Period of Fastest Growth	Period from Inception to Maturity (Years)	Stage of Life Cycle
General store	1800–1840	100	Declining
Single-line store	1820–1840	100	Mature
Department store	1860–1940	80	Mature
Variety store	1870–1930	50	Declining
Corporate chain	1920–1930	50	Mature
Discount store	1955–1975	20	Mature
Conventional supermarket	1935–1965	35	Mature/declining
Shopping centre	1950–1965	40	Mature
Gasoline station	1930–1950	45	Mature
Convenience store	1965–1975	20	Mature
Home improvement centre	1965–1980	15	Late growth
Superspecialists	1975–1985	10	Mature
Warehouse clubs	1990–?	5 (projected)	Late growth
Computer-assisted retailing	1990–?	7 (projected)	Early growth
Hypermarkets	1990–1992	3	Mature/declining
Factory outlets	1990–?	5 (projected)	Early growth

SOURCE: Adapted from J. B. Mason and M. L. Mayer, *Modern Retailing: Theory and Practice*, fifth ed. (Burr Ridge, IL: Richard D. Irwin, 1990), p. 25.

and shrinkage (or theft of merchandise). Each of these trends represents a significant threat; however, if managed well, each could represent an exciting opportunity.

Information Technology

Today's retailers must be comfortable with the use of information technology. As noted in the chapter opener, information technology in the form of the Internet offers a new type of nonstore retailing. Even traditional forms of retailing have felt the impact of advances in information technology because in the last decade changing technology has made numerous retail innovations possible, including:[27]

- Computerized checkout counters equipped with scanners and voice synthesizers that recite merchandise price.
- Automatic teller machines (ATMs) at banks.
- Electronic shopping systems such as videotex.
- Computerized-assisted design (CAD) to plan store layouts.
- Store catalogs on videodiscs.
- Home shopping through cable television.
- Electronic data interchange (EDI) between retailers and their suppliers.
- Interactive computer-based kiosks.

Many retailers have discovered that technology is a now a competitive tool in retailing. For example, EDI enables retailers to be more effective in the practice of relationship marketing. As noted in Chapters 7 and 12, it is not uncommon for retailers to use sophisticated scanner technology as an information source for placing orders and communicating with vendors using EDI.

But EDI is not the only way technological advancement is being adopted by Canadian retailers in their efforts to be competitive. Interactive kiosks are being used in stores to collect market information, build databases, provide customer information,

MARKETPLACE APPLICATION

International Retailers Discover a Tough Canadian Market

Home Depot entered Canada in February 1994, when it purchased 75 percent of Toronto-based Aikenhead's from Molson Cos. Ltd. It will open eight instead of nine stores in 1995, and half of the planned 10 stores in 1996. Company officials say sales have not met expectations and cite the economy, cultural factors, and different labor laws as reasons for this slower than expected rate of growth.

Home Depot is not alone. Several other U.S.-based retailers have made a retreat of one kind or another. Atlanta-based Petstuff, whose new parent, PETsMart Inc. of Phoenix, Ariz., decided it wasn't time to move into Canada, and Minneapolis, Minn.-based Target stores, which sent scouting teams to Canada, ultimately stayed away, as well.

Douglas Tigert, retail analyst and professor at Babson College in Wellesley, Mass., says U.S. retailers are seeing more competition than they bargained for when they first stepped across the border. Real estate, wage, and operational costs that are higher than they are in the U.S., as well as a market that is less populous and has fewer discretionary dollars, are all reasons why "American retailers won't ever do the same sales per square foot (here) as they do in the U.S.," Tigert adds.

1. In your opinion, what impact have U.S.-based retailers had on Canadian consumers?

2. Do you believe Canadian retailers can survive if more international retailers decide to enter the Canadian retail market?

SOURCE: James Pollock, "Canada Tougher Than U.S. Stores Thought," *Marketing*, July 3/10, 1995), p. 4.

and to dispense coupons (see Chapter 7). To provide fast and additional service to shoppers, Kmart and Consumers Distributing use interactive kiosks, where product information can be called up on a computer screen. CD-ROM technology is also being used by retailers to enable shoppers to manipulate images on-screen to view a mix and match of various choices such as clothing garments, and wall colours and upholstery.[28]

Changing Demographics

There are several demographic characteristics that are likely to affect the future of Canadian retailing. Among these characteristics are a slowdown of population growth, the aging of the population, and increased education levels. The exact impact of these changes is unknown; however, most marketing experts believe these changes will result in increased competition for market share and thus increased growth in international retailing, a shift in the types of products and services demanded, and an increased demand for quality service. Because increased demand for quality service has become such a dominant trend in recent years, Chapter 19 discusses this topic in detail.

Increasing Competition

In recent years, Canadian retailers have faced increasing domestic-based competition and an onslaught of U.S.-based retailers. Although the Canadian market may be much tougher than U.S. retailers thought (see the accompanying Marketplace Application box), the recent arrival of Wal-Mart, Toys "Я" Us, Home Depot, and other retailers has forced Canadian retailers to adjust to meet the challenge.

To stay competitive, Canadian retailers are investing in more sophisticated scanner-based data collection networks, building relationships with suppliers in an effort to reduce costs, redefining product lines, reassessing store location decisions and renovating stores, and improving—and in some cases establishing for the first time—customer service programs. Given the rapid speed with which these changes are being made, it is clear that many Canadian-based retailers are able to respond to the challenge.

The Shrinkage Problem

A long-standing, growing problem in retailing is **shrinkage,** or theft of merchandise by customers and employees. Shrinkage costs Canadian retailers hundreds of millions of dollars annually. This cost is ultimately passed on to consumers in the form of higher prices. To combat shrinkage, retailers have become more aggressive in their use of such approaches as guards, detectives, employee awareness programs, and magnetic detectors.

LEARNING CHECK

1. Market share is usually fought out before the _____ stage of the retail life cycle.

2. What is shrinkage?

LEARNING OBJECTIVE REINFORCEMENT

1. Understand the value created by retailing. Retailing provides value to the individual consumer and is important to the economy as a whole. Retailers create value for consumers by performing three basic functions: a transactional function, a logistical function, and a facilitating function. Also, retailing has a significant economic impact. Retail sales in Canada are estimated to reach $249 billion in 1999. The retail sector also employs over 1.8 million people in Canada, or approximately 15 percent of the total employed labour force. Some of Canada's top retailers, such as the Hudson's Bay Company, Zellers, and Kmart Canada, each had sales in the billions in 1996. Their sales levels surpass even the GNP of several small nation–states.

2. Describe the life cycle of retail stores. The process of growth and decline that retail outlets experience is described by the retail life cycle. The first stage, early growth, is the emergence of a retail concept, with a sharp departure from existing competition. In the next stage, accelerated development, both market share and profit achieve their greatest growth rates. At this stage, companies tend to focus on the distribution element of the retail mix. The third stage is the maturity phase. New retail forms enter in the maturity phase, stores try to maintain their market share, and price discounting occurs. The challenge facing retailers at this stage is to delay entering the decline stage in which market share and profit fall rapidly. To prevent decline, retailers need to find creative ways of discouraging their customers from moving to alternative retail forms.

3. Explain the impact of future challenges in Canadian retailing. Retailing in Canada is in a constant state of change. There are four trends that are, in part, responsible for this constant state of change. These are: information technology, changing demographics, increasing competition, and shrinkage (or theft of merchandise).

KEY TERMS AND CONCEPTS

CHAPTER QUESTIONS AND APPLICATIONS

1. How has Wal-Mart altered the nature of retailing in Canada?

2. Discuss the impact of the growing number of dual-income households on *(a)* nonstore retailing and *(b)* the retail mix.

3. How does *value added* affect a store's competitive position?

4. In retail pricing, retailers often take a mark down. Explain why a retailer would mark down a product.

5. What are the similarities and differences between the product (Chapter 10) and retail life cycles?

6. How would you classify Wal-Mart in terms of its position on the retail positioning matrix?

7. According to the retail life cycle, what will happen to factory outlet stores?

8. In Figure 13–3 Kinney Shoes was placed on the retail positioning matrix. What strategies should Kinney follow to move itself into the same position as Birks?

9. Breadth and depth are two important components in distinguishing among types of retailers. Discuss the breadth and depth implications of the following retailers *(a)* Wal-Mart, *(b)* Dell Computers, and *(c)* Lands' End.

10. The text discusses the development of teleshopping and Internet shopping in Canada. How does the development of each of these retailing forms agree with the implications of the retail life cycle?

APPLICATION CASE 13-1
WHY ARE YOU TREATING ME LIKE THIS?

Kim Shaw purchased a very expensive pair of shoes she had been admiring for several weeks in the window of Designer's Shoe Shop. Kim was a student and although she worked at a part-time job she had to save for several weeks before being able to afford to purchase the shoes.

After wearing the shoes only once, Kim noticed a rip on the heel of one of the shoes. Kim was certain the rip had not been the result of her mistreatment of the shoe because there was no evidence of a scrape or cut. Instead, it appeared as if the leather on the heel ripped as the result of being pulled too tightly in the manufacturing process. Kim was disappointed but not concerned because she assumed Glen Maher, the owner/manager of Designer's Shoe Shop, would replace her shoes with another pair. Kim and other members of her immediate family had been fairly regular shoppers for many years at Designer's Shoe Shop and at a clothing store owned by Glen Maher.

Less than two weeks after the purchase, Kim returned the shoes to Designer's Shoe Shop and approached Glen Maher with her complaint. When she politely asked if she could replace the shoes with another pair, Glen's response was, "No way! These are very exclusive shoes. I purchased them in Italy so I can't simply return them for replacement."

Kim was shocked by Glen's reaction, not so much by what he said but the way in which he said it. In response, she tried to negotiate alternative solutions such as returning the shoes to the supplier herself or having them repaired at Glen's expense. These suggestions only angered Glen. He reiterated his position and said, "Look, I can't help you! I'm not in the business of selling used shoes. It's your problem not mine."

Kim was disappointed in Glen's attitude and told several friends and family members about her plight. Upon hearing the story, most of these folks advised her to seek a more satisfactory response to her complaint. To attempt such a response, Kim's mother Doris volunteered to approach Glen on the matter.

When approached by Doris, Glen's response was one of absolute anger. In a very negative tone, he restated his position to Doris. News of Glen's behaviour angered Kim's father Larry. Larry was not the type to complain to retailers, but in this case he was of the opinion that Glen was being unreasonable. Larry approached Glen but they could only agree on one thing: The issue would have to be settled in small claims court.

Rather than go that route, Kim decided to have the shoes repaired. Within a week, the shoes were repaired for a cost of $20—a small price to pay given how much she paid for the shoes.

Kim and her parents have since told many people about Glen's failure to stand behind his products. Moreover, the family has vowed never to shop at a store owned by Glen Maher.

QUESTIONS:
1. Were Kim's requests realistic given the situation?
2. Evaluate the outcomes of the encounter for Kim, and for the store owner.
3. If you were a retail service consultant reviewing a videotape of the encounters described in this case, what suggestions would you offer for avoiding such a situation in the future?
4. Is it reasonable for customers to expect small independent retailers to provide the same level of service as they would expect from corporate chains?

APPLICATION CASE 13-2
IKEA: INVENTING A WAY OF DOING BUSINESS

IKEA has invented a way of retailing furniture that can only be implemented with the aid of a sophisticated logistics system that involves multiple cooperative relationships. For one thing, IKEA makes the consumer an active partner. The consumer transports the product home and does the final assembly, eliminating two of the most cumbersome aspects of the traditional furniture business. IKEA's stores are a combination of gallery and warehouse. Products are displayed in rooms that are fully furnished, allowing the consumer to visualize how they look in a home setting. Products are stored in flat cartons, which the consumer picks up and takes home right away, the ultimate in convenience and speed. IKEA will even rent out automobile roof racks! This approach to retailing eliminates many of the costs associated with traditional approaches, allowing lower prices for the consumer.

Other significant cost savings have been achieved by IKEA because of its sophisticated logistics system. IKEA has developed a global network of low-cost, high-quality suppliers who work exclusively or largely for IKEA, and receive orders for large volumes of standardized components designed and engineered by IKEA. In return for cooperating, suppliers receive technical and engineering support, assistance in securing finances, management training and development, and a host of specialized services designed to integrate them into the IKEA way of doing business.

To coordinate the flow of product, suppliers ship components to one of 15 IKEA distribution centres where the components are assembled into cardboard cartons complete with instructions for final assembly. The entire IKEA network, from checkout terminals in the stores to distribution centres and suppliers, is linked through one of the world's most sophisticated electronic data interchange (EDI) systems.

QUESTIONS:

1. From the consumer's point of view, what makes IKEA's approach to retailing an attractive alternative to traditional furniture shopping?
2. What are the key success factors for IKEA?
3. What kind of information would be ideal for IKEA to include in its EDI system?

SOURCE: Adapted from Joseph R. D'Cruz and Alan M. Rugman, "Developing International Competitiveness: The Five Partners Model," *Business Quarterly,* (Winter, 1993), pp. 60–72.

Understanding Integrated Marketing Communications

Direct Marketing

Communication

Sales

Promotion

Personal Selling

advertising

Public Relation

Integrated Marketing Communications: An Overview

THE TREND TOWARD INTEGRATED MARKETING COMMUNICATIONS

Communicating with customers used to be much simpler. Most marketers usually bought some television, radio, or newspaper ads, and perhaps offered the consumer some coupons every now and then. But today's marketplace has fractured into smaller and smaller segments, requiring new techniques to help business communicate with consumers. Most marketers still use traditional advertising, but many are also adding new ways to reach the consumer. In doing so, some are starting to think about the integrated use of communications to extend and maximize their budgets and to ensure that their target audience receives a consistent message. This is what integrated marketing communications (IMC) is all about.

IMC has now become one of the hottest marketing watchwords of the 1990s. One survey of marketing executives showed that integrated marketing communications will be the most important factor in shaping marketing strategy over the next decade. But interestingly enough, many small businesses have practiced an integrated approach to communications for many years.

Why? With limited budgets, many small businesses were forced to look for effective communications solutions—they didn't care if it was advertising, public relations, or sales promotion. Most larger organizations, on the other hand, with more resources and departmental structures, failed to see the value of integration. Today's fragmented market, increased competition, and greater concern over the costs of marketing communications have forced these large organizations to rethink their strategies. Many are embracing

347

IMC. One expert believes organizations are more conscious of getting measured results from their communications dollars. This is what an IMC approach can offer.

One problem with integration is that many traditional communications techniques are being combined with existing as well as newer techniques, creating confusion about what to call some of these new forms of communications activities. For example, is an infomercial a 30-minute television advertisement, a direct marketing communications technique, or a combination of both? Is an electronic, interactive information shelf display for Benylin considered advertising or point-of-purchase sales promotion? Academics may argue about what to call these techniques, but practitioners view them as powerful communications techniques that will be more effective in influencing a target audience's attitudes and behaviour.[1]

In this chapter, we will discuss the concept of marketing communications. We will examine the role of marketing communications and how the marketing communications process works. You will be introduced to the major marketing communications techniques available to marketers, and, of course, to the concept of integrated marketing communications. Finally, we will highlight the elements that must be included in an integrated marketing communications plan, and what factors influence the composition of the marketing communications mix to be used in a plan.

MARKETING COMMUNICATIONS

Marketing communications, sometimes called promotion, is an important element of the marketing mix. **Marketing communications** are marketer-initiated communications directed to target audiences in order to influence attitudes and behaviours. This includes every element of the marketing mix. For example, a product's design sends a message. The same is true of a product's package. Distribution channels are a form of communication; a product sold in a discount store may communicate a different message than a similar product sold in an upscale department store. The price of a product also sends a message; to some consumers, a low price may signal poor quality, while a higher price may mean higher quality.

The five major marketing communications techniques or categories that we will focus on are: advertising, public relations (PR), sales promotion, direct marketing communications (DMC), and personal selling. To communicate effectively with its target audience, an organization may have to rely on a combination of these five major techniques. An organization's **marketing communications mix** (sometimes called the promotional mix) is the combination of the techniques or categories it chooses to use.

The Role of Marketing Communications

The role of marketing communications is simple: to influence or affect the behaviour of the intended target audience. Figure 14–1 demonstrates the role of marketing communications in achieving three broad objectives: (1) to *inform* the target audience, (2) to *persuade* the target audience, and (3) to *remind* the target audience. It also shows that each of the five marketing communications techniques can play a role in achieving these objectives.

Informing the target audience about a product and its benefits is an important marketing communications function. If a potential customer is not aware of a product there is no chance that he or she will buy it. But while having an informed potential customer

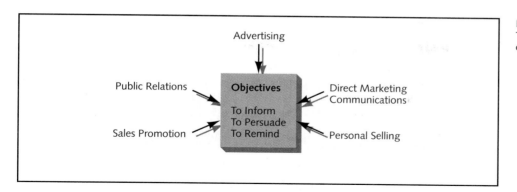

FIGURE 14–1
The role of marketing communications.

is a necessary condition for purchase, it is not sufficient. The potential customer must be given a reason, or be persuaded, to buy. Finally, once the purchase is made, the customer must be reminded about the benefits they enjoyed by using the product. In essence, the customer may have purchased the product, but is still susceptible to competitors' messages about their products. Marketing communications after the sale is important to ensure the customer feels good about the purchase and will become a repeat purchaser.

An Overview of the Marketing Communications Mix

As mentioned earlier, to communicate effectively with its target audience an organization may have to rely on a combination of five major marketing communications techniques. An organization's marketing communications mix can be comprised of advertising, public relations (PR), sales promotion, direct marketing communications (DMC), and personal selling. While separate chapters are devoted to discussing these major techniques, here we want to provide a brief overview of each technique. Each can play a role in informing, persuading, and reminding a target audience.

Advertising. **Advertising** is any paid form of nonpersonal communication about an organization, good, service, or idea by an identified sponsor. The *paid* aspect of this definition is important, because the time or space for the advertising message normally must be bought. A full-page, four-colour ad in *Châteline,* for example, costs about $30,000, while a full-page, four-colour ad in *L'Actualité* costs about $12,000. An occasional exception to paid advertising is the *public-service announcement,* where the advertising time or space is donated. Advertising normally involves the use of major media such as television, radio, magazines, and newspapers; however, new ways to advertise are being developed all the time. Chapter 15 discusses advertising in detail.

Public Relations. **Public relations (PR)** involves communications activities designed to influence the perceptions, opinions, and beliefs about an organization among its relevant publics including customers, employees, shareholders, government, and the general public. The goal of PR is to create a positive image about an organization, its products, services, or people. There are costs associated with the PR function (e.g., staff) but, unlike advertising, an organization does not pay for any PR time or space in the media, commonly referred to as *publicity.* While publicity is an important PR tool, other PR techniques are also available to an organization that will allow them to effectively communicate with its target audience(s). These will be discussed in Chapter 15.

An advertiser can reach over 200,000 Canadians with a paid ad in *Cosmo*.

COSMOPOLITAN IS A UNIVERSAL LANGUAGE.

In more than 80 countries, in 12 languages and 28 editions. Whether you need to tell your story universally or locally, from Sydney to Siena to Stuttgart to Seattle, there is no better way to reach young women than Cosmopolitan. Call Seth Hoyt at (212) 649-3282.

COSMOPOLITAN. THE LARGEST SELLING YOUNG WOMEN'S MAGAZINE IN THE WORLD.

A publication of Hearst Magazines, a division of The Hearst Corporation. © 1991 The Hearst Corporation.

Sales Promotion. **Sales promotion** is a short-term inducement of value offered to arouse interest in buying a good or service. Sales promotions can be offered to ultimate consumers (consumer sales promotions) as well as to intermediaries (trade sales promotions). Examples of consumer sales promotions include coupons, deals, samples, sweepstakes, and rebates. Examples of trade sales promotions include allowances and discounts and cooperative advertising. Chapter 16 discusses sales promotions in detail.

Direct Marketing Communications. **Direct marketing communications (DMC)** involves communicating directly with target customers to encourage an "immediate" response by telephone, mail, electronic means, or personal visit. DMC methods include direct mail, direct-response advertising (broadcast and print), and telemarketing. The goal of seeking an "immediate" response from the customer is what differentiates DMC from the other marketing communications methods. Direct marketing communications is a fast growing segment in the marketing communications field because it can provide marketers with direct, immediate, and measurable results. The development of consumer databases has also helped spawn its growth. DMC will be discussed in Chapter 16.

Personal Selling. **Personal selling** is defined as the two-way flow of communication between buyer and seller, designed to influence a person's or a group's purchase decision. Unlike advertising, personal selling is usually face-to-face communication between the source (sender) and the receiver. However, selling by telephone, or telemarketing, is growing in popularity. Chapter 17 discusses the role of personal selling in the marketing communications mix.

LEARNING CHECK

1. Marketing communications can be defined as _____.

2. Marketing communications are designed to achieve three broad objectives. What are they?

3. What are the five major marketing communications techniques?

Face-to-face sales presentation.

FIGURE 14–2
The marketing communications process.

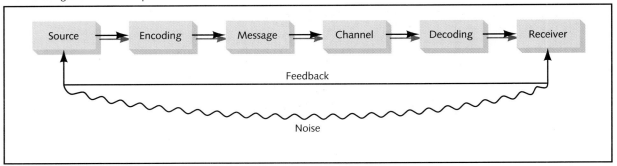

The Marketing Communications Process

Communication is the process of establishing shared meaning. Six elements are necessary for communication to occur: a source, a message, a channel, a receiver, and the processes of encoding and decoding.[2] Figure 14–2 demonstrates how the marketing communications process works.

The marketer is the **source** of the communication or the message sender. **Encoding** is the process of selecting words, pictures, and other symbols in order to transmit the intended message. The **message** is the idea to be conveyed by the source. The **channel** is the means by which the message is conveyed. The channel could be the media (e.g., television, radio, etc.) or it could be a salesperson standing outside your door. **Decoding** is the process by which the **receiver**—the intended target for the message—deciphers or interprets the message. Decoding is performed by the receiver according to his or her own frame of reference, that is, his or her values, beliefs, and attitudes.[3]

Figure 14–2 shows a line labelled feedback. **Feedback** is the communication flow from the receiver back to the source and indicates whether the message was decoded and understood as intended. Chapter 15 reviews approaches called *pretesting* that ensure that advertisements are decoded properly. Also shown in Figure 14–2 is something called noise. **Noise** is any distraction or distortion during the communications process that prevents the message from being effectively communicated. Noise can be a simple error, such as a printing mistake that affects the meaning of a newspaper ad. Noise can also include competing messages and distractions like a telephone call during a salesperson's presentation.

In the ad on page 353, Lexus is the source of the message. The ad appeared in a magazine (the channel). How would you interpret (decode) this advertisement? The picture and the text in the advertisement show that the source's intention is to introduce a unique product and position Lexus as a company in "the relentless pursuit of perfection"—a position the source believes will appeal to the upper-income readers of the magazine.

The marketing communications process is not always successful. Errors in communication can happen several ways. The source may not have adequately encoded the message, a properly encoded message may be sent through the wrong channel and never make it to the receiver, the receiver may not properly decode the message, or finally, feedback may be so delayed or distorted that it is of no use to the source or sender.

Although marketing communications appears easy to perform, truly effective communications can be very difficult. Another requirement for effective communication is that the source (sender) and the receiver have a shared **field of experience**—similar understanding and knowledge. Some of the better-known marketing communications

A source, a channel, and a message.

problems have occurred when Canadian and U.S. companies have taken their messages to cultures with different fields of experience. Many misinterpretations are merely the result of bad translations. For example, General Motors made a mistake when its "body by Fisher" claim was translated into Flemish as "corpse by Fisher."[4]

Integrated Marketing Communications

Until recently, most organizations used a departmental or functional approach to marketing communications. Departments were often established that specialized in one communications technique such as advertising, public relations, sales promotion, and so forth. Each department often worked separately and with little regard to the others' activities. Because of the lack of coordination and communication between departments, sometimes conflicting messages were created and disseminated to the target audience. Moreover, organizations lost opportunities to combine techniques that could have improved the effectiveness of their communications and maximized their finite communications budgets.

Integrated marketing communications (IMC) involves the integrated and coordinated use of all forms of communication reaching the target audience so that consistency in the message is achieved and communications resources are maximized. IMC is a new way of looking to the whole, where organizations once only saw parts. It involves defining the organization's communications needs and selecting the best solutions from the full range of communications techniques available.[5]

Figure 14–3 contrasts the departmental or functional approach to marketing communications and the IMC approach. With the IMC approach, an integrated plan is often developed by a coordinating marketing communications department, with input from each functional area. All departments know who the target audience is, what the communications objectives are, and what the basic communications theme will be. Each department will be assigned communications responsibilities based on its abilities to achieve the communications objectives. The departments execute their part of the plan, working closely with one another to ensure effective implementation.

FIGURE 14–3
Departmental approach vs. IMC approach.

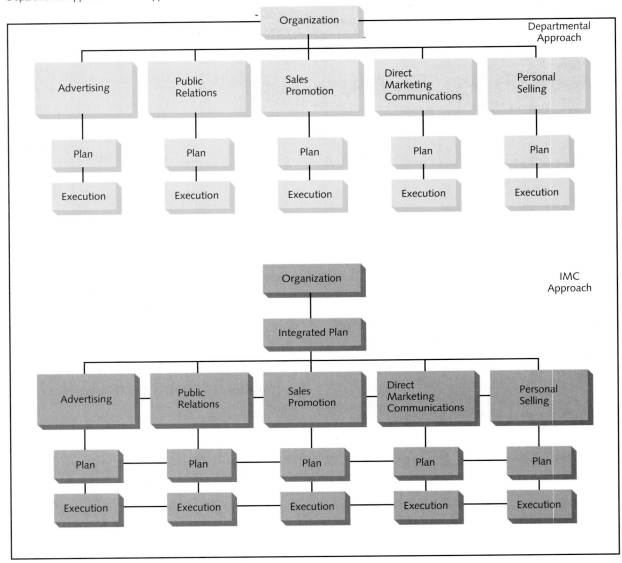

LEARNING CHECK

1. What are the six elements required for communication to occur?

2. A difficulty for Canadian companies using marketing communications in foreign markets is that the audience does not share the same _____.

3. What is integrated marketing communications?

I. Target Audience
II. Marketing Communications Objectives
III. Marketing Communications Budget
IV. Marketing Communications Theme
V. Marketing Communications Mix
VI. Execution
VII. Control and Evaluation

FIGURE 14–4
The integrated marketing communications plan.

THE INTEGRATED MARKETING COMMUNICATIONS (IMC) PLAN

Most often, an organization's IMC plan can be found as part of its overall marketing plan. Usually contained in the marketing mix section of the marketing plan (Chapter 2), an IMC plan details the marketing communications activities that will be undertaken in order to help achieve the organization's marketing objectives. Figure 14–4 shows the elements that must be part of an IMC plan.

Target Audience

Effective marketing communications begins with a well-defined target audience. Essentially, an organization must know who it wants to communicate with and why. The target audience may be current customers, prospects (e.g., competitors' customers), or those who might influence a buying decision. The target audience can consist of ultimate consumers, or organizational buyers (including intermediaries), or both. The organization's marketing plan should detail the target market, or the groups of consumers toward which the organization directs its marketing effort.

While the IMC plan is usually an integral component of an organization's overall marketing plan, as noted above, it also can be a separate or stand-alone document. If it is separate, details on the target audience must be spelled out and must be consistent with the target market information found in the marketing plan. Details might include where the target audience is located (geographically), demographic and psychographic descriptions, media habits, and purchase behaviour.

Marketing Communications Objectives

The broad marketing communications objectives—to inform, to persuade, and to remind—must be translated into more specific and measurable objectives that will form the basis of the IMC plan. The objectives could focus on:

- Establishing a product image.
- Differentiating the product.
- Encouraging product trial.
- Stimulating demand.
- Establishing, modifying, or reinforcing attitudes.
- Developing sales leads.
- Developing repeat purchase behaviour.
- Stimulating impulse buying.

The marketing communication objectives flow logically and are linked to the overall marketing objectives set by the organization. For example, suppose the Canadian government wants to increase by 10 percent the number of tourists coming to Canada in 1997. With that specific marketing objective, those responsible for marketing communications must then determine how many people must be reached and influenced by the marketing communications mix in order to ensure achievement of the marketing objective. In this case, the communications objectives might be stated as: "To reach 20 million prospects with 5 messages during the spring of 1997 in order to stimulate interest in Canada as a vacation spot" or "To increase from 15 percent to 25 percent consumer awareness and interest in Canada as a vacation spot." With an IMC plan, each element of the marketing communications mix will have its own specific objective(s). Collectively, these objectives must be consistent and mutually reinforcing.

Marketing Communications Budget

After establishing the communications objectives, an organization must decide how much to spend on the effort. Determining the ideal amount for a communications budget is difficult. There are several methods that can be used to set the budget, including percentage of sales, competitive parity, all you can afford, and objective and task.

Percentage of Sales. In the **percentage of sales budgeting** approach, funds are allocated to marketing communications as a percentage of past or anticipated sales, in terms of either dollars or units sold. A common budgeting method,[6] this approach is often stated in terms such as, "Our marketing communications budget for this year is 3 percent of last year's gross sales." The advantage to this approach is obvious: It's simple and provides a financial safeguard by tying the budget to sales. However, there is a fallacy in this approach in that the assumed causal relationship between sales and marketing communications is reversed. In theory, marketing communications should determine sales levels, rather than sales levels determining marketing communications expenditures. Using this method, an organization might reduce its marketing communications budget because of a downturn in past sales or an anticipated downturn in future sales—situations in which it may need marketing communications the most.

Competitive Parity. A second common approach to set marketing communications budgets, **competitive parity budgeting,** matches either competitors' absolute levels of spending or the proportion per point of market share. This approach has also been referred to as *matching competitors* or *share of market*. It is important to consider the competition in budgeting.[7] Consumer responses to marketing communications are affected by competing marketing communications, so if a competitor runs 30 radio ads each week and a sales promotion once a month, it may be more difficult for a firm to effectively communicate with the consumer with only five radio messages and a sales promotion once a year.[8] The competitor's budget level, however, should not be the only determinant in setting an organization's marketing communications budget. The competition might have different marketing communications objectives, which require a different level of communications expenditures.

All You Can Afford. Common to many small businesses is **all you can afford budgeting,** in which money is allocated to marketing communications only after all other budget items are covered. As one company executive said in reference to this budgeting process, "Why, it's simple. First I go upstairs to the controller and ask how much they can afford to give this year. He says a million and a half. Later, the boss comes to me

FIGURE 14–5
The objective and task approach.

Objectives	
1. To increase awareness among college students for the new CD-player cleaning kit. Awareness at the end of one semester should be 20 percent of all students, up from the existing 0 percent today.	
2. To have 1 percent of those students buy the kit through the use of a $2 coupon inducement.	

Tasks	Costs
Advertisements once a week (with in-ad coupon) for a semester in 500 college papers	$240,000
Coupon redemption/handling costs	40,000
Weekly radio advertising on nationally syndicated "Top 40" program	25,000
Three monthly, full-page ads in *Audio* magazine	9,000
Total budget	$314,000

and asks how much we should spend, and I say, 'Oh, about a million and a half.' Then we have our budget."[9] Fiscally conservative, this approach has little else to offer. Using this budget philosophy, a company acts as though it doesn't know anything about a marketing communications–sales relationship or what its communications objectives are.

Objective and Task. The best approach to budgeting is **objective and task budgeting,** whereby an organization determines its marketing communications objectives, outlines the tasks to accomplish these objectives, and determines the communications cost of performing these tasks.[10]

This method takes into account what the organization wants to accomplish and requires that the objectives be specified.[11] Strengths of the other budgeting methods can be integrated into this approach because each previous method's strength is tied to the objectives. For example, if the costs are beyond what the organization can afford, objectives are reworked and the tasks revised. The difficulty with this method is the judgment required to determine the tasks needed to accomplish objectives. Figure 14–5 shows a sample part of an integrated marketing communications plan with objectives, tasks, and budget outlined. The total amount to be budgeted is $314,000. If the organization can afford only $200,000, the objectives must be reworked, tasks redefined, and the total budget recalculated.

Marketing Communications Theme

As we saw in Chapter 2, an organization will attempt to "position" its product in the market in a certain way. The desired positioning must then be effectively communicated to the target audience. While the overall marketing mix must be designed to support and reinforce the intended positioning, marketing communications plays an integral role here. The organization creates a basic "positioning theme" that is delivered to the market largely through marketing communications activities. The theme sets the tone for the specific messages that will be created for various advertising, public relations, sales promotion, direct marketing communications, and personal selling activities. In short, the theme is the umbrella from which all other messages are created.

For example, to position itself as a long-lasting battery, Duracell uses a simple positioning theme: "No other battery lasts longer, stronger." This theme is used in all of Duracell's marketing communications. While the specific message content may vary depending on the different communications techniques, the messages will be consistent with the general theme. The creating of basic message content and message appeals are discussed in more detail in Chapter 15.

MARKETPLACE APPLICATION

Pepsi Uses Integrated Marketing Communications Approach in Honduras

New owners and an aggressive integrated marketing communications campaign has put the pep back into Pepsi in Honduras, doubling market share in less than a year and catching Coca-Cola off guard. Mariposa Corp. of Guatemala injected new life into the sluggish Pepsi franchise by boosting communications expenditures by 30 percent, making Pepsi the pick of a new generation of Honduran cola drinkers. Daniel Alvarez, Pepsi's marketing manager, says marketing is the most important thing in Honduras. People consume what they see, hear, or read about. So Pepsi launched a massive communications campaign with a common theme, "Try Pepsi Today." On television, radio, and in the newspapers—all the time, people are reading, hearing, and seeing, "Try Pepsi Today." To further heighten Pepsi's image, the company sponsors town fairs and concerts and helps support schools and colleges. Pepsi is also the official sponsor of the country's number one soccer team. The company has also taken charge of publicity, increased merchandising efforts, and undertaken major sampling programs in the streets. Twenty shiny new trucks painted with the Pepsi logo have also been added to the fleet and are seen daily by consumers as they wind through the narrow streets. And the campaign is working. Market share has shot up 20–30 percent in just nine months. Along with the integrated marketing communications effort, the company has focused on better service to vendors. The company also made an investment in refrigeration. The number of coolers has risen from 800 to 4,000—a key move in a sweltering country where most pop is drunk lukewarm.

1. What other marketing communications tools could Pepsi consider for its integrated marketing communications effort?

2. Pepsi's current theme, "Try Pepsi Today," will have to be modified sooner or later. Why? And, what could be a reasonable follow-up theme?

SOURCE: Adapted from Andrea Mandel Campbell, "Hondurans Drink Up Aggressive Pepsi Promo Push," *Marketing,* August 5, 1996, p. 6.

Marketing Communications Mix

An organization must be able to select the appropriate marketing communications mix that is both affordable and effective in achieving stated communications objectives. It is also critical that the mix is carefully integrated and mutually reinforcing. Many factors influence the composition of the marketing communications mix including: the characteristics of each technique, the target audience, stage of the product's life cycle, characteristics of the product, and decision stage of the buyer.

Characteristics of the Techniques. Each marketing communications technique has its own unique characteristics, including particular strengths and weaknesses (see Figure 14–6). Marketers have to understand these strengths and weaknesses in order to select appropriate techniques. In general, the marketer will find some techniques are better suited than others in achieving particular stated objectives.

For example, if an organization wants to reach a wide audience quickly and make them aware of its product, advertising would be a viable option to consider. Advertising can also be attention-getting and can communicate specific product benefits to prospective buyers. Advertising allows the organization to control what it wants to say and when. However, advertising has high absolute costs in terms of production and placement. Also, if the advertising is not direct-response in nature, there is often a lack of direct feedback that makes it difficult to know if, and how well, the message was received.

While advertising may be viewed with skepticism, public relations is often viewed as a more credible source of information. An organization can also deliver more infor-

Attention-getting ad.

FIGURE 14–6   Strengths and weaknesses of marketing communications techniques.

	Strengths	*Weaknesses*
Advertising	• Efficient in reaching large numbers of people • Attention-getting	• High absolute costs • Difficult to receive good feedback • Often viewed by consumers with skepticism
Public Relations	• Credibility • Can provide more information than through ads	• Difficult to secure media cooperation
Sales Promotion	• Effective in stimulating sales in short run • Very flexible	• Easily abused by consumers • Easily duplicated by competitors
Direct Marketing Communications (DMC)	• Direct, immediate, and measurable results • Precision targeting • Easily complements other communications techniques	• Some consumers reluctant to buy via DMC
Personal Selling	• Personal feedback • Very persuasive • Can select audience • Can give complex information	• Extremely expensive per exposure • Message may be inconsistent

mation to its target audiences through public relations than advertising. However, some public relations activities such as publicity often require media support which may be difficult to secure.

Sales promotions can stimulate sales by offering an incentive to buy. However, sales gains may be temporary, and if used continually, sales promotions can lose their effectiveness. Direct marketing communications (DMC) can provide direct, immediate, and measurable results. DMC can also offer precision targeting and can complement other techniques such as personal selling. However, unless the company is known by the consumer, there may be a reluctance to buy via direct marketing communications.

Lastly, personal selling allows the seller to see or hear the potential buyer's reaction to the message. A salesperson can also tightly control to whom the presentation is made. However, personal selling is very expensive per exposure and different salespeople can change the message so that consistency of the message to all customers may be lost.

Target Audience. The marketing communications mix will be affected by the intended target audience. As we noted earlier, the target audience can consist of ultimate consumers, or organizational buyers including intermediaries, or both. The mix used in each of these cases will vary in scope and nature. For example, if the intended audience is the ultimate consumer, a manufacturer may rely more heavily on advertising and consumer sales promotion. If the intended audience is the intermediary, a manufacturer will use personal selling as a major component of the mix.

If the intended audience is the intermediary, a manufacturer is likely to use a **push strategy,** directing the mix (personal selling and trade sales promotion, for example) to the intermediaries to gain their cooperation in ordering and stocking the product and to market it to the ultimate consumer. Using a push strategy, the channel member "pushes" the product to the consumer (see Figure 14–7).

FIGURE 14–7
Push vs. pull strategy.

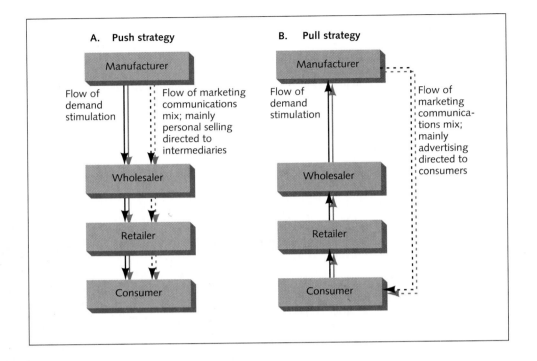

With the ultimate consumer as the target, a manufacturer will tend to use a **pull strategy,** directing the mix (advertising and consumer sales promotion, for example) toward the consumers to induce them to ask the intermediaries for the product. Seeing demand from the ultimate consumer, the intermediaries demand it from the manufacturer. Thus, with a pull strategy, the consumer "pulls" the product through the channel.

If an organization wants to reach both ultimate consumers and intermediaries, a combination of push–pull strategy will be used. The mix will be developed and the budget allocated to reflect the relative importance of the target audiences (i.e., ultimate consumers and intermediaries). Many Canadian consumer goods firms are allocating greater percentages of their budget toward intermediaries. In some cases, as much as 60 percent of the budget is being allocated to personal selling and trade sales promotions designed to reach the intermediaries, while only 40 percent is spent on advertising, consumer sales promotions, and direct marketing communications directed towards the ultimate consumers.[12]

Product Life Cycle. All products have a product life cycle (Chapter 10), and the composition of the marketing communications mix often changes over the four life cycle stages, as shown for Purina Puppy Chow in Figure 14–8.

Introduction stage Informing consumers in an effort to increase their level of awareness is the primary communications objective in the introduction stage of the product life cycle. In general, all the marketing communications techniques may be part of the mix at this time, although the use of specific mix elements during any stage depend on the product and situation. Stories on Purina's new nutritional dog food are placed in *Dog World* magazine, trial samples are sent to registered dog owners in ten major cities, advertisements are placed during reruns of the TV show "Lassie," and the sales force (personal selling) begins to approach supermarkets to get orders. Advertising is particularly important as a means of reaching as many people as possible to build up aware-

FIGURE 14–8
Marketing communications mix over the product life cycle of Purina Puppy Chow.

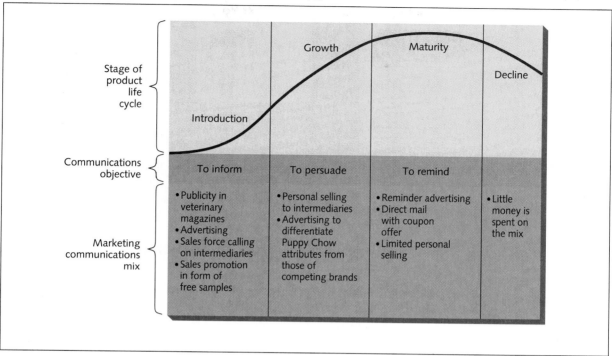

ness and interest. Public relations activities may even begin slightly before the product is commercially available.

Growth stage The primary communications objective during the growth stage is to persuade the consumer to buy the product—Purina Puppy Chow—rather than substitutes, so it is necessary to gain brand preference and solidify distribution. Sales promotion assumes less importance in this stage, and public relations is not a factor because it depends on the novelty of the product. The primary component of the mix is advertising, which stresses brand differences. Personal selling is used to solidify the channel of distribution. For consumer products such as dog food, the sales force calls on wholesalers and retailers in hopes of increasing inventory levels and gaining shelf space. For industrial products, the sales force often tries to get contractual arrangements to be the sole source of supply for the buyer.

Maturity stage In the maturity stage, the need is to maintain existing buyers, and advertising's role is to remind buyers of the product's existence. A direct marketing communications technique such as a direct mail coupon offered to dog owners might be used to maintain loyal buyers. The sales force at this stage will also seek to satisfy intermediaries, offering them allowances and discounts as an incentive to continue to stock the product.

Decline stage The decline stage of the product life cycle is usually a period of phase-out for the product, and little money is spent on marketing communications.

Characteristics of the Product. The proper blend of the elements in the marketing communications mix also depends on the type of product. Three specific

Purina Puppy Chow: a product in the maturity stage of its life cycle.

IBM Thinkpad, a complex and expensive product.

characteristics should be considered: complexity, risk, and ancillary services. *Complexity* refers to the technical sophistication of the product and hence the amount of understanding required to use it. It's hard to provide much information in a one-page magazine ad or 30-second television ad, so the more complex the product, the greater the emphasis on personal selling.

Another characteristic to consider is the degree of *risk* represented by the product's purchase. Risk for the buyer is the cost in financial terms (such as a few thousand dollars spent for an IBM ThinkPad portable computer), or social or physical terms. A hair transplant procedure might represent all three risks—it may be expensive, people can see and evaluate the purchase, and there may be a chance of physical harm. Although advertising helps, the greater the risk, the greater the need for personal selling.

The level of *ancillary services*—service or support after the sale—required by a product also affects the type of mix used. This consideration is common to many industrial products and consumer purchases. Who will repair your automobile or VCR? Advertising and public relations can help establish the seller's reputation. However, personal selling is essential to build buyer confidence and provide evidence of customer service.

Decision Stage of the Buyer. Knowing the customer's stage of decision making can also affect the composition of the marketing communications mix.

Prepurchase stage In the prepurchase stage advertising and public relations are more helpful than personal selling, because advertising and public relations (notably publicity) inform the potential customer of the existence of the product and the seller. Sales promotion in the form of free samples can also play a role to gain low-risk trial. When a salesperson calls on the customer after heavy advertising or public relations, there is some recognition of what the salesperson represents. This is particularly important in industrial settings, in which sampling of the product may not be possible. Direct marketing communications techniques, such as direct mail or direct-response television advertising, could also be used to encourage prospects to phone for more information on the product or to mail a request for a sample. Telemarketing may also be used.

Purchase stage At the purchase stage the importance of personal selling is highest, whereas the impact of advertising and public relations is lowest. Sales promotion in the form of coupons, deals, point-of-purchase displays, and rebates can be very helpful in encouraging demand. Direct marketing communications techniques such as direct mail or telemarketing are also useful at this stage.

Postpurchase stage In the postpurchase stage the salesperson is still important. In fact, the more personal contact after the sale, the more the buyer is satisfied. Advertising is also important to assure the buyer that the right purchase was made. Advertising and personal selling help reduce the buyer's postpurchase anxiety.[13] Sales promotion in the form of coupons can also be used to help encourage repeat purchases from satisfied first-time users.

Creating and placing an ad—part of the plan execution (a pull strategy ad).

Execution

The Integrated Marketing Communications plan will not be successful unless it is put into action. Depending on the nature of the marketing communications mix, the organization may have to create ads, purchase media time and space, begin the sales promotion programs, and deploy the sales force. If appropriate, public relations activities and direct marketing communications programs will also have to be executed. The plan elements have to be well coordinated and executed on a timely basis. However, some elements of the plan may have to be executed before others. For example, the ad program may precede the sales force deployment in order to ensure that the salespeople are not calling on "cold customers." Like the overall marketing plan, execution of the IMC plan requires good internal communications; the scheduling of precise tasks, assignment of responsibilities, and deadlines; and organizational support for the plan.

Control and Evaluation

An organization must establish ways to control and evaluate the success or failure of the IMC plan and its basic components. Having well-defined objectives allows for proper control and evaluation. An organization could evaluate the success of its advertising by running tests to see if the target audience noticed the ads. It may monitor its consumer sales promotion activities by counting the number of coupons redeemed, or measure the effectiveness of personal selling by examining the number of new accounts opened. Researchers might test the impact of public relations activities by asking consumers about their attitudes toward the organization both before and after the PR program, to determine its effectiveness. The organization can easily test the impact of its direct marketing communications program by measuring consumer response (e.g., inquiries, purchases, etc.). Whatever the control and evaluation procedures are, they must be spelled out in the plan. As with the overall marketing plan, if results are not as predicted, corrective actions must be taken.

LEARNING CHECK

1. What are the seven elements that must be part of an IMC plan?

2. What are the four methods for setting a marketing communications budget?

3. Explain the difference between a push and a pull strategy.

Should Everyone Have a Right to Use Marketing Communications

Professional marketers realize there are legal and ethical issues associated with the use of marketing communications. In many cases, there are laws and regulations concerning what types of goods, services, or ideas that can and cannot be communicated to a target audience. Most marketers understand what is legal and what is illegal when it comes to marketing communications. But some marketing communications may be technically legal but raise significant ethical questions. For example, many suggest that tobacco companies use marketing communications to convey an image that smoking is glamorous. Similarly, beer manufacturers are accused of using lifestyle ads that appeal to youth. Some groups are even questioning the use of marketing communications by religious groups or others who aspouse a particular philosophy. For example, Australia's most elaborate advertising billboard—a giant three-dimensional volcano—doesn't sell soft drinks or hamburgers. Instead, it markets a controversial religion. The 330-square-meter billboard, including a five-meter-high television screen, advertises L. Ron Hubbard's 1950 book *Dianetics,* the foundation stone of the Church of Scientology. The volcano is expected to occupy the site for six years, and the TV screen will show commercials for Dianetics. Telephone numbers and details on how to obtain copies of *Dianetics* will be flashed during the ads. A "testing centre" near the billboard is available for people to go and receive an evaluation by Scientologists. Many Australians are uncomfortable with the Church of Scientology and their use of this marketing communications campaign. It may be legal, many suggest, but it is not ethical for the Church of Scientology to market its philosophy in this manner.

1. What do you think about this situation?

2. Some suggest that if the communications do not advocate hate or violence, everything else is OK. Comment.

SOURCE: Adapted in part from "Aussie Volcano Spews Scientology Doctrine," *Marketing,* August 5, 1996, p. 6.

LEGAL AND ETHICAL ISSUES IN MARKETING COMMUNICATIONS

Over the years many consumers have been misled—or even deceived—by some forms of marketing communications. Examples include sweepstakes in which gifts were not awarded and advertisements whose promises were great until the buyer reads the small print. While deceptive or misleading marketing communications are illegal in Canada, they do continue to occur.

Marketing communications targeted at special groups such as children and the elderly raise ethical concerns. For example, providing free product samples to children in elementary schools, or linking product lines to TV programs and movies, has led to questions about the need for various restrictions on marketing communications activities. Although there are many federal and provincial rules and regulations governing marketing communications practices in Canada, some observers believe more regulation is needed.

More formal regulation of marketing communications activities would be very expensive to police and enforce. As a result, there are increasing efforts by advertising agencies, trade associations, and marketing organizations at self-regulation. By imposing standards that reflect the values of society on marketing communications, marketers can facilitate the development of new techniques, minimize regulatory constraints and restrictions, and help consumers gain confidence in the communications efforts used to influence their purchases. Today, more than ever, marketing executives must make sound ethical judgments about the use of existing and new communications practices and not simply adhere to the technical letters of the law.

LEARNING OBJECTIVE REINFORCEMENT

1. Define marketing communications. Marketing communications, sometimes called promotion, are marketer-initiated communications directed to target audiences in order to influence attitudes and behaviours.

2. Understand the role of marketing communications in an organization. The role of marketing communications is simple: to influence or affect the behaviour of the intended target audience. Marketing communications are designed to achieve three broad objectives: to inform the target audience, to persuade the target audience, and to remind the target audience.

3. List the five techniques that can comprise a marketing communications mix. To communicate effectively with its target audience, an organization may have to rely on a combination of five major techniques: advertising, public relations (PR), sales promotion, direct marketing communications (DMC), and personal selling. An organization's marketing communications mix (sometimes called its promotional mix) is the combination of the techniques or categories it chooses to use.

4. Explain the marketing communications process. Communication is the process of establishing shared meaning. For communication to occur six elements are necessary: a source, a message, a channel, a receiver, and the processes of encoding and decoding. The marketer is the source of the communication or the message sender. Encoding is the process of selecting words, pictures, and other symbols in order to transmit the intended message. The message is the idea to be conveyed by the source. The channel is the means by which the message is conveyed. Decoding is the process by which the receiver—the intended target for the message—deciphers or interprets the message. Feedback is the communication flow from the receiver back to the source and indicates whether the message was decoded and understood as intended. Noise is any distraction or distortion during the communications process that prevents the message from being effectively communicated.

5. Define integrated marketing communications. Integrated marketing communications (IMC) involves the integrated and coordinated use of all forms of communication reaching the target audience so that consistency in the message is achieved and communications resources are maximized. It involves defining the organization's communications needs and selecting the best solutions from the full range of communications techniques available.

6. Outline the components of an integrated marketing communications plan. The basic components that must be part of any IMC plan include: (1) definition of target audience, (2) marketing communications objectives, (3) marketing communications budget, (4) marketing communications theme, (5) marketing communications mix, (6) execution, and (7) control and evaluation.

7. Explain the methods used for setting a marketing communications budget. There are several methods that can be used to set a communications budget, including: (1) percentage of sales budgeting, wherein funds are allocated to marketing communications as a percentage of past or anticipated sales, in terms of either dollars or units sold; (2) competitive parity budgeting, which is matching competitors' absolute levels of spending or the proportion per point of market share; (3) all you can afford budgeting, in which money is allocated to marketing communications only after all other budget items are covered; and (4) objective and task budgeting, wherein an organization determines its marketing communications objectives, outlines the tasks to accomplish these objectives, and determines the communications cost of performing these tasks.

8. Outline the factors that influence the composition of the marketing communications mix. An organization must be able to select the appropriate marketing communications mix that is both affordable and effective in achieving stated communications objectives. It is also critical that the mix is carefully integrated and mutually reinforcing. Many factors influence the composition of the marketing communications mix including: (1) the characteristics of each technique, (2) target audience, (3) stage of the product's life cycle, (4) characteristics of the product, and (5) decision stage of the buyer.

KEY TERMS AND CONCEPTS

marketing communications p. 348
marketing communications mix p. 348
advertising p. 349
public relations (PR) p. 349
sales promotion p. 350
direct marketing communications (DMC) p. 350
personal selling p. 351

communication p. 352
source p. 352
encoding p. 352
decoding p. 352
receiver p. 352
feedback p. 352
noise p. 352
field of experience p. 352

integrated marketing communications (IMC) p. 353
percentage of sales budgeting p. 356
competitive parity budgeting p. 356
all you can afford budgeting p. 356
objective and task budgeting p. 357
push strategy p. 359
pull strategy p. 360

CHAPTER QUESTIONS AND APPLICATIONS

1. Marketing communications are designed to achieve three broad objectives. What are they?

2. After listening to a recent sales presentation, Mary Smith signed up for membership at the local health club. On arriving at the facility, she learned there was an additional fee for racquetball court rentals. "I don't remember that in the sales talk; I thought they said all facilities were included with the membership fee," complained Mary. Describe the problem in terms of the marketing communications process.

3. Explain how the marketing communications techniques used by an airline would differ if the target audience was (a) consumers who travel for pleasure or (b) corporate travel departments that select airlines to be used by company employees.

4. Fisher-Price Company, long known as a manufacturer of children's toys, has introduced a line of clothing for children. Outline an integrated marketing communications plan to get this product introduced to the marketplace.

5. Many insurance companies sell health insurance plans to companies. In these companies the employees pick the plan, but the set of offered plans is determined by the company. Recently, Blue Cross, a health insurance company, ran a television ad stating, "If your employer doesn't offer you Blue Cross coverage, ask why." Explain the strategy behind the advertisement.

6. Assume you're responsible for developing a marketing communications plan for a new snowboard you and your business partner just developed. What should you learn about your target audience first?

7. Interview a few local retailers. Ask them if they know about integrated marketing communications. Do they use IMC? If not, ask why not?

8. In your interviews with local retailers (question 7), ask them what methods they use to set their marketing communications budget. Ask them why they have chosen that particular method and whether or not they think it is effective.

APPLICATION CASE 14-1
VITALITY HEALTH FOOD STORE

Vitality Health Food Store will open for business in the fall of 1997. It will be an independently owned retail store run by Jon Carter, a university graduate with a degree in business. It will be located in a strip mall in a growing, upscale, suburban neighbourhood. Carter decided to open the business because of his interest in health food and because of the impressive growth that has occurred in the sector over the past decade (9 percent annually). Vitality has no other specialty health food stores to compete with in its trade area. However, many supermarkets in the area do offer some health food sections in their stores in response to consumer demand for health food.

Carter has projected sales of $500,000 for his first year of business, which is about average for a store of this type and size. He has also allocated about $25,000 for marketing communications activities, using a pecentage of sales budgeting approach. His basic marketing strategy is to penetrate the market by positioning the store as the one-stop shop for consumers' health food needs. Customer service, convenience, and variety will be integral elements of the marketing strategy. Carter and all of the store's employees will be knowledgeable, friendly, and committed to the concept of "relationship marketing."

Carter conducted some research on the health food shopper. He has determined that his primary (potential) customer will have the profile outlined in Exhibit 1. He selected his location given the numbers of potential customers within close proximity to the store who fit the profile. But Carter realizes that customers must be made aware of the store, and must be persuaded to visit and make purchases. Moreover, those cus-

EXHIBIT 1 Profile of Potential Shopper.

Demographics:	Female; aged 25–49, college educated; working in professional occupations; earning over $30,000 per year
Lifestyle:	Health and fitness oriented; environmentally conscious; concerned about preservatives and additives in food
Benefits sought:	Want to deal with knowledgeable people when shopping for health food; are prepared to pay higher prices for better health food
Media habits:	Most likely to read consumer magazines, the Sunday edition of the newspaper, listen to FM radio, and watch late-night television

tomers must be reminded to return and encouraged to become regular shoppers. He knows marketing communications must play a major role if the business is to be successful.

QUESTIONS

1. Given Vitality's marketing objectives (i.e., $500,000 in sales), formulate 2–3 primary marketing communications objectives that would be appropriate for the store to pursue.
2. What should be the basic "theme" communicated by Vitality to its target audience?
3. What would be the most appropriate marketing communications mix for Vitality given the communications objectives, target audience, and budget?
4. How can Vitality track the impact of its marketing communications?

APPLICATION CASE 14-2
NATIONAL COMMUNITY TREE FOUNDATION

In the 1990 Green Plan, the Government of Canada made clear its commitment to providing a safe and healthy environment for present and future generations. A key part of the Green Plan is a programme called Tree Plan Canada. It recognizes the fundamental importance of our rural and urban forests in addressing the problem of global warming and improving the quality of life for all Canadians. The National Community Tree Foundation (NCTF) was formed as a nonprofit, (non-governmental) organization to manage the Tree Plan Canada programme and to ensure that its objectives became realities. The fundamental purpose of the NCTF is "to foster and encourage

the planting and care of trees in and around more than 5,000 cities, towns, and villages by 1998.

Tree planting is certainly not a new idea in this country. The forestry sector plants millions of trees each year. But virtually all of these trees are planted to compensate for the effects of timber harvesting or forest fires. So the first hurdle facing the Foundation was to educate Canadians that they too had an important role to play in planting new trees in urban and rural areas. If NCTF's objectives were to be achieved within the timeframe specified, then average Canadians would have to be motivated to plant trees in and around their communities. But

Canadians would only plant trees if they understood the benefits of trees as an integral part of the ecosystem. The public's affinity for trees and forests was a good starting point, with their aesthetic appreciation and a belief in the "goodness of green."

What was still needed was crystal-clear communication of the solid science that makes trees vital to human survival. Canadians needed to know, or be reminded, that trees are the lungs of the earth, filtering the air we breathe and removing pollutants. NCTF wanted Canadians to appreciate that a mature tree keeps on cleaning and cleaning, at no charge, for many decades. But if the message was only seen as a lesson, NCTF would lose its audience—just providing boring facts about an issue that people believed they already understand simply would not work. NCTF allocated an initial $420,000 for marketing communications activities designed to create public awareness and public involvement (a call to action).

QUESTIONS

1. Given the challenges facing NCTF, what marketing communications techniques would you recommend the Foundation to use?
2. Besides the initial target audience of "average adult Canadians," who else should NCTF target to become involved with the programme?
3. What type of creative theme would prompt Canadians to action?

SOURCE: Adapted from Canadian Advertising Success Stories, Cassies II, Canadian Congress of Advertising, 1995. Used with permission.

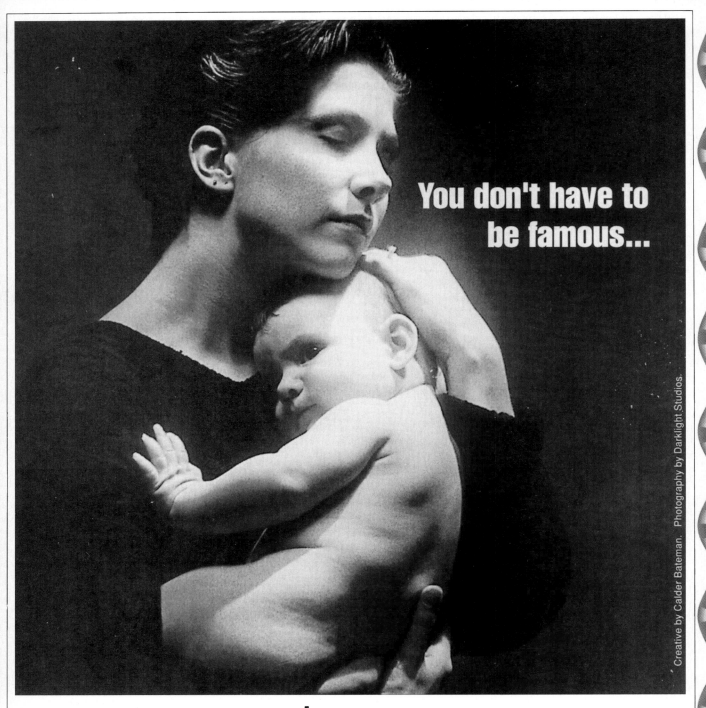

You don't have to be famous...

You only have to be human.

It's funny how democratic a disease can be. It can come from any place and affect hundreds, then thousands of people unexpectedly in a short time. Women are 17% of new HIV/AIDs cases in Alberta – and rising. Young people are 25%, with cases all across Alberta. Every community needs to find its solutions. Every person needs to understand and we all need to talk about it.

Abstinence remains an option

Creative by Calder Bateman. Photography by Darklight Studios.

This message was created as part of a province–wide HIV/AIDS prevention campaign for young adults.
For more information call the provincial AIDS Program at 427-0836 (toll free through the RITE line).

Advertising and Public Relations

ALBERTA AIDS ADS AIM TO CHANGE BEHAVIOUR

With messages such as, "If you drink to get lucky, your luck might have run out" and "More women are buying condoms. It's not taboo. It's smart," the Alberta government's AIDS campaign doesn't mince words. According to Rick McHutchion of Alberta Health's provincial AIDS program, the ad campaign uses a novel approach. The goal is not to increase knowledge, but to get people to apply their knowledge in the heat of the moment.[1]

Visually, the campaign is stark and lean. The six 30-second television spots use little action or dialogue. Some of the messages and images are so explicit that they're aired after 9 P.M. The campaign's five newspaper spots are also minimalist, with few containing more than 25 words. The ads were developed using input from focus groups. But the biggest obstacle wasn't reaching the target audience, it was convincing bureaucrats and politicians that the campaign should be run. The provincial government was reducing funding for public programs and services, and the campaign was not an easy sell, according to McHutchion.

Eventually the government was convinced it was the right time and direction for the campaign. About $125,000 was budgeted for production and another $150,000 was allocated for the media buy. Donations of air time and newspaper space effectively doubled the value of the media purchases. The print ads run in seven dailies and 40 weeklies, and the TV spots run on commercial and community stations across the province.[2]

Successful advertising is a challenge. Advertising typically has only a few seconds to communicate its message. It must be the right message and it must reach the right audience. In this chapter we will discuss advertising. Later in the chapter, we will also discuss the concept of public relations. In the case of Alberta Health, their AIDS ad campaign was given additional support by the media, which provided some air time and ad space at no cost, a form of public relations called *public-service announcements.* Both advertising and public relations can be integral components of an organization's integrated marketing communications plan.

DEFINING ADVERTISING

Chapter 14 described **advertising** as any *paid* form of *nonpersonal* communication about an organization, good, service, or idea by an identified sponsor. Two terms are highlighted: *paid* distinguishes advertising from public relations, where there is no payment to media, and *nonpersonal* separates it from personal selling.

TYPES OF ADVERTISEMENTS

As you look through any magazine, the number of advertisements and the varying themes can be overwhelming. Advertisements are prepared for different purposes, but they basically consist of two types: product and institutional. These two types can be further classified on the basis of whether they are designed to get the consumer to take immediate action (direct response) or to influence future purchases or actions by the consumer (delayed response).

Product Advertisements

Focusing on selling a good or service, **product advertisements** take three forms: pioneering (or informational), competitive (or persuasive), and reminder.

Used in the introductory stage of the life cycle, *pioneering advertisements* tell people what a product is, what it can do, and where it can be found. The key objective of a pioneering ad, such as that for the Sony MiniDisc recorder/player, is to inform the target market. Properly developed informative ads have been found to be interesting, convincing, and effective, according to consumer judgment.[3]

Advertising that promotes a specific brand's features and benefits is *competitive advertising.* The objective of such a message is to persuade the target market to select the firm's brand rather than that of a competitor. An increasingly common form of competitive advertising is comparative advertising, which shows one brand's strengths relative to those of competitors.[4] Some research suggests that one-third of all television commercials are comparative ads.[5] Firms that use comparative advertising must be able to support their claims in order to meet government as well as self-regulatory requirements established by the Canadian Code of Advertising Standards.

Reminder advertising is used to reinforce previous knowledge of a product. Reminder advertising is good for products that have achieved a well-recognized position and are in the mature phase of their product life cycle. Another type of reminder ad, reinforcement, is used to assure current users they made the right choice. One example: "Aren't you glad you use Dial. Don't you wish everybody did?"

Institutional Advertisements

The objective of **institutional advertisements,** sometimes called *corporate advertising,* is to build goodwill or an image for an organization, rather than promote a specific

Example of a pioneering ad.

good or service. Institutional advertising has been used by Bank of Montreal, General Motors, and Molson to build confidence in the company name. Often this form of advertising is used to support public relations activities.[6] Four alternative forms of institutional advertisements are often used:

1. *Advocacy advertisements* state the position of a company on an issue. Molson runs an extensive advertising campaign encouraging the responsible use of alcohol.

2. *Pioneering institutional advertisements,* like the pioneering ad category for products discussed earlier, are used for a new announcement about what a company is, what it can do, or where it is located. Canada Trust uses a pioneering institutional ad campaign to better position itself in the personal banking market in Canada using the theme "thinking like a customer," as shown in the accompanying ad.

3. *Competitive institutional advertisements* communicate the advantages of one product class over another and are used in markets where different product classes compete for the same buyers. The Dairy Farmers of Canada runs ads with the objective of increasing demand for milk as it competes against other types of beverages.

4. *Reminder institutional* advertisements, like the corresponding product ads, simply bring the company's name to the attention of the target market again.

Direct-Response and Delayed-Response Advertising

While advertising is classified as product or institutional, both types can be further classified as either direct-response or delayed-response advertising. **Direct-response advertising** (product or institutional) seeks to motivate the customer to take immediate action. A television ad wanting you to call an 800 number and order a product now is a direct-response ad. In Chapter 16, we will discuss direct-response advertising as an important direct marketing communications (DMC) technique used by many marketers today.

An example of a
pioneering institutional ad.

Delayed-response advertising, on the other hand, presents images and/or information designed to influence the consumer in the near future when making purchases or taking other actions. Most national automobile advertising, for example, is delayed-response in nature; advertisers do not expect you to drop everything and run to your car dealer immediately to buy a car.

LEARNING CHECK

1. What is the difference between pioneering and competitive ads?

2. What is the purpose of institutional advertising?

3. What is direct-response advertising?

DEVELOPING THE ADVERTISING PROGRAM

Because media costs are high, advertising decisions must be made carefully, using a systematic approach. Paralleling the planning, implementation, and control steps described in the marketing management process (Chapter 2), the advertising decision process is divided into developing, executing, and evaluating the advertising program (Figure 15–1). Development of the advertising program focuses on the *four Ws:*

FIGURE 15–1
The advertising decision process.

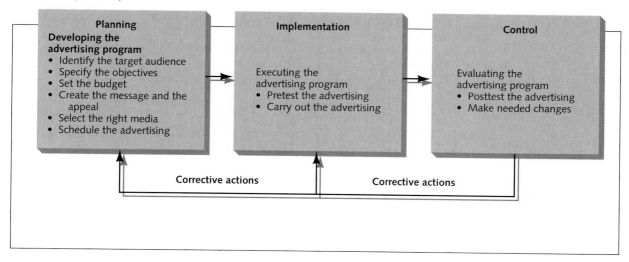

• *Who* is the target audience?
• *What* are the advertising objectives, the amounts of money that can be budgeted for the advertising program, and the kind of message to use?
• *When* should the advertisements be run?
• *Where* should the advertisements be run?

Identifying the Target Audience

As we discussed in Chapter 14, identifying the target audience is critical for successful communications. To the extent that time and money permit, the target audience for the advertising program is the target market for the firm's product. Generally, the target audience will have been determined during the planning stages for the integrated marketing communications plan. However, the more the firm knows about its target audience's profile, the easier it is to develop an advertising program. An important aspect of the planning phase for advertising is determining the media habits of the target audience. For example, if a firm wanted to reach you with its ads, it would need to know what TV shows you watch and what magazines you read.

Specifying Advertising Objectives

As we saw in Chapter 14, the three broad communications objectives of marketing communications are: to inform, to persuade, and to remind the target audience. At the advertising level, the objectives usually become more specific. One framework advertisers can use to set advertising objectives is the **hierarchy of effects model.** This model suggests that there is a sequence of stages a prospective buyer goes through from initial awareness of a product to eventual action (either trial or adoption of the product).[7] The stages include:

• *Awareness.* The consumer's ability to recognize and remember the product or brand name.

- *Interest.* An increase in the consumer's desire to learn about some of the features of the product or brand.
- *Evaluation.* The consumer's appraisal of the product or brand on important attributes.
- *Trial.* The consumer's actual first purchase and use of the product or brand.
- *Adoption.* Through a favourable experience on the first trial, the consumer's repeated purchase and use of the product or brand.

Although sometimes an objective for an advertising program involves several steps in the hierarchy of effects, it often focuses on a single stage. No matter what the specific objective might be, from building awareness to increasing repeat purchases, advertising objectives should possess three important qualities:

1. They should be designed for a well-defined target audience.
2. They should be measurable.
3. They should cover a specific time period.

Setting the Advertising Budget

After setting the advertising objectives, an organization must decide how much to spend. Determining the ideal amount for an ad budget is difficult because there is no precise way to measure the exact results of spending advertising dollars. However, the methods used to set the overall integrated marketing communications plan budget can be used to set the specific ad budget. Those methods discussed in Chapter 14 include: percentage of sales budgeting, competitive parity budgeting, all you can afford budgeting, and objective and task budgeting. As with the IMC budget, the best approach to setting the ad budget is the objective and task approach.

Creating the Message and the Appeal

The central element of an advertising program is designing the message that the intended audience will see (as in magazines, newspapers, and TV) or hear (as in radio and TV) and the message's basic appeal. The message content and basic appeal are largely driven by the basic positioning strategy determined by the organization, and must be consistent with the overall message theme as set through the integrated marketing communications planning process. The specific message and appeal must be designed to execute the desired positioning and mutually reinforce the theme of the overall IMC plan.

Message Content. Every advertising message is made up of both informational and persuasive elements. These two elements, in fact, are so intertwined that it is sometimes difficult to tell them apart. For example, basic information in many ads such as the product name, benefits, features, and price are presented in a way that tries to attract attention and encourage purchase. On the other hand, even the most persuasive advertisements have to contain at least some basic information to be successful. Importantly, the message content must stress the product's ability to deliver on benefits deemed important to a prospective buyer.

Message Appeal. Once advertisers determine message content, or what will be said, they must then determine how it will be said, or the message appeal. Information and persuasive content must be combined in the form of an appeal to provide the basic reason for the consumer to act. Although the marketer can use many different types of appeals, common advertising appeals include fear appeals, sex appeals, and humorous appeals.

Fear appeals suggest to the consumer that he can avoid some negative experience through the purchase and use of a product, or through a change in behaviour. Insurance companies often try to show the negative effects of premature death on the relatives of those who don't carry enough life or mortgage insurance. Food producers encourage the purchase of low-fat, high-fibre products as a means of reducing cholesterol levels and the possibility of a heart attack.[8] When using fear appeals, the advertiser must be sure that the appeal is strong enough to get the audience's attention and concern, but not so strong that it will lead them to "tune out" the message.

In contrast, *sex appeals* suggest to the audience that the product will increase the attractiveness of the user. Sex appeals can be found in almost any product category, from automobiles to toothpaste. Unfortunately, many commercials that use sex appeals are only successful at gaining the attention of the audience; they may have little impact on how consumers think, feel, or act. Some advertising experts even argue that such appeals get in the way of successful communication by distracting the audience from the purpose of the ad.

Humorous appeals imply either directly or more subtly that the product is more fun or exciting than competitors' offerings. Like fear and sex appeals, humour appeals are widely used in advertising and can be found in many product categories. Unfortunately for the advertiser, humour tends to wear out quickly, thus boring the consumer. Eveready ads, featuring the Energizer battery bunny, frequently change to avoid this advertising "wear-out."

Creating the Right Ad. The "creative" people in the organization doing the advertising, or its advertising agency, have the responsibility to create attention-getting, memorable, and believable advertising. The creative efforts involve determining specific message content and use of an appropriate appeal.

In recent years, advertisers have become more concerned about the effectiveness of advertising. The debate over reasons for the success or failure of advertising programs usually comes down to a discussion of the ad itself or the media (e.g., magazine, television, or radio). Canadian research has found that only one in five new advertising campaigns are successful. Of those that fail, poorly designed ads account for almost 80 percent of failures while media problems account for only 20 percent.

Poor campaigns usually involve one or more of the following problems: failure to make brand linkage (the association of the creative idea with the brand), lack of persuasive communication, inappropriate strategy, or poor use of media. Better-performing ads tended to use mnemonic or brand linkage, relevance or consistency to historic image, uniqueness in a category, newsworthiness, and humour. What didn't appear to affect ad performance was energy level, use of music, use of animals, plot involvement, or soft versus hard sell.

The research also suggests that poor ad quality cannot be offset with heavy media buying. In other words, if the advertising is bad, advertisers cannot spend double on media to make it better.[9] Thus, the production quality of ads is often just an important as the ad message itself. But, creating quality advertisements is a complex process. Performing artwork, layout, and production for the ads can be costly and time-consuming. A high-quality 30-second TV commercial can cost $150,000 to produce.

LEARNING CHECK

1. What are the five stages of the hierarchy of effects model?

2. What are the characteristics of good advertising objectives?

Humourous appeals are used frequently in advertising.

Does your dad have a hard time breathing, especially at night? Breathe Right strips will help him breathe easier by holding open his nasal passages. So give him Breathe Right strips for Father's Day and have a happy father every day. Breathe Right strips. In cough and cold sections everywhere.

Breathe Right nasal strips

Improves Breathing By Reducing Nasal Airflow Resistance

Drug-free *greatly pulls open nasal passages*

10 Med/Lg Nasal Dilators

Manufacturer's Coupon | Expires 12/31/95

Save 50¢

CONSUMER: Limit one coupon per purchase as specified on the face of this coupon. No other coupon may be used in conjunction with this coupon. RETAILER: You are authorized to act as our agent and redeem this coupon at face value plus 8 cents handling, in accordance with our redemption policy, copies available upon request. Void if copied and where prohibited, licensed and regulated. Good only in U.S.A. Cash value 1/100 cent. Send properly redeemed coupons to: CNS, Inc., P.O. Box 390268, El Paso, TX 88539-0268.

0039

5 57145 51050 0

Happy Father's Day.

Selecting the Right Media

In addition to determining the right message and appeal, every advertiser must select the right media in which to place its advertisements. The *advertising media,* or the means by which the message is communicated to the target audience, include television, radio, magazines, newspapers, and outdoor, as well as other options. The "media selection" decision should be made on the basis of the target audience, type of product, nature of the message,

FIGURE 15–2 The language of the media buyer.

Term	What It Means
Reach	The number of different people exposed to an advertisement.
Rating	The percentage of households in a market that are tuned to a particular TV show or radio station.
Frequency	The average number of times an individual is exposed to an advertisement.
Gross rating points (GRPs)	Reach multiplied by frequency.
Cost per thousand (CPM)	The cost of advertising divided by the number of thousands of individuals or households that are exposed.

campaign objectives, available budget, and costs of alternative media. In 1995, over $8 billion was spent on advertising in the major media in Canada. About 23 percent of the total was spent on newspaper ads, 21 percent on television, 10 percent on yellow pages, 9 percent on outdoor, 9 percent on radio, and about 5 percent on magazine ads.[10]

Choosing a Medium and a Vehicle within That Medium. In deciding where to place advertisements, an organization has several media to choose from and a number of alternatives, or vehicles, within each medium. Often advertisers use a mix of media forms and vehicles to maximize the exposure of the message to the target audience while at the same time minimizing costs. These two conflicting objectives of maximizing exposure and minimizing costs are of central importance to media planning.

Basic Media Terms. Media buyers speak a language of their own, so all advertisers involved in selecting the right media for their campaigns must be familiar with some common terms used in the advertising industry. Figure 15–2 shows the most common terms used in media decisions.

Because advertisers try to maximize the number of individuals in the target market exposed to the message, they must be concerned with reach. **Reach** is the number of different people exposed to an advertisement. The exact definition of reach sometimes varies among alternative media. Newspapers often use reach to describe their total circulation or the number of different households that buy the paper. Television and radio stations, in contrast, describe their audience using the term **rating**—the percentage of households in a market that are tuned to a particular TV show or radio station. In general, advertisers try to maximize reach in their target market at the lowest cost.

Although reach is important, advertisers are also interested in exposing their target audience to a message more than once. This is because consumers often do not pay close attention to advertising messages, some of which contain large amounts of relatively complex information. When advertisers want to reach the same audience more than once, they are concerned with **frequency,** the average number of times a person in the target audience is exposed to a message or an advertisement. Greater frequency is desirable, like greater reach.

When reach is multiplied by frequency, an advertiser will obtain a commonly used reference number called **gross rating points (GRPs).** To obtain the appropriate number of GRPs to achieve an advertising campaign's objectives, the media planner must balance reach and frequency. For example, a firm could have one ad plan that will reach 30 percent of Canadian households 5 times (on average) for a total of 150 GRPs, or it could have another plan that reaches 50 percent of Canadian households 3 times (on average) for a total of 150 GRPs. Which is better? While the reach is the same in both plans, one plan gives greater frequency. If the costs are the same, the plan with the greater frequency

FIGURE 15–3   Advantages and disadvantages of major advertising media.

Medium	Advantages	Disadvantages
Television	Reaches extremely large audience; uses picture, print, sound, and motion for effect; can target specific audiences.	High cost to prepare and run ads; short exposure time and perishable message; difficult to convey complex information.
Radio	Low cost; can target specific audiences; ads can be placed quickly; can use sound, humour, and intimacy effectively.	No visual excitement; short exposure time and perishable message; difficult to convey complex information.
Magazines	Can target specific audiences; high-quality colour; long life of ad; ads can be clipped and saved; can convey complex information.	Long time needed to place ad; limited control of ad position; relatively high cost; competes for attention with other magazine features.
Newspapers	Excellent coverage of local markets; ads can be placed and changed quickly; ads can be saved; quick consumer response; low cost.	Ads compete for attention with other newspaper features; can't control ad position on page; short life span; can't target specific audiences.
Direct mail	Best for targeting specific audiences; very flexible (3D, pop-up ads); ad can be saved; measurable; no competition with editorial matter.	Relatively high cost; audience often sees it as "junk mail."
Outdoor	Low cost; local market focus; high visibility; opportunity for repeat exposures.	Message must be short and simple; low selectivity of audience; criticized as traffic hazard, eyesore.

SOURCES: C. L. Bovée and W. F. Arens, *Contemporary Advertising,* fourth edition, (Burr Ridge, IL: Richard D. Irwin, 1992), pp. 437–44; and W. G. Nickels, J. M. McHugh, and S. M. McHugh, *Understanding Business* third edition (Burr Ridge, IL: Richard D. Irwin, 1993), p. 332.

would be more desirable. But often costs are not the same, so media planners must consider the comparative costs of various ad plans, usually on a cost per thousand basis. **Cost per thousand (CPM)** refers to the cost of reaching 1,000 individuals or households with an advertising message in a given medium (M is the Roman numeral for 1,000).

Advertisers with a finite ad budget cannot maximize both reach and frequency. With a fixed budget, reach and frequency are inversely related. If one goes up, the other goes down. In such situations, it is becoming more common for companies to trade some reach for greater frequency. In other words, advertisers will consciously decide to reach fewer customers but to communicate with them more frequently. Striking a balance between reach and frequency is important, but so is the overall weight (GRPs) of a campaign. Canadian research shows that ad campaigns with fewer than 100 GRPs per week media weight are far less effective than those between 100 and 125 GRPs.[11]

Different Media Alternatives

Figure 15–3 summarizes the advantages and disadvantages of the important advertising media. All, except direct mail, will be described in more detail in this chapter. We will examine direct mail in detail in Chapter 16 as a dominant direct marketing communications tool. However, you should remember that it is an advertising medium and is often used by companies that are not direct marketers.

Television. Television is a valuable medium because it communicates through both sight and sound. In addition, television is the only medium that can reach 99 percent of the homes in Canada.[12] On average, Canadian adults watch about 25 hours of TV a week.

Television's major disadvantage is cost. The price of a 30-second commercial during prime time can be as high as $28,000 on CTV, a private English network, and over $17,000 on Radio-Canada, the CBC French television network.[13] Because of these

TV storyboards lead to commercials, which communicate with sight and sound.

high charges, some advertisers have reduced the length of their commercials from 30 seconds to 15 seconds. This practice, referred to as *splitting 30s,* reduces costs but can also restrict the amount of information and emotion that can be conveyed.[14] Another problem with television is the likelihood of wasted coverage—having people outside the target audience see the advertisement. In recent years, the cost and wasted coverage problems of TV have been reduced through the introduction of cable TV. Advertising time is often less expensive on cable channels than the major networks. In addition, cable TV offers many specialty channels with very narrowly defined audiences such as MuchMusic, TSN, YTV, CBC Newsworld, and Chinavision, the first national Chinese-language network in Canada.

Advertisers are also trying new ways to improve the effectiveness of their television advertising. In Chapter 16, we will discuss the use of direct-response television advertising as well as program-length commercials called *infomercials.*

Radio. There are over 700 radio stations broadcasting in Canada; about 51 percent are AM stations and 49 percent are FM stations. Combined, these stations reach 95 percent of all Canadians age 12 and over.[15] The major advantage of radio is that it is a segmented medium—there are many different stations with different programming formats designed to attract certain market segments (e.g., country stations, hard rock stations). The average adult in Canada, aged 18 or over, tunes in to radio about 23 hours per week. Radio is also a portable medium with good out-of-home reach, particularly during drive time.

The disadvantage of radio is that it has limited use for products that must be seen. Another problem is the ease with which consumers can tune out a commercial by switching stations. Radio is also a medium that must compete for people's attention as they engage in other activities such as driving, working, or relaxing. Peak listening time for radio in Canada is between 6 A.M. and 9 A.M.

Magazines. There are over 500 consumer magazines in Canada, as well as several important general business magazines.[16] The marketing advantage of this medium is the great number of special-interest publications that appeal to narrowly defined segments. Skiers read *Ski Canada* magazine, craftspeople subscribe to *Crafts Plus,* pet owners buy *Pets* magazine, gardeners peruse *Canadian Gardening,* and expectant mothers in Quebec read *Mon Bébé.* Each magazine's readers often represent a unique customer profile. *The Hockey News* has a distinctively male, sports-oriented audience, so a hockey equipment manufacturer that places an ad in *The Hockey News* knows it is reaching the desired target audience. In addition to the distinct audience profiles of magazines, good colour reproduction is an advantage that allows magazines to create strong images.[17]

The cost of advertising in national magazines is a disadvantage. The cost of a full-page, four-colour ad in *Maclean's* is over $26,000. But many national publications publish regional editions (*Maclean's* publishes 13), which reduce absolute cost and wasted coverage. In addition to cost, a limitation of magazines is their infrequency. At best, magazines are printed on a weekly basis, with many specialized publications appearing only monthly or less often.

High technology is arriving in magazine ads. Cardboard pop-up ads have been used by Dodge trucks, for example. Revlon offered actual samples of eye shadow in fashion magazines, and if you read *Architectural Digest* you could even smell a Rolls-Royce interior using a special scent strip. And for something new? Interactive disk ad inserts! Apple Canada inserted a DOS-formatted 3.5-inch diskette into 28,000 subscriber and newsstand copies of *Profit* magazine. The disk provides users a sample of Apple's graphical user interface. The interactive element of the diskette allows readers to explore Apple technology.[18] *Canadian Business* magazine offers Corporate 500 data on a diskette insert, around which ad space is available.

Newspapers. Newspapers are an important local medium with excellent reach potential. There are over 100 daily newspapers and about 900 weekly community newspapers in Canada. The average paid circulation for the dailies is over 5 million copies, and the average weekly circulation for the weeklies is 9 million. Household penetration of the dailies is 63 percent. About 65 percent of Canadians read a weekly paper.[19] Dailies allow advertisements to focus on specific current events, such as a 24-hour sale. Community newspapers can be used by local retailers and other businesses with a good degree of certainty of reaching customers in their trade area. Local retailers often use newspapers as their primary advertising medium.

Newspapers are rarely saved by the purchaser, so companies are generally limited to ads that call for immediate customer action, or direct response (although customers can clip and save ads they want). Companies also cannot depend on newspapers for colour reproduction as good as that in most magazines.

National advertising campaigns rarely include this medium except in conjunction with local distributors of their products. In these instances both parties often share the advertising cost, using a cooperative advertising program.

Outdoor. A very effective medium for reminding consumers about your product is outdoor advertising. The most common form of outdoor advertising, called *billboards,* often results in good reach and frequency and has been shown to increase purchase rates.[20] The visibility of this medium is good supplemental reinforcement for well-known products, and it is a relatively low-cost, flexible media alternative. A company can buy space just in the desired geographic market. A disadvantage to billboards, however, is that no opportunity exists for lengthy advertising copy. Also, a good billboard depends on traffic patterns and sight lines. In many areas, environmental laws have limited the use of this medium. To overcome some of the problems faced by street-level billboards, mall posters are available at 400 shopping centres across Canada and are

An example of a catchy billboard ad.

designed to reach pedestrian traffic coming to and leaving the malls. Transit shelter advertising is also available in many markets.

If you ever lived in a metropolitan area, chances are you might have seen another form of outdoor advertising, transit advertising (not be to confused with transit shelter ads). This medium includes messages on the interiors and exteriors of buses, subway cars, and taxis. As the use of mass transit grows, transit advertising may become increasingly important. Selectivity is available to advertisers, who can buy space by neighbourhood or bus route. Total-paint buses are also available, buses that may be totally painted on the outside to carry an advertising message. One disadvantage to this medium is that the heavy travel times, when audiences are the largest, are not conducive to reading advertising copy. People are standing shoulder to shoulder on the subway, hoping not to miss their stop, and little attention is paid to the advertising.

Other Media. As traditional media have become more expensive and cluttered, advertisers have been attracted to a variety of nontraditional advertising options called *place-based media*. Messages are placed in locations that attract a specific target audience, such as airports, doctors' offices, health clubs, bars, theatres (where ads are played on the screen before the movies are shown), elevators, the Jumbotron at SkyDome, and even public bathroom stalls. Other new media options include *product placement*—paying to have a brand-name product used in a movie or even in video games. Another new venue for advertisers is on the Internet. Many companies have set up their own advertising sites on the World Wide Web hoping to reach the millions of consumers who go on-line everyday.

Selection Criteria. Choosing among these alternative media is difficult and hinges on several factors. First, knowing the media habits of the target audience is essential to deciding among the alternatives. Second, product attributes occasionally necessitate that certain media be used. For example, if colour is a major aspect of the product appeal, radio is excluded. Newspapers allow advertising for quick action to confront competitors, and magazines are more appropriate for complicated messages because the reader can spend more time reading the message. The final factor in selecting a

MARKETPLACE APPLICATION

New Forms of Outdoor Media

There's more to outdoor media these days than traditional billboards and transit advertising. Here are just a
few examples of new outdoor media available to advertisers in Canada. Pedal Power Promotions, a Halifax-
based company, offers companies a chance to advertise
on its bike-stands located across Atlantic Canada. Each
bike-stand has double-sided ad space available. Ads are
printed on a durable surface and covered by Lexan for
weather protection. The company will also move the
ads from one location to another or store them for reuse
at a later date. In Montreal, outdoor advertisers have
two new options. Logi-Pub offers advertisers nine-foot-
wide-by-seven-foot-high electronic signboards with
high resolution, full-colour display and video capabilities. Place des Arts now offers advertisers the opportunity to reach eight million pedestrians who travel
through its underground passageway each year. The

walkway features 70 illuminated panels and 15 triangu-
lar, cubic, and wall-mounted display cases.

Urban Outdoor Trans Ad of Toronto offers painted
murals featuring Clear Focus window film for use on
storefront windows. This permits full visibility through a
building's windows for those inside. Cleslok Outdoor,
also a Toronto-based company, offers 30 backlit vertical
boards in the Toronto area, the only ones in Canada.

1. What is the primary role of traditional and these
   new forms of outdoor media?
2. Some advertisers are worried that there are just too
   many advertising options, and consumers may be
   turned off and tuned out. Comment.

SOURCE: Adapted from Gail Chiasson, "New Ways to Reach People
Where They Don't Live," *Marketing*, July 22/29, 1996, p. 16.

medium is cost. When possible, alternative media are compared using a common denominator that reflects both reach and cost—a measure such as CPM.

Scheduling the Advertising

There is no correct schedule to advertise a product, but three factors must be considered. First is the issue of *buyer turnover,* which is how often new buyers enter the market to buy the product. The higher the buyer turnover, the greater is the amount of advertising required. A second issue in scheduling is the *purchase frequency;* the more
frequently the product is purchased, the less repetition is required. Finally, companies
must consider the *forgetting rate,* the speed with which buyers forget the brand if advertising is not seen.

Setting schedules requires an understanding of how the market behaves. Most
companies tend to follow one of three basic approaches:

1. *Steady ("drip") schedule.* When seasonal factors are unimportant, advertising
   is run at a steady or regular schedule throughout the year.
2. *Flighting ("intermittent") schedule.* Periods of advertising are scheduled between periods of no advertising to reflect seasonal demand.
3. *Pulse ("burst") schedule.* A flighting schedule is combined with a steady
   schedule because of increases in demand, heavy periods of competitive advertising, or introduction of a new product.

For example, products such as dry breakfast cereals have a stable demand throughout the
year and would typically use a steady schedule of advertising. In contrast, products such
as snow skis and suntan lotions have seasonal demands and receive flighting-schedule
advertising during the seasonal demand period. Some products such as toys or auto-

An ad to stimulate
seasonal demand.

mobiles require pulse-schedule advertising to facilitate sales throughout the year and during special periods of increased demand (such as holidays or new car introductions). Some evidence suggests that pulsing schedules are superior to other advertising strategies.[22]

LEARNING CHECK

1. You see the same ad in *Time* and *Maclean's* magazines and on billboards and TV. Is this an example of reach or frequency?

2. What is the most selective medium available?

3. What factors must be considered when choosing among alternative media?

EXECUTING THE ADVERTISING PROGRAM

As shown earlier in Figure 15–1, executing the advertising program involves pretesting the advertising message and actually carrying out the advertising program. By evaluating advertising efforts, marketers can try to ensure that their advertising expenditures are not wasted.[23] Evaluation is usually done at two separate times: before and after the advertisements are run in the actual campaign. Several methods used in the evaluation process at the stages of idea formulation and message development will be discussed here. Posttesting methods are reviewed in the section on evaluation.

Pretesting Advertising

To determine whether the advertisement communicates the intended message or to select among alternative versions of the advertisement, **pretests** are conducted before the advertisements are placed in any medium.

Portfolio Tests. Portfolio tests are used to test message alternatives. The test ad is placed in a portfolio with several other ads and stories, and consumers are asked to read through the portfolio. Afterward subjects are asked for their impressions of the ads on several evaluative scales, such as from "very informative" to "not very informative."

Jury Tests. Jury tests involve showing the ad to a panel of consumers and having them rate how they liked it, how much it drew their attention, and how attractive they thought it was. This approach is similar to the portfolio test in that consumer reactions are obtained. However, unlike the portfolio test, a test advertisement is not hidden within other ads.

Theatre Tests. Theatre testing is the most sophisticated form of pretesting. Consumers are invited to view new television shows or movies in which test commercials are also shown. Viewers register their feelings about the advertisements either on hand-held electronic recording devices used during the viewing or on questionnaires afterward.

Carrying Out the Advertising Program

The responsibility for actually carrying out the advertising program can be handled in one of three ways, as shown in Figure 15–4. The *full-service agency* provides the most complete range of services, including market research, media selection, message

FIGURE 15–4   Alternative structures of advertising agencies used to carry out the advertising program.

Type of Agency	Services Provided
Full-service agency	Does research, selects media, develops message, and produces artwork
Limited-service agency	Specializes in one aspect of creative process; usually provides creative production work; buys previously unpurchased media space
In-house agency	Provides range of services, depending on company needs

development, artwork, and production. Agencies that assist a client by both developing and placing advertisements are usually compensated by receiving 15 percent of media costs. However, many advertising agencies are now charging a straight fee for service, since the commission-based system has come under attack by advertisers. The credibility of the agency's advice to increase advertising expenditures is often called into question when the agency gains additional compensation as the ad budget increases.

A *limited-service agency* specializes in one aspect of the advertising process, such as providing creative services to develop the advertising copy or buying previously unpurchased media space. Limited-service agencies that deal in creative work are compensated by a contractual agreement for the services performed. Finally, *in-house agencies* made up of the company's own advertising staff may provide full services or a limited range of services.

EVALUATING THE ADVERTISING PROGRAM

The advertising decision process does not stop with executing the advertising program. The advertisements must be posttested to determine whether they are achieving their intended objectives, and results may indicate that changes must be made in the advertising program.

Posttesting Advertising

An advertisement may go through **posttests** after it has been shown to the target audience to determine whether it accomplished its intended purpose. Five approaches common in posttesting are:[24]

Aided Recall (Recognition–Readership).   After being shown an ad, respondents are asked whether their previous exposure to it was through reading, viewing, or listening. The Starch test, shown in the accompanying photo, uses aided recall to determine the percentage who remember seeing a specific magazine ad (*noted*), who saw or read any part of the ad identifying the product or brand (*seen–associated*), and who read at least half of the ad (*read most*). Elements of the ad are then tagged with the results, as shown in the picture.

Unaided Recall.   A question such as, "What ads do you remember seeing yesterday?" is asked of respondents without any prompting to determine whether they saw or heard advertising messages.

Attitude Tests.   Respondents are asked questions to measure changes in their attitudes after an advertising campaign, such as whether they have a more favourable attitude toward the product advertised.[25]

Starch scores on advertisement.

Inquiry Tests. Additional product information, product samples, or premiums are offered to an ad's readers or viewers. Ads generating the most inquiries are presumed be the most effective.

Sales Tests. Sales tests involve studies such as controlled experiments (e.g., using radio ads in one market and newspaper ads in another and comparing the results) and consumer purchase tests (measuring retail sales that result from a given advertising campaign). The most sophisticated experimental methods today allow a manufacturer, a distributor, or an advertising agency to manipulate an advertising variable (such as schedule or message) through cable systems and observe subsequent sales effects by monitoring data collected from checkout scanners in supermarkets.[26]

MAKING NEEDED CHANGES

Results of posttesting the advertising copy are used to reach decisions about changes in the advertising program. If the posttest results show that an advertisement is doing poorly in terms of awareness or cost efficiency, it may be dropped and other ads run in its place in the future. On the other hand, sometimes an advertisement may be so successful it is run repeatedly or used as the basis of a larger advertising program. The Chevy truck ad campaign "like a rock" is a good example.

Important Changes in Advertising and Society

Advertising has been attacked by critics with accusations that it is often misleading, manipulates children, debases language, creates materialism, and perpetuates stereotyping of women and minorities. Canadian research shows that consumers do have some negative feelings toward advertising. In particular, most Canadians believe it does manipulate children and that it is often misleading. One study found that almost 70 percent of consumers surveyed wanted more regulation on advertising; over 40 percent wanted alcohol advertising banned, and 30 percent wanted all children's advertising banned.[27]

Several aspects of advertising are changing, given the interests and concerns of society. The first is advertising to children. There are both tighter government regulations and self-regulatory guidelines set by advertising organizations to control advertising directed toward children. For instance, Quebec does not allow any advertising directed toward children. The Canadian Code of Advertising Standards sets specific guidelines for advertisers who do advertise to children outside Quebec. YTV, a youth specialty channel in Canada, does not accept commercials between Monday and Friday, 9:00 A.M. to 3:30 P.M., prime viewing times for preschoolers. In addition, there are no commercial messages allowed during any program for children under five years of age.

The second change involves a move toward more realistic advertising. This includes the realistic depiction of women and minorities and the use of situations that reflect reality (e.g., divorce and death). Realistic portrayals of women and minorities are not only desirable but fundamental in a modern marketplace. Such initiatives are socially desirable and can only help improve the consumer's image of advertising in the long run.

The use of advertising by professionals (e.g., lawyers, dentists, accountants) is another area where change is occurring. Many professional bodies are relaxing their restrictions on the use of advertising. Most professionals and consumers appear to want such liberalization of professional services advertising.[28]

LEARNING CHECK

1. Explain the difference between pretesting and posttesting of advertising messages.

2. What is the difference between aided- and unaided-recall posttests?

ETHICS INSIGHT

Public Relations: Who/What Should We Believe?

Many organizations realize that most consumers view public relations, particularly news-oriented publicity, as more credible than advertising per se. As such, many organizations have turned to well-managed public relations programs in order to influence the perceptions that relevant publics have toward them or their causes. Many organizations disseminate information that will cast them only in the best possible light, or ensure that their view on a particular issue is conveyed to the public. However, there is growing concern that the public relations function is being used to disseminate misinformation, or at least, an outrageous distortion of reality. Take, for example, the battle over salmon farming in British Columbia. On one side, opponents to salmon farming are using publicity to suggest that the farmed salmon are raised on artificial hormones and antibodies. They also argue that the mostly Atlantic salmon raised

in offshore pens compete with and threaten Pacific salmon species. The B.C. Salmon Farmers Association is countering with a public and community relations blitz that they feel addresses the misinformation campaigns by its opponents. For now, the B.C. government has imposed a moratorium on new salmon farming sites pending environmental review. For the consumer, it is a question of who/what to believe.

1. What are the dangers when organizations with conflicting views on an issue market their positions via public relations activities?
2. What role does the media play in this situation?

SOURCE: Adapted, in part from Michael McCullough, "Salmon Farmers Aim to Remake Their Image," *Marketing*, August 5, 1996, p. 2.

PUBLIC RELATIONS

As defined in Chapter 14, **public relations (PR)** involves communications activities designed to influence the perceptions, opinions, and beliefs about an organization among its relevant publics, including customers, employees, shareholders, government, and the general public. The goal of PR is to create a positive image about an organization, its products, services, or people. PR differs from advertising, which involves the use of paid media.

Public Relations Tools

Public relations can be used in a variety of situations to support other marketing communications initiatives. PR can be used to obtain news coverage about new products, or about new uses for existing products. PR can be used to counter negative coverage resulting from product recalls, product tamperings, and other crisis communications situations. Finally, PR can be used to create or enhance the favourable image of a corporation in the minds of customers and employees. Specifically, PR can involve the use of any of the following tools and tactics.[29]

Publicity. **Publicity** involves the creation and dissemination of information about a company or product in order to obtain favourable media coverage. Publicity usually takes the form of news releases, news conferences, press kits, or informational documents. The goal of publicity is to have the media tell the company's story. Publicity is used in positive situations such as new product launches, as well as in negative marketing situations such as product failure cases. Nonprofit organizations like Alberta Health's AIDS program discussed in the chapter opener, rely heavily on publicity to spread their messages. PSAs (public service announcements), where free space or time is donated by the media is a common use of publicity for these organizations.

Special Events Sponsorship. A growing area of marketing public relations involves the creation or support, and publicizing of company-sponsored seminars, conferences, sports competitions, entertainment events, or other celebrations. The goal of events sponsorship is to create a forum in which to disseminate company information

An example of public-service activities; Molson Breweries "Take Care" campaign.

or to create brand identification to members of the target audience. College sports events such as the CIAU hockey and football championships are sponsored by Coca-Cola and General Motors. Volvo sponsors professional men's tennis and leverages that activity by sponsoring club-level, grassroots tournaments. Volvo has found that for every dollar it spends on sponsoring an event, it gets back seven times as much in terms of equivalent media time.[30]

Public-Service Activities. Public-service activities include establishing or supporting community-based initiatives that benefit the well-being of society. Ciba-Geigy Canada sponsors Health & Welfare Canada's Quit 4 Life Program, which encourages teens to quit smoking. Labatt and Molson Breweries both sponsor responsible use of alcohol initiatives. Cause-related marketing (CRM) is another way for a company to get involved in public-service activities.

Collateral Materials. Annual reports, brochures, newsletters, or video presentations about the company and its products are also PR activities. These materials provide information to target publics and often generate publicity. Newsletters, for example, have been found to build company and brand awareness.[31]

Good public relations activities should be planned and made part of an organization's integrated marketing communications effort. For example, The Body Shop of Canada sponsors a public-service campaign to stop violence against women. This program is part of The Body Shop's overall communications strategy to generate a positive corporate image for the company and its products.[32]

LEARNING OBJECTIVE REINFORCEMENT

1. Explain how advertising can be classified. Advertising can be classified as either product or institutional, and can be further classified in terms of whether it is seeking a direct-response or delayed-response from the consumer. Product advertisements take three forms: pioneering, competitive, and reminder. Institutional ads are of these three types plus one more: advocacy.

2. Understand the four W's of developing an advertising program. Development of an advertising program focuses on the four W's: (1) Who is the target audience? (2) What are the advertising objectives, the amounts of money that can be budgeted for the advertising program, and the kind of message to use? (3) When should the advertisements be run? and (4) Where should the advertisements be run.

3. Outline the importance of the advertising message and the types of appeals that can be used by advertisers. The central element of an advertising program is designing the message for the intended target audience. The message must execute the organization's desired product position and mutually reinforce the organization's overall message theme as set through the integrated marketing communications planning process. The most common message appeals are fear, sex, and humour.

4. Explain the factors considered in selecting the right media. Every advertiser must select the right media to place its advertisements. The "media selection" decision should be made on the basis of the target audience, type of product, nature of message, campaign objectives, available budget, and costs of alternative media.

5. Recognize the terms used by media buyers. The most common terms used in media decisions are: reach (the number of different people exposed to an advertisement), frequency (the average number of times an individual is exposed to an advertisement), rating (the percentage of households in a market that are tuned to a particular TV show or radio station), gross rating points—GRPs (reach multiplied by frequency), and cost per thousand—CPM (the cost of advertising divided by the number of thousands of individuals or households that are exposed).

6. Understand the three basic approaches to scheduling advertising. Scheduling advertising must take into account buyer turnover, purchase frequency, and the rate at which consumers forget. The three basic scheduling approaches are: (1) steady (drip) schedule, where ads are run at a steady or regular schedule throughout the year because seasonal factors are unimportant; (2) flighting (intermittent) schedule, where periods of advertising are scheduled between periods of no advertising to reflect seasonal demand; and (3) pulse (burst) schedule, where a flighting schedule is combined with a steady schedule because of increases in demand, heavy periods of competitive advertising, or introduction of a new product.

7. Explain how advertising is evaluated before and after it is run. Advertising is evaluated before and after the ad is run. Pretesting can be done with portfolio, jury, or theatre tests. Posttesting is done on the basis of aided recall, unaided recall, attitude tests, inquiry tests, and sales tests.

8. Define public relations and why it is used. Public relations (PR) involves communications activities designed to influence the perceptions, opinions, and beliefs about an organization among its relevant publics including customers, shareholders, government, and the general public. The goal of PR is to create a positive image about an organization, its products, services, or people.

9. Outline the tools of public relations. PR can involve the use of any of the following tools: (1) publicity, (2) special events sponsorship, (3) public-service activities, and (4) collateral materials such as annual reports and newsletters.

KEY TERMS AND CONCEPTS

advertising p. 372
product advertisements p. 372
institutional advertisements p. 372
direct-response advertising p. 373
delayed-response advertising p. 374

hierarchy of effects p. 375
reach p. 379
rating p. 379
frequency p. 379
gross rating points p. 379

cost per thousand p. 380
pretests p. 385
posttests p. 386
public relations p. 389
publicity p. 389

CHAPTER QUESTIONS AND APPLICATIONS

1. How does competitive product advertising differ from competitive institutional advertising?

2. Suppose you are the advertising manager for a new line of children's fragrances. Which media would you use to advertise this new product?

3. You have recently been promoted to the director of advertising for the Timkin Tool Company. In your first meeting with Mr. Timkin, he says, "Advertising is a waste! We've been advertising for six months now and sales haven't increased. Tell me why we should continue." Give your answer to Mr. Timkin.

4. A large life insurance company has decided to switch from using a strong fear appeal to a humorous approach. What are the strengths and weaknesses of such a change in message strategy?

5. Some national advertisers have found that they can have more impact with their advertising by running a large number of ads for a period and then running no ads at all for a period. Why might such a flighting schedule be more effective than a steady schedule?

6. Which medium has the lowest cost per thousand?

Medium	Cost	Audience
TV show	$5,000	25,000
Magazine	2,200	6,000
Newspaper	4,800	7,200
FM radio	420	1,600

7. The Toro company has a broad product line. What timing approach would you recommend for the advertising of (a) the lawn mower line, and (b) the new line of lawn and garden furniture?

8. What are two advantages and disadvantages of the advertising posttests described in the chapter?

9. There is an old saying that "you pay for advertising, but you pray for PR." Explain.

APPLICATION CASE 15-1
LYSOL

L&F is a North American business unit of the Kodak Corporation. An important brand for L&F is the Lysol product line. Most Canadian consumers are familiar with Lysol Spray, but L&F wants to increase sales of not only the spray product, but the entire line of Lysol products. It is attempting to develop a strategy in Canada in order to market more of the entire line of Lysol products.

Lysol, primarily the spray, has a long brand heritage in Canada. The disinfectant benefit of the product is very distinctive. In the early 1990s, Lysol spray had 44 percent household penetration in Canada, but the other Lysol products—Lysol Basin, Tub & Tile Cleaner; Lysol Toilet Bowl Cleaner; and Lysol Liquid (All-Purpose) Cleaner—had much lower penetration. With little existing synergy between the products within the line, L&F wanted to bring these disparate products together. In doing so, L&F could achieve economies of scale in terms of marketing expenses. The company believed that by combining the marketing budgets for the four separate products, it could achieve a greater impact on the market. It was felt that one way to link the products together was through the unifying benefit of disinfection.

L&F wanted to achieve greater market penetration with all four products. However, the overall household cleaning product category was not growing and in some areas was actually declining. Some industry people felt that one reason for this was that many households were cleaning less. They also felt that the recession was impacting on sales in the category. Therefore, new growth for Lysol would have to come at the expense of existing competitors.

While all competitors were using advertising and couponing, the intensity of the battle was at the shelf level. Competitive firms were literally battling it out for shelf space in order to capture market share. This meant that trade sales promotions were being used extensively, often in the form of price discounting. L&F felt it shouldn't get more involved in trade discounts because of the squeeze it put on margins. It did believe, however, that limited use of consumer coupons should be part of its overall consumer-focused marketing communications activity.

L&F believed that the Lysol brand probably had a rather tired personality. The company wanted to give it a 1990s contemporary, interesting, and even provocative image. The problem was that to most consumers, household cleaning products were really an uninteresting category. As such, building consumer awareness of the entire line would not be possible without increasing the level of consumer involvement. The question was how to create interest or involvement with the product line. A way had to be found to demonstrate the line and to have consumers pay attention.

L&F knew that timing would be important. For example, interest in the category would be highest just before or during traditional spring cleaning time in Canada, which ran between late February to early May. Interest would also be high again in late fall or early winter. But if the product line itself could not be made interesting or more involving, even good timing wouldn't help.

L&F had to determine an appropriate creative message for the consumer, select an appropriate communications medium, and consider other ways to build sales and market share for the line.

QUESTIONS

1. What would be the most appropriate communications medium for L&F to use in order to communicate with its market?
2. What would be a creative way to build consumer involvement with the product line? What would be the specific message and execution?
3. Besides the specific communications medium you recommended to L&F in question #1, what other marketing communications activities would you recommend to build sales and market share for the Lysol line?
4. What type of communications schedule would you recommend L&F use during the year?

*This case information was supplied by the Television Bureau of Canada (TVB). We gratefully acknowledge the support of the TVB. Used with permission.

APPLICATION CASE 15-2
METRO TORONTO WORKS DEPARTMENT

In recent years there has been a pronounced increase in the public's awareness of environmental issues. Yet the perceived magnitude of some of the problems was so overwhelming that many people weren't modifying their behaviour, thinking that one person could hardly make a difference. Moreover, in Metro Toronto, there was both ignorance and uncertainty as to the range of environmental or waste management services offered by the Metro Toronto Works Department. While the Blue Box Recycling programme had high visibility (a walk through the neighbourhood on collection days would show many blue containers by the curbside), other initiatives of the Works Department were less well known.

Metro Toronto Works Department wanted Metro residents to become part of the solution. This meant continuous education about what was and what wasn't recyclable through the Blue Box programme, and raising awareness of other less familiar programmes. But increased participation in waste management programmes would only happen if residents perceived them to be simple and convenient rather than time consuming and complex.

The Department determined that an advertising and public relations campaign would be necessary to generate awareness and encourage increased household participation in the waste management programmes. The campaign would focus on all waste management programmes including Blue Box Recycling, Backyard Composting, Water Efficiency, and Household Hazardous Waste Disposal. Seasonal projects (such as summer lawn watering reduction and Christmas tree recycling) and special events (such as Environmental Days and Waste Reduction Week) also had to be highlighted. The Department decided no scare tactics would be used. The campaign would be a positive one. Citizens would be encouraged to participate and shown that their cooperation was necessary, easy, and meaningful. The thrust of the campaign would rest on the premise that, although the magnitude of environmental waste was huge, every single one of us, every single day, could make small contributions that, when added together, become significant.

QUESTIONS

1. Given the campaign's objective, what would you recommend as the primary media choice for Metro Works?
2. What would be the basic message appeal you would recommend to encourage residents to participate?
3. What public relations activities would you recommend for Environmental Days and Waste Reduction Week?

SOURCE: Adapted, in part, from Canadian Advertising Success Stories, Cassies II, Canadian Advertising Congress, 1995. Used with permission.

Mountain Blackberry
Orchard Peach
CLEARLY CANADIAN
Summer Strawberry
CLEARLY CANADIAN.
Wild Cherry
CLEARLY CANADIAN.
Country Raspberry
CLEARLY CANADIAN.

Sales Promotion and Direct Marketing Communications

AFTER READING THIS CHAPTER YOU WILL BE ABLE TO:

1. Understand the role of sales promotion in an integrated marketing communications plan.

2. Outline the types of consumer sales promotions available to a marketer.

3. Outline the types of trade sales promotions available to a marketer.

4. Explain the role of direct marketing communications in an integrated marketing communications plan.

5. Appreciate the variety of direct marketing communications tools available to the marketer.

THE CLEAR BENEFITS OF SALES PROMOTION

Clearly Canadian Beverages, a Vancouver-based company, has been a leading player in the new-age beverage category over the past several years. The new-age beverage market includes healthful carbonated or noncarbonated flavoured waters and other beverages sold as alternatives to alcohol or soft drinks. Many experts suggest that Clearly Canadian has been successful because of its pricing, packaging, distribution, positioning, formulating, and financing as well as its ability to respond quickly to changing market conditions. But others suggest its success can be attributed to effective use of both consumer and trade sales promotions. In fact, a large portion of Clearly Canadian's multi-million dollar integrated marketing communications budget is dedicated to sales promotion activities.

In order to maintain awareness, create excitement, and encourage consumers to buy Clearly Canadian products, the company relies heavily on sampling in major mall locations and at air shows, where it participates as a corporate sponsor. It also runs point-of-purchase sweepstakes in which consumers can win Clearly Canadian merchandise. In order to motivate and encourage its salespeople and trade partners to move more product through the pipeline, Clearly Canadian offers an incentive program to all those who exceed their distribution and product presence objectives. These sales promotion activities, combined with the use of regional ad campaigns, have helped the company generate high levels of brand awareness and real bottom-line sales results.[1]

In this chapter, we will discuss two important forms of marketing communications: sales promotion and direct marketing communications. We will discuss the various sales promotion and direct marketing communications techniques available to market-driven organizations, and their respective roles in an organization's integrated marketing communications plan.

SALES PROMOTION

As defined in Chapter 14, **sales promotion** is a short-term inducement of value offered to arouse interest in buying a good or service. Sales promotions offered to ultimate consumers are called **consumer sales promotions.** For example, a consumer might receive a rebate for making a purchase. Sales promotions directed to intermediaries are referred to as **trade sales promotions.** For instance, a retailer could receive a price discount for purchasing a specific quantity of a product within a specified period.

The Importance of Sales Promotion

At one time, sales promotion was considered a supplemental marketing communications tool. But more recently the use of sales promotion has increased, and so has its perceived importance to marketers. In fact, in Canada, more money is spent on sales promotion than on advertising.[2] There are several reasons for this. For one, many marketers are looking for measurable results from their marketing communications efforts. Sales promotion is viewed as an effective tool in this regard. Consumers and the trade (e.g., retailers) have become more value conscious and thus more responsive to sales promotion activities.

Some suggest that the use of sales promotion has grown because it has become contagious. In other words, many marketers are simply responding to the increased use of sales promotion by competitors. Finally, the availability of technology such as computerized scanning equipment has also served as a stimulus for the growth of sales promotion.

While sales promotions have grown in use and in stature, they are rarely used in isolation or as stand-alones. In an integrated marketing communications plan, sales promotion activities work in conjunction with other communications, supporting and reinforcing the overall plan. For example, consumer sales promotions usually must be advertised and can add to the effectiveness of advertising (e.g., an ad with a coupon may gain a better response than an ad without a coupon), while trade promotions can support or enhance an organization's personal selling efforts.

Consumer Sales Promotions

There are a variety of consumer sales promotion techniques available to a market-driven organization. Each kind of consumer sales promotion has its advantages and disadvantages. Moreover, some consumer sales promotion techniques tend to be more effective than others in achieving particular objectives. As the use of consumer sales promotion has increased, marketers have developed methods for selecting and assessing the impact of various techniques. Figure 16–1 provides a summary overview of the alternative consumer sales promotion tools.

A study of consumer sales promotions showed that the most frequently used techniques were, in descending order: coupons, cents-off promotions, refunds, premiums, samples, and sweepstakes.[3]

FIGURE 16–1 Consumer sales promotion alternatives.

Kinds of Consumer Sales Promotion	Objectives	Advantages	Disadvantages
Coupons	Stimulate demand; increase trial	Encourage retailer support	Consumers delay purchases
Deals	Increase trial; retaliate against competitor's actions	Reduce consumer risk	Consumers delay purchases; perceived product value reduced
Premiums	Build goodwill	Attract consumers with free or reduced-price merchandise	Consumers buy for premium, not product
Contests	Increase consumer purchases; build business inventory	Encourage consumer involvement with product	Require creative or analytical thinking
Sweepstakes	Encourage present customers to buy more; minimize brand switching	Get customer to use product and store more often	Sales drop after sweepstakes
Samples	Encourage new product trial	Low risk for consumer	High cost for company
Continuity programs	Encourage repeat purchases	Help create loyalty	High cost for company
Point-of-purchase displays	Increase product trial; provide in-store support for other promotions	Provide good product visibility	Hard to get retailer to allocate high-traffic space
Rebates	Encourage customers to purchase; stop sales decline	Effective at stimulating demand	Easily copied; steal sales from future; reduce perceived product value

Coupons. **Coupons** are typically printed certificates giving the bearer a saving or a stated price reduction when they purchase a specific product. Coupons can be used to stimulate demand for mature products or promote the early trial of a new brand. In 1995, over 17 billion coupons were distributed in Canada, including direct-to-consumer and retailer-initiated coupons. Consumers redeemed more than 268 million of these coupons, which had an average face value of 68 cents. This means that Canadians saved over $180 million on products as a result of using coupons.[4]

Studies show that when coupons are used, a company's market share does increase during the period immediately after they are distributed.[5] There are indications, however, that couponing can reduce gross revenues by lowering the price paid by already-loyal consumers.[6] Therefore, manufacturers and retailers are particularly interested in coupon programs directed at potential first-time buyers.

Coupons can be distributed in several ways. A popular method is through the *free-standing insert* (FSI), a preprinted coupon (sometimes contained in an ad) placed into a separate publication, such as a newspaper. Another technique used by retailers, called retailer in-ad coupons, appear in the retailers' regular weekly newspaper or flyer advertisements. Coupons can also be distributed in-store. On-shelf couponing uses a dispenser mounted near the manufacturer's or retailer's particular product, while point-of-sale or checkout coupons can be dispensed at the cash register to very targeted buyers.

Deals. **Deals** are short-term price reductions, commonly used to increase trial among potential customers or to retaliate against a competitor's actions. There are two basic types of deals: cents-off deals and price-pack deals. *Cents-off deals* offer a brand at less than a regular price, and the reduced prices are generally marked directly on the label

Friday's attracts new
buyers with coupons.

or package. Cents-off deals can be very effective, even more so than coupons in stimulating short-term sales.

Price-pack deals offer consumers something extra such as "20 percent more for the same price," or "two packages for the price of one." Price-pack deals can be very effective in retaliating against or preempting a competitor's actions. For example, if a rival manufacturer introduces a new cake mix, the company could respond with a price-pack deal (e.g., 2 for 1), building up the stock on the kitchen shelves of cake mix buyers and making the competitor's introduction more difficult. Marketers must be careful not to overuse deals, however. If consumers expect a deal, they may delay a purchase until the deal occurs. Moreover, frequent deals may erode the perceived value of the brand to the consumer.

Premiums. **Premiums** are items offered free or at a significant savings as incentives to buy a product. A premium offered at below its normal price is known as *self-liquidating* because the cost charged to the consumers covers the cost of the item. Offering premiums at no cost or at low cost encourages customers to return frequently or to use more of the product. However, the company must be careful that the consumer doesn't buy just the premium.

Contests. With **contests,** consumers apply their analytical or creative thinking to try to win a prize. Most often a consumer submits an entry to be judged by a panel. Many companies use contests not only to increase consumer purchases, but to obtain the names and addresses of consumers for use in direct marketing communications programs. Gillette's Cavalcade of Sports 25-week hockey pool contest awarded a $1 million weekly cash prize to each week's winner.

Sweepstakes. A **sweepstakes** also requires participants to submit some kind of entry form, but are purely games of chance requiring no analytical or creative effort by the consumer. *Reader's Digest* and Publisher's Clearing House are two of the better-known sweepstakes. Canada has federal and provincial regulations covering sweepstakes, contests, and games regarding fairness, to ensure that the chance of winning is represented honestly, and to guarantee that the prizes are awarded.

Many organizations use contests or sweepstakes to get customers to buy or use their products more often.

Samples. Another common consumer sales promotion is **sampling,** or offering the product free or at a greatly reduced price. Often used for new products, sampling puts the product in the consumer's hands. A trial size—that is, a package that is smaller than the regular package size—is generally offered. If consumers like the sample, it is hoped they will remember and buy the product. Coty Canada launched its Universo fragrance for men with an extensive sampling program in theatres that were running Coty's 30-second commercial about the product.[7] Kimberly-Clark used sampling to promote its UltraTrim diapers. It undertook a personally addressed sample mailing to 235,000 Canadian households using a database of mothers provided primarily by Welcome Wagon. The sampling program was backed up by TV advertising developed specifically for the Canadian market, as well as newspaper and magazine ads with coupons.[8]

Sampling is also used to support established products. Pepsi, for example, has used sampling in the hope of converting Coca-Cola drinkers. Pepsi also used free samples to attract new customers.

Continuity program: GM's credit card.

Continuity Programs. Continuity programs are a consumer sales promotion tool used to encourage and reward repeat purchases by acknowledging each purchase made by a consumer and offering a premium as purchases accumulate. Trading stamps, which were first used by supermarkets and gas stations in the 1960s and 1970s, are an example. More recently airlines and hotels have used frequent-flyer and frequent-traveler programs to reward loyal customers. Even GM has a continuity program—a credit card that allows consumers to accumulate up to $3,500 in "points" toward the purchase of a new Chevrolet, Pontiac, Oldsmobile, Buick, or Cadillac.[9] (For an example of another continuity program, read the Marketplace Application box.)

A gravity-feed bin that doubles as a point-of-purcahse display.

Point-of-Purchase Displays. In a store aisle, you often encounter a sales promotion called a *point-of-purchase display.* These product displays take the form of advertising signs, which sometimes actually hold or display the product, and are often located in high-traffic areas near the cash register or the end of an aisle. The accompanying picture shows gravity-feed bins that Nabisco uses for its animal crackers; it helps ensure product freshness, provides storage, and captures the consumer's attention as an end-of-aisle, point-of-purchase display.[10] A recent survey of retailers found that 87 percent plan to use more point-of-purchase materials in the future, particularly for products that can be purchased on impulse.[11]

Some studies estimate that two-thirds of a consumer's buying decisions are made in the store. This means that grocery product manufacturers want to get their message to you at the instant you are next to their brand in your supermarket aisle—perhaps through a point-of-purchase display. At many supermarkets this may be done through the VideOcart. Sitting on the handlebar of your supermarket shopping cart, the VideOcart's liquid crystal display (LCD) screen will remind you twice per aisle about products next to your cart that you might consider buying. The displays on your screen are triggered by transmitters on the store shelves and can be updated by satellite connections with the manufacturer.

Rebates. Another consumer sales promotion tool, the cash **rebate,** offers the return of money based on proof of purchase. This technique has been used heavily by car manufacturers facing increased competition. Computer companies like Apple have also used rebates effectively in selling PCs to ultimate consumers. When a rebate is offered on lower-priced items such as detergent or dog food, the time and trouble of mailing in the proof-of-purchase to get the rebate check means that many buyers—attracted by the rebate offer—never take advantage of it. However, this "slippage" is less likely to occur with frequent users of rebates.[12]

LEARNING CHECK

1. Which consumer sales promotion tool is most common for new products?

2. What is the difference between a coupon and a deal?

3. The return of money based on proof of purchase is called a _____.

$ MARKETPLACE APPLICATION

Pepsi-Cola Canada's Continuity Program . . . The Right (Pepsi) Stuff

In 1996, Pepsi-Cola Canada Beverages officially unveiled "Pepsi-Stuff"—a unique continuity or consumer-loyalty program where consumers collect points off especially marked packages of Pepsi, Diet Pepsi, and Pepsi Max and redeem them for merchandise from the Pepsi stuff catalogue. It's one of the largest consumer-loyalty programs ever run by a packaged-goods company in Canada, and a leading-edge example of youth-targeted marketing. In fact, the breadth, scale, and intensity of this massive consumer outreach dwarfs any previous effort made by the company—including the Pepsi Challenge. Pepsi figured out a long time ago that the youth market was pivotal to success in the soft drink business. It is now making sure that every teen in Canada knows about the Pepsi Stuff program. Over a six-month period, more than 460 million points will be in circulation on more than 17.5 million packages of Pepsi products, with $92 million in premiums available to consumers. And to help consumers swap the best Pepsi Stuff for points, 12 million Pepsi Stuff catalogues have been distributed in-pack and in-store. That's one catalogue for nearly every two Canadians.

The Pepsi Stuff program is supported by a new TV, radio, direct mail, and transit advertising campaign, as well as a massive in-store point-of-purchase drive. The simple theme line running throughout the integrated marketing communications campaign is "Pepsi Stuff . . . Drink it, Get it." Pepsi suggests that among other benefits, the Pepsi Stuff program adds value to a soft-drink purchase in an innovative and youth-relevant way. "Providing value to loyal drinkers is the very foundation of our organization," states Jeff Lobb, vice-president of marketing at Pepsi-Cola Canada Beverages. "With Pepsi Stuff, teens can actually taste, see, feel, and experience value every time . . . and that works for us and them," adds Lobb.

1. If you were a regular Coke drinker, would the Pepsi Stuff program motivate you to switch to Pepsi?
2. What is the possible down side of the Pepsi Stuff program?

SOURCE: Adapted from Jeff Lobb, "The Right (Pepsi) Stuff," *Marketing*, July 8, 1996, p. 15.

Trade Sales Promotions

Some of the consumer sales promotions discussed already can also be directed toward intermediaries such as wholesalers, retailers, or distributors. Trade sales promotions help push products through the marketing channel. Because of this, they have grown in importance to marketers. In fact, more sales promotion dollars are directed toward intermediaries than ultimate consumers. A survey by the Association of Canadian Advertisers (ACA) of its membership revealed that 60 percent of ACA members' marketing communications budgets went toward trade sales promotions.[13] Three major trade sales promotion techniques that are unique to intermediaries are: allowances and discounts, cooperative advertising, and training and motivation of distributors' sales forces.

Allowances and Discounts. Trade sales promotions often focus on maintaining or increasing inventory levels in the channel of distribution. An effective method for encouraging such increased purchases by intermediaries is the use of **allowances and discounts.** However, overuse of these "price reductions" can lead to retailers' changing their ordering patterns in the expectation of such offerings. Although there are many variations that manufacturers can use with discounts and allowances, three common approaches include the merchandise allowance, the case allowance, and the finance allowance.[14]

Reimbursing a retailer for extra in-store support or special featuring of brands is a *merchandise allowance.* Performance contracts between the manufacturer and the trade member usually specify the activity to be performed, such as a picture of the product in a newspaper with a coupon good at only one store. The merchandise allowance then consists of a percentage deduction from the list case price ordered during the promotional period. Allowances are not paid by the manufacturer until it sees proof of performance (such as a copy of the ad placed by the retailer in the local newspaper).

A second common trade promotion, a *case allowance,* is a discount on each case ordered during a specific time period. Such an allowance is usually deducted from the invoice. A variation of the case allowance is the "free goods" approach, whereby retailers receive some amount of the product free based on the amount ordered, such as one case free for every 10 cases ordered.[15]

A final type of allowance and discount, the *finance allowance,* involves paying retailers for financing costs or financial losses associated with consumer sales promotions. This trade promotion is regularly used and has several variations. One type is the floor stock protection program—manufacturers give retailers a case allowance price for products in their warehouse, which prevents shelf stock from running down during the promotional period. Also common are freight allowances, which compensate retailers that transport orders from the manufacturer's warehouse.

Cooperative Advertising.
Resellers often perform the important function of promoting the manufacturer's products at the local level. One common trade sales promotional activity is to encourage both better quality and greater quantity in the local advertising efforts of resellers through **cooperative advertising.** This is a program by which a manufacturer pays a percentage of the retailer's local advertising expense for advertising the manufacturer's products.

Usually the manufacturer pays a percentage, often 50 percent, of the cost of advertising up to a certain dollar limit, which is based on the amount of the purchases the retailer makes of the manufacturer's products. In addition to paying for the advertising, the manufacturer often furnishes the retailer with a selection of different ad executions, sometimes suited for several different media. A manufacturer may provide, for example, several different print layouts as well as a few broadcast ads for the retailer to adapt and use.[16]

Training and Motivation of Distributors's Sales Forces.
One of the many functions the intermediaries perform is customer contact and selling for the producers they represent. A manufacturer's success often rests on the ability and motivation of the reseller's sales force to represent its products.

Thus it is in the best interest of the manufacturer to help train and motivate the reseller's sales force. Because the reseller's sales force is often less sophisticated and knowledgeable about the products than the manufacturer might like, training can increase sales performance. Training activities include producing manuals and brochures to educate the reseller's sales force. The sales force then uses these aids in selling situations. Other activities include national sales meetings sponsored by the manufacturer and field visits to the reseller's location to inform and motivate the salesperson to sell the product.

Often the manufacturer will sponsor sales contests to motivate the sales force to increase their sales performance. These contests offer good performers the chance to receive cash prizes, gifts, or trips. Sometimes a manufacturer will not sponsor a sales contest but will instead offer incentives in the form of *push money,* or *spiffs,* to encourage salespeople to "push" the manufacturers' products. Some of the gifts can come in the form of *specialty advertising* items that carry the manufacturer's name or logo, such as pens, memo pads, or day planners. The importance of including training and motivational programs into an organization's integrated marketing communications plan is becoming more widely recognized by marketers.[17]

LEARNING CHECK

1. Trade sales promotions often focus on _____ or _____ inventory levels in the channel of distribution.

2. What is a case allowance?

3. What is push money?

DIRECT MARKETING COMMUNICATIONS

As you read in Chapter 14, **direct marketing communications (DMC)** involves communicating directly with target customers to encourage an "immediate" response by telephone, mail, electronic means, or personal visit. DMC methods include direct mail, direct-response advertising (broadcast and print), and telemarketing. The goal of seeking an "immediate" response from the customer is what differentiates DMC from the other marketing communications methods. Because a direct response is sought, results are measurable and marketers can determine the effectiveness of DMC more so than with most other forms of marketing communications. In fact, one study suggests that the results of a direct-response television ad should be known within 90 minutes of its airing, since the majority of those who will respond to the ad will do so within this time frame.[18]

Because of its immediacy and its measurable results, direct marketing communications is one of the fastest growing forms of marketing communications. As we saw in Chapter 7, information technology in marketing has helped spawn the growth of DMC. The development of databases containing demographic, media, and consumption profiles of customers has enabled marketers to deploy a variety of direct marketing communications methods.

Most organizations, including those using direct channels (direct marketers) and those using intermediaries, now use DMC methods to reach their customers. These organizations include manufacturers, wholesalers, retailers, and nonprofit groups. DMC methods are used to reach both ultimate consumers and organizational consumers (the trade) and are often an integral component of an integrated marketing communications plan. Organizations have turned to DMC for two basic reasons:

1. To solicit a direct and immediate response from prospects or customers.
2. To maintain and enhance customer relationships (relationship marketing).

There are a variety of DMC tools available to the market-driven organization. These include direct mail, direct-response television advertising, direct-response radio advertising, direct-response print advertising, telemarketing, and electronic direct marketing communications. Let's examine each of these methods in some detail.

Direct Mail

While new forms of direct marketing communications have developed in recent years—such as telemarketing, fax marketing, and teleshopping—direct mail is still expected to be the primary DMC tool into the next decade. **Direct mail** includes any form of communication addressed to customers or prospects through public or private delivery services. It can range in complexity from a simple flyer to a package containing a letter, brochure, video, and response card. The response rates, on a per thousand basis, is usually higher for direct mail than other marketing communications methods. This is why many firms, large and small, have turned to this DMC method.

Example of direct mail piece.

Many firms rely on direct mail as their only communications tool. Consumer product companies such as book and record clubs, publishers, and some insurance companies use direct mail as their only way to communicate to customers and prospects. However, other organizations such as General Motors and American Express are now including direct mail as part of their overall integrated marketing communications effort. Many business-to-business marketers also use direct mail, including IBM, Xerox, and many commercial banking institutions. Some of the advantages and disadvantages of direct mail are listed in Figure 16–2.

Using Direct Mail. To be effective in using direct mail, marketers must begin with appropriately selected targets, both customers and prospects. Many marketers work from their own in-house databases which contain lists and profiles of their customers. Others buy or rent lists from companies known as list brokers. Many of these brokerage firms will custom develop a list based on the type of customer being sought by the particular marketer. These brokerage firms will often have information on customers who have bought from other marketers via direct mail and will use this information to screen potential targets. These so-called *compiled lists* can be expensive, however, and many firms will instead buy or rent lists of names and addresses of potential customers selected from magazine subscription or organizational directory lists. In doing so, they risk losing some precision in terms of targeting.

An organization may combine the lists of in-house customers and various purchased or rented lists to develop a comprehensive mailing list. In most cases, the firm will use computers to merge the lists and delete any repeated names through a purging process. The marketer must then develop the offer and determine how to present it to the customer using formats such as brochures, personalized letters, and so forth. In general, many organizations will test the offer and the format of the direct mail piece, either using focus groups or a small test mailing. Based on the response, the firm will either make changes or go with the tested piece.

The next important step in the direct mail process is to deal promptly with the customer or prospect responses. The company must have inventory, order filling, shipping, and billing capabilities to meet the demand. Customers must receive what they ordered at the price they ordered it and within a reasonable time frame. Finally, the company

FIGURE 16–2   Advantages and disadvantages of direct mail.

Advantages	Disadvantages
Flexibility (in message and format)	High cost per exposure
Selectivity of intended audience	Delivery delays
Intensive coverage of the target audience	Can be perceived as "junk mail"
Ability to measure effectiveness	

must be prepared to deal with customer complaints, make adjustments, deal with returns, and ensure customer satisfaction. Most companies that attract customers through direct mail wish to maintain ongoing relationships with them over time (relationship marketing). Keeping an up-to-date and comprehensive database allows a company to build such one-to-one relationships with their customers.

Direct-response Television Advertising

As we saw in Chapter 15, advertising can be classified as being either delayed-response or direct-response in nature. Whereas delayed-response advertising is designed to influence the consumer in the near future when making a purchase, direct-response advertising seeks to motivate the customer to take immediate action. **Direct-response television advertising** has become a popular DMC method. Direct-response television advertising can come in one of three forms: (1) direct-response ads, (2) infomercials, and (3) home shopping channels.

Typically, direct-response television advertisements are ads with an 800 telephone number and an address for placing an order or requesting information. The ads can be 30, 60 or 90 seconds in length. The ads are often persuasive, usually urging the customer to phone right away.

The newest development in direct-response television advertising is the **infomercial.** The infomercial is a program-length commercial (usually 30 minutes) that seeks to prompt an immediate response from the consumer. The infomercial often mixes information and entertainment, and makes ongoing requests for consumers to call a toll-free number for further information or to order a product or service.

Originally infomercials were seen only on late-night cable stations and often featured get-rich-quick schemes. But infomercials have become more mainstream and are being used to market many of the top brands in the marketplace. Marketers see infomercials as a way to stand out in a cluttered television advertising environment. A 30-second commercial is more likely to get lost in the clutter than a 30-minute one. Moreover, infomercials allow marketers to convey more information to the consumer. Infomercials also guarantee a prompt means for measuring results. Finally, information obtained from those requesting information or ordering a product can be used to develop a database. This database, in turn, can assist in the development of an organization's overall integrated marketing communications plan.

Volvo and Saturn, for example, have used infomercials successfully. Information obtained from consumers via the infomercials were used to better match particular prospects to specific makes and models, and to allow local dealerships to do follow-up communications (e.g., telemarketing, direct mail) with customers in their areas. But do infomercials work? One study found that 81 percent of the adult viewing audience watches infomercials and that 5 percent bought products or requested more information as a result of the infomercials.[19]

Home shopping channels (discussed in Chapter 13) are another form of direct-response television advertising. Television programs or entire channels are dedicated to selling goods and services to the consumer in the comfort of their home. Some home shopping channels, like QVC and the Canadian Home Shopping Network (CHSN), broadcast 24 hours a day, seven days a week. Viewers are offered a variety of products to buy, all of which they can order via an 800 number. With the coming of two-way, interactive television, many experts believe this form of direct marketing communication will grow in magnitude and become a major form of DMC.

Infomercials are growing in popularity.

Direct-response Radio Advertising

Direct-response radio advertising allows the marketer to obtain immediate feedback from consumers. The listener hears the ad and is asked to telephone or write the company for more information or to order the product or service. Because radio is a highly segmented media, marketers can direct their ads to a narrowly defined target. Radio time can also be relatively inexpensive compared to other forms of direct marketing communications. However, a listener who hears the commercial while driving may not be able to remember or record a telephone number or address.

Direct-response Print Advertising

Direct-response print ad.

Newspapers and magazines also offer an opportunity for direct marketing communications, known as **direct-response print advertising.** Consumers can respond to ads carrying an address, order form, coupon, or telephone number. The consumer could be asked to purchase or request additional information. Magazines offer the prospect of using *reader-response cards*—inserted cards in magazines that allow consumers to request further information from the advertiser. As we mentioned in Chapter 15, a new form of inserts are interactive diskettes that contain information about an organization or its products or services. Several firms have used these diskettes, including Merrill Lynch and Apple Canada.

Telemarketing

Telemarketing is an interactive DMC method that uses the telephone to initiate, develop, and enhance relationships with customers. Marketers can use *outbound* telemarketing to sell directly to consumers and businesses, while *inbound* toll-free 800 numbers can be used to receive orders from television and radio ads or direct mail campaigns.

Telemarketer in action.

On a cost-per-contact basis, telemarketing is less expensive than personal selling, but it can be more expensive than broadcast advertising or direct mail. Often telemarketing is combined with other direct marketing communications methods. For example, *telemail* combines telemarketing efforts with a direct-mail campaign. An organization using telemail will usually send out well-targeted letters to customers or prospects and then follow up with a personal telephone call. The telemail method has proven to be more effective than direct mail or telemarketing used alone.[20]

Telemarketing is very popular in both consumer and business marketing. General Electric, for example, uses telemarketing to generate and qualify sales leads for its sales force. Many consumers appreciate the offers they receive by telephone. Properly designed and targeted telemarketing provide many customer benefits such as increased convenience. However, the explosion of unsolicited telephone marketing has angered a large number of consumers who object to what they call "junk phone calls" and the invasion of privacy. The Canadian Direct Marketing Association, whose member companies represent 80 percent of direct marketing sales in Canada, has mandated that its members comply with the consumers' right to privacy and honour consumers who request not to be called. The federal and provincial governments are considering even tougher regulations with regard to "do not call" requests made by consumers. (For an ethical discussion on telemarketing; see Ethics Insight box.)

Electronic Media

Several forms of direct marketing communications are available besides broadcast media. Although not as widely used as the DMC methods already discussed, interactive computers, interactive kiosks, and fax marketing are becoming part of the DMC arsenal.

For one, consumers and marketers can now communicate directly with each other through telephone lines and a personal computer using interactive computer services. As we saw in Chapter 13, Prodigy is one of the largest computer-based shopping and information services available. Also, remember the Internet? Many marketers are

ETHICS INSIGHT

All is Not Right with Telemarketing

Telemarketing does not have a good image with most consumers. In fact, survey after survey shows that the majority of consumers asked feel telemarketing is an invasion of privacy, an offensive way to market, and a waste of consumer's time. Why are many Canadians turned off by telemarketers? In some cases, there are telemarketers who engage in illegal and deceptive practices as well as unethical behaviour. For example, take the case of a telemarketing company who phones consumers and tells them they have won prizes. The consumers are then asked to pay the shipping and handling costs for the prizes; the cost of which greatly exceeds the real costs of shipping and handling as well as the value of the prize. In another case, consider telemarketing company representatives who lead consumers to believe they are volunteers requesting donations for a charity. In fact, they are paid fundraisers who are working on commission. What about a telemarketer who uses telemail programs where a consumer receives a direct mail piece and is asked to phone an 800 number for further information. Unknown to the consumer, the telemarketer uses an automatic number identification or caller ID intrusion system that identifies the incoming caller's number without their knowledge or consent. If the consumer does not buy the product or service initially, the company now has the consumer's telephone number and begins recalling the consumer in an attempt to sell them. The telemarketer also has an opportunity to capture and sell consumers' unlisted telephone numbers. In many cases, they are telemarketers who are simply guilty of deception, legally, and in other cases, engaging in unethical, but perhaps not illegal practices. This has not only tarnished the image of reputable telemarketers, but all other professional marketers.

1. Do you have any personal experiences with a telemarketer who has engaged in an illegal or unethical practice? Elaborate.

2. What can be done about these unethical telemarketers?

reaching their customers directly via the World Wide Web system. Firms such as BMW and Panasonic attempt to communicate directly with customers in cyberspace, providing information on new products and services.

Interactive kiosks, usually located in retail stores (Chapter 7) are also a new electronic direct marketing communications tool. These kiosks use touch-screen technology and allow consumers to access information of interest. Some of the kiosks include catalogues of products and direct toll-free numbers for placing orders.

Fax machines allow people to transmit and receive documents by telephone. The use of a fax machine as a direct marketing communications tool has been restricted primarily to business marketing. Marketers who sell to other businesses now routinely accept customer orders by fax. They will also use the fax to send requested information to customers as per their requests. Others, however, use the fax to send unsolicited information to prospective customers. Like unsolicited telemarketing, some business firms do not appreciate "junk fax messages."

LEARNING OBJECTIVE REINFORCEMENT

1. Understand the role of sales promotion in an integrated marketing communications plan. For many marketers, sales promotion has become an important part of their integrated marketing communications plan. It is used when marketers are seeking measurable results from their marketing communications efforts. Sales promotions, however, are rarely used in isolation. Instead, sales promotion activities work in conjunction with other communications, supporting and reinforcing the overall plan. For example, consumer sales promotions usually must be advertised and can add to the effectiveness of advertising, while trade promotions can support or enhance an organization's personal selling efforts.

2. Outline the types of consumer sales promotions available to a marketer. There are a variety of consumer sales promotion techniques available to a marketer. The most common ones include: coupons, deals, premiums, contests, sweepstakes, samples, continuity programs, point-of-purchase displays, and rebates.

3. Outline the types of trade sales promotions available to a marketer. The three major trade sales promotion techniques are allowances and discounts, cooperative advertising, and training and motivation of distributors' sales forces.

4. Explain the role of direct marketing communications in an integrated marketing communications plan. DMC methods are used to reach both ultimate consumers and organizational consumers (the trade) and are often an integral component of an integrated marketing communications plan. The role of DMC in an integrated marketing commu-

nications plan is (1) to solicit a direct and immediate response from prospects or customers, and (2) to maintain and enhance customer relationships (relationship marketing). Because a direct response is sought, results are measurable and marketers can determine the effectiveness of DMC more so than with most other forms of marketing communications.

5. Appreciate the variety of direct marketing communications tools available to the marketer. There are a variety of DMC tools available to the marketer including: direct mail, direct-response television advertising (including infomercials and home shopping channels), direct-response radio advertising, direct-response print advertising, telemarketing, and electronic media such as interactive computers, interactive kiosks, and fax marketing.

KEY TERMS AND CONCEPTS

sales promotion p. 398
consumer sales promotion p. 398
trade sales promotion p. 398
coupons p. 399
deals p. 399
premiums p. 400
contests p. 400

sweepstakes p. 400
sampling p. 401
rebate p. 402
allowances and discounts p. 403
cooperative advertising p. 404
direct marketing communications (DMC) p. 405

direct mail p. 405
direct-response television advertising p. 407
infomercial p. 407
direct-response radio advertising p. 408
direct-response print advertising p. 408
telemarketing p. 408

CHAPTER QUESTIONS AND APPLICATIONS

1. Identify the sales promotion tools that might be useful for *(a)* Tastee Yogourt—a new brand introduction, *(b)* 3M self-sticking Post-It notes, and *(c)* Wrigley's spearmint gum.

2. Why has sales promotion grown in importance as a marketing communications tool?

3. Does your family use coupons? Why or why not? What factors affect coupon redemption?

4. Why should marketers avoid overusing deals?

5. Are there any problems with a manufacturer using push money, or spiffs, to encourage a dealer's or distributor's salespeople to "push" the manufacturer's products?

6. What distinguishes direct marketing communications from other forms of marketing communications? Why has it grown in popularity?

7. What are the advantages and disadvantages of direct mail?

8. What types of products would benefit most from using an infomercial?

9. The Toronto Raptors basketball team has asked you to advise them as to which sales promotion techniques could best improve home game attendance? What will you tell them?

10. What do you think should be done to eliminate "junk telemarketing" and "junk fax marketing"?

APPLICATION CASE 16–1
PROMOTING CALLMALL™ & VISTA 350*: A HIGH-TECH SERVICE INTRODUCTION

BACKGROUND

It was August. The final technical issues were identified and would be eliminated in the next manufacturing run. Working forward with dates, this meant an early November launch was possible. This was as late as was logically feasible and there was still a fear of *getting lost in the Christmas rush*. Since this was the first introduction of the Vista 350 and CallMall in North America, the budget for marketing would be liberal, but not excessive.

Now we were down to the wire. Given the November date, this meant that depending on what marketing communication tools were used, decisions would have to be made in two weeks to get production started. What would be the lowest cost option to meet the objectives? What marketing communications concepts should be implemented?

INDUSTRY, COMPANY, AND PRODUCT/SERVICE

The New Brunswick Telephone Company, Limited (NBTel), is an acknowledged world leader in telecommunications. It invests in people and technology. Serving more than 300,000 customers in New Brunswick, NBTel's expertise is in developing and delivering local and long distance telephone services, wireless services, advanced network services, and interactive multimedia applications that provide a competitive advantage to businesses and enrich the day-to-day lives of consumers.

Known as an innovator and pace setter in the industry, NBTel has had many "firsts" to its credit. For example, NBTel was the first telephone company in Canada to introduce community calling service, call display, and province-wide Internet access service on both a dial-up and dedicated-access basis. NBTel Mobility's Caller Pays service is also a first in Canada. TalkMail™, a universal voice-messaging service provided to customers along with their basic local telephone service, and CallMall™, a joint venture with Northern Telecom (Nortel) that provides customers with access to home-based banking, shopping, and information services, are both world firsts.

The Vista 350 is one of the newest phone sets available with features such as: 8-line, back-lite display screen, message waiting light, speaker phone, caller's log, and a directory of names and numbers. What makes the phone most unique is the ADSI-based display that allows connection with a computer server and the downloading of information based on the customer's request.

The two services offered with the set were CallMall and QuickAds.

- CallMall is a customer-initiated connection to a computer that allows the customer to see, read, and hear information, and to complete transactions for banking and catalogue shopping.
- QuickAds allow customers to select categories of interest. Ads are then displayed on the phone based on these categories.

The telephone would be rented monthly and the additional CallMall and QuickAds services were added at no cost. Other services such as name display and call answer were also available at a monthly charge.

THE MARKET

The first launch was set for Monoton, NB. It represented about 50,000 households. The market is about one-third French with the balance English speaking. It is a smaller town with a mix of service, logistics, and manufacturing industries—a good representation of the rest of Canada, which was the longer term plan for marketing CallMall and Vista 350.

OBJECTIVES

There were two objectives:

1) 10+ percent overall penetration of the service before year end, with excellent retention on each install.
2) 80+ percent local awareness of the new services.

ADVERTISING AND PROMOTION OPTIONS

Everything was on the table; however, the plan had to be approved and should meet the objectives at the lowest cost. The options included:

- News conference.
- Free trials.
- Commercials—TV and/or radio.
- Billboards.
- Mail—targeted or mass marketed, traditional or a "gimmick."
- Multiple locations for distribution channels.

To achieve the aggressive penetration targets, a good marketing communication strategy and plan had to be devised and implemented. There was a concern with a free trial because all sets returned would have to be refurbished, adding cost to an already expensive set.

The decision was now in the hands of the launch team. What was the strategy and plan of action?

YOUR TASK:

1. Refer to Figure 16–1. Identify and discuss the advantages and disadvantages of sales promotions not identified by NBTel as promotional options.
2. Prepare a list of strategy and action plan ideas for the launch team. Make sure your suggestions are consistent with the objectives, constraints, etc. discussed in the case.

---

*Trademark of Nortel, NBTel licensed user.
SOURCE: This case was prepared by Mervyn Hann of NBTel as a basis for classroom discussion, and is not meant to illustrate either effective or ineffective management. Used with permission.

APPLICATION CASE 16-2
RECRUITING VOLUNTEER BUSINESS EXECUTIVES FOR CORPORATE FUNDRAISING: USING SALES PROMOTIONS AND DIRECT MARKETING COMMUNICATIONS

How does an unknown performing arts centre, perceived to be an amateur, community theatre, attract corporate support in a cost-effective manner? Just ask Bill Murray.

Bill Murray was the Audience and Business Development Officer for a newly opened nonprofit performing arts centre located in a major suburb of Vancouver, British Columbia. Bill's primary objectives were to increase the Centre's corporate profile in the surrounding business community, and to recruit business executives who would volunteer their time for corporate fundraising.

The performing arts centre had been open two years and most of the events presented in the theatre were local amateur productions of theatre, dance, and music. Other events booked into the Centre were non-performance related, such as seminars, workshops, and conferences.

Unfortunately, there were not enough local performing and non-performing events to generate the rental and ticket sale revenues required by the Centre to break even. As well, the Centre had an image of being a "community theatre" as opposed to a "professional–regional" performing arts centre.

To address the issues of revenue shortfalls and poor quality image, the Board of Directors decided to put on its own professional theatre and children's music series. The theatre series consisted of five professional theatrical productions per year. Each production ran for 14 days, whereby the Centre produced three of the productions in house and purchased two touring productions. The children's series consisted of five children's entertainers who performed two shows per day running over a three-day period. Both the theatre and the children's music series were sold on annual season subscriptions or by single tickets.

To ensure the Centre could afford to present these potentially riskier but more profitable professional programs, the Board of Directors needed to attract corporate support from the local business community.

BILL'S SOLUTION

An integrated direct marketing communications strategy was developed and employed over a 12-month period. The four-step strategy was as follows:

1) *Introduce the Centre and its key personnel to the local business community.* The Centre joined the suburb's 525-member Chamber of Commerce. Along with Bill, the Centre's General Manager and the Board's President made a presentation to the Chamber members at one of its business luncheons.
2) *Invite the business community to the Centre's professional theatre productions.* All 525 business executives

who were members of the Chamber were invited to opening night performances of the Centre's first two theatrical productions. The invitations were designed so that invitees attending had to fill out information about themselves and their company, and then provide it to the box office officials upon their arrival. Box office staff then issued a pair of tickets for the best house seats, two free refreshment tickets, and a special reception name tag allowing them to attend a backstage cast reception. To assess the level of excitement and appreciation towards the Centre, Bill mingled with attendees prior to the performance, during intermission, and at the post-show reception.

3) *Recruit business executive attendees to become involved in the volunteer corporate fundraising campaign.* Bill recruited a Campaign Chair from the invited attendees. Then on behalf of the Campaign Chair, Bill sent a letter to all attendees asking them to attend a corporate fundraising campaign meeting. At the campaign meeting, those who attended were officially recruited to be on the Centre's corporate fundraising team. Team members received a volunteer appreciation gift, a bronze key chain in the shape of the Centre's ticket stub.

4) *Implement the corporate fundraising campaign.* Fundraising team members were each asked to identify 10 companies as potential corporate supporters. The Centre, on the volunteer's behalf, mailed these 10 identified company executives information on the corporate campaign and the Centre's operations. The volunteers followed up with a personal phone call and/or visit to encourage their 10 identified companies to financially support the Centre.

RESULTS

The following results were associated with Bill' corporate fundraising campaign:

- Of the 525 invitations sent out, 64 business executives accepted and attended the theatrical production (a response rate of 12%).
- Of the 64 business executives, 20 were recruited to be volunteers for the corporate fundraising campaign (a response rate of 31%).
- Of the 200 companies identified and approached by the 20 member fundraising team, 110 companies (a response rate of 55%) gave an average financial donation of $105, for a total of $11,500.

- Of the 20 volunteers, 15 purchased corporate theatre subscriptions for the next theatre season, which amounted to $3,600 in revenue (a response rate of 75%).
- The campaign also identified six companies interested in sponsoring Centre events the following season. Five of these companies became sponsors and contributed a total of $30,000.

Bill was very pleased with the results of his fundraising strategy. He estimated the direct costs associated with this strategy (mailings, stationery, etc.) to be $1,500. More important perhaps than the revenues associated with the strategy to date, Bill believed a number of marketing relationships had been formed that would serve to ensure the continued success of the Centre for many years to come.

QUESTIONS:

1. Refer to Figure 16–1. What type(s) of sales promotion were used?
2. Critically assess the strengths and weaknesses of Bill's solution. Identify sales promotions not incorporated in Bill's solution that you believe could enhance the effectiveness of the campaign.
3. What feature of Bill's solution qualifies it as a form of direct marketing communications?
4. Review the response rates reported above for the first four results items. Why did the response rates increase?

SOURCE: Prepared by Lloyd Salomone, President of Precision Target Marketing Ltd., Fredericton, N.B. Used with permission. Names and locations have been disguised. This case serves as a basis for discussion rather than an illustration of either effective or ineffective handling of an administrative situation.

CHAPTER 17

Personal Selling and Sales Management

AFTER READING THIS CHAPTER YOU WILL BE ABLE TO:

1. Understand the importance of personal selling in today's competitive environment.

2. Explain the distinction between traditional selling and relationship selling.

3. Describe three types of personal selling.

4. Describe the stages in the personal selling process.

5. Specify the functions and tasks in the sales management process.

RELATIONSHIP SELLING: A NEW DIMENSION OF PROFESSIONAL PERSONAL SELLING

When you think of the word *salesperson,* does it conjure up an image of a fast-talking, back-slapping, joke-telling salesman? If so, marketing experts will tell you that the modern professional salesperson is nothing like that. Today's sales professionals are considered a vital link between the customer and the organization. Therefore, today's salesperson is often a highly trained professional who is given the responsibility of attracting and cultivating customer relationships.

Several trends have had a significant impact on the complexity of personal selling and sales management in the 1990s:

- Intense foreign competition.
- Rising customer expectations.
- Increasing buyer expertise.
- Developments in computer technology and communications.
- Influx of women and minorities into sales careers.
- Growing emphasis on controlling costs.[1]

To successfully adapt to these trends, market-driven organizations have broadened the concept of personal selling. There is an increased emphasis on an approach to selling which is referred to as *relationship selling.* **Relationship selling** is the practice of building ties to customers through a salesperson's attention and commitment to customer needs over time. Relationship selling involves mutual respect and trust among buyers and sellers. It focuses on creating long-term customers, not a one-time sale.[2]

417

Salespeople who practise relationship selling deliver customer value by easing the buying process and by offering instructions, information, and advice. Customer value is also created by those salespeople who follow through after the sale to ensure that customers are satisfied and to find out whether they need further assistance. To be successful at relationship selling, a salesperson really needs to have: an understanding of customers' needs, sound knowledge of the company's products, effective communication skills, and a desire to ensure customer satisfaction after the sale.

This chapter examines the scope and significance of personal selling and sales management in marketing. It describes the distinction between traditional selling and the relationship selling approach, highlights the many forms of personal selling, and outlines the selling process. Finally, the functions of sales management are described.

SCOPE AND SIGNIFICANCE OF PERSONAL SELLING AND SALES MANAGEMENT

Chapter 14 described personal selling and management of the sales effort as part of a firm's marketing communications mix. Although it is important to recognize that personal selling is a useful approach for communicating with present and potential buyers, it is much more. Take a moment to answer the questions in Figure 17–1. As you read on, compare your answers with those in the text.

Personal selling requires a two-way flow of communications between a buyer and a seller—often in a face-to-face encounter—designed to influence a person's or group's purchase decision. However, with advances in telecommunications, personal selling also takes place over the telephone, as well as through teleconferencing and interactive computer links between buyers and sellers.

Personal selling remains a highly human-intensive activity despite the use of technology. Accordingly, salespeople and the technology adopted to aid the sales process must be managed. **Sales management** consists of planning the selling program and implementing and controlling the personal selling effort of the firm. Numerous tasks are involved in managing personal selling, including setting objectives; organizing the sales force; recruiting, training, and compensating salespeople; and evaluating the performance of individual salespeople.

Everyone Sells

There are over 1 million people classified as salespeople in Canada working in a variety of sales positions. They work as manufacturing sales agents, real estate brokers, stockbrokers, salesclerks in retail stores, and more.

FIGURE 17–1
Personal selling and sales management quiz.

1. About how much does it cost for a consumer product salesperson to make a single sales call? (check one)

   $100 _____ $150 _____ $200 _____
   $125 _____ $175 _____ $225 _____

2. "A salesperson's job is finished when a sale is made." True or false? (circle one)

   True   False

3. On average, sales training programs devote about what percentage of time to sales techniques? (check one)

   20% _____   40% _____   60% _____
   30% _____   50% _____   70% _____

It could be said, however, that everyone sells. Almost every interaction between two or more people can influence a person's or group's decision making. Moreover, every occupation that involves customer contact requires an element of personal selling. For example, doctors, lawyers, accountants, bankers, and company personnel recruiters perform sales-related activities, whether or not they know and acknowledge it.

It could be said that many key executives are their organization's most visible salesperson, and indeed many key executives in major Canadian companies have significant sales and marketing experience in their work history. Thus, selling often serves as a stepping-stone to top management positions, as well as being a career path in itself.

Most entrepreneurs and managers of small organizations report that they spend most of their time actively selling their ideas, goods, and services. Even when these individuals are able to remove themselves from day-to-day sales activities, many choose to remain active in the process of personal selling because it allows them to remain close to their customers.

Dave Nichol, the creator of Loblaw's President's Choice brand, is now a familiar face to many Canadians as a visible salesperson for Cott Corp.

Personal Selling in Marketing

Personal selling serves three major roles in a firm's overall marketing effort. First, salespeople are the critical link between the firm and its customers. This role requires that salespeople match company interests with customer needs to satisfy both parties in the exchange process. Second, salespeople *are* the company in a consumer's eyes. They represent what a company is or attempts to be and are often the only personal contact a customer has with the company. Third, personal selling may play a dominant role in a firm's marketing communications efforts. This situation typically arises when a firm uses a push strategy (see Chapter 14).

As discussed in Chapter 1, we believe truly market-driven organizations will embrace the seven imperatives for marketing success. (See Figure 1–6, Chapter 1.) Given the nature and scope of personal selling, an organization cannot truly embrace the seven imperatives unless its salespeople are committed to the imperatives—on the frontline, in the field—because the actions of salespeople are what provide customers with a sense of the seller's commitment to a market-driven philosophy.

As discussed in the introduction to this chapter, market-driven organizations have broadened the concept of personal selling by implementing a kind of selling known as relationship selling. These organizations have realized the importance of the sixth imperative for marketing success—they *practise relationship marketing.* Relationship selling is one way in which organizations can implement the relationship marketing concept. This type of selling is a totally different approach from the traditional selling approach. Figure 17–2 provides a comparison of relationship selling to traditional selling. Relationship selling is an effective way of developing long-term, cost-effective links with individual customers for mutual benefit. The effectiveness of relationship selling has been well documented by the research conducted by several organizations.[3]

LEARNING CHECK

1. What is personal selling?

2. What is involved in sales management?

3. What is relationship selling?

FIGURE 17–2   Relationship selling versus traditional selling.

Relationship Selling	Traditional Selling
• Selling is a service. • Selling is helping. • Buyers want a trusted salesperson. • The follow-through is number one. • Great sellers truly care. • "We"-oriented. • Long-term oriented.	• Selling is a contest. • Selling is persuading. • Buyers are liars. • The close is number one. • Great sellers are manipulators. • "Me"-oriented. • Short-term oriented.

SOURCE: Adapted from Jim Cathcart, "Traditional vs. Relationship Selling," *The Selling Advantage,* February 1990, pp. 1–2; Thomas N. Ingram and Raymond W. LaForge, *Sales Management Analysis and Decision Making,* 2nd edition, The Dryden Press, 1992, p. 161

THE MANY FORMS OF PERSONAL SELLING

Personal selling assumes many forms, based on the amount of selling done and the amount of creativity required to perform the sales task. Broadly speaking, three types of personal selling exist: order taking, order getting, and sales support activities.[4] Figure 17–3 compares order getters and order takers to illustrate some important differences between them.

Order Taking

Typically, an **order taker** processes routine orders or reorders for products that were already sold by the company. The primary responsibility of order takers is to preserve an ongoing relationship with existing customers and maintain sales. Two types of order takers exist. *Outside order takers* visit customers and replenish inventory stocks of resellers, such as retailers or wholesalers. For example, Frito-Lay salespeople call on supermarkets, neighbourhood grocery stores, and other establishments to ensure that the company's line of snack products (such as Doritos and Tostitos) is in adequate supply.

Inside order takers, also called *order clerks* or *salesclerks,* typically answer questions, take orders, and complete transactions with customers. Many retail clerks are inside order takers, as are people who take orders from buyers by telephone. Order takers, for the most part, do little selling in a conventional sense and engage in little problem solving with customers. They often represent simple products that have few options, such as confectionery items, magazine subscriptions, and highly standardized industrial products.

FIGURE 17–3   Comparing order takers and order getters.

Basis of Comparison	Order Takers	Order Getters
Objective	Handle routine product orders or reorders	Identify new customers and sales opportunities
Purchase situation	Focus on straight rebuy purchase situations	Focus on new buy and modified rebuy purchase situations
Activity	Perform order processing functions	Act as creative problem solvers
Training	Require significant clerical training	Require significant sales training
Source of sales	Maintain sales volume	Create new sales volume

Order Getting

An **order getter** sells in a conventional sense and identifies prospective customers, provides customers with information, persuades customers to buy, closes sales, and follows up on customers' use of a product or service. Like order takers, order getters can be inside (an automobile salesperson) or outside (an IBM salesperson). Order getting involves a high degree of creativity and customer empathy and typically is required for selling complex or technical products with many options, so considerable product knowledge and sales training are necessary.

Order getting is an expensive process.[5] It is estimated that the median direct cost of a single sales call for an industrial product is $198.67; for a consumer product, $210.43; and for a service, $193.58. (What amount did you check for question 1 in Figure 17–1?) The direct annual cost for a "typical" salesperson, with compensation and field expenses (including travel, entertainment, food, and lodging), is $52,594 for industrial products, $48,659 for consumer products, and $48,461 for services. These costs illustrate why telephone selling (telemarketing), with a significantly lower cost per call (in the range of $20 to $25) and little or no field expense, is so popular today.

Sales Support Personnel

Sales support personnel augment the selling effort of order getters by performing a variety of services. For example, **missionary salespeople** do not directly solicit orders but rather concentrate on performing other marketing activities and introducing new products. They are used extensively in the pharmaceutical industry, where they persuade physicians to prescribe a firm's product. Actual sales are made through wholesalers or directly to pharmacists who fill prescriptions. A **sales engineer** is a salesperson who specializes in identifying, analyzing, and solving customer problems and brings know-how and technical expertise to the selling situation, but often does not actually sell products and services. Sales engineers are popular in selling industrial products such as chemicals and heavy equipment.

In many situations, firms engage in **team selling,** the practice of using an entire team of professionals in selling to and servicing major customers.[6] Team selling is used when specialized knowledge is needed to satisfy the different interests of individuals in a customer's buying centre. For example, a selling team might consist of a salesperson, a sales engineer, a service representative, and a financial executive, each of whom would deal with a counterpart in the customer's firm. Team selling takes different forms. In **conference selling,** a salesperson and other company resource people meet with buyers to discuss problems and opportunities. In **seminar selling,** a company team conducts an educational program for a customer's technical staff, describing state-of-the-art developments.

LEARNING CHECK

1. What is the principal difference between an order taker and an order getter?

2. What is team selling?

A Xerox Corporation
advertisement featuring
team selling.

THE PERSONAL SELLING PROCESS: BUILDING RELATIONSHIPS

Selling, and particularly order getting, is a complicated activity that involves building buyer–seller relationships. Although the salesperson–customer interaction is essential to personal selling, much of a salesperson's work occurs before this meeting and continues after the sale itself. The **personal selling process** consists of six stages: prospecting, preapproach, approach, presentation, close, and follow-up (Figure 17–4).

Prospecting

Personal selling begins with *prospecting*—the search for and qualification of potential customers.[7] There are three types of prospects. A *lead* is the name of a person who may be a possible customer. A *prospect* is a customer who wants or needs the product. If an individual wants the product, can afford to buy it, and is the decision maker, this individual is a *qualified prospect.*

Leads and prospects are generated using several sources. For example, advertising may contain a coupon or a toll-free number to generate leads. Some companies use exhibits at trade fairs, professional meetings, and conferences to generate leads or prospects. Another approach for generating leads is through *cold canvassing* in person or by telephone. Although the refusal rate is high with cold canvassing, this approach can be successful.

Because of the development and growth in database marketing (see Chapter 7), prospecting has become a little easier, and often the response rates are much higher since the databases allow for greater precision when targeting. But cold canvassing is often criticized by consumers as an intrusion on their privacy. As we saw in Chapter 16, many trade associations have codes of ethics for dealing with this issue, such as adhering to consumers' "do not call," "do not mail," or "do not visit" requests. Also,

FIGURE 17-4 Stages and objectives of the personal selling process.

Stage	Objective	Comments
Prospecting	Search for and qualify prospects	Start of the selling process; prospects produced through advertising, referrals, and cold canvassing.
Preapproach	Gather information and decide how to approach the prospect	Information sources include personal observation, other customers, and own salespeople.
Approach	Gain prospect's attention, stimulate interest, and make transition to the presentation	First impression is critical; gain attention and interest through reference to common acquaintances, a referral, or product demonstration.
Presentation	Begin converting a prospect into a customer by creating a desire for the product or service	Different presentation formats are possible; however, involving the customer in the product or service through attention to particular needs is critical; important to deal professionally and ethically with prospect scepticism, indifference, or objections.
Close	Obtain a purchase commitment from the prospect and create a customer	Salesperson asks for the purchase; different approaches include the trial close and assumptive close.
Follow-up	Ensure that the customer is satisfied with the product or service	Resolve any problems faced by the customer to ensure customer satisfaction and future sales possibilities.

greater government regulation of such practices is being considered. For example, under proposed CRTC regulations, telemarketers will be required to inform consumers that they have the right to say no to such solicitations.[8]

Preapproach

Once a salesperson has identified a qualified prospect, preparation for the sale begins with the preapproach. The *preapproach* stage involves obtaining further information on the prospect and deciding on the best method of approach. Activities in this stage include finding information on who the prospect is, how the prospect prefers to be approached, and what the prospect is looking for in a product or service. For example, a stockbroker will need information on a prospect's discretionary income, investment objectives, and preference for discussing brokerage services over the telephone or in person. Identifying the best time to contact a prospect is also important.

Approach

The *approach* stage involves the initial meeting between the salesperson and prospect, where the objectives are to gain the prospect's attention, stimulate interest, and build the foundation for the sales presentation itself and the basis for a working relationship.[9] The first impression is critical at this stage, and it is common for salespeople to begin the conversation with a reference to common acquaintances, a referral, or even the product or service itself. Which tactic is taken will depend on the information obtained in the prospecting and preapproach stages.

The approach stage is very important in international settings. In many societies outside Canada, considerable time is devoted to nonbusiness talk designed to establish a rapport between buyers and sellers. For instance, it is common that two or three meetings occur before business matters are discussed in the Middle East and Asia.

Presentation

The *presentation* is at the core of the order-getting selling process, and its objective is to convert a prospect into a customer by creating a desire for the product or service. Three major presentation formats exist: stimulus–response format, formula selling format, and need-satisfaction format.

Stimulus–Response Format. The **stimulus–response presentation** format assumes that given the appropriate stimulus by a salesperson, the prospect will buy. A counter clerk at McDonald's is using this approach when she asks whether you'd like an order of french fries or a dessert with your meal. The counter clerk is engaging in what is called *suggestive selling.* Although useful in this setting, the stimulus–response format is not always appropriate, and for many products a more formalized format is necessary.

Formula Selling Format. A more formalized presentation, the **formula selling presentation** format, is based on the view that a presentation consists of information that must be provided in an accurate, thorough, and step-by-step manner to inform the prospect. A popular version of this format is the *canned sales presentation,* which is a memorized, standardized message conveyed to every prospect.[10] Canned sales presentations can be advantageous when the differences between prospects are unknown or with novice salespeople who are less knowledgeable about the product and selling

Prospecting at trade shows is becoming popular for many organizations.

process than experienced salespeople. Although it guarantees a thorough presentation, it often lacks flexibility and spontaneity.

Need–Satisfaction Format. The stimulus–response and formula selling formats share a common characteristic: the salesperson dominates the conversation. By comparison, the **need-satisfaction presentation** format emphasizes probing and listening by the salesperson to identify needs and interests of prospective buyers. Once these are identified, the salesperson tailors the presentation to the prospect and highlights product benefits that may be valued by the prospect.

The need-satisfaction format, which emphasizes problem solving, is the most consistent with the marketing concept. Two selling styles are associated with this format. **Adaptive selling** involves adjusting the presentation to fit the selling situation, such as knowing when to offer solutions and when to ask for more information. **Consultative selling** focuses on problem identification, where the salesperson serves as an expert on problem recognition and resolution.[11] Both styles are used for industrial products such as computers and heavy equipment. Many consumer service firms such as brokerage and insurance firms and consumer product firms like Xerox Canada and Gillette also subscribe to these selling styles.

Handling Objections. A critical concern in the presentation stage is handling objections. *Objections* are excuses for not making a purchase commitment or decision. Some objections are valid and are based on the characteristics of the product or service or price. However, many objections reflect prospect scepticism or indifference. Whether valid or not, experienced salespeople know that objections do not put an end to the presentation. Rather, techniques can be used to deal with objections in a courteous, ethical, and professional manner. Six techniques used to deal with objections are shown in Figure 17–5.

Close

The *closing* stage in the selling process is when a purchase commitment is obtained from the prospect. This stage is the most difficult because the salesperson must determine when the prospect is ready to buy. Telltale signals indicating a readiness to buy

---

1. *Acknowledge and convert the objection.* This technique involves using the objection as a reason for buying. For example, a prospect might say, "The price is too high." The reply: "Yes, the price is high because we use the finest materials. Let me show you . . ."
2. *Postpone.* The postpone technique is used when the objection will be dealt with later in the presentation: "I'm going to address that point shortly. I think my answer would make better sense then."
3. *Agree and neutralize.* Here a salesperson agrees with the objection, then shows that it is unimportant. A salesperson would say, "That's true and others have said the same. However, they concluded that issue was outweighed by the other benefits."
4. *Accept the objection.* Sometimes the objection is valid. Let the prospect express such views, probe for the reason behind it, and attempt to stimulate further discussion on the objection.
5. *Denial.* When a prospect's objection is based on misinformation and clearly untrue, it is wise to meet the objection head on with a firm denial.
6. *Ignore the objection.* This technique is used when it appears that the objection is a stalling mechanism or is clearly not important to the prospect.

SOURCE: Based on Ronald D. Balsley and E. Patricia Birsner, *Selling: Marketing Personified* (Hinsdale, IL: Dryden Press, 1987), pp. 261–63.

FIGURE 17–5
Techniques used to deal with objections.

$ MARKETPLACE APPLICATION

Global Selling: Honing Your Cultural Ear

By the year 2000, the economy of East Asia—spanning from Japan to Indonesia—will almost equal that of North America and total about four-fifths of the European Community economy. The marketing opportunities in East Asia are great, but effective selling in these countries will require a keen cultural ear. Seasoned global marketers know that in many Asian societies it is impolite to say no, and *yes* has multiple meanings.

Yes in Asian societies can have at least four meanings. It can mean that listeners are simply acknowledging that a speaker is talking to them even though they don't understand what is being said, or it can mean that a speaker's words are understood but not agreed with. A third meaning of *yes* conveys that a presentation is understood but other people must be consulted before

any commitment is possible. Finally, *yes* can also mean that a proposal is understood and accepted. However, experienced negotiators also note that this *yes* is subject to change if the situation is changed.

This one example illustrates why savvy salespeople are sensitive to cultural underpinnings when engaged in cross-cultural sales negotiations.

1. How should salespeople cope with the challenges of cross-cultural sales negotiations?

SOURCES: Based on P. R. Cateora, *International Marketing*, 8th ed. (Burr Ridge, IL: Richard D. Irwin, 1993), p. 145; L. Kraar, "Asia 2000," *Fortune*, October 5, 1992, pp. 111–42; C. R. Ruthstrom and K. Matejka, "The Meanings of 'Yes' in the Far East," *Industrial Marketing Management*, vol. 19, 1990, pp. 191–92; and S. Frank, "Global Negotiating," *Sales & Marketing Management*, May 1992, pp. 64–69.

include body language (prospect reexamines the product or contract closely), statements ("This equipment should reduce our maintenance costs"), and questions ("When could we expect delivery?").

The close itself can take several forms. Three closing techniques are used when a salesperson believes a buyer is about ready to make a purchase: trial close, assumptive close, and urgency close. In a *trial close,* the prospect is asked to make a decision on some aspect of the purchase: "Would you prefer the blue or the grey model?" An *assumptive close* entails asking the prospect to make choices concerning delivery, warranty, or financing terms under the assumption that a sale has been finalized. An *urgency close* is used to commit the prospect quickly by making reference to the timeliness of the purchase: "The low-interest financing ends next week," or, "That is the last unit we have in stock." Of course, these statements should be used only if they accurately reflect the situation; otherwise, such claims would be unethical. When a prospect is clearly ready to buy, the *final close* is used and a salesperson asks for the order.[12]

Knowing when the prospect is ready to buy becomes even more difficult in cross-cultural buyer–seller negotiations where societal customs and language play a large role. Read the accompanying Marketplace Application to understand the multiple meanings of *yes* in Japan and other societies in the Far East.

Follow-Up

The selling process does not end with the closing of a sale; rather, professional selling requires customer follow-up. The *follow-up* stage includes making certain the customer's purchase has been properly delivered and installed and difficulties experienced with the use of the item are addressed. Attention to this stage of the selling process solidifies the buyer–seller relationship. Moreover, research shows that the cost and effort to obtain repeat sales from a satisfied customer is roughly half of that necessary to gain a sale from a new customer.[13] In short, today's satisfied customers become tomorrow's qualified prospects or referrals. (What was your answer to question 2 in the quiz?)

LEARNING CHECK

1. What are the six stages in the personal selling process?

2. What is the distinction between a lead and a qualified prospect?

3. Which presentation format is most consistent with the relationship marketing concept? Why?

THE SALES MANAGEMENT PROCESS

Selling must be managed if it is going to contribute to a firm's overall objectives. Although firms differ in the specifics of how salespeople and the selling effort are managed, the sales management process is similar across firms. Sales management consists of three interrelated functions: sales plan formulation, sales plan implementation, and evaluation and control of the sales force (Figure 17–6).

Sales Plan Formulation

Formulating the sales plan is the most basic of the three sales management functions. The **sales plan** is a statement describing what is to be achieved and where and how the selling effort of salespeople is to be deployed. Formulating the sales plan involves three tasks: setting objectives, organizing the sales force, and developing account management policies.

Setting Objectives. Setting objectives is central to sales management because this task specifies what is to be achieved. In practice, objectives are set for the total sales force and for each salesperson. Selling objectives can be output-related and focus on dollar or unit sales volume, number of new customers added, and profit. Alternatively, they can be input-related and emphasize the number of sales calls and selling expenses. Output- and input-related objectives are used for the sales force as a whole and for each salesperson. A third type of objective that is behaviourally related is typically specific

FIGURE 17–6
The sales management process.

SOURCE: Based on G. A. Churchill, Jr., N. M. Ford, and O. C. Walker Jr., *Sales Force Management,* 4th ed. (Burr Ridge, IL: Richard D. Irwin, 1993), pp. 11–12.

FIGURE 17–7   The case for using company salespeople versus independent agents.

Criteria	Case for Company Sales Force	Case for Independent Agents
Control	Company selects, trains, supervises, and can use multiple rewards to direct salespeople.	Agents are equally well selected, trained, and supervised by the representative organization.
Flexibility	Company can transfer salespeople, change customer selling practices, and otherwise direct its own sales force.	Little fixed cost is present with agents; mostly there are variable costs; therefore, firm is not burdened with overhead.
Effort	Sales effort is enhanced because salespeople represent one firm, not several; firm loyalty is present; there is better customer service because salespeople receive salary as well as commission	Agents might work harder than salespeople because compensation is based soley on commissions; customer service is good, since it builds repeat business.
Availability	Knowledgeable agents might not be available where and when needed.	Entrepreneurial spirit of agents will make them available where a marketing opportunity exists.

for each salesperson and includes her product knowledge, customer service, and selling and communication skills. Increasingly, firms are also emphasizing knowledge of competition as an objective, since salespeople are calling on customers and should see what competitors are doing.[14]

Whatever objectives are set, they should be precise and measurable and specify the time period over which they are to be achieved. Once established, these objectives serve as performance standards for the evaluation of the sales force—the third function of sales management.

Organizing the Sales Force. Establishing a selling organization is the second task in formulating the sales plan. Three questions are related to organization. First, should the company use its own sales force, or should it use independent agents such as manufacturer's representatives (see Figure 17–7)? Second, if the decision is made to employ company salespeople, then should they be organized according to geography, customer type, or product or service? Third, how many company salespeople should be employed?

The decision to use company salespeople or independent agents is based on an analysis of economic and behavioural factors. An economic analysis examines the costs of using both types of salespeople and is a form of break-even analysis.

If a company elects to employ its own salespeople, then it must choose an organizational structure based on geography, customer, or product (Figure 17–8). A *geographical structure* is the simplest organization, where Canada, or indeed the globe, is first divided into regions and each region is divided into districts or territories. Salespeople are assigned to each district with defined geographical boundaries and call on all customers and represent all products sold by the company. The principal advantage of this structure is that it can minimize travel time, expenses, and duplication of selling effort. However, if a firm's products or customers require specialized knowledge, then a geographical structure is not suitable.

When different types of buyers have different needs, a *customer organizational structure* is used. In practice this means that a different sales force calls on each separate type of buyer. For example, Firestone Tire & Rubber has one sales force that calls

Customer organization

- General Sales Manager
  - Sales Manager Auto industry
  - Sales Manager Farm and construction equipment
  - Sales Manager Government and military
    - District Sales Manager
    - District Sales Manager
    - District Sales Manager
      - Individual salespeople

Product organization

- General Sales Manager
  - Divisional Sales Manager Product A
  - Divisional Sales Manager Product B
    - Eastern Regional Sales Manager
    - Western Regional Sales Manager
      - District Sales Manager
      - District Sales Manager
      - District Sales Manager
        - Individual salespeople

Geographical organization

- General Sales Manager
  - Eastern Regional Sales Manager
  - Western Regional Sales Manager
    - District Sales Manager
    - District Sales Manager
    - District Sales Manager
      - Individual salespeople

Downsizing at Goodie Soups*

Goodie Soups, a strong regional company that specialized in canned and packaged soup mix products, decided several years ago to expand into new geographic areas within the Canadian market. Although Goodie serviced all its current customers with its own sales force, it was considering the elimination of its current sales force system which consisted of 12 salespeople. Under this system, each salesperson was assigned to a geographic territory. Each territory had at least 60 retailers who were to be visited by the salesperson on a regular basis.

To expand into new areas as planned and to be competitive, sales managers at Goodie realized that operating costs would have to be significantly reduced. John Witt, Goodie's V.P. of sales, believed there was only one solution. His solution called for the establishment of a major account management system. This system would

result in a downsized sales force. In fact, this system would replace the existing 12 salespeople with a sales force of only three key account representatives. Witt believed that it would be more economical for Goodie to focus exclusively on high-volume wholesalers and retailers. According to Witt, "We just can't afford the luxury of providing personalized service to low-volume accounts. We need to focus our efforts and begin building strong relationships with major account buyers."

1. Is this company acting ethically if it replaces its current sales force with a small team of key account representatives?

2. Discuss the advantages and disadvantages of major account management.

*All names and places have been disguised.

on its own dealers and another that calls on independent dealers, such as gasoline stations. The rationale for this approach is that more effective, specialized customer support and knowledge is provided to buyers. However, this structure often leads to higher administrative costs and some duplication of selling effort, since two separate sales forces are used to represent the same products.

A variation of the customer organizational structure is **major account management** (also known as *key account management*), the practice of using team selling to focus on important customers so as to build mutually beneficial, long-term, cooperative relationships.[15] Major account management often involves teams of sales, service, and technical personnel who work with purchasing, manufacturing, engineering, logistics, and financial executives in customer organizations. This recent innovation, which often assigns company personnel to a customer account, results in "customer specialists" who can provide exceptional service. At the same time, it suffers from the same disadvantages of the typical customer sales organization.

When specific knowledge is required to sell certain types of products, then a *product organization* is used. For example, Procter & Gamble has a sales force that sells household cleaning products and another that sells food products. The primary advantage of this structure is that salespeople can develop expertise with technical characteristics, applications, and selling methods associated with a particular product or family of products. However, this structure also produces high administrative costs and duplication of selling effort, since two company salespeople call on the same customer.

In short, there is no one best sales organization for all companies in all situations. Rather, the organization of the sales force should reflect the marketing strategy of the firm.

The third question related to sales force organization involves determining the size of the sales force. For example, why does Frito-Lay have about 10,000 salespeople who call on supermarkets and grocery stores to sell snack foods? The answer lies in an analysis of the number of accounts (customers) served, the frequency of calls on accounts, the length of an average call, and the amount of time a salesperson can devote to selling.

Developing Account Management Policies. The third task in formulating a sales plan is to develop **account management policies** specifying whom salespeople should contact, what kinds of selling and customer service activities should be engaged in, and how these activities should be carried out.[16] These policies might state which individuals in a buying organization should be contacted, the amount of sales and service effort that different customers should receive, and the kinds of information salespeople should collect before or during a sales call.

Sales Plan Implementation

The sales plan is implemented through several specific tasks. The three major tasks involved in implementing a sales plan are sales force recruitment and selection, sales force training, and sales force motivation and compensation.

Sales Force Recruitment and Selection. Effective recruitment and selection of salespeople is one of the most crucial tasks of sales management. It entails finding people who match the type of sales position required by a firm. Recruitment and selection practices would differ greatly between order-taking and order-getting sales positions, given the differences in the demands of these two jobs. Therefore, recruitment and selection begin with a carefully crafted job analysis.

A **job analysis** is a written description of what a salesperson is expected to do, and therefore it differs among firms.[17] Figure 17–9 shows a job analysis for building materials salespeople—an order-getting sales position. This analysis identifies eight

FIGURE 17–9 Job analysis for an order-getting salesperson.

Job Factor	Activities
Assisting and working with district management	Assisting district sales management in market surveys, new product evaluations, etc. Preparing reports on territorial sales expenses Managing a sales territory within the sales expense budget Using district management to make joint sales calls on customers
Customer service	Arranging credit adjustments on incorrect invoicing, shipping, and order shortages Informing customers of supply conditions on company products Assisting customers and prospects in providing credit information to the company
Personal integrity and selling ethics	Representing company products at their true value Working within the merchandising plans and policies established by the company Investigating and reporting customer complaints
Direct selling	Knowing correct applications and installations of company products Making sales presentations that communicate product benefits Handling sales presentations
Developing relationships with customers	Maintaining a friendly, personal relationship with customers Using equipment to strengthen the business relationship with customers Providing customers with technical information on company products
Keeping abreast of market conditions	Keeping customers informed of market conditions that affect their businesses Keeping the company informed of market conditions
Meeting sales objectives	Identifying the person with authority to make the purchasing decision Closing the sale and obtaining the order Selling company products at a volume that meets or exceeds expectations
Maintaining complete customer records	Maintaining customer records that are complete and up to date Checking customers' inventory and recommending orders

L. M. Lamont and W. J. Lundstrom, "Defining Industrial Sales Behavior: A Factor Analytic Study," *1974 Combined Proceedings* (Chicago: American Marketing Association, 1974), pp. 493–98; by permission of the American Marketing Association.

major job factors and describes important activities associated with each. Note particularly the frequent mention of customer service functions and relationship building and the specific reference to personal integrity and selling ethics.

Firms use a variety of methods for evaluating prospective salespeople. Personal interviews, reference checks, and background information provided on application blanks are the most frequently used methods.[18]

Sales Force Training. Whereas recruitment and selection of salespeople is a one-time event, sales force training is an ongoing process that affects both new and seasoned salespeople. Sales training covers much more than selling practices. On average, training programs devote 35 percent of time to product information, 30 percent to sales techniques, 25 percent to market and company information, and 10 percent to other topics, including ethical practices.[19] (What was your answer to question 3 on the quiz?)

Training salespeople is an expensive and time-consuming process.[20] The direct cost of training a new industrial product salesperson (excluding salary) is $22,236 and training takes eight months. Training a new consumer product salesperson costs $11,616 and takes five months, and training new salespeople in service industries costs $14,501 and takes seven months. On-the-job training is the most popular type of training, followed by individual instruction by experienced salespeople. Formal classes and seminars taught by sales trainers are also growing in popularity.

Sales Force Motivation and Compensation. A sales plan cannot be successfully implemented without motivated salespeople. Research on salesperson motivation suggests that (1) a clear job description, (2) effective sales management practices, (3) a sense of achievement, and (4) proper incentives or rewards will produce a motivated salesperson.[21]

Pay is an important motivating factor, which means that close attention must be given to how salespeople are financially rewarded for their efforts. Salespeople are paid using one of three plans: straight salary, straight commission, or a combination of salary and commission. Under a *straight salary compensation plan* a salesperson is paid a fixed fee per week, month, or year. With a *straight commission compensation plan* a salesperson's earnings are directly tied to the sales or profit generated. A *combination compensation plan* contains a specified salary plus a commission on sales or profit generated. Obviously each plan has its advantages and disadvantages and is particularly suited to certain situations (Figure 17–10).

Of course, nonmonetary rewards are also given to salespeople for meeting or exceeding objectives. These rewards include trips, honour societies, distinguished salesperson awards, and letters of commendation.[22] Some unconventional rewards include the new pink Cadillacs, fur coats, and jewellery given by Mary Kay Cosmetics to outstanding salespeople.

Effective recruitment, selection, training, motivation, and compensation programs combine to create a productive sales force. Ineffective practices often lead to costly sales force turnover. U.S. and Canadian firms experience an annual 27 percent turnover rate, which means that about one of every four salespeople is replaced each year. The expense of replacing and training a new salesperson, including the cost of lost sales, can be as high as $75,000.[23] Moreover, new recruits are often less productive than established salespeople.

Sales Force Evaluation and Control

The final function in the sales management process is evaluating and controlling the sales force. It is at this point that salespeople are assessed as to whether sales objectives were met and account management policies were followed. Both quantitative and behavioural measures are used.

FIGURE 17–10 Comparison of different compensation plans.

	Straight Salary	Straight Commission	Combination
Frequency of use	12%	5%	83%
Especially useful	When compensating new salespeople; when a firm moves into new sales territories that require developmental work; when salespeople need to perform many nonselling activities	When highly aggressive selling is required; when nonselling tasks are minimized; when company cannot closely control sales force activities	When sales territories have relatively similar sales potentials; when firm wishes to provide incentive but still control sales force activities
Advantages	Provides salesperson with maximum amount of security; gives sales manager large amount of control over salespeople; easy to administer; yields more predictable selling expenses	Provides maximum amount of incentive; by increasing commission rate, sales managers can encourage salespeople to sell certain items; selling expenses relate directly to sales resources	Provides certain level of financial security; provides some incentive; selling expenses fluctuate with sales revenue; sales manager has some control over salesperson's nonselling activities
Disadvantages	Provides no incentive; necessitates closer supervision of salespeople's activities; during sales declines, selling expenses remain at same level	Salespeople have little financial security; sales manager has minimum control over sales force; may cause salespeople to provide inadequate service to smaller accounts; selling costs less predictable	Selling expenses less predictable; may be difficult to administer

SOURCE: Adapted from G. A. Churchill, Jr., N. M. Ford, and O. C. Walker, Jr., *Sales Force Management Planning, Implementation, and Control*, 4th ed. (Burr Ridge, IL: Richard D. Irwin, 1993), p. 591.

Quantitative Assessments. Quantitative assessments are based on input- and output-related objectives set forth in the sales plan. Input-related measures focus on the actual activities performed by salespeople, such as those involving sales calls, selling expenses, and account management policies. The number of sales calls made, selling expense related to sales made, and the number of reports submitted to superiors are the most frequently used input measures.

Output measures focus on the results obtained and include sales produced, accounts generated, profit achieved, and orders produced compared with calls made. Dollar sales volume, last year/current year sales ratio, the number of new accounts, and sales of specific products are the most frequently used measures when evaluating salesperson output.[24]

Behavioural Evaluation. Less quantitative behavioural measures are also used to evaluate salespeople. These include subjective and often informal assessments of a salesperson's attitude, product knowledge, selling and communication skills, appearance, and demeanour. Even though these assessments are highly subjective, they are frequently considered, and in fact inevitable, in salesperson evaluation.[25] Moreover, these factors are often important determinants of quantitative outcomes.

LEARNING CHECK

1. What are the three types of selling objectives?

2. What three factors are used to structure sales organizations?

3. Sales training typically focuses on what two sales-related issues?

LEARNING OBJECTIVE REINFORCEMENT

1. Understand the importance of personal selling in today's competitive environment. For many organizations personal selling plays a dominant role in its marketing communications efforts. Moreover, salespeople *are* often viewed as the company in a consumer's eyes. Therefore, sales professionals are considered a vital link between the customer and the organization. Today's salesperson is often a highly trained professional who is given the responsibility of attracting and cultivating customer relationships.

2. Explain the distinction between traditional selling and relationship selling. Relationship selling is the practice of building ties to customers through a salesperson's attention and commitment to customer needs over time. Relationship selling involves mutual respect and trust among buyers and sellers. It is a "we"-oriented kind of selling which focusses on creating long-term customers, not a one-time sale.

A traditional selling approach is a "me"-oriented approach to selling which focusses on short-term sales objectives with little concern for customers' needs over time.

3. Describe three types of personal selling. Three types of personal selling exist: order-taking, order-getting, and sales support activities. Each type differs from the other in terms of actual selling done and the amount of creativity required to perform the job. Order takers process routine orders or reorders for products that were already sold by the company. Order getters sell in a conventional sense and identify prospective customers, provide customers with information, persuade customers to buy, close sales, and follow-up on customers' use of a product or service. Sales support personnel augment the selling process of order getters by performing a variety of services such as providing technical expertise.

4. Describe the stages in the personal selling process. The personal selling process consists of six stages: prospecting, preapproach, approach, presentation, close, and follow-up.

Prospecting is the search for and qualification of potential customers. Once a salesperson has identified a qualified prospect, preparation for sale begins with the *preapproach stage* which involves obtaining further information on the prospect and deciding on the best method of approach. The *approach stage* involves the initial meeting between the salesperson and prospect, where the objectives are to gain the prospect's attention, stimulate interest, and build the foundation for the sales presentation itself and the basis for a working relationship. The *presentation stage* involves the contact with the customer which is designed to convert the prospect into a customer by creating a desire for the product or service. The *closing stage* in the personal selling process is when a purchase commitment is obtained from the prospect. The selling process does not end with the closing of a sale; rather, professional selling requires customer *follow-up*. This stage includes making certain the customer's purchase has been properly delivered and installed and difficulties experienced with the use of the item are addressed.

5. Specify the functions and tasks in the sales management process. Sales management consists of three interrelated functions: sales plan formulation, sales plan implementation, and evaluation and control of the sales force. The first function, sales plan formulation, involves three tasks: setting objectives, organizing the sales force, and developing account management policies. The major tasks involved in the second function, sales plan implementation, are sales force recruitment and selection, sales force training, and sales force motivation and compensation. The final function in the sales management process, evaluating and controlling, involves the assessment of salespeople to determine whether sales objectives were met and account management policies were followed. Both quantitative and behaviourial measures are used.

KEY TERMS AND CONCEPTS

relationship selling p. 417
personal selling p. 418
sales management p. 418
order taker p. 420
order getter p. 421
missionary salespeople p. 421
sales engineer p. 421

team selling p. 421
conference selling p. 421
seminar selling p. 421
personal selling process p. 422
stimulus–response presentation p. 424
formula selling presentation p. 424
need-satisfaction presentation p. 425

adaptive selling p. 425
consultative selling p. 425
sales plan p. 427
major account management p. 430
account management policies p. 431
job analysis p. 431

CHAPTER QUESTIONS AND APPLICATIONS

1. Why should relationship selling be a practice of interest to marketing managers?

2. Bree Benson is a new sales representative for the Charles Schwab brokerage firm. In searching for clients, Bree purchased a mailing list of subscribers to the *Financial Post*

and called them all regarding their interest in discount brokerage services. She asked if they had any stocks and if they had a regular broker. Those people without a regular broker were asked about their investment needs. Two days later Bree called back with investment advice and asked if they would like to open an account. Identify each of Bree's actions in terms of the stages of selling (see Figure 17–4).

3. Where would you place each of the following sales jobs on the order-taker/order-getter continuum shown below? *(a)* Burger King counter clerk, *(b)* automobile insurance salesperson, *(c)* IBM computer salesperson, *(d)* life insurance salesperson, and *(e)* shoe salesperson.

Order taker	Order getter

4. Which type of personal selling—order getting, order taking, or support—is the most likely to be taken over by interactive computer networks between buyers and sellers? Why?

5. When is it appropriate for firms to engage in *team selling?* Identify several products or services that would normally be sold using a team-selling approach.

6. Suppose someone said to you, "The only real measure of a salesperson's performance is the amount of sales produced." How might you respond?

7. Jon Winston is the president of a Canadian-based supplier of component parts for both mainframe and personal computers. Jon has decided to restructure his company sales force in order to develop long-term relationships with buyers. To accomplish this objective Jon has decided to adopt a customer organizational structure. Jon's new structure will require two sales forces, one that will sell to buyers of components used in mainframe computers and one that will sell exclusively to buyers of parts for personal computers. Does this type of organizational structure seem to be appropriate? What are the disadvantages of having a separate sales force for different types of customers?

8. U.S. and Canadian firms experience an annual sales force turnover rate of 27 percent. Does this turnover rate seem too high? Why or why not? What can sales force managers do in order to reduce turnover rates?

9. An increasing number of Canadian firms are using telemarketing as a means of selling products. How might the popularity of telemarketing be explained?

10. Suppose someone said to you, "In today's competitive environment it just does not make sense to employ a company sales force. Independent agents are always the best alternative because the firm is not burdened with the expense of overhead." How might you respond?

APPLICATION CASE 17–1
BORDEN PAPERS LTD.

Garry Walters sells paper products to large institutional and government accounts for Borden Papers Ltd. As a sales representative, Garry is responsible for calling on all customers in his southwestern Ontario territory.

In a recent performance review with his sales manager, Dianne Bently, Garry was informed of his less than satisfactory sales performance. Prior to this review Garry was not aware that his performance was less than what Dianne expected. In the past, according to Dianne, Garry had demonstrated above average effort. Furthermore, Garry's call reports indicated he was calling on more accounts than all of Borden's 15 other salespeople and his share of sales to low-volume buyers was slightly above average.

Now, however, Dianne was concerned about Garry's performance because his sales to large-volume buyers was among the lowest at Borden. Dianne believed Garry was having difficulty obtaining a purchase commitment from these possible accounts because he was not handling the *closing stage* of the selling process properly.

In an effort to confirm her belief, Dianne asked Garry to explain his approach to closing the sale with major account buyers.

"It's easy, Dianne, I'm a straight shooter. I almost always hit them with, 'Are you interested in placing a large order today?' Isn't this the best way to do it? This approach protects me from wasted selling time because buyers normally respond with an excuse for not placing an order. These buyers will never buy our products."

In response to this explanation, Dianne responded, "I know what your problem is, Garry."

QUESTIONS:
1. What is Garry's problem?
2. Why might Garry be experiencing this problem?
3. Would you recommend training as a solution to Garry's problem? If so, what specific techniques would you recommend?

APPLICATION CASE 17–2
THE SALES MANAGEMENT SEMINAR: "RELATIONSHIPS AND SALES FORCE PERFORMANCE"

While having dinner at the end of the first day of their two-day sales management seminar, Dee Smith and Ross Nichson were discussing the content of the day's seminar. Their employer, Investment Mutual Inc., now requires all its senior sales managers to attend this seminar.

Dee Smith: I don't understand why in this age of cost cutting, we are forced to attend this seminar. No matter the fancy talk or the seminar leader's Ph.D., this stuff has nothing to do with the real world. A salesperson's job is really simple—they sell the company's financial products. There is only one factor that really counts and that is money. If you offer enough money the sales job will get done.

Another thing, what is all this talk about building quality relationships? My salespeople don't have enough time to identify new leads let alone spend time building relationships. When I was in the field, I knew when I had a good relationship with my clients. It was either a good relationship or a bad one, and I was bright enough to avoid those clients that didn't like me.

Ross Nichson: Well, Dee, I don't know. I think I've learned a lot of really useful stuff today. When we return to the office next week I'm going to try some of the things we learned. When I first started in sales, my first boss was big into build-

ing relationships—both within his sales force and with customers. He expected me to build relationships with customers and he made a great effort to have a quality working relationship with me. I recall many informal meetings with him when he would seek my opinion on such things as the company's reward system and its system of territory assignment. He really made me feel as if he cared.

I've got to believe that we can use these performance and relationship factors to help our salespeople reach their potential.

Dee Smith: I think you're losing it, Ross. Let's change the topic. I need some coffee.

QUESTIONS:
1. On the basis of the conversation between Dee Smith and Ross Nichson, what kind of sales manager do you think each is?
2. Do you think that sales managers can have much impact on the performance of individual salespeople?
3. If you were hiring a new sales manager at Investment Mutual, what specific hiring criteria would you use? Would you want your sales managers to attend sales management seminars on topics such as relationship development and sales performance factors?

Understanding the Expanded Settings for Marketing

CHAPTER 18

Global and International Marketing

AFTER READING THIS CHAPTER YOU WILL BE ABLE TO:

1. Understand the factors that have helped shape a new global arena.

2. Describe why market-driven organizations enter foreign markets.

3. Explain the difference between global marketing and international marketing.

4. Outline the sequence of decisions in entering foreign markets.

5. Understand the importance of assessing the political, economic, and cultural conditions of foreign markets.

6. Outline the alternative modes of entering foreign markets.

7. Explain the use of a standardized and customized marketing mix when entering foreign markets.

TOKYO DISNEYLAND AND EURODISNEY: LESSONS IN ENTERING FOREIGN MARKETS

Disney's experiences in taking its theme parks abroad highlight both the opportunities and dangers of entering foreign markets. Before entering the Japanese market, Disney's research showed that Japanese children loved the Disney characters, 30 million people lived within 30 miles of the proposed site, and Japanese households had plenty of discretionary income to buy tickets. From its start, Tokyo Disneyland was a huge success. Today, more than a decade later, it averages more annual guests than the original Disneyland.

Contrast this experience with EuroDisney. Located 20 miles east of Paris, EuroDisney opened its doors in 1992. Research showed the theme park would be accessible to households from all 12 European Community countries, and that European children loved the Disney characters. But research also showed two special concerns: compared to Tokyo, the weather was worse, and there were fewer households in the immediate area with high discretionary incomes.

Nonetheless, because Paris is the tourist capital of Europe this location was chosen over a sunny Spanish alternative. Disney also didn't count on a European recession, and the French not appreciating its aggressive marketing campaigns. A year after its launch, the European recession and the bad winter weather caused EuroDisney to fall a million visitors short of its projections. Now EuroDisney has switched to soft-sell ads stressing the themes of kids and fun, targets French history teachers to get their classes to learn American history at EuroDisney, and is using cold-weather themes like ice skating and Finnish reindeer to attract visitors.[1]

Tokyo Disneyland, a Disney success in a foreign market.

Disney's experience illustrates the practical benefits and difficulties of entering foreign markets. In this chapter we will discuss exactly what global and international marketing are and why firms would enter foreign markets. We will also discuss the importance of assessing foreign markets for possible entry, describe alternative means of entry, and explain how marketing plans can be successfully developed for these markets.

A NEW GLOBAL ARENA

As we stated in Chapter 1, whether they like it or not most organizations find themselves competing in a global arena. Today markets for many products and services are global in scope rather than local, regional, or national. The realities of this new global arena means that organizations must view the world as a potential marketplace and be prepared to search for opportunities around the globe. If they do not, they risk losing those opportunities abroad as well as losing their home markets to foreign competitors who come to compete in their backyard.

Advances in travel, communications, and technology have helped shape a new global arena. But two other factors in the late 20th century have had a significant impact on the development of a more globalized marketplace. One is an international agreement called the **General Agreement on Tariffs and Trade (GATT).**

In 1948, GATT was established to liberalize global trade and place it on a secure basis, thereby contributing to economic growth and development and to the welfare of the world's people.[2] GATT assists in reducing trade barriers around the world and in creating more favourable conditions for global trade. Since it was established, this agreement has helped build global trade from $60 billion to over $4 trillion annually.

The second factor which has had significant impact on the development of a global marketplace is free trade among nations. In recent years a number of countries with similar economic objectives have formed transnational trade groups or signed trade agreements for the purpose of encouraging free trade among member nations and enhancing their individual economies. Two of the most recent and best-known examples are the European Community (EC) and the North American Free Trade Agreement (NAFTA). We will discuss these agreements further later in this chapter.

IMPORTANCE OF GLOBAL TRADE

All nations and regions of the world do not participate equally in global trade. Global trade flows reflect interdependencies among industries, countries, and regions and manifest themselves in country, industry, company, and regional exports and imports.

The total value of global trade has grown an average of 13 percent per year since 1970 and, as mentioned, currently exceeds $4 trillion. A global perspective on global trade views exports and imports as complementary economic flows: A country's imports affect its exports and its exports affect its imports.[3] Every nation's imports arise from the exports of other nations. As the exports of one country increase, its national output and income rise, which in turn leads to an increase in the demand for imports. This nation's greater demand for imports stimulates the exports of other countries. Increased demand for exports of other nations energizes their economic activity, resulting in higher national income, which stimulates their demand for imports. In short, imports affect exports and vice versa. This phenomenon is called the **trade feedback effect** and is one argument for free trade among nations.

Continually rising consumer income in Japan, Taiwan, South Korea, Hong Kong, and other Asian and Pacific Rim countries, fueled by their growth in exports, has prompted a demand for goods and services from Canada and the United States. Many North American companies are benefiting from rising consumer incomes in Asia and the Pacific Rim, including General Motors, which exports cars to Taiwan; Johnson & Johnson, with its robust business for lotions and shampoos in South Korea; and Kodak, which dominates the $1 billion film market for professional photography in Japan.

Where does Canada fit in? Canada is a trading nation; we export close to 25 percent of our **gross domestic product (GDP)**—the monetary value of all goods and services produced in a country during one year. Almost every Canadian is affected by global trade and Canada's trading activities. The effects vary from the products we buy (Samsung computers from Korea, Waterford crystal from Ireland, wine from France) to those we sell (Ganong chocolates to Japan, Moosehead beer to Sweden), and the additional jobs and improved standards of living that can result from global trade. So global trade is not only important for the Canadian firms that see opportunities to prosper, it is also important because of consumer welfare and the thousands of jobs it creates.

While Canada trades with dozens of other countries, the three largest importers of Canadian goods and services are the United States (accounting for close to 75 percent),

Ganong seeks opportunities in foreign markets like Japan.

Japan, and the United Kingdom. These countries are also the top three exporters to Canada, with both Japan and the U.K. enjoying a trade surplus, and the United States suffering a trade deficit with our country.

BENEFITS AND DIFFICULTIES IN ENTERING FOREIGN MARKETS

The GATT agreement and transnational trading groups have helped create opportunities for market-driven organizations to compete in foreign markets. Organizations choosing to enter these markets can achieve many benefits, but they can also encounter many difficulties.

Benefits of Entering Foreign Markets

The main reason for organizations to enter foreign markets is to exploit a better business opportunity in terms of increased sales and profits. Either firms are limited in their home country or their opportunities are greater in foreign countries. Some firms get a large portion of their sales revenues from foreign markets, including MacMillan Bloedal (57 percent), Chrysler Canada (60 percent), and the Royal Canadian Mint (80 percent).[4]

Royal Canadian mint markets its investment coins in dozens of countries around the world.

Many organizations find themselves with little room for growth in their domestic market. Competition may increase and leave a smaller portion of the pie to enjoy, or demand may shift to a newer, better product. The economic environment in the home country may be undesirable because of higher taxes or a recession. It would seem logical to turn to other markets in any of these cases.

Hence foreign markets may offer an opportunity for growth. A product that is mature and facing dwindling sales at home may be new and exciting on other countries. For example, France's Sodima, whose Yoplait yogourt was in the mature phase of its product life cycle at home, was happy to license its product to General Mills for sale in

1. To counter adverse economic factors in the home market.
2. To extend a product's life cycle.
3. To reduce or avoid competition.
4. To enhance economies of scale in production and marketing.
5. To dispose of inventories.
6. To export (and import) new technology.
7. To increase profits or shareholder well-being.

FIGURE 18–1
Key reasons to enter foreign markets.

North America, where yogourt sales were growing rapidly. Similarly, McDonald's Canada is encouraged by its sales in Russia, where the hamburger market is in the early stage of the product life cycle and competition is less intense than in Canada. Volvo cannot sell enough of its cars in its own domestic Swedish market, so it must obtain foreign sales in order to achieve necessary production and marketing economies of scale. Figure 18–1 summarizes the main reasons why Canadian organizations may consider entering foreign markets.

Difficulties of Entering Foreign Markets

Is entering foreign markets easy? Not the least. Some experts believe successful entry into foreign markets takes time, money, and persistence. One consultant suggests that Canadian firms wishing to enter the Japanese market—one of the toughest in the world—may take at least 25 years to achieve the same success found at home.[5]

Although entering foreign markets involves the same principles of domestic marketing discussed throughout the book, those principles must be applied with care. For example, greater efforts may be required to research foreign markets to properly identify target markets, competition, distribution systems, and so forth. Campbell Soup, a company with 60 percent market share in the North American wet soups category, lost $30 million in Great Britain when it initially entered that market. The problem was that Campbell's didn't clearly communicate that the soup was condensed, and consumers saw it as a poor value compared to the larger cans stocked next to it. Later in this chapter, we will discuss ways to increase the chances of successful entry into foreign markets.

DIFFERENCE BETWEEN GLOBAL AND INTERNATIONAL MARKETING

As defined in Chapter 1, **international marketing** is marketing across national boundaries. Many firms operate on an international level, but the number of foreign markets in which they compete and their level of participation in those markets may vary greatly. Moreover, some organizations have committed themselves to becoming truly global in scope. These **global corporations** (global marketers) are firms that look at the entire world as one market and conduct research and development, manufacturing, and marketing activities wherever they can best be done. National boundaries and regulations are largely irrelevant to global corporations. They run their businesses and make decisions on the basis of all possible choices in the world, not simply favouring domestic options because they are convenient.

Many corporations have had to become global in nature because of the globalization of the industries or markets in which they compete. A **global industry** (global market) is

FIGURE 18–2   Sequence of decisions in entering foreign markets.

Assess the foreign marketing environment	Evaluate ways to enter a foreign market	Tailor the marketing plan to the foreign country
Political conditions Economic conditions Cultural conditions →	Exporting Licensing Joint venture Direct ownership →	Select the country Establish the marketing organization Design and implement the marketing plan

one in which the competitive positions of organizations in given local or national markets are affected by their overall global positions. In other words, an organization's competitiveness in one country is affected by its competitiveness in other countries and vice versa. Telecommunications, automobiles, pharmaceuticals, electronics, banking, and computers are examples of global industries.

Whether an organization decides to compete internationally in just one foreign market or as a global participant on every continent, a sequence of decisions must precede their successful entry into those markets. These decisions, outlined in Figure 18–2, are discussed in more detail throughout the remainder of the chapter.

LEARNING CHECK

1. Two factors that have had a significant impact on the development of a more globalized marketplace are _____ and _____.

2. What is the trade feedback effect?

3. What are the reasons why a firm might enter a foreign market?

ASSESSING THE FOREIGN MARKETING ENVIRONMENT

When attempting to make a decision about whether or not to enter foreign markets, and/or which one to enter, market-driven organizations assess the marketing environments of foreign countries very carefully. As we saw in Chapter 3, an *environmental scan* examines five forces in the marketing environment (social, economic, technological, competitive, and regulatory).

In this section, we will focus on three key environmental variables—political, economic, and cultural—that can affect marketing in foreign countries in strikingly different ways from those of domestic markets. Market-driven organizations considering marketing efforts in new countries undertake a serious environmental scan in order to assess opportunities and threats in those foreign markets.

Political Conditions

The difficulties in assessing the political conditions of a country lie not only in identifying the current condition but also in estimating how long those conditions will last. Some companies use analyses ranging from computer projections to intuition to assess a country's political conditions. The dimensions being evaluated include political stability, trade barriers, trade incentives, and transnation trade groups.

ETHICS INSIGHT

Fair Trade and Protectionism

Global trade is enhanced when there is free and fair trade among nations. Nevertheless, the governments of many countries continue to practice protectionism. The principal economic argument for protectionism is that it preserves jobs, protects a nation's political security, discourages economic dependency on other countries, and encourages the development of domestic industries. Still, tariffs and quotas, the principal trade barriers used by protectionists, discourage global trade and often result in higher domestic prices on goods and services produced by protected industries. Currently, there are beer import tariffs in Canada, rice import tariffs in Japan, sugar import quotas in the United States, and automobile quotas in many European countries. Each interferes with the global trade of these products. Regional trade agreements such as those found in the provisions of the European Community and the North American Free Trade Agreement may also pose a situation where member nations can obtain preferential treatment in tariffs and quotas, whereas nonmember nations cannot. For some, protectionism, in its many forms, raises some ethical questions.

1. Is protectionism, no matter how applied, an ethical practice?

2. Is it ethical for countries to use protectionism even if it means consumers in those countries may have to pay higher prices for goods and services?

Political Stability. Billions of dollars have been lost by companies in the Middle East as a result of wars and changes in government. Holiday Inn was badly hurt during the war in Lebanon. Petroleum firms lost vast sums throughout the Iran–Iraq and Gulf wars. Losses like these encourage careful selection of stable countries not likely to be suddenly at war.

When instability is suspected, companies do everything they can to protect themselves against losses. They will limit their trade to exporting products into the country, minimizing investments in new plants in the foreign economy. Currency will be converted as soon as possible. Many firms are now reluctant to expand operations in Hong Kong, currently a British crown colony, because of uncertainties about what will happen after 1997, when it reverts to China. Similarly, billions of dollars of investments are on hold by Western firms waiting to see what kind of political stability is in store in Russia and Latin America.

Trade Barriers. While free and fair trade among nations has increased, governments of many countries continue to engage in economic protectionism. *Protectionism* is the practice of shielding one or more sectors of a country's economy from foreign competition through the use of trade barriers, most notably tariffs and quotas. *Tariffs,* which are a government tax on goods and services entering a country, primarily serve to raise prices on imports. (See the Ethics Insight box for a discussion on protectionism.)

A *quota* is a restriction placed on the amount of product allowed to enter or leave a country. Quotas can be mandatory or voluntary, and may be legislated or negotiated by governments. Import quotas seek to guarantee domestic industries' access to a certain percentage of their domestic market. The best-known quota concerns the mandatory or voluntary limits on foreign automobiles in many countries. Less visible quotas apply to the importation of many other products such as electronic and agricultural products. Research shows that tariffs and quotas discourage global trade and often result in higher prices on the goods and services produced by protected industries.[6]

FIGURE 18–3   Significance of NAFTA and EC

	Percentage of World Total	
Measure	NAFTA	EC
Population	7	6
Gross national product	27	28
Total exports	16	38
Grain production	19	9

Foreign governments can also impose other barriers or initiate other actions against foreign marketers. A government may not allow its currency to be converted into other currencies *(blocked currency)*. A government can refuse to have dealings with another country and *boycott* that country's products to express disapproval for past actions. Or, a host country could actually take over a foreign company or assets through *expropriation.*

One way to measure a country's attitude toward trade is to examine the restraints the country puts on it. If tariffs, quotas, and government bureaucracy are plentiful and restrictive, chances are the country is not very receptive to foreign involvement in its economy. Canada, however, is seen by many nations as a country that actively encourages trade.

Trade Incentives.   Just as countries can discourage trade through trade barriers, they can also encourage it by offering investment incentives, helping in site location, and providing other services. Hungary offers a five-year "tax holiday"—a period during which no corporate taxes will be assessed—to encourage foreign firms to develop manufacturing facilities there. In addition, a country or group of countries can establish equitable standards to enable foreign products to compete fairly in their domestic markets, the topic discussed next.

Transnation Trade Groups.   Many countries have formed economic ties through the development of transnation trade groups. The two largest trade group agreements are NAFTA (North American Free Trade Agreement) and EC (European Community), mentioned earlier. The importance of these two groups is huge, as shown by the percentage of the global total for various measures of economic activity (see Figure 18–3). A brief look at the NAFTA and EC situations illustrates both the potential upside and downside of such transnation agreements.

On the upside, the NAFTA agreement rolls back 20,000 separate tariffs over the next 10 to 15 years between participating nations (Canada, United States, and Mexico) and will reduce dairy and textile quotas, thereby making many imported and domestic products cheaper to Canadian consumers. NAFTA will also increase jobs in industries like telecommunications, banking, and high technology. But with Mexican wage rates about one-sixth of those in Canada, and with much less stringent employment and environmental rules, some economists suggest Canada will lose manufacturing jobs in industries like automobiles and home appliances.[7]

The EC agreement reduced most of the barriers to the free flow of goods, services, capital, and labour across the national borders of the participating nations. The 12 European Community nations are: Great Britain, Ireland, Denmark, Belgium, the Netherlands, Luxembourg, Germany, France, Italy, Greece, Portugal, and Spain (see Figure 18–4). With this agreement, participating countries each believe they will be better off economically. The collective economic size of the 12 nations that make up the EC gives it great international significance.

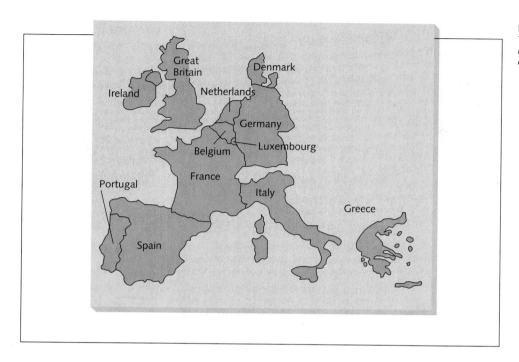

FIGURE 18–4
The 12-member countries of the European Community.

The size of the EC market is one reason many firms are increasing their marketing activities in EC countries. A second reason is that even large corporations in major countries can no longer survive by competing only in their domestic market if they are in global industries.

Other transnation trade groups (both formal and informal) that will represent important markets as we move into the next century include the seven European Free Trade Agreement (EFTA) countries (Austria, Switzerland, Norway, Sweden, Finland, Iceland, and Turkey); and the four "Little Dragons" (Hong Kong, Singapore, South Korea, and Taiwan).

Economic Conditions

When assessing foreign markets to enter, marketers must carefully examine the country's stage of economic development, the country's economic infrastructure, consumer income, and currency exchange rates.

Stage of Economic Development. There are over 200 countries in the world today, each of which is at a slightly different stage of its economic development. However, they can be classified into two major groupings that will help a marketer better understand their needs:

- *Developed countries* have somewhat mixed economies. Private enterprise dominates, although they have substantial public sectors as well. Canada, the United States, Japan, and most of Western Europe can be considered developed.
- *Developing countries* are in the process of moving from an agricultural to industrial economy. There are two subgroups within the developing category: (1) those that have already made the move and (2) those that remain locked in a preindustrial economy. Countries such as Poland, Hungary, Israel, Venezuela,

Pacific Rim consumers are
seeing retailers and brand
names from around the
globe.

and South Africa fall into the first group. In the second group are Pakistan, Sri Lanka, Tanzania, and Chad, where living standards are low and improvement will be slow. One-third of the world's population is in this second group.

The stage of economic development significantly affects other economic factors, as discussed below.

Economic Infrastructure. The **economic infrastructure**—a country's communication, transportation, financial, and distribution systems—is a critical consideration in determining whether to try to market to a country's consumers and organizations. Poor economic infrastructure is why many North American and European manufacturers of consumer goods have generally avoided China. But producers of primary goods (e.g., wheat and coal) and industrial product manufacturers are marketing in China. Companies in the transportation and communications fields are doing particularly well in selling products and services needed to develop China's infrastructure. This will eventually pave the way for more consumer goods manufacturers to serve China more effectively.

Parts of the infrastructure that North Americans or Western Europeans take for granted can be huge problems elsewhere, not only in developing countries but even in former Soviet-bloc nations where such infrastructure is assumed to be in place. Communications is an example. There are few international telephone lines going into Russia, so overseas dialing can take hours. In Warsaw it is not uncommon to dial a half dozen times before connecting with the desired number—the other five are busy or wrong numbers, because of the antiquated system. In Moscow, *Reader's Digest* learned to send its material by registered mail in plain brown envelopes—or by private delivery services—because attractive packages tend to get "lost" in the Russian postal system.[8] These communications problems have led to billions of dollars of investment to upgrade telecommunications and postal systems in Eastern European nations.

Even the legal system can cause problems. Emerging markets such as Indonesia and China lack a written, legal framework for business, so transactions in these nations rely more heavily on personal relationships. Also, because private property did not exist under communism, the legal red tape involved in obtaining title to buildings and land for new manufacturing operations has been a huge problem for Western firms trying to conduct business in former Soviet-bloc nations.

Consumer Income. A global or international marketer selling consumer goods also must consider what the average per capita income is among a nation's consumers and how the income is distributed. Per capita income is less than $200 annually in some of the developing countries. However, a country's distribution of income is also important, as it may give a more reliable picture of a country's purchasing power. Because consumers in some developing countries may have subsidies for food, housing, and health care, firms take great care in interpreting local economic data. That is why India holds increasing interest for marketers. And while the average annual wage in China is less than $1,000, many Chinese have second jobs or bonuses not reported as income. With heavily subsidized housing, a large proportion of a Chinese consumer's income is disposable.[9]

Currency Exchange Rates. Fluctuations in exchange rates among the world's currencies are of critical importance in international marketing. Such fluctuations affect everyone—from international vacationers to global corporations. But in seeking to protect their investments, global corporations face even more frantic currency exchange problems than individual tourists. For example, global corporations have foreign currency traders whose job goes on 24 hours a day. Currency fluctuations can wipe out a firm's profit from regular operations, so decisions on when to buy or sell foreign currencies are critical. For example, in one four-year period in the 1980s, Kodak lost about $500 million because of currency fluctuations.

Cultural Conditions

Marketers seeking to enter foreign markets must understand the foreign nation's society and its culture. This is critical because the culture of a country will influence what needs consumers have and how they go about satisfying them. One way to examine a society's culture is to conduct **cross-cultural analysis,** the study of similarities and differences among consumers in two or more nations or societies.[10] A thorough cross-cultural analysis involves an understanding and appreciation of the values, customs, symbols, and language of other societies.

Values. As we saw in Chapter 5, *values* represent personally or socially preferable modes of conduct or states of existence that are enduring. Understanding the basic values of a given society is important when evaluating foreign markets. For example:[11]

- A door-to-door salesman would find selling in Italy impossible because it is improper for a man to call on a woman if she is home alone.
- McDonald's does not sell hamburgers in its restaurants in India because the cow is considered sacred by almost 85 percent of the population.
- Germans have not been overly receptive to the use of credit cards such as Visa or Mastercard and installment debt to purchase goods and services. Indeed, the German word for debt, *Schuld,* is the same as the German word for guilt.
- In the Arab world and Latin American countries, business-to-business negotiations are a social event where bargaining is an integral part of any transaction. Efforts to adhere to a strict agenda and impersonalize the negotiations could be viewed as an insult.

These examples illustrate how cultural values can influence behaviour in different societies. Cultural values shape individual values, which in turn affect attitudes toward consumption and the relative importance assigned to specific attributes of goods and services.

Customs. **Customs** are the norms and expectations about the way people do things in a specific country. Clearly, customs can vary significantly from country to country. Some customs that might be considered unusual to Canadians include the following.[12]

- In France, men wear more than twice the amount of cosmetics that women do.
- Japanese women give Japanese men chocolates on Valentine's Day.
- Businesspeople in Middle Eastern and Latin American countries prefer to negotiate within inches of their colleagues; Canadians who find this difficult can offend their potential associates and ruin a possible agreement.

Customs can also relate to nonverbal behaviour of individuals in different cultural settings. For example, in many European countries it is considered impolite not to have both hands on the table in business meetings. Direct eye contact is viewed positively in North and Latin America but negatively in Japan. Casual touching is also inappropriate in Japan, while men often hold hands in Middle Eastern countries as a sign of friendship.[13] Companies operating in foreign markets have come to realize that sensitivity to the customs of a country can make the difference between success and failure. Colgate-Palmolive, General Electric, and Honda place a high priority on cross-cultural training relating to customs.[14]

Cultural Symbols. **Cultural symbols** are things that represent ideas and concepts to a society or nationality. Symbols and symbolism play an important role in cross-cultural analysis because different cultures ascribe different meanings to things. So important is the role of symbols that a field of study, called **semiotics,** has emerged that examines the correspondence between symbols and their role in the assignment of meaning for people. By adroitly using cultural symbols, marketers can tie positive symbolism to their goods and services to enhance their attractiveness to consumers. However, improper use of symbols can spell disaster. A culturally sensitive marketer will know that Canadians are superstitious about the number 13 and Japanese feel the same way about the number 4. Shi, the Japanese word for four, is also the word for death. Knowing this, golf ball manufacturers do not sell golf balls in packages of four in Japan.

Cultural symbols can evoke deep feelings as well. In an ad campaign Coca-Cola Company turned the Eiffel Tower into the familiar Coca-Cola bottle. No problems. But when Coca-Cola turned the marble columns in the Parthenon, which crowns Athens' Acropolis, into Coca-Cola bottles, the Greeks were outraged. They refer to the Acropolis as the "holy rock," and a government official said that the Parthenon is an "international symbol of excellence" and "whoever insults the Parthenon insults international culture." Coca-Cola apologized for the ad.[15]

Marketers are also sensitive to the fact that the country of origin or the manufacturer of products and services can symbolize superior or poor quality in some countries. For example, Russian consumers believe products made in Japan and Germany are superior in quality to products from North America and the United Kingdom, while Japanese consumers believe Japanese products are superior to those made in Europe and North America.

Language. Marketers should know not only the native tongues of countries in which they market their products and services, but also the nuances and idioms of a language. Even though about 100 official languages exist in the world, anthropologists estimate that at least 3,000 different languages are spoken.[16] There are nine official languages spoken in the 12-nation European Community, and Canada has two official languages (English and French). Fifteen major languages are spoken in India alone, although English is the official language.

English, French, and Spanish are the principal languages in global diplomacy and commerce. However, the best language to communicate with consumers is their own, as any seasoned global or international marketer will attest. Unintended meanings of brand names and messages have ranged from the absurd to the obscene. For instance:[17]

- When an advertising agency set out to launch Procter & Gamble's successful Pert shampoo in Canada, it turned out that the name means "lost" in French. Procter & Gamble substituted the brand name Pret, which means "ready."
- The Vicks brand name common in Canada is German slang for sexual intimacy; therefore, Vicks is called Wicks in Germany.

To avoid errors, experienced global or international marketers use *back translation,* whereby a translated word or phrase is retranslated into the original language by a different interpreter.

Reader's Digest learned important lessons that apply to most firms entering foreign markets when it launched its Russian and Hungarian editions. For those lessons, see the Marketplace Application box.

Cultural Ethnocentricity. The tendency for people to view their own values, customs, symbols, and language favourably is well known. However, the belief that aspects of one's culture are *superior* to another's is called **cultural ethnocentricity** and is a sure impediment to successful global or international marketing. Cultural ethnocentricity can often result in stereotyping others, including their behaviours, and result in a superficial understanding of and virtually no appreciation for the culture of another people.

An outgrowth of cultural ethnocentricity exists in the purchase and use of goods and services produced outside of a country. Marketers are acutely aware that certain groups within countries disfavour imported products, not on the basis of price, features, or performance, but purely because of their foreign origin. **Consumer ethnocentrism** is the tendency to believe that it is inappropriate, indeed immoral, to purchase foreign-made products.[18] Ethnocentric consumers believe that buying imported products is wrong because such purchases are unpatriotic, harm domestic industries, and cause domestic unemployment. The prevalence of consumer ethnocentrism in the global marketplace is unknown. However, one study indicated that 5 percent of consumers in the United Kingdom and France, and 6 percent in Germany said that knowing a product was made in their country was the single most important factor in considering the purchase of a product.[19]

Values, customs, symbols, and language combine to create unique qualities of different cultures. Understanding cultural differences and similarities will become even more important as artificial boundaries between societies crumble with the decline in economic protectionism and the increase in freer trade. Successful global or international marketers will recognize (1) the potential for using cultural factors in devising their marketing strategies, and (2) the importance of anticipating cultural changes and linking these changes to consumption patterns.

LEARNING CHECK

1. What are examples of trade barriers and trade incentives that global or international marketers should consider when undertaking marketing activities in a new country?

2. What is a country's economic infrastructure?

3. Semiotics involves the study of _____.

MARKETPLACE APPLICATION

Reader's Digest Offers Advice for Entering Foreign Markets

Reader's Digest successfully launched Russian and Hungarian editions of its magazine. The Reader's Digest Association, Inc., learned some valuable lessons along the way. They suggest firms entering foreign markets should:

1. Understand the market, its culture, and business environment. For example, Russians may not arrive at work until 10:00 A.M.—not because they're lazy, but because they've been up since 5:00 A.M. standing in long lines shopping for food. So a big tote bag with a *Reader's Digest* logo in Russian was a hit as a giveaway at the news conference product launch.
2. Use traditional Western marketing techniques—with a dose of common sense. Direct mail is almost unknown in Hungary, so it can be very effective, but the quality of mailing lists is likely to be bad.

3. Stick to a back-to-basics approach. Do marketing research early to uncover any surprises.
4. Pay relentless attention to details. This gets down to such details as making sure your video plays in the host's country's technical format and double-checking your translations with someone whom you trust—and who understands the local idiom.
5. Communicate, communicate, communicate. State things simply in all communications and put key items in writing to avoid misunderstandings. Talk frequently to be sure there's an easy, nonthreatening avenue for open communications.

1. Is there any other advice you can offer marketers entering foreign markets, in terms of analyzing and understanding the culture in those markets?

SOURCE: Adapted from Carole M. Howard, "Reader's Digest Meets Eastern Europe," *Express*, Spring 1992, pp. 28–31.

EVALUATING WAYS TO ENTER A FOREIGN MARKET

Once an organization has decided to enter a foreign market, it must select a means of entry. The option chosen depends on the organization's willingness and ability to commit financial, physical, and managerial resources. As Figure 18–5 demonstrates, the amount of financial commitment, risk, and profit potential increases as the organization moves from exporting to direct ownership. Host countries not only seek the benefits of additional products available for sale, but are often even more interested in the number of good jobs available for local workers. Figure 18–5 shows that local employment increases significantly as an organization's financial commitment increases.

Exporting

Exporting is producing goods in one country and selling them in another country. This option allows an organization to make the fewest changes in product, organization, and even corporate goals. Host countries usually do not like this practice, because it provides less local employment than alternative means of entry.

Indirect exporting is a firm's selling its domestically produced goods in a foreign country through an intermediary. It involves the least commitment and risk, but will probably return the least profit. This kind of exporting is ideal for the company that has no overseas contacts but wants to market abroad. The intermediary is often a broker or an agent that has the marketing know-how and the resources necessary for the effort to succeed.

FIGURE 18–5
Alternative ways to enter
a foreign market.

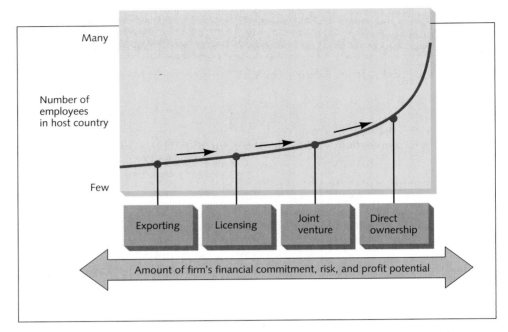

Direct exporting is a firm's selling its domestically produced goods in a foreign country without intermediaries. Most companies become involved in direct exporting when they believe their volume of sales will be sufficiently large and easy to obtain so that they do not require intermediaries. For example, the exporter may be approached by foreign buyers that are willing to contract for a large volume of purchases. Direct exporting involves more risk than indirect exporting for the company, but also opens the door to increased profits.

Licensing

Under licensing, a company offers the right to a trademark, patent, trade secret, or other similarly valued items of intellectual property in return for a royalty or a fee. The advantages to the company granting the license are low risk and a capital-free entry into a foreign country. The licensee gains information that allows it to start with a competitive advantage, and the foreign country gains employment by having the product manufactured locally.

There are some serious drawbacks to this mode of entry, however. The licensor forgoes control of its product and reduces the potential profits gained from it. In addition, while the relationship lasts, the licensor may be creating its own competition. Some licensees are able to modify the product somehow and enter the market with product and marketing knowledge gained at the expense of the company that got them started. To offset this disadvantage, many companies strive to stay innovative so that the licensee remains dependent on them for improvements and successful operation. Finally, should the licensee prove to be a poor choice, the name or reputation of the company may be harmed.

Two variations of licensing, local manufacturing and local assembly, represent alternative ways to produce a product within the foreign country. With local manufacturing, a Canadian company may contract with a foreign firm to manufacture products according to stated specifications. The product is then sold in the foreign country or exported back to Canada. With local assembly, the Canadian company may contract with a firm in a foreign country to assemble (not manufacture) parts and components that have been shipped to that country. In both cases, the advantage to the foreign country is the employment of its people, and the Canadian firm benefits from the lower wage rates in the foreign country.

Joint Venture

When a foreign company and a local firm invest together to create a local business, it is called a **joint venture.** These two companies share ownership, control, and profits of the new company. Investment may be made by having either of the companies buy shares in the other or by creating a third and separate entity.

The advantages of this option are twofold. First, one company may not have the necessary financial, physical, or managerial resources to enter a foreign market alone. Second, a government may require or strongly encourage a joint venture before it allows a foreign company to enter its market.

The disadvantages arise when the two companies disagree about policies or courses of action for their joint venture or when governmental bureaucracy bogs down the effort. For example, Canadian firms often prefer to reinvest earnings gained, whereas some foreign companies may want to spend those earnings. Or a Canadian firm may want to return profits to Canada, while the local firm or its government may oppose this—the problem now faced by many joint ventures in Eastern Europe.

Direct Ownership

The biggest commitment a company can make when entering a foreign market is **direct ownership,** a domestic firm's actually investing in and owning a foreign subsidiary or division. Examples of direct ownership are Toyota's automobile plant in Ontario and Hyundai's plant in Quebec. Many Canadian-based corporations are also switching to this mode of entry. For example, Alcan opened a $30 million recycling plant in Worrington, England, and Ganong Brothers Chocolates opened a new plant in Thailand.

Many firms participate in a number of foreign markets, simultaneously using a variety of modes of entry for different countries. Remember W.K. Buckley Ltd. (Buckley's Mixture) from Chapter 10? Buckley has entered several foreign markets in different ways. The company uses direct exporting for the United States market, indirect exporting for Australia, a joint venture in China, and a licensing agreement for Holland.[20]

Buckley's uses a number of ways to enter foreign markets.

LEARNING CHECK

1. What mode of entry could a company follow if it has no previous experience in marketing in foreign countries?

2. How does licensing differ from joint venture?

TAILORING THE MARKETING PLAN TO THE FOREIGN COUNTRY

Marketing plans may have to be adjusted for foreign markets, not simply be duplicates of those at home. Three basic steps in adapting marketing plans for foreign markets are (1) selecting a country for entry, (2) establishing the most effective organization for marketing on a foreign level, and (3) designing the marketing plan to fit the market's needs.

Selecting the Country for Entry

In choosing a country for its foreign marketing efforts, a company must evaluate many factors, following these steps:

1. *Specify the marketing objectives.* These objectives should be achievable yet challenging. Profit levels, return on investment (ROI), sales, and competitive positions are all areas for which objectives are delineated.
2. *Choose a single- or a multiple-country strategy.* Choosing to enter a single country or several countries in a region is based on the product or products being sold and the sales potential. If several adjacent countries all want the same size or style of product, the marketing and production economies of scale may suggest a multiple-country strategy.
3. *Specify the candidate countries or regions to consider.* Alternative countries or regions that meet both the stated objectives and the economic profile needed for success should be listed as potential candidates.
4. *Estimate the ROI for each of the candidates.* To estimate the ROI, a company must project the size of the market, the expected revenues, the expenses, and the profits for each candidate country or region.
5. *Select one or more countries or regions to enter.* The preceding analysis screens the candidates to provide a list of one or more countries or regions that appear most likely to achieve the firm's objectives for its foreign marketing plan.

Granted, these are all estimates and include some room for error. However, they will provide the necessary framework to enable the firm to make a knowledgeable choice among countries and regions.

Establishing the Marketing Organization

After selecting a country for entry, the firm must establish an appropriate marketing organization. Its goal is to respond to the different needs of foreign markets yet take advantage of the experience and knowledge of domestic marketers. Some alternative marketing organizations are discussed.

Export Department. When a company is simply exporting its goods, it typically does so through an export department. Made up of a manager and perhaps several assistants, this group handles the necessary paperwork.

Foreign Subsidiary. A wholly owned foreign subsidiary commonly has its own head of operations, who reports directly to the company president. Sales of Apple's Macintosh computer in Japan were slow until Apple established a subsidiary there. Sales began rising when the subsidiary developed a Japanese-language operating system for the Macintosh and announced that much of its software would use the new system.

International Division. When international sales become substantial or when modes of entry other than simple exporting are added, a company usually expands to include an international division. This division can be either geographically-based or product-based. The movement of products as well as their marketing is then handled by this group.

Ford targets Latin American markets.

Worldwide Products Division. A worldwide products division is used when a company decides that it is no longer a company conducting international marketing, but rather a global corporation that markets throughout the world. Like an international division, this structure can be divided into regions, with each division responsible for all products within a region, or it can be divided by products, with each division responsible for all markets where its product is sold. Most likely this structure is accompanied by a management base recruited from around the world.

Designing and Implementing the Marketing Plan

A global or international marketer goes through the same steps in designing a marketing plan for a foreign country as they would for their domestic market. An additional critical decision is whether or not the marketing mix used in the domestic market should be maintained or modified for the foreign market(s). Only after careful research can the marketer make this decision.

Standardized Marketing Mix. At one extreme, a company can use a **standardized marketing mix.** In this case, the same marketing mix is used for every market. If a firm believes the way the product is used and the needs it satisfies are universal, it will use a standardized marketing mix. If complete standardization is possible it can mean substantial savings for the company in terms of production and marketing. It can also allow for the possibility of global branding (Chapter 10). Coca-Cola is one of the few companies that has been able to operationalize a fairly standardized marketing mix around the world.

Customized Marketing Mix. At the other extreme is a **customized marketing mix,** where the marketer adjusts or modifies the marketing mix for each market. If a firm believes the way the product is used and the needs it satisfies are unique to each country, a customized marketing mix is used. Customizing the mix means greater costs. But many marketers believe that adapting the mix to fit the needs, values, customs, language, and purchasing power of a target country will lead to greater market share and, overall, increased profitability.

Most often, companies do not completely standardize or completely customize their marketing mix. In general, companies look to standardize where possible and customize where necessary. This strategy, sometimes called a "hybrid approach," is most commonly used. McDonald's uses a hybrid approach. Although it has standardized much of its menu, it gives a degree of flexibility to franchises to allow for local customer preferences in their countries.

For example, McDonald's in Germany has beer on its menu, and its restaurants in Japan offer saki. And, while it uses the same general advertising theme in most countries, the ads are done in the language of the host country.

As mentioned earlier, only through careful research can a marketer determine the proper marketing mix for a given country.

Product. The product may be sold in foreign markets in one of three ways: in the same form as in the domestic market, with some adaptations, or as a totally new product.

- *Extension.* Selling the same product in other countries is an extension strategy. It works well for products like Coca-Cola, Wrigley's gum, General Motors cars, and Levi's jeans. However, it didn't work for Jell-O (a more solid gelatin was preferred to the powder in England) or Duncan Hines (which was seen as too moist and crumbly to eat with tea in England).
- *Adaptation.* Changing a product in some way to make it more appropriate for a country's climate or preferences is an adaptation strategy. Heinz baby food offers strained lamb brains for Australians and strained brown beans in the Netherlands. Exxon sells different gasoline blends based on each country's climate.
- *Invention.* Designing a product to serve the unmet needs of a foreign nation is an invention strategy. This is probably the strategy with the most potential, since there are so many unmet needs, yet it is actually the least used. National Cash Register has followed a reverse invention strategy by introducing crank-operated cash registers in some developing nations that have unreliable or inaccessible electric power.

In foreign markets—as in domestic ones—nothing succeeds like quality products that satisfy consumer needs and wants at reasonable prices. Honda motorcycles, Caterpillar construction equipment, Canon cameras, and Black & Decker power tools are examples.

Price. Most foreign countries use a cost-plus pricing strategy. For global or international firms this can mean their products are priced higher than the local goods. Why? Global or international products must include not only the cost of production and selling, but also tariffs, transportation and storage costs, and higher payments to intermediaries.

Dumping is a firm's selling a product in a foreign country below its domestic price. This is most often done to build a share of the market by pricing at a competitive level. Another reason is that the products being sold may be surplus or cannot be sold domestically, and are therefore already a burden to the company. The firm may be glad to sell them at almost any price.

Some pharmaceutical firms sell penicillin, for example, at a lower price in foreign countries than at home. They justify this by saying that R&D costs are not included in foreign prices. Japan has been accused of following a dumping strategy for some of its products in Canada and the United States.

An unusual pricing dimension of global or international marketing is **counter-trade**—using barter rather than money. Although countertrade accounts for only about 10–15 percent of world trade, it is growing in importance. An example was when Boeing sold ten 747 jet aircraft to Saudi Arabia in return for crude oil valued at 10 percent below posted world prices.

An unpleasant aspect of pricing is **bribery,** the practice of giving or promising something of value in return for a corrupt act. This is a common practice in many countries to reduce red tape and make sales. Although in many countries bribery is an accepted business practice in some foreign sales, it is officially illegal in all countries.

Marketing Communications. Various aspects of marketing communications may have to be changed to reflect the differences in foreign markets. Advertising programs provide examples. Because values differ substantially from country to country, a product that is a luxury in one country may be a necessity in another. Creative messages in advertisements must then be designed to directly address the peculiarities within each market.

A recent study evaluating advertising across 16 countries found that only 5 percent of the ad campaigns studied were totally standardized, 5 percent were totally customized for the local market, and 90 percent were hybrid approaches where the advertising agencies tailored the umbrella strategy to the local market.[21] Regardless of the strategy, marketers have some strong "do" guidelines when advertising in foreign countries.[22]

- *Do* use TV commercials in which visuals are dominant over commercials that are "copy-heavy."
- *Do* enhance TV commercials with music—a powerful device that cuts across many cultures.
- *Do* test unique, distinctive approaches to see that they meet the basic rules and good taste guidelines of a culture.
- *Do* use brand symbols, trademarks, or logos—where possible—when the brand has stature and the symbol is meaningful.

Research also carries some other warnings: (1) a brilliant slogan in one language rarely translates to another with the same power and precision, so be careful, and (2) trying to please everyone in a culture and offend no one often gives bland, ineffective ads, just as it does domestically.

Where there is a common language, many TV and print ads can be used both domestically and in a common-language country. For example, Australia markets Australian vacations to Canadians while Canada markets Canadian vacations to Australians—both using domestic ad campaigns in the other country.

Distribution. A global or international marketer must establish a channel of distribution to meet the goals it has set. Figure 18–6 outlines the channel through which a product manufactured in one country must travel to reach its destination in a foreign country. The first step involves the seller; its headquarters is the starting point and is responsible for the successful distribution to the ultimate consumer.

A common language helps Australia market itself to Canadian tourists.

The next step is the channel between the two nations, moving the product from the domestic market to the foreign market. Intermediaries that can handle this responsibility include resident buyers in the foreign country, independent merchant wholesalers who buy and sell the product, and agents who bring buyers and sellers together.

Once the product is in the foreign nation, that country's distribution channels take over. Foreign channels can be very long or surprisingly short, depending on the prod-

FIGURE 18–6 Foreign marketing channel of distribution.

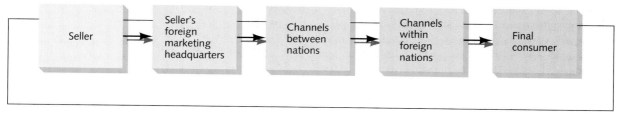

uct line. In Japan fresh fish go through three intermediaries before getting to a retail outlet. Conversely, shoes go through only one intermediary. In other cases the channel does not even involve the host country. P&G sells its soap door-to-door in the Philippines because there are no alternatives in many parts of that country. The sophistication of the distribution channel increases with the economic development of the country. Supermarkets facilitate selling products in many nations, but they are not popular or available in many others where low incomes, culture, and lack of refrigeration dictate shopping on a daily rather than a weekly basis.

LEARNING CHECK

1. What are three product strategies used when marketing in foreign countries?

2. What is dumping?

3. What is countertrade?

LEARNING OBJECTIVE REINFORCEMENT

1. Understand the factors that have helped shape a new global arena. Several factors have created a new global arena, including advances in travel and communications. But two other factors have had a significant impact on the development of a more globalized marketplace: the General Agreement on Tariffs and Trade (GATT) and free trade among nations.

2. Describe why market-driven organizations enter foreign markets. There are several key reasons why market-driven organizations enter foreign markets: (1) to counter adverse economic factors in the home market, (2) to extend a product's life cycle, (3) to reduce or avoid competition, (4) to enhance economies of scale in production and marketing, (5) to dispose of inventories, (6) to export (and import) new technology, and (7) to increase profits or shareholder well-being.

3. Explain the difference between global marketing and international marketing. International marketing is simply marketing across national boundaries. Many firms participate in foreign markets; however, their level of participation is not as extensive as a global marketer. These global marketers, or global corporations, look at the entire world as one market and conduct research and development, manufacturing, and marketing activities wherever they can best be done. National boundaries and regulations are largely ir-

relevant to global corporations. They run their businesses and make decisions on the basis of all possible choices in the world.

4. Outline the sequence of decisions in entering foreign markets. Essentially, the sequence of decisions include: (1) assess the foreign marketing environment, specifically the political, economic, and cultural conditions, (2) evaluate ways to enter a foreign market (e.g., exporting, licensing, etc.), and (3) tailor a marketing plan to the foreign country.

5. Understand the importance of assessing the political, economic, and cultural conditions of foreign markets. Successful marketing in domestic markets requires knowledge of the marketing environment. Similarly, success in foreign markets is often tied to how well the marketer understands those foreign markets. Conducting an environment scan and focusing on the political, economic, and cultural conditions of foreign markets allows the marketer to properly identify both opportunities and threats in those markets. The marketing environment in foreign countries can be strikingly different from those of domestic markets. Marketers need to discover if the foreign markets differ, and if so, in what ways.

6. Outline the alternative modes of entering foreign markets. The four basic modes of entry into foreign markets are exporting (direct or indirect), licensing, joint ventures, and direct ownership. The relative difficulty, as well as the amount of commitment, risk, and profit potential increases in moving from exporting to direct ownership.

7. Explain the use of a standardized and customized marketing mix when entering foreign markets. When entering foreign markets, a marketer can use, at one extreme, a standardized marketing mix—that is, the same marketing mix is used for every market. A standardized marketing mix is used if a firm believes the way the product is used and the needs it satisfies are universal. Standardization can mean substantial savings, and can allow for the possibility of global branding. At the other extreme is a customized mar-

keting mix, where the marketer adjusts or modifies the marketing mix for each market. A customized marketing mix is used if a firm believes the way the product is used and the needs it satisfies are unique to each country. Customizing the mix means greater costs, but adapting the mix to fit the needs, values, customs, language, and purchasing power of a target country may result in greater market share and increased profitability. Most often, companies do not completely standardize or completely customize their marketing mix. In general, companies look to standardize where possible and customize where necessary. This strategy is called a "hybrid approach."

KEY TERMS AND CONCEPTS

General Agreement on Tariffs and Trade (GATT) p. 440–441
trade feedback effect p. 441
gross domestic product (GDP) p. 441
international marketing p. 443
global corporation p. 443
global industry p. 443
economic infrastructure p. 449

cross-cultural analysis p. 450
customs p. 450
cultural symbols p. 451
semiotics p. 452
cultural ethnocentricity p. 452
consumer ethnocentrism p. 452
exporting p. 453
joint venture p. 455

direct ownership p. 455
standardized marketing mix p. 457
customized marketing mix p. 457
dumping p. 458
countertrade p. 459
bribery p. 459

CHAPTER QUESTIONS AND APPLICATIONS

1. A manufacturer of shoes has decided to enter a foreign market and has selected China. The manufacturer's assumption is that with such a large population, a lot of shoes can be sold. Why might China be a good or bad market opportunity?

2. What is the difference between an international marketer and a global corporation?

3. What steps do some countries take to discourage trade? Why might they do this?

4. As a novice, what alternative mode of entry would you use to enter a foreign market? Why?

5. Knowing that owning Western goods is a status symbol in Russia, what goods might you want to sell there?

6. Ask some of your friends if they prefer to buy Canadian products over products manufactured in another country. If yes, ask them why. If no, ask them why not. Write up a brief report outlining your findings.

7. What are three product strategies a marketer can use in foreign market introductions? Which strategy has the

most potential? Why? Can you think of any reverse inventions that might be successful?

8. Because English is the official language in Australia, many Canadian companies might select this market as an easy one to enter. Other companies, however, believe that this similarity in language could make it even harder to successfully engage in foreign trade there. Who's right? Why?

9. Coca-Cola is sold worldwide. In some countries Coca-Cola owns the manufacturing facilities; in others it has signed contracts with licensees. When selecting a licensee in each country, what factors should Coca-Cola consider?

10. What specific advice would you give to a group of Canadian executives planning to negotiate a business transaction with Latin American executives?

11. What specific factors are impediments to using a standardized marketing mix in every country in which a company markets?

APPLICATION CASE 18-1
THE COCA-COLA COMPANY: JAPAN

The Coca-Cola Company is the world's largest carbonated soft drink producer. The company sells over 10 billion cases of soft drinks worldwide. Approximately 75 percent of the company's soft drink revenues and 80 percent of soft drink operating income arise from sales outside North America. These statistics are not surprising since Coke and Coca-Cola are among the world's best-known trademarks.

The Coca-Cola Company is clearly a global enterprise. Four of the world's top five carbonated soft drinks are sold by the company. These brands are Coca-Cola/Coca-Cola Classic, Diet Coke/Coca-Cola Light, Fanta, and Sprite. The company captures 45 percent of the worldwide market for carbonated soft drink flavour segments: cola, orange, and lemon-lime. One of the reasons for Coca-Cola's worldwide presence is its extensive, efficient, and effective bottling network. This bottling network, which includes company-owned bottlers, joint ventures with established bottlers in various countries, and franchised bottlers, allows for Coca-Cola/Coca-Cola Classic to be distributed in 195 countries, Fanta and Sprite in 164 countries, and Diet Coke/Coca-Cola Light in 117 countries.

The Coca-Cola Company sold its products in Japan as early as the 1920s. However, it did not establish a formal Japanese subsidiary until 1957. Since that time, the company has built a dominant position in the Japanese soft drink market. For example, Coca-Cola is sold in 1 million stores and some 700,000 vending machines in Japan. The Coca-Cola Company captures 32 percent of all carbonated and noncarbonated soft drinks sold in Japan. It is estimated that the Coca-Cola brand captures 70 percent of the $1.65 billion Japanese cola market, while Coca-Cola Light captures 20 percent. In contrast, Pepsi-Cola captures less than 10 percent of this market. Industry executives estimate that advertising spending for the Coca-Cola brand is $80 million compared to $16 million for Pepsi-Cola.

The successful entry into Japan by the Coca-Cola Company and its subsequent performance provides valuable insights into global and international marketing in general and the need to consider cultural issues in particular. For instance, company executives emphasize that adaptation to the local culture manifests itself in numerous ways. Its management practices focus on censensus and group-building consistent with Japanese values. Customs such as lifetime employment for Japanese employees are adopted. Efforts to localize consumer communications also are evident in the language used in advertising and the group settings featuring consumption of the product.

QUESTIONS

1. How are the collectivist aspects of Japanese culture incorporated into the Coca-Cola Company's management and marketing practices in Japan?
2. After watching the videotape featuring television commercials for Coca-Cola in Japan, what similarities do you see with Coca-Cola commercials in Canada?

APPLICATION CASE 18-2
MCDONALD'S RESTAURANTS OF CANADA GOES TO MOSCOW

George Cohon, chairman, president, and CEO of McDonald's Restaurants of Canada had a vision that went beyond the borders of Canada. He believed that the 290 million people living in the now former Soviet Union would be interested in the McDonald's concept. Cohon's dream of expansion actually began when he played host to a Soviet delegation at the Montreal Olympics in 1976. He followed up these contacts hoping to send mobile units to the 1980 Moscow Games, but because of the Olympic boycott he put the dream on hold. When Mikhail Gorbachev introduced the concepts of *glasnost* and *perestroika* to the Soviet Union and the world, Cohon once again saw an opportunity. Gorbachev's economic reforms would allow for joint ventures between Soviets and foreign companies. In April 1988, Cohon negotiated a 49/51 percent joint venture with the food service administration of the Moscow City Council. The agreement called for the development of 20 restaurants and a huge food-processing complex.

The McDonald's Restaurants of Canada and Moscow City Council joint venture involved two major departures from McDonald's normal practice: The joint venture was with an organization and not an individual and the deal involved the development of a processing plant. All of McDonald's restaurants have historically depended on local suppliers for its food. However, the low quality and reliability of Soviet farm produce created the need for vertical integration—control over the manufacturing of the food required for the restaurants. Sourcing food locally and setting up its own processing facilities would be a big task. McDonald's persuaded some of its largest suppliers to help out in improving the quality and productivity of selected Soviet farms and to assist in building the processing plant.

European meat experts introduced new feed programs for the local cattle. Potato growers and processors from the Netherlands introduced strains preferred for frozen french fries and provided a system for processing them. Bakers from the U.S., Canada, Sweden, and Germany developed the bun and pie systems. Dairy experts from Sweden set up a pasteurization process for a country where bacteria levels in milk were often six times higher than those permissible in the West. To construct the 10,000 sq. metre processing facility called McComplex, McDonald's used a Finnish company with a long history of dealing with the Soviets.

Although McComplex gave it control over the manufacturing of hamburger patties, buns, french fries, and fixings, McDonald's still needed to depend on a farm and food system renowned for its inefficiency for its beef, flour, potatoes, and vegetables. Moreover, McDonald's had committed itself to operate with rubles. This currency was inconvertible and thus any imports would have to be paid in hard currency generated with the Soviet system, or by diverting money directly from McDonald's Restaurants of Canada. The processing plant cost $40 million—almost 10 times the cost of the first restaurant—and was paid for in hard cash.

Cohon is betting that someday the ruble will become a convertable currency. He argues that the joint venture is a long-term project and that he wanted the people of Moscow to be able to buy food at the restaurant in rubles, not be treated like second-class citizens. In contrast, Pizza Hut, with two locations in Moscow, allows only those with hard currency to eat inside its reataurants. People paying in rubles can buy food there, but they have to eat the product outside.

In addition to the concerns of the quantity and quality of supplies, the joint venture also had to deal with Soviet bureaucracy. Approvals to move the project ahead were long in coming and often caused frustration. One bright spot was that young Muscovites were eager to work at the restaurants.

McDonald's received over 25,000 applications for the roughly 700 positions available at the first restaurant. McDonald's picked the best and many were sent for training at the Institute of Hamburgerology in Toronto and to Hamburger University at McDonald's world headquarters in Oak Brook, Illinois.

The McComplex was completed on schedule and on January 31, 1990, the largest McDonald's restaurant in the world opened its doors. Its Gorky Street location was just 10 minutes from Red Square. The multi-level, 700-seat restaurant would serve approximately 50,000 customers a day, making it not only the largest restaurant in the system, but the busiest. Demand forced the restaurant to almost double its staff. However, many people suggest that the success of the first restaurant should be put into perspective: There is demand for any quality good in Moscow and the people of this city often waited in long lines to buy any food that might be available. Indeed, the experts suggest, in these circumstances McDonald's would be successful.

The political uncertainty in Russia, however, has some experts suggesting that McDonald's may have jumped the gun. Still, the joint venture moves forward with the opening of its second and third restaurants and a new office tower. Cohon suggests the "long view" is McDonald's approach and that Russia needs what McDonald's can provide—organizational infrastructure, technology transfer, managerial talent, agricultural improvement, and import substitution.

QUESTIONS

1. Why was McDonald's Restaurants of Canada so interested in securing a joint venture operation in Moscow?
2. With the disintegration of the Soviet Union and the prospect of Russia falling back in the hands of communist hard-liners, many wonder about McDonald's bold move into Moscow. Was being the "first in" a real advantage for McDonald's Restaurants of Canada?
3. What is the risk for McDonald's operating on a rubles-only basis?

THE DANIELS CORPORATION
AND CFRB AM 1010
Present

Toronto
TASTE 96

*A Benefit For Second Harvest
In Aid Of Hunger Relief*

THE VAUGHAN ESTATES OF SUNNYBROOK

2075 BAYVIEW AVENUE.

CHAPTER 19

Services and Nonprofit Marketing

AFTER READING THIS CHAPTER YOU WILL BE ABLE TO:

1. Outline the four unique elements of services.

2. Explain the service continuum.

3. Describe the important dimensions of service quality.

4. Understand the important role of internal marketing in service organizations.

5. Explain the importance of branding a service.

6. Understand the concept of capacity management in services marketing.

7. Explain nonprofit marketing and the four basic types of nonprofit marketing.

8. Outline the unique aspects of nonprofit marketing.

BATTLING HUNGER IN OUR HOMETOWN

Second Harvest is a charitable nonprofit organization located in Toronto. Its mission: to locate and collect surplus perishable food and deliver it to social service agencies and community organizations in Metro Toronto that feed the hungry. It is not a food bank; it handles perishable food only, and it does not warehouse food. It serves as a link between surplus food—food that would otherwise go to waste—and organizations that provide food to people in need. It is estimated that over 150,000 people depend on emergency food programs every month in Toronto. Ironically, while people are going hungry, more than 20 percent of all food produced in this country is wasted.

Second Harvest operates with a small staff and a core of volunteers. It does not charge the recipient organizations for the food it supplies. Second Harvest is supported by some public funds, grants, and private donations. It currently has over 500 food donors and delivers food to more than 80 recipient organizations. In 1996, it delivered over 1.3 million pounds of food to these organizations—food that otherwise would have been wasted.

Second Harvest attempts to inform and educate the community that hunger does exist in the City of Toronto and in other cities and towns across the nation. It seeks out volunteers willing to provide time, money, or food so it can continue to serve those in need. Second Harvest spreads its message mainly through the use of public relations activities such as public-service announcements, news releases, and newsletters. With the help of corporate sponsors, it also holds an annual fund raiser called Toronto Taste. Attendees pay to sample the creations of many of Toronto's top chefs. About one third of Second Harvest's funding now comes from this special event. Toronto Taste not only provides needed funding to keep Second Harvest operating; it also creates broad public awareness of Second Harvest and its basic mission.[1]

Second Harvest is an example of a nonprofit service organization. While the marketing of services by for-profit organizations is unique and challenging, marketing a nonprofit service organization is even more formidable. In this chapter we will first discuss how services differ from traditional products (goods), how consumers purchase and evaluate services, and the important aspects of managing the marketing mix for services. We will then focus on nonprofit marketing, what it is, and why it is different than for-profit marketing. You will see how marketing can be applied successfully in both services and nonprofit marketing settings.

UNIQUENESS OF SERVICES

As defined in Chapter 1, **services** are activities, deeds, or other basic intangibles offered for sale to consumers in exchange for money or something else of value. Services have become one of the most important components of the Canadian as well as world economy. In Canada, over 60 cents out of every consumer dollar is spent on buying services. Seven out of 10 Canadians work in the service sector. In other words, more Canadians are doing things (performing services) than making things (producing goods). Experts predict that nearly all new employment in the future will be created by the service sector. They suggest that if current trends continue, almost all Canadians will be working in services by 2025.[2] Much of this employment is expected to be created by small service companies, particularly those offering personal, professional, and informational services.

Currently, new types of services are emerging all the time. These include grocery shopping services, pet-sitting and pet-walking services, house-watching services, voice mail and voice messaging services, and even a fax message service. CompuFax, of Downsview, Ontario, offers automated fax services that eliminate the need for manual faxing and can send out any number of faxes, however long and varied, at a cost per page less than that of a postage stamp. Besides being able to send out the same fax to numerous customers simultaneously, CompuFax also offers two other services. Fax on demand enables customers to use their Touch-Tone phones to request information on a variety of products and services. A computer program at CompuFax reads the request and fills the order in seconds without a manual operator. The company will also set up an interactive program for a client. The targets for the services are financial institutions, insurance companies, publishers, and high-tech industries.[3]

The Four I's of Services

There are four unique elements to services: intangibility, inconsistency, inseparability, and inventory. These four elements are referred to as the **four I's of services.**

Intangibility. Services are intangible; that is, they can't be held, touched, or seen before the purchase decision. In contrast, before purchasing a traditional product, a consumer can touch a box of laundry detergent, kick the tire of an automobile, or sample a new breakfast cereal. A major marketing need for services is to make them tangible or show the benefits of using the service.[4] American Express emphasizes the year-

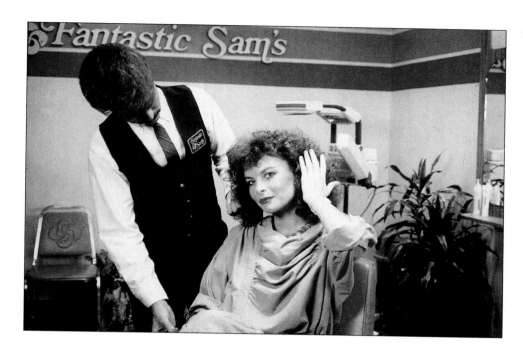

Services are people.

end summary of charges it sends you, and a leading insurance company says, "You're in good hands with Allstate."

Inconsistency. Marketing services is challenging because the quality of a service is often inconsistent. Since many services depend on the people who provide them, their quality of service can vary with each person's capabilities and the day-to-day performance of the same individual. Inconsistency is much more of a problem in services than it is with tangible goods. Tangible products can be of good or bad quality, but with modern production lines the quality will at least be consistent.

On the other hand, one day the Toronto Maple Leafs look great, possible Stanley Cup winners, and the next day lose by 10 goals. Or a cello player with the Vancouver Symphony may not be feeling well and give a less-than-average performance. Whether the service involves tax assistance at Ernst & Young or guest relations at the Sheraton, organizations attempt to reduce inconsistency through standardization and training.[5] Standardization through automation is becoming increasingly popular, as, for example, in the use of ATMs by the banking industry.

Inseparability. A third difference between services and goods, related to problems of consistency, is inseparability. In most cases the consumer cannot (and does not) separate the service from the deliverer of the service or the setting in which the service occurs. For example, to receive an education, a person may attend a university. The quality of the education may be high, but if the student has difficulty parking, finds counseling services poor, or sees little opportunity for extracurricular activity, he may not be satisfied with the educational experience.

Inventory. Inventory of services is different from that of goods. Inventory problems exist with goods because many items are perishable and, as noted in Chapter 12, there are costs associated with handling inventory. With services, inventory carrying costs

FIGURE 19–1   Inventory carrying costs in services.

are more subjective and are related to **idle production capacity,** or availability of the service provider when there is no demand. The inventory cost of a service is the cost of reimbursing the person used to provide the service along with any needed equipment. If a physician is paid to see patients but no one schedules an appointment, the fixed cost of the idle physician's salary is a high inventory carrying cost. In some service businesses, however, the provider of the service is on commission (a Merrill Lynch stockbroker) or is a part-time employee (a counterperson at McDonald's). Then, the inventory carrying costs can be significantly lower or nonexistent: The idle production capacity is cut back through reduction of hours or there is no salary to pay because of the commission compensation system.

Figure 19–1 shows a sliding scale of inventory carrying costs represented on the high side by airlines and hospitals and on the low end by real estate agents and hairstylists. The inventory carrying cost of airlines is high because of high-salaried pilots and very expensive equipment. In contrast, real estate agents and hairstylists work on commission and need little expensive equipment to conduct business.

The Service Continuum

The four I's differentiate services from goods in most cases, but many companies are not clearly service-based or good-based organizations. Is IBM a computer company or a service business? Does MacLean Hunter provide only goods when it publishes *Marketing* magazine, or does it consider itself a service because it presents up-to-date business information? As companies look at what they bring to the market, there is a range from the tangible to the intangible or good-dominant to service-dominant offerings referred to as the **service continuum** (Figure 19–2).

Teaching, nursing, and the theatre are intangible, service-dominant activities, and intangibility, inconsistency, inseparability, and inventory are major concerns in their marketing. Salt, neckties, and dog food are tangible goods, and the problems represented by the four I's are not relevant in their marketing. However, some businesses are a mix of intangible service and tangible good factors. A clothing tailor provides a service but also a good, the finished suit. How pleasant, courteous, and attentive the tailor is to the customer is an important component of the service, and how well the clothes fit is an important part of the good. As shown in Figure 19–3, a fast-food restaurant is about half tangible goods (the food) and half intangible services (courtesy, cleanliness, speed, convenience).

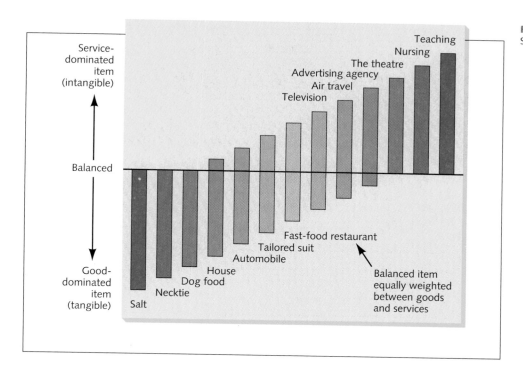

FIGURE 19–2
Service continuum.

LEARNING CHECK

1. What are the four I's of services?

2. Would inventory carrying costs for an accounting firm employing chartered accountants be *(a)* high, *(b)* low, or *(c)* nonexistent?

3. To eliminate inconsistencies, organizations rely on _____ and _____.

PURCHASING A SERVICE

Because of their intangible nature, it is generally more difficult for consumers to evaluate services before purchase than it is to evaluate goods (see Figure 19–3). Tangible goods such as clothes, jewelry, and furniture have *search* qualities, such as colour, size, and style, which can be determined before purchase. But rarely can a consumer inspect, try out, or test a service in advance. This is because some services such as restaurants and child care have *experience* qualities, which can only be discerned after purchase or consumption. Other services provided by specialized professionals such as medical diagnosis and legal services have *credence* qualities, or characteristics that the consumer may find impossible to evaluate even after purchase and consumption.[6]

The experience and credence qualities of services force consumers to make a prepurchase examination of the service by assessing the tangible characteristics that are part of, or surround, the service.[7] In other words, consumers will evaluate what they cannot see by what they can see. For example, you might consider the actual appearance of the dentist's office, or its physical location when making a judgment about the possible quality of dental services that might be supplied there. Market-driven service

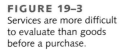

FIGURE 19–3
Services are more difficult to evaluate than goods before a purchase.

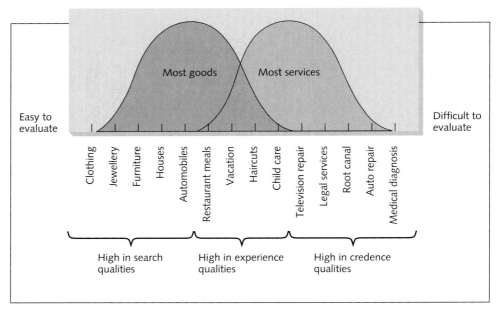

organizations go to great lengths to ensure that the tangible aspects of the services convey the appropriate image and serve as surrogate indicators of the intangible service to be provided. Proper management of the tangible aspects of services is sometimes called *impression management.*

Service marketers must also recognize that because of the uncertainty created by experience and credence qualities, consumers turn to personal sources of information such as early adopters, opinion leaders, and reference group members during the purchase decision process.[8] Accordingly, services marketers must ensure customer satisfaction in order to ensure positive word-of-mouth referral.

POSTPURCHASE EVALUATION

Once a consumer tries a service, how does she evaluate it? Primarily by comparing expectations about the service with the actual experience she has with the service. Differences between a consumer's expectations and experience are identified through **gap analysis.** This type of analysis asks consumers to assess their expectations and experiences on various dimensions of service quality. Expectations are influenced by word-of-mouth communications, personal needs, past experience, and marketing communications activities, while actual experiences are determined by the way an organization delivers the service.

One popular instrument developed by researchers to measure service quality and to conduct gap analysis is called SERVQUAL.[9] Researchers measure consumers' expectations and their actual service experience using a multi-item instrument. Consumers are asked to rate the importance of various dimensions of service quality and to score the service in terms of their expectations and actual experience. SERVQUAL provides the services marketer with a consumer rating of service quality and an indication of where improvements can be made.

FIGURE 19–4 Dimensions of service quality.

Dimension and Definition	Questions Used to Assess
Tangibles: Appearance of physical facilities, equipment, personnel, and communications materials	Do our employees dress appropriately?
Reliability: Ability to perform the promised service dependably and accurately	Did we perform the service right the first time?
Responsiveness: Willingness to help customers and provide prompt service	Do our employees provide you with prompt service?
Assurance: Respectful, considerate personnel who listen to customers and answer their questions	Do our employees treat you courteously? Do they answer all your questions?
Empathy: Knowing the customer and understanding their needs; approachable and available	Do our employees understand your needs? Are our operating hours convenient for you?

SOURCE: Adapted from A. Parasuraman, Leonard L. Berry, and Valarie A. Zeithaml, "More on Improving Service Quality Measurement," *Journal of Retailing,* Spring 1993, pp. 140–47; and R. Kenneth Teas, "Expectations, Performance, Evaluation, and Consumers' Perceptions of Quality," *Journal of Marketing,* October 1993, pp. 18–34.

Researchers using SERVQUAL have found that consumers judge service quality along five key dimensions: tangibles, reliability, responsiveness, assurance, and empathy (see Figure 19–4 for definitions and illustrations of these dimensions).[10] However, the relative importance of these various dimensions of service quality has been found to vary by type of service.[11] Services marketers must understand what dimensions consumers use in judging service quality, recognize the relative importance of each dimension, find out how they rate in terms of service quality, and take actions to deliver service quality that is consistent with consumer expectations. As a consumer, you play an important role in ensuring organizations deliver service quality. However, as the Ethics Insight box points out, sometimes consumers do not provide the feedback necessary to improve service quality.

LEARNING CHECK

1. What are the differences between search, experience, and credence qualities?

2. What is gap analysis?

3. An instrument or approach used to measure service quality is _____?

MANAGING THE MARKETING OF SERVICES

Just as the unique aspects of services necessitate changes in the consumer's purchase process, the marketing management process requires special adaptation.[12] In services marketing the employee often plays a central role in attracting, building, and maintaining relationships with customers.[13] This aspect of services marketing has led to a new concept: *internal marketing.*[14]

Internal marketing is based on the notion that in order for a service organization to serve its customers well, it must care for and treat its employees like valued customers. In short, the organization must focus on its employees, or internal market, before successful marketing plans can be directed at customers.[15] Internal marketing involves creating an organizational climate in general, and jobs in particular, that lead to the right service personnel performing the service in the right way. The organization must train and motivate all its employees to work together to provide service quality

Consumer's Role in Improving Service Quality

Research has shown that many consumers are reluctant to provide feedback to services organizations about their perceptions of the quality of the organization's services. One study found that only one in 27 service customers offers feedback that may be important in improving service quality.

Most services marketers want to know if customers are happy or satisfied with the services they provide. Many try a variety of methods (e.g., customer response or comment cards) to obtain or encourage customer feedback. However, most consumers do not take the time to provide this feedback even if they are unhappy or dissatisfied with the service quality provided. In general,

most consumers, if unhappy, will simply not return. And, while they will not take the time to tell the organization about their unhappiness, they will take the time to tell their friends and/or co-workers. The question is, why?

1. If you have a problem with an organization that markets a service, whether it is inconvenient hours or rude employees, wouldn't it be better to tell the organization?

2. Is it ethical for you to complain about a service organization to your friends without informing the organization about your dissatisfaction?

3. How can the situation be improved?

and customer satisfaction. Research has shown that service organizations that want to be truly customer-oriented must be employee-oriented. One services marketer has stated that "unhappy personnel create unhappy customers."[16]

In addition to employees, services organizations must also focus on the proper management of the marketing mix. Let's discuss the special nature of the marketing mix for services.

Product (Service)

To a large extent, the concepts of the product component of the marketing mix discussed in Chapters 9 and 10 apply equally well to Cheerios (a good) and to American Express (a service). Yet there are three aspects of the product/service element of the mix that warrant special attention: exclusivity, brand name, and capacity management.

Exclusivity. One favourable dimension in a new product is its ability to be patented. A patent gives the manufacturer of a product exclusive rights to its production. A major difference between products and services is that services cannot be patented. Hence the creator of a successful fast-food chain could quickly discover the concept being copied by others. Domino's Pizza now sees competitors copy its quick delivery advantage, the service which propelled Domino's to success.

Branding. An important aspect in marketing goods is the branding strategy used. However, because services are intangible, the brand name or identifying logo of the service organization is particularly important in consumer decisions because it is more difficult to describe what is being provided.[17] Many companies in the financial services industry in Canada, such as banks, trust companies, brokerage firms, and insurance companies, are now using branding, or are strengthening their existing branding efforts, in order to distinguish themselves in the minds of the consumers. Canada Trust and Bank of Montreal are two prime examples. Strong brand names and symbols are important for services marketers not only for differentiation purposes but also for con-

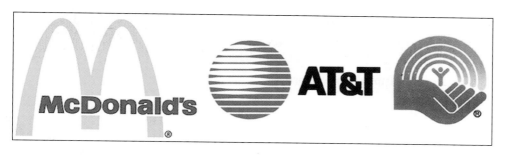

Brand names and logos create service identities.

veying an image of quality. A service firm with a well-established brand reputation will also find it easier to market new services than firms without such brand reputations.[18]

Capacity Management. A key distinction between goods and services is the inseparability of services. To buy and simultaneously use the service, the customer must be present at the service delivery site. For example, a patient must be in the dental chair to "buy" a root canal, and a guest must be in a hotel to "buy" an accommodation. So the product/service component of the mix must be made available to the consumer by managing demand. This is referred to as **capacity management.**

Service organizations must manage the availability of the offering to (1) smooth demand over time so that demand matches capacity and (2) ensure that the organization's assets are used in ways that will maximize the return on investment (ROI).[19] Figure 19–5 shows how a hotel tries to manage its capacity during the high and low seasons. Differing price structures are assigned to each segment of consumers to help moderate or adjust demand for the service. Airline contracts fill a fixed number of

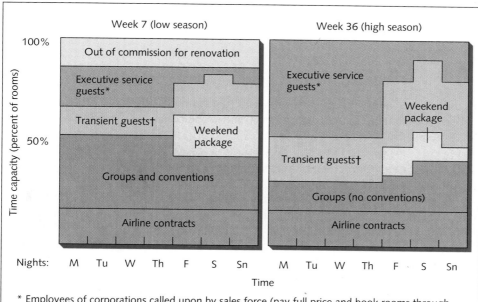

FIGURE 19–5
Balancing capacity management.

* Employees of corporations called upon by sales force (pay full price and book rooms through special reservations line).
† Individual customers paying full price but reserving rooms via publicized telephone number or by just "walking in."

$ MARKETPLACE APPLICATION

Synchromarketing: Adjusting Demand and Supply

One of the Four I's that can be very problematic for the services marketer is the inability to inventory service capacity. Idle capacity is always a problem, but perhaps more difficult is the inability to handle peak load demands. The synchronizing of demand and supply must occur in order to overcome idle capacity problems and to ensure customer satisfaction.

The key in synchromarketing is adjusting supply to match demand and adjusting demand to meet supply. In other words, it means working both sides of the street—altering the timing of consumer demand and exerting better control over the supply. The services marketer must avoid excess capacity as well as situations where excess demand goes unsatisfied. In order to better match demand and supply, the following methods can be considered by services marketers: (1) market similar services to target segments having different demand patterns, (2) market service extras or price reductions during nonpeak times, (3) train personnel to perform multiple tasks, (4) hire part-time employees during peak times, (5) educate consumers to use services during nonpeak times, (6) charge higher prices during peak times, and (7) increase customer participation in service delivery during peak times to increase efficiency.

Communications can play a key role in synchromarketing. Use of media should be tied to capacity. Services marketers can communicate to customers about nonpeak times and encourage them to use the service during those times. They can also communicate that service extras or other incentives like price reductions are available at certain times. It is also important to stop marketing communications activities when demand is already exceeding capacity.

1. Are there any other ways that a services marketer can better synchronize demand and supply?

rooms throughout the year. In the slow season, when more rooms are available, tour packages at appealing prices are used to attract groups or conventions, such as an offer for seven nights in Orlando at a reduced price. Weekend packages are also offered to buyers. In the high-demand season, groups are less desirable because guests who will pay high prices travel to Florida on their own.

Pricing

In the service industries, price is often referred to in various ways. Hospitals refer to charges; consultants, lawyers, physicians, and accountants to fees; airlines to fares; and hotels to rates.

Setting Prices. Two common methods of pricing services are cost plus percentage-of-cost and target ROI pricing.

Cost plus percentage-of-cost pricing, discussed in Chapter 11, entails charging a customer for the cost of providing the service plus an additional fixed percentage. Professional service organizations such as accounting firms charge a fee based on a billable rate. The billable rate is the cost of the accountant (salary, benefits, training, and overhead) plus a markup. This pricing is common to most professional service organizations such as law, medicine, and consulting.

In *target ROI pricing,* the price for the service is based on a targeted ROI. This method of setting price is common in capital-intensive services such as airlines or public utilities.

Role of Pricing. Pricing plays two essential roles: to affect consumer perceptions and to be used in capacity management. Because of the intangible nature of services, price can indicate the quality of service. Would you be willing to risk a $10 dental

Service marketers need to stress assurances of satisfaction in their ads.

surgery? Or a $50 divorce lawyer? Studies have shown that when there are few well-known cues by which to judge a product, consumers use price.[20]

The capacity management role of price is also important to movie theatres, hairstylists, restaurants, and hotels. Many service businesses use **off-peak pricing,** which consists of charging different prices during different times of day or days of the week to reflect variations in demand for the service. For example, restaurants offer luncheon specials, and movie theatres offer matinee prices.

Marketing Communications

In services marketing, most organizations rely on marketing communications to show consumers the benefits of purchasing the service. Advertising can be effective to demonstrate attributes such as availability; location; consistent quality; efficient, courteous service; and assurances of satisfaction.[21] Public relations also plays a role in conveying a proper image and in helping to support a firm's positioning strategy.[22] Public relations tools such as events sponsorship or public-service activities are very popular among service firms. This is particularly true for professional services companies that are often restricted in how they use marketing communications by their professional governing bodies.

Personal selling also plays an important role in services marketing. It has been said that when a consumer buys a service, he is buying the person selling the service.

Deloitte & Touche uses multiple locations to serve its clients.

Personal selling is valuable not only in attracting customers but in retaining them. Increasingly, many service marketers are following the path set by packaged goods firms, that is, they are developing integrated marketing communications plans.[23]

Distribution

Distribution is a major factor in developing service marketing strategy because of the inseparability of services from the producer. Rarely are intermediaries involved in the

The impact of technology in services marketing.

distribution of a service; the distribution site and service deliverer are the tangible components of the service.

Historically in professional services marketing, little attention has been paid to distribution. But as competition grows, the value of convenient distribution is being recognized. Hairstyling chains, legal firms, tax preparation companies, and accounting firms (such as Deloitte & Touche) use multiple locations for the distribution of services. In the banking industry, customers of participating banks using the Interac system can access any one of thousands of automated teller machines across Canada.

SERVICES IN THE FUTURE

What can we expect from the services industry in the future? Technology, a significant trend that has affected product (goods) marketing, is also impacting the services sector and will continue to do so in the future. The importance of relationship marketing and the technologies to pursue it will be applied more broadly in the service sector in the future. It has often been argued that relationship marketing in the services sector has been based on the notion that the employee is responsible for relationship building, at a very personal level. While employees will continue to be integral in cultivating long-term relations with customers, the advent of database and relationship marketing technologies will help enhance and solidify the personal efforts of service employees. For example, a computer support system at Toronto Dominion Bank now allows employees who interface with customers to deliver the full capabilities of the bank.

Consumers will put increased demand on services companies, expecting greater convenience, responsiveness, and access. Technology will play a large role in satisfying those demands. Just as some product marketers are leveraging technology as a competitive advantage, so too will the service marketer. One service expert suggests that service firms that can balance "high tech with high touch" will be successful in the future.[24]

As deregulation of service industries increases and entry barriers drop, the services market will become increasingly more competitive. Like product marketers before them, service firms will have to expend greater efforts to develop distinctive branding and positioning strategies. Services marketers will look to the experience of product marketers when making strategic marketing and management decisions. This can be valuable, since much of what is known about product marketing can be applied to services marketing.

But services marketing and management can be different, especially as the degree of intangibility increases. Service firms will have to recognize the differences and be prepared to develop marketing and management strategies beyond those currently used by product marketers. For example, one important area of distinction is the relative importance of the employee (as the provider and the service), especially in highly intangible, high-contact services. In this case, superior employee performance may be a source of competitive advantage for service firms, more so than in product marketing. But to leverage employees as a competitive advantage will take an innovative corporate culture that provides training, motivation, and employee empowerment. The challenge for services organizations in the future, according to Peter Drucker, will be how to organize and motivate their workers and how to provide them with dignity in their work.[25]

LEARNING CHECK

1. How does a movie theatre use off-peak pricing?

2. Smoothing demand is the focus of _____ management.

3. Does a lawyer use cost plus percentage-of-cost or target return on investment pricing?

NONPROFIT MARKETING

As we saw in Chapter 1, **nonprofit organizations** are organizations that operate without the intent of earning profit. They provide or market goods, services, and ideas to their target markets but do not seek profit. Nonprofit organizations operate in the public and private sector and include such diverse operations as public schools, churches, political parties, government agencies, and charitable organizations. Many nonprofit organizations do provide or market services and face many of the same challenges confronting for-profit services marketers. But, as we will discuss shortly, there are several characteristics unique to nonprofit organizations that set them apart from a typical for-profit services organization.

The relevance of marketing in the context of nonprofit organizations was highlighted 30 years ago in a landmark article entitled, "Broadening the Marketing Concept."[26] The authors proposed that marketing was a broad, societal activity that encompassed more than commercial or for-profit enterprises. They believed that marketing could and should be applied to nonprofit settings. While some marketers still have problems with this concept, many nonprofit organizations have embraced marketing, and have improved their operations accordingly.

Four Types of Nonprofit Marketing

There are four basic types of nonprofit marketing: person marketing, place marketing, organization marketing, and idea marketing.

Person Marketing. **Person marketing** involves the use of marketing activities designed to influence the target market's attitudes and behaviour toward a person. The most notable example is political campaigns, where politicians market themselves to get voter support.

Place Marketing. **Place marketing** involves the use of marketing activities designed to influence a target market's attitudes and behaviour toward a particular place. The objective may be to attract tourists, convention business, or new industries. While successful place marketing may yield financial rewards for a particular location, the marketing activities are usually undertaken by nonprofit organizations such as tourist bureaus or industrial development commissions. For example, Tourism Canada, a federal government agency, spends millions of dollars each year to attract tourists to this country. Businesses and communities enjoy the economic spin-off that results from increased tourism, but Tourism Canada is a nonprofit (government) organization.

Organization Marketing. **Organization marketing** involves the use of marketing activities in order to attract members, donors, participants, and volunteers to a particular organization. As we saw in the chapter opener, Second Harvest attempts to attract volunteers, as well as surplus food and financial donors. While it is true that for-profit organizations can also market themselves to enhance their images, we focus here on organization marketing by nonprofit entities.

Idea Marketing. **Idea marketing** (sometimes called *social marketing*) involves the marketing of a cause or idea to a given target market. The causes or ideas can be broad and diverse, and may include public health issues such as smoking, alcohol, or drug use, and environmental issues such as protecting the wilderness, animal rights, or the plight of endangered species.

Uniqueness of Nonprofit Marketing

Nonprofit organizations face many of the same challenges as for-profit marketers. These challenges include identifying and satisfying a target market, and the struggle to become more market-driven. Nonprofit organizations that provide services also have much in common with for-profit services marketers who must manage the four unique elements of services: intangibility, inconsistency, inseparability, and inventory, as discussed earlier in the chapter. But nonprofit marketing is different than for-profit marketing in several unique ways, including:

1. The providers of funds *(donors)* to a nonprofit organization are often different from users *(clients)* of its goods or services. This means that the organization has two major target markets: donors and clients, each with different needs.
2. The lack of a profit objective can make it difficult to identify a practical measure of success. For example, some human services organizations may have to define their objectives in terms of numbers of people served or helped by the organization. Second Harvest measures its success in terms of how much food it recovers and redistributes to the agencies feeding the hungry.
3. Nonprofit marketing generally involves nonfinancial exchanges in which the marketer is not asking the target market to exchange money for goods and services. For example, Alberta Health's AIDS prevention campaign (Chapter 15) seeks to change people's sexual behaviour. Various programs seek to stop people from smoking, or drinking and driving. Aside from fundraising efforts, most political marketing involves nonfinancial exchanges.

An example of nonprofit marketing.

IF YOU KNEW HOW MANY DOLPHINS DIED TO MAKE THIS TUNA SANDWICH, YOU'D LOSE YOUR LUNCH.

Over 6 million dolphins were killed by tuna fleets in the eastern tropical Pacific over the last 30 years.

These dolphins weren't killed for food or for use in any product. They were killed purely to increase net profits.

It was just these dolphins' bad luck that schools of large, profitable yellowfin tuna often swim below dolphin herds. And in the late '50s, fishermen realized that if they could snare the dolphins, they could net tons and tons of the tuna below.

First, the dolphins are chased and herded with speedboats, helicopters, and underwater explosives. Then, an enormous net is set around the herd and drawn closed at the bottom.

Exhausted and entangled in the nets, many dolphins suffocate. Some are literally crushed to death.

The Marine Mammal Protection Act of 1972 has helped. But it hasn't helped enough. Over 100,000 dolphins continue to die each year at the hands of the tuna industry.

Please donate your time or money to Greenpeace so we can continue our efforts to save the dolphins. If you must eat canned tuna, buy only Albacore or chunk white tuna which isn't caught "on dolphins."

Better yet, don't buy any tuna at all. It will only leave a bad taste in your mouth.

GREENPEACE
1436 U Street, Washington, DC 20009

4. Many nonprofit organizations are involved in marketing controversial issues or ideas. Few people question the mission and objectives of the local landscaping company. Nonprofit marketers, on the other hand, occasionally find themselves marketing controversial programs such as family planning or sex education. While for-profit marketers worry about getting their message across to their target markets, nonprofit marketers, especially those marketing ideas or causes, must worry about being counterattacked by groups that disagree with them.

5. Nonprofit organizations enjoy tax exemptions not available to for-profit organizations, creating tax-advantaged competition. Some nonprofit organizations operate just like a for-profit organization. The on-site gift shop owned by the Victoria General Hospital in Halifax operates in basically the same manner as the gift shops on nearby Spring Garden Road. The hospital uses the income generated by the gift shop to help defray its overall operational costs. But some for-profit operators often argue that nonprofit organizations that compete directly with them have unfair advantages because the nonprofits are exempt from a variety of taxes. This situation is likely to become more controversial as more nonprofit organizations engage in commercial activities to supplement their other sources of income.

MANAGING THE MARKETING OF NONPROFIT ORGANIZATIONS

As you know, marketing management is the process of planning, implementing, and controlling the organization's marketing effort. Nonprofit organizations, like for-profit organizations, must manage their marketing efforts. What we want to focus on here are the target market and the marketing mix of the nonprofit organization.

Target Market

As we mentioned earlier, with many nonprofit organizations the target market consists of two separate and distinctive groups: *clients,* the people who receive the goods and services, and *donors,* the people and organizations who donate time and money to support the organization. Understanding who the clients are and why they need the organization goes to the core or mission of the many nonprofit organizations. However, it is equally important for those organizations to understand the donors—who they are and why they donate. Serving these two groups effectively can be a challenge.

The Marketing Mix

In light of the differences between clients and donors, the marketing mix offered to one target market can be quite different from the mix it offers the other. Red Cross, for example, has one target market comprised of people who benefit from their disaster relief services, and another consisting of people who donate time and money to support the other. This should be kept in mind as we examine the components of the marketing mix below.

March is Red Cross Month
Millions of Canadians benefit from the programs and services of the Canadian Red Cross every year.

Only through the generous assistance of people like you – volunteers, blood donors, and financial supporters – can the Red Cross continue to help people in need. You *can* make a difference. Contact your local Red Cross branch or call 1-800-668-2866 to make a donation.

Canadian Red Cross

Product. As is the case with services marketing, many of the concepts of product development and product management discussed in Chapters 9 and 10 also apply to nonprofit marketing. The product must meet the needs of the target market, and must be managed effectively as market conditions change. However, many nonprofit organizations market services or ideas that may be more difficult to define for the organization and the consumer. For example, when marketing the concept of family planning in China, the product is not family planning, the product is population control. Like services marketers, nonprofit organizations can benefit from having strong brand names and symbols. Nonprofit organizations with well-established (brand) reputations have an easier time marketing than those without such brand reputations.

As changes occur in the marketing environment, nonprofit organizations, like their for-profit counterparts, may have to adjust their product offerings or delete those that have reached the end of their product life cycle. Sometimes, modifying or repositioning the product may be feasible. New products should follow the new product development process discussed in Chapter 9. The Lung Association of Canada, for example, after accomplishing its original mission of battling against tuberculosis, had to broaden its mission to include other lung diseases such as asthma and lung cancer.

Pricing. Pricing in a nonprofit setting must be viewed broadly. Price, in many cases, must be evaluated in terms of what you are asking clients and donors to give up. The cost might be money, but it might be time, pleasure, freedom, or convenience. Food banks that need volunteers to help serve meals ask people to give time. Clients must find ways to get to the food bank in order to receive the goods, which may involve a cost to them. Campaigns against drinking and driving ask people to forego the freedom of driving after drinking. Recycling programs that ask people to separate their recoverable materials ask them to give up the convenience of tossing everything in the trash. If nonprofit organizations ask for too much, the consumer may not respond. Just because some nonprofit organizations may deal in "free services," clients and donors will

The Lung Association of Canada; a nonprofit organization that works to fight lung diseases.

still perceive "costs" in dealing with them. As such, nonprofit organizations must examine the clients' and donors' perspective with regard to the psychic costs versus psychic benefits associated with the organization. If clients or donors find that the psychic costs of being associated with the organization outweigh the benefits, the nonprofit organization will not be successful.

Marketing Communications. While some nonprofit organizations have developed well-financed integrated marketing communications plans, most still rely on public relations to get their message out to their target audiences. As we saw in Chapter 15, publicity, in particular—usually in the form of public-service announcements (PSAs)—is often the key communications technique used by nonprofit organizations. But the use of special events such as concerts and telethons are also growing in popularity as nonprofit organizations attempt to communicate more effectively with their target audiences, both clients and donors. Some groups are also finding that videos and newsletters are good vehicles to build consumer awareness and interest in the organization. The use of volunteers to engage in personal selling and fundraising in their communities is showing some resurgence, as well.

As with for-profit organizations, the key to successful marketing communications is knowing the target audience and delivering the right message. A systematic and integrated approach to marketing communications as spelled out in Chapter 14 is applicable to nonprofit organizations.

Distribution. Distribution of goods and services is conceptually similar, whether or not the provider seeks a profit. The tactics employed by the nonprofit organization may differ somewhat because established channels of distribution generally do not exist for nonprofit groups. Moreover, many nonprofit organizations (e.g., universities, hospitals, museums) serve clients and donors from a fixed location. It is often difficult to enhance the delivery system when the location cannot be changed. Some nonprofit organizations, like many for-profit services marketers, are overcoming that hurdle by developing satellite locations, or adjusting their hours of operation to suit client needs. Some universities, for example, deliver courses at an organization's place of business so the organization's employees do not have to go on campus.

A more difficult situation is in which, in many cases, nonprofit organizations are not marketing goods or services, so the customer does not experience any distribution in a real sense. For example, if you donate to the United Way, United Way does not provide you with a good or service in return. Instead your money gets channelled to various social agencies that deliver services to their clients. You receive the satisfaction of helping others, but not a tangible product in the exchange process. Because of this, many nonprofit organizations attempt to communicate with contributors to show them where their money has gone, and how efficiently it was used. Research shows that nonprofit organizations that can demonstrate efficient use of resources are able to secure more donors and a higher average donation.[27]

LEARNING CHECK

1. What is nonprofit marketing?

2. What are the four types of nonprofit marketing?

3. Many nonprofit organizations have two target markets: _____ and _____.

LEARNING OBJECTIVE REINFORCEMENT

1. Outline the four unique elements of services. Services have four unique elements: intangibility, inconsistency, inseparability, and inventory. Intangibility refers to the difficulty in communicating service benefits. Inconsistency refers to the difficulty in providing the same level of quality each time a service is purchased. Inseparability means that service deliverers represent the service quality, and inventory costs for services are related to the costs of maintaining production capacity.

2. Explain the service continuum. Many companies are not clearly service-based or goods-based organizations. As companies look at what they bring to the market, there is a range from tangible to the intangible, or good-dominant to service-dominant, offerings referred to as the service continuum.

3. Describe the important dimensions of service quality. There are various dimensions of service quality. Five important dimensions identified by researchers are: tangibles (appearance of physical facilities, equipment, personnel, and communications materials), reliability (ability to perform the promised service dependably and accurately), responsiveness (willingness to help customers and provide prompt service), assurance (respectful, considerate personnel who listen to customers and answer their questions), and empathy (knowing the customers and understanding their needs, and being approachable and available).

4. Understand the important role of internal marketing in service organizations. In services marketing, the employee often plays a central role in attracting, building, and maintaining relationships with customers. Internal marketing is based on the notion that in order for a service organization to serve its customers well, it must care for and treat its employees like valued customers. In short, it must focus on its employees, or internal market, before successful programs can be directed at customers. Internal marketing involves creating an organizational climate in general, and jobs in particular, that lead to the right service personnel performing the service in the right way. Training and motivating all employees to work together to provide service quality and customer satisfaction is an important aspect of internal marketing.

5. Explain the importance of branding a service. Because services are intangible, branding a service is particularly important in order to differentiate the service and to convey an image of quality. The brand name or identifying logo helps "tangiblize" the service for the consumer.

6. Understand the concept of capacity management in services marketing. The inseparability of production and consumption of services means capacity management is important in services marketing. Capacity management involves smoothing demand to meet capacity. Essentially, the services firm tries to adjust or synchronize demand for its service in order to maximize the use of its resources.

7. Explain nonprofit marketing and the four basic types of nonprofit marketing. Nonprofit organizations are organizations that operate without the intent of earning profit. They provide or market goods, services, and ideas to their target markets but do not seek profit. Nonprofit organizations operate in the public and private sector and include such diverse operations as public schools, churches, political parties, government agencies, and charitable organizations. There are four basic types of nonprofit marketing: person marketing, place marketing, organization marketing, and idea marketing. Person marketing involves the use of marketing activities designed to influence the target market's attitudes and behaviour toward a person (e.g., a politician). Place marketing involves the use of marketing activities designed to influence a target market's attitudes and behaviour toward a particular place (e.g., a vacation destination). Organization marketing involves the use of marketing activities in order to attract members, donors, participants, and volunteers to a particular organization (e.g., Second Harvest). Idea marketing (sometimes called social marketing) involves the marketing of a cause or idea (e.g., animal rights) to a given target market.

8. Outline the unique aspects of nonprofit marketing. Nonprofit marketing is different than for-profit marketing in several unique ways, including: (1) the providers of funds (donors) to a nonprofit organization are often different from users (clients) of its goods or services, resulting in two major target markets each with different needs; (2) the lack of a profit objective can make it difficult to identify a practical measure of success; (3) nonprofit marketing generally involves nonfinancial exchanges in which the marketer is not asking the target market to exchange money for goods and services; (4) many nonprofit organizations are involved in marketing controversial issues or ideas; and (5) nonprofit organizations enjoy tax exemptions not available to for-profit organizations, creating tax-advantaged competition.

KEY TERMS AND CONCEPTS

services p. 468
four I's of services p. 468
idle production capacity p. 470
service continuum p. 470
gap analysis p. 472

internal marketing p. 473
capacity management p. 475
off-peak pricing p. 477
nonprofit marketing p. 480

person marketing p. 481
place marketing p. 481
organization marketing p. 481
idea marketing p. 481

CHAPTER QUESTIONS AND APPLICATIONS

1. Explain how the four I's of services would apply to a branch office of the Royal Bank.

2. Idle production capacity may be related to inventory or capacity management. How would the pricing component of the marketing mix reduce idle production capacity for *(a)* a car wash, *(b)* a stage theatre group, and *(c)* a university?

3. What are the search, experience, and credence qualities of an airline for the business traveller and the pleasure traveller? What qualities are most important to each group?

4. This chapter showed that consumers judge service quality along five key dimensions: tangibles, reliability, responsiveness, assurance, and empathy. Indicate the "one" dimension which is most important to you in judging service quality of each of the following services: *(a)* physicians, *(b)* banking, *(c)* car rental companies, and *(d)* dry cleaning.

5. The text suggests that internal marketing is necessary before a successful marketing plan can be directed at consumers. Why is this particularly true for service organizations?

6. Outline the capacity management strategies that an airline must consider.

7. Draw the channel of distribution for the following services: *(a)* a restaurant, *(b)* a hospital, and *(c)* a hotel.

8. What tactics could nonprofit organizations like charities use to attract more volunteers?

9. A children's hospital has asked you to prepare a plan to attract large-gift donors (e.g., individuals who will contribute more than $5,000). How would you prepare and execute the plan?

10. Health and Welfare Canada has hired you as a communications consultant. They want you to devise a basic marketing communications theme that would encourage young adults to stop smoking. Come up with a basic theme and why you think it would be effective.

APPLICATION CASE 19-1
WORLD WIDE AIRLINES (A)

World Wide Airlines is a multi-country airline carrier operating in Canada. It provides services, both by itself and in cooperation with other airlines, to almost any destination on the globe. On January 16, 1996, Mr. Arthur Overstreet, the manager of customer relations for the airline, returned from his Caribbean vacation to a pile of letters on his desk. On top of the pile was a letter with a note on it from Mr. Toole, the president of the airline. The note said simply, "Arthur, look after this."

QUESTIONS:

1. Do you think Dr. Ross was justified in writing the letter? Why?
2. How would you have handled the series of events if you were: (a) Dr. Ross or (b) an airline employee?
3. Explain the importance of the following as they affect the service provided to Dr. and Mrs. Ross: (a) tangibles, (b) responsiveness, (c) empathy, (d) reliability, (e) assurance.
4. What do you think Dr. Ross expects from the writing of this letter?
5. As Mr. Overstreet, the manager of customer relations, what would you do? What factors would you take into consideration in making your decision?

January 11, 1996

Mr. Harry M. Toole
President & CEO
World Wide Airlines Ltd. (WWA)

Dear Sir:
"Never has so little been done by so few for so many."

I am writing to you to object to the dreadful and completely unsatisfactory service my wife and I received lately from your airline. Without question, I can say that in over 30 years of flying, service levels have reached a new low.

I would like to quote from your own words in the December issue of WWA News for Members, in which you state: "The restructuring gave us a new start. We intend to make the most of it." You also go on to say: "Your loyalty did too. Customers like you are the lifeblood of our business—and the future of our airline. We will never forget that. We never will."

Sir, I think you must suffer from short-term memory loss, because this is not the company with which I flew. The kind of treatment my wife and I received is best used in my Marketing classes as examples of what customer service should *not* be.

I have just returned from a month-long trip to Australia using a combination of your airline and Koala Air. As you are aware, your company provides part-way service and Koala carries passengers the rest of the way.

The following is a listing of my complaints regarding service levels provided by WWA:

1. While in Honolulu on the outward leg, I called the toll-free number for WWA to try to secure seats with leg room, a process necessitated by my 6′7″ frame. I have had problems with preassignment before and understood that it might be a problem. My problem, however, was that the staff person involved was overtly belligerent and argumentative. He informed me that since I was "a Koala passenger" he could do nothing for me. He made it very clear that Koala was assigned certain seats and that was that. For your information, I had no such problem with the Koala representative.
2. On the return leg from Honolulu, a flight which leaves for Vancouver at 1 A.M. or so, the passengers were assaulted with a never-ending series of useless announcements such that sleep was impossible. For example, on several occasions a crew member announced that seat belts should be buckled while sleeping. The trouble is that the announcement was made with such frequency that sleep was impossible.

3. On the trip eastward from Vancouver, the check-in staff were very helpful. This fortuitous event was wiped away very quickly by the attitude of the cabin crew. I was seated in the first row behind business class. When I boarded the airplane, the overhead lockers in rows 4–5 were filled with crew baggage. I asked one male crew member if he could put a bag in the front lockers and was informed in no uncertain terms that the area was "reserved for business class passengers," this despite the fact that there was room for the bag. In addition, several other passengers remarked about the unfriendly attitude of more than one of the crew members. I remembered from your newsletter that employees now own a substantial portion of the company. I pity the other shareholders if this kind of behaviour is what is to be expected.

4. On arrival in Montreal, and only after running at high speed from one end of the airport to the other, I was informed that the flight was an hour late. I have no problem with weather delays; however, I was then informed that the flight was overbooked and the passengers were asked to volunteer to step down until the next day. I volunteered my boarding passes, made a call home to have someone pick up the luggage which was already on the flight, and then one minute from departure was informed that my seats were not needed any longer. Needless to say, there was no baggage room on the plane when I boarded. In addition, it was almost standing room only, with one passenger sitting on a stool in the cockpit.

Now as if this were not enough, even though I had already decided to send this letter the end was not in sight. When we arrived home, my wife's suitcase had disappeared. Not only did this bag contain over $3000 in clothing and jewellery, but it contained all of the pictures and negatives from our vacation in Australia—a fitting end perhaps to over $6000 in airfares and the most frustrating series of flights on record. To make matters worse, the baggage staff trying to trace this luggage seems to exhibit a complete lack of concern regarding our predicament. In frustration, I finally stated that all I wanted was for someone to indicate in any manner whatsoever that this matter was being given some priority. I have been promised return calls which never came; I have been left on hold for over 10 minutes while someone checked the file. I am tired of the process completely.

I have been a loyal customer of your airline for years, but I can tell you as surely as I write this letter that I will be going to your competitors for future travel. I will leave the delightful experience to your many other loyal customers who seem to have lower definitions of adequate service than do I.

Sincerely,

Bill Ross
Professor of Marketing & ex-frequent flyer

APPLICATION CASE 19-2
WORLD WIDE AIRLINES (B)

It was now March 1 and Dr. Ross had not received a reply to his complaint letter of January 11 (see World Wide Airlines (A)). He concluded that the lack of attention to his letter regarding poor service was just another example of the poor service attitude of World Wide Airlines. On March 3, a letter from Mr. Overstreet was delivered to his office.

QUESTIONS:

1. Does this letter satisfactorily address Dr. Ross' complaint? Explain.

2. What amount, if any, should be sent to Dr. Ross as reimbursement for suffering? $50, $100, $200, some other amount? Why?

3. As Mr. Overstreet, is there anything else you would have done?

March 3, 1996

Dear Dr. Ross:

Thank you very much for your recent communication.

It is our policy to treat passenger concerns very seriously and we endeavour to investigate each situation in depth so that we may react in a responsible manner. Your comments certainly indicate that the service you received on your recent journey fell short of the level we intend for our customers and we would ask that you accept our sincere apologies. Passenger opinion is extremely valuable in assessing our performance and we have taken the liberty of forwarding your observations to the appropriate manager for information and action. I will not elaborate on the points you have raised; you offer them in a constructive sense and we intend to act responsibly.

Our foremost objective is to provide airline performance that will be a source of pride for both our customers and employees, by achieving a high and consistent standard of service and reliability. Senior management are committed to this goal and we are all striving to build a better airline.

In the interest of good customer relations, we enclose a travel credit which is valid for any of our scheduled flights in the coming year.

Thank you for taking the time to share your feedback and impressions. Your continued support is very important to us and we will do our best to ensure all future travels on World Wide Airlines are satisfactory in every respect.

Yours truly,

A. Overstreet
Customer Relations

APPLICATION CASE 19-3
SECOND HARVEST

Second Harvest is a charitable nonprofit organization that began in Toronto in 1985. Its mission: to locate and collect surplus perishable food and deliver it to social services agencies and community organizations in Metro Toronto that feed the hungry. Second Harvest is not a food bank; it handles perishable food only and it does not warehouse food. It serves as a link between surplus food—food which would otherwise go to waste—and organizations that provide food to people in need. Many social service agencies and community organizations have difficulty keeping up with the demand for emergency food assistance. In Toronto, it is estimated that over 154,000 people depend on emergency food programs each month. Most of those people are single women and children. Ironically, while people are going hungry, more than 20 percent of all food produced in North America is wasted.

Second Harvest's basic day-to-day operations are conducted out of a small office under the direction of an Executive Director, working with a small staff, and primarily a core group of volunteers. Using a small fleet of trucks donated by good corporate citizens. Second Harvest retrieves surplus food from any industry, group, or individual who regularly or occasionally has excess food including food producers, farmers, retailers, wholesalers, restaurants, hospitals, production houses, and organizers of special events. It then delivers this food to a variety of agencies or organizations including drop-ins or soup kitchens, food pantries or food banks, residences or shelters, and subsized housing developments. In 1996, Second Harvest picked up and delivered more than 1 million pounds of food.

This food consisted of bread, baked goods, dairy products, produce, beverages, meat, snack foods, and prepared foods.

Second Harvest has also been involved with several self-help initiatives, including the publication of a cookbook which contains inexpensive, easy-to-prepare recipes designed to help those on a fixed income who need to stretch their food dollars. Second Harvest also plays a role as an advocate for change in public policy as it pertains to hunger and poverty.

In order to achieve its objectives. Second Harvest attempts to create awareness of the organization and its efforts through public relations activities including PSAs, news releases, newsletters, and special events. One of its major events is an annual fundraiser called Toronto Taste, where attendees pay to sample the food dishes created by Toronto chefs. Second Harvest also participates in hospitality industry trade shows where it hopes to create greater awareness of its activities, and to increase its food donor base. It also has a public relations firm which donates its time and talent in order to help heighten Second Harvest profile in the community.

QUESTIONS
1. How can Second Harvest motivate more individuals and organizations to donate to their cause?
2. What specific marketing communication tools would you recommend that Second Harvest use to reach those prospective donors?
3. What are some unique sources of surplus food that Second Harvest could tap into?

Beemaid Honey Ltd.

Paul Belisle's normally jovial face was creased with worry as he looked at a memo from his vice president of marketing, Rick Rees, in May 1995. Belisle, president of Beemaid Honey Ltd. of Winnipeg, had just finished reviewing Rees' assessment of company sales in the important German market. Sales had started to fall dramatically in 1993 when, unknown to Beemaid, a German competitor had begun packaging an inferior local honey in a bottle that was a direct copy of Beemaid's packaging. Two years of legal battles had stopped the copycat but the damage to Beemaid's market position in its standard creamed clover honey seemed nearly irreparable. Rees was suggesting the company's new honey-based mustards and barbecue sauce might be introduced to the German market and make up for lost sales. He wanted to go ahead and take these products to the important ANUGA trade show later in the year and introduce them to the German marketplace. Belisle knew introducing a new product was an expensive and possibly difficult proposition. What information did he need before deciding on whether or not to market his mustards and barbecue sauce in Germany?

THE COMPANY AND ITS PRODUCTS

Beemaid Honey Ltd. was founded as a farm-based cooperative in 1959 to market the products of beekeepers in Alberta and Manitoba. In early 1995 the company was owned by some 400 beekeepers in Canada's three prairie provinces and operated plants in Winnipeg and Edmonton. Annual sales were just over $20 million and 50 people were employed in the processing operations at the two plants. On a typical day the company turned out over 20,000kg of premium quality honey.

The firm prided itself on the quality of its products. The company's owner/beekeepers collected raw honey in 45-gallon drums and delivered it to the Winnipeg or Edmonton plants. A half day of testing determined whether the product was acceptable. On acceptance, the raw honey was graded for moisture level, pollen count, flavour, and colour. Colour and moisture are particular indicators of quality, with colour influenced by the type of flower from which the honeybees have collected their nectar. Clover- and alfalfa-based honey is generally very white and has a mild flavour. Buckwheat-based honey is normally darker with a much stronger flavour and aroma. Moisture content is also important: The drier the honey, the higher the quality and price. Most of Beemaid's honey originated in clover, alfalfa, and canola fields and was light with a low moisture content.

Beemaid produced two basic products, pure liquid honey and creamed honey. Producing consumer-ready honey was not a difficult process. The raw product is melted in a "hot room" and pumped through filters to remove dirt, pieces of wax, or bee parts. After pasteurization, liquid honey is bottled and product destined to become creamed honey placed in a cool room to harden. Creamed honey is simply a liquid product to which natural honey crystals are added. Crystallization is a natural process that takes place with all honeys over time. The resulting creamed product is much easier to ship and has a longer shelf life.

Belisle wanted Beemaid to become a food company, not simply a honey producer. As such, he had diversified the product line to include not only traditional creamed and liquid honey but new products such as *Hot n' Spicy Honey Mustard and Honey Bar Bee Q Sauce* (see Appendix A for a listing of Beemaid's major product lines). These had been successfully introduced into the North American market and were the products Rick Rees proposed using to revitalize Beemaid's German market.

BEEMAID'S EXPORT OPERATIONS

Beemaid had exported since its founding. Canadian beekeepers produce approximately 35 million kilograms of honey per annum. Despite the fact that Canadians are the second largest per capita consumers of honey in the world, Canadian consumption is only 20–25 million kilograms yearly. As a result, Canadian honey processors have traditionally been major players in the world marketplace. In 1995 Beemaid exported to 30 countries with over one-third of its sales coming from the export market.

The United States was Beemaid's primary export market, accounting for nearly two-thirds of the firm's exports. The U.S. had been largely ignored by Beemaid until the mid 1980s as a result of an unwritten understanding that cooperatively owned Beemaid would not compete with the Iowa-based Sioux Honey Association, another cooperative and the largest supplier in the U.S. market. Competition in the Canadian market from Chinese producers and slow growth in other export markets gradually forced Beemaid into the U.S.

In entering the U.S. market, Beemaid decided to concentrate on building an identifiable brand name. California was chosen as the test market and in 1986 the firm embarked on a three-year program that saw their product climb to the number one spot in some market segments. This was accomplished by a massive in-store sampling program which focused on Beemaid's quality and taste as well as their unique 16 oz., beehive-shaped plastic squeeze bottle. At that time American firms packaged all their product in glass jars. The easy to handle Canadian squeeze bottle was a hit.

After initial success in California, the company embarked on a systematic market research program to determine what part of the U.S. should be their next target. After wading through masses of research on consumption trends and taste preferences, the company decided on Florida and Texas. Florida was a success. However, Beemaid's experience in Texas served to teach the company a lesson in how important traditional loyalties can be in the food market. Despite a program that saw Beemaid's products demoed in almost every store in the state, the company was virtually shut out of the market by locally manufactured Burleson's. Whatever the merits of Beemaid, Texans wanted honey made in Texas, not Canada. Despite the Texas setback, by 1995 Beemaid was established in 20 states in all regions.

While the company pursued brand name sales in the U.S., their strategy in Europe and the Far East was to concentrate on the private label market. They did not feel the firm was large enough to absorb the costs associated with establishing a brand image in markets such as Japan and Germany. In Germany, for example, the company worked with a German partner, Breitshamer and Ulrich Co., that shipped German manufactured 500ml glass jars, tops, and labels to Beemaid's Winnipeg plant where they were filled with creamed honey and shipped back to Germany. Similar arrangements existed with firms in Sweden, France, and Switzerland. While labels used in European markets featured Canada and the maple leaf prominently, Beemaid was unknown.

Germany is one of the largest honey markets in the world and Germans are the product's largest per capita consumer. German beekeepers produce less than one-quarter of the country's annual consumption of just over 100,000 tonnes and total imports are roughly 90,000 tonnes per annum. Most imports are of lower grade honey shipped in bulk form from China, Argentina, and Mexico. Canada is one of the few countries shipping a high quality product in a consumer-ready pack. Virtually all honey sold at retail was packaged in a standard 500ml glass jar which sold for anywhere from CDN$2.99 to $5.49, depending on the brand. Companies competed on taste and quality, with packaging virtually a non-issue.

Germany, as part of the European Union, levied a 26 percent tariff on imported honey. This was part of the reason Beemaid used German packaging materials for its products. With duty remission possible on European Union-made components and the glass jars making up one-third of the cost of the final product, it was cost effective for the firm to ship empty bottles thousands of kilometres to Winnipeg to be filled. Germany's tough environmental laws were another factor. Manufacturers are ultimately responsible for recycling or reusing a high percentage of their packaging materials. Companies sign agreements with the German government which includes minimum recycle/reuse targets and the government charges firms an environmental fee depending on the packaging they use. Fees for easy to reuse or recycle glass were substantially lower than those for plastics. Numerous other restrictions concerning weights and measures and labelling also apply.

Food retailing in Germany was highly concentrated. Giant firms such as Tengelman (sales of CDN$30 billion) dominated the market. Each chain operated stores of various sizes from the equivalent of a Canadian 7-Eleven convenience store up to giant hypermarkets. Competition at the retail level was fierce as the German consumer was becoming much more conscious of the value–price relationship and demanding high quality at increasingly lower prices. High taxes and new surcharges to pay for the rebuilding of the former East Germany had made the German shopper much less ready to pay the very high prices which had characterized the German market since the end of WW II. German retailers had increasingly responded to the demands for more variety and lower prices by searching for new product offerings overseas and bypassing traditional importers. Dealing direct with the manufacturer allowed the retailers to reduce their costs.

As Paul Belisle studied Rick Rees' memo (see Appendix B for the full text), Rick stuck his head in the door. "What do you think, Paul? I think ANUGA might be our best opportunity to launch the mustard and barbecue products in the near future. The show is huge and buyers will be there from throughout Germany." Belisle nodded, "You're right. Let's meet this afternoon and see if we can sort this out. I'd at least like to know what information we need to make a good decision on what to do with mustards and barbecue sauce in Germany."

QUESTIONS FOR DISCUSSION

1. What types of market information will Beemaid require before they decide whether to market mustards and barbecue sauce in Germany?

2. Where can such information be accessed?

3. Product adaptation could be critical to the successful introduction of Beemaid's mustards and barbecue sauce in Germany. What features of these products might need to be changed for the German market?

4. Should the company examine the possibility of abandoning private label and developing the Beemaid brand in Germany? Why or why not?

5. What impact might Germany's environmental laws have on the introduction of mustards and barbecue sauce?

APPENDIX A   Beemaid Honey Ltd. typical export products.

Product	Packaging
Honey Bar Bee Q Sauce	250ml plastic squeeze bottle
Hot n'Spicy Mustard	250ml plastic squeeze bottle
Clover Liquid Honey	16oz. PETG jar, 12oz. plastic beehive squeeze bottle, 16oz. plastic squeeze bottle.
Clover Cream Honey	12oz. plastic tub, 16oz. plastic beehive squeeze bottle, 500ml glass jar
Clover Cinnamon Honey	12oz. plastic beehive squeeze bottle
Raw Natural Liquid Honey	2lb. plastic squeeze bottle, 6lb. plastic bottle
International Gourmet Honey Mustard (Belgian or French)	250ml plastic squeeze bottle

APPENDIX B   Rick Rees' memo to Paul Belisle.

May 10, 1995

To   : Paul Belisle

From   : Rick Rees

Subject   : German Market

I think we should get together sometime this week to discuss the German market. As you know our standard lines of clover honey have done very poorly in the last 24 months due to the copycat. Despite our best efforts I think it may be a long time before sales of traditional products recover and I would like to boost sales in the market by introducing our mustard and barbecue products. The ANUGA trade show will be held in Cologne this October and I think this might be an excellent opportunity to introduce the new product. Your thoughts?

Clean Windows, Inc.*

It was January 1995. Terry Gill and John Kelly, partners of Clean Windows, Inc. (CW), were contemplating a marketing strategy for expanding their operations in the window cleaning market. Both were full-time students in the second year of their degree programs at the University of New Brunswick. They were committed to their studies and realized that their chosen strategy must allow them to complete their degree programs within the next two years.

They were optimistic that CW had the opportunity to grow very rapidly. Their optimism appeared justified, given the growth they had experienced in both residential and commercial contracts since they commenced operations in July 1994 (see Figure 1). Mr. Kelly attributed this growth to the "current lack of serious competition in the greater Fredericton area."

When questioned about balancing schoolwork and the responsibilities of his business, Mr. Gill commented:

> We know we have a really great concept here, but our study schedule could result in a lack of attention to customer demands and administrative details. I think that we can pull it off, but we need to make the right choices and develop an appropriate marketing strategy. John and I even considered franchising as our means of growth because we have to grow to maximize profitability.

INITIAL STRATEGY

Operations commenced June 20, 1994, with enough equipment for two cleaners. Initially, all labour activity was completed by Mr. Gill and Mr. Kelly. Business was relatively slow the first

FIGURE 1   Monthly cleaning gross revenue.

Month	Residential	Commercial	Total
July	$1,377	$ 37	$1,414
August	2,175	45	2,220
September	1,990	1,423	3,413
October	1,402	2,509	3,911
November	315	1,021	1,336
December	0	896	896

SOURCE: Company records.

*This case was prepared and revised by Dr. E. Stephen Grant, University of New Brunswick, assisted by G. T. Clarke and K. Dunphy. Copyright 1997.

Names of companies and people have been disguised. Some quantitative data have been adjusted, but relationships of data have been maintained. This case serves as a basis for discussion rather than an illustration of either effective or ineffective handling of an administrative situation.

two months (see Figure 1), as most of the owners' time was spent cleaning windows, not on marketing and management activity. Advertising in these months was limited to the purchase of business cards and a direct mail campaign. The business cards were an important asset for business contacts, but the mailout resulted in limited success. It was thought that this was due to poor timing.

One thousand five hundred photocopied flyers were distributed just prior to a long weekend in July. Both partners and employees delivered the flyers to private residences in the downtown area and to a few upscale neighbourhoods.

By the end of July a display ad was run in the business directory section of the local newspaper and free airtime was received on a local radio station interested in assisting student businesses. Unfortunately, neither of these two media proved successful. Lawn signs and T-shirts displaying the company logo and phone number were purchased. These media, combined with word of mouth, accounted for close to 85 percent of all new cleaning contracts.

These forms of marketing communications were responsible for business growth in August and September. With this additional business, the need for extra staff became apparent. By August, six cleaners were employed. An increase in demand through September and October was experienced, but it became difficult for both partners to cope with the increased volume as university commenced in September. By then, employment had decreased to two full-time employees who were responsible for reducing the partners' workload.

In early November, Mr. Gill and Mr. Kelly realized that the two full-time employees were not working out as anticipated. The decision was made to lay off both employees. This left only the partners to resume the labour-intensive duties of window cleaning. This was very difficult, since both maintained a rigorous cleaning schedule in addition to a full course load.

With the summer quickly approaching, both partners agreed that this strategy would have to be reconsidered.

COMPETITION

When questioned about the competition, Mr. Kelly commented:

> There is only one firm that cleans residential windows, but we don't see them as a serious competitor. We know that they do have some business, but they cannot have much. We have phoned them several times, but our calls were never returned. There are two firms that service only commercial accounts. One of these firms cleans high-rise buildings only, but they operate out of Moncton, which is more than a two-hour drive. The other is a local firm; they are not equipped to clean high-rises but they have a very significant share of the local commercial market. We are certain that we can compete with them; almost all of our commercial clients have experienced their service and have expressed relief that there is now an alternative available.

Mr. Kelly had obtained information on all three of these competitors (see Figure 2). Fredericton had a number of maid and janitorial service companies. Most of these firms cleaned windows; however, none cleaned external window surfaces, and they cleaned interior window surfaces on an irregular basis.

Although Fredericton offers only a relatively small potential market size, both partners are certain that there is an attractive opportunity in both the residential and the commercial market.

Many customers have indicated they would use CW's service again. One customer stated that she had seen the lawn sign and then decided to request CW's service. Unable to find the phone number (a business number was obtained in September), she claimed to have driven more than 50 miles before finding the lawn sign that she needed to find the number.

Mr. Gill believed that the most profitable opportunity would be to service what he calls high-rise buildings (all those that require staging). He estimates that there are more than 350 such buildings in the Fredericton area.

FIGURE 2 Competition in Fredericton window cleaning market.

Company	Customer Type*	Bonded	Liability Insurance	Estimated Price
City Window Cleaners	Residential	?	?	?
Mr. Windows	Commercial	Yes	Yes	$15/hr
Gormay Cleaners	Commercial—high-rise buildings only	No	Yes	$40/hr
Other (janitorial and maid services)	Commercial⁺ and residential⁺	NA	NA	NA

* Residential customers are defined as single dwellings only, all other accounts are defined as commercial.
† Clean only interior window surfaces.
? = unavailable.
SOURCE: Telephone directory and telephone enquiries.

COST DATA

Cost data are given in Figures 3 and 4. All costs for 1994 (see Figure 3) were actual, based on the costs incurred to date. Costs for 1995 (see Figure 4) have been estimated by the partners. Transportation costs have been excluded. A small van belonging to Mr. Kelly's father had been used and John was confident that this vehicle would be available for at least another year. Although CW incurs no rental fee for the use of this van, fuel would have to be purchased.

All estimated costs were believed to be reasonably accurate. However, the pricing of window contracts had been much more arbitrary. Mr. Kelly sees the pricing decision as being of key importance to CW's long-term profitability. To date, prices have been based on an estimated completion time for each potential contract.

The time estimate is multiplied by a charge-out rate of $15/hour per cleaner. Mr. Kelly confessed that the decision to use $15 per hour was arbitrary; however, he was confident that it was competitive and fair. This was thought to be the same charge-out rate used by Mr. Windows (see Figure 2). Mr. Kelly had difficulty deciding what to charge in the future. Although he believed their price was competitive, he had a hunch that many customers expected a lower charge-out rate given their status as students. He believed it was a serious issue and realized that many customers selected CW because of the altruistic satisfaction they received from supporting a student venture.

FIGURE 3 Actual costs—1994.

Variable Costs	Per Hour	
Wages		
One two-person crew	(2 × $5.50 each)	$11.00/hour
Supplies		
Fuel	$ .75	
Cleaning fluids	.50	
Cleaning materials	.90	2.15
Total variable costs		$13.15

Fixed Costs	Per Month
Insurance (liability)	$ 15.00
Telephone	55.00
Advertising	110.00
Bank charges	25.00
Equipment depreciation	10.00
Total fixed costs	$215.00

SOURCE: Company records.

FIGURE 4 Estimated costs—1995.

Variable Costs	Per Hour	
Wages		
One two-person crew	(2 × $5.70 each)	$11.40/hour
Supplies		
Fuel	$ .80	
Cleaning fluids	.50	
Cleaning materials	.90	2.20
Total variable costs		$13.60

Fixed Costs	Per Month
Insurance (liability)	$ 20.00
Telephone	60.00
Advertising	200.00
Bank charges	30.00
Equipment depreciation	20.00
Total fixed costs	$330.00

SOURCE: Company estimates.

Enough equipment (ladders, staging, buckets, etc.) to operationalize three two-person crews had been acquired. It was estimated that additional equipment would cost $300 per crew, but it was uncertain whether or not it would be necessary to hire additional crews.

Additional investment would be necessary in order to clean high-rise buildings. Staging that would allow one person to safely manoeuvre up and down the side of a high-rise would cost approximately $4,500.

THE MARKET

Mr. Gill had evaluated the Fredericton market and concluded that it was sizable enough to allow CW to realize satisfactory profits. He had collected select statistics at the university's library (see Figure 5). Although Mr. Gill was uncertain how many households and commercial customers were likely to use his services, he was certain that his competitors were not satisfying the current demand.

In the past, CW's window contracts were largely concentrated within a small geographic area. Both partners were uncertain why this phenomenon existed. Mr. Kelly questioned, "Is this because our lawn signs were displayed more often in this area? Are these people different, or is it related to other, undetermined causes?"

THE FUTURE

The partners faced a number of important decisions. They had to decide whether or not their current strategy was appropriate for the situation. If it was not, they would have to agree on appropriate changes. These changes would have to be made in light of both partners' commitment to expansion. They believed they could create a student-owned franchise operation similar to College Pro Painters and University Painters. However, they were uncertain how they should proceed.

They would need to make some decisions very soon. Exams finished in April, and they anticipated that April and May would be extremely busy months, given that many people under-

FIGURE 5 Selected characteristics—Fredericton, NB.

Dwelling characteristics	
Single detached house	10,230
Apartment, five or more storeys	275
Movable dwelling	50
All other types	5,890
Total number of occupied private dwellings	16,445
Population characteristics	
By industry division	
All industries	24,095
Primary industries (SIC divisions A, B, C, and D)	440
Manufacturing industries (division E)	1,290
Construction industries (division F)	1,160
Transportation, storage, communication, and other utility industries (divisions G and H)	1,895
Trade industries (divisions I and J)	4,435
Finance, insurance, and real estate industries (divisions K and L)	950
Government service industries (division N)	4,565
Other service industries (divisions M, O, P, Q, and R)	9,365
Not applicable	480
Total labour force 15 years and over	24,570

SOURCE: Statistics Canada, Cat. 94-107 and 108, 1986.

take an effort in the spring to clean their homes and businesses. They realized there would be little time available for analysis and strategic planning after late March. Time would be spent hiring employees, selling, cleaning, and perhaps even studying for final exams.

QUESTIONS

1. How can the market (commercial and residential) for window cleaning be segmented?

2. What types of marketing communications activities would you suggest CW, Inc., use? How can the firm encourage repeat usage of its service?

3. How feasible is the venture?

4. Would you recommend that the partners attempt to sell franchise agreements? Explain.

Constant Creation Gourmet Cuisine

In July 1991 Greg Brooks, founder, president and, to date, only full-time employee of Constant Creation Gourmet Cuisine, felt his company had reached a plateau. The firm's line of dessert and hot sauces had been sold direct to the consumer at craft and gift shows since 1983. Mr. Brooks realized the growth potential of this channel was limited and was seeking new avenues for expansion.

THE COMPANY

After Greg Brooks finished his BSc. in Psychology at Acadia University in 1976 he worked in several food-related businesses, including catering. In 1978 Brooks and his wife, Maryse Hudon, opened the Appletree Landing restaurant in Canning, Nova Scotia. The restaurant catered to the tourist trade and opened on a seasonal basis. Appletree Landing featured a range of high quality desserts, including cheese cake selections topped by sauces developed in house by Brooks and Hudon. The popularity of these sauces, which included brandied cherry, wild blueberry rum, and maple cream, was such that Brooks began selling them to customers at the restaurant.

In 1983 Brooks became convinced that Appletree Landing's dessert sauces could be the basis of a separate business. In November of that year he made up gift packs of four sauces and took them to the three-day Christmas at the Forum craft show in Halifax, Nova Scotia. He sold his entire inventory in two hours and Constant Creation Gourmet Cuisine was born.

In its first full year of operation the firm sold $13,000 worth of product. This doubled each year until 1987 when the economic slowdown of the late 1980s began to take its toll. While growth slowed after 1987, sales continued to rise and were predicted to reach $130,000 by the end of 1991. The company was marginally profitable although sales tended to cluster around the Christmas period and timing of cash flows was a major problem. Brooks and Hudon operated both their restaurant and Constant Creation until 1989 when the restaurant reached the stage it could be sold for a profit. From that point the couple concentrated their energies on Constant Creation.

THE PRODUCT

In 1991 the company's sauce line totalled 20 items. They ranged from Raspberry Sauce with Grand Marnier through Fire From Within, a Caribbean style hot sauce to be used sparingly by those with cast iron digestive systems (see Appendix A). The product line was split evenly between fruit-based dessert sauces and ethnic hot sauces. The recipes for each had been invented by Brooks and Hudon and featured 90 percent locally grown ingredients from the Annapolis Valley of Nova Scotia. These were supplemented by high quality imported products such as all natural pectin from Denmark. No additives, preservatives, or stabilizers were used and wherever possible organically grown produce was incorporated. To further develop the all natural, healthy image, refined sugar, oils, and salt were also removed from all products.

The sauces were available in 65ml or 250ml glass bottles with attractive labels professionally designed in 1990. Production took place in a 300 sq. ft. facility added to the back of Brooks' home. In 1990 total production was 10,000 65ml bottles and 15,000 250ml bottles. Sales were evenly split between the dessert and hot sauces. Projections for 1991 were 12,000 65ml bottles and 18,000 250ml bottles. Maximum production capacity of the existing plant and equipment was approximately 200,000 bottles per annum.

MARKETING COMMUNICATIONS AND CHANNELS OF DISTRIBUTION

Brooks' initial approach to the condiments market was direct to the end user through local and regional craft shows. Eight years later this approach had not changed significantly. While the firm had entered the central Canadian market as early as 1984 the approach was the same, direct to the consumer sales through events such as "One of a Kind" in Toronto and the Ottawa Christmas Craft Show. In 1991 direct to the consumer sales still accounted for 70 percent of the company's receipts (see Figure 1) and Brooks was spending upward of 100 days per year manning booths at craft and gift shows. A limited wholesale trade had, however, resulted from participation in wholesale trade shows. The firm's products were sold at wholesale prices to approximately 40 specialty food stores and gift shops and by firms producing gift baskets. Typical outlets were "Jennifer's of Nova

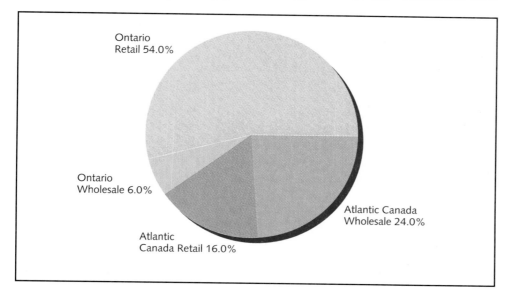

FIGURE 1
Constant creation 1991 sales by region.

Scotia" in Halifax and Peggy's Cove, Nova Scotia, and "Alive and Well" in Toronto, Ontario. Brooks was unsure whether the wholesale trade was worth the effort as, in his words, "you need 10 times the production to make the same profit."

The company had tried and rejected several manufacturer's agents in Ontario and Quebec. Brooks felt Constant Creation's product line was most successful when the full range of sauces was presented to the consumer. While the agents had initially promised to market the product on this basis, each had ended up marketing a limited number of the best-selling sauces.

Brooks positioned his products to appeal to the up-market gourmand looking for something unique. The all natural aspect of the sauces typically attracted younger, upper-middle class consumers looking for something different to use in home food preparation. The sauces were not marketed as Nova Scotian or Atlantic Canadian regional products in an effort to ensure they had the widest possible appeal. The company did not advertise outside the trade show circuit.

Direct competition for Constant Creation's products was limited. No specialty or regional manufacturer produced a range of all natural sauces similar to Constant Creation's. On the national level Loblaws' President's Choice line of ethnic sauces provided indirect competition. The President's Choice product, however, was sold through different channels (i.e., national chain stores) and could not match Constant Creation's ingredient and quality claims.

THE CANADIAN SPECIALTY FOODS INDUSTRY

The Canadian Association of Specialty Foods defines its members' products as "premium quality foods of some uniqueness with good presentation and select distribution." Constant Creation's products met this definition and the company was typical of the Canadian specialty foods industry. Over one-third (36%) of the industry consisted of companies with specialty food sales of less than $100,000 and only 30 percent of companies had sales of more than $1.0 million. Three-quarters of the firms in the sector had fewer than 50 employees and 34 percent had fewer than 10 people on staff. The range of products manufactured in the sector was large al-

FIGURE 2
Most popular specialty foods produced by Canadian manufacturers (expressed as % of industry members producing each product).

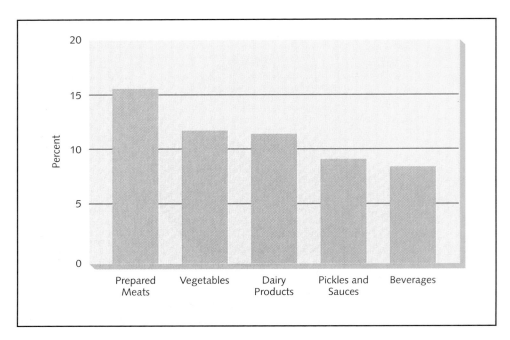

though the majority clustered in five product groups: prepared meats, vegetables, dairy products, pickles and sauces, and beverages (see Figure 2).

Established for eight years, Constant Creation was becoming something of a grandfather in a fast changing industry. Less than half (45%) of the firms in the sector were more than 10 years old and 35 percent had less than five years of experience. Atlantic Canadian firms tended to mirror the experience in the rest of the country but differed in one important aspect, export orientation. While only 44 percent of Ontario firms and 34 percent of companies in western Canada were exporters, 64 percent of Atlantic Canadian companies had entered the international market. The small size of the region and the proximity to populous New England forced many companies to look south.

The specialty food consumer tended to be a well-off baby boomer looking for a high quality, nutritious, and unique product. Most were concerned with the presence of additives and preservatives but still demanded freshness. In the early 1990s the specialty food market was growing at a real rate of roughly 10 percent per annum. New products were in constant demand and manufacturers were obliging, despite a 90 plus percent failure rate for new product introductions. In 1990 the fastest growing product areas were snack foods (rice cakes, bagel chips, pita crisps) and condiments (primarily seafood and ethnic sauces).

Distribution of specialty foods in Canada was complex (see Appendix B). The specialty food distributor dominated the market and tended to "push" products through the system. The small size of most specialty food manufacturers precluded heavy advertising or other brand awareness activities. As a result most sales promotion was used at the store level and included recipes, sampling, and retailer education. Few, if any, manufacturers used Constant Creation's direct to the consumer approach.

OPPORTUNITIES

In July 1991 Brooks felt a threshold had been reached with his current methods of marketing communications and distribution. To decide how best to grow the business he looked at three possibilities: increased emphasis on the wholesale market, exporting, and development of a custom manufacturing business.

As noted earlier Brooks had been dissatisfied with previous attempts to increase sales in the wholesale market. His experience with manufacturers' agents had not been good and he was concerned with the smaller profit margins available. While his direct costs to produce most of his products were only 35 percent of the wholesale price, he was still attracted to the much higher gross margins available in the direct to the consumer trade. Nevertheless, the fact he had considerable excess production capacity made the wholesale market worth another close look.

At the invitation of the federal government's International Trade Centre in Halifax, Brooks had participated in a New Exporters to Border States (NEBS) mission to Boston earlier in 1991. This brief introduction to the New England market had intrigued him with the significant opportunity it presented but there appeared to be many problems. New labelling regulations under consideration by the USFDA might require major, and costly, changes to Constant Creation's labels. American regulations on the import of sugar and products containing high levels of sugars were complex and might also affect the potential of the company's products in the U.S. market. Finally Constant Creation would face direct competition from many small American companies. While Brooks was confident his products were equal or better in terms of quality and presentation, American firms had several cost advantages that could have the effect of pricing Constant Creation out of the market. The 250ml glass jars that Brooks bought from a Halifax distributor for $0.30, for example, were available in New England for the equivalent of $0.18.

A third avenue open to Constant Creation could be a custom product service. For a fee Brooks could develop a unique product in house for a customer and package it using labels of Brooks' or the customer's design. He felt the minimum order quantity for this service might be as low as $600 if the customer used one of Constant Creation's standard recipes. The service would be targeted at small outlets, such as gift shops, which would like to offer something unique to their customers.

QUESTIONS FOR DISCUSSION

1. Evaluate Constant Creation's current distribution system. What are the basic challenges in developing a distribution strategy?

2. What internal and external factors should Brooks take into consideration in deciding how he will expand his firm?

3. Should the marketing mix, other than the distribution issue (i.e., product, price, marketing communications) be modified in any way?

4. Evaluate each of the options Brooks has identified. Are there other options which might be considered?

APPENDIX A   Constant Creation Product/Price List

Product	Wholesale (65 ml)	Sugg. Retail (65ml)	Wholesale (250ml)	Sugg. Retail (250 ml)
Raspberry/Grand Marnier Sauce	$1.95	$3.95	$3.95	$ 7.95
Wild Blueberry Rum Sauce	1.50	2.75	3.25	5.95
Triple Cherry Jubilee	1.50	2.75	3.25	5.95
Peach Melba Sauce	1.50	2.75	3.25	5.95
Chocolate Kahlua Sauce	2.15	3.95	5.65	9.95
Maple Cream Coulis	2.50	4.95	7.95	11.95
Triple Sec Cranberry Sauce	1.50	2.75	3.25	5.95
Orange Sauce Supreme	1.50	2.75	3.25	5.95
Spiced Mulled Wine Mix	1.50	2.75	3.25	5.95
Mexican Summer Salsa	1.50	2.95	3.25	5.95
Szechuan Hot Sauce	1.50	2.95	3.25	5.95
Cajun Sauce With Red Wine	1.50	2.95	3.25	5.95
Indian Chutney	1.50	2.95	3.25	5.95
Caribbean Pepper Sauce	1.50	2.95	3.25	5.95
Hot Lemon Sauce	1.50	2.95	3.25	5.95
Atlantic Cocktail Sauce	1.50	2.95	3.25	5.95
Mandarin Plum Sauce	1.50	2.95	3.25	5.95
Thai Satay Sauce	1.50	2.95	3.25	5.95
Fire From Within	2.15	3.95	3.95	7.95
Madras Curry Concentrate	1.50	2.95	3.25	5.95

APPENDIX B   Specialty Food Distribution in Canada

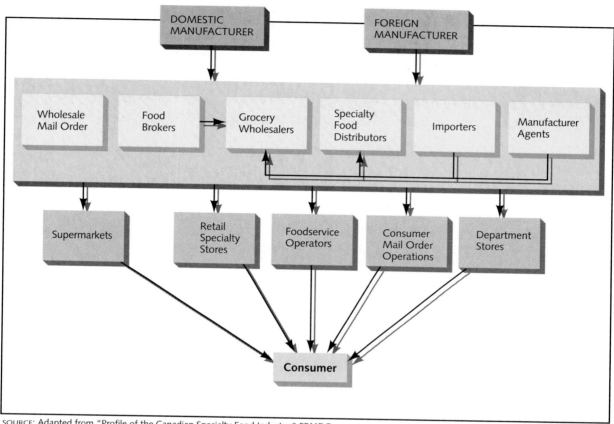

SOURCE: Adapted from "Profile of the Canadian Specialty Food Industry," FPMDC.

The Canadian and U.S. Retail Sectors: The Same or Different?*

THE IMPORTANCE OF RETAILING

Historically retail trade has been a large contributor to the economies of both Canada and the U.S. In 1994 retail sales topped $206 billion in Canada and passed $2.2 trillion in the U.S., numbers which correspond closely with the population ratio of approximately 10:1 between the two countries. Given the geographical proximity, a variety of cultural similarities, and the political push toward increased free trade between the two countries it appears that a viable way for Canadian retailers to expand operations and increase sales would be to identify and target additional consumer segments within the U.S. market.

THE QUESTION

But is this really as easy as it sounds? If we look at the statistics of cross border retail operations this strategy becomes questionable. As of the early 1990s 29 Canadian retailers had entered the U.S. market, however, only eight of these were successful (Mason, et al., 1993). As students of business we have to ask ourselves why this may be the case. Why do Canadian firms have so much trouble entering the U.S. market?

THE FACTS

To address this question it seems that the most logical place to start is with a comparison of the U.S. and Canadian retail sectors themselves. Perhaps, despite the superficial similarities we all observe between the two countries, there are subtle differences in the way business is done that impacts Canadian retailers' ability to do business in the U.S.

THE CONSUMER

Where do consumers spend their money?

Trends in personal consumption expenditures suggest that the retailing sector is getting a decreasing share of the consumer dollar. Primarily due to changes in consumer lifestyles, we

---

* This case was prepared by Shelley M. Rinehart, University of New Brunswick, Saint John, and Deborah Zizzo, University of Oklahoma. Used with permission.
Based on: Rinehart, Shelley M. & Zizzo, Deborah. (1995) "The Canadian and US Retailing Sectors: Important Changes over the Past 60 Years." *Journal of Retailing and Consumer Services,* 2(1), 33–47.

have seen a steady increase in expenditures directed toward the services sector and durable goods while expenditures on semi- and non-durable goods have grown much more slowly (see Figure 1). In fact, the services sector currently accounts for well over 50 percent of consumer expenditures in both Canada and the U.S. What does this mean for the retailing sector? This trend translates into increasingly intense competition for every retail dollar the consumer is willing to spend.

How much money do consumers spend?

Over the past 60 years personal disposable income has grown faster in Canada than in the U.S. However, despite having more money to allocate to retail purchasing, real retail sales per capita grew at 1.4 percent per year in both Canada and the U.S. and per capita expenditures were roughly equivalent for the two countries (see Figure 2). Well . . . so far so similar! Let's look at some store characteristics.

THE STORE

How many stores?

Despite the common public outcry that we are becoming "overstored," in both Canada and the U.S. the number of stores has increased only by about 1 percent per year over the past 60 years while the population for both countries has grown at slightly higher rates. In fact, for both countries the number of stores per person has actually decreased from 1930 levels (see Figure 3). Interestingly, Canada has historically serviced more people with fewer stores than has the U.S.

How big are the stores?

Categorizing by number of employees we see that "medium sized stores", those with 20–99 employees have increased their portion of total retail sales over the past 50 years, despite the fact that they account for less than 10 percent of the retail establishments in both countries. This trend is also evident when the data is categorized in terms of sales volume. In Canada, the percentage of sales accounted for by mid-range retailers increased, primarily at the expense of the very largest of stores. The trend was a little different in the U.S., where the mid-range retailers gained ground at the expense of the smaller operations.

What kind of stores are they?

Since the early 1930s scholars and business people alike have predicted that eventually "chain stores would take over the world" (Knapp, 1931; Palmer, 1931). While chain stores have certainly experienced significant growth, both in terms of store numbers and sales, over the past 60 years the changes are not quite as dramatic as expected. In both Canada and the U.S. the number of chain stores as a percentage of total stores has grown rather steadily over that time (see Figure 4). However, when we look at the percentage of total sales accounted for by chain stores we see very different patterns emerge between the two countries (see Figure 5). In Canada, as late as 1988, independent retail operations accounted for 60 percent of total retail sales. While this represents a fall from 1930 levels, the historical pattern of decline has not been either as steady or dramatic as that experienced by U.S. based independent retailers.

BACK TO THE QUESTION(S)

How do we explain the difference in success rates of cross-participating retailers?

1. What are the differences between the Canadian and U.S. retailing environment?
2. What consumer, market, economic, or environmental factors may contribute to these differences?

3. What impact are these differences likely to have on cross-participating retailers?
4. Do you think that in the future the Canadian and U.S. retailing environments will become more similar or different? Why?
5. Do you think that U.S. cross-participators will continue to enjoy 100 percent success rates as they expand their business endeavors in the Canadian market?

REFERENCES

Knapp, H. (1931). "The Coming Battle of the Chains," in Bloomfield, D. (ed.), *Selected Articles on Trends in Retail Distribution,* The Handbook Series III, Vol 3. The H. W. Wilson Company, New York, pp. 340–344.

Mason, J. B., Mayer, M., Ezell, H., Laroche, M., and MacDougall, G. (1993). *Canadian Retailing.* Richard D. Irwin, Burr Ridge, Illinois.

Palmer, J. (1931). "What About Chain Stores," in Bloomfield, D. (ed.), *Selected Articles on Trends in Retail Distribution,* The Handbook Series III, Vol 3. The H. W. Wilson Company, New York, pp. 2221–2246.

FIGURE 1 Personal consumption expenditures—Canada and U.S. in constant dollars (1947–1991).

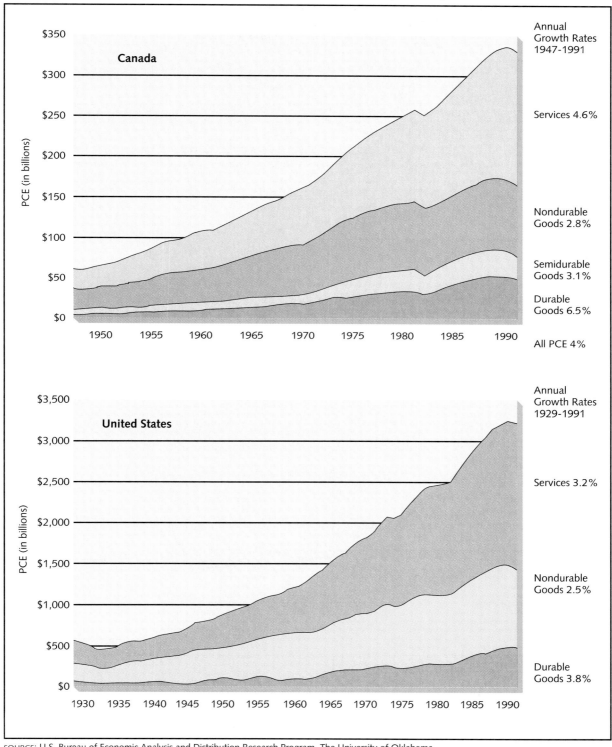

SOURCE: U.S. Bureau of Economic Analysis and Distribution Research Program, The University of Oklahoma.

FIGURE 2   Retail sales per capita—Canada and U.S. in constant dollars (1929–1991).

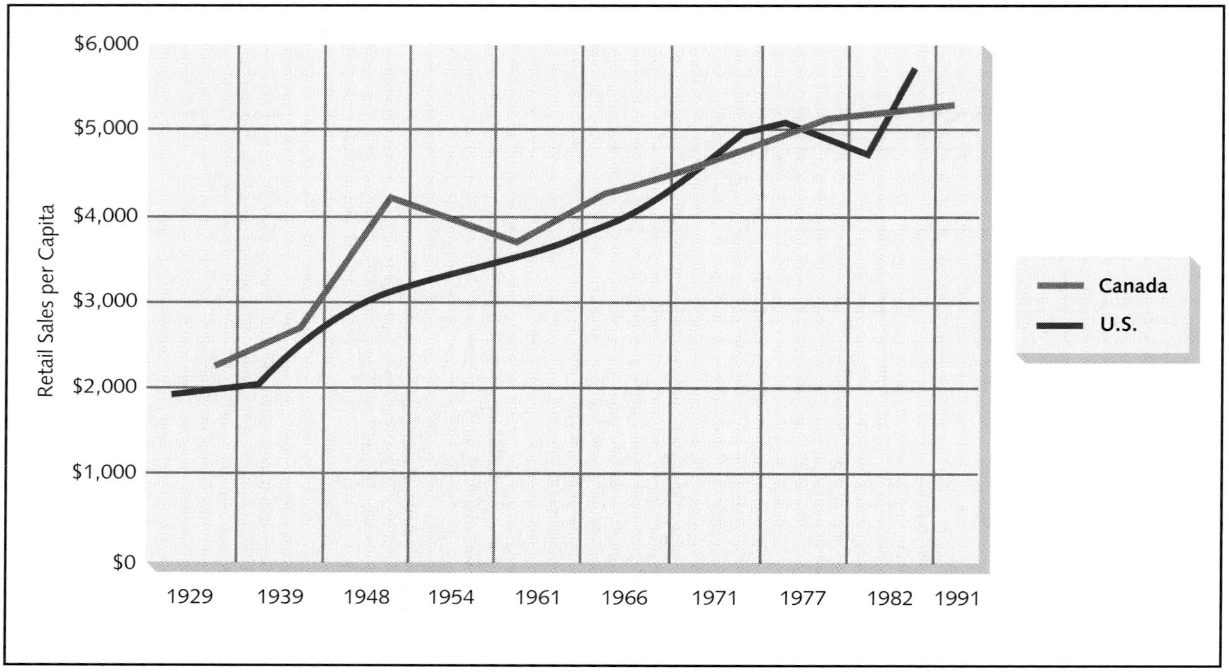

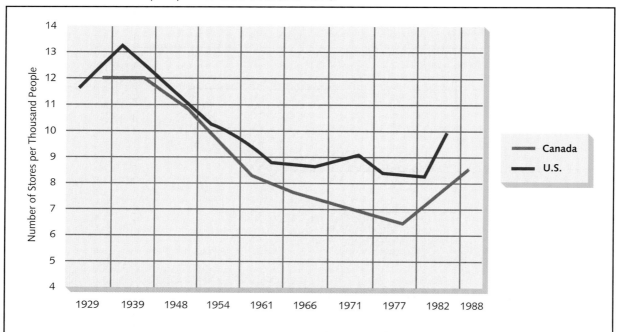

SOURCE: Statistics Canada, U.S. Bureau of Economic Analysis and Distribution Research Program, The University of Oklahoma.

FIGURE 3   Number of stores per capita—Canada and U.S. (1929–1988).

SOURCE: Statistics Canada, U.S. Bureau of Economic Analysis and Distribution Research Program, The University of Oklahoma.

FIGURE 4 Chain stores as a percent of all stores—Canada and United States

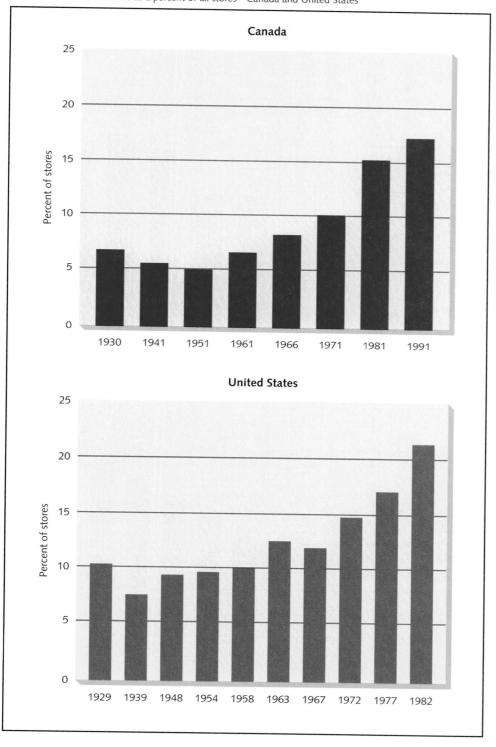

FIGURE 5 Chain store sales as a percent of all store sales—Canada and United States

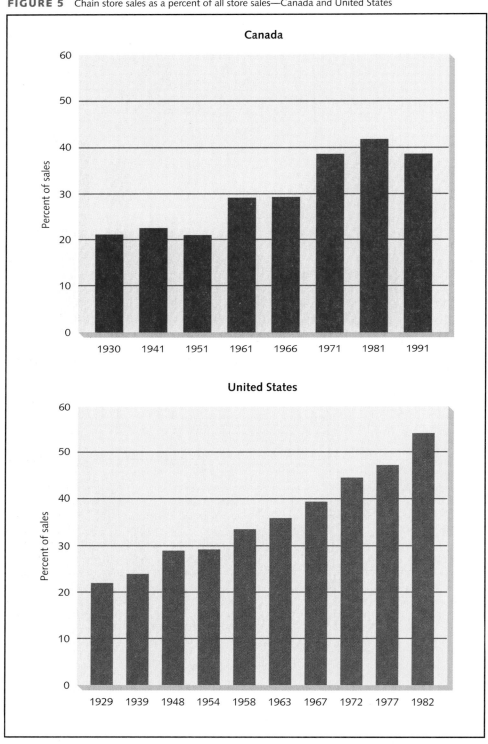

National Hockey League

The National Hockey League traces its beginnings to November 22, 1917, and as such is the second oldest league of the four major team sports in North America, with only professional baseball pre-dating it. Throughout its history, the NHL has been recognized for its ideas and innovations. For example, the NHL was the first major sports league to introduce a play-off system, one that has been adopted by all other major sports. However, historically, the NHL and many of the team owners had a negative mindset toward marketing. Marketing was actually considered unseemly. The general approach was to simply open the doors at the arenas and wait for the customers to come. But with NHL costs, particularly player salaries, on the rise, the NHL needs a bigger audience, both at the games and on television. The League now recognizes it needs to market itself. The culture at the top is now more market-driven. NHL Commissioner Gary Bettman, the former vice president of the NBA (National Basketball Association), leads the new marketing effort of the NHL.

The League is heavily involved in product licensing, while corporate involvement and sponsorship in the NHL is also a priority with the League. Several teams have built new arenas and have attracted major corporate sponsors to be associated with the new complexes (e.g., General Motors Place, home of the Vancouver Canucks, and the Molson Centre, home to the Montreal Canadiens). The NHL is also looking at the European market. ESPN, for example, is broadcasting NHL games on prime-time Swedish TV, and Europe is seen as a good market for licensing. In an effort to improve the entertainment value of the game for television viewers, the League has improved on how the games are televised, from the use of different camera angles to a computer-enhanced puck that is easier to follow.

Marketing professional hockey in the United States has become a little easier with entertainment giants Disney and Blockbuster Entertainment as the League's Anaheim and Miami franchisees. Blockbuster offers NHL merchandise in its video outlets across Canada and the U.S. Cross marketing possibilities with Disney appear endless. For example, the Mighty Ducks new arena, The Pond, is close to Disneyland, so vacation packages and other tie-ins with the theme park are certain. The NHL believes that other strong franchisees in the U.S., including Denver and Phoenix, will help sell the game to a new generation of fans and ensure its long-term prosperity. The National Hockey League hopes that with great players and great teams, consumers will support and patronize professional hockey as a wholesome form of entertainment.

QUESTIONS FOR DISCUSSION

1. What is the "product" that the National Hockey League is really marketing to prospective fans? Who is the NHL competing with in terms of fan attendance?

2. How does marketing "hockey" differ from marketing a consumer product like breakfast cereal?

3. Do some thinking or some research. Find out the basic demographic characteristics of the hockey fan. Why is it important for the NHL to know the basic profile of the hockey fan?

Glossary

above-, at-, or below-market pricing Pricing based on what the market price is.

account management policies Policies that specify whom salespeople should contact, what kinds of selling and customer service activities should be engaged in, and how these activities should be carried out.

adaptive selling A need-satisfaction sales presentation involving adjusting the presentation to fit the selling situation.

advertising Any paid form of nonpersonal communication about an organization, good, service, or idea by an identified sponsor.

advocacy advertisements Institutional advertisements that state the position of a company or an issue.

allowances and discounts A type of trade sales promotion technique used to encourage increased purchases by intermediaries.

all you can afford budgeting Allocating funds to marketing communications only after all other budget items are covered.

anchor stores Well-known national or regional stores that are located in regional shopping centres.

approach stage In the personal selling process, the initial meeting between the salesperson and the prospect, where the objectives are to gain the prospect's attention, stimulate interest, and build the foundation for the sales presentation.

attitudes Learned predispositions to respond to an object or a class of objects in a consistent manner.

average revenue The average amount of money received for selling one unit of a product.

baby boomers The generation of Canadians born between 1946 and 1964.

back translation The practice of retranslating a word or phrase into the original language by a different interpreter to catch errors.

barriers to entry Business practices or conditions that make it difficult for a new firm to enter the market.

behavioural segmentation A way of segmenting markets based on consumers' behaviour with or toward a product.

beliefs A consumer's subjective perception of how well a product or brand performs on different attributes; these are based on personal experience, advertising, and discussions with other people.

bidders list A list of firms believed to be qualified to supply a given item.

blended family Two families from prior marriages merged into a single household as spouses remarry.

brand equity The added value a given brand name provides a product beyond the product's functional benefits.

brand extension The practice of using a current brand name to enter a completely different product class.

brand loyalty A favourable attitude toward and consistent purchase of a single brand over time.

brand name Any word or device (design, shape, sound, or colour) that is used to distinguish one organization's products from a competitor's.

branding Activity in which an organization uses a name, phrase, design, or symbol, or a combination of these, to identify its products and distinguish them from those of a competitor.

breadth of product line The variety of different items a store or wholesaler carries.

break-even analysis An analysis of the relationship between total revenue and total cost to determine profitability at various levels of output.

break-even point (BEP) Output quantity at which total revenue and total cost are equal and beyond which profit occurs.

bribery The practice of giving or promising something of value in return for a corrupt act.

buildup forecast Summing the sales forecasts of each of the components to arrive at a total forecast.

business analysis Stage of the new product process in which the features of the product are specified together with the marketing strategy needed to commercialize it and the necessary financial projections are made.

business firms Privately owned organizations that serve customers in order to earn a profit.

buy classes Groups of three specific buying situations organizations face; new buy, straight rebuy, and modified rebuy.

buying centre The group of persons within an organization who participate in the buying process and share common objectives, risks, and knowledge important to that process.

buying objectives Goals set by the participants in the buying process to help them achieve their organization's objectives; for a business firm, usually to increase profits through reducing costs or increasing revenues.

capacity management Managing the demand for a service so that it is available to consumers.

category killers Specialty discount outlets that focus on one product category such as electronics or business supplies at very competitive prices.

cause-related marketing Tying the charitable contributions of a firm directly to the customer revenues produced through the marketing of one of its products.

census metropolitan areas Geographic areas with a labour market of 100,000 or more people.

central business district The oldest retail setting; the community's downtown area.

channel The means by which a message is conveyed (e.g., media).

channel captain A marketing channel member that coordinates, directs, and supports other channel members; may be a manufacturer, wholesaler, or retailer.

code of ethics An organization's formal statement of its ethical principles and rules of conduct.

cognitive dissonance The feeling of postpurchase psychological tension or anxiety about the purchase decision.

cognitive moral development People progress through three distinct phases of moral development: preconventional, conventional, and postconventional.

commercialization The final phase of the new product process, in which the product is positioned and launched into full-scale production and sales.

communication The process of establishing shared meaning; six elements—source, message, channel, receiver, and the processes of encoding and decoding—are required for communication to occur.

community shopping centre A retail location that typically has one primary store (usually a department store branch) and 20 to 40 smaller outlets, and serves a population base of about 100,000.

company forecast (see sales forecast)

comparative advertisements Advertisements that show one brand's strengths relative to those of its competitors.

competition The set of alternative organizations that could provide a product to satisfy a specific market's needs.

Competition Act Federal legislation designed to protect competition and consumers in Canada.

competitive advertisements Advertisements that demonstrate a specific brand's features and benefits.

competitive institutional advertisements Institutional advertisements that promote the advantages of one product class over another and are used in markets where different product classes compete for the same buyer.

competitive parity budgeting Matching the competitors' absolute level of communications spending or the proportion per point of market share.

concentrated marketing A market segmentation strategy where a marketer decides to seek a large share of just one segment of the total market, tailoring the elements of the marketing mix specifically to attract that segment.

conference selling A form of team selling in which a salesperson and other company resource people meet with buyers to discuss problems and opportunities.

consultative selling A need-satisfaction sales presentation in which the salesperson focuses on problem definition and serves as an expert on problem recognition and resolution.

consumer behaviour Actions of a person to purchase and use products, including the mental and social processes that precede and follow these actions.

consumer ethnocentrism The tendency to believe that it is inappropriate, indeed immoral, to purchase foreign-made products.

consumer goods Products purchased by the ultimate consumer.

consumer purchase decision process The stages a buyer passes through in making choices about which products to buy.

consumer sales promotions Sales promotions offered to ultimate consumers (e.g., coupons).

consumer socialization The process by which people acquire the skills, knowledge, and attitudes necessary to function as consumers.

consumerism A movement to increase the influence, power, and rights of consumers in dealing with institutions.

contests A sales promotion technique where consumers apply their analytical or creative thinking to try to win a prize.

continuity programs Sales promotions used to encourage and reward repeat purchases by acknowledging each purchase made by a consumer and offering a premium as purchases accumulate.

continuous innovation Introduction of new products that require no new learning to use.

contracting A strategy used during the decline stage of the product life cycle in which a company contracts the manufacturing or marketing of a product to another firm.

convenience goods Items that the consumer purchases frequently and with a minimum of shopping effort.

cooperative advertising Advertising programs in which a manufacturer pays a percentage of the retailer's local advertising expense for advertising the manufacturer's products.

corporate chain A type of retail ownership in which a single firm owns multiple outlets.

cost of goods sold Total cost of the products sold during a specified time period.

cost per thousand (CPM) The cost of reaching 1,000 individuals or households with an advertising message in a given medium. (M is the Roman numeral for 1,000).

cost-plus pricing A method of pricing that merely adds an amount—a markup—to all costs.

countertrade Using barter rather than money in making global or international marketing.

coupons Typically, printed certificates giving the bearer a saving or a stated price reduction when they purchase a specific product.

cross-cultural analysis The study of similarities and differences between consumers in two or more nations or societies.

cue A stimulus or symbol perceived by the consumer.

cultural ethnocentricity The belief that aspects of one's culture are superior to another's.

cultural symbols Things that represent ideas and concepts to a society or nationality.

culture The set of values, ideas, and attitudes of a homogeneous group of people that are transmitted from one generation to the next.

customary pricing A method of pricing based on a product's tradition, standardized channel of distribution, or other competitive factors.

customer service The ability of a logistics system to satisfy users in terms of time, dependability, communications, and convenience.

customer value The combination of benefits received by customers that includes quality, price, convenience, on-time delivery, and both before-sale and after-sale service.

customized marketing mix The use of a different marketing mix by an organization when entering foreign markets.

customs Norms and expectations about the way people do things in a specific country.

data The facts and figures pertinent to a problem, composed of primary and secondary data.

database marketing An organization's effort to collect demographic, media, and consumption profiles of customers in order to target them more effectively.

deal A sales promotion that offers a short-term price reduction.

deceptive pricing A practice by which prices are artificially inflated and then marked down under the guise of a sale; illegal under the Competition Act.

decline stage The fourth and last stage of the product life cycle, when sales and profitability decline.

decoding The process by which the receiver deciphers or interprets the message sent by the source or message sender.

delayed-response advertising Advertising intended to influence the consumer in the near future, rather than right away, in making purchases or taking other actions.

deletion A strategy of dropping a product from the product line, usually in the decline stage of the product life cycle.

delivered pricing The practice of refusing a customer delivery of an article on the same trade terms as other customers in the same location.

demand curve The summation of points representing the maximum quantity of a product consumers will buy at different price levels.

demographics The study of the characteristics of a human population including size of population, growth rate, geographical distribution, age, gender, marital status, education, ethnicity, income, and so forth.

demographic segmentation A way to segment consumer markets based on population characteristics such as age, gender, income, and so forth.

depth interviews Detailed individual interviews with people relative to a research project.

depth of product line The assortment of each item a store or wholesaler carries.

derived demand Sales of a product (typically industrial) that result from the sales of another item (often consumer).

desk jobber (see drop shipper).

development Phase of the new product process in which the idea on paper is turned into a prototype; includes manufacturing and laboratory and consumer tests.

differentiated marketing A market segmentation strategy whereby a marketer will target more than one segment and design separate marketing mixes for each.

differentiation positioning Positioning that avoids direct competition by stressing unique aspects of the product.

diffusion of innovation The process by which people receive new information and accept new ideas and products.

direct channel A marketing channel in which a producer and an ultimate consumer interact directly with each other.

direct mail Any form of communication addressed to customers or prospects and delivered through public or private delivery services.

direct marketing communications (DMC) Communicating directly with target customers to encourage an immediate response by telephone, mail, electronic means, or personal visit; methods include direct mail, direct-response advertising, and telemarketing.

direct ownership A domestic firm's actually investing in and owning a foreign subsidiary or division.

direct-response advertising Advertising that seeks to motivate consumers to take immediate action, such as a TV ad asking consumers to call a telephone number to place an order.

direct-response print advertising A form of direct marketing communications using newspapers and magazines designed to obtain direct response from readers.

direct-response radio advertising A form of direct marketing communications that allows the marketer to obtain immediate feedback from consumers through the use of radio.

direct-response television advertising A form of direct marketing communications where the television advertiser seeks to motivate the customer to take immediate action (e.g., direct-response ads, infomercials, and home shopping channels).

discontinuous innovation Introduction of new products that require totally new consumption patterns.

discounts Reductions from list price that a seller gives a buyer as a reward for some buyer activity favourable to the seller.

discretionary income The money that remains after taxes and necessities have been paid for.

disposable income The money a consumer has left after taxes to use for necessities such as food, shelter, and clothing.

distinctive competencies An organization's unique resources and special skills that form the basis for the organization's sustainable competitive advantage.

diversification A strategy that requires an organization to expand into new products and new markets.

drive A need that moves an individual to action.

dual distribution An arrangement in which a firm reaches buyers by employing two or more different types of channels for the same basic product.

dumping A firm's selling a product in a foreign country below its domestic price.

durable good An item that lasts over an extended number of uses.

dynamically continuous innovation Introduction of new products that disrupt the consumer's normal routine but do not require learning totally new behaviours.

early adopters The 13.5 percent of the population who are leaders in their social setting and act as an information source on new products for other people.

early majority The 34 percent of the population who are deliberate and rely on personal sources for information on new products.

economic infrastructure A country's communication, transportation, financial, and distribution systems.

economy The income, expenditures, and resources that affect the cost of running an organization or a household.

80/20 rule The principle that 80 percent of an organization's sales are generated by 20 percent of its customers.

elastic demand A situation where a percentage decrease in price produces a larger percentage increase in quantity demanded, thereby actually increasing sales revenue.

electronic data interchange (EDI) An interactive computer network that connects manufacturers with suppliers, distributors, and retailers so that they can share information.

encoding The process of selecting words, pictures, and other symbols in order to transmit the intended message.

environmental scanning The process by which market-driven organizations continually acquire information on events outside their organizations in order to identify and interpret potential trends that can impact on their business.

ethics The moral principles and values that govern the actions and decisions of an individual or a group.

ethical climate An aspect of organizational culture that describes the decision processes used to determine whether dilemmas are ethical or unethical.

euro-branding The strategy of using the same brand name for the same product across all countries in the European Community.

evaluative criteria Both the objective and subjective attributes of a brand important to consumers when evaluating different brands or products.

evoked set The group of brands a consumer would consider acceptable out of the set of brands in the product class of which she is aware.

exchange The trade of things of value between a buyer and a seller so that each is better off than before.

exclusive distribution A distribution strategy whereby a producer sells its products or services in only one retail outlet in a specific geographical area.

expense-to-sales ratio A form of ratio analysis in which the specific costs or expenses for a sales representative are expressed as a percentage of sales revenue.

experience curve pricing A method of pricing in which price often falls following the reduction of costs associated with the firm's experience in producing or selling a product.

experiment Obtaining data by manipulating factors under tightly controlled conditions to test for cause and effect.

exporting Producing goods in one country and selling them in another country.

failure fee A penalty payment made to a retailer by a manufacturer if a new product does not reach predetermined sales levels.

family branding (see multiproduct branding).

family life cycle The concept that each family progresses through a number of distinct phases, each of which is associated with identifiable purchasing behaviours.

feedback The communication flow from receiver back to sender; indicates whether the message was decoded and understood as intended.

field of experience A person's understanding and knowledge; to communicate effectively, a sender and a receiver must have a shared field of experience.

FOB (free on board) Designation for the point on the transportation route at which the seller stops paying transportation costs.

FOB origin pricing A method of pricing in which the title to goods passes to the buyer at the point of loading.

focus group An informal session of 6 to 10 current or potential users of a product in which a discussion leader seeks their opinions on the firm's or a competitor's products.

follow-up stage The phase of the personal selling process that entails making certain that the customer's purchase has been properly delivered and installed and that any difficulties in using the product are promptly and satisfactorily addressed.

form of ownership Who owns a retail outlet. Alternatives are independent, corporate chain, cooperative, or franchise.

formula selling presentation The selling format that consists of providing information in an accurate, thorough, and step-by-step manner to persuade the prospect to buy.

four I's of services Four unique elements to services; intangibility, inconsistency, inseparability, and inventory.

franchising A contractual agreement with a parent company that allows an individual or a firm (the franchisee) to operate a certain type of business under an established name and according to specific rules.

frequency The average number of times a person in the target audience is exposed to a message or advertisement.

gap analysis An evaluation tool that compares expectations about a particular service with the actual experience a consumer has with the service.

General Agreement on Tariffs and Trade (GATT) An international treaty intended to liberalize global trade.

generation X The label given to Canadians aged 20–29.

generic brand A branding strategy that lists no product name, only a description of contents.

global brand Using the same brand name and positioning for a product in all markets worldwide.

global corporation A business firm that looks at the entire world as one market and conducts research and development, manufacturing, financing, and marketing activities wherever they can best be done.

global industry One in which the competitive positions of organizations in given local or national markets are affected by their overall global positions; also known as a *global market.*

green marketing Marketing efforts to produce, market, and reclaim ecologically or environmentally sensitive products.

gross domestic product The monetary value of all goods and services produced in a country during one year.

gross income The total amount of money earned in one year by a person, household, or family unit.

gross margin Net sales minus cost of goods sold.

gross rating points (GRPs) A reference number for advertisers, created by multiplying reach by frequency.

growth stage The second stage of the product life cycle, characterized by rapid increases in sales and by the appearance of competitors.

harvesting A strategy used during the decline stage of the product life cycle in which a company continues to offer a product but reduces support costs.

head-to-head positioning Competing directly with competitors on similar product attributes in the same target market.

hierarchy of effects The sequence of stages a prospective buyer goes through from initial awareness of a product to eventual action (either trial or adoption of the product). The stages include awareness, interest, evaluation, trial, and adoption.

horizontal conflict Disagreements between intermediaries at the same level in a marketing channel.

hypermarket A large store (over 200,000 square feet) offering a mix of food products and general merchandise.

idea generation A phase of the new product process in which a firm develops a pool of concepts as candidates for new products.

idea marketing The marketing of a cause or idea to a given target market; *sometimes called social marketing.*

idle production capacity A situation where a service provider is available but there is no demand.

inconsistency A unique element of services: variation in service quality because services are delivered by people with varying capabilities.

indirect channel A marketing channel in which intermediaries are situated between the producer and consumers.

industrial firm An organizational buyer that in some way reprocesses a good or service it buys before selling it again.

industrial goods Products used in the production of other products for ultimate consumers.

inelastic demand A situation where a small percentage decrease in price produces a smaller percentage increase in quantity demanded.

infomercial Program-length advertisement, often 30 minutes long, that seeks to prompt an immediate response from the consumer.

innovators The 2.5 percent of the population who are venturesome and highly educated, use multiple information sources, and are the first to adopt a new product.

inseparability A unique element of services: the fact that a service cannot be separated from the deliverer of the service or the setting in which the service occurs.

institutional advertisement Advertisements designed to build goodwill or an image for an organization, rather than market a specific good or service.

intangibility A unique element of services: the fact that services cannot be held, touched, or seen before the purchase decision.

integrated marketing communications (IMC) The integrated and coordinated use of all forms of communications reaching the target audience so that consistency in the message is achieved and communications resources are maximized.

intensive distribution A distribution strategy whereby a producer sells goods or services in as many outlets as possible in a geographic area.

internal marketing The notion that in order for a service organization to serve its customers well, it must care for and treat its employees like valued customers; focusing efforts on its internal market (employees) before successful marketing plans can be directed at customers.

international marketing Marketing across national boundaries.

intertype competition Competition between dissimilar types of retail outlets brought about by scrambled merchandising.

introduction phase The first stage of the product life cycle, in which sales grow slowly and profit is low.

inventory (1) Physical material purchased from suppliers, which may or may not be reworked and is available for sale to customers. (2) A unique element of services: the need for and cost of having a service provider available.

involvement The personal, social, and economic significance of a purchase to a consumer.

job analysis A written description of what a salesperson is expected to do.

joint venture An arrangement in which a foreign company and a local firm invest together to create a local business.

just-in-time (JIT) An inventory control system that maintains very low inventory levels because stock is constantly being ordered and delivered as it is being sold.

laggards The 16 percent of the market who have fear of debt, use friends for information sources, and accept ideas and products only after they have been long established in the market.

late majority The 34 percent of the population who are skeptical, are below average in social status, and rely less on advertising and personal selling for information than do innovators or early adopters.

laws Society's values and standards that are enforceable in the courts

lead time Lag from ordering an item until it is received and ready for use.

learning Those behaviours that result from (1) repeated experience and (2) thinking.

level of service The degree of service provided to the customer by the retailer: self, limited, or full.

licensing A contractual agreement whereby a company allows another firm to use its brand name, patent, trade secret, or other property for a royalty or fee.

lifestyle People's mode of living, identified by how they spend their time and resources (activities), what they consider important in their environment (interests), and what they think of themselves and the world around them (opinions).

logistics management Organizing the cost-effective flow of raw materials, in-process inventory, finished goods, and related information from point of origin to point of consumption to satisfy customer requirements.

loss-leader pricing Deliberately pricing a product below its customary price to attract attention to it.

macromarketing The aggregate flow of a nation's goods and services to benefit society.

maintained markup The difference between the final selling price and retailer cost; also called *gross margin*.

major account management The practice of using team selling to focus on important customers to build mutually beneficial, long-term, cooperative relationships.

make–buy decision An evaluation of whether a product or its parts will be purchased from outside suppliers or built by the firm.

manufacturer branding A branding strategy in which the brand name for a product is designated by the producer, using either a multiproduct or a multibranding approach.

marginal analysis Study of allocating resources in order to balance incremental revenues of an action against incremental costs.

marginal revenue The change in total revenue obtained by selling one additional unit.

markdown Reduction in retail price usually expressed as a percentage, equal to the amount reduced divided by the original price and multiplied by 100.

market People with the desire and ability to buy a specific product.

market development A strategy of marketing existing products to new markets.

market-driven organization An organization in which customer needs are paramount and form the basis upon which the organization is built; an organization that seeks to discover and satisfy customer needs with a totally integrated organizational effort.

market modifications Attempts to increase product usage by creating new use situations, finding new customers, or altering the marketing mix.

market penetration A strategy that represents an organization's decision to pursue growth with existing products within existing markets.

market potential Maximum total sales of a product by all firms to a segment under specified environmental conditions and marketing efforts of the firms (also called *industry potential*).

market segmentation Aggregating prospective buyers into groups, or segments, that (1) have common needs and (2) will respond similarly to a specific marketing offer.

market segments The groups that result from the process of market segmentation; a relatively homogeneous collection of prospective buyers.

market share The ratio of sales revenue of a firm to the total sales revenue of all firms in the industry, including the firm itself.

market testing A phase of the new product process in which prospective consumers are exposed to actual products under realistic or simulated purchase conditions to see if they will buy.

marketing The process of planning and executing the conception, pricing, communications, and distribution of products to create exchanges that satisfy individual and organizational objectives.

marketing audit A comprehensive, unbiased, periodic review of an organization's marketing management efforts designed to identify new problems and opportunities that warrant a plan of action to improve performance.

marketing channel People and firms involved in the process of making a good or service available for use or consumption by consumers or industrial users.

marketing communications Marketer-initiated communications directed to target audiences in order to influence attitudes and behaviour.

marketing communications mix The combination of the communications techniques or categories an organization chooses to use to communicate to its target audiences; could consist of advertising, public relations, sales promotion, direct marketing communications, and personal selling.

marketing environment Social, economic, technological, competitive, and regulatory forces, at home and abroad, that shape the organization's marketing process.

marketing management The process of planning, implementing, and controlling the organization's marketing effort.

marketing mix The offer designed to appeal to the target market; consists of product, price, marketing communications, and distribution elements.

marketing plan The written plan of action developed as a result of the marketing planning process.

marketing research The process of defining a marketing problem and opportunity, systematically collecting and analyzing information, and recommending actions to improve an organization's marketing activities.

marketing strategy Selecting a target market and developing a marketing mix to satisfy that market's need and achieve the organization's marketing objectives; outlines the target markets sought, intended positioning, and specific details of the marketing mix.

marketing tactics The detailed day-to-day operational decisions essential to the overall success of a marketing strategy.

markup The amount added to the cost of goods sold to arrive at a selling price, expressed in dollar or percentage terms.

mature market Market consisting of people over age 50.

maturity phase The third stage of the product or retail life cycle, in which market share levels off and profitability declines.

merchandise line The number of different types of products and the assortment a store carries, distinguished by breadth and depth.

message The information sent by a source to a receiver in the communications process.

method of operation How and where a retailer provides services; the alternative approaches are an in-store or a nonstore format (mail, vending, computer-assisted, or teleshopping).

micromarketing How an individual organization directs its marketing activities and allocates its resources to benefit its customers.

mission An organization's defined purpose.

mission statement A statement that defines the organization's purpose—what it wants to accomplish; defines what type of customer it wishes to serve, the specific needs of customers, and the means or technology by which it will serve these needs; clarifies the nature of existing products, markets, and functions the organization presently provides.

missionary salespeople Sales support personnel who do not directly solicit orders but rather concentrate on performing promotional activities and introducing new products.

mixed branding A branding strategy in which the company may market products under its own name and that of a reseller.

modified rebuy An organizational buying situation in which the users, influencers, or deciders seek to change the product specifications, price, delivery schedule, or supplier.

motivation The energizing force that causes behaviour that satisfies a need.

multibranding A manufacturer's branding strategy in which a distinct name is given to each of its products.

multiple-zone pricing Pricing products the same when delivered within one of several specified zones or geographical areas, but with different prices for each zone depending on demand, competition, and distance; also called *zone-delivered pricing*.

multiproduct branding A branding strategy in which a company uses one name for all products; also called *blanket* or *family branding*.

need-satisfaction presentation A selling format that emphasizes probing and listening by the salesperson to identify needs and interests of prospective buyers.

new buy An organization's first-time purchase of a good or service, characterized by greater potential risk.

new product process The sequence of activities a firm uses to identify market opportunities and convert them to a salable good or service. There are seven steps: new product strategy, idea generation, screening and evaluation, business analysis, development, testing, and commercialization.

new product strategy development The phase of the new product process in which a firm defines the role of new products in terms of overall growth objectives.

noise Any distraction or distortion during the communications process that prevents the message from being effectively communicated.

nonprofit organizations Organizations that operate without the intent of earning profit.

North American Free Trade Agreement (NAFTA) An agreement signed by Mexico, the United States, and Canada to lift many trade barriers.

North American Industry Classification System (NAICS) A system that provides common industry definitions to facilitate the measurement of economic activity in the three member countries of NAFTA.

objective and task budgeting A budgeting approach whereby the company (1) determines its market's communications objectives, (2) outlines the tasks to accomplish these objectives, and (3) determines the communications cost of performing these tasks.

objectives Specific measurable goals an organization seeks to achieve and by which it can measure its performance.

observation Watching, either in person or by mechanical means, how people actually behave.

odd–even pricing Setting prices a few dollars or cents under an even number, such as $19.95.

off-peak pricing Charging different prices during different times of the day or days of the week to reflect variations in demand for the service.

off-price retailing Selling brand-name merchandise at lower than regular prices.

opinion leaders Individuals who exert direct or indirect social influence over others.

order cycle time (see lead time)

order getter A salesperson who sells in a conventional sense and engages in identifying prospective customers, providing customers with information, persuading customers to buy, closing sales, and following on customer experience with the good or service.

order taker A salesperson who processes routine orders and reorders for products that have already been sold by the company.

organization marketing Organization marketing involves the use of marketing activities in order to attract members, donors, participants, and volunteers to a particular organization.

organizational buyers Units such as industrial firms, wholesalers, retailers, or other entities that buy goods and services for their own use or for resale.

organizational buying behaviour The decision-making process that organizations use to establish the need for products and identify, evaluate, and choose among alternative brands and suppliers.

organizational buying criteria The factors on which buying organizations evaluate a potential supplier and what it wants to sell—the objective attributes of the supplier's products and services and the capabilities of the supplier itself.

organizational culture The shared values, beliefs, and purpose of employees that affect individual and group behaviour.

organizational marketing The marketing of goods and services to profit and nonprofit organizations for use in the creation of goods and services that they then produce and market to other organizational customers as well as ultimate consumers.

original markup The difference between retailer cost and initial selling price.

outsourcing Contracting work that formerly was done in-house by employees—such as those in marketing research, advertising, and public relations departments—to small, outside firms.

packaging The container in which a product is offered for sale and on which information is communicated.

parallel development An approach to new product development that involves the simultaneous development of the product and production process.

penetration pricing Pricing a product low in order to discourage competition from entering the market.

perceived risk The anxieties felt by the consumer because he cannot anticipate the outcome of making a purchase but sees that there might be negative consequences.

percent of sales budgeting Allocating funds to marketing communications as a percentage of past or anticipated sales, in terms of either dollars or units sold.

perception The process by which an individual selects, organizes, and interprets information to create a meaningful picture of the world.

perceptual map A graph displaying consumers' perceptions of product attributes across two or more dimensions.

person marketing The use of marketing activities designed to influence the target market's attitudes and behaviour toward a person.

personal selling The two-way flow of communications between a buyer and a seller, often in a face-to-face encounter, designed to influence a person's or a group's purchase decision.

personal selling process Sales activities occurring before, during, and after the sale itself, consisting of six stages:

(1) prospecting, (2) preapproach, (3) approach, (4) presentation, (5) close, and (6) follow-up.

personality A person's consistent behaviours or responses to recurring situations.

physical distribution management Organizing the movement and storage of a finished product until it reaches the customer.

pioneering advertisements Advertisements that tell what a product is, what it can do, and where it can be found.

pioneering institutional advertisements Institutional advertisements about what a company is or can do or where it is located.

place marketing The use of marketing activities designed to influence the target market's attitudes and behaviour toward a place.

point-of-purchase displays Displays located in high-traffic areas in retail stores, often next to checkout counters.

product Anything that is offered to a market for acquisition, use, or consumption and satisfies an individual or organizational need (includes goods, services, ideas, places, and people).

product-driven organization An organization whose central concern is making and creating products; an organization that believes a good product will create its own demand.

psychographic segmentation A way of segmenting markets according to personality or lifestyle.

public relations Communications activities designed to influence the perceptions, opinions, and beliefs about an organization among its relevant publics including customers, employees, shareholders, government, and the general public.

posttests Tests conducted after an advertisement has been shown to the target audience to determine whether it has accomplished its intended purpose.

power centre A large strip mall with multiple anchor (or national) stores, a convenient location, and often a supermarket.

preapproach stage The stage of the personal selling process that involves obtaining further information about a prospect and deciding on the best method of approach.

predatory pricing Selling products at a low price to injure or eliminate a competitor.

premium A sales promotion that consists of offering merchandise free or at significant savings over retail.

prestige pricing Setting a high price so that status-conscious consumers will be attracted to the product.

pretests Tests conducted before an advertisement is placed to determine whether it communicates the intended message or to select between alternative versions of the advertisement.

price The money or other consideration exchanged for the purchase or use of a good, an idea, or a service.

price elasticity of demand The percentage change in quantity demanded relative to a percentage change in price.

price lining Setting the price of a line of products at a number of different specific pricing points.

pricing constraints Factors that limit a firm's attitude in the price it may set.

pricing objectives Goals relating to the role of price in an organization's marketing and strategic plans.

primary data Facts and figures that are newly collected for a research project.

private branding Selling of products under the name of a wholesaler or retailer rather than under the manufacturer's name.

product advertisements Advertisements that focus on selling a good or service and take three forms: (1) pioneering (or informational), (2) competitive (or persuasive), and (3) reminder.

product cannibalism A firm's new product gaining sales by stealing them from its other products.

product class An entire product category or industry.

product development A strategy of developing new products in existing markets.

product form Variations of a product within a product class.

product life cycle The life of a product over four stages: introduction, growth, maturity, and decline.

product line A group of products closely related because they satisfy a class of needs, are used together, are sold to the same customer group, are distributed through the same outlets, or fall within a given price range.

product mix The number and variety of product lines offered by a company.

product modifications Strategies of altering a product characteristic, such as quality, performance, or appearance.

product positioning The place a product occupies in a consumer's mind relative to competitors.

production goods Products used in the manufacturing of other items that become part of the final product.

profit A business firm's reward for the risk it undertakes in offering a product for sale; the money left over after a firm's total expenses are subtracted from its total revenues.

profit responsibility The view that companies have a single obligation, which is to maximize profits for owners or stockholders.

profitability analysis Measuring the profitability of a firm's products, customer groups, sales territories, channels of distribution, and order sizes.

prospecting stage In the personal selling process, the search for and qualification of potential customers.

protocol In the new product development process, an early statement that identifies a well-defined target market; specifies customers' needs, wants, and preferences; and states what the product will be and do.

publicity The creation and dissemination of information about a company or product in order to obtain favourable media coverage.

pull strategy Directing the marketing communications mix to ultimate consumers to encourage them to ask the intermediaries for the product.

push strategy Directing the marketing communications mix to channel members or intermediaries to gain their cooperation in ordering and stocking a product.

qualitative research A form of research that does not allow making statistical inferences or quantitative statements but is useful for hypothesis generation for quantitative research.

quality The features and characteristics of a product that bear on its ability to satisfy customers' needs.

quantitative research Research based on numerical scores or measurements that can be used to draw conclusions about a population through statistical inference.

rating (TV or radio) The percentage of households in a market that are tuned to a particular TV show or radio station.

reach The number of different people exposed to an advertisement.

reactive strategies New product strategies that result in new product development as a defensive response to competitors' new items.

rebate A sales promotion in which money is returned to the consumer based on proof of pruchase.

receivers People—such as consumers—who read, hear, or see a message sent by a source in the communication process.

reciprocity An industrial buying practice in which two organizations agree to purchase products from each other.

reference group People to whom a person looks as a basis for self-appraisal or source of personal standards.

regional shopping centres Suburban malls with up to 100 stores that typically draw customers from a 5- to 10-mile radius, usually containing one or two anchor stores.

regulation The federal and provincial laws placed on a business with regard to the conduct of its activities.

relationship marketing An organization's effort to develop a long-term cost-effective link with individual customers for mutual benefit.

relationship selling The practice of building ties to customers based on a salesperson's attention and commitment to customer needs over time.

reliability The ability of research results to be replicated under identical environmental conditions.

reminder advertisements Advertisements used to reinforce previous knowledge of a product.

replenishment time (see lead time)

repositioning Changing the place a product occupies in a consumer's mind relative to competitive offerings.

reseller A wholesaler or retailer that buys physical products and resells them again without any processing.

retail life cycle A concept that describes a retail operation over four stages: early growth, accelerated development, maturity, and decline.

retail positioning matrix A framework for positioning retail outlets in terms of breadth of product line and value added.

retailing All the activities that are involved in selling, renting, and providing goods and services to ultimate consumers for personal, family, or household use.

retailing mix The strategic components that a retailer manages, including goods and services, physical distribution, and communications tactics.

return on investment (ROI) The ratio of after-tax net profit to the investment used to earn that profit.

reverse marketing The effort by organizational buyers to build relationships that shape suppliers' products, services, and capabilities to fit a buyer's needs and those of its customers.

sales-driven organization An organization that emphasizes the role of the sales force to find consumers for products that they produce best, given their existing resources; an organization that believes any product can be sold if enough selling effort is used.

sales engineer A salesperson who specializes in identifying, analyzing, and solving customer problems and who brings technological expertise to the selling situations, but often does not actually sell goods and services.

sales forecast What one firm expects to sell under specified conditions for the uncontrollable and controllable factors that affect sales.

sales management Planning, implementing, and controlling the personal selling effort of the firm.

sales plan A statement describing what salespeople are to achieve and where and how their selling effort is to be deployed.

sales promotion A short-term inducement of value offered to arouse interest in buying a good or service.

sampling (marketing research) Selecting representative elements from the chosen population under investigation.

sampling (sales promotion) A sales promotion technique whereby a consumer is offered a product free or at a greatly reduced price.

scrambled merchandising Offering several unrelated product lines in a single retail store.

screening and evaluation The phase of the new product process in which a firm uses internal and external evaluations to eliminate ideas that warrant no further development effort.

sealed-bid pricing A method of pricing whereby prospective firms submit price bids for a contract to the buying agency at a specific time and place, with the contract awarded to the qualified bidder with the lowest price.

secondary data Facts and figures that have already been recorded before the start of the research project at hand.

selective distribution A distribution strategy whereby a producer sells its products in a few retail outlets in a specific geographical area.

self-regulation An industry's policing itself rather than relying on government controls.

seminar selling A form of team selling in which a company team conducts an educational program for a customer's technical staff, describing state-of-the-art developments.

semiotics The field of study that examines the correspondence between symbols and their role in the assignment of meaning for people.

service continuum A range from the tangible to the intangible or good-dominant to service-dominant offerings available in the marketplace.

services Activities, deeds, or other basic intangibles offered for sale to consumers in exchange for money or something else of value.

shelf life The time a product can be stored before it spoils.

shopping goods Products for which the consumer will compare several alternatives on various criteria.

shrinkage A term used by retailers to describe theft of merchandise by customers and employees.

situational influences Temporary conditions or settings that occur at the time and place of a particular purchase that can affect the decision process; they are not part of the product nor part of the inherent characteristics of the consumer.

skimming pricing A high initial price attached to a product to help a company recover the cost of development.

slotting fee Payment by a manufacturer to place a new product on a retailer's shelf.

social audit A systematic assessment of a firm's objectives, strategies, and performance in the domain of social responsibility.

social classes The relatively permanent and homogeneous divisions in a society of people or families sharing similar values, lifestyles, interests, and behaviour.

social forces The characteristics of the population, its values, and its behaviour.

social responsibility The idea that organizations are part of a larger society and are accountable to society for their actions.

specialty goods Products that a consumer will make a special effort to search out and buy.

standardized marketing mix The use of the same marketing mix by an organization when entering foreign markets.

statistical inference Drawing conclusions about a population from a sample taken from that population.

stimulus–response presentation A selling format that assumes the prospect will buy if given the appropriate stimulus by a salesperson.

straight commission compensation plan A compensation plan in which salespeople's earnings are directly tied to their sales or profit generated.

straight rebuy An organization's reordering of an existing good or service from the list of acceptable suppliers, generally without checking with the various users or influencers.

straight salary compensation plan A compensation plan where the salesperson is paid a fixed amount per week, month, or year.

strategic alliances Agreements between two or more independent firms to cooperate for the purpose of achieving common objectives.

strategic channel alliances A practice whereby one firm's marketing channel is used to sell another firm's products.

strategic planning The process by which an organization examines its capabilities and the changing marketing environment in order to identify its mission, objectives, and strategies for growth.

strip location A cluster of stores that serves people who live within a 5- to 10-minute drive in a population base of under 30,000.

subcultures Subgroups within the larger, national culture with unique values, ideas, and attitudes.

subliminal perception Seeing or hearing messages without being aware of them.

support goods Items used to assist in the production of other goods and services.

surveys A method used to generate primary data by asking consumers questions and recording their responses.

sustainable competitive advantage A strength, relative to competitors, to be used in the markets the organization serves or the products it offers.

sweepstakes A sales promotion technique that requires participants to submit some kind of entry form but are purely games of chance requiring no analytical or creative effort by the consumer.

SWOT An acronym that refers to a simple, effective technique an organization can use to appraise its internal strengths and weaknesses and external opportunities and threats.

target market One or more specific groups of consumers toward which an organization directs its marketing efforts.

target profit pricing A method of pricing that begins with a specific profit objective and then determines a product's prices based on the expected number of units to be sold.

team selling Using a group of professionals in selling to and servicing major customers.

technology An environmental force that refers to inventions or innovations from applied science or engineering research.

telemarketing An interactive form of direct marketing communications that uses the telephone to initiate, develop, and enhance relationships with customers.

test marketing The process of offering a product for sale on a limited basis in a defined area to gain consumer reaction to the actual product and to examine its commercial viability and the marketing program.

tied selling A seller's requirement that the purchaser of one product also buy another product in the line.

time poverty Condition resulting from the growth in dual-income families as the number of tasks to do expands while the time to do them shrinks.

top-down forecast Subdividing an aggregate forecast into its principal components.

total logistics cost All expenses associated with transportation, materials handling and warehousing, inventory, stockouts, and order processing.

total revenue The total amount of money received from the sale of a product.

trade feedback effect The effect of a country's imports on its exports and of its exports on its imports.

trade name The commercial name under which a company does business.

trademark Legal identification of a company's exclusive rights to use a brand name or trade name.

trade sales promotions Sales promotions directed to intermediaries (e.g., allowances and discounts).

trend extrapolation Extending a pattern observed in past data into the future.

ultimate consumers People who use the goods and services purchased for a household.

undifferentiated marketing A market segmentation strategy where a marketer decides not to distinguish between any segments and goes after the market as a whole using one marketing mix (also known as *mass marketing*).

uniform delivered pricing A geographical pricing practice in which the price the seller quotes includes all transportation costs.

unitary demand elasticity A situation where the percentage change in price is identical to the percentage change in quantity demanded.

unsought goods Products that the consumer does not know about or knows about and does not initially want.

usage rate Quantity of a product consumed or amount of patronage during a specific time period; a measure that varies significantly among different customer groups.

Valdez Principles Guidelines that encourage firms to focus attention on environmental concerns and corporate responsibility.

validity The degree to which research has actually measured what it was intended to measure.

value Specifically, the ratio of perceived quality to price (value = perceived benefits/price).

value analysis A systematic appraisal of the design, quality, and performance requirements of an industrial purchase to reduce purchasing costs.

value consciousness Consumer concern for obtaining the best quality, features, and performance for a given price of a product or service.

value-based pricing A method of pricing that involves increasing perceived product or service benefits while maintaining or decreasing prices or simply lowering prices on standard items consumers buy with regularity.

values Personally or socially preferable modes of conduct or states of existence that are enduring.

vertical conflict Disagreement between different levels in a marketing channel.

vertical marketing systems Professionally managed and centrally coordinated marketing channels designed to achieve channel economies and maximum marketing impact.

warehouse A location, often decentralized, that a firm uses to store, consolidate, age, or mix stock; to house product-recall programs; or to ease tax burdens.

warranty A statement indicating the liability of the manufacturer for product deficiencies.

word of mouth The influence people have on each other through face-to-face conversations.

youth market The market consisting of consumers aged 10–19.

Endnotes

CHAPTER 1

1. Regis McKenna, "Marketing is Everything," *Harvard Business Review,* January–February 1991, pp. 65–79.
2. Shelby D. Hunt and John J. Burnett, "The Macromarketing/Micromarketing Dichotomy: A Taxonomical Model," *Journal of Marketing,* Summer 1982, pp. 9–26.
3. Adapted from "AMA Board Approves New Marketing Definition," *Marketing News,* March 1, 1985, p. 1.
4. Annual Report (Fairfield: General Electric Company, March 1991).
5. Frederick E. Webster, Jr., "The Changing Role of Marketing in the Corporation," *Journal of Marketing,* October 1992, pp. 1–17.
6. Walter van Waterschoot and Christophe Van den Bulte, "The 4P Classification of the Marketing Mix Revisited," *Journal of Marketing,* October 1992, pp. 83–93.
7. "Iceberg Vodka on the Rock," *Marketing,* January 30, 1995, p. 4.
8. William Winston, "Value Marketing: The Marketing Tool for the Year 2000," *Journal of Customer Service in Marketing and Management,* vol. 1, no. 1, 1995, pp. 2–8.
9. Michael Tracy and Fred Wiersema, "Customer Intimacy and Other Value Disciplines," *Harvard Business Review,* January–February 1993, pp. 84–93.
10. Thomas D. Kuczmarski, *Innovation: Capturing and Cultivating New Ideas for the Competitive Edge* (Chicago: American Marketing Association, 1995).
11. Regis McKenna, "Marketing is Everything," pp. 65–79.
12. Adapted from David Shani and Sujana Chalasani, "Exploiting Niches Using Relationship Marketing," *Journal of Consumer Marketing,* Summer 1992, pp. 33–421.
13. Frederick E. Webster, Jr., "The Changing Role of Marketing in the Corporation," pp. 1–17.
14. Regis McKenna, "Marketing is Everything," pp. 65–79.

CHAPTER 2

1. Kenneth J. Cook, *AMA Complete Guide to Strategic Planning for Small Business* (Chicago: American Marketing Association, 1994).
2. J. Stanco, *Utilizing the Strategic Marketing Organization* (New York: The Haworth Press Inc., 1996).
3. Godfrey Golzen, "Outspoken Nestlé Chairman Keeps Finger on the Button," *Marketing,* April 3, 1995, p. 6.
4. H. Igor Ansoff, "Strategies for Diversification," *Harvard Business Review,* September–October 1957, pp. 113–24. Also see, Alan J. Magrath, *Marketing Strategies for Growth in Uncertain Times* (Chicago: American Marketing Association, 1995).

5. Fred Weir, "Third Golden Arches Dawns on Moscow Horizon," *The Mail-Star,* July 6, 1993, p. B–6.
6. Arthur A. Thompson, Jr. and A. J. Strickland III, *Strategic Management,* 7th ed. (Burr Ridge, IL: Richard D. Irwin, 1993), pp. 87–90.
7. Mary T. Curren, Valerie S. Folkes, and Joel H. Sheckel, "Explanations for Successful and Unsuccessful Marketing Decisions: The Decision Maker's Perspective," *Journal of Marketing,* April 1992, pp. 18–31.
8. Robert Howard, "The CEO as Organizational Architect," *Harvard Business Review,* September–October 1992, pp. 107–21; and Christopher Bartlett and Sumantra Ghosal, "Matrix Management: Not a Structure, a Frame of Mind," *Harvard Business Review,* July–August 1990, pp. 138–45.
9. Betsy Spethmann, "Category Management Multiples," *Advertising Age,* May 11, 1992, p. 42, "Focus on Five Stages of Category Management," *Marketing News,* September 28, 1992, pp. 17, 19.
10. Philip Kotler, *Marketing Management,* 7th ed. (Englewood Cliffs, NJ: Prentice Hall, 1991), pp. 691–92.
11. J. Byrne, R. Brandt, and O. Port, "The Virtual Corporation," *Business Week,* February 8, 1993, pp. 98–103.
12. Jon Katzenbach and Douglas Smith, "The Discipline of Teams," *Harvard Business Review,* March–April 1993, pp. 111–20.
13. Don Frey, "Learning the Ropes: My Life as a Product Champion," *Harvard Business Review,* September–October 1991, pp. 46–56.
14. Thomas J. Peters and Robert H. Waterman, Jr., *In Search of Excellence: Lessons from America's Best-Run Companies* (New York: Harper & Row, 1982).
15. Tim Falconer, "A Classic Comes of Age," *Marketing,* September 13, 1993, pp. 1, 3.
16. Philip Kotler, William Gregor, and William Rogers, "The Marketing Audit Comes of Age," *Sloan Management Review,* Winter 1977, pp. 25–43.
17. Stanley J. Shapiro and V. H. Kirpalani, *Marketing Effectiveness: Insights from Accounting and Finance* (Boston: Allyn & Bacon, 1984).

CHAPTER 3

1. Roger Sauve, *Canadian People Patterns* (Saskatoon: Western Producer Prairie Books, 1993); Statistics Canada, *Market Research Handbook,* cat. 63–224 (Ottawa, 1996).
2. Douglas Bell, "Immigration Trends Shape Demand," *Marketing,* May 21, 1993, p. 29.

3. Brian Briggs and Ray Bollman, "Urbanization in Canada," *Social Trends,* Summer 1991, pp. 8–12.

4. Jim McElgunn "TV Must Get Serious, Says Angus Reid," *Marketing,* November 4, 1991, p. 4.

5. Douglas Bell, "Immigration Trends Shape Demand," p. 29.

6. Julia Moulden, "Even Greener Marketing," *Marketing,* February 8, 1993, pp. 1, 3.

7. Statistics Canada, *Market Research Handbook,* cat. 63–224 (Ottawa, 1996); Statistics Canada, *Selected Income Statistics,* cat. 93–331 (Ottawa, 1996); and Raymond Chow, "China's Middle Class Embracing the Supermarket," *Maine Sunday Telegram,* November 26, 1995; p. 5F.

8. "BMW Puts a Backseat Driver on a Chip," *Business Week,* July 30, 1990, p. 20.

9. Michael Porter, *Competitive Strategy* (New York: Free Press, 1980).

10. Stan Sutter, "Molson Pours into U.S.," *Marketing,* January 25, 1993, p. 1.

11. "The Best and Worst Deals of the '80s," *Business Week,* January 15, 1990, pp. 52–62.

CHAPTER 4

1. Adapted from information supplied by Seagram Canada, Montreal, 1995. Used with permission.

2. For a discussion of the definition of ethics, see Gene Laczniak and Patrick E. Murphy, *The Higher Road: A Path to Ethical Marketing Decisions* (Boston: Allyn & Bacon, 1992), Chapter 1.

3. Verne E. Henderson, "The Ethical Side of Enterprise," *Sloan Management Review,* Spring 1982, pp. 37–47.

4. M. Boomer, C. Gratto, J. Grauander, and M. Tuttle, "A Behavioral Model of Ethical and Unethical Decision Making," *Journal of Business Ethics* 6 (1987), pp. 265–80.

5. "Just How Honest Are You?" *Inc.,* February 1992, p. 104.

6. "Business Week/Harris Poll: Is an Antibusiness Business Backlash Building?" *Business Week,* July 20, 1987, p. 71; and "Looking to Its Roots," *Time,* May 27, 1987, pp. 26–29.

7. "What Bosses Think about Corporate Ethics," *The Wall Street Journal,* April 6, 1988, p. 21

8. N. Craig Smith and John A. Quelch, *Ethics in Marketing* (Homewood, IL: Richard D. Irwin, 1993).

9. For a comprehensive review on marketing ethics, see John Tsalikis and David J. Fritzche, "Business Ethics: A Literature Review with a Focus on Marketing Ethics," *Journal of Business Ethics,* 8 (1989), pp. 695–743.

10. Adapted from information supplied in Arthur Andersen & Co, SC's *Business Ethics Program*; see also O. C. Ferrell and John Fraedrich, *Business Ethics: Decision Making and Cases,* 2nd edition (Boston: Houghton Mifflin Company, 1994), Chapter 5.

11. O. C. Ferrell and Larry Gresham, "A Contingency Framework for Understanding Ethical Decision Making in Marketing," *Journal of Marketing* 49, Summer 1985, pp. 87–96.

12. Leonard J. Brooks, "Corporate Codes of Ethics," *Journal of Business Ethics* 8 (1989), pp. 117–29.

13. Ralph E. Anderson, Joseph F. Hais, Jr. and Alan J. Bush, Professional Sales Management; 2nd edition (New York: McGraw-Hill, 1992).

14. Adapted from Mark Stevenson, "Waste Not," *Canadian Business,* January 1994, pp. 20–26.

15. Avil Menon, "Cause-Related Marketing: A Coalignment of Marketing Strategy and Corporate Philanthropy," *Journal of Marketing,* July 1988, pp. 58–74. The examples given are found in this article and "McD's Ties to World Cup," *Advertising Age,* April 13, 1992, p. 17. See also Scott M. Smith and David S. Alcorn, "Cause Marketing: A New Direction in the Marketing of Corporate Responsibility," *The Journal of Consumer Marketing,* Summer 1991, pp. 19–35.

16. These steps are adapted from J. J. Carson and G. A. Steiner, *Measuring Business Social Performace: The Corporate Social Audit* (New York: Committee for Economic Development, 1974); see also E. M. Epstein, "The Corporate Social Policy Process: Beyond Business Ethics, Corporate Social Responsibility, and Corporate Social Responsiveness," *California Management Review,* Spring 1987, pp. 99–114.

17. Rajib N. Sanyal and Joao S. Neves, "The Valdez Principles: Implications for Corporate Social Responsibility," *Journal of Business Ethics* 10 (1991), pp. 883–90.

18. For a listing of unethical consumer practices, see Robert E. Wilkes, "Fraudulent Behavior by Consumers," *Journal of Marketing,* October 1978, pp. 67–75; see also Catherine A. Cole, "Research Note: Determinants and Consumer Fraud," *Journal of Retailing,* Spring 1989, pp. 107–20.

19. "Coupon Scams Are Clipping Companies," *Business Week,* June 15, 1992, pp. 110–11; Paul Bernstein, "Cheating—The New National Pastime?" *Business,* October–December 1985, pp. 24–33; and "Video Vice: 1 in 10 Copy Videotapes Illegally," *USA Weekend,* Febuary 9–11 1990, p. 18.

20. Julia Moulden, "Even Greener Marketing," *Marketing,* February 8, 1993, pp. 1, 3; and "Consumers Keen on Green but Marketers Don't Deliver," *Advertising Age,* June 29, 1992, pp. S–2, S–4.

21. Stan Sutter, "The Challenge of the 1990's," *Marketing,* July 3, 1989, p. 2; and Derek Stevenson, "Buying Green," *Canadian Consumer,* Febuary 1991, p. 47.

22. Julia Moulden (reference cited).

CHAPTER 5

1. "Shoppers Less Loyal, More Thrifty," *Marketing,* June 14, 1993, p. 14.

2. Jo Marney, "Food Still First with Many People," *Marketing,* May 1991, p. 17.

3. F. G. Crane and T. K. Clarke, *Consumer Behaviour in Canada: Theory and Practice,* 2nd ed. (Toronto: Dryden, 1994).

4. Stephen J. Hoch and John Deighton, "Managing What Consumers Learn from Experience," *Journal of Marketing,* April 1989, pp. 1–20.

5. Narasimhan Srinivasan and Brian T. Ratchford, "An Empirical Test of a Model of External Search for Automobiles," *Journal of Consumer Research,* September 1991, pp. 233–42; and Julie L. Ozanne, Merrie Brucks, and Dhruv Grewal, "A Study of Information Search Behavior During the Categorization of New Products," *Journal of Consumer Research,* March 1992, pp. 452–63.

6. William E. Warren, "Demographic and Psychographic Dimensions as Predictors of Information Sources Used in Making a Consumer Decision," *Journal of Promotion Management,* 1 (1991), pp. 43–55.

7. F. G. Crane and T. K. Clarke, *Consumer Behaviour in Canada: Theory and Practice.*

8. John A. Howard, *Consumer Behavior in Marketing Strategy* (Englewood Cliffs, NJ: Prentice Hall, 1989), pp. 176–77, 361.

9. For a discussion of the involvement construct, see F. G. Crane and T. K. Clarke, *Consumer Behaviour in Canada: Theory and Practice,* pp. 376–401.

10. J. Paul Peter and Jerry C. Olson, *Consumer Behavior: Marketing Strategy Perspectives,* 3rd ed. (Burr Ridge, IL: Richard D. Irwin, 1993), pp. 239–41.

11. Del Hawkins, Roger J. Best, and Kenneth J. Coney, *Consumer Behavior: Implications for Marketing Strategy,* 5th ed. (Burr Ridge, IL: Richard D. Irwin, 1992), pp 441–42; Peter and Olson, p. 420.

12. Russell Belk, "Situational Variables and Consumer Behavior," *Journal of Consumer Research,* December 1975, pp. 157–63.

13. For a discussion on situational influences, see F. G. Crane and T. K. Clarke, *Consumer Behaviour in Canada: Theory and Practice,* pp. 403–23.

14. This perspective on motivation and personality is based on Hawkins, Best, and Coney, Chapter 10.

15. K. H. Chung, *Motivational Theories and Practices* (Columbus, OH: Grid, 1977). See also A. H. Maslow, *Motivation and Personality* (New York: Harper & Row, 1970).

16. Arthur Kopenen, "The Personality Characteristics of Purchases," *Journal of Advertising Research,* September 1960, pp. 89–92.

17. Joel B. Cohen, "An Interpersonal Orientation to the Study of Consumer Behavior, *Journal of Marketing Research,* August 1967, pp. 270–78.

18. Terry Clark, "International Marketing and National Character: A Review and Proposal for an Integrative Theory," *Journal of Marketing,* October 1990, pp. 66–79.

19. For further reading on subliminal perception, see F. G. Crane and T. K. Clarke, "Subliminal Perception" in *Advertising, Law and Social Sciences,* ed., Jack P. Lipton and Bruce Dennis Sales (New York: Plenum Publishing, 1994), pp. 129–154.

20. Robert Settle and Pamela Alreck, "Reducing Buyers Sense of Risk," *Marketing Communications,* January 1989, pp. 34–40; and G. R. Dowling, "Perceived Risk: The Concept and Its Management," *Psychology and Marketing,* Fall 1986, pp. 193–210.

21. See Hawkins, Best, and Coney, pp. 263–81; and David Loudon and Albert J. Della Bitta, *Consumer Behavior,* 3rd ed. (New York: McGraw-Hill, 1988), pp. 437–74.

22. "Shoppers Less Loyal, More Thrifty," *Marketing,* June 14, 1993, p. 14.

23. Gordon Allport, "Attitudes," in *Readings in Attitude Theory and Measurement,* ed. Martin Fishbein (New York: John Wiley & Sons, 1968), p. 3.

24. Peter and Olson, pp. 195–98. See also Richard J. Lutz, "Changing Brand Attitudes through Modification of Cognitive Structure," *Journal of Consumer Research,* 2 (1975), pp. 49–59.

25. Henry Assael, *Consumer Behavior and Marketing Action,* 3rd ed. (Boston: Kent Publishing, 1990), p. 275.

26. Russell Belk, "Possessions and the Extended Self," *Journal of Consumer Research,* September 1988, pp. 139–68.

27. *The VAL 2 Segmentation System* (Menlo Park: CA: SRI International, 1989).

28. Adapted from *The Goldfarb Segments: A Marketing Tool* (Toronto: Goldfarb Consultants, March 1992).

29. Laurence F. Feick and Linda Price, "The Market Maven: A Diffuser of Marketplace Information," *Journal of Marketing,* January 1987, pp. 83–97; and Peter H. Block, "The Product Enthusiast: Implications for Marketing Strategy," *Journal of Consumer Marketing,* Summer 1986, pp. 51–61.

30. Crane and Clarke, *Consumer Behaviour in Canada,* p. 152.

31. F. G. Crane, and T. K. Clarke, "The Identification of Evaluative Criteria and Cues Used in Selecting Services," *Journal of Services Marketing,* Spring 1988, p. 53–59.

32. Crane and Clarke, *Consumer Behaviour in Canada,* p. 446–448.

33. Damo Darlin, "Although U.S. Cars Are Improved, Imports Still Win Quality Survey," *The Wall Street Journal,* December 12, 1985, p. 27.

34. Crane and Clarke, *Consumer Behaviour in Canada,* pp. 152–53.

35. Terry L. Childers and Akshay R. Rao, "The Influence of Familial and Peer-Based Reference Groups on Consumer Decisions," *Journal of Consumer Research,* September 1992, pp. 198–211.

36. "Honda Revs Up a Hip Cycle Campaign," *The Wall Street Journal,* July 31, 1989, p. B1.

37. George P. Moschis, *Consumer Socialization* (Lexington, MA: Lexington Books, 1987).

38. Patrick E. Murphy and William A. Staples, "A Modernized Family Life Cycle," *Journal of Consumer Research,* June 1979, pp. 12–22.

39. Sidney C. Bennett and Elnora W. Stuart, "In Search of Association Between Personal Values and Household Decision Processes: An Exploratory Analysis," *AMA Educators Conference Proceedings* (Chicago: American Marketing Association, 1989), pp. 259–64.

40. Crane and Clarke, *Consumer Behaviour in Canada,* p. 136.

41. See Robert B. Settle and Pamela L. Alreck, *Why They Buy* (New York: John Wiley & Sons, 1989), pp. 197–219.

42. Milton Yinger, "Ethnicity," *Annual Review of Sociology* 11 (1985), pp. 151–80.

43. Adapted from François Vary, "Quebec Consumer Has Unique Buying Habits," *Marketing,* March 23, 1992, p. 28. See also "Today's Media Are More Than Messages," *Marketing,* May 13, 1991, p. 6.

CHAPTER 6

1. Interview courtesy of Steve Whitacer, Honeywell, MICRO SWITCH Division.

2. Adapted from Peter LaPlaca, "From the Editor," *Journal of Business & Industrial Marketing,* Summer 1992, p. 3.

3. Peter LaPlaca, "From the Editor," *Journal of Business & Industrial Marketing,* Summer 1988, p. 3.

4. Statistics Canada, *Market Research Handbook,* cat. 63-224 (Ottawa, 1995).

5. The North American Industry Classification System Proposed Industry Classification Structure, (Washington, DC: Office of Management and Budget, July 26, 1995).

6. An argument that consumer buying and organizational buying do not have important differences is found in Edward F. Fern and James R. Brown, "The Industrial/Consumer Marketing Dichotomy: A Case of Insufficient Justification," *Journal of Marketing,* Spring 1984, pp. 68–77. Other writers do draw distinctions between the two types of buying. See, for example, Robert W. Eckles, *Business Marketing Management* (Englewood Cliffs, NJ: Prentice Hall, 1990), p. 6; and Robert W. Haas, *Business Marketing Management* (Boston: PWS-Kent Publishing Company, 1992), p. 31.

7. Figure 6–2 is based on Robert Reeder, Edward G. Brierty, and Betty Reeder, *Industrial Marketing,* 2nd ed. (Englewood, NJ: Prentice Hall, 1991), pp. 8–22; Robert W. Eckles, *Business Marketing Management* (Englewood Cliffs, NJ: Prentice Hall, 1990), p. 20–26; Frank G. Bingham Jr., and Barney T. Raffield III, *Business to Business Marketing Management* (Burr Ridge, IL: Richard D. Irwin, 1990), pp. 6–14; Michael D. Hutt and Thomas W. Speh, *Business Marketing Management,* 3rd ed. (Hinsdale, IL: Dryden Press, 1989), p. 6–12; and Michael H. Morris, *Industrial and Organizational*

Marketing (Columbus, OH: Merrill Publishing Company, 1988), pp. 21–28.

8. Daniel H. McQuiston and Rockney G. Walters, "The Evaluative Criteria of Industrial Buyers: Implications for Sales Training," *Journal of Business & Industrial Marketing,* Summer to Fall 1989, pp. 65–75.

9. David L. Blenkhorn and Peter M. Banting, "How Reverse Marketing Changes Buyer–Seller Roles," *Industrial Marketing Management,* August 1991, pp. 185–90; and Michael R. Leenders and David L. Blenkhorn, *Reverse Marketing: The New Buyer–Supplier Relationship* (New York: Free Press, 1988).

10. J. William Semich and Somerby Dowst, "How to Push Your Everyday Supplier into World Class Status," *Purchasing,* August 17, 1989, p. 76.

11. Richard N. Cardozo, Shannon H. Shipp, and Kenneth Roering, "Proactive Strategic Partnerships: A New Business Markets Strategy," *Journal of Business & Industrial Marketing,* Winter 1992, pp. 51–63.

12. Steve McDaniel, Joseph G. Ormsby, and Alicia Greshma, "The Effect of JIT on Distributors," *Industrial Marketing Management,* May 1992, pp. 145–49.

13. Shirley Cayer, "Welcome to Caterpillar's Quality Institute," *Purchasing,* August 16, 1990, pp. 81–84.

14. Mary C. LaForge and Louis H. Stone, "An Analysis of the Industrial Buying Process by Means of Buying Center Communications," *Journal of Business & Industrial Marketing,* Winter–Spring 1989, pp. 29–36.

15. "Where Three Sales a Year Make You a Superstar," *Business Week,* February 17, 1986, pp. 76–77.

16. Bingham and Raffield, p. 11.

17. Thomas V. Bonoma, "Major Sales: Who Really Does the Buying?" *Harvard Business Review,* May–June 1982, pp. 111–19.

18. Huang Quanya, Richard Andrulis, and Chen Tong, *A Guide to Successful Business Relations with the Chinese* (New York: The Haworth Press, 1994).

19. Julia M. Bristor, "Influence Strategies in Organizational Buying: The Importance of Connections to the Right People in the Right Places," *Journal of Business-to-Business Marketing* I (1993), pp. 63–98.

20. These definitions are adapted from Frederick E. Webster, Jr., and Yoram Wind, *Organizational Buying Behavior* (Englewood Cliffs, NJ: Prentice Hall, 1972), p. 6.

21. Arch G. Woodside and Nyrem Vyas, *Industrial Purchasing Strategies: Recommendations for Purchasing and Marketing Managers* (Lexington, MA: Lexington Books, 1987).

22. James R. Stock and Paul H. Zinszer, "The Industrial Purchase Decision for Professional Services," *Journal of Business Research,* February 1987, pp. 1–16.

23. Patrick J. Robison, Charles W. Faris, and Yoram Wind, *Industrial Buying and Creative Marketing* (Boston: Allyn & Bacon, 1967).

24. For a study on the buy-class framework that documents its usefulness, see Erin Anderson, Wujin Chu, and Barton Weitz, "Industrial Purchasing: An Empirical Exploration of the Buy-Class Framework," *Journal of Marketing,* 1987, pp. 71–86. For a study not supporting the buy-class framework, see Joseph A. Bellizzi and Philip McVey, "How Valid is the Buy-Grid Model?" *Industrial Marketing Management,* February 1983, pp. 57–62.

25. Tony L. Henthorne, Michale S. LaTour, and Alvin J. Williams, "How Organizational Buyers Reduce Risk," *Industrial Marketing Management,* February 1993, pp. 41–48.

26. Gerald Levitch, "Sitting Pretty," *Marketing,* June 21, 1993, pp. 1, 3.

27. Ibid.

28. Ibid.

29. Ibid.

CHAPTER 7

1. Adapted from Dale Burger, "Pushing Creativity to the Limit," *Computing Canada,* May 24, 1995 (Willowdale, Ont: Plesman Publications Ltd.), p. 37.

2. Robert A. Peterson, *Marketing Research,* 2nd ed. (Burr Ridge, IL: Richard D. Irwin, 1988), pp. 2–3.

3. "New Marketing Research Definition Approved," *Marketing News,* January 2, 1987, pp. 1, 14.

4. Calvin L. Hodock, "The Decline and Fall of Marketing Research in Corporate America," *Marketing Research,* June 1991, pp. 12–22.

5. Ken Riddell, "Shoppers Add Life to Pop Market," *Marketing,* July 26, 1993, p. 2.

6. Patrick E. Murphy and Gene R. Laczniak, "Emerging Ethical Issues Facing Marketing Researchers," *Marketing Research,* June 1992, pp. 6–11.

7. This section on advantages and disadvantages of cross tabulations was adapted from Roseann Maguire and Terry C. Wilson, "Banners or Cross Tabs? Before Deciding, Weigh Data—Format, Pros, Cons," *Marketing News,* May 13, 1983, pp. 10–11.

8. For a discussion on marketing research as a continuous process, see Eugene Del Vecchio, "Marketing Research as a Continuous Process," *Journal of Consumer Research,* Summer 1990, pp. 13–19.

9. Robert A. Peterson, *Marketing Research,* 2nd ed.

10. W. Steven Perkins and Ram C. Rao, "The Role of Experience in Information Use and Decision Making by Marketing Managers," *Journal of Marketing Research,* February 1990, pp. 1–10.

11. Howard Schlossberg, "Marketers Moving to Make Data Bases Actionable," *Marketing News,* February 18, 1991, p. 8.

CHAPTER 8

1. "Reebok High Steppers," *Fortune,* July 1, 1991, p. 84.

2. Jean Sherman, "No Pain, No Gain," *Working Women,* May 1987, p. 92; "Can Reebok Sprint Even Faster?" *Business Week,* October 6, 1986, pp. 74–75; and "Sneakers That Don't Specialize," *Business Week,* June 6, 1988, p. 146.

3. "Reebok's Pump Is Patent-Primed," *Business Week,* November 9, 1992, p. 52; Edward C. Baig, "Products to Watch: Reebok Pump," *Fortune,* January 1, 1990, p. 97; and "Where Nike and Reebok Have Plenty of Running Room," *Business Week,* March 11, 1991, pp. 56–60.

4. Example supplied by Allison Scolieri, Goldfarb Consultants, Toronto, March 10, 1992.

5. James Pollock, "Ault Whips Up the Dairy Industry with PurFiltre," *Marketing,* March 13, 1995, p. 2.

6. F. G. Crane and T. K. Clarke, "Attitudes toward Milk: A Canadian View," *British Food Journal,* November–December, 1989, pp. 6–9.

7. *Simmonds 1990 Study of Media and Markets: Restaurants, Stores, and Grocery Shopping Poll* (New York: Simmonds Market Research Bureau, Inc., 1990), pp. 0001–0003.

8. Marshall Greenberg and Susan Schwartz McDonald, "Successful Needs/Benefits Segmentation: A User's Guide," *Journal of Consumer Marketing,* Summer 1989, pp. 29–36.

9. George S. Day, *Market-Driven Strategy* (New York: Free Press, 1990), p. 168.

10. A. Ries and J. Trout, *Positioning: The Battle for Your Mind* (New York: McGraw-Hill, 1981).

CHAPTER 9

1. Definitions within this classification are from Committee on Definitions, *Marketing Definitions: A Glossary of Marketing Terms* (Chicago: American Marketing Association, 1960).
2. Ibid.
3. Brian Dumaine, "Closing the Innovation Gap," *Fortune,* December 2, 1991, pp. 56–62.
4. Brenton R. Schlender, "How Sony Keeps the Magic Going," *Fortune,* February 24, 1992, pp. 76–84.
5. Dumaine, p. 56.
6. F. G. Crane and T. K. Clarke, *Consumer Behaviour in Canada: Theory and Practice,* 2nd ed. (Toronto: Dryden, 1994).
7. Clare Ansberry, "Eastman Kodak is Pulling Plug in Its Ultralife," *The Wall Street Journal,* April 10, 1990, pp. B1, B2.
8. Laura Medcalf, "Analyst Suggests Red Dog has Already had Its Day," *Marketing,* April 10, 1995, p. 2.
9. "Smokeless Cigarette Test Turns to Ashes," *Boston Globe,* March 1, 1989, p. 43.
10. Claire Poole, "Sweating It Out," *Forbes,* October 16, 1989, p. 274.
11. R. G. Cooper and E. J. Kleinschmidt, "Major New Products: What Distinguishes the Winners in the Chemical Industry?" *Journal of Product Innovation Management,* March 1993, pp. 90–111.
12. *New Products Management for the 1980s* (Booz, Allen & Hamilton, Inc., 1982).
13. "Masters of Innovation: How 3M Keeps Its New Products Coming," *Business Week,* April 10, 1989, pp. 58–63.
14. *Marketing,* June 7, 1993, p. 2.
15. Laura Medcalf, "Of Ice and Men," *Marketing,* July 26, 1993, pp. 1, 3.
16. "P&G Rewrites the Marketing Rules," *Fortune,* November 6, 1989, pp. 34–38.
17. Gail Chiasson, "A Sobering Mouthwash Pitch," *Marketing,* June 28, 1993, p. 2.
18. Ibid.
19. "Masters of Innovation," *Business Week,* April 10, 1989, pp. 58–63; and P. Ranganath Nayak and John M. Ketteringham, *Breakthroughs!* (New York: Rawson Associates, 1986), pp. 50–73.
20. Dumaine, p. 57; Schlender, p. 78.
21. Brian Dumaine, "Corporate Spies Stoop to Conquer," *Fortune,* November 7, 1988, 68–76.
22. Susan Caminiti, "What the Scanner Knows About You," *Fortune,* December 3, 1990, pp. 51–52.
23. Sak Onkvisit and John J. Shaw, *Product Life Cycles and Product Management* (New York: Quorum Books, 1989), p. 26.
24. Paul Ingrassia, "Industry is Shopping Abroad for Good Ideas to Apply to Products," *The Wall Street Journal,* April 29, 1985, p. 1.
25. "Step by Step with Nike," *Business Week,* August 13, 1990, pp. 116–17.
26. Melvin Prince, "Choosing Simulated Test Marketing Systems," *Marketing Research,* September 1992, pp. 14–16; and Christopher Power, "Will It Sell in Podunk? Hard to Say," *Business Week,* August 10, 1992, pp. 46–47.
27. "Pinning Down Costs of Product Introductions," *The Wall Street Journal,* November 26, 1990, p. B1.
28. "How Managers Can Succeed through Speed," *Fortune,* February 13, 1990, pp. 54–59.
29. Ibid.
30. W. Christopher Musselwhite, "Time-Based Innovation: The New Competitive Advantage," *Training and Development,* January 1990, pp. 53–56.

CHAPTER 10

1. James Pollock, "The Taste of Success," *Marketing,* January 23, 1995, pp. 11, 13.
2. David M. Gardner, "Product Life Cycle: A Critical Look at the Literature," in *Review of Marketing 1987,* ed. Michael Houston (Chicago: American Marketing Association, 1987), pp. 162–94.
3. Joseph Pereira, "Name of the Game: Brand Awareness," *The Wall Street Journal,* February 14, 1991, pp. B1, B4.
4. "The Sun Chip Also Rises," *Advertising Age,* April 27, 1992, pp. S–2, S–6; and "Gillette to Launch Women's Sensor," *Advertising Age,* February 10, 1992, p. 36.
5. Orville C. Walker, Jr., Harper W. Boyd, Jr., and Jean-Claude Larréché, *Marketing Strategy* (Burr Ridge, IL: Richard D. Irwin, 1992), p. 251.
6. "HDTV Coming of Age," *Maine Sunday Telegram,* May 30, 1993, p. 7A.
7. Lawrence P. Feldman and Albert L. Page, "Harvesting: The Misunderstood Market Exit Strategy," *Journal of Business Strategy,* Spring 1985, pp. 79–85.
8. William Qualls, Richard W. Olshavsky, and Ronald E. Michaels, "Shortening of the PLC—An Empirical Test," *Journal of Marketing,* Fall 1981, pp. 76–80.
9. The terms *high-* and *low-learning life cycles* were developed by Chester R. Wasson, *Dynamic Competitive Strategies and Product Life Cycles* (Austin, TX: Austin Press, 1978).
10. John Bissell, "What New Age Beverages Could Learn From Coolers," *Brandweek,* September 27, 1993, p. 20.
11. Everett M. Rogers, *Diffusion of Innovations,* 3rd ed. (New York: Free Press, 1983).
12. S. Ram and Jagdish N. Sheth, "Consumer Resistance to Innovation: The Marketing Problem and Its Solution," *Journal of Consumer Marketing,* Spring 1989, pp. 5–14.
13. Lara Mills, "Big Send-Off for Diet Pepsi," *Marketing,* January 30, 1995, p. 4.
14. James Pollock, "Mr. Christie Watches His Waistline with Low-fat Extensions," *Marketing,* January 30, 1995, p. 4.
15. "Modified Screwdrivers May Prevent Slips," *The Wall Street Journal,* December 19, 1990, p. B1.
16. Alecia Swasy, "How Innovations at P&G Restored Luster to Washed Up Pert and Made It No. 1," *The Wall Street Journal,* December 6, 1990, pp. B1, B6; and "Tossing Its Head at P&G, Helene Curtis Styles Itself No. 1 in the Hair-Care Market," *The Wall Street Journal,* November 19, 1992, pp. B1, B16.
17. Elaine Underwood, "Retro Brands: Tastykake and Ritz Get a Legacy Look by Returning to Ghosts of Packages Past," *Adweek Marketing,* October 4, 1991, p. 18; and *Marketing,* June 7, 1993, p. 3.
18. Cyndee Miller, "Beef, Pork Industries Have Met the Enemy—and It's Chicken," *Marketing News,* August 5, 1991, pp. 1, 7.
19. "Et Tu, Brut?" *Consumer Reports,"* March 1992, p. 203; and John B. Hinge, "Critics Call Cuts in Package Size Deceptive Move," *The Wall Street Journal,* February 5, 1991, pp. B1, B8.
20. "Xerox Fights Trademark Battle," *Advertising Age,* April 27, 1992, p. I–29.
21. David A. Aaker, *Managing Brand Equity* (New York: Free Press, 1991).

22. Ibid.

23. Tim Falconer, "Hockey Hype," *Marketing,* March 22, 1993, pp. 1, 3.

24. James Pollock, "Taste of Success," pp. 11, 13.

25. "Ruffles Makes Waves in Israel," *Advertising Age,* November 23, 1992, p. J–12.

26. Daniel L. Doden, "Selecting a Brand Name That Aids Marketing Objectives," *Advertising Age,* November 5, 1990, p. 34.

27. Kim Robertson, "Strategically Desirable Brand Name Characteristics," *Journal of Consumer Marketing,* Fall 1989, pp. 61–71.

28. David A. Aaker and Kevin Lane Keller, "Consumer Evaluations of Brand Extensions," *Journal of Marketing,* January 1990, pp. 27–41.

29. "Baby Boom in Toiletries Hits J&J," *Advertising Age,* January 21, 1991, p. 16; and J&J Sets Nighttime Tylenol," *Advertising Age,* February 18, 1991, pp. 1, 46.

30. Warren Keegan, Sandra Moriarty, and Tom Duncan, *Marketing* (Englewood Cliffs, NJ: Prentice Hall, 1992), p. 467.

31. "Low Threat Labels," *Marketing,* June 14, 1993, p. 9.

32. Carl McDaniel and R. C. Baker, "Convenience Food Packaging and the Perception of Product Quality," *Journal of Marketing,* October 1977, pp. 57–58.

33. "P&G to Tout Recycled Packages," *Advertising Age,* April 19, 1990, p. 42; and "Heinz to Unveil Recyclable Bottle for Its Ketchup," *The Wall Street Journal,* April 4, 1990, p. B3.

34. "Germany's New Packaging Laws: The 'Green Dot' Arrives," *Business America,* February 24, 1992, pp. 36–37; and "The Last to Go Green: U.S. Lags in Eco-Labeling," *Business International,* March 30, 1992, pp. 93–94.

35. John A. Quelch, "The Procter & Gamble Company: The Lenor Refill Package," Harvard Business School Case N9-592-016; "Procter & Gamble Inc.: Downy Enviro-Pak," University of Western Ontario Case 9-90-A006; and "Downy Refill Makes a Splash on Shelves," *Advertising Age,* July 8, 1991, p. 16.

36. Sonia L. Nazario, "Microwave Packages That Add Crunch to Lunch Also Pose Chemical Risks," *The Wall Street Journal,* March 1, 1990, pp. B1, B6.

37. Robert E. Wikes and James B. Wilcox, "Limited versus Full Warranties: The Retail Perspective," *Journal of Retailing,* Spring 1981, pp. 65–77.

CHAPTER 11

1. Interview with Kimberly R. Grant. Used with permission.

2. Adapted from Kent B. Monroe, *Pricing: Making Profitable Decisions,* 2nd ed. (New York: McGraw-Hill, 1990), Chapter 4. See also David J. Curry, "Measuring Price and Quality Competition," *Journal of Marketing,* Spring 1985, pp. 106–17.

3. Joseph B. White, "Value Pricing Is Hot as Shrewd Consumers Seek Low-Cost Quality," *The Wall Street Journal,* March 12, 1991, pp. A1, A5; and *Marketing News,* January 1, 1991, p. 1.

4. Numerous studies have examined the price–quality value relationship. See, for example, Jacob Jacoby and Jerry C. Olson, eds., *Perceived Quality* (Lexington, MA: Lexington Books, 1985); Kent B. Monroe and William B. Dodds, "A Research Program for Establishing the Validity of the Price–Quality Relationship," *Journal of the Academy of Marketing Science,* Spring 1988, pp. 151–68; and Roger A. Kerin, Ambuj Jain, and Daniel J. Howard, "Store Shopping Experience and Consumer Price–Quality–Value Perceptions," *Journal of Retailing,* Winter 1992, pp. 235–45. For a thorough review of the price–qual-

ity–value relationship, see Valarie Z. Zeithaml, "Consumer Perceptions of Price, Quality, and Value," *Journal of Marketing,* July 1988, pp. 2–22.

5. Barbara J. Coe, "Shifts in Industrial Pricing Objectives," *AMA Educators' Conference Proceedings* (Chicago: American Marketing Association, 1988), pp. 9–14. See also Barbara Coe, "Strategy in Retreat: Pricing Drops Out," *Journal of Business & Industrial Marketing,* Winter–Spring 1990, pp. 5–26.

6. "Pepsi, Coke Say They're Loyal to NutraSweet," *The Wall Street Journal,* April 22, 1992, p. B1.

7. "Made Just for Him," *Time,* April 16, 1990, p. 49.

8. Michael Garry, "Dollar Strength: Publishers Confront the New Economic Realities," *Folio: The Magazine for Magazine Management,* February 1989, pp. 88–93; Cara S. Trager, "Right Price Reflects a Magazine's Health Goals," *Advertising Age,* March 9, 1987, pp. 5–8ff; and Frank Bruni, "Price of Newsweek? It Depends," *Dallas Times Herald,* August 14, 1986, pp. S1, S20.

9. Kent B. Monroe, *Pricing: Making Profitable Decisions,* 2nd ed. (New York: McGraw-Hill, 1990), pp. 24–26. See also David W. Nylen, *Marketing Decision-Making Handbook* (Englewood Cliffs, NJ: Prentice Hall, 1990), pp. G237–G239.

10. For illustrations of break-even analysis that document its use and versatility, see Thomas L. Powers, "Break-Even Analysis with Semi-fixed Costs," *Industrial Marketing Management,* February 1987, pp. 35–41; and "Break-Even Analysis," *Small Business Report,* August 1986, pp. 22–24.

11. See, for example, V. Kumar and Robert P. Leone, "Measuring the Effect of Retail Store Promotions on Brand and Store Substitution," *Journal of Marketing Research,* May 1988, pp. 178–85.

12. Robert C. Blattberg and Scott A. Neslin, *Sales Promotion: Concepts, Methods, and Strategies* (Englewood Cliffs, NJ: Prentice Hall, 1990); and Kent B. Monroe, *Pricing: Making Profitable Decisions,* 2nd ed. (New York: McGraw-Hill, 1990).

13. For an excellent review of bundle pricing, see Joseph P. Guiltinan, "The Pricing Bundling of Services: A Normative Framework," *Journal of Marketing,* April 1987, pp. 74–85; and Thomas T. Nagle, *The Strategy and Tactics of Pricing* (Englewood Cliffs, NJ: Prentice Hall, 1987), pp. 170–72.

14. For a discussion on the experience curve, see William W. Alberts, "The Experience Doctrine Reconsidered," *Journal of Marketing,* July 1989, pp. 36–49.

15. "IBM's Personal-Computer Strategy: At Any Price," *The Economist,* October 10, 1992, pp. 82, 84.

16. "Store-Brand Pricing Has to Be Just Right," *The Wall Street Journal,* February 14, 1992, p. B1.

17. For a review of quantity discounts, see George S. Day and Adrian B. Ryans, "Using Price Discounts for a Competitive Advantage," *Industrial Marketing Management,* February 1988, pp. 1–14; and James B. Wilcox, Roy D. Howell, Paul Kuzdrall, and Robert Britney, "Price Quantity Discounts: Some Implications for Buyers and Sellers," *Journal of Marketing,* July 1987, pp. 60–70.

18. Michael Levy and Charles Ingene, "Retailers Head Off Credit Cards with Cash Discounts," *Harvard Business Review,* May–June 1983, pp. 18–22.

19. Rockney G. Walters, "An Empirical Investigation in Retailer Response to Manufacturer Trade Promotions," *Journal of Retailing,* Summer 1989, pp. 258–72; and Ronald C. Curhan and Robert J. Kopp, "Obtaining Retailer Support for Trade Deals: Key Success Factors," *Journal of Advertising Research,* December–January 1987–1988, pp. 51–60.

CHAPTER 12

1. Adapted from *Canadian Business* (October 1995), p. 16.
2. For an extensive review of industrial channel and distribution systems, see E. Raymond Corey, Frank V. Cespedes, and V. Kasturi Rangan, *Going to Market: Distribution Systems for Industrial Products* (Boston: Harvard Business School Press, 1989).
3. Michael D. Hutt and Thomas W. Speh, *Business Marketing Management,* 4th ed. (Hinsdale, IL: Dryden Press, 1992), pp. 314–15.
4. James D. Hlavacek and Tommy J. McCuistion, "Industrial Distributors—When, Who, and How?" *Harvard Business Review,* March–April 1983, pp. 96–101.
5. John A. Quelch, "Why Not Exploit Dual Marketing?" *Business Horizons,* January–February 1987, pp. 52–60. See also Gary L. Frazier and Tassaddug A. Shervani, "Multiple Channels of Distribution and Their Impact on Retailing," in *The Future of U.S. Retailing,* ed. Robert A. Peterson (New York: Quorum Books, 1992), pp. 217–37.
6. "Looks Like Hot Summer for Iced Tea," *Advertising Age,* May 4, 1992, p. 4.
7. The examples are described in "GM Says Sales Arm Plans to Distribute Saab Cars in Canada," *The Wall Street Journal,* May 10, 1990, p. B2; and Rustan Kosenko and Don Rathz, "The Japanese Channels of Distribution: Difficult but Not Insurmountable," *AMA Educators' Conference Proceedings* (Chicago: American Marketing Association, 1988), pp. 233–36.
8. For research on similarities and differences among agents, merchant wholesalers, and sales offices and branches, see James R. Moore, Donald W. Eckrich, and Vijay Bhasim, "Industrial Channels Design and Structure: An Empirical Investigation," *Journal of Midwest Marketing,* Fall 1988, pp. 87–98; and Ronald D. Michman, "Managing Structural Changes in Marketing Channels," *Journal of Business & Industrial Marketing,* Summer–Fall 1990, pp. 5–14.
9. For research on manufacturer's agents, see Donald M. Jackson and Michael E. d'Amico, "Products and Markets Served by Distributors and Agents," *Industrial Marketing Management,* February 1989, pp. 27–33.
10. Louis W. Stern and Adel I. El-Ansary, *Marketing Channels,* 4th ed. (Englewood Cliffs, NJ: Prentice Hall, 1991).
11. "Clothing Makers Don Retailers' Garb," *The Wall Street Journal,* July 13, 1989, p. B1.
12. Frank V. Cespedes, "Channel Management Is General Management," *California Management Review,* Fall 1988, pp. 98–120.
13. This exhibit is based on discussions in "Mass Market Transforms PC Retailing," *The Wall Street Journal,* December 18, 1990, p. B1; "More Computer Marketers Taking the Direct Approach," *Marketing News,* October 26, 1992, p. 6; and "A Surprise Lift for Computer Retailers," *Business Week,* October 4, 1992, pp. 63–64.
14. Carla Rapoport, "You Can Make Money in Japan," *Fortune,* February 12, 1990, pp. 84–92; and "Avon Launches a $90 Million Offer to Buy Back Shares in Japanese Unit," *The Wall Street Journal,* September 15, 1992, p. B4.
15. Philip Kotler, *Marketing Management,* 7th ed. (Englewood Cliffs, NJ: Prentice Hall, 1991), p. 568; and Michael R. Czinkota and Jon Woronoff, *Unlocking Japanese Markets* (Chicago: Probus Publishing Co., 1991), pp. 92–97.
16. "Gillette Tries to Nick Schick in Japan," *The Wall Street Journal,* February 4, 1991, pp. B3, B4.
17. For examples of channel conflict, see Allan J. Magrath and Kenneth G. Hardy, "Avoiding the Pitfalls in Managing Distribution Channels," *Business Horizons,* September–October 1987, pp. 29–33; and Rogert J. Calantone and Jule B. Gassenheimer, "Overcoming Basic Problems between Manufacturers and Distributors," *Industrial Marketing Management,* August 1991, pp. 215–21.
18. "Heinz Struggles to Stay at the Top of the Stack," *Business Week,* March 11, 1985, p. 49.
19. Studies that explore the dimensions and use of power and influence in marketing channels include Gul Butaney and Lawrence H. Wortzel, "Distributor Power versus Manufacturer Power: The Customer Role," *Journal of Marketing,* January 1988, pp. 52–63; Kenneth A. Hunt, John T. Mentzer, and Jeffrey E. Danes, "The Effect of Power Sources on Compliance in a Channel of Distribution: A Causal Model," *Journal of Business Research,* October 1987, pp. 377–98; and F. Robert Dwyer and Jule Gassenheimer, "Relational Roles and Triangle Dramas: Effects on Power Play and Sentiments in Industrial Channels," *Marketing Letters 3* (1992), pp. 187–200.
20. Definition provided by the Council of Logistics Management, Chicago, 1986. Emphasis added.
21. Elizabeth Edwardson, "Workers at L. L. Bean Busy as Santa's Elves Filling Christmas Orders," *Minneapolis Star Tribune,* December 23, 1992, p. 5D.
22. John J. Coyle, Edward J. Bardi, and C. John Langley, Jr., *The Management of Business Logistics,* 5th ed. (St. Paul, MN: West Publishing, 1992), pp. 85–90.
23. Coyle, Bardi, and Langley, p. 90.
24. George Stalk, Philip Evans, and Lawrence Shulman, "Competing on Capabilities: The New Rules of Corporate Strategy," *Harvard Business Review,* March–April 1992, pp. 57–69 (especially pp. 61–62). Also see Hank Gilman, "Rural Retailing Chains Prosper by Combining Service, Sophistication," *The Wall Street Journal,* July 2, 1984, p. 1.

CHAPTER 13

1. Based on a personal interview with Keith Dunphy. Used with permission.
2. Peter Bloch, Nancy Ridgeway, and Daniel L. Sherrell, "Extending the Concept of Shopping: An Investigation of Browsing Activity," *Journal of the Academy of Marketing Science,* Winter 1989, pp. 13–22; Alan J. Bash and E. Stephen Grant, "The Potential Impact of Recreational Shoppers on Mall Intercept Interviewing: An Exploratory Study, *Journal of Marketing–Theory and Practice,* Fall 1995, pp. 73–83.
3. *Canadian Markets* (Toronto: The Financial Post, 1994), pp. 26–40; Statistics Canada, *Market Research Handbook,* cat. 63–224 (Ottawa, 1993), p. 170; and Statistics Canada, *Employment Statistics,* cat 72–002 (Ottawa, 1993).
4. Derek Stevenson, "Cross-Border Dispute," *Canadian Consumer,* July–August 1991, pp. 8–15.
5. "World's Top Stores," *Marketing,* March 1, 1993, p. 18.
6. Jennifer S. Stack and Joseph E. McKendrick, "Franchise Market Expands As Rest of Economy Slumps," *Marketing News,* July 6, 1992, p. 11.
7. Robert E. Bond and Christopher E. Bond, *The Source Book of Franchising Opportunities* (Burr Ridge, IL: Dow Jones-Irwin, 1991).
8. Bob Mackin, Jr., "Designer Coffee a Hot Item on the West Coast," *Marketing,* June 28, 1993, p. 12.

9. Angela Kryhul, "Superstore Concept Expands."

10. Helen Keeler, "Shopping a la Carte: Everything You Want to Know about Catalogue Shopping," *Canadian Consumer,* November–December 1991, pp. 25–27.

11. Statistics Canada, *Market Research Handbook,* cat. 63-224 (Ottawa, 1993), p. 105.

12. "Trade Exec's 'Crystal-Ball' Outlook for the 1990s," *Vending Times,* December 1989, pp. 1, 3, 8.

13. Phil Fitzell, "Opening the Floodgates," *Beverage World,* January 1990, pp. 48–58.

14. Based on correspondence with Michael MacNeil, NBTel. Used with permission.

15. David Fryxell, "How to Succeed in Executive Shopping," *Link-Up,* March–April 1992, pp. 8–10; Gary Robins, "On-Line Service Update," *Stores,* February 1990, pp. 24–29; and "Computer Formats Spur Variety in ER," *Discount Store News,* July 3, 1989, p. 116.

16. The following discussion is adapted from William T. Gregor and Eileen M. Friars, *Money Merchandising: Retail Revolution in Consumer Financial Services* (Cambridge, MA: Management Analysis Center, Inc., 1982).

17. William Lazer and Eugene J. Kelley, "The Retailing Mix: Planning and Management," *Journal of Retailing,* Spring 1961, pp. 34–41.

18. Francis J. Mulhern and Robert P. Leon, "Implicit Price Bundling of Retail Products: A Multiproduct Approach to Maximizing Store Profitability," *Journal of Marketing,* October 1991, pp. 63–76.

19. Barry Brown, "Edmonton Makes Size Pay Off in Down Market," *Advertising Age,* January 27, 1992, pp. 5–4.

20. Eric Peterson, "Power Centers! Now!" *Stores,* March 1989, pp. 61–66; and "Power Centers Flex Their Muscle," *Chain Store Age Executive,* February 1989, pp. 3A, 4A.

21. Pierre Martineau, "The Personality of the Retail Store," *Harvard Business Review* 36 (January–February 1958), p. 47.

22. Howard Barich and Philip Kotler, "A Framework for Marketing Image Management," *Sloan Management Review,* Winter 1991, pp. 94–104; Susan M. Keaveney and Kenneth A. Hunt, "Conceptualization and Operationalization of Retail Store Image: A Case of Rival Middle-Level Theories," *Journal of the Academy of Marketing Science,* Spring 1992, pp. 165–75; and James C. Ward, Mary Jo Bitner, and John Barnes, "Measuring the Prototypicality and Meaning of Retail Environments," *Journal of Retailing,* Summer 1992, p. 194. For a review of the store image literature, see Mary R. Zimmer and Linda L. Golden, "Impressions of Retail Stores: A Content Analysis of Consumer Images," *Journal of Retailing,* Fall 1988, pp. 265–93.

23. Mary Jo Bitner, "Servicescapes: The Impact of Physical Surroundings on Customers and Employees," *Journal of Marketing,* April 1992, pp. 57–71.

24. Jans-Benedict Steenkamp and Michel Wedel, "Segmenting Retail Markets on Store Image Using a Consumer-Based Methodology," *Journal of Retailing,* Fall 1991, p. 300; and Philip Kotler, "Atmosphere as a Marketing Tool," *Journal of Retailing,* Winter 1973–74, p. 61.

25. *Marketing,* June 21, 1993, p. 2.

26. William R. Davidson, Albert D. Bates, and Stephen J. Bass, "Retail Life Cycle," *Harvard Business Review,* November–December 1976, pp. 89–96.

27. Avijit, Ghosh, *Retail Management,* 2nd Edition (Fort Worth, TX: The Dryden Press, 1994), p. 123.

28. John Torella, "All the World's a Retail Stage: In-store Drama Offers a Real Payback," *Marketing,* (July 31/August 7, 1995), p. 14.

CHAPTER 14

1. Hy Haberman, "Toward a New Discipline," *Marketing,* March 6, 1995, p. S4; and Scott Hume, "Integrated Marketing: Who's in Charge Here?" *Advertising Age,* March 22, 1993, p. 3.

2. Ibid.

3. F. G. Crane and T. K. Clarke, *Consumer Behaviour in Canada: Theory and Practice,* 2nd ed. (Toronto: Dryden 1994) pp. 287–298.

4. F. G. Crane and T. K. Clarke, *Consumer Behaviour in Canada: Theory and Practice,* p. 114.

5. This discussion of IMC is based on Don E. Schultz, Stanley I. Tannenbaum, and Robert F. Lauterborn, *Integrated Marketing Communications* (Chicago: NTC Business Books, 1993); and Don E. Schultz, "Integrated Marketing Communications: Maybe Definition Is in the Point of View," *Marketing News,* January 18, 1993, p. 17.

6. For a discussion on models used to set communications budgets, see Gail L. Stautamoyer and Jay D. Lindquist, "Promotion Decision Models: A State of the Art Review," *Journal of Promotion Management,* vol. 2, no. 3/4, 1994, pp. 1–35.

7. Kusum L. Ailawadi, Paul W. Farris, and Mark E. Parry, "Share and Growth Are Not Good Predictors of the Advertising and Promotion/Sales Ratio," *Journal of Marketing,* January 1994, pp. 86–97.

8. Ailawadi, Farris, and Parry, pp. 86–97; and James A. Schroer, "Ad Spending: Growing Market Share," *Harvard Business Review,* January–February 1990, pp. 44–48.

9. Daniel Seligman, "How Much for Advertising?" *Fortune,* December 1956, p. 123. Also see F. G. Crane, "The Promotion Intelligence Quotient of Small Business Owners," *Journal of Small Business & Entrepreneurship,* July–September 1992, pp. 14–18.

10. James E. Lynch and Graham J. Hooley, "Increasing Sophistication in Advertising Budget Setting," *Journal of Advertising Research,* February–March 1990, pp. 67–75.

11. Jimmy D. Barnes, Brenda J. Muscove, and Javad Rassouli, "An Objective and Task Media Selection Decision Model and Advertising Cost Formula to Determine International Advertising Budgets," *Journal of Advertising* 11, no. 4 (1982), pp. 68–75.

12. Ken Riddell, "Advertising Sees Share of Pie Dwindling," *Marketing,* January 7, 1994, p. 2; and Ken Riddell, "The Need for Leadership," *Marketing,* June 14, 1993, p. 15.

13. F. G. Crane and T. K. Clarke, *Consumer Behaviour in Canada: Theory and Practice,* 2nd ed., (Toronto: Dryden 1994), pp. 237–238, 346.

CHAPTER 15

1. Adapted from Terry Bullick, "Alberta AIDS Ads Aim to Change Behaviour," *Marketing,* March 1995, p. 2.

2. Ibid.

3. William K. Darley & Robert E. Smith, "Advertising Claim Objectivity: Antecedents and Effects," *Journal of Marketing,* October 1993, pp. 100–113.

4. Naveen Donthu, "Comparative Advertising Intensity," *Journal of Advertising Research,* November 1992, pp. 53–58.

5. Jennifer Lawrence, "P&G Ads Get Competitive," *Advertising Age,* February 1, 1993, p. 14; and Jerry Gotlieb and Dan Sorel, "The Influence of Type of Advertising, Price, and Source

Credibility on Perceived Quality," *Journal of the Academy of Marketing Science,* Summer 1992, pp. 253–260.

6. For a discussion of institutional or corporate advertising, see F. G. Crane, "The Need for Corporate Advertising in the Financial Services Industry: A Case Study Illustration," *Journal of Services Marketing,* vol. 4, no. 2 (1990), pp. 31–37.

7. F. G. Crane and T. K. Clarke, *Consumer Behaviour in Canada: Theory and Practice,* 2nd ed., (Toronto: Dryden 1994) pp. 383, 436–437.

8. Bob Garfield, "Allstate Ads Bring Home Point about Mortgage Insurance," *Advertising Age,* September 11, 1989, p. 120; and Judann Dagnoli, " 'Buy or Die Mentality' Toned Down in Ads," *Advertising Age,* July 19, 1993, p. 8.

9. Gail Chiasson, "Tracking Shows Why Most Ads Fail," *Marketing,* July 19, 1993, p. 8.

10. Canadian Media Directors' Council (CMDC), *Media Digest* (Toronto, 1994–95), p. 7

11. Gail Chiasson, "Tracking Shows Why Most Ads Fail."

12. Canadian Media Directors' Council, *Media Digest,* p. 9.

13. Ibid., p. 11.

14. Surenda N. Singh and Catherine Cole, "The Effects of Length, Content, and Repetition on Television Commercial Effectiveness," *Journal of Marketing Research,* February 1993, pp. 91–104. For a discussion on how to improve the effectiveness of 15-second ads, see Kenny Chan and Rajender K. Garg, "A Scripty-Theoretic Perspective on the Communication Effectiveness of 'Pool-Out' 15-Second Television Commercials," *Journal of Promotion Management,* vol. 1, no. 4, (1993) pp. 67–88.

15. Canadian Media Directors' Council, *Media Digest,* p. 19.

16. Ibid., p. 29.

17. Julia Collins, "Image and Advertising," *Harvard Business Review,* January–February 1989, pp. 93–97.

18. "Apple Launches Disk Ad Inserts," *Marketing,* March 22, 1993, p. 2.

19. Canadian Media Directors' Council, *Media Digest,* pp. 22–25.

20. "Out of Home in Evolution," *Marketing,* January 30, 1995, pp. 15–16; and Arch G. Woodside, "Outdoor Advertising as Experiments," *Journal of the Academy of Marketing Science,* Summer 1990, pp. 229–37.

21. Beng Soo Ong and David Meri, "Should Product Placement in Movies be Banned," *Journal of Promotion Management,* vol. 2, no. 3/4 (1994) pp. 159–176.

22. Sehoon Park and Minhi Hahn, "Pulsing in a Discrete Model of Advertising Competition, *Journal of Marketing Research,* November 1991, pp. 397–405.

23. John Dalla Costa, "Shattering Marketing Myths," *Marketing,* April 3, 1995, p. 11; and "Professor Claims Corporations Waste Billions on Advertising," *Marketing News,* July 6, 1992, p. 5.

24. The discussion of posttesting is based on Courtland L. Bovee and William F. Arens, *Contemporary Advertising,* 4th ed. (Burr Ridge, IL: Richard D. Irwin, 1994), p. 209.

25. David A. Aaker and Douglas M. Stayman, "Measuring Audience Perceptions of Commercials and Relating Them to Ad Impact," *Journal of Advertising Research,* August–September 1990, pp. 7–17; and Ernst Dichter, "A Psychological View of Advertising Effectiveness," *Marketing Management* 1, no. 3 (1992), pp. 60–62.

26. George E. Belch and Michael A. Belch, *Introduction to Advertising and Promotion,* 2nd ed. (Burr Ridge, IL: Richard D. Irwin, 1993), pp. 702–703: and Laurence N. Gold. "The Evolution of Television Advertising-Sales Measurement: Past,

Present, and Future," *Journal of Advertising Research,* June–July 1988, pp. 19–24.

27. F. G. Crane, "Consumers' Attitudes toward Advertising: A Canadian Perspective," *International Journal of Advertising* 10 (1991), pp. 111–16.

28. F. G. Crane, Carolyn Meacher, and T. K. Clarke, "Lawyers' Attitudes toward Legal Services Advertising in Canada, *International Journal of Advertising,* 8 (1989) pp. 71–78.

29. Joe Marconi, *Image Marketing: Using Public Perception to Create Market Share and Awareness* (Chicago: American Marketing Association, 1996).

30. This discussion on PR was based, in part, on Mark Clemente, *The Marketing Glossary* (New York: AMACOM, 1992), pp. 283–285.

31. Howard Schlossberg, "Sports Marketing," *Journal of Promotion Management,* 1 (1991), pp. 119–22.

32. *Marketing,* January 25, 1993, p. 11.

33. Lara Mills, "Strategic's Body Shop Campaign Wins Double Gold," *Marketing,* March 20, 1995, p. 9.

CHAPTER 16

1. *Annual Report* (Vancouver, Clearly Canadian Beverage Corporation, 1995).

2. Keith McIntyre, "Sometimes, Smaller is Better," *Marketing,* Nov. 28, 1994, p. 14.

3. "Donnelly Marketing's 14th Annual Survey of Promotional Practices," *Promo,* May 1992, p. 24.

4. *1995 Review of Couponing Trends,* (Markham, Ontario: NCH Promotional Services, January 1996).

5. Kapil Bawa and Robert W. Shoemaker, "Analyzing Incremental Sales from a Direct-Mail Coupon Promotion," *Journal of Marketing,* July 1989, pp. 66–78.

6. Roger A. Strang. "Sales Promotion—Fast Growth, Faulty Management," *Harvard Business Review,* July–August 1976, pp. 115–24.

7. Gail Chiasson, "Men's Fragrance Market Gets a Couple of New Players," *Marketing,* March 27, 1995, p. 4.

8. James Pollock, "The Poop on Ultra Diapers," *Marketing,* November 22, 1993, p. 4.

9. Glenn Heitsmith, "Credit Cards Form Hub of Loyalty Programs," *Promo,* October 1992, pp. 30, 56.

10. "New Handy Snack Display is Dandy," *Marketing News,* October 9, 1987, p. 15.

11. Cyndee Miller, "P-O-P Gains Followers As 'Era of Retailing' Dawns," *Marketing News,* May 14, 1990, p. 2.

12. Marvin A. Jolson, Joshua L. Wiener, and Richard B. Rosecky, "Correlates of Rebate Proneness," *Journal of Advertising Research,* February–March 1987, pp. 33–43.

13. Keith McIntyre, *Marketing.*

14. George E. Belch and Michael A. Belch, *Introduction to Advertising and Promotion,* 2nd ed. (Burr Ridge, IL: Richard D. Irwin, 1993) pp. 613–618.

15. Ibid., p. 613.

16. Ibid., p. 617–618; and G. A. Marken, "Firms Can Maintain Control over Creative Co-op Programs," *Marketing News,* September 28, 1992, pp. 7, 9.

17. Jerry White, "Integrated Marketing," *Marketing,* June 14, 1993, p. 15.

18. Aldo Cundari, "Power and Information," *Marketing,* March 6, 1995, p. S9.

19. Jo Marney, "The Lowdown on Infomercials," *Marketing,* January 23, 1995, p. 18.

20. Rosalee Courage, "Getting Through the Prospect's Door with Tele/Mail," *Journal of Promotion Management,* vol. 1, no. (1991) pp. 85–88.

CHAPTER 17

1. Thayer C. Taylor, "How the Game Will Change in the 1990s," *Sales & Marketing Management,* June 1989, pp. 52–61.

2. For different perspectives on relationship selling, see Robert F. Dwyer, Paul H. Schuer, and Sejo Oh, "Developing Buyer–Seller Relationships," *Journal of Marketing,* April 1987, pp. 11–27; Lawrence A. Crosby, Kenneth R. Evans, and Deborah Cowles, "Relationship Quality in Services Selling: An Interpersonal Influence Perspective," *Journal of Marketing,"* July 1990, pp. 68–81; and Barry J. Farber and Joyce Wycoff, "Relationships: Six Steps to Success," *Sales & Marketing Management,* April 1992, pp. 50–56.

3. See Thomas N. Ingram and Raymond W. LaForge, *Sales Management Analysis and Decision Making,* 2nd edition, (The Dryden Press, 1992), pp. 161–162, for a discussion of the trend toward and effectiveness of relationship selling.

4. For a perspective on types of selling, see Thomas R. Wotruba, "The Evolution of Personal Selling," *Journal of Personal Selling & Sales Management,* Summer 1991, pp. 1–12.

5. "1992 Sales Manager's Budget Planner," *Sales & Marketing Management,* June 22, 1992, pp. 68, 73.

6. Cathy Hills, "Making the Team," *Sales & Marketing Management,* February 1992, pp. 55–57.

7. Marvin A. Jolson and Thomas R. Wotruba, "Prospecting: A New Look at This Old Challenge," *Journal of Personal Selling & Sales Management,* Fall 1992, pp. 59–66.

8. James Pollock, "In Pursuit of Privacy," *Marketing,* January 4, 1993, pp. 1, 4.

9. Gerrard Macintosh, Kenneth A. Anglin, David M. Szymanski, and James W. Gentry, "Relationship Development in Selling: A Cognitive Analysis," *Journal of Personal Selling & Sales Management,* Fall 1992, pp. 23–34.

10. For a variation on the "canned presentation," see Marvin A. Jolson, "Canned Adaptiveness: A New Direction for Modern Salesmanship," *Business Horizons,* January–February 1989, pp. 7–12.

11. Research on these formats can be found in Barton A. Weitz, Harish Sujan, and Mita Sujan, "Knowledge, Motivation, and Adaptive Behavior: A Framework for Improving Selling Effectiveness," *Journal of Marketing,* October 1986, pp. 174–91; Thomas W. Leigh and Patrick F. McGraw, "Mapping the Procedural Knowledge of Industrial Sales Personnel: A Script-Theoretic Investigation," *Journal of Marketing,* January 1989, pp. 16–34; David M. Szymanski, "Determinants of Selling Effectiveness: The Importance of Declarative Knowledge to the Personal Selling Concept," *Journal of Marketing,* January 1988, pp. 64–67; and Rosann L. Spiro and Barton A. Weitz, "Adaptive Selling: Conceptualization, Measurement, and Normological Validity," *Journal of Marketing Research,* February 1990, pp. 61–69.

12. An extensive listing of closing techniques is found in Robin T. Peterson, "Sales Representative Perceptions on Various Widely Used Closing Tactics," *AMA Educators' Conference Proceedings* (Chicago: American Marketing Association, 1988), pp. 220–24.

13. William A. O'Connell and William Keenan, Jr., "The Shape of Things to Come," *Sales & Marketing Management,* January 1990, pp. 36–41.

14. See, for example, Troy A. Festervand, Stephen J. Grove, and Eric Reidenbach, "The Sales Force as a Marketing Intelligence System," *Journal of Business & Industrial Marketing,* Winter 1988, pp. 53–60; Douglas M. Lambert, Howard Marmorstein, and Arun Sharma, "Industrial Salespeople as a Source of Market Information," *Industrial Marketing Management* 19 (1990), pp. 141–48; and Lawrence B. Chonko, John F. Tanner, and Ellen Reid Smith, "The Sales Force's Role in International Marketing Research and Marketing Information Systems," *Journal of Personal Selling & Sales Management,* Winter 1991, pp. 69–79.

15. For an extended treatment of major account management, see Jerome A. Colletti and Gary S. Turbridy, "Effective Major Account Management," *Journal of Personal Selling & Sales Management,* August 1987, pp. 1–10; and Richard Cardozo and Shannon Shipp, "New Selling Methods Are Changing Industrial Sales Management," *Business Horizons,* September–October 1987, pp. 23–28.

16. Several variations of the account management policy grid exist. See, for example, Gilbert A. Churchill, Jr., Neil M. Ford, and Orville C. Walker, Jr., *Sales Force Management: Planning, Implementation, and Control,* 4th ed. (Burr Ridge, IL: Richard D. Irwin, 1993), p. 249; and David W. Cravens, Thomas N. Ingram, and Raymond W. LaForge, "Evaluating Multiple Channel Strategies," *The Journal of Business & Industrial Marketing,* Fall 1991, pp. 37–48.

17. For research on job analyses, see William C. Montcrief III, "Selling Activity and Sales Position Taxonomies for Industrial Salesforces," *Journal of Marketing Research,* August 1986, pp. 261–70.

18. Neil M. Ford, Orville C. Walker, Jr., Gilbert A. Churchill, Jr., and Steven W. Hartley, "Selecting Successful Salespeople: A Meta-Analysis of Biographical and Psychological Selection Criteria," in *Review of Marketing 1987,* ed. Michael J. Houston (Chicago: American Marketing Association, 1988), pp. 90–131.

19. Earl D. Honeycutt, Jr., Clyde E. Harris, Jr., and Stephen B. Castleberry, "Sales Training: A Status Report," *Training and Development Journal,* May 1987, pp. 42–47.

20. Churchill, Ford, and Walker, p. 530; and Douglas J. Dalrymple and William L. Cron, *Sales Management,* 4th ed. (New York: John Wiley & Sons, 1992), p. 444.

21. See, for example, William L. Cron, Alan J. Dubinsky, and Ronald E. Michaels, "The Influence of Career Stages on Components of Salesperson Motivation," *Journal of Marketing,* January 1988, pp. 78–92; and Walter Kiechel III, "How to Manage Salespeople," *Fortune,* March 14, 1988, pp. 179–80.

22. "Types of Employee Awards," *Sales & Marketing Management,* June 22, 1992, p. 73.

23. For statistics and research on salesperson turnover, see "Turnover Rates by Industry Group," *Sales & Marketing Management,* June 22, 1992, p. 71; and René Y. Darmon, "Identifying Sources of Turnover Costs: A Segmental Approach," *Journal of Marketing,* April 1990, pp. 46–56. See also Edward F. Fern, Ramon A. Avila, and Dhruv Grewal, "Salesforce Turnover: Those Who Left and Those Who Stayed," *Industrial Marketing Management* 18 (1989), pp. 1–9; and Thomas R. Wotruba and Pradeep K. Tyagi, "Met Expectations and Turnover in Direct Selling," *Journal of Marketing,* July 1991, pp. 24–35.

24. Erin Anderson and Richard L. Oliver, "Perspectives on Behavior-Based versus Outcome-Based Salesforce Control Systems," *Journal of Marketing,* October 1987, pp. 76–88; and Daniel A. Sauers, James B. Hunt, and Ken Bass, "Behavioral Self-Management as a Supplement to External Sales Force Controls,"

Journal of Personal Selling & Sales Management, Summer 1990, pp. 17–28.

25. Jerry McAdams, "Rewarding Sales and Marketing Performance," *Management Review,* April 1987, pp. 33–38. See also Gilbert A. Churchill, Jr., Neil M. Ford, Steven W. Hartley, and Orville C. Walker, Jr., "The Determinants of Salesperson Performance: A Meta-Analysis," *Journal of Marketing Research,* May 1985, pp. 103–18.

CHAPTER 18

1. Walter Roessing, "Japan's New Focus on Fun," *Northwest World Traveler,* International Edition, September 1992, pp. 68–72; and Richard Corliss, "Viola! Disney Invades Europe. Will the French Resist?" *Time,* April 20, 1992, pp. 82–84.

2. *General Agreement on Tariffs and Trade: What It is, What It Does.* (Geneva, Switzerland: GATT Information and Media Relations Division, 1990), pp 1–3.

3. This discussion is based on Karl E. Case and Ray C. Fair, *Principles of Economics* (Englewood Cliffs, NJ: Prentice Hall, 1989), p. 930.

4. *The Financial Post 500* (Toronto: The Financial Post Company, 1992).

5. Kenichi Ohmae, "Planting for a Global Harvest," *Harvard Business Review,* July–August 1989, pp. 136–45.

6. Robert Z. Lawrence and Robert E. Litan, "Why Protectionism Doesn't Pay," *Harvard Business Review,* May–June 1987, pp. 60–67.

7. "The Barriers Come Tumbling Down," *Time,* August 17, 1992, pp. 15–16; David Aikman and Laura Lopez, "MEGAmarket," *Time,* August 10, 1992, pp. 43–44; and Paul Magnusson, "Free Trade? They Can Hardly Wait," *Business Week,* September 24, 1992, pp. 24–25.

8. Carole M. Howard, "Reader's Digest Meets Eastern Europe," *Express Magazine,* Spring 1992, pp. 28–31.

9. James Sterngold, "The Awakening Chinese Consumer," *The New York Times,* October 11, 1992, pp. F1, F6.

10. Vern Terpstra and Kenneth David, The Cultural Environment of International Business, 3rd ed. (Cincinnati: South-Western Publishing, 1991).

11. These examples are adapted from Terpstra and David; and Sergey Frank, "Global Negotiating," *Sales and Marketing Management,* May 1992, p. 64–69.

12. See Terpstra and David; and "Valentine's Day in Japan: Ladies Don't Expect a Gift," *The Christian Science Monitor,* February 13, 1989, p. 6.

13. Roger E. Axtell, *"Do's and Taboos around the World,* compiled by the Parker Pen Company (New York: John Wiley & Sons, 1985).

14. Joann S. Lublin, "Younger Managers Learn Global Skills," *The Wall Street Journal,* March 31, 1992, p. B1.

15. "Greeks Protest Coke's Use of Parthenon," *Dallas Morning News,* August 17, 1992, p. D4.

16. Terpstra and David, pp. 24–25.

17. These examples are adapted from Terpstra and David, p. 21; David A. Ricks, Jeffrey S. Arpan, and Marilyn Y. Fu, "Pitfalls in Advertising Overseas," *Journal of Advertising Research,"* December 1974, p. 48; and David A. Ricks, "Products That Crashed into the Language Barrier," *Business and Society Review,* Spring 1983, pp. 46–50.

18. Terence A. Shimp and Subhash Sharma, "Consumer Ethnocentrism: Construction and Validation of the CETSCALE," *Journal of Marketing Research,* August 1987, pp. 280–89.

19. Nancy Giges, "Europeans Buy Outside Goods, but Like Local Ads," *Advertising Age,* April 27, 1992, pp. I–1, I–26.

20. James Pollock, "A Taste of Success, *Marketing,* January 23, 1995, pp. 11, 13.

21. Alan T. Shao, "Standardized Advertising Campaigns: Impediments Encountered by European Agencies," *Journal of Promotion Management,* 1, no. 2, 1993, pp. 39–52.

22. "Global Advertising: Standardized or Multi-Cultural?" *Journal of Advertising Research,* July–August, 1992.

CHAPTER 19

1. *Annual Reports* (Toronto: Second Harvest, 1991–95).

2. Herbert G. Grubel and Michael A. Walker, *Service Industry Growth,* The Frasier Institute, 1989.

3. *Marketing,* June 14, 1993, p. 2.

4. Leonard Berry, "Big Ideas in Services Marketing," *Journal of Consumer Marketing,* Spring 1986, pp. 47–51.

5. Frederick F. Reichheld and W. Earl Sasser Jr., "Zero Defections: Quality Comes to Services," *Harvard Business Review,* September–October 1990, pp. 105–11; "Standardization Services Run Gamut from Mufflers to Wills," *Marketing News,* April 10, 1987, pp. 17, 43; and Valarie A. Zeithaml, Leonard Berry, and A. Parasuraman, "Communication and Control in the Delivery of Service Quality," *Journal of Marketing,* April 1988, pp. 35–48.

6. Valarie A. Zeithaml, "How Consumer Evaluation Processes Differ Between Goods and Services," in *Marketing of Services,* ed. James H. Donnelly and William R. George (Chicago: American Marketing Association, 1981), pp. 186–190.

7. Keith B. Murray, "A Test of Services Marketing Theory: Consumer Information Acquisition Activities, *Journal of Marketing,* January 1991, pp. 10–25.

8. Ibid.

9. A. Parasuraman, Leonard L. Berry, and Valarie A. Zeithaml, "More on Improving Service Quality Measurement, *Journal of Retailing,* Spring 1993, pp. 140–47.

10. A. Parasuraman, Valarie A. Zeithaml, and Leonard L. Berry, "Reassessment of Expectations as Comparison Standard in Measuring Service Quality: Implications for Further Research," *Journal of Marketing,* January 1994, pp. 111–124; and R. Kenneth Teas, "Expectations, Performance Evaluation, and Consumers' Perceptions of Quality," *Journal of Marketing,* October, 1993, pp. 18–34.

11. J. Joseph Cronin Jr. and Steven A. Taylor, "Measuring Service Quality: A Reexamination and Extension," *Journal of Marketing,* July 1992, pp. 55–68.

12. Leonard L. Berry, Jeffrey S. Conant, and A. Parasuraman, "A Framework for Conducting a Services Marketing Audit," *Journal of the Academy of Marketing Science,* Summer 1991, pp. 255–68.

13. Patriya Tansuhaj, Donna Randall, and Jim McCullough, "A Services Marketing Management Model: Integrating Internal and External Marketing Functions," *Journal of Services Marketing,* Winter 1988, pp. 31–38.

14. Christian Gronoos, "Internal Marketing: Theory and Practice," in *Services Marketing in a Changing Environment,* ed. T. Bloch, G. D. Upah, and V. A. Zeithaml (Chicago: American Marketing Association, 1984), pp. 41–47.

15. Ibid.

16. F. G. Crane, *Professional Services Marketing: Strategy and Tactics* (New York: The Haworth Press, 1993).

17. Dan R. E. Thomas, "Strategy is Different in Service Businesses," *Harvard Business Review,* July–August 1978, pp. 158–65.

18. Sundar G. Bharadwaj, P. Rajan Varadarajan, and John Fahy, "Sustainable Competitive Advantage in Services Industries: A Conceptual Model and Research Propositions," *Journal of Marketing,* October 1993, pp. 83–99.

19. Christopher Lovelock, *Services Marketing* (Englewood Cliffs, NJ: Prentice Hall, 1991), pp. 122–27.

20. Kent B. Monroe, "Buyers Subjective Perceptions of Price," *Journal of Marketing Research,* February 1973, pp. 70–80; and Jerry Olson, "Price as an Informational Cue: Effects on Product Evaluation," in *Consumer and Industrial Buying Behavior,* ed. A. G. Woodside, J. N. Sheth, and P. D. Benett (New York: Elsevier-North Holland Publishing, 1977), pp. 267–86.

21. See F. G. Crane, *"Professional Services Marketing: Strategy and Tactics;* and William R. George and Leonard L. Berry, "Guidelines for the Advertising of Services," *Business Horizons,* July–August 1981, pp. 52–56.

22. William Mindak and Seymour Fine, "A Fifth P: Public Relations," in *Marketing of Services,* ed., James H. Donnelly and William R. George (Chicago: American Marketing Association, 1981), pp. 71–73.

23. F. G. Crane, *Professional Services Marketing: Strategy and Tactics.*

24. Leonard Berry, "Big Ideas in Services Marketing."

25. Stan Sutter, "Advertising That's a Step Ahead of the Times," *Marketing,* January 25, 1993, p. 7.

26. Philip Kotler and Sidney J. Levy, "Broadening the Marketing Concept," *Journal of Marketing,* January 1969, p. 10.

27. James W. Harvey and Kevin F. McCrohan, "Service Value for Nonprofits," in *Add Value to Your Service,* ed., Carol Surprenant (Chicago: American Marketing Association, 1987) pp. 119–22.

Photo Credits

CHAPTER 1

p. 2, Timothy G. Lewis; p. 5 (left), Courtesy Rollerblade, Inc.; **p. 5** (right), Courtesy Johnson & Johnson; **p. 6,** Robert Burroughs; **p. 11,** Courtesy of Department of Economic Development & Tourism, Province of New Brunswick; **p. 12,** Courtesy of Sport Chek; **p. 17,** Courtesy Coca-Cola Ltd. "Powerade®, Fruitopia®, and Coca-Cola®" are used with permission.; **p. 18,** Courtesy of Chrysler Canada; **p. 19,** Courtesy GE Medical Systems; **p. 20,** Courtesy of Toyota Canada; **p. 21,** Courtesy of Compusearch; **p. 22,** Courtesy The Body Shop; **p. 23,** Ken Kerbs.

CHAPTER 2

p. 28, Courtesy of *Foodservice* and *Hospitality* magazine, published by Kostuch Publications Ltd.; **p. 32,** Peter Charlesworth/SABA; **p. 34,** Courtesy McDonald's Corporation; **p. 38,** Courtesy of Volvo; **p. 41,** Sharon Hoogstraten; **p. 44** (top), Courtesy Domino's Pizza, Inc.; **p. 44** (bottom), Courtesy Dodge Division of Chrysler Corporation; **p. 45,** Courtesy General Motors Corporation.

CHAPTER 3

p. 64, Courtesy Avon Products, Inc.; **p. 70,** Photo: O. Toscani. Courtesy of Benetton; **p. 71** (top), Sharon Hoogstraten; **p. 71** (bottom), Sharon Hoogstraten; **p. 73,** Courtesy Hyatt Hotels Corporation; **p. 74,** Michael Greenlar; **p. 76,** Greg Wolff.

CHAPTER 4

p. 86, Courtesy of Joseph E. Seagram & Sons Ltd.; **p. 95,** Courtesy of Terra Choice Environmental Services Inc.; **p. 96,** Bruce McAllister/Stock Imagery.

CHAPTER 5

p. 102, Chuck Keeler/Tony Stone Images; **p. 105,** Courtesy of Volkswagen Canada; **p. 109,** Used with permission of Michelin North America, Inc. All rights reserved.; **p. 111** (top), Sharon Hoogstraten; **p. 111** (middle), Courtesy Canadian Standards Association; **p. 111** (bottom), Courtesy Good Housekeeping; **p. 117,** Courtesy of Dairy Farmers of Ontario; **p. 122,** Greg Wolff.

CHAPTER 6

p. 128, Courtesy Honeywell's MICRO SWITCH Division; **p. 134,** Courtesy Alcan Aluminum Ltd.; **p. 135,** Courtesy of OSRAM SYLVANIA INC.; **p. 136,** Courtesy Harley-Davidson Motor Company; **p. 138** (left), Courtesy Honeywell's MICRO SWITCH Division; **p. 138** (right), Courtesy Honeywell's MICRO SWITCH Division; **p. 139,** Janet Gill/Tony Stone Images; **p. 143,** Voyles.

CHAPTER 7

p. 150, Courtesy of O'Hara Systems, Inc.; **p. 157,** Steve Smith/Outline; **p. 158,** Courtesy Fisher-Price; **p. 161,** Bob Daemmrich; **p. 162,** Courtesy Shoppers Drug Mart; **p. 166,** Courtesy of Eaton's and *Apparel Industry Magazine* (May, 1994)/Photography by Peter Power.

CHAPTER 8

p. 184, AP/Wide World Photos; **p. 186,** Courtesy Coca-Cola Ltd. "Powerade®, Fruitopia®, and Coca-Cola®" are used with permission.; **p. 189,** Used with permission of Clairol, Inc.; **p. 191,** Courtesy of Ault Foods Limited; **p. 192,** Sharon Hoogstraten; **p. 193,** Courtesy Matsushita Consumer Electronics Co.; **p. 194** (all), Used with permission of Apple Computer, Inc.; **p. 198,** David Harry Stewart/Tony Stone Images.

CHAPTER 9

p. 208, Courtesy of Sursun International Ltd.; **p. 212,** Courtesy Norwegian Cruise Line; **p. 214,** Courtesy Tiffany & Co.; **p. 215,** Courtesy of Sony Electronics Inc.; **p. 216,** Ray Marklin; **p. 217,** Sharon Hoogstraten; **p. 219,** Courtesy Labatt Breweries; **p. 221,** Courtesy Frito-Lay Inc.; **p. 223,** Courtesy The Procter & Gamble Company; **p. 227** Virtuality Visette® 2 Headset.

CHAPTER 10

p. 232, Courtesy of W.K. Buckley Ltd.; **p. 236,** Courtesy Cantel; **p. 239,** Courtesy of QMA; **p. 241,** Sharon Hoogstraten; **p. 242,** ® registered trademarks of Coca-Cola Ltd., appear courtesy of Coca-Cola Ltd.; **p. 245,** Courtesy NHL Enterprises, L.P.; **p. 246,** Courtesy Elite Foods Ltd.; **p. 250,** Sharon Hoogstraten; **p. 251,** Courtesy The Procter & Gamble Company.

CHAPTER 11

p. 258, Courtesy of Kimberly Grant; **p. 265,** Courtesy H.J. Heinz Company; **p. 266,** Sharon Hoogstraten; **p. 271,** Courtesy of Cantel; **p. 274,** Mug Shots/The Stock Market; **p. 277,** Courtesy The Toro Company; **p. 278,** Courtesy Canadian Tire Corporation, Limited.

CHAPTER 12

p. 294, UPS and UPS shield design are registered trademarks of United Parcel Service of America, Inc. Used by permission.; **p. 305,** Courtesy H&R Block Tax Services, Inc.; **p. 308,** Courtesy Warner-Lambert Company; **p. 314,** Courtesy Rapistan Demag Corp.

CHAPTER 13

p. 322, © Joy Cummings/UNB Audio Visual Services; **p. 327,** Chuck Keeler/Tony Stone Images; **p. 330,** Courtesy L.L. Bean, Inc.; **p. 332,** Permission granted by CompuServe Inc.; **p. 336,** Courtesy of West Edmonton Mall.

CHAPTER 14

p. 346, Courtesy of Crispin Prebys; **p. 350,** Courtesy Cosmopolitan; **p. 351,** Voyles; **p. 353,** Courtesy Lexus; **p. 358,** Courtesy American Express; **p. 361,** Greg Wolff; **p. 362,** Courtesy of International Business Machines Corporation; **p. 363,** Courtesy SmithKline Beecham.

CHAPTER 15

p. 370, Courtesy of Alberta Health, Provincial AIDS Program; **p. 373,** Courtesy Sony Electronics Inc.; **p. 374,** Courtesy Canada Trust; **p. 378,** Courtesy CNS, Inc.; **p. 381,** Courtesy Ford Motor Company; **p. 383,** Courtesy of Dairy Farmers of Ontario; **p. 384,** Courtesy Tecnica; **p. 387,** Reprinted with permission from Hanes Hosiery, a division of Sara Lee Corporation and Roper Starch Worldwide; **p. 390,** Courtesy Molson Breweries.

CHAPTER 16

p. 396, Courtesy Clearly Canadian Beverages; **p. 400,** Courtesy Friday's; **p. 401,** Courtesy Canada Trust; **p. 402** (top), Courtesy General Motors Corporation; **p. 402** (bottom), Ray Marklin; **p. 406,** Courtesy Dundee Resorts; **p. 408** (top), Photo courtesy of © 1996 American Harvest, Inc.; **p. 409,** Bruce Ayres/Tony Stone Images.

CHAPTER 17

p. 416, David Bloch Photography; **p. 419,** Courtesy of Dave Nichol; **p. 422,** Courtesy Xerox Corporation; **p. 424,** Courtesy National Housewares Manufacturers Association.

CHAPTER 18

p. 438, Corbis-Bettmann; **p. 440,** AP/Wide World Photos; **p. 442,** Courtesy Ganong Bros., Limited; **p. 442,** Courtesy Royal Canadian Mint; **p. 448,** Steven Rothfeld; **p. 451,** Tony Craddock/Tony Stone Images; **p. 452,** Courtesy Reader's Digest Inc.; **p. 455,** Courtesy of W.K. Buckley Ltd.; **p. 457,** Courtesy Ford Motor Company; **p. 460,** Courtesy Australian Tourist Commission.

CHAPTER 19

p. 466, Courtesy of Second Harvest; **p. 469,** Courtesy FS Concepts; **p. 475** (left), Courtesy McDonald's Corporation; **p. 475** (middle), Courtesy AT&T; **p. 475** (right), Courtesy United Way of America; **p. 477,** Courtesy ITT Sheraton Canada; **p. 478,** Courtesy of Deloitte & Touche LLP; **p. 479,** Courtesy Toronto Dominion Bank; **p. 481,** Sharon Hoogstraten; **p. 482,** Courtesy Greenpeace; **p. 483,** Courtesy of Canadian Red Cross; **p. 484,** Courtesy of Canadian Lung Association.

Name Index

Company Index

Subject Index